AF333674

PETER CLAPHAM SHEPPARD

HIS LIFE AND WORK

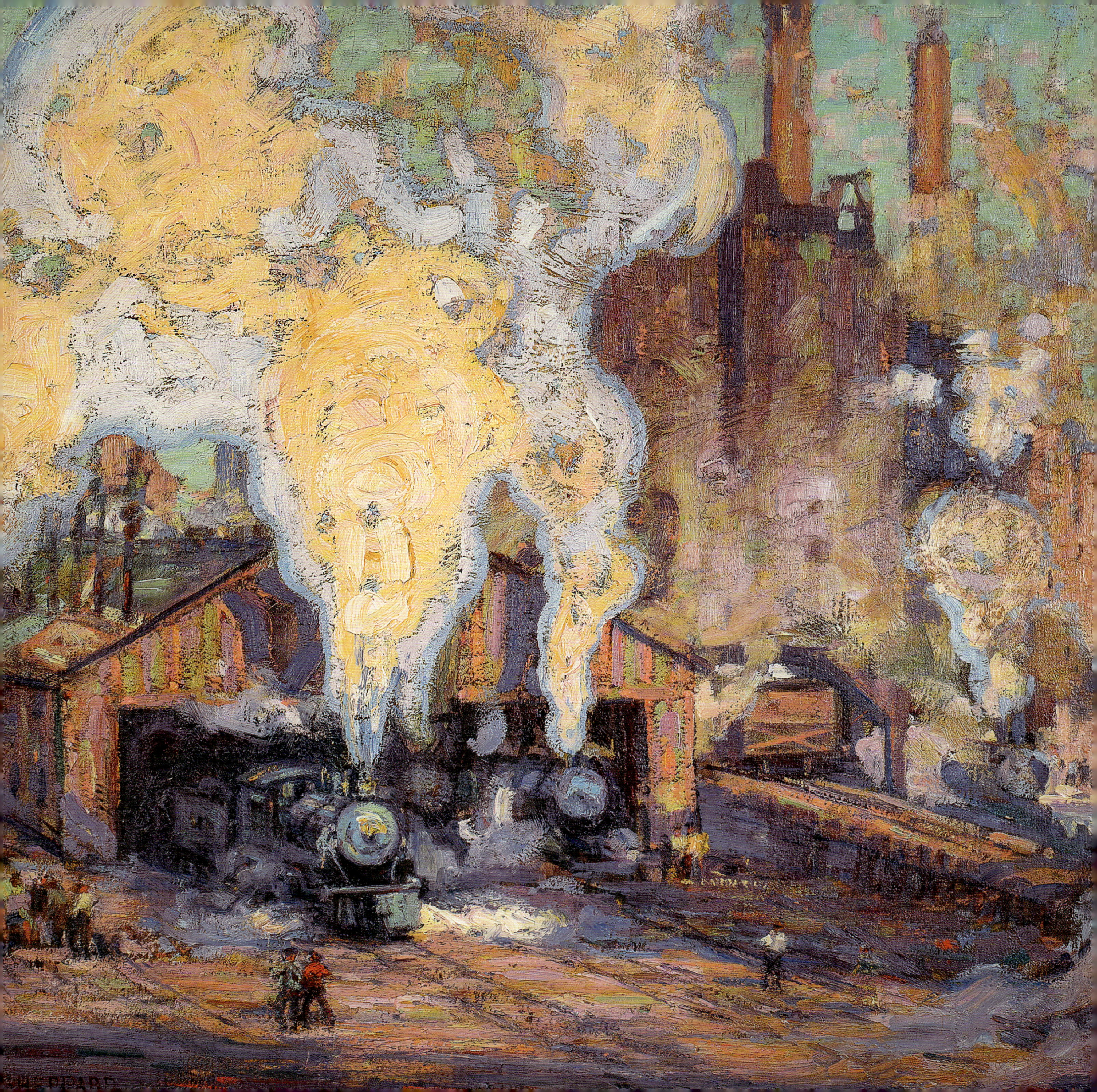

PETER CLAPHAM SHEPPARD

HIS LIFE AND WORK

TOM SMART

Foreword by Louis Gagliardi

Firefly Books

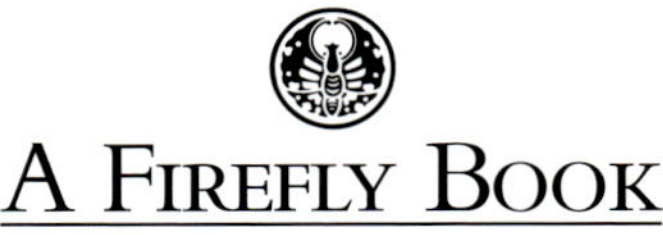

A Firefly Book

Published by Firefly Books Ltd. 2018

Text copyright © Tom Smart 2018

Foreword copyright © Louis Gagliardi 2018

All rights reserved. No part of this publication may be reproduced, stored in
a retrieval system, or transmitted in any form or by any means, electronic,
mechanical, photocopying, recording or otherwise, without the prior written
permission of the Publisher.

First printing

Library of Congress Control Number: 2018931797

Library and Archives Canada Cataloguing in Publication
Smart, Tom, author
    Peter Clapham Sheppard : his life and work / Tom Smart ; foreword by
Louis Gagliardi.

Includes bibliographical references and index.
ISBN 978-0-228-10078-2 (hardcover)

    1. Sheppard, Peter Clapham, 1879-1965. 2. Sheppard, Peter Clapham,
1879-1965--Criticism and interpretation. 3. Painters--Canada--Biography.
I. Title.

ND249.S493S63 2018   759.11   C2018-900511-4

Published in the United States by
Firefly Books (U.S.) Inc.
P.O. Box 1338, Ellicott Station
Buffalo, New York 14205

Published in Canada by
Firefly Books Ltd.
50 Staples Avenue, Unit 1
Richmond Hill, Ontario L4B 0A7

Cover and interior design: George A. Walker

Printed in China

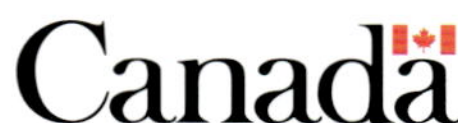

We acknowledge the financial support of the Government of Canada.

FRONT COVER
*The Bridge Builders, Construction,
Bloor Street Viaduct.*
1915. Oil on canvas, 147.3 x 101.6 cm.

FRONTISPIECE
The Engine Home.
1919. Oil on canvas, 84 x 91.4 cm.

Pages 6 and 7
Snowstorm, Montreal.
1921. Oil on panel, 21.6 x 26.7 cm.

BACK COVER
Lower New York (detail).
1921–22. Oil on canvas, 122 x 89 cm.

*Remembering speechlessly we seek the great forgotten
language, the lost lane-end into heaven, a stone,
a leaf, an unfound door.*

—Thomas Wolfe, *Look Homeward, Angel*

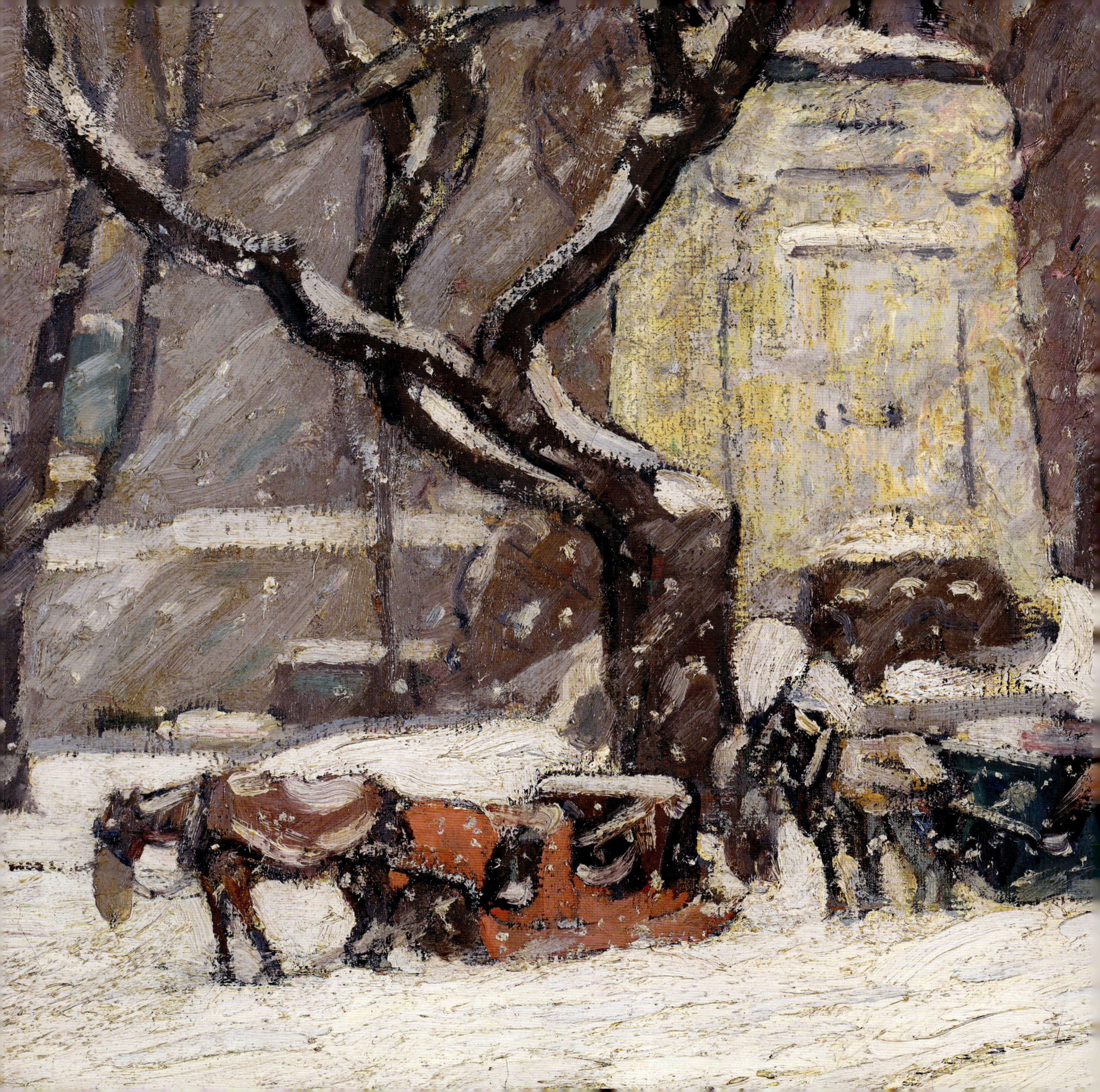

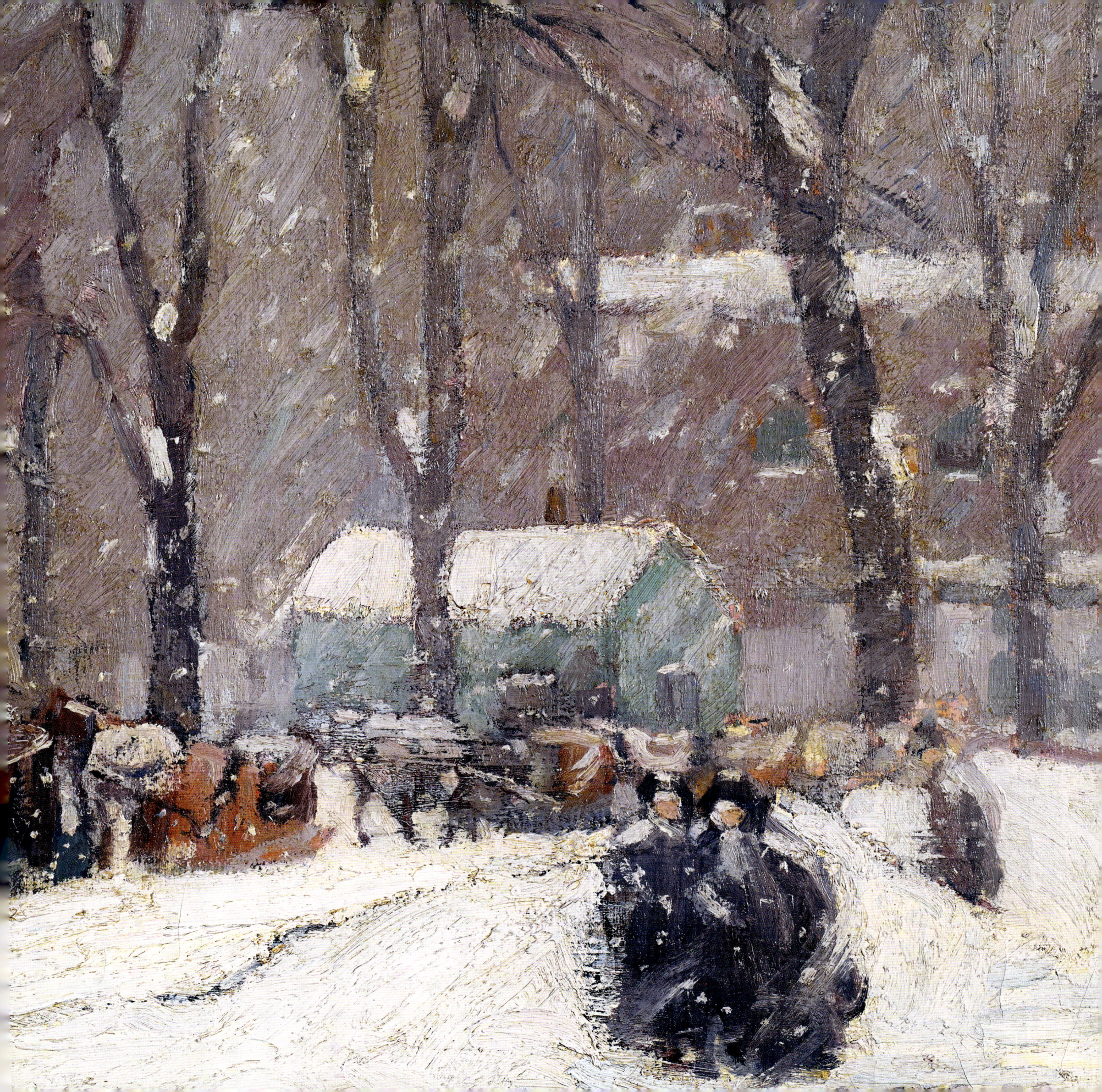

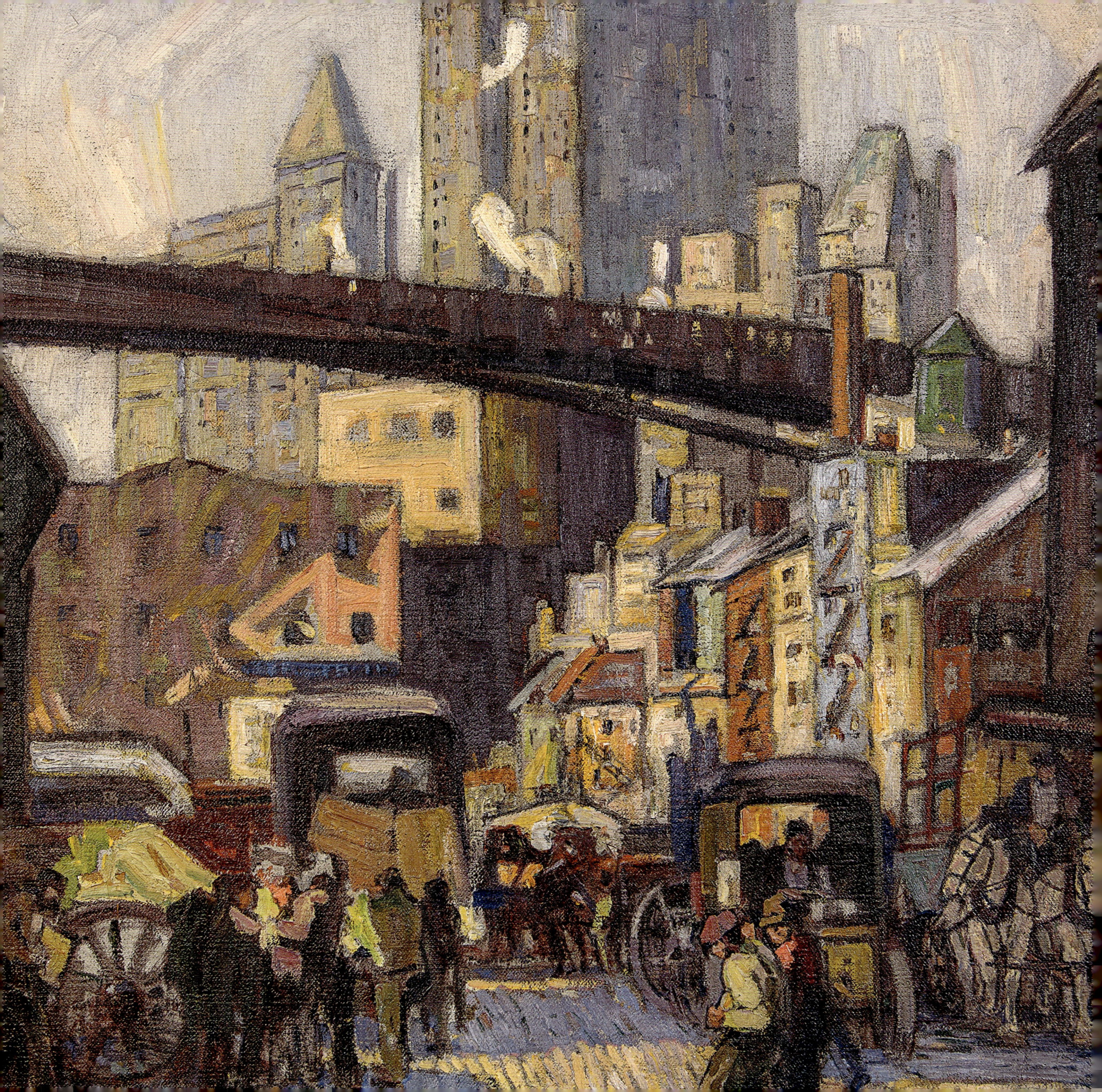

To the memory of Peter Clapham Sheppard, whom I never knew but whose
spirit has been a constant companion these last thirty years. This book fulfills an
unspoken but deeply felt covenant to honour him and to render gratitude.
To Bernice Fenwick Martin, who altered the course of my life forever, this work is
testament to the unshaken faith and beautiful friendship given. Her steadfast love
and admiration for P.C. Sheppard inspired this quest. It is to her that I owe this
transformative journey of knowledge, resolution, and validation.
And last but not least, to Ugo Gagliardi: my first and best friend, my constant
light and teacher, my precious brother, evermore.

— Louis Gagliardi

Lower New York (detail).
1921–22. Oil on canvas,
122 x 89 cm.

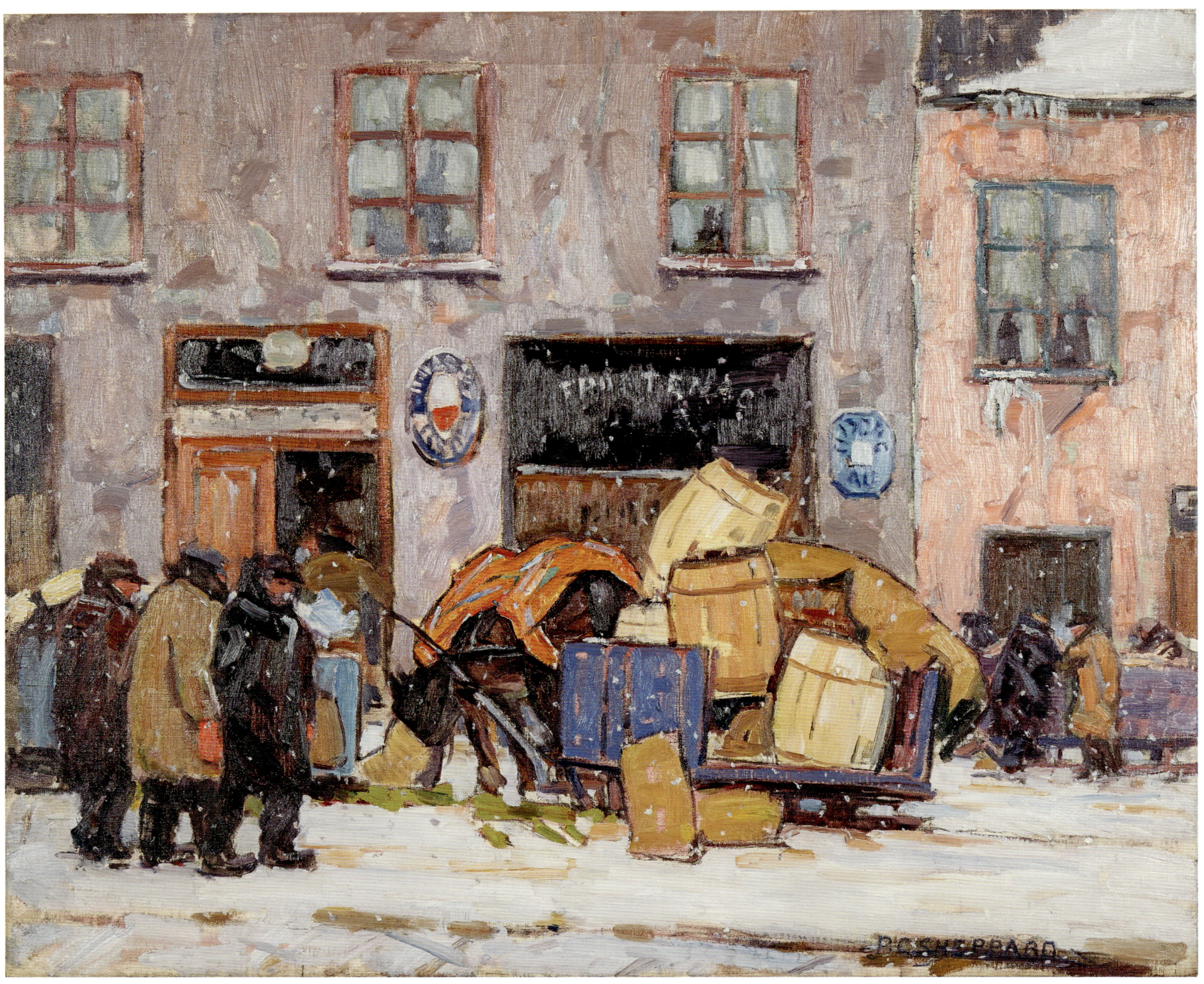

The Inn Yard.
1926–27. Oil on canvas,
91.4 x 76 cm.

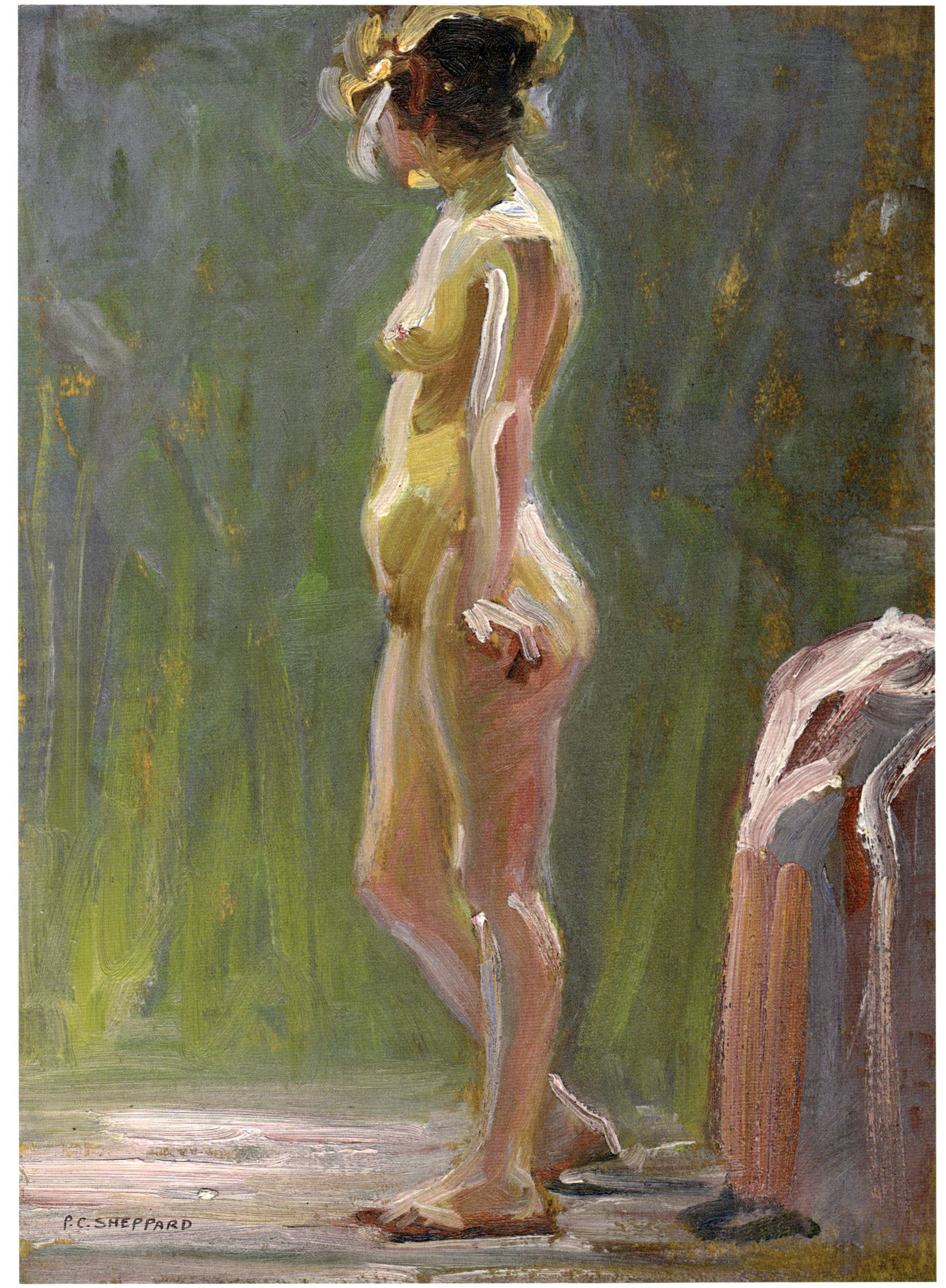

Study from Life.
1912. Oil on panel,
35.6 x 24.8 cm.

Contents

15 Acknowledgements, Tom Smart
17 Acknowledgements, Louis Gagliardi
19 Foreword
25 Introduction: Invisibility

CHAPTER ONE: Beginnings

Commercial Artwork
36 An elusive portrait
38 Transition in Canadian art from "old simplicity"
      to "modern efficiency"
38 Conflicting dates of birth
40 A working artist
40 "Fine" and "commercial" art

CHAPTER TWO: Transition

Fine Art
46 A fine art student, 1911 and 1912
50 The Ontario Society of Artists, 1911
51 Early works: Fine art before 1912
64 An art education
65 Influential instructors at the Ontario College of Art
68 William Cruikshank: Respect for tradition
69 George Agnew Reid: The expressive properties of colour
72 J.W. Beatty: The importance of drawing and composition
76 Student work at the Ontario College of Art, after 1912
87 First Nations model: Thundercloud
87 Other student work, to 1914
90 A graduate of OCA, 1914

CHAPTER THREE: The City as Subject

Artists Doing Distinctly Canadian Work
95 The Studio Building and the winds of change, 1914–15
96 Patriotic fervour
97 Sketchbooks, 1916
103 Construction of the Bloor Street/
       Prince Edward Viaduct, 1915
110 Making a living as an artist, 1917 onward
114 Arrival of the circus, 1919
118 The Group of Seven

CHAPTER FOUR: Working Beyond Toronto

New York and Montreal
123 Transition, 1920s
123 New York influences
129 Montreal
131 New York City, 1923–24
135 Influence of John Sloan
144 Old Store, Craig Street, 1925
147 British Empire Exhibition, 1925
151 A "radical" in Montreal, 1925–27
154 Other cabstands
163 Interlude: Oil sketches on wood panels, 1920s

CHAPTER FIVE: Toronto

Return to Toronto, 1929
196 Painted panels and sketchbooks of the 1930s
208 A calculated risk–taker
208 Toronto Ward paintings, 1930s
210 Louisa Street and Elizabeth Street
    sketches and paintings, early 1930s
221 Impartial eclecticism, 1934
221 In the company of "good pictures"
225 A kind of retirement
226 Visibility

229 **Notes to the Text**
232 **Exhibition History**
233 **Image Credits**
234 **Selected Bibliography**
235 **Index**

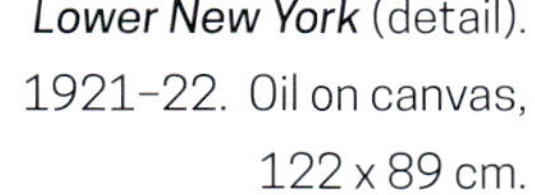

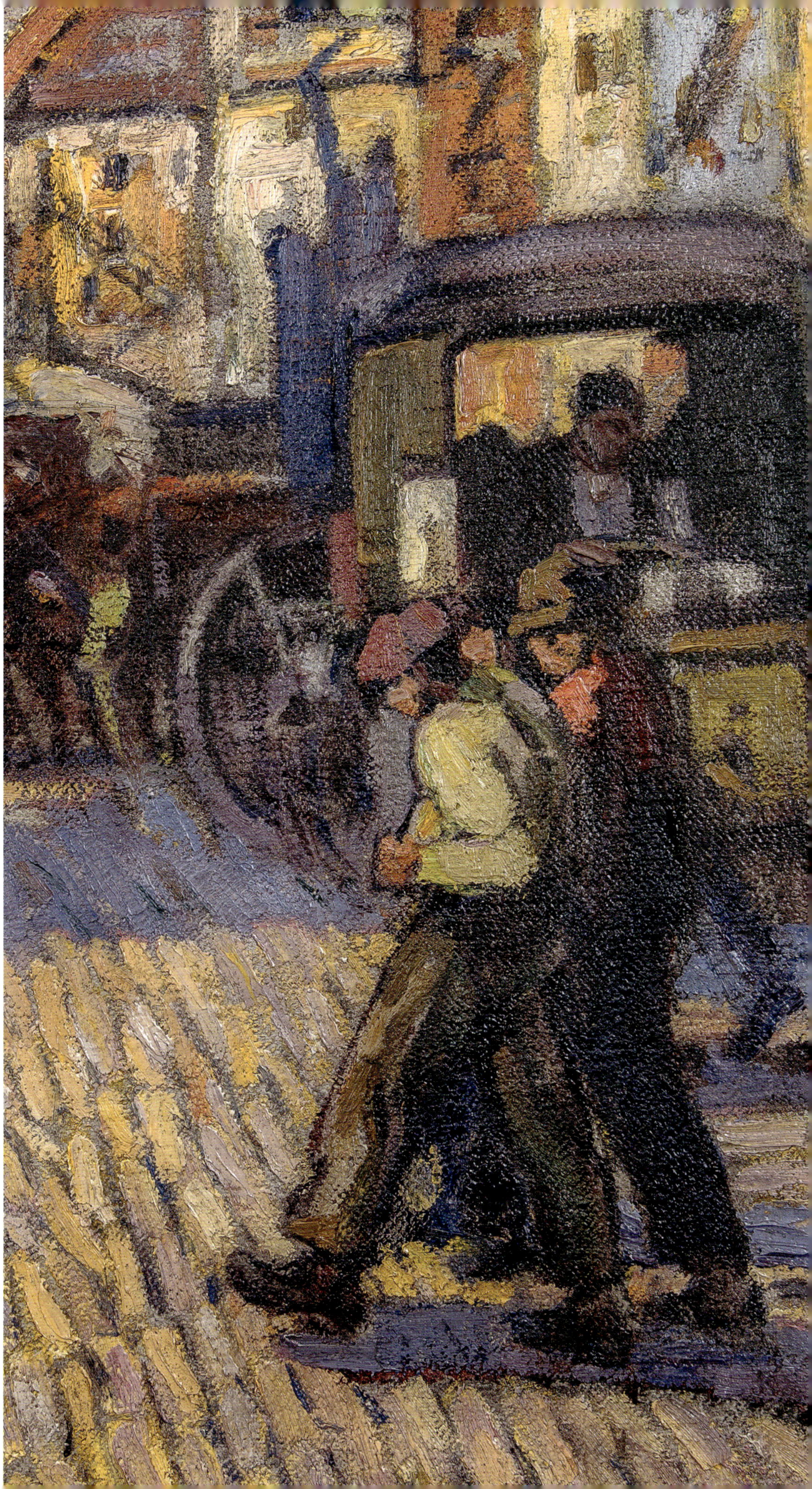

Lower New York (detail).
1921–22. Oil on canvas,
122 x 89 cm.

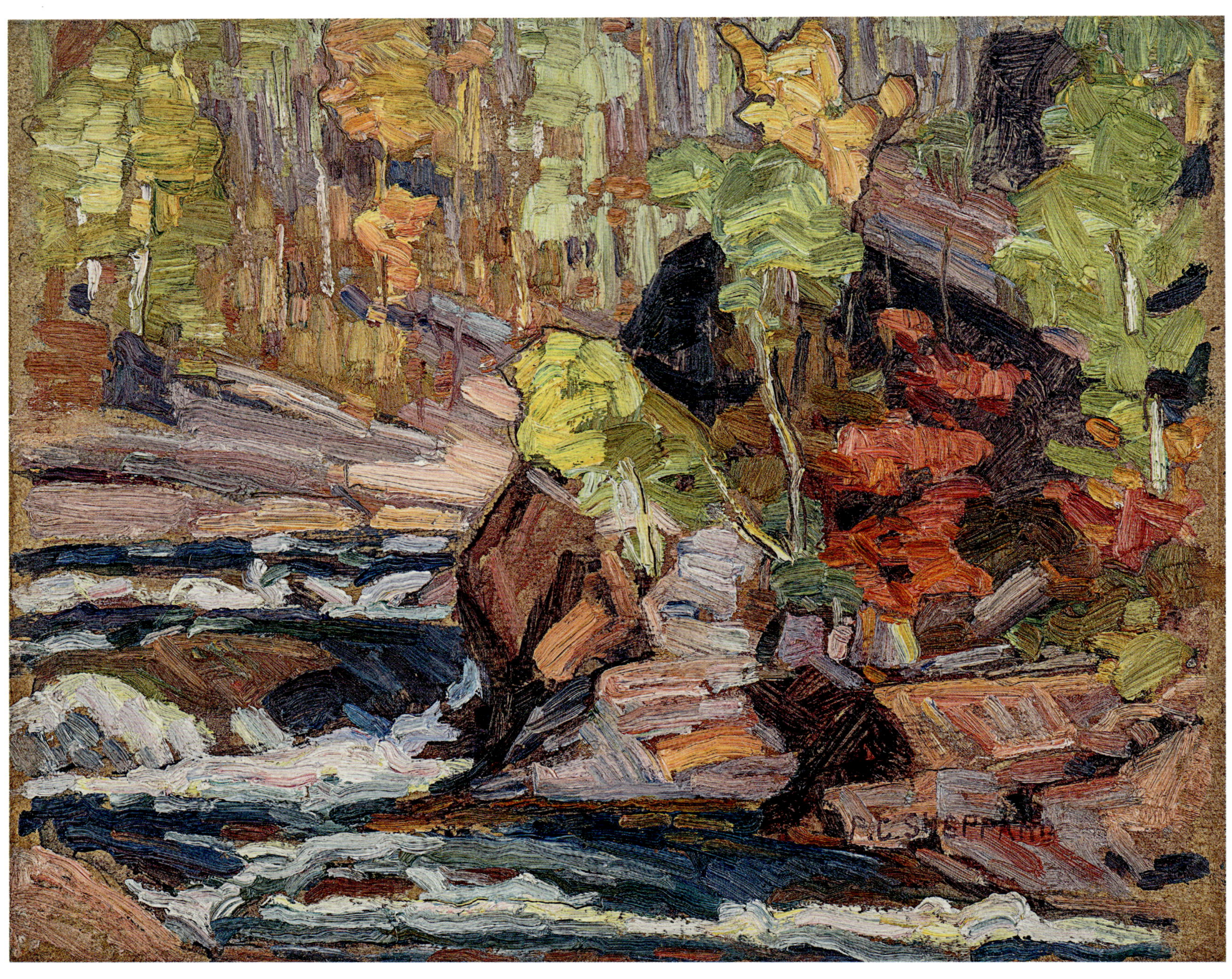

Autumn Landscape.
1922. Oil on board,
21.6 x 26.7 cm.

Acknowledgements

My thanks to the many people who provided me with assistance as I researched and wrote this book. In particular, I am grateful to Louis Gagliardi, whose passion about the life and art of Peter Clapham Sheppard proved infectious. He welcomed me into the artist's archive he has established, and was generous in sharing its contents with me, and patient with my many questions. I would also like to express my appreciation to the staff at the City of Toronto Archives, the Art Gallery of Ontario, the National Gallery of Canada and Casa Loma. George and Michelle Walker were instrumental in preparing the manuscript for publication, for designing this book and for liaising with the staff at Firefly Books, Lionel Koffler and Michael Worek, to see it through to publication. I am appreciative of the work of Chandra Wohleber, who edited the manuscript with such care and sensitive appreciation for the art, and of Allegra Robinson, who did careful and thorough work on the proofs. Susan was with me on this journey of discovery, keeping me on the path that brought Sheppard and his art to light, and for this I am most thankful.

— Tom Smart

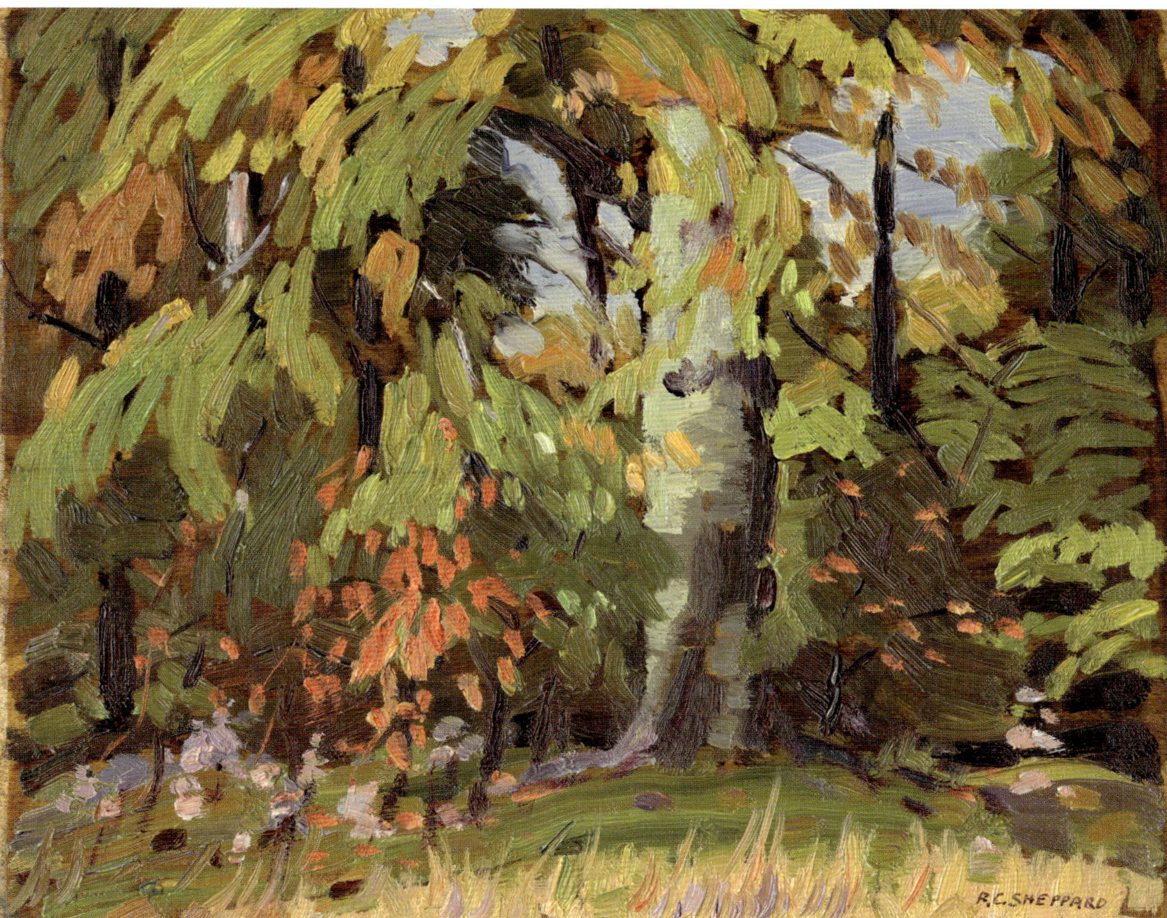

October.
1924. Oil on panel,
21.6 x 26.7 cm.

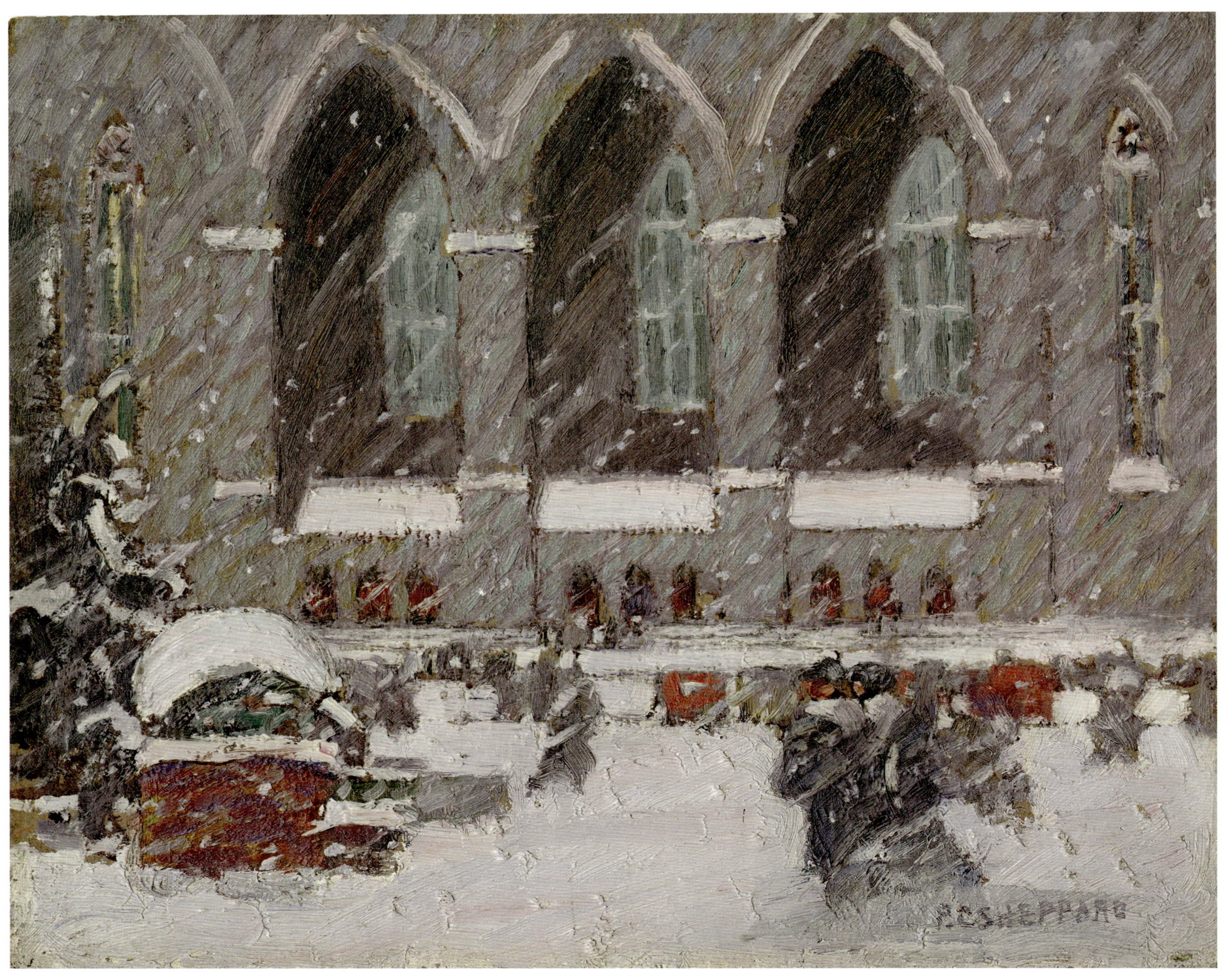

Snowstorm, Montreal.
c. 1921. Oil on panel,
21.6 x 26.7 cm.

Acknowledgements

It is to Tom Smart and Ross King that I owe the lion's share of gratitude and recognition for breathing new life into the forgotten art of Peter Clapham Sheppard. The depth of their perception and their profound familiarity with artistic quality made them the first modern champions of the artist. I shall always cherish the memory of that full day when we three were immersed in viewing the artworks, taking a break only to enjoy my mother's pizza. No one had seen this critical mass of artworks in fifty years and I am happy that the honour went to them.

My beloved wife, Marlene, through her love and patient support, gave me the strength and resolution I needed to pursue this inspiring, life-altering labour. Her loss, in 2006, was an utter devastation and, in the words of Tennyson, made "hollow, hollow, hollow all delight." It has been my goal, in large part, to honour her memory and so I have continued, even though it would have been easy to stop. I know she would be proud of me and, especially, of our two children, Emily and Vincent, through whom she lives and breathes.

I am forever thankful to my parents, Vincenzo and Lucia, and to my brother, Ugo. A lifetime of their unwavering patience, unconditional love, and boundless generosity has nurtured and defined me.

My efforts over the last thirty years, to confer upon Sheppard the recognition he deserves, have introduced me to many friends and new acquaintances. I met Elaine and Christopher George as a result of pursuing an important canvas by Sheppard, *Lower New York*, over ten years ago, and their friendship has made all the difference to me. Their enthusiastic support of my dreams for the artist, as well as their wisdom and willingness in giving advice, have positively affected the quality of my time and work. I owe them my immense gratitude.

Many people provided timely and valuable services to help furnish this book. George Nanowski, conservator and friend, expertly liberated most of these artworks from layered dirt and distress, the result of decades of oblivion. Don Miller and Daniel Dabrowski professionally photographed the canvases and sketches with expert, sensitive eyes and technical brilliance. Sally and Emmett Maddix brought their peerless experience to framing these works and, in so doing, engendered the perfect aesthetic encounter.

I wish to acknowledge the following for their professionalism and assistance: Martha Kelleher; Laszlo Cser of Restorart; Camilla Marking, Picture Library, National Gallery, London; Linda Morita, the librarian at the McMichael Canadian Art Collection; Raven Amiro and Phillip Dombowski of the National Gallery of Canada; Tracy Mallon-Jensen, Cindy Brouse, Donald Rance, Marilyn Nazar and Christopher Ocean of the Art Gallery of Ontario; Victoria Sigurdson and Scott Hillis at the Hoover Library, Ontario College of Art & Design University; Dan LaCaprara; Rob Cowley; Linda Rodeck; Sonya de Lazzer of the Riverbrink Art Museum; the wonderful team at the City of Toronto Archives; the courteous and efficient staff at Archives Ontario; Lani Wilson, Curator at the Government of Ontario Art Collection; Allan Walker and Christopher Coutlee in Special Collections at the Toronto Reference Library.

Of vital importance to the design and publication of this book: George A. Walker, whose talent and advice walked me through this enjoyable learning curve. His wife, Michelle Walker, was also extremely helpful in organizing us all. Chandra Wohleber had the formidable task of editing the manuscript and did so with a keen professional eye and graciousness. Allegra Robinson contributed sensitive and careful work on the proofs. Lionel Koffler and Michael Worek of Firefly Books facilitated the journey from manuscript to book with expertise, goodwill and patience.

In the final phase of image proofing, I appreciated the friendly welcome of Joe Kotler and James Li at Moveable Inc. While there, it was the technical expertise, professionalism and gentle manner of Maria Victoria B. Verzosa that deserve praise and gratitude. It is she who imparted that last sensitive touch to renew the forgotten treasures to life and, with this book, to preserve them for posterity.

Lorena, my dear Cio-Cio San, renewed my life with love from which all hope and ecstasies spring.

And finally, but in truth primarily, to dear Vincent Van Gogh, whence it all began: to him I owe the steadfast passion that has governed my entire life, a life which has been filled with love, the consolation of beauty, the pursuit of knowledge, and identity. *Une poignée de main bien de cœur.*

— Louis Gagliardi

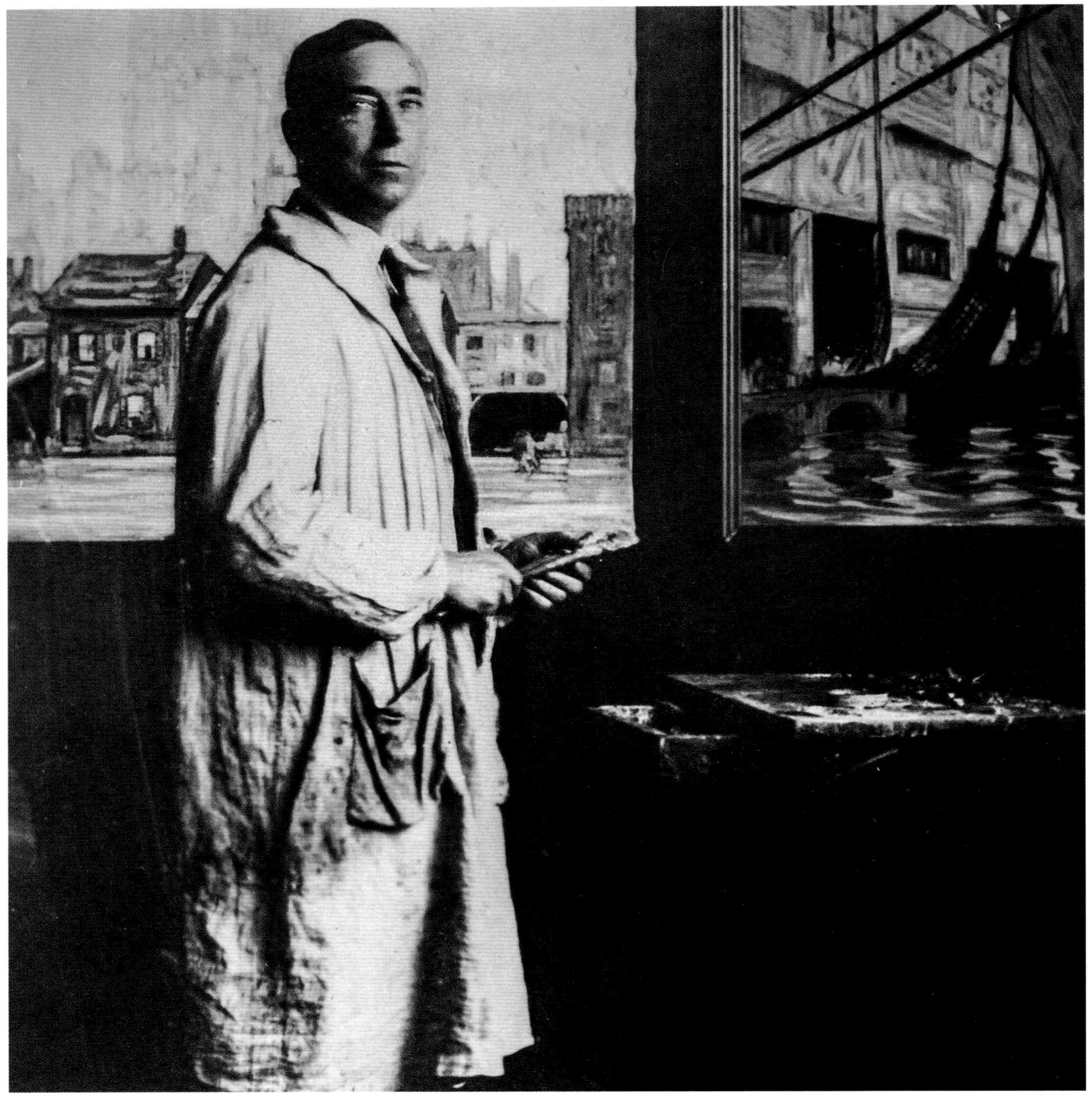

Sheppard at work in his Toronto studio, with paintings in the background: *Three Old Houses, Louisa Street* (left) and *Sea Port/Ocean Freighter* (right), c. 1929–30.

Foreword

A new verse is about to be written into the narrative of Canada's visual art history and it is unveiled here for the first time in the text and images that follow. It is timely, too, befitting Canada's recent sesquicentennial celebration and the consequent re-examination of our history, culture, and identity.

The Victorian art and social critic John Ruskin wrote that one of the three autobiographies of a great nation, indeed, the most important, is the book of its art. Surely a proud and dynamic country such as ours has more to offer in the way of its pictorial history than the oft-repeated account of the belauded Group of Seven. There *were* others, such as Peter Clapham Sheppard, who also belonged to that first generation of modernist artists who, together, established a nationalistic art movement that emerged with our nation's identity: itself forged out of the crucible of the First World War. Many deserving men and women of that epoch slipped through those cracks of history into which destinies are often obscured or forever lost — an injustice made worse by the near impossibility now of gathering a critical mass of their artworks for the purpose of survey, scholarship, and public appreciation.

But a separate fate played out for Peter Clapham Sheppard as the reader shall see and read here.

Spanning an historic century of tumult, waste, and loss and through the confluence of three lives, a rich trove of his artistic output is preserved for us. This collection is, quite possibly, the last best kept secret in historical Canadian art and provides an alternative visual time capsule of our past. For these reasons precisely, Sheppard is uniquely positioned at this moment in our cultural history: now, more than ever, is it important to further define and advance the story of Canadian art outside of the Group of Seven. This book, therefore, is both an unveiling of and a homecoming for a deserving homegrown talent whose time has rightfully returned.

P.C. Sheppard is not, and never was, a follower of the prevailing Group of Seven, as is the judgment summarily imposed on so many Canadian artists ever since; nor should he be cast as a subtenant in the culture. His is a soon-to-be rediscovered legacy, that of a Canadian modernist in the early 20th century utilizing the same creative ambition and stylistic tools, as did his famous friends, but in a direction different from that of the landscape-driven group.

Sheppard's powerful works come alive as images of the city, raw and authentic, peopled by those whose lives were tied to it. His prodigious output presents rich groundwork from which new discussions will be generated. This book now provides that opportunity.

Of particular interest to today's art lovers, curators, and scholars are Sheppard's captivating depictions of Toronto, New York, and Montreal; namely, *Arrival of the Circus* (Toronto, 1919); *The Waterfront* (New York City, 1922); *Lower New York* (1922); *The Tramp* (New York City, 1921); *The Cabstand, Montreal, Dominion Square* (1926); *The Market, November* (Montreal, 1929); *The Bloor Street Viaduct* (Toronto, 1915), along with many others. This latter picture is described by author Tom Smart as a "national treasure." Bravura impressionist paintings such as *The Engine Home* (1919) are unmatched in the visual lexicon of Canadian art. *Early Snow, Montreal* (1925) was one of a select group of paintings that proudly represented Canada at the Wembley and Paris exhibitions during the 1920s.

Artworks such as these, as well as the formidable works by Sheppard in the collections of the National Gallery of Canada and the Art Gallery of Ontario, are destined for the Canadian visual canon. The artist should now be celebrated as one of our very best.

A well-deserved and exciting future awaits him and it is my ardent belief that the journey will be launched with this foundational and critical biography of the artist presently before you.

— Louis Gagliardi, MSEd
Curator of the Peter Clapham Sheppard Collection

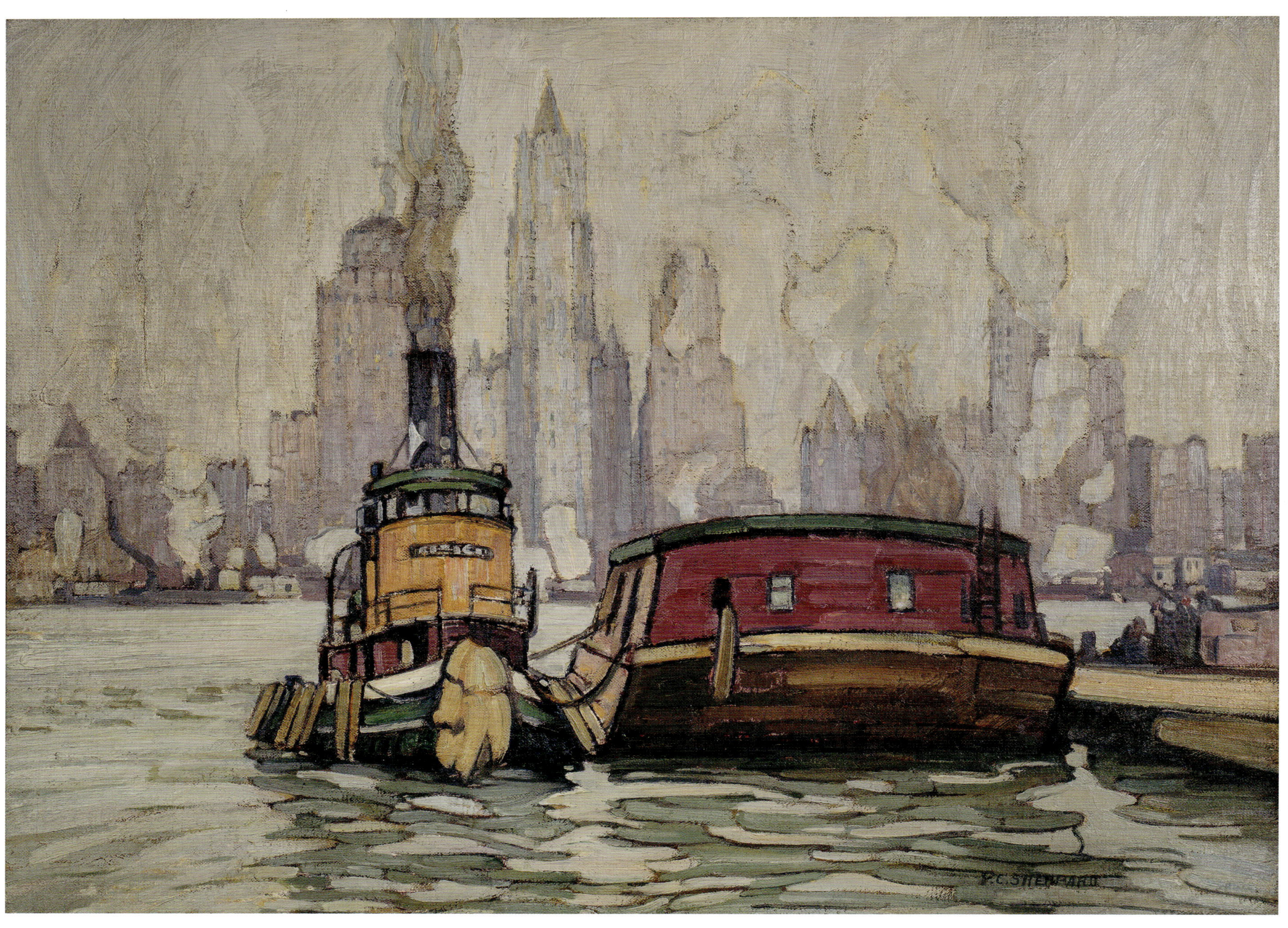

The Waterfront, New York City.
1922. Oil on canvas,
89 x 122 cm.

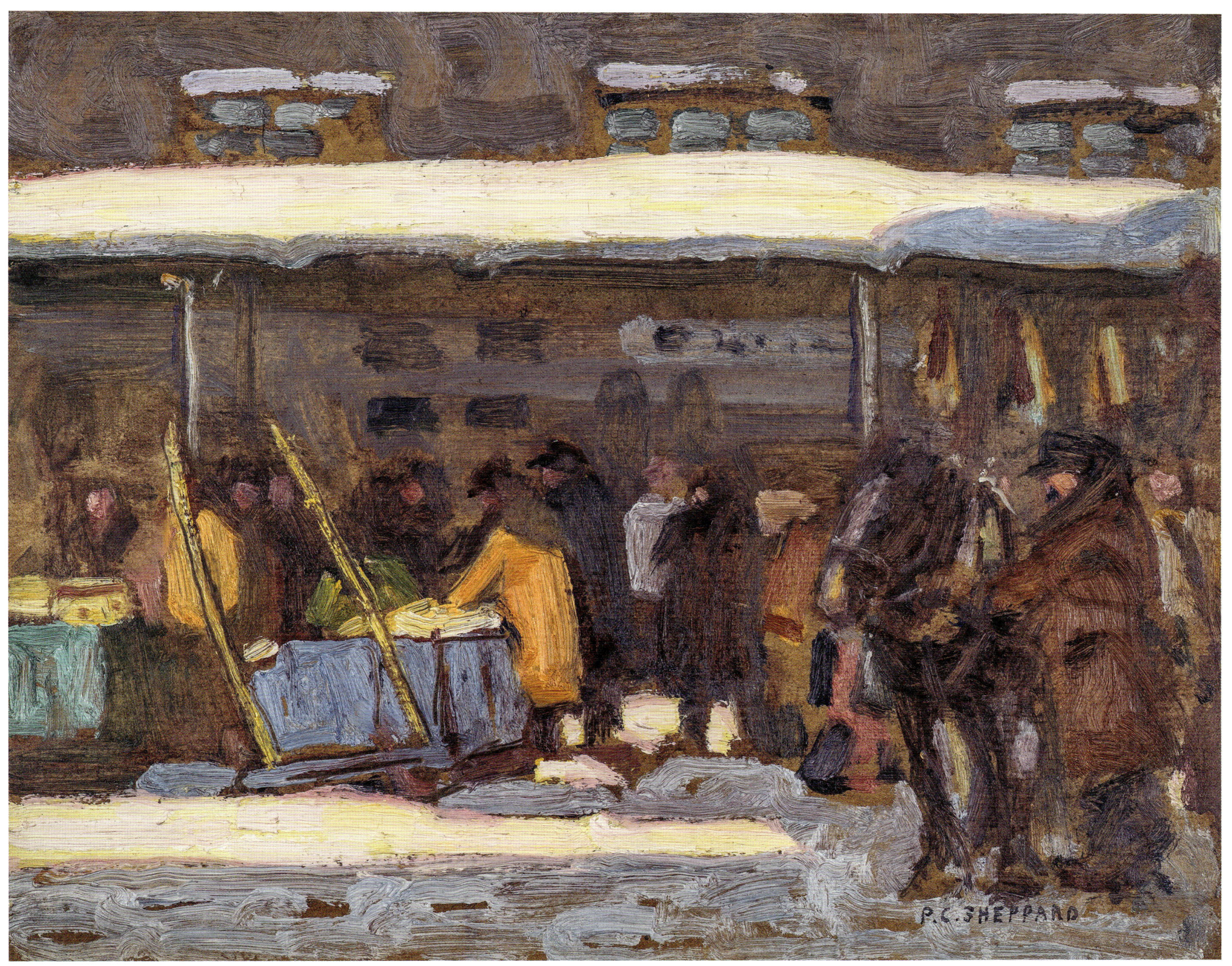

Market, Montreal.
1926. Oil on panel,
21.6 x 26.7 cm.

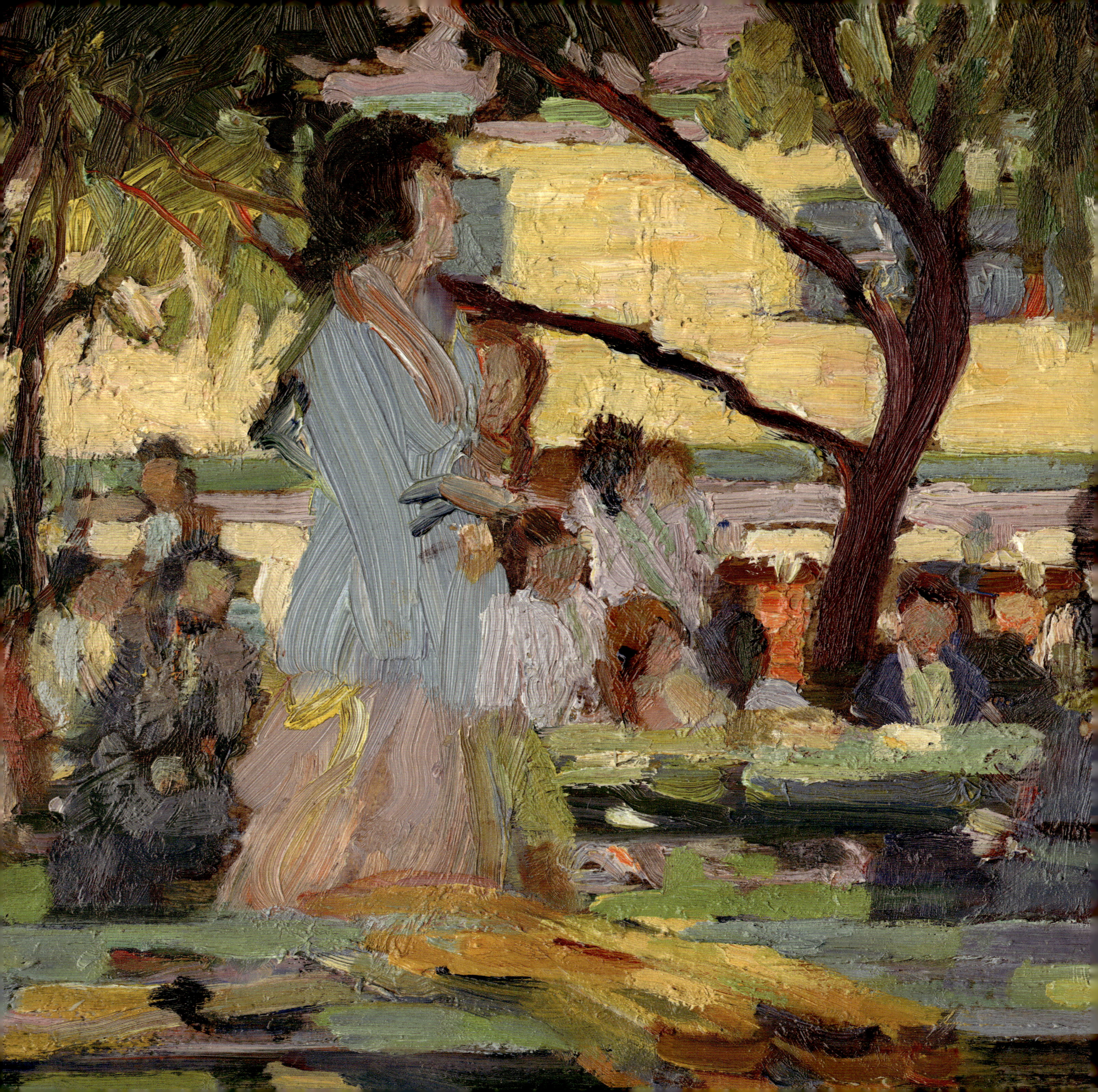

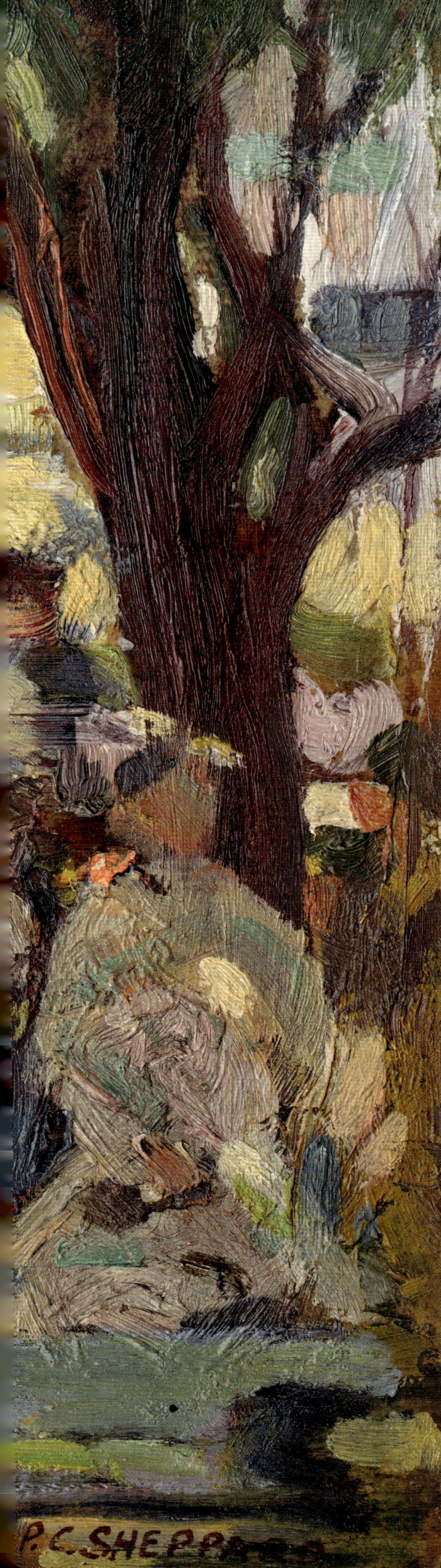

The Promenade.
1919. Oil on panel,
21.6 x 26.7 cm.

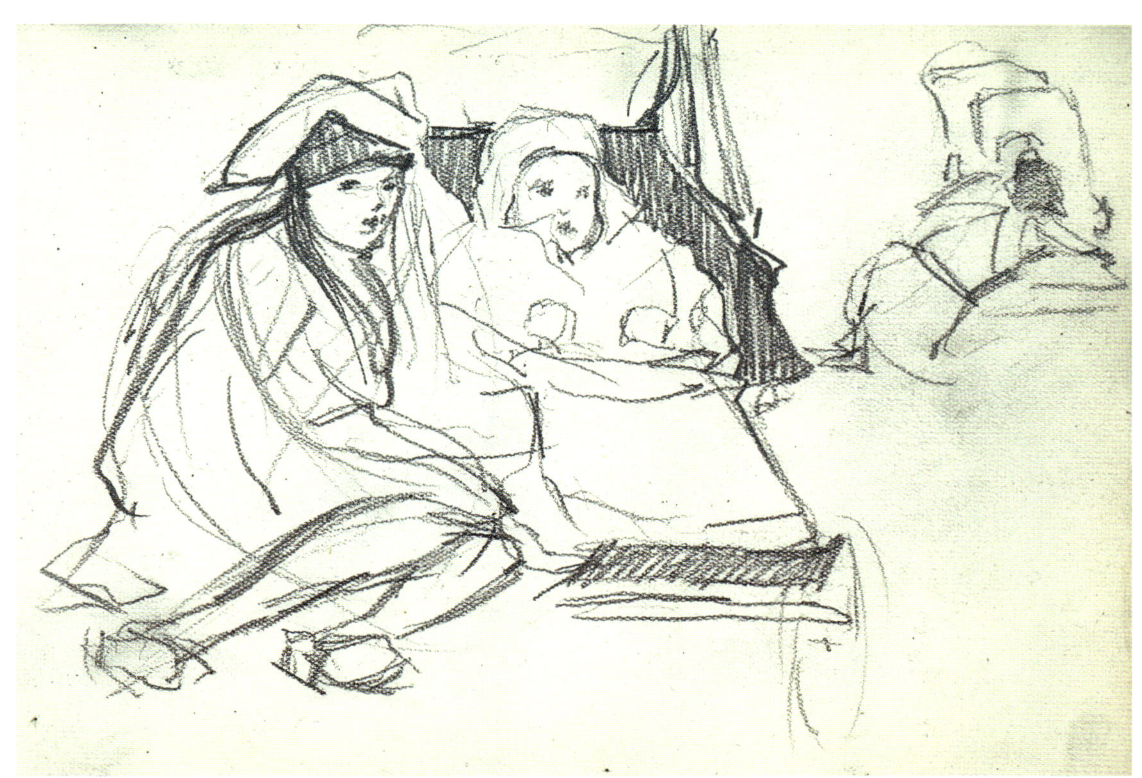

Figure with Child in Pram.
c. 1916. Graphite on paper,
22.2 x 14 cm.

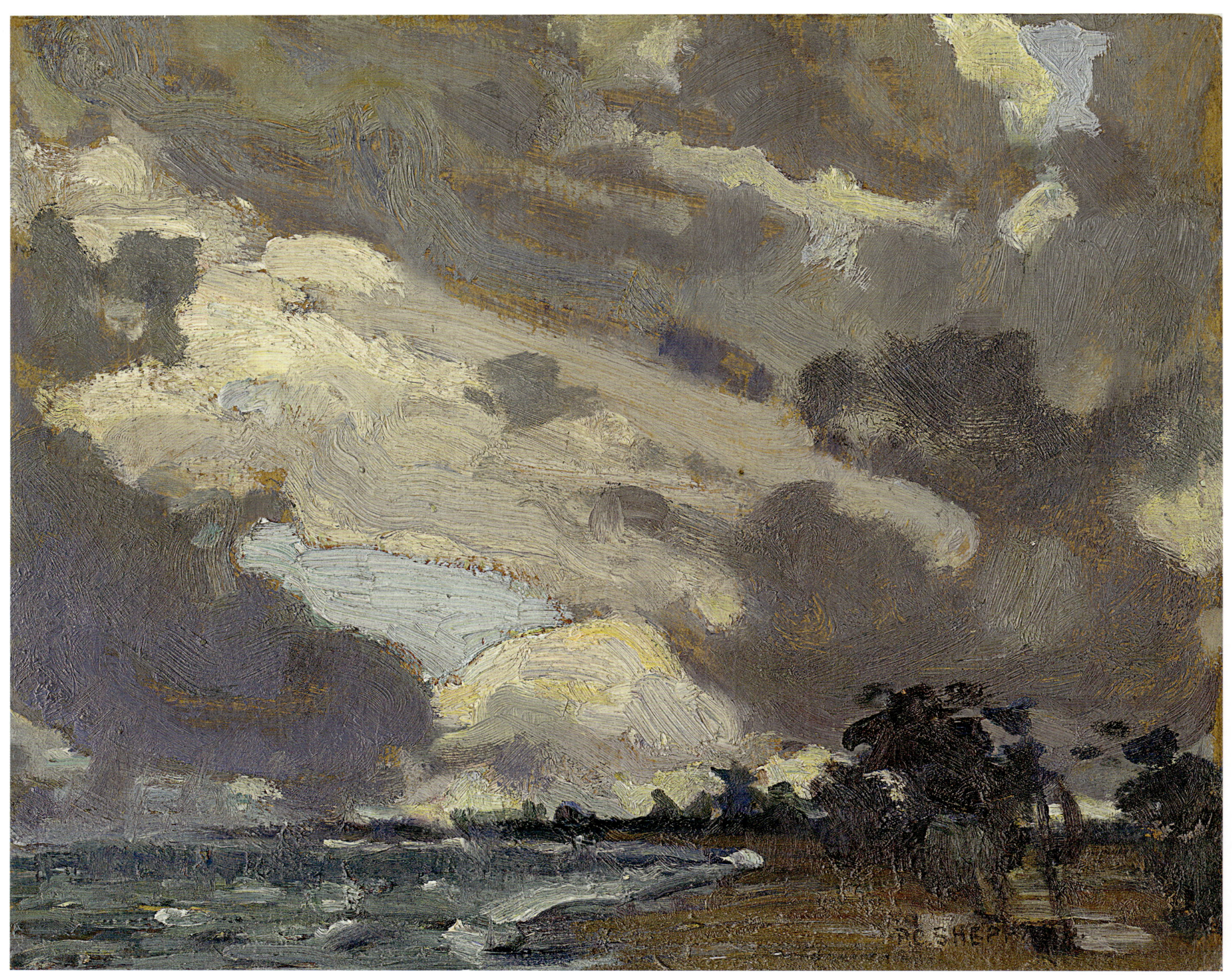

Cloudscape.
1934. Oil on board,
21.6 x 26.7 cm.

Introduction

INVISIBILITY

You can easily vanish into the wilderness. Trees, rocks and lakes might turn immediately from picturesque elements of a benign landscape into threats, even monsters that could swallow you whole, making you disappear. A frightful myth of carnivorous land is part of the foundation of Canada's national identity. This story is told with a cast of diverse characters ranging from ghosts to heroic artists who meet mysterious deaths on inland lakes. Other versions of the narrative extol the virtues of being absorbed into wilderness forests and lakes, the better to channel the energies of the wilderness that animate them and us and, often, to represent them in paint. The common thread of the myths is that there is much to learn from a seemingly inscrutable nature. The journey of discovery, while risky, has its rewards. You might be exposed to awe-inspiring vistas, be confronted with deeply embedded fears and phobias, be made to feel puny and insignificant, or perhaps even be exalted when apparently cast into the presence of divinity. Nature teaches lessons in many different ways and by means of a variety of languages. However, its classroom is ridden with perils, the worst being death if you fail some of its tests.

The bush has claimed many a Canadian artist. As creative muse, it has cast a spell on generations who found in representing and interpreting it potent means of self-expression and collective identity. Paintings, resulting from artists' creative encounters, have stood for many things. National identity is likely at the top of the list. Our Group of Seven, along with Emily Carr and their acolytes, constitute an acute phenomenon in 20th-century painting, especially in the art made before mid-century: symbols of identity that continually transmute and morph as the decades go by. Even today, the work of these artists and that of others who fell under their spell has a mystifying hold over the national imagination.

The strength of the enchantments of the Group of Seven and their associates has had its disadvantages, too, because from their art a kind of unintended orthodoxy emerged. As stylistic mavericks, they brought to the Canadian imagination European modernist approaches to painting, which they conscripted to interpreting the nature of Canada. The success of their project has been proven in its durability and meaningfulness across the century and down to the present. But an unintended consequence of their longevity and continual reinvention is that other artists have gone unnoticed. So powerful is the brilliance radiating from *their* work that many other artists are either in their shadow or rendered formless next to their incandescence. In effect they are invisible.

It is too easy to say that this invisibility is due to the lesser quality of their art. The work is seen as lacking the properties that propelled their contemporaries' art to prominence. To a modest extent this may well be true. As orthodoxies go, though, there is also an element of exclusionism that has kept an agreed-upon canon pure and undiluted: an unfair turn of events for artists who, although accomplished in their own right, found themselves overlooked and their painted expressions cast as unimportant. In essence, they became unseen, shunted to the side by the forces that conspired against them. The reasons for invisibility are actually complex and varied. The fact remains that those who worked in the penumbra of current trends and public taste or who were relegated there by tastemakers and trendsetters, through no fault of their own, and not through the quality of their art, drifted from public consciousness and were forgotten.

This phenomenon describes the fate of Canadian Peter Clapham Sheppard, a lifelong professional figurative artist and urban and landscape painter. He was a contemporary of the members of the Group of Seven and may well even have been a friend of Tom Thomson. His career path traced the same trajectory as theirs in a formative time — a time when an ambitious artist could balance the needs and requirements of so-called commercial art with a fine art practice in order to make a career and a living. Sheppard adapted some of the most up-to-date modes, conventions and idioms in his work, and at the same time made use of his training in a centuries-old curriculum of art instruction based on drawing and painting from the human figure. His was a life and art that continually oscillated between the modern and the historical, between creative risk-taking and

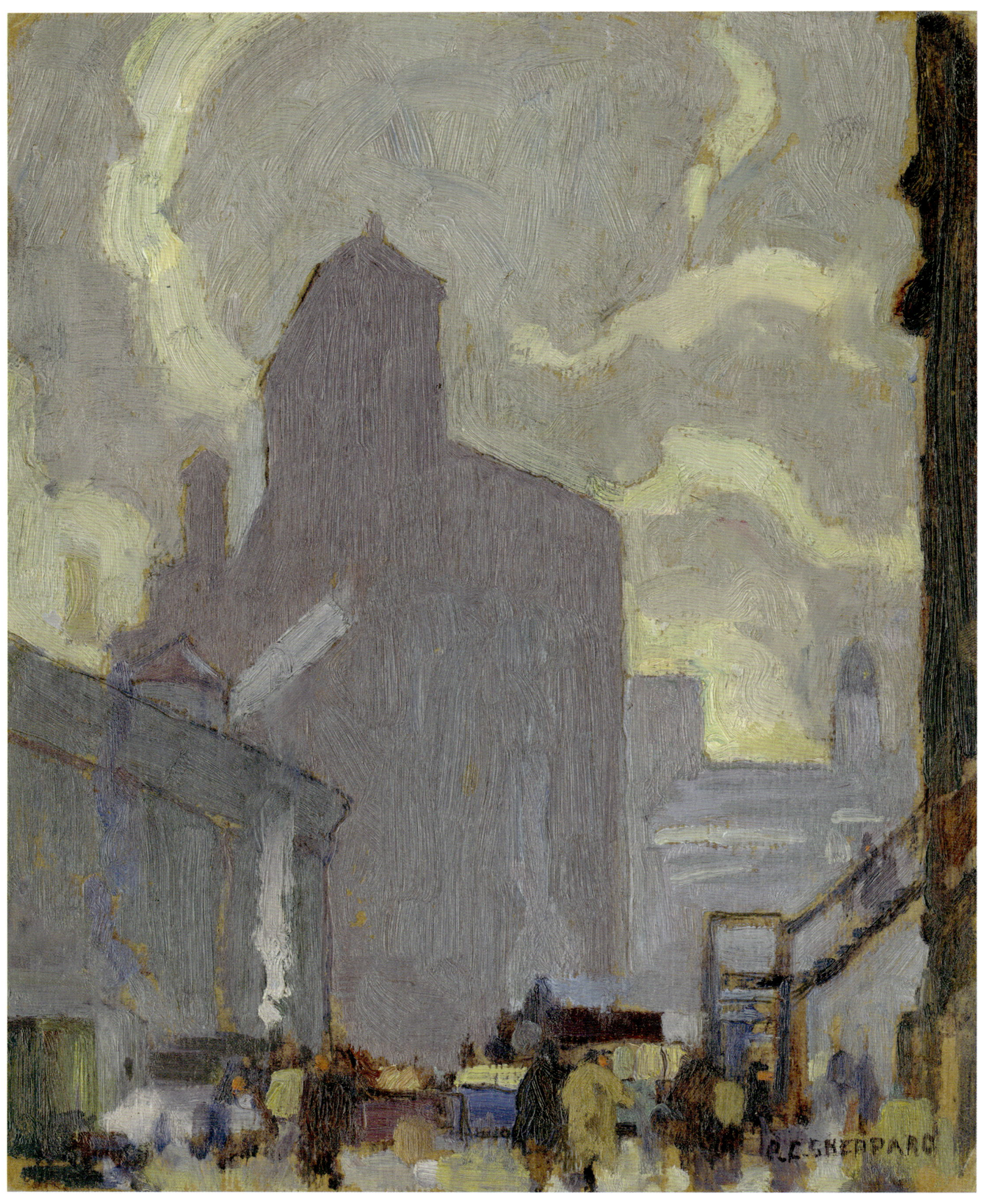

Construction.
1916. Oil on panel,
26.7 x 21.6 cm.

working within the clearly defined parameters of convention. A journeyman lithographer and a curious chronicler of daily life in and around the parks, avenues and dockyards of Toronto, Montreal and New York City, Sheppard had one eye on the past and the other on the future, which he interpreted as industrial growth; he expressed this artistically.

In the years since his death in 1965, traces of Sheppard and his work have grown ever more faint, receding from the public eye, gradually fading from the memories of all but a few close friends. The closest was one of his former young students, a painting companion and friend, Bernice Fenwick Martin, who gathered up and preserved his studio contents and became their curator after he passed away. Largely due to her efforts and those of Louis Gagliardi, an educator and passionate arts patron who assumed control of the Sheppard archive from Bernice, this legacy has been preserved. The works of art in the archive — predominantly paintings and drawings — along with a modest collection of historical documents, letters, postcards and other fragments constitute a record of this creative life.

Yet by no means is this archive comprehensive or complete. There are no diaries, no volumes of correspondence, and very few published secondary sources. With no biographies and no autobiography, the only comprehensive record of Sheppard's life is his art — a potentially rich primary source, unconventional, eloquent and mute at the same time. It traces the life of a mind and imagination expressed as art, but it is silent on motivations, influences, sources, encounters or derivations. At best, it is a circumstantial archive that compels me to trust-fall into the world he defined through art and plumb its depths for clues about the man. I want to draw him back to visibility, to conjure him whole from the fragmentary evidence of his art.

Sheppard first came to my attention when Louis walked into my office at the McMichael Canadian Art Collection in 2006 and showed me a photographic album of this artist's work. Until then I had not heard of Sheppard. Louis' visit was intended to introduce me to an early Canadian painter and contemporary of many members of the Group of Seven who may well have suffered the professional fate of working in the shadow that they cast during their lives and after their deaths.

Louis showed me the substantial collection of the artist's works of art he had acquired from Bernice. This body of work provides a portrait of an artist whose practice was a part of his times. Louis indicated strongly that his wish was to lay a foundation for future art history studies that would be more inclusive and more fully representative of the times in which Sheppard worked as a professional artist.

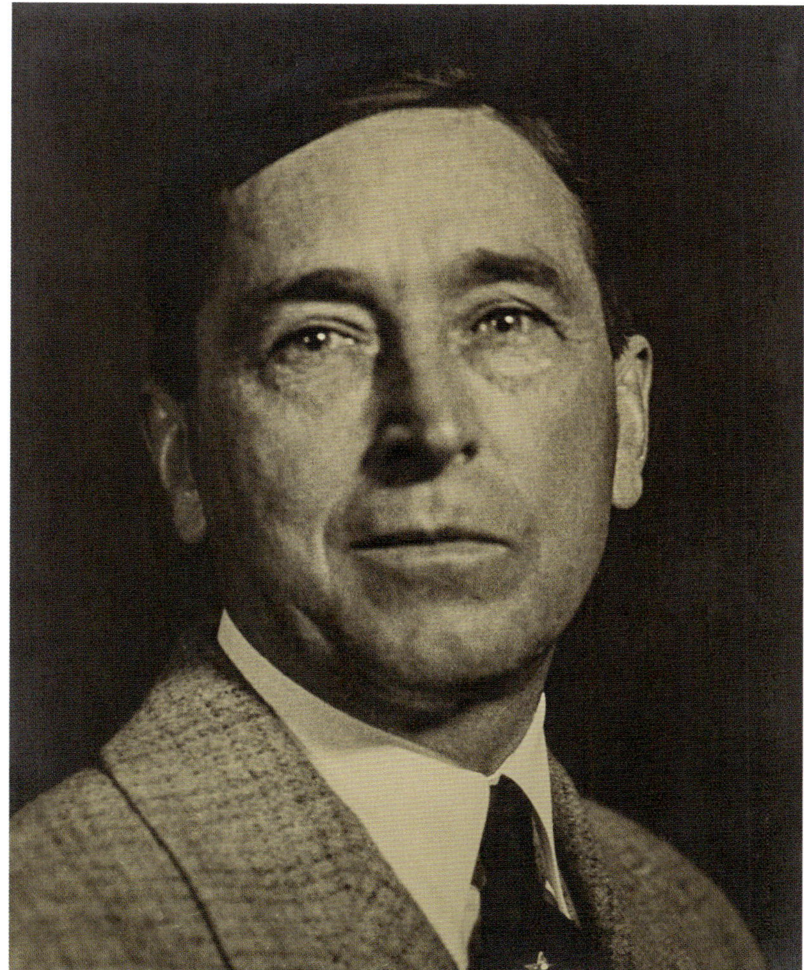

Peter Clapham Sheppard, 1930.

To an eye seeing Sheppard's art for the first time, more than a century after it was made, its magic, much like that of the work of his contemporaries, is its unmistakable immediacy. It gives the illusion that its author has captured the moment and arrested it until curious eyes reanimate the pages or panels, causing the images to spring to life uncannily. The effect of immediacy also creates a sense of intimacy, not only with the times portrayed (now long past), but also with the artist who set them down. The lively sketched lines or expressive brushstrokes are windows into the mind and thoughts of this obscured artist. Their apparent immediacy gives the attentive viewer a sense of privileged access across the decades to the personality of the artist himself.

My intimation is that Sheppard saw himself as a viewer — an observer on the sidelines — of his society and also as its chronicler. The description of a gang of men building a viaduct's gigantic pier, a depiction of the arrival of a circus troupe, or the painted study of a woman sitting contemplatively on a park bench: these all give evidence of someone who was comfortable in the role of watcher. He described what he saw without a heavy-handed interpretive gloss, turning what he viewed into an emblem of a time or a

visual poem. It is this quality that gives his work its timeless dynamism. I felt an instant connection with the artist even though a century of upheaval separated us.

In the succeeding decade, that initial, highly charged sense of connection has persisted. This is due entirely to the energy that emanates from the art itself. What I know of Sheppard is almost entirely the result of what I see in the art and decipher from its arcane, at times hermetic visual language, whose grammar is line and tone, light and mass, texture and space, colour and form. I studied the many paintings and drawings during several successive visits to the Sheppard archive. These were always times of unrushed study accompanied by commentary and conversations that Louis and I had over the works of art.

A portrait study on a wooden panel would elicit a sense of astonishment at the vividness of the palette, the energy of the brushstrokes and the vivacity with which the model has been rendered. Leafing through one of the dozens of sketchbooks would stimulate thoughts on the kind of training Sheppard must have received and the debt he surely owed one or another of his teachers. Or the quick studies would serve as remarkable time capsules that, as if by magic, reincarnated the souls he had clandestinely sketched as they sat pensively in a park, looked out over the lakeshore or went about their business, oblivious to the man on the periphery with a sketchbook and a keen eye capturing them for eyes such as mine looking down at these pages a century later.

The larger paintings on canvas or board give wider fields for Sheppard to display his talents and imagination as he interpreted the evidence of rapid industrial and social growth expressed in ambitious infrastructure projects, or in the bustling activity of the ports. What the evidence of the art reveals in the several hundreds of paintings, oil sketches and drawings that are preserved in the archive, is that Sheppard identified deeply with the urban centres of Toronto, Montreal and New York City; with their people, with the environments around them and with the expansiveness of economic ambitions. These are his subjects. It is as if he were telling the viewer that in some manner each and every subject he put his mind and brush to was emblematic of his rich imagination and of his absolute identification with the society he lived in. In his subjects he is visible.

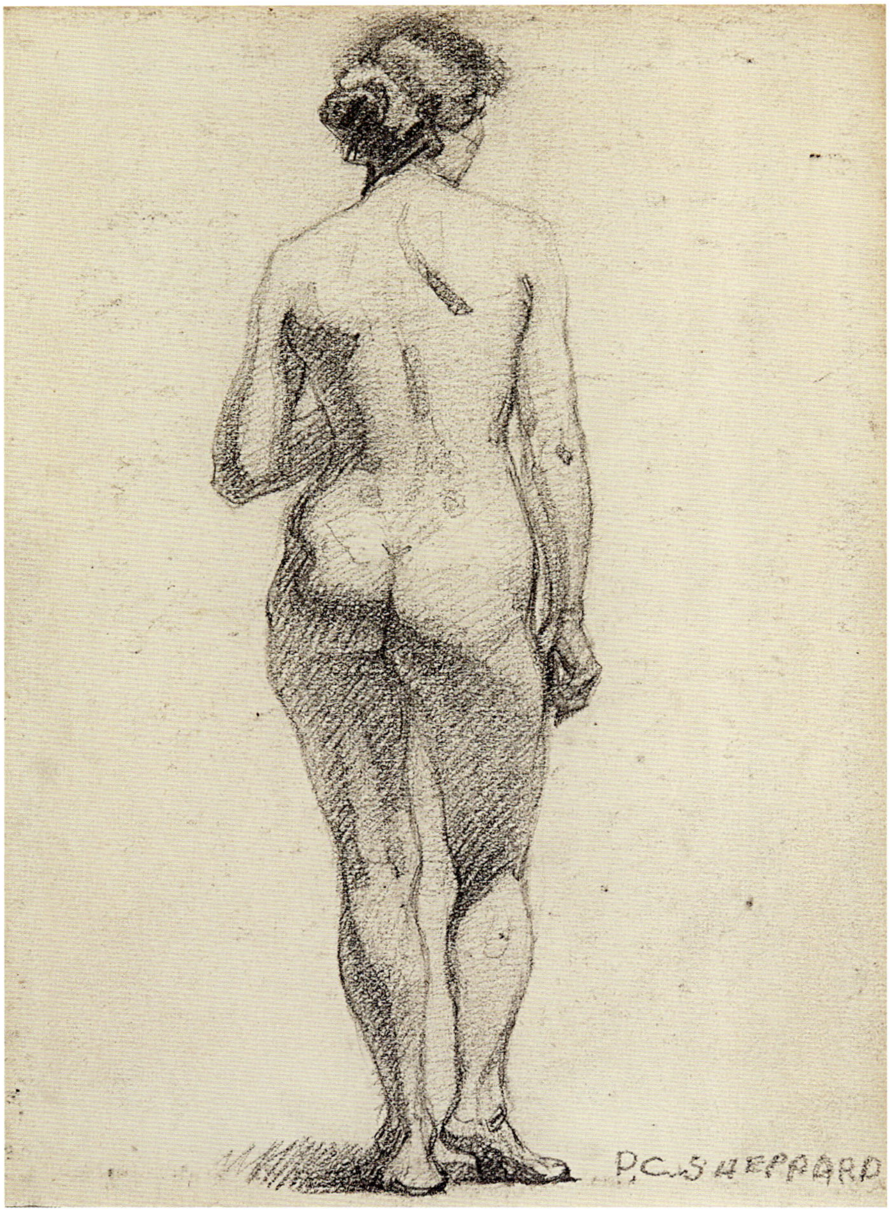

Study from Life.
1912. Pencil,
12.7 x 9 cm.

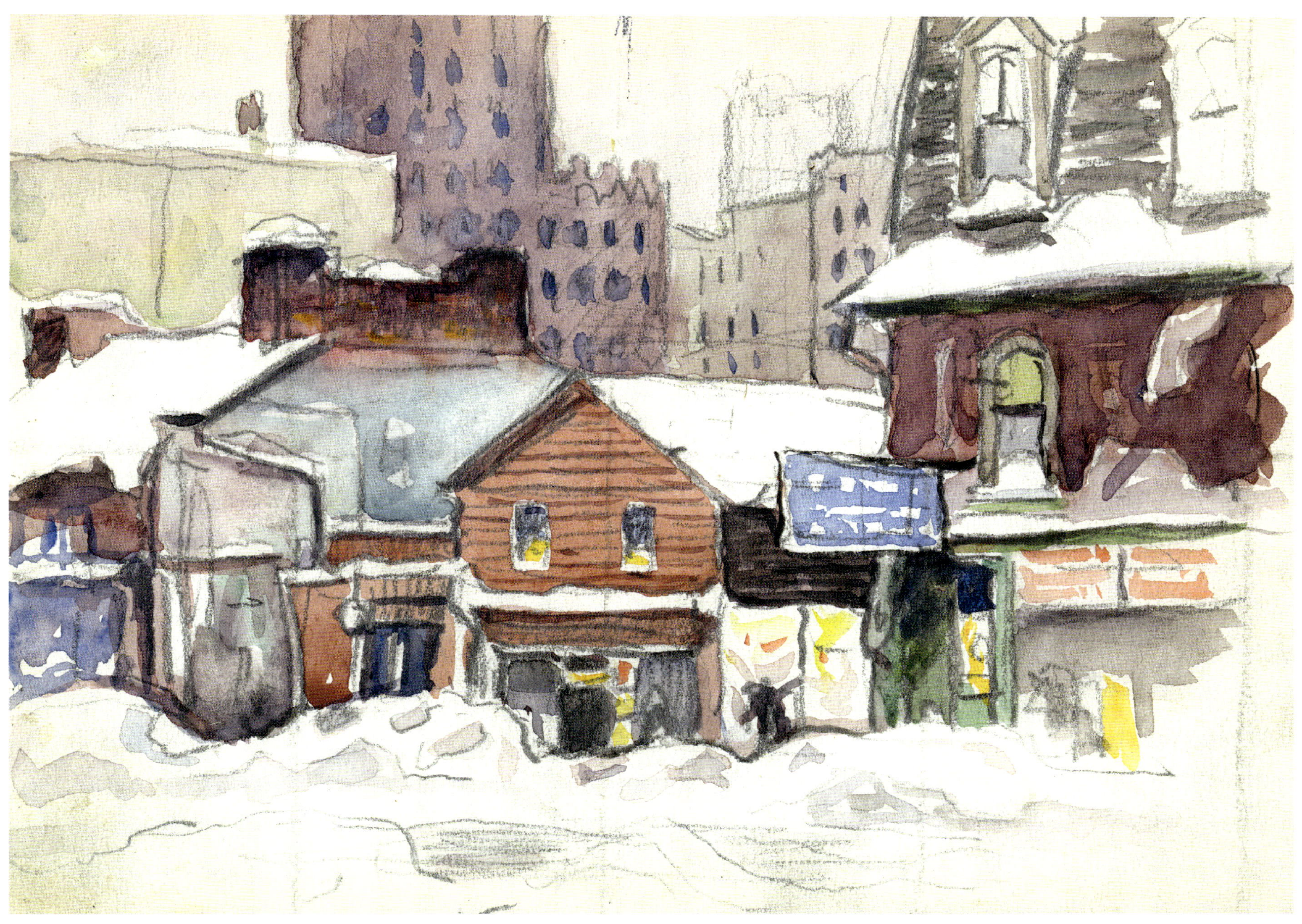

The Ward.
1930–31. Watercolour,
12.7 x 17.8 cm.

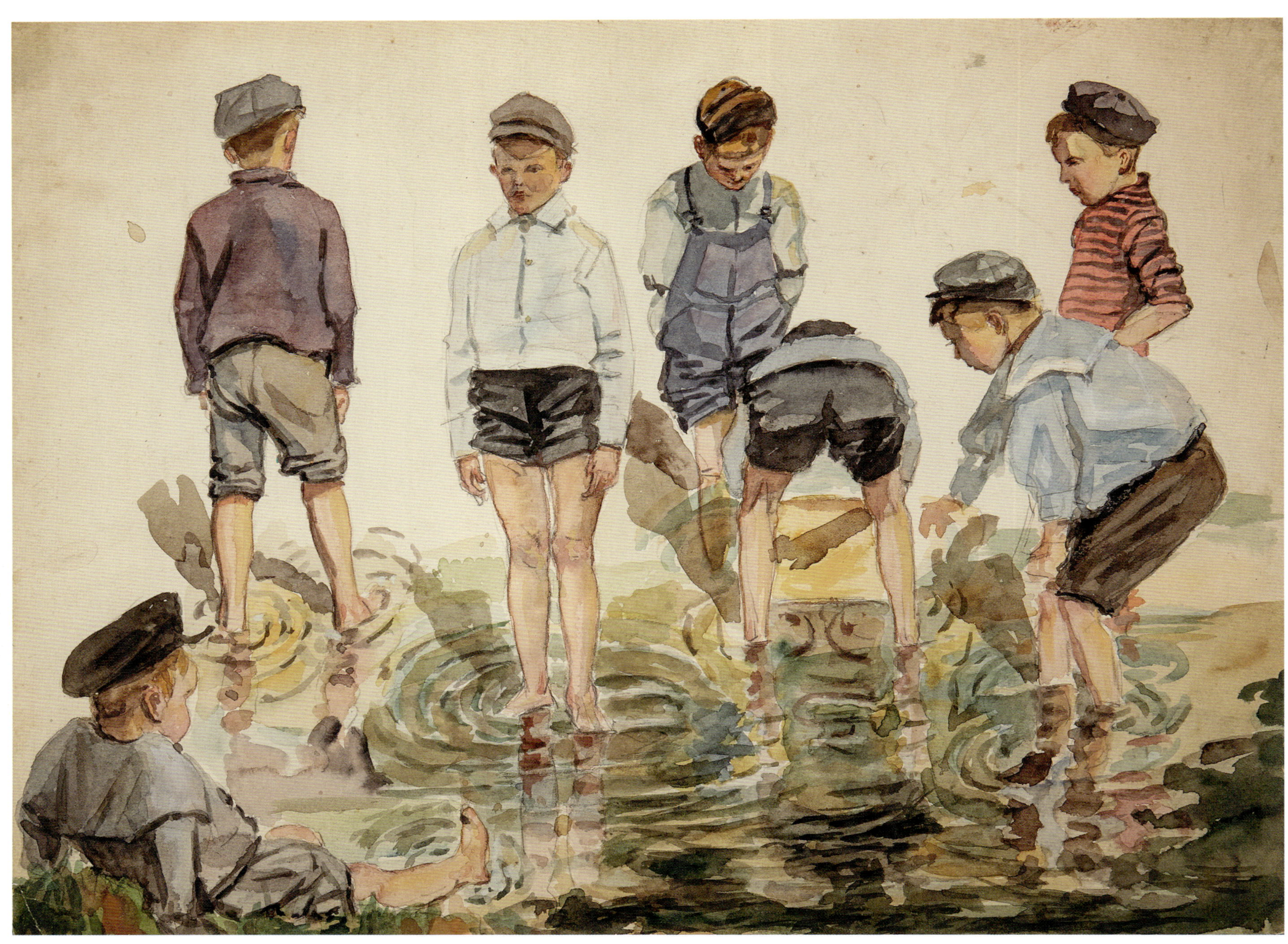

Boys by a Pond.
c. 1900. Watercolour,
25 x 33.7 cm.

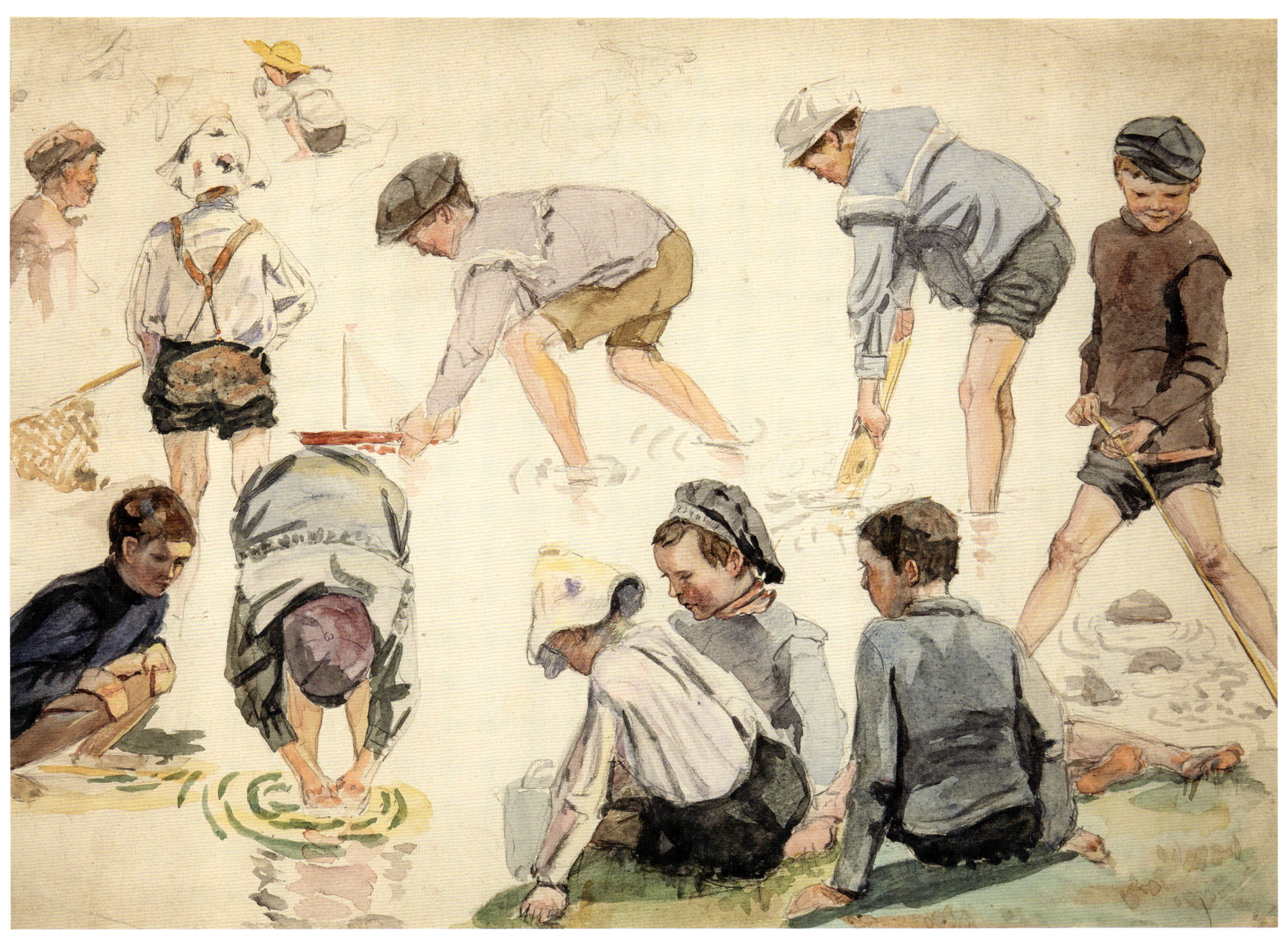

Boys Playing.
c. 1900. Watercolour,
25 x 33.7 cm.

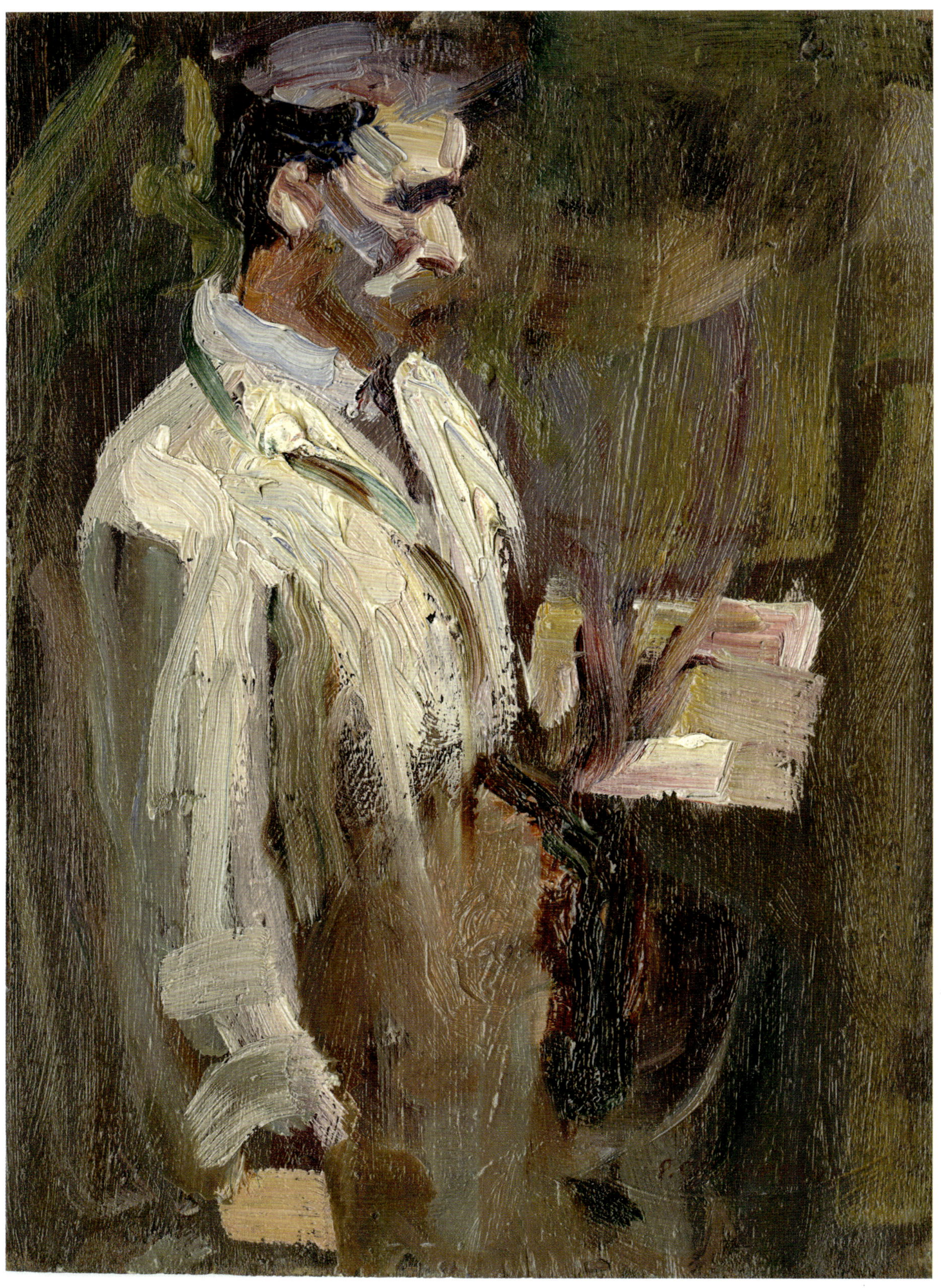

The Artist.
c. 1910–12. Oil on panel,
22.2 x 15.9 cm.

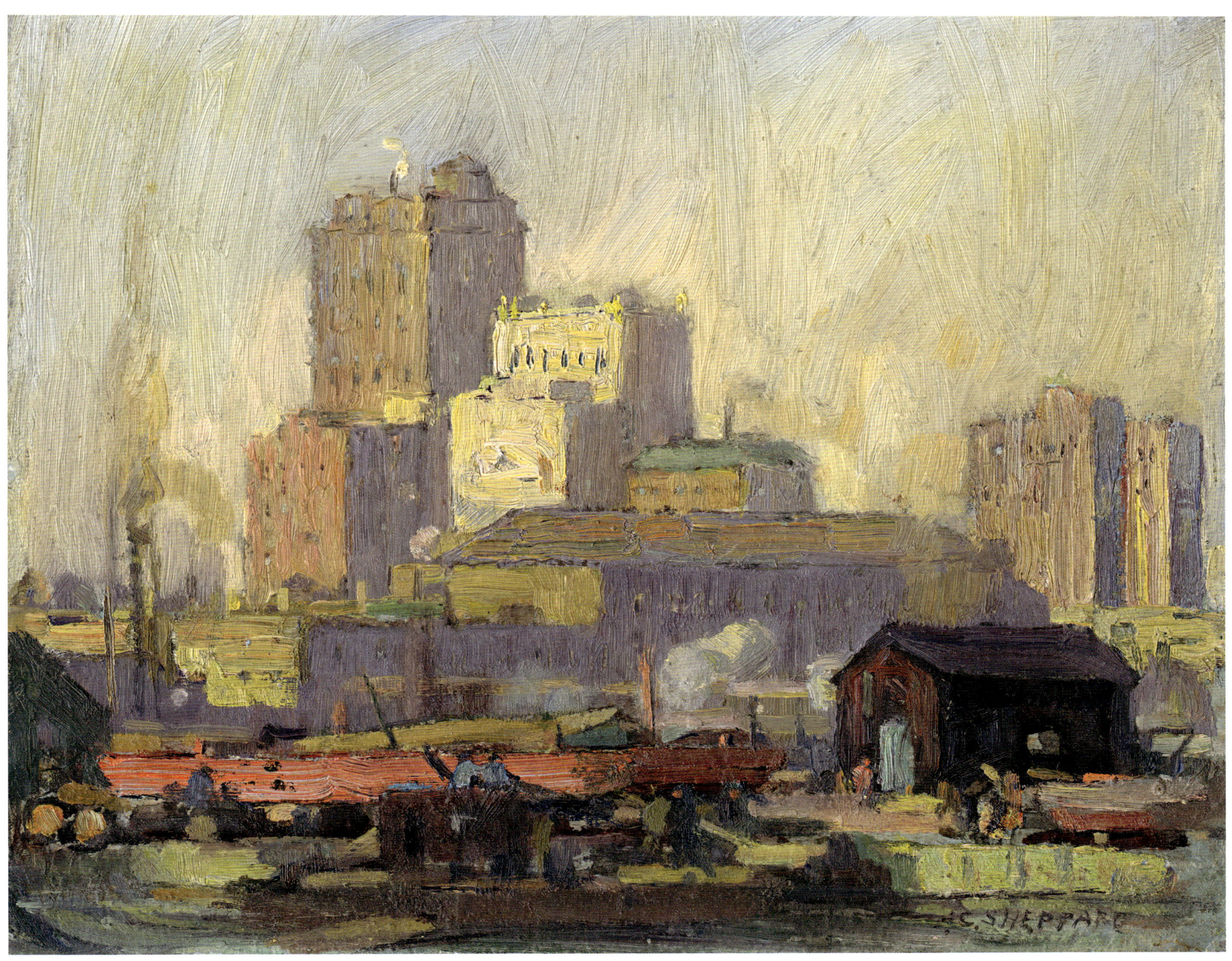

The City.
c. 1925. Oil on panel,
21.6 x 26.7 cm.

The Engine Home (detail).
1919. Oil on canvas,
84 x 91.4 cm.

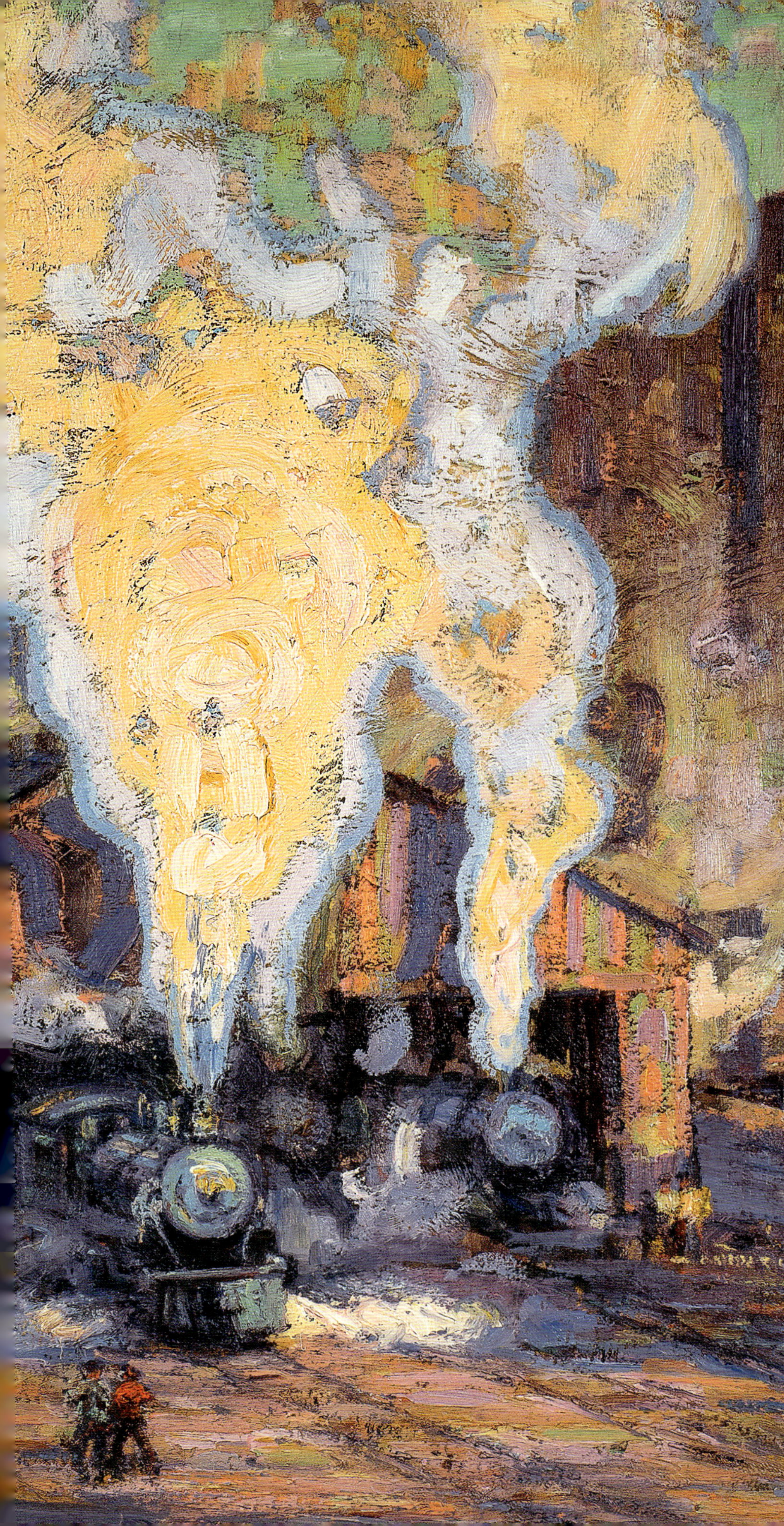

CHAPTER ONE

Beginnings

Commercial Artwork

AN ELUSIVE PORTRAIT

A very brief biography remains among Sheppard's papers. Compiled by Bernice, it provides little factual information. Nevertheless, the sketch suggests a narrative arc to Sheppard's life: "He served his apprenticeship in lithography," we are told by Bernice, "while still a young boy, with the predecessors of Rolph, Clark, Stone Ltd., and became one of the best commercial lithographers in Canada …"[1] Yet, Bernice felt that even the phrase describing commercial endeavours needed a qualifier attached to it because she offers that he worked as a commercial artist, "only as a means of livelihood, as he was wholly dedicated to fine art, scorning the commercial and paint[ing] the subjects he loved most, constantly seeking to express the unusual in strong, vigorous patterns of singing color and bold design."

Brief as it is, Bernice's sketch has laid the foundation for this book by noting an arc and a focus for his biography. Sheppard was formed artistically in the realm of commercial arts associated with the printing industry, which gave him opportunities to develop his innate talents and hone his craft. A college education in art offered opportunities in the emerging context of fine arts in Toronto and in the professional societies that were established to support artists early in the 20th century. A growing confidence, fuelled by critical recognition, prompted Sheppard to travel to New York City and Montreal, where he stretched himself creatively and defined an artistic path that sustained him to his retirement.

Sheppard's life's story was also propelled by the dynamic tension between "commercial" and "fine" arts. Straddling both channels of the art world in Canada in order to make it as a successful fine artist in the early 20th century, Sheppard (like so many of his peers) had to find ways to reconcile personal expression with commerce. The general assumption was that the two branches never touched — that you would be hard pressed to find the ingredients of "fine" expression in work made for the trades, and that commercial success was unlikely to be found in works of creative expression. "Commercial" art was never "infected" with the values of aesthetics, form and poetry that characterized expressions of the soul. Sheppard, Bernice tells us, was perhaps better than most of his peers when it came to working at high levels of performance in both spheres, and he was equally successful at keeping the two worlds distinct, at arm's length from each other.

"He worked tirelessly seven days a week and many evenings," Bernice boasts, "creating many important gallery canvases in his studio and sketching outdoors, which he loved, and was a kin with all of nature." She adds: "His creed was to observe and paint the world around him, without becoming a participator in the passing scene. He believed artists should be … apart, and not let themselves become involved with things which tend to distract from their creative work."

Little is said yet much is inferred in this compact statement, the hallmark of an approach to painting that was sorely tested in the early decades of the 20th century, exactly when Sheppard was plying his trade and expressing his soul. Bernice reveals that Sheppard was an aesthetic purist, that he obeyed the laws of art. His fealty was to the work of art, to its inner necessities and to the elements of its making. Colour, light, line, texture, composition, balance: all the formal elements of pictorialism and the conventions that surround them were where Sheppard's loyalty lay. The fine arts had a code of best practices, and Sheppard, Bernice implies, worked within its parameters with integrity and diligence.

Unfortunately, the context in which he and an entire cohort worked was changing, frequently in disruptive ways that left the notions of pictorialism's integrity in shards. Unmoored from the values that had formed him as an artist, Sheppard found refuge in the pure pursuit of painting scenes. As Bernice reminds us, an observer "of the world around him who did not let [himself] become involved with those things that tend to distract from their creative work," Sheppard clung to a notion of professional integrity that became an artifact even while he was still alive. Sheppard, Bernice perhaps unintentionally admits, became a victim of art that was self-expressive, self-referential, representational and uninterested in forces that lay outside the boundaries at the edges of the frames. Sheppard did not engage with his subjects, as modernism demanded of its artists. He steadfastly maintained a posture of objective and passive *disengagement* with the world and his subjects. He applied a conventional orderliness to the chaos of nature and the unruliness of the urban maelstrom in front of his easel and to the ideas that swirled around the academic principles to which he clung.

Laudatory, affectionate and maybe even a tad bitter in tone, although direct and short, Bernice's description has a truth to it. This written statement constitutes the longest encapsulation of Sheppard's life that has come down to us. Yet as honest as Bernice's eulogy may be, I would like to tease out the biases it betrays. The rest is silence; there are no other written accounts of Sheppard's life. There is virtually nothing else to provide more knowledge to a researcher hoping to construct a coherent and complete biography of this artist.

The artworks are the only primary sources that can be consulted in the search for this man. The secondary sources — exhibition catalogues in which his work is mentioned or illustrated, newspaper reviews, listings in the *City of Toronto Directory* and scant mentions in the literature of the time — contribute a few details such as addresses and job records, and they add some context for appreciating the man's accomplishments, but really all we have with which to form an impression of Sheppard's life is what can be translated from the artwork itself. The foundations of this biography are built on what can be deciphered from the evidence of his art and supported by the clues in the circumstantial, contextual and secondary sources that, although perhaps unreliable, do help to frame a narrative that is as close as we can get to the truth.

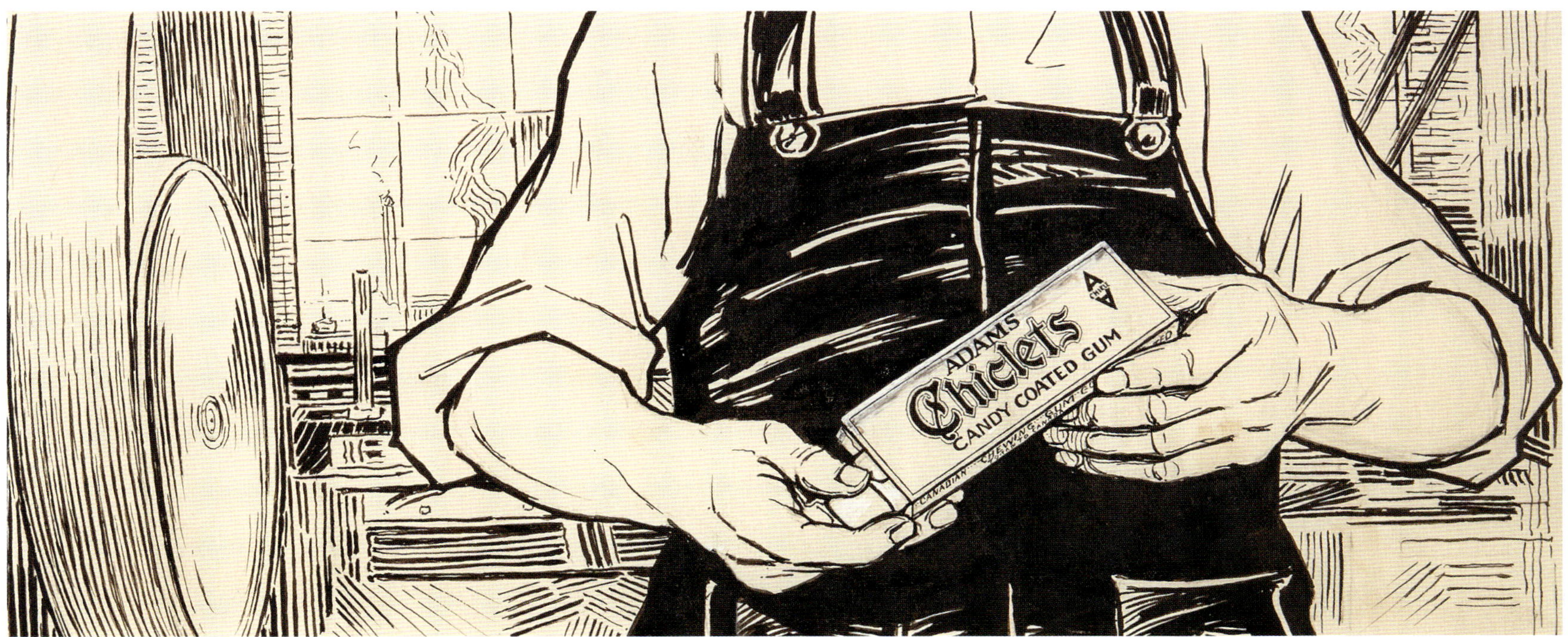

Chiclets Advertisement.
c. 1900. Ink drawing,
11.4 x 26 cm.

TRANSITION IN CANADIAN ART FROM "OLD SIMPLICITY" TO "MODERN EFFICIENCY"

In 1947, writing on the occasion of the 75th anniversary of the Ontario Society of Artists, its venerable president, landscape painter, graphic designer and teacher L.A.C. Panton (1894–1954), claimed that in 1872 (a mere seven years before Sheppard was born), when the OSA was established, "Canada … proved very barren soil in which to plant the tender roots of a native art." "The eighteen seventies," he went on, "were a decade in which Canadian life and ideas were undergoing a subtle yet profound change." In his view, the "culture of the cabin was giving way to the culture of the college." A new, young, dynamic generation was emerging from the few colleges in Upper Canada, and they felt the stirrings of "an ambition to fulfill their destiny as a nation, great in mind and spirit as well as in geographical extent." In short, Panton saw this generation as "awakening to the realization of their own potentialities as the builders of a new and nobler life. Hope and expectation were in the air." And this air was purified by the changes that marked the times as the pioneers passed on the legacy of Confederation to the next generation. It was a time of transformation and disruption as the "old simplicity" gave way to "modern efficiency."[2] In broad strokes and in a narrative that was both prosaic and nostalgic, Panton described the Toronto into which Sheppard, a future member of the OSA, was born and grew up. It was a time of expansion and promise for the industrious small town on the banks of Lake Ontario, in an area long regarded as a meeting place for First Nations travelling down the Credit, Humber and Don Rivers to gather as a community in and around the ravines and dunes on the lakeshore. These same hills were mined by settlers for their clay, which was easily fired into the red or yellow bricks that were used to build neat houses in places called "Cabbagetown," "the Ward" and "the Annex," houses built for recent immigrants from England, Scotland, Ireland and countries of central and eastern Europe.

Was it as simple a time as Panton suggests? Likely not. It was a hardscrabble existence in Toronto (also known as "Hogtown") for its Upper Canadian settlers, but also one where industriousness saw rewards in the progress defined by a neat compass-point grid of streets, avenues and alleys that marked the boundaries of wards and townships in the fertile headwaters that penetrated central and southern Ontario. Hard work was a virtue to be cultivated as fully as the farmlands that lay on the town's outskirts — a town that seemed continually to be pushing itself farther and farther north, west and east of the lakeshore.

CONFLICTING DATES OF BIRTH

The facts tell us that Sheppard's father, William (1844–1924), was a brick maker, as was William's father, John. Yet even in birth, the record is elusive because all the official biographies, slim though they may be and consisting of not much more than sheets enumerating accomplishments in an artist file, give Peter Clapham Sheppard's year of birth as 1882[3] or 1881[4]. However, the official registration of his birth declares unequivocally that he came into the world in York, Ontario, on October 21, *1879*, the son of William Sheppard and Jesse Ford (1846–December 26, 1912), who lived at 16 Beverley Street.[5]

Why the discrepancy between the official date of 1879 and the recorded dates (used even by the artist himself) of 1882 and 1881? This is where truth becomes vague, and the portrait not more than a sketch because no explanation appears anywhere in the primary or secondary material that I have been able to reconstitute and consult. All through his life Sheppard created an impression, whether deliberately or not, that he was two or three years younger than he actually was. The question is never satisfactorily answered either in fact or through circumstance. Perhaps Sheppard preferred to create a life — his biography — as a self-authored construction based on a distant

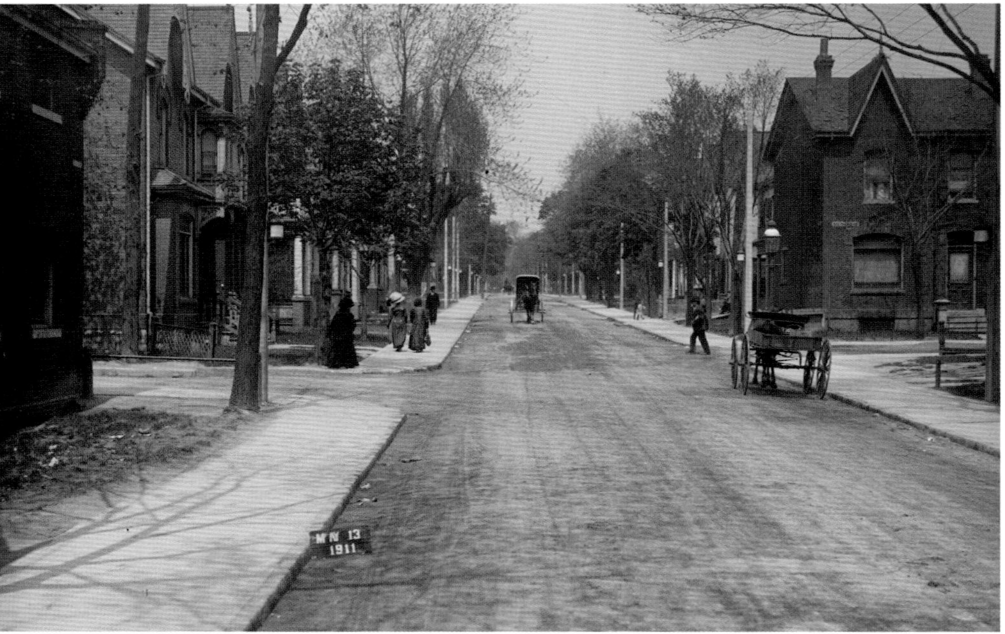

Looking north up Beverley Street, Toronto, 1911. Sheppard lived here briefly with his parents when he was an infant.

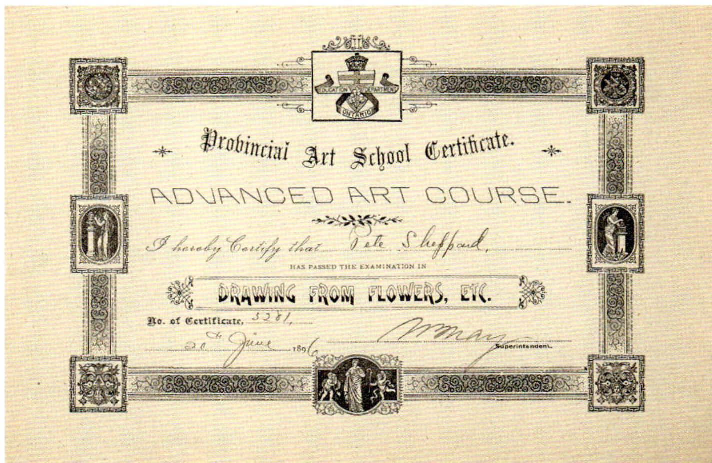

Peter Sheppard's certificate from the Provincial Art School, 1896.

relationship to fact for purposes that are entirely personal. Notwithstanding the question around his birth year, young Peter arrived into a family that already included two daughters: Adelaide, born in 1873, and Mary, born in 1878. Eventually, Peter would also have a brother, Charles, born in 1882, and a third sister, Jessie, born in 1886.

Very little is known about Peter's early years, beyond the fact that his parents moved from their Beverley Street home sometime before 1892, the year his father's name appears as the owner of a house at 8 Belmont Street,[6] and as "a tile maker" employed by the brick-making firm run by John Sheppard, who lived next door at 6 Belmont Street, along with a Peter Sheppard, most likely John's son or brother (and thus our subject's uncle or great-uncle).[7] In a contemporary advertisement, John Sheppard is described as a "Manufacturer of brick and drain tile" at the address of 982–992 Yonge Street, and at 22 Belmont Street, just down the block from John and William's homes.[8]

Peter C. Sheppard appears in the *City of Toronto Directory* of 1897.[9] In 1896, when he was 17 years old, he was employed as an "artist" at Barclay, Clark & Co., a commercial lithography company whose plant was situated at 26–28 Lombard Street in the growing city's commercial core. The young man must certainly have displayed talent to be employed at one of the city's more respected and progressive printing houses. His talent was also recognized on June 20, 1896, when he received a certificate recognizing his passing an examination in "drawing from flowers, etc." from the Provincial Art School.[10] A very early watercolour, possibly from around this time, survives in the archive. Its subject is an old church at Yonge Street and Davenport Road just a couple

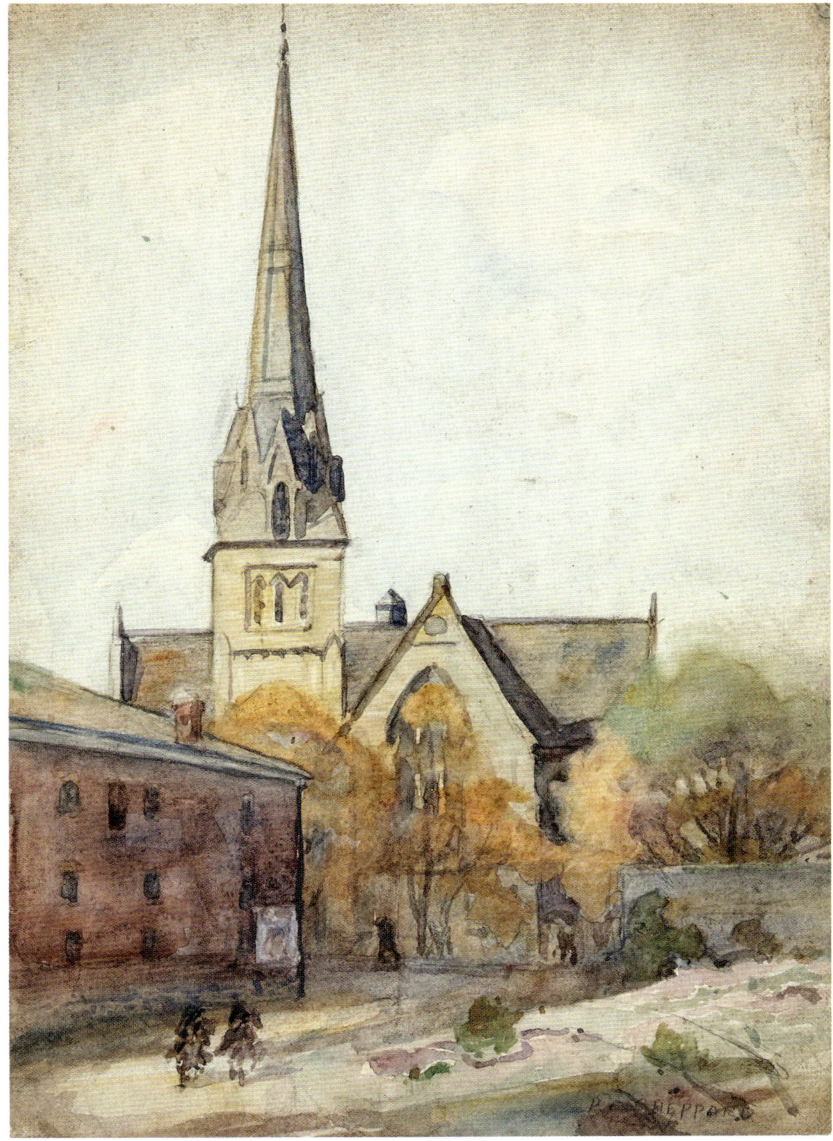

Old Church (Yonge St. and Davenport Rd., Toronto).
c. 1895. Watercolour,
28 x 19 cm.

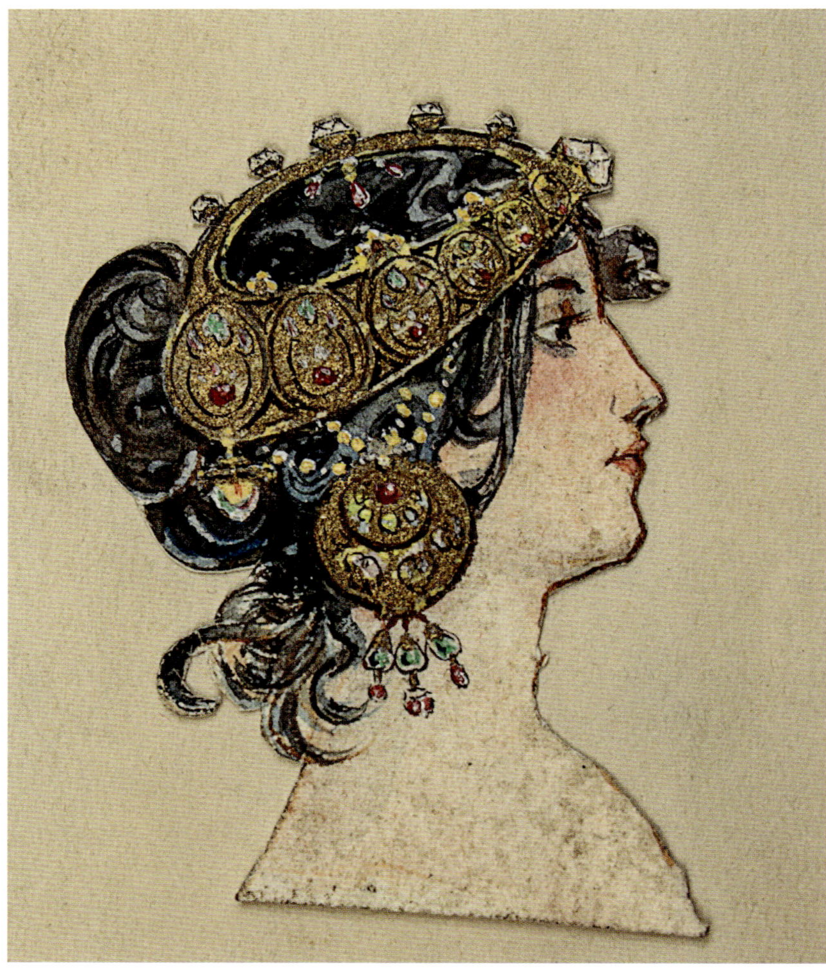

Profile Portrait.
c. 1904. Watercolour,
14 x 8 cm.

of blocks directly south of his home. It is enticing to imagine that the scene documents a view Sheppard saw every day from his front step or window. An early work, the watercolour is dependent on its precise line drawing to define the architecture and suggest perspective. And yet in spite of its evident technical weaknesses, it conveys a subtle moodiness animated by the figures on horseback shown in silhouette in the foreground. Although described in sepia tones to underline an old-world charm, the view would have been illustrative of contemporary Toronto painted through the lens of a nostalgic older English landscape mode.

A WORKING ARTIST

Sheppard's role as an artist in the commercial printing world was divided among several specialized trades, particularly those performed in his employment at Barclay, Clark & Co., and included foreman, pressman and transferor. Although his name does not appear on the *City of Toronto Assessment Roll* (different from the *City of Toronto Directory*), Sheppard would have worked alongside a tight crew of artists that included Otto Phaendtner, Herman Trott, George Goldike, William Durand, Herbert Currie, H.E. Shiner, A. Mueller and D.R. (or S.K.) Pendleton, all artists whose accomplishments have been lost to memory and time.[11] In 1900, Sheppard's occupation was listed as "lithographer" (although he may have been an apprentice at this trade), and his religion as Methodist.[12]

As a junior artist for a commercial lithographer, Sheppard would have been a busy if perhaps unimportant employee in one of a growing number of businesses that brought artists, engravers, lithographers and printers together in a single operation to satisfy the public's increasing appetite for single-sheet commercial prints. As a business sector, printing on paper quickly developed as a profitable enterprise in Toronto, which could accommodate a vast array of printing firms. What began as a lucrative business printing views and landscapes in the 1870s evolved into all manner of printed material designed for popular consumption, such as advertisements, labels, playbills, calendars, cards and ephemera. In the late 19th and early 20th centuries this translated into employment opportunities for engravers and artists, among them Sheppard.[13]

"FINE" AND "COMMERCIAL" ART

Sheppard arrived on the Toronto artistic stage in the late 1890s, a propitious time for an ambitious and eager young artist seeking a career in a field that was divided roughly into two categories: "fine" and "commercial" art. Fine art based its value on aesthetic principles — art for art's sake. Pictorialism was its primary purpose; artists painted pictures of scenes that interpreted historical, religious or mythological subjects, or painted still lifes, all with the purpose of edifying the mind and providing decoration. In contrast, commercial art was directly linked to promoting sales through visual means: advertisements, labelling, printed illustrations, magazines and many other formats.[14]

The printing arts industry — that is, "commercial" art, had undergone a transformation in the last quarter of the 19th century when individual illustrators,

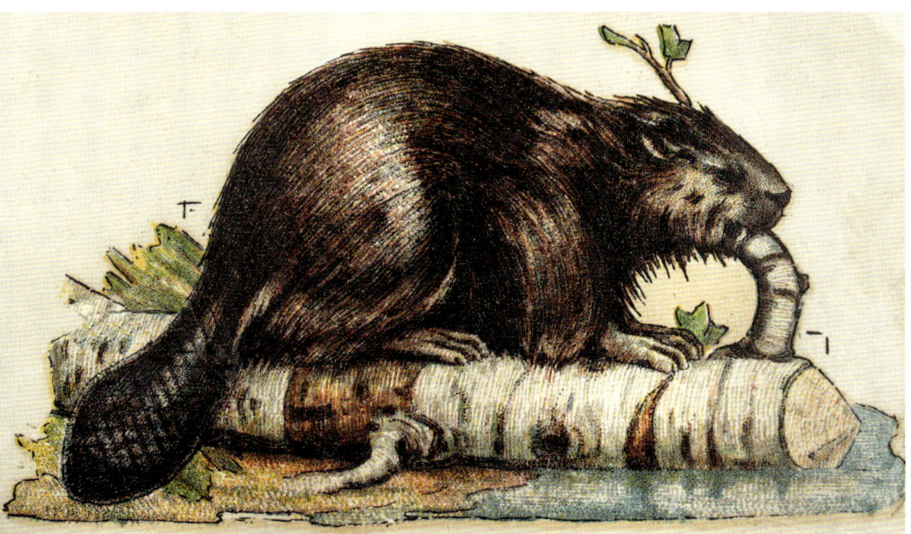

Commercial Illustration.
c. 1900. Watercolour,
7.5 x 13 cm.

the graphic arts industry developed and technical processes sped up, the increasing demand for images led to the growth of the trade of illustrators, a third artistic caste which was sequestered from the higher-status artists by being seen as aiding in commercial production, not in the elevated calling of creating pure art. As artists increasingly became employed as illustrators, and as engravers and lithographers for commercial presses, their status changed to a level of perceived inferiority, and their work was not accepted as an art

engravers, lithographers, and then printers, photographers and photo-engravers joined forces across Europe and North America to establish fully integrated operations where all elements of design, production and printing existed under one roof. This incorporation of traditionally separate enterprises led to the formation of the modern graphic arts industry, whose business was based on reproducing art in printed and published formats that were circulated to mass audiences.[15]

Although the merger of separate trades led to a profitable business model, the marriage of disciplines was not fully embraced within the graphic arts industry. A rivalry soon formed between the "fine" and "commercial" aspects of the industry. On the one hand, the fine artists (who saw their work as part of a tradition whose roots were in academic art or in the advancement of European-based modes) considered themselves of a higher status of specialization, certainly above the lower caste of labourers who toiled in the commercial categories of printer, engraver and lithographer. Changes wrought by industrialization included the redefinition of artistic production. Where in the mid-19th century artists whose work was produced and disseminated in commercial enterprises were considered to be part of the industrial trades, by the century's end they were careful to self-define as artist-craftsmen. As

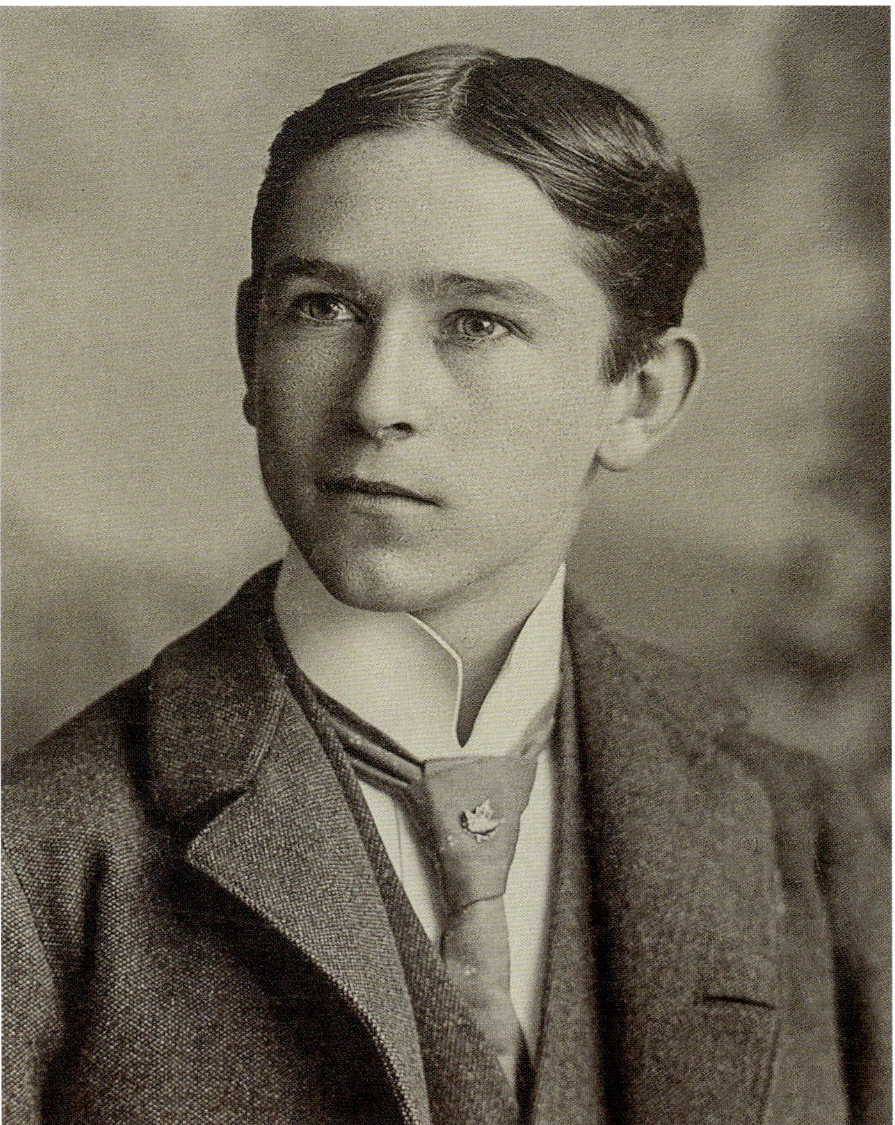

The artist as a young man, c. 1895.

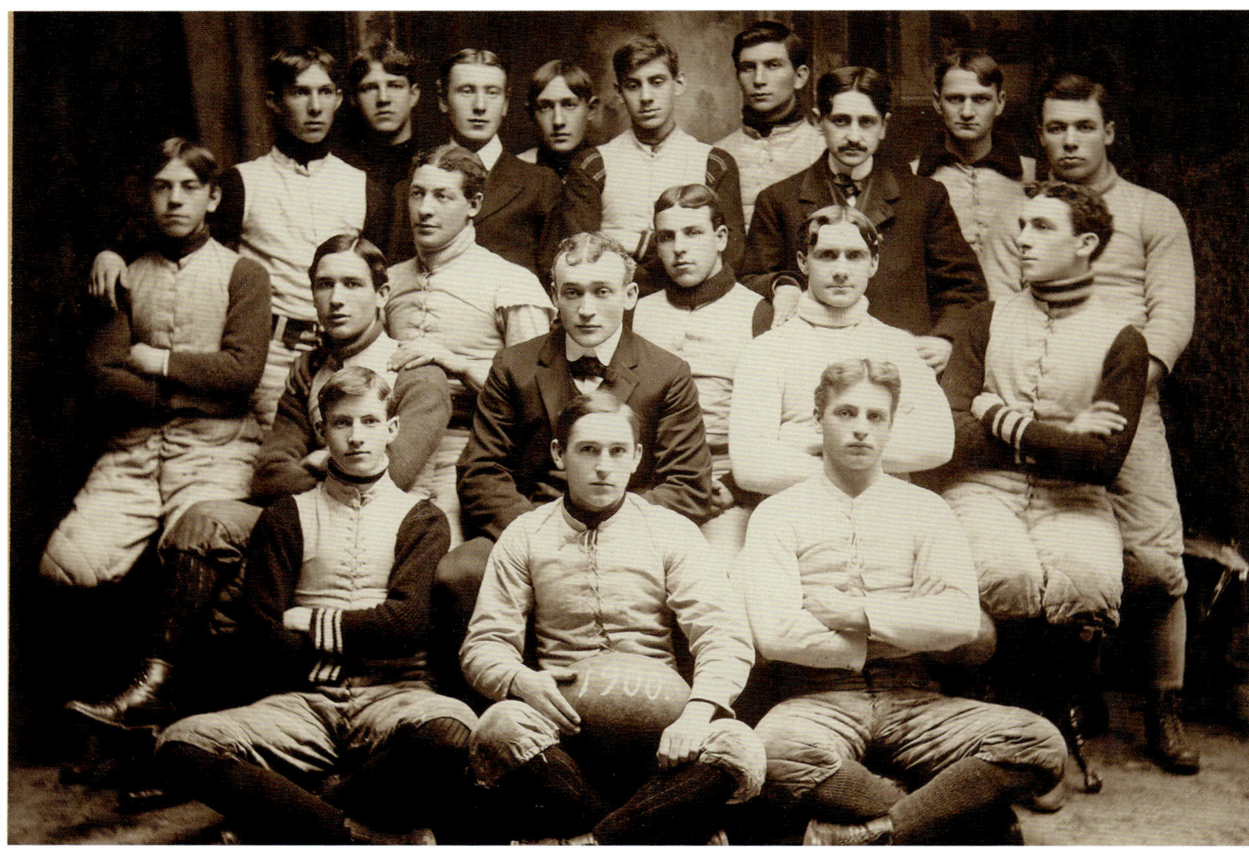

Victoria Rugby Football Club Champions, Toronto Rugby League, 1900–01. Sheppard is front row, centre.

form. Illustration was seen as an impure art because industrial patrons commissioned it. Fine art was considered a more noble pursuit because of the freedom of expression that lay at its heart.[16]

This is the fraught and uncertain artistic terrain that as a young, impressionable artist Sheppard would have had to negotiate if he wanted to make a living as an artist, particularly in early-20th-century Toronto, a city dominated by the Methodist value of self-sufficiency through hard, manual work. In fact, the division of art into the two distinct categories, and the resulting tensions and prejudices between them, lies at the heart of the development of Canadian art across the century. In truth, the commercial graphic arts firms occupied an important place in the development of Canadian art, allowing generations of artists to survive *as artists* because they earned a steady income from commercial art. They balanced the economic requirement of having a working relationship with commercial art with the inner compulsion to be expressive and creative as fine artists.

Despite the commercial nature of a graphic arts firm such as Barclay, Clark & Co., art remained central to the whole operation; success (or failure) was dependent on the creativity of the artists in a firm's employ. It was good business to hire and retain artists who had talents both as creative thinkers and as skilled technicians able to translate ideas into images for reproduction. Indeed, many artists exhibited few qualms about toiling in graphic arts enterprises and at the same time working independently as fine artists. Theirs was a confidence set in the bedrock of fine art talents and technical skills, which mitigated any lingering doubts that the graphic, industrial work was inferior

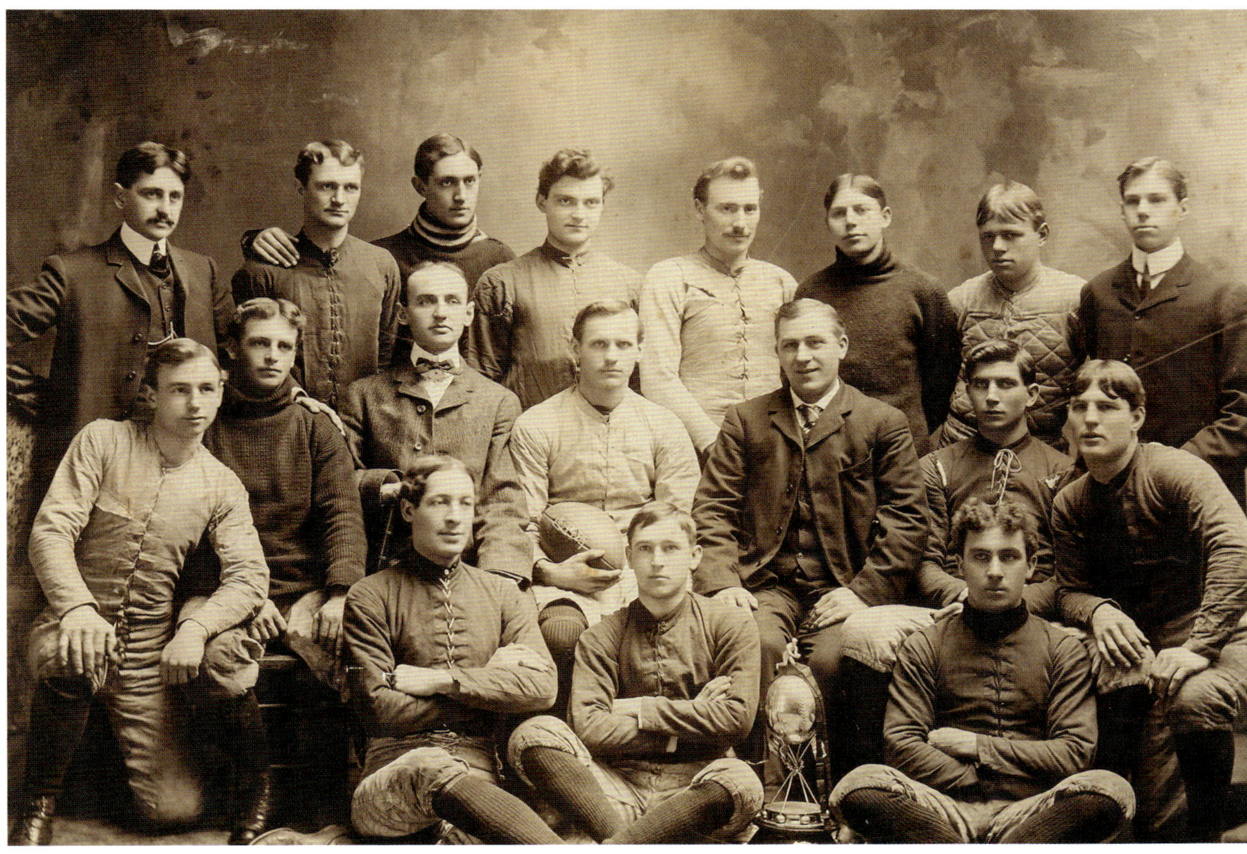

Victoria Rugby Football Club, 1903. Sheppard is front row, centre.

in status. Artists who became successful outside the commercial art world often seamlessly worked in commercial enterprises as well, and they were not considered to be acting in a contradictory or compromising manner.[17] Others had difficulty reconciling the distinction and chose either to abandon forays into the fine arts, or to reject the responsibilities and security of the day job for the freedom and risks of working entirely as a self-employed artist, dependent on satisfying the tastes of the collecting public or the requirements of patrons.[18]

This relationship between art and commerce defined Canada's cultural community, and none more so than Toronto's, for decades into the 20th century. Artists submitted their work to selection committees for the annual exhibitions of the Royal Canadian Academy and the Ontario Society of Artists, and buttressed this activity with commercial work. Fred Challener (1869–1959) worked for the lithographic firm Rolph, Clark, Stone Ltd.; C.W. Jefferys (1869–1951) was an art teacher and well-known newspaper illustrator; and J.W. Beatty (1869–1941) augmented his fine art practice with earnings as a teacher and as a cartoonist for, among other publications, the *Canadian Magazine*.[19] Indeed, what artist and designer Albert Robson (1882–1939) said about the situation in 1932 validated the close, interdependent relationship that the two worlds had to each other, a situation that nurtured young Sheppard, and in which he developed as an artist. Robson averred that, "The commercial studios proved to be ... fertile training ground[s] that developed a number of landscape painters and represent a movement from commercial art to painting that was, to a degree, peculiar to Toronto."[20] Sheppard is one perfect example of this.

The Gasworks (detail).
c. 1912. Oil on board,
21.5 x 26.7 cm.

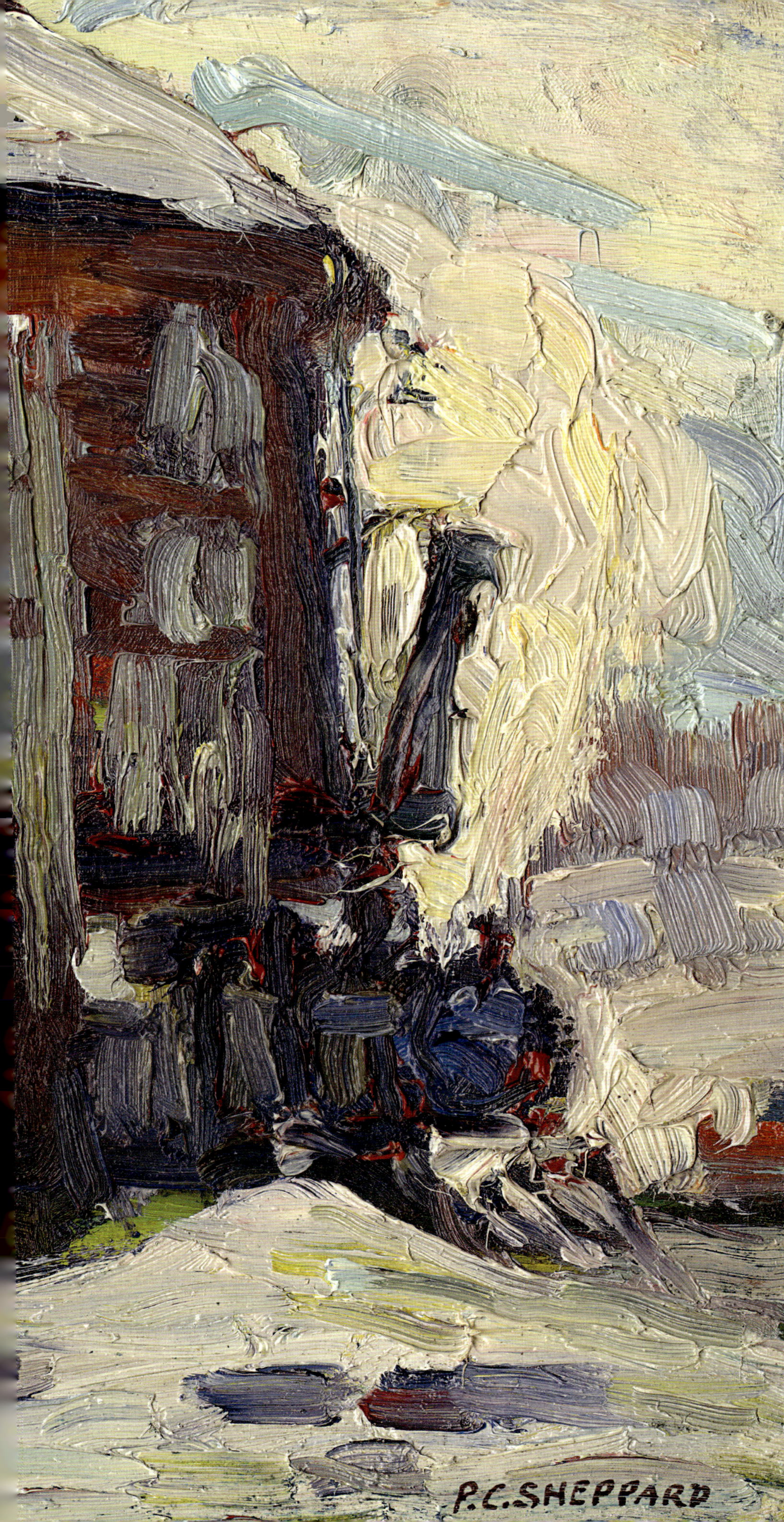

CHAPTER TWO

Transition

Fine Art

A FINE ART STUDENT, 1911 AND 1912

In 1911 and 1912 Peter Sheppard toiled by day as a lithographer and then with what precious little time remained after the workday, made his way to his drawing bench, called a "donkey," at the art school, then known as the Ontario College of Art. At this time Sheppard, although in his early 30s, lived with his parents at 81 Summerhill Avenue. Their home was part of an enclave on the crest of an eons-old edge of the lakefront, but in the early 20th century it offered a view of the ever-growing cityscape rippling up to the escarpment from the lakeshore.[21] In 1913, the family moved a few doors west to 63 Summerhill Avenue, closer to Yonge Street, the city's main north-south thoroughfare.

In the course of research in the Sheppard archive, I come across a plastic box containing undated drawings, paintings and prints, most of which appear to be from a portfolio of Sheppard's earliest artwork, likely dating before the time he lived on Summerhill Ave, but there is also a batch of material that was certainly intended for the commercial trade. These early paintings and drawings from this portfolio include a watercolour inscribed *Calton Hill Cemetery, Edinboro* [*sic*] (right), an early testament of Sheppard trying his hand at this difficult medium. This view from Scotland may have been copied from a reproduction, as there's no evidence of Sheppard having travelled to Scotland around this time. It is similar in style to his undated *Old Church* (Yonge St. and Davenport Rd.) (see page 39) discussed earlier: both are watercolour sketches (on paperboard panel) that give the impression of having been made in the open air, despite that being unlikely in the Edinboro [*sic*] scene. They capture the effects of light in the landscape with balanced washes to describe clouds and sky, and a controlled brushwork in *Old Church* delineates the trees and branches. Another picture, of a building (possibly a hotel) with horse carriage garages on its ground floor, is more evidence of an artist struggling with a new medium.

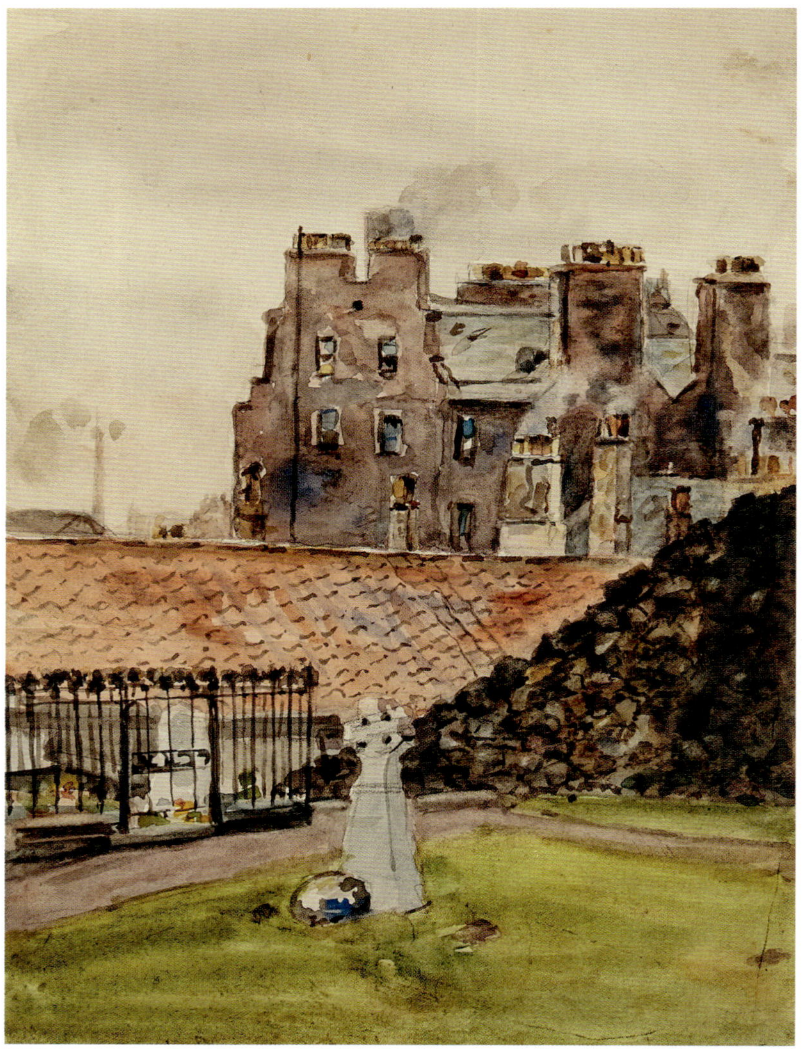

Calton Hill Cemetery, Edinboro [*sic*].
c. 1895. Watercolour,
25 x 17 cm.

What interests me, however, beyond these early watercolours, is the drawings that were clearly made for the commercial trade. Sheppard may have held a number of roles in the lithography shop, but he appears to have distinguished himself as a graphic illustrator. Going through the stack of material, I see drawings on tracing paper of a child playing on a hobby horse and another of a girl with gift boxes standing next to a dog, both elements of a printed advertisement. An ink drawing of a workman holding a packet of Adams Chiclets Candy Coated Gum (see page 37) displays a fine, confident handling of the brush and inks to describe the man's arms and hands — difficult subjects for even the most talented draftsman. I linger over a pencil drawing of a farming woman, basket in hand, helping with the harvest (see page 65). The model is gaily posed, smiling out at the viewer (or prospective customer) in a composition that gives way to a horse-drawn thresher behind her. Farther down in the box, I unearth a watercolour portrait of an elderly man wearing a pith helmet (see page 65). If this compact character study was intended as a commercial illustration, it has a remarkably fresh individuality and unique sensibility, beyond the usual. There is a rare vitality in the model's

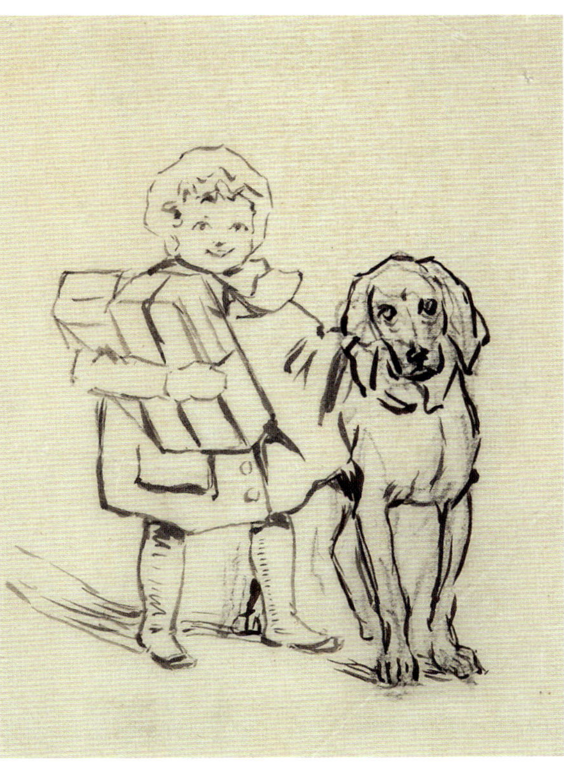

Girl with Dog and Gifts.
c. 1898. Drawing,
14 x 9.5 cm.

quizzical gaze and in the slightly upturned mouth that peeks out from behind the substantial walrus moustache.

Near the bottom of this portfolio of material there is an array of paintings and drawings that are evidence of a remarkably agile watercolour illustrator working at a high level of accomplishment. Among them are a miniature watercolour of a beaver (see page 41), and a cameo profile watercolour painting of a woman in an elaborate headdress (see page 40), with the inked inscription "Sketch/Clark Litho Co," a curious notation because this is the only extant piece from Clark Lithographing Co.[22]

The portfolio includes a naturalistic painting of a rainbow trout at the centre of the composition with vignettes around it. There are also two very fine watercolours of multiple studies of boys playing in a pond (see pages 30–31). The figures are wonderfully alive. By the time Sheppard made these undated watercolour paintings he had developed a fine ease with the medium, especially for depicting figures. The vitality of the studies suggests that Sheppard made the paintings in the open air; maybe he found a comfortable perch near the pond and spent what was no doubt a pleasant afternoon catching the life around the pond as the boys launched toy boats, caught minnows, made dams and rafts or just cooled their feet on a hot day.

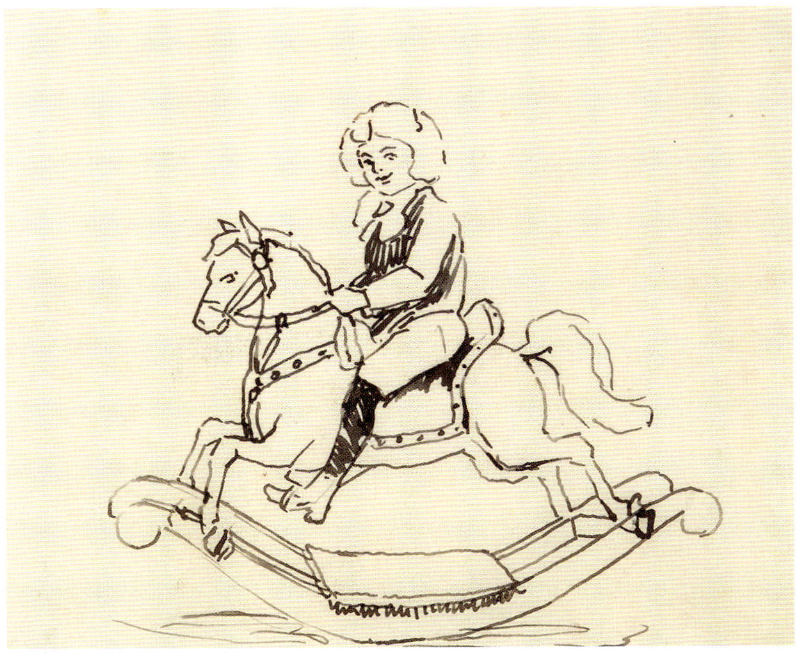

Child on a Hobby Horse.
c. 1898. Drawing,
14 x 14 cm.

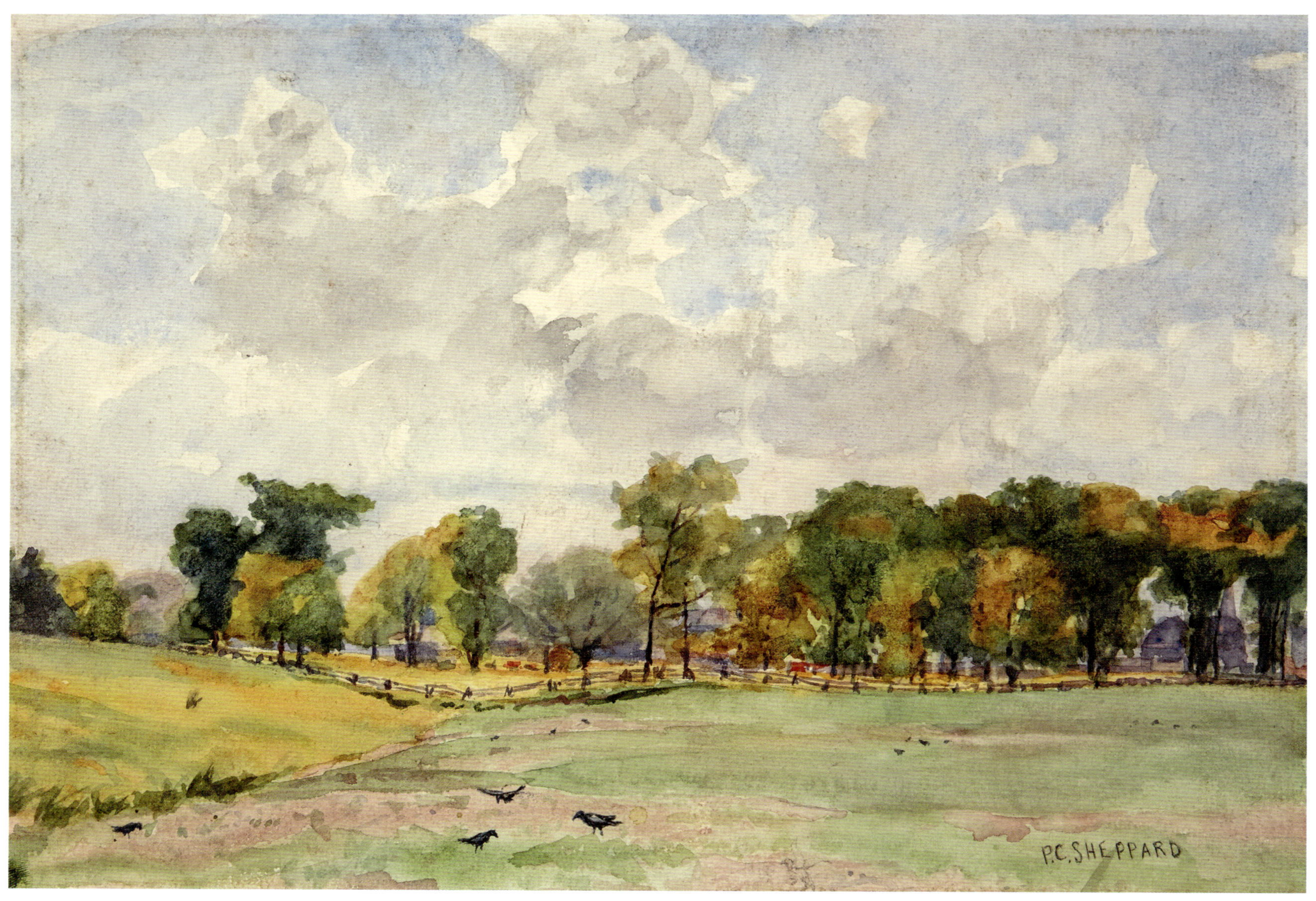

Field and Crows.
c. 1895. Watercolour,
19 x 27.3 cm.

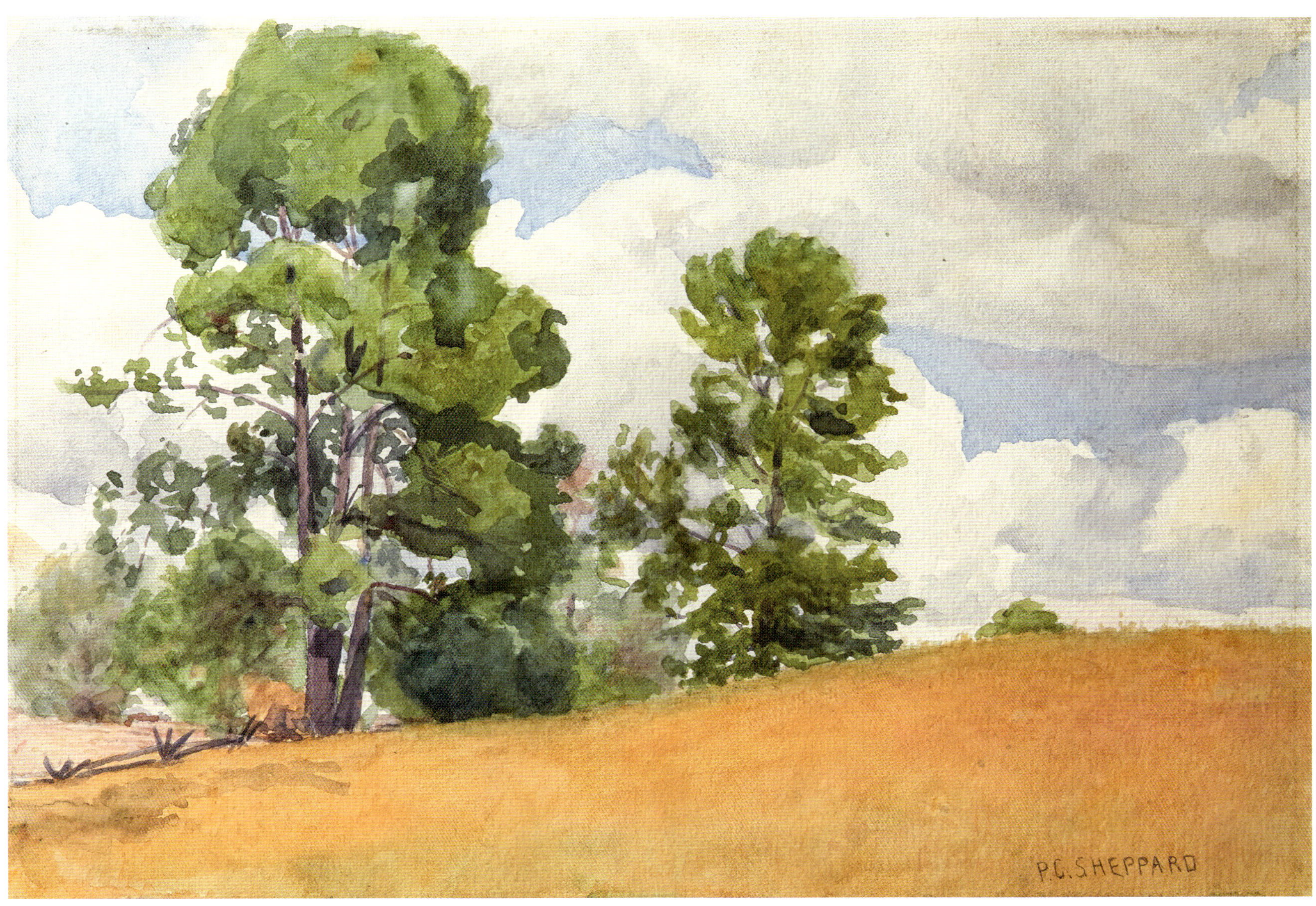

Field and Trees.
c. 1895. Watercolour,
19 x 27.3 cm.

Even though these works are over a century old, their youthful subjects having passed away, they show that Sheppard had the uncommon gift of capturing in paint that rarest of essences: life. Looking at the watercolours and drawings today, I am struck by the sympathetic treatment of the young fellows. Where does the magic of his painting lie? In the way they are drawn? In the way the shadows fall on the figures, throwing their expressions and gestures into such expressive relief? In the uncanny way the artist captures boyish movement and the innate inquisitiveness of these subjects as they explore all there was to explore in this pond? To my eye, Sheppard achieves magic in all aspects of these tender, innocent portraits that capture life and a moment in time so perfectly.

The archive holds a sketchbook in which Sheppard drew studies of nudes sometime around 1912, when he was living at 63 Summerhill Avenue. This hand-held sketchbook is filled with rapidly drawn figure studies of models casually posed in light and dark shading. The clear, modest drawings (right and pages 51–53) reveal how he carefully delineated general shapes in graphite by rendering three or four tones. The figures show the artist's skilled understanding of anatomy, composition and proportion, and his ability to indicate how light moves across a model's surfaces. Sheppard brought to his work, however modest and private, a level of humanity that is evident in the liveliness with which the models are depicted in graphite on the paper. In virtually all the sketches in the book, his elegant line and sensitivity to tonal modulations express ease of craft and fluency with the visual language of figuration.

THE ONTARIO SOCIETY OF ARTISTS, 1911

The outcome of Sheppard's early forays into self-taught sketching and watercolour, done before he was a student at the Ontario College of Art, was that he had works exhibited in the 1911 annual show of the Ontario Society of Artists.[23] Sheppard was in good company at the OSA of 1911. A photograph of the group of exhibitors (see page 55) in that year's salon includes Lawren Harris, Robert Gagen, Mabel Johnston, George Agnew Reid, Frank Johnston, C.W. Jefferys, J.W. Beatty, Mary H. Reid and J.E.H. MacDonald, along with the venerable Edmund Wyly Grier, among others.

The OSA always felt the need to defend itself from its critics for being both reactionary and forward thinking at the same time. This paradox seems to have been bred into the organization from its earliest days. Part of its genetic code was to advocate for the visual arts by creating proper institutions to enable professional artists to paint, exhibit and perhaps even make a living in the fine arts. The association was born in 1872 in an effort to facilitate the exhibiting of contemporary art in Toronto. At that time, the city had no public or private picture galleries. Artists depended upon recommendations from peers, commissions, private showings and even plain old good luck to garner sales of their work. To buy a painting, a client could call on an artist directly or visit the Upper Canada Provincial Exhibition, where works of art were awarded prizes alongside mercantile or farm products.

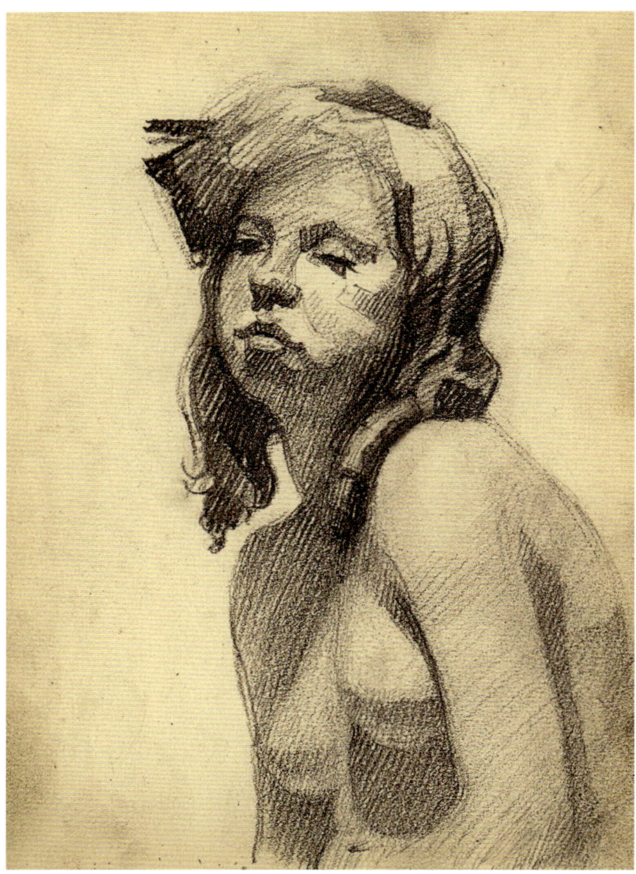

Studies from Life, OCA.
c. 1912. Graphite,
17.7 x 12.7 cm.

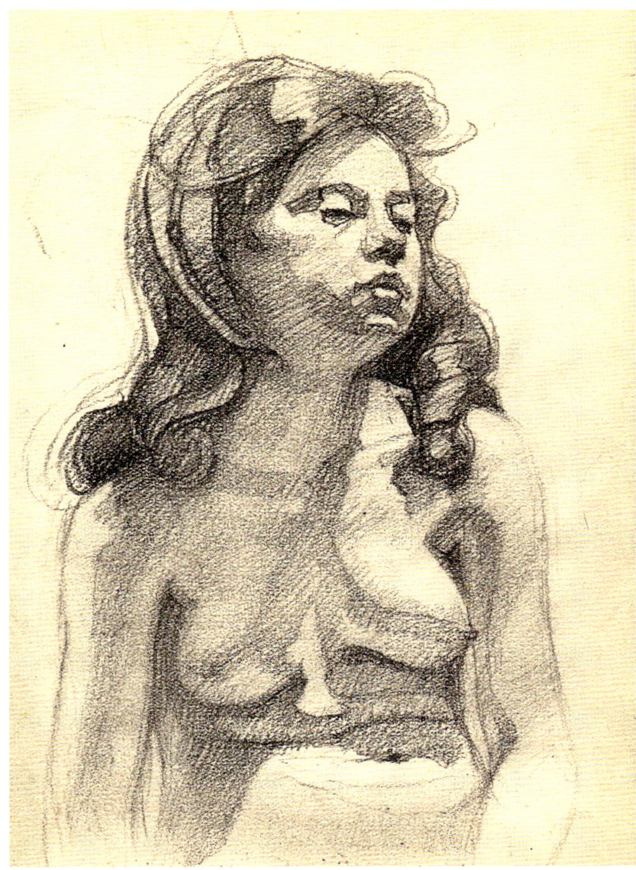

Studies from Life, OCA.
c. 1912. Graphite,
17.7 x 12.7 cm.

In the early 1870s, the OSA fulfilled a meagre mission of teaching art to art teachers at the Normal School, a school in which high school graduates were trained to be teachers, and of continuing the school's practice of exhibiting art in one of its classrooms. In 1873 it carried out its aim of fostering the creation and exhibition of original art in the province by producing its first annual juried exhibition, at which more than 100 works of art were sold, some of them to the Ontario government, which wanted to assemble a provincial art collection for exhibition in the parliament buildings. In the ensuing years of the late 19th century, the OSA successfully lobbied the government to open a publicly supported school of art and design, and to continue acquiring a collection of art from artists across the province that would eventually be housed and exhibited in a proper museum.

At the same time, the OSA opened its own art gallery and continued holding annual juried exhibitions, a practice that eventually became the art exhibition of the Canadian National Exhibition. In 1912 the OSA was instrumental in lobbying for funds that allowed for the founding of what would later become the Ontario College of Art.[24]

Even in its earliest days, the OSA struggled to defend itself on two fronts. It propelled painters to define a national art reflecting some of the modernist precepts emanating from Europe, while at the same time it defended itself against charges of being too conservative and too provincial. The stresses on the organization and the internal debates that ensued gave the society a kind of creative frisson that fostered innovation while also preserving past practices and modes.

Sheppard became a member of the OSA at a fortunate time, in 1911, when its president, society painter Edmund Wyly Grier (1862–1957), noted in his address to the members that its annual exhibition, "shows that we are not narrow or partisan in our conception of what is acceptable in theme or what is admirable in treatment; so that the most diverse types of pictorial expression are represented on our walls, and the young and vigorous aspirant meets with as generous treatment as is accorded to the veterans of the fraternity."[25] Sheppard, then 32 years old, seemed to have had one foot pointed to the future and another treading in the past, while eking out a living as a lithographer. He epitomized the ideal "young and vigorous aspirant" for whom the OSA was poised to provide the confidence to march forward into the new century to define a national art.

EARLY WORKS: FINE ART BEFORE 1912

Sheppard's earliest paintings and drawings show his willingness to experiment. Aware of the contemporary currents in painting, Sheppard displayed precociousness in his interpretation of several different manners. He moved almost effortlessly between inherited, perhaps outmoded styles, and the fresh air of up-to-date modernism blowing into Canada from France and the United States.

Among the early works of art in the archives is an etching in sepia ink of an old tugboat (see page 56), which dates from around 1910, when Sheppard was 31 years old. It is clearly delineated; the emphasis is on the contour of the boat and capturing its outline. The deft handling of lines, a skill ideally suited to etching, conveys shape and volume. Although there are some dark tones, the print is a lively testament to Sheppard's agility with line, and to his keen sense of observation. The open foreground indicates that the subject was drawn

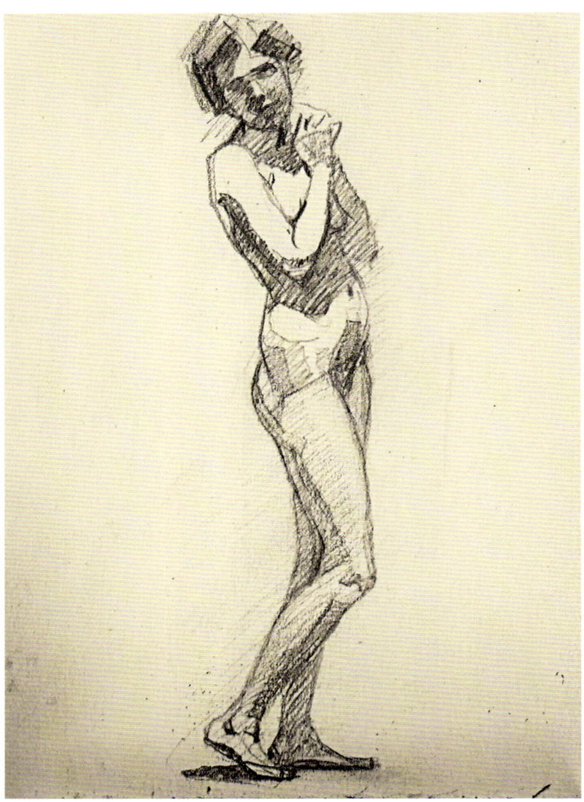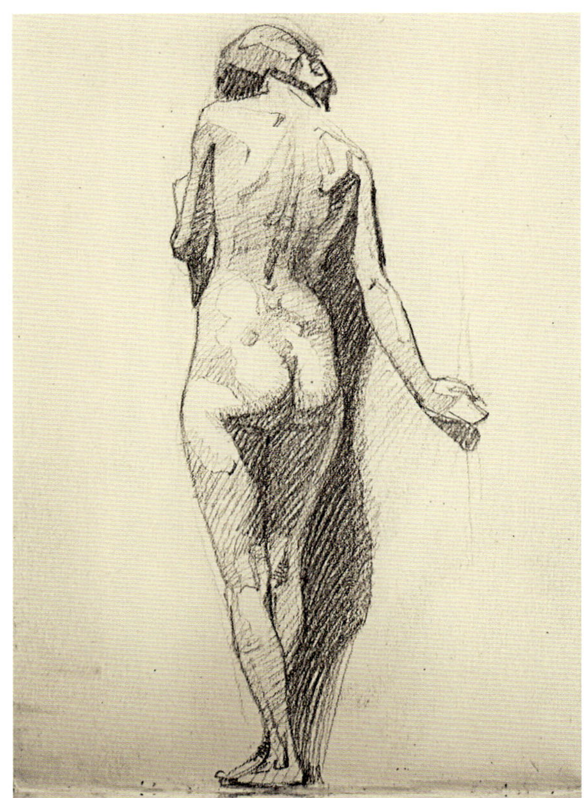

Studies from Life, OCA.
c. 1913. Pencil,
12.7 x 9 cm.

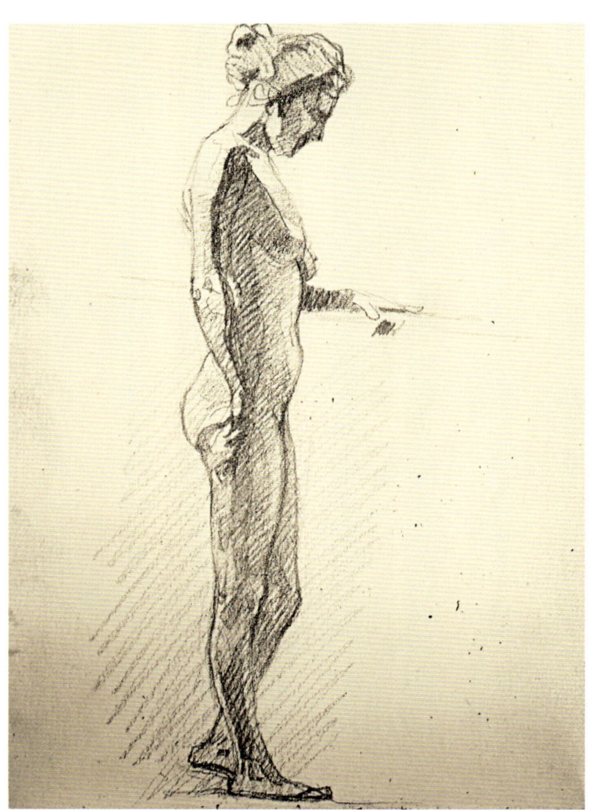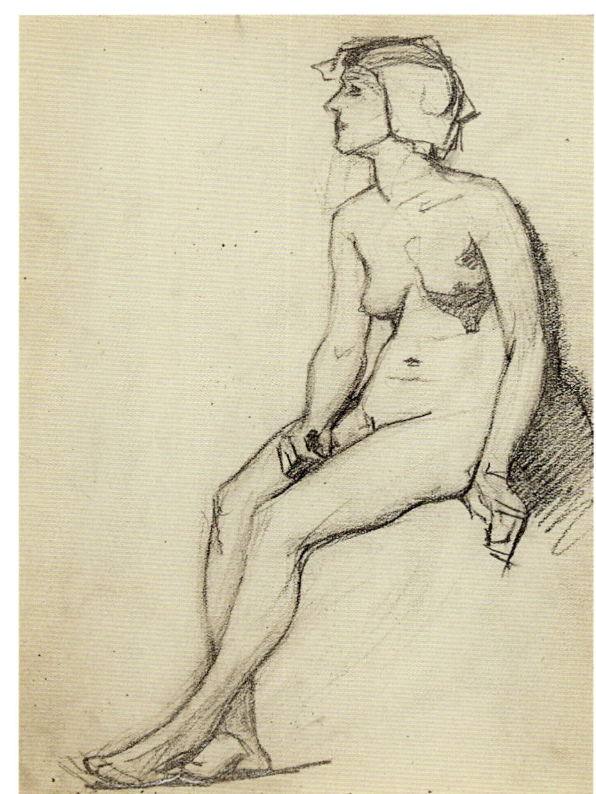

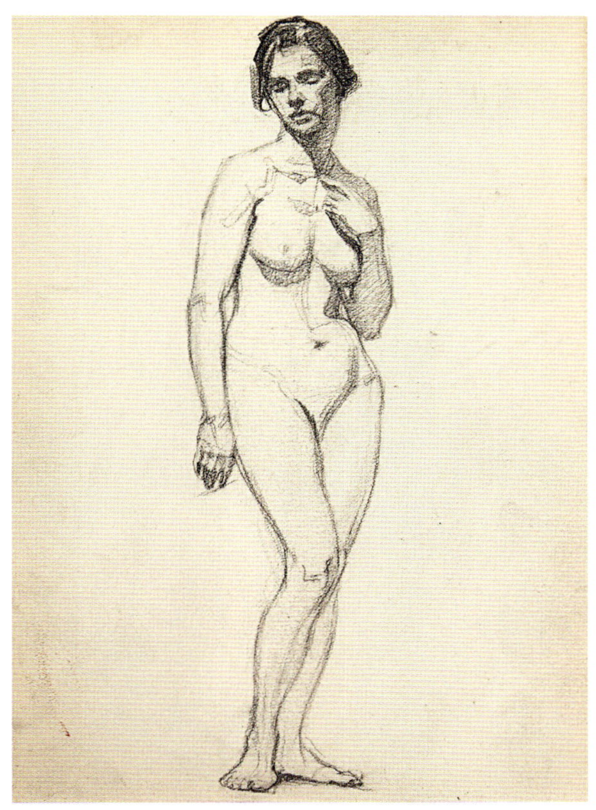
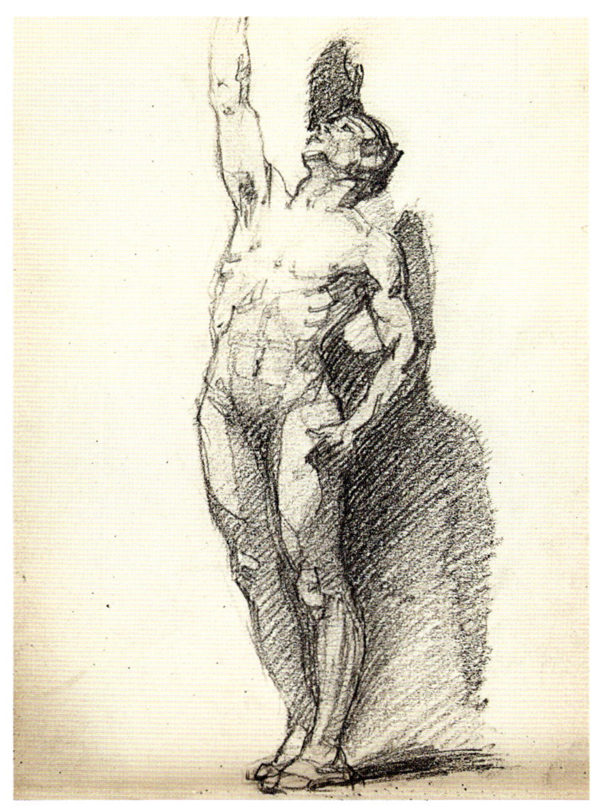
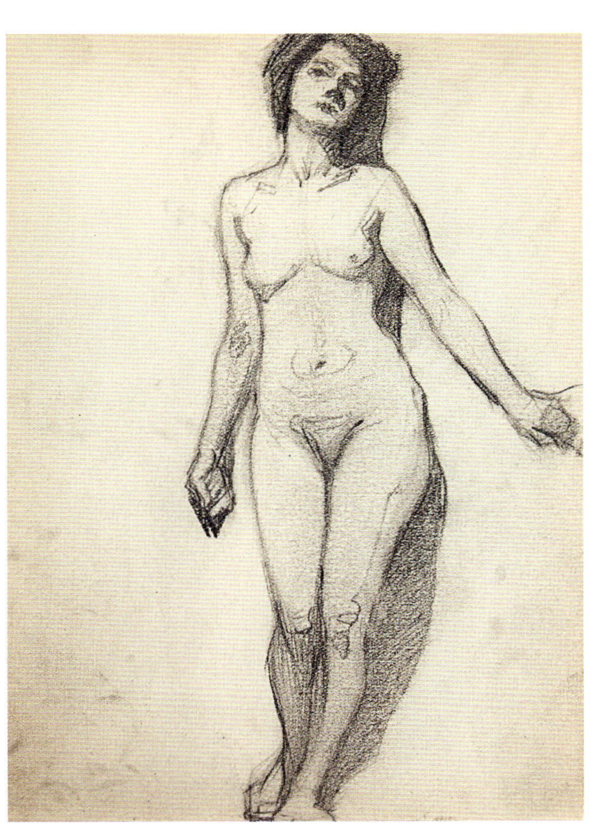
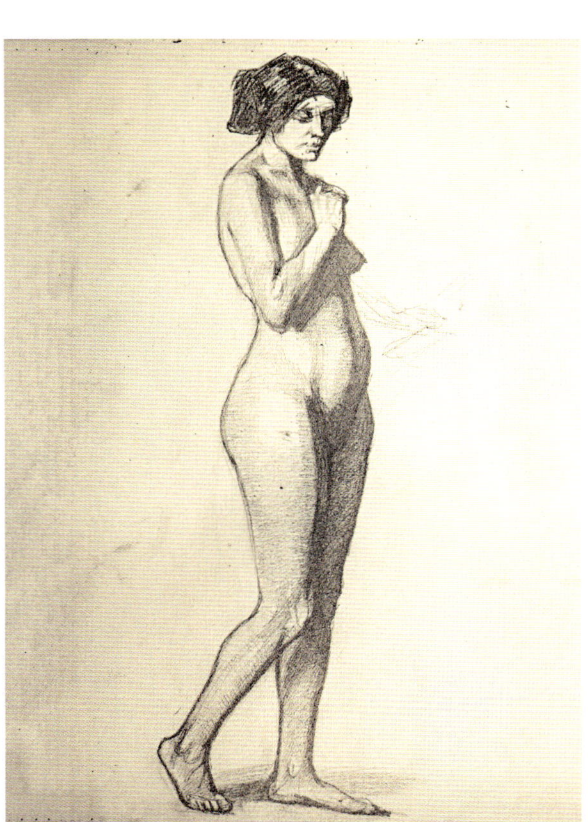

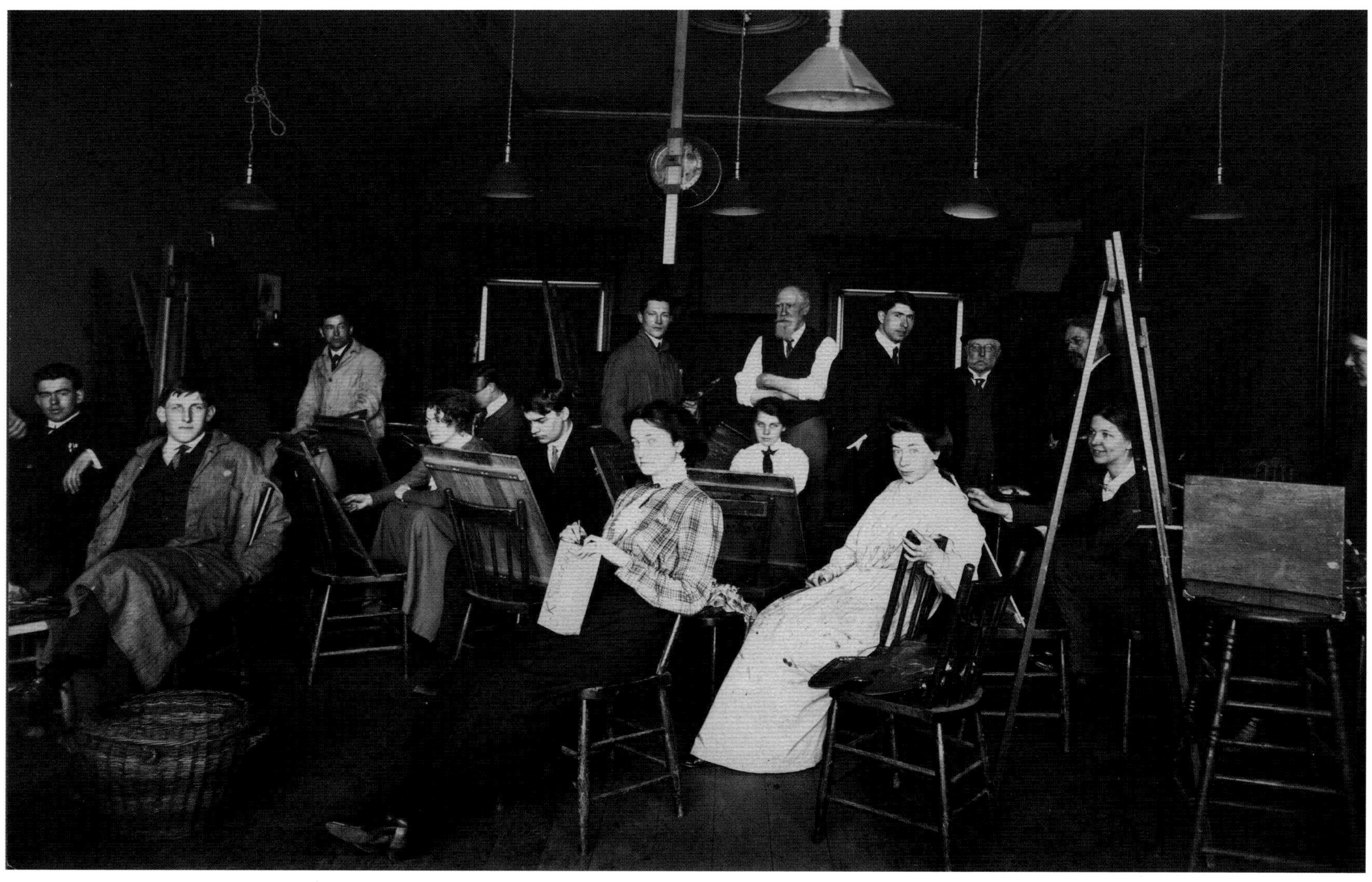

Life drawing class, Ontario School of Art, the Grange, 1911. Sheppard is third from left.

from life. Perhaps Sheppard found the beached tug on the shores of Lake Ontario. But what this modest print reveals is that Sheppard possessed skill; he could draw well, and it is not too much of a leap to assume that this served him well in his job as a lithographer. It also introduces a subject that would capture his attention and imagination and test his skills over the remainder of his career: boats. In the archive collection there is a common thread of interpreting boats in the water, boats in harbour, docked vessels, boats in dry dock being repaired, ocean steamers, cargo boats and even the canoe. Sheppard was inordinately attracted to floating vessels and watercraft, subjects that evidently gave him much inspiration and were an endless source of expressive possibilities throughout his entire career.

Death of Virginia, (see page 57) dating from around 1910, a drawing likely made to be transferred onto an etching plate, portrays the moment when Virginia's father, Verginius, stabs his daughter to protect her chastity and uphold her freedom before she is enslaved by Marcus Claudius. Sheppard has depicted the scene in a very finely delineated manner that captures its

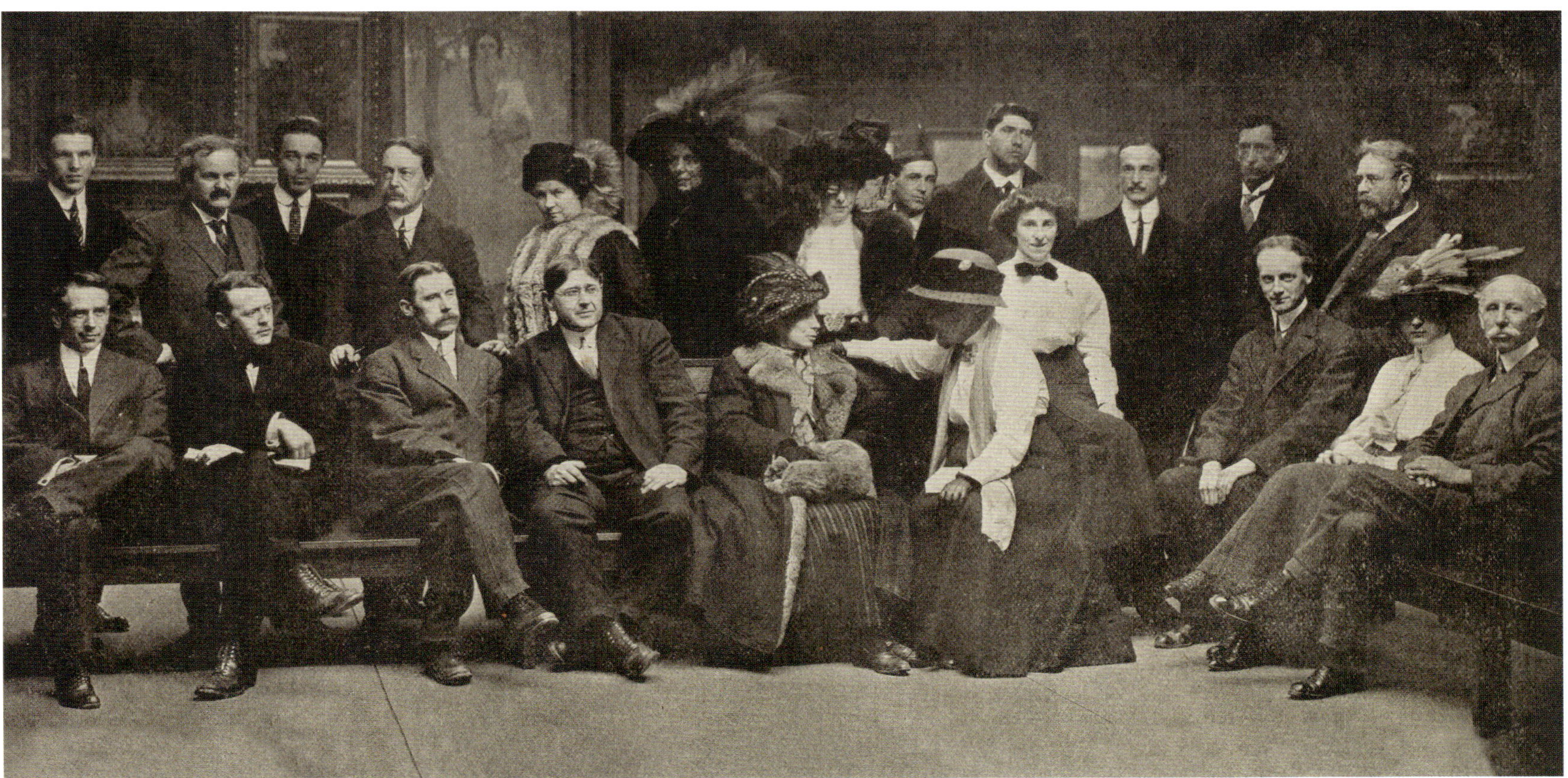

Exhibitors at the Ontario Society of Artists' Exhibition, 1911. Sheppard is standing, fifth from right, back row. Standing, left to right: W. S. Broadhead, Owen Staples, L. S. Harris, Robert Gagen, Mrs. Mabel A. Johnston, Miss Henrietta Vickers , Mrs. J. E. Elliot, P. C. Sheppard, F. R. Halliday, H. S. Palmer, W. C. Johnston, G. A. Reid. Seated, left to right: T.W. McLean, Francis H. Johnston, C. W. Jefferys, J. W. Beatty, Miss Harriet Ford, Mrs. M. H. Reid, Miss Minnie Kallymeyer, J. E. H. MacDonald, Miss Mary E. Wrinch, E. Wyly Grier.

tragedy through the relationship of father and daughter and the gestures of the figures, particularly their hands. The drawing is rendered in an intricate play of lines to convey tone, volume, anatomy and gestures. The composition reinforces the tragic theatricality of the subject while also leading the eye in and through the classical landscape of the Roman Forum.

I also come across what appears to be another early print by Sheppard of the actor Lionel Braham (1879–1947), best known for his portrayal of Spirit of Christmas Present in the 1938 film version of *A Christmas Carol,* in the costume robes of a bishop or cardinal. This print (see page 57) was made with the Ben Day process and then lithographed. Sheppard's contemporary Tom Thomson (1877–1917) was adept at employing this commercial printing technique. Sheppard displays his skill with the process in the evident ease with which he creates the folds and textures of the costume's fabrics and laces. Although the actor's proportions are strangely elongated, nevertheless, the print is a testament to the young artist's technical range.

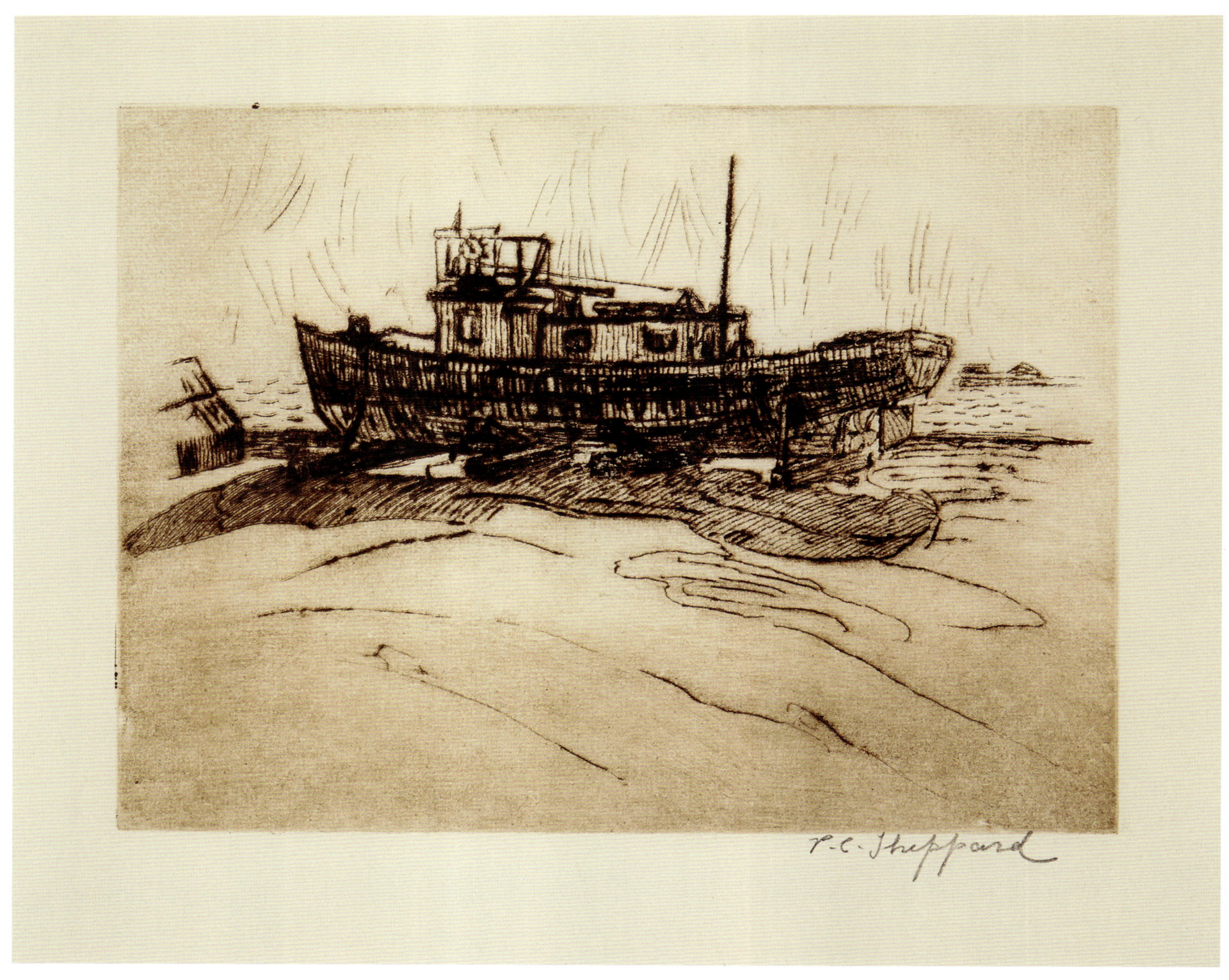

Tugboat.
c. 1910. Etching,
15 x 20.3 cm.

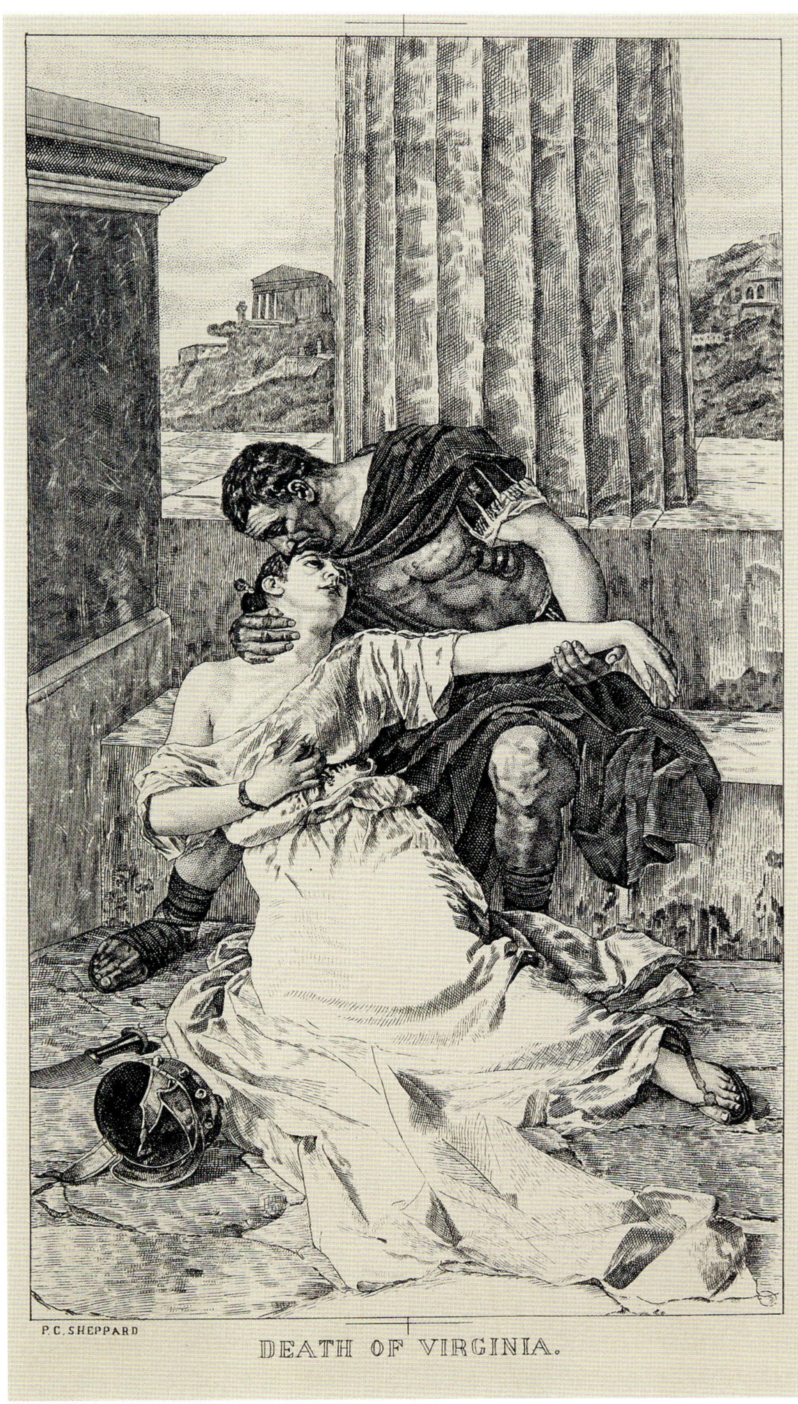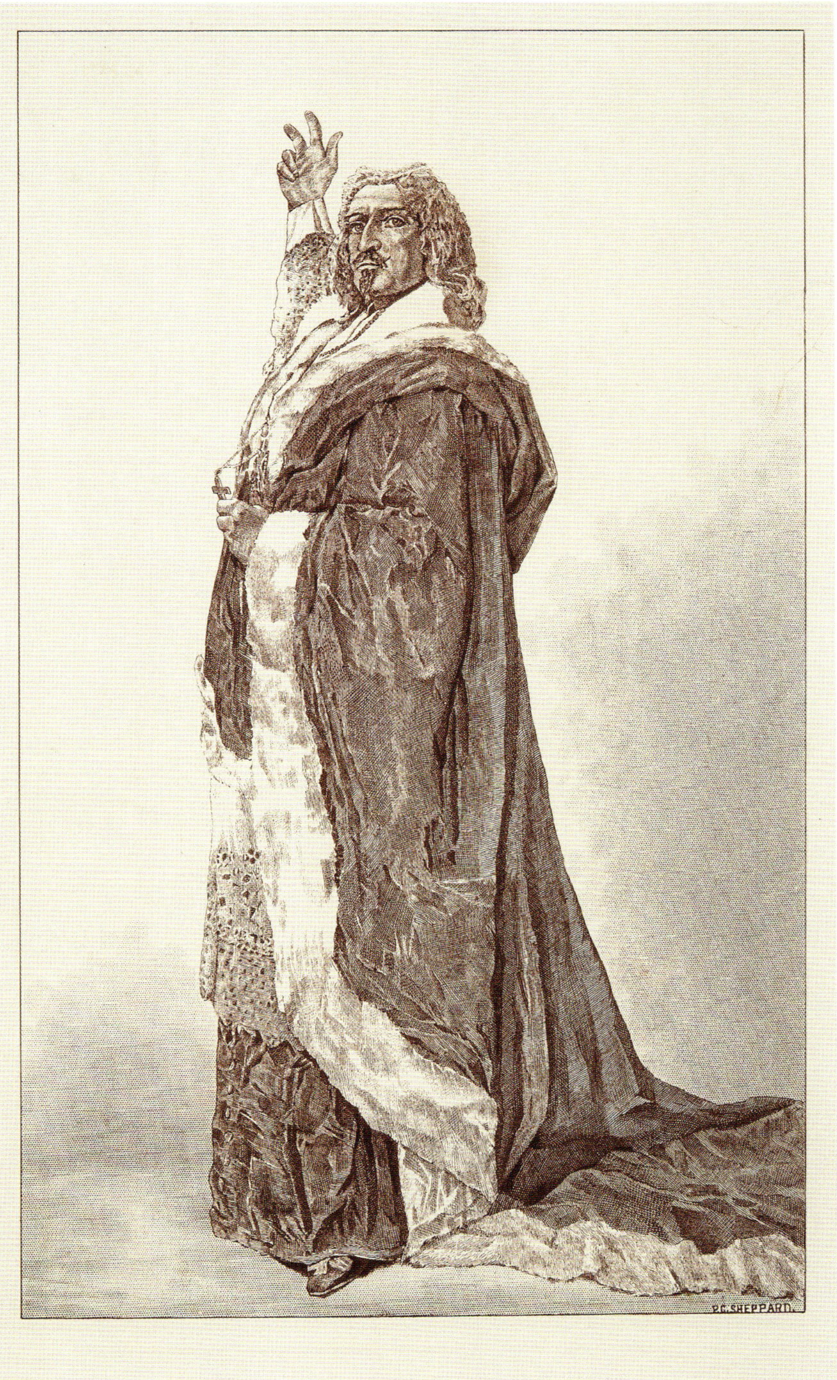

Death of Virginia.
c. 1910. Drawing,
26 x 15.5 cm.

Lionel Braham.
c. 1910. Lithograph,
26 x 15.5 cm.

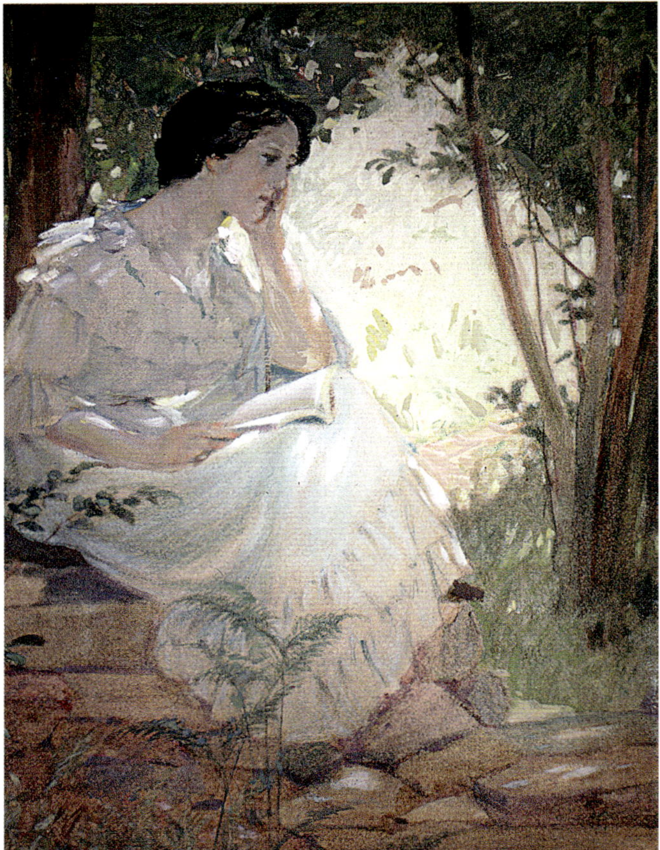

Reading.
By George Agnew Reid.
1900. Pastel on paper,
59.7 x 44.5 cm.

The archive also contains several modestly sized works, one a profile portrait of a man (possibly Tom Thomson) in the bow of a canoe (see page 74), and another depicting a woman in a blue dress seated on a bench under the shade of a tree (see page 59). The model, looking out at the viewer, sits in the shadow of a leafy branch while the sunshine illuminates the middle ground behind her. Compositionally, the elements are symmetrically arranged in an orderly, theatrical tableau, establishing a pleasing rhythm of darks and lights on the canvas. In these respects the painting shows a similarity to George Agnew Reid's *Reading* (above). Sheppard, it appears, might have set his sights on emulating this very painting, or on measuring his technique against that

demonstrated by the elder painter, who was soon to become one of his instructors at OCA. This early work points to an artist identifying with one of the leading Toronto painters of the day and working to adopt his style, whose roots can be traced to Impressionism.

Sheppard took a second stab at similar subject matter in his contemporaneous *Woman in the Garden, the Grange* (see page 60). This painting is gorgeously rendered in a palette of dappled brushstrokes, all the better to give a tangible impression of light filtering through the canopy of trees and bushes. The young woman is posed in a garden thicket, cradled by two branches. The painting indicates that Sheppard saw himself more as an Impressionist than as a Tonalist — he was interested more in capturing the effects of light on the subject than in rendering a perfectly formed figure. The painting is an essay on the light illuminating the shaded thicket and the figure in it. Sheppard has used a palette of green and yellow-greens. The composition's mauve foreground sets up a stage in which the figure is placed, and beautiful rhythms are established by brushstrokes that lie in a richly coloured background.

In these early paintings, Sheppard explores the expressive potential of a subject defined by a figure posed in a garden. This is also seen in his large-format painting *In the Garden* (see page 61), which was exhibited in the 1912 OSA show. It is a nearly life-sized portrait of a young girl standing in a sunlit garden. By setting the face in shadow, Sheppard has chosen to describe the model in a generalized manner — the forms are not volumetric; instead, the body is flattened with emphasis on the play of light and shadow as planes of colour interact in a gentle, dynamic rhythm. The overall effect is of a radiant, understated beauty. His impressionistic portrait of a woman sewing on a park bench from around 1912 (see page 68) presents a moody variation on the theme of a woman in a sunlit garden. The fine study is an essay in light falling on the figure, highlighted by intense whites that make the eye want to squint. The leaves surrounding the figure create a framing device with the shaded background throwing the brightly rendered figure into relief. Dabs of paint establish visual interest while also intensifying the dazzling light effects.

Sheppard did not solely apply his method to figure studies. He also interpreted the landscape through the Impressionist mode. *The Gasworks* of 1912 (see page 63) is a remarkable, understated winter study of the ice-encrusted cylindrical building, which appears to have been painted on the spot. Given the evidence of freezing temperatures, it is not surprising that the painting reflects a rapid execution, one that is entirely suited to capturing the effects of the weather and light as they are traced on the building. In fact, the paint

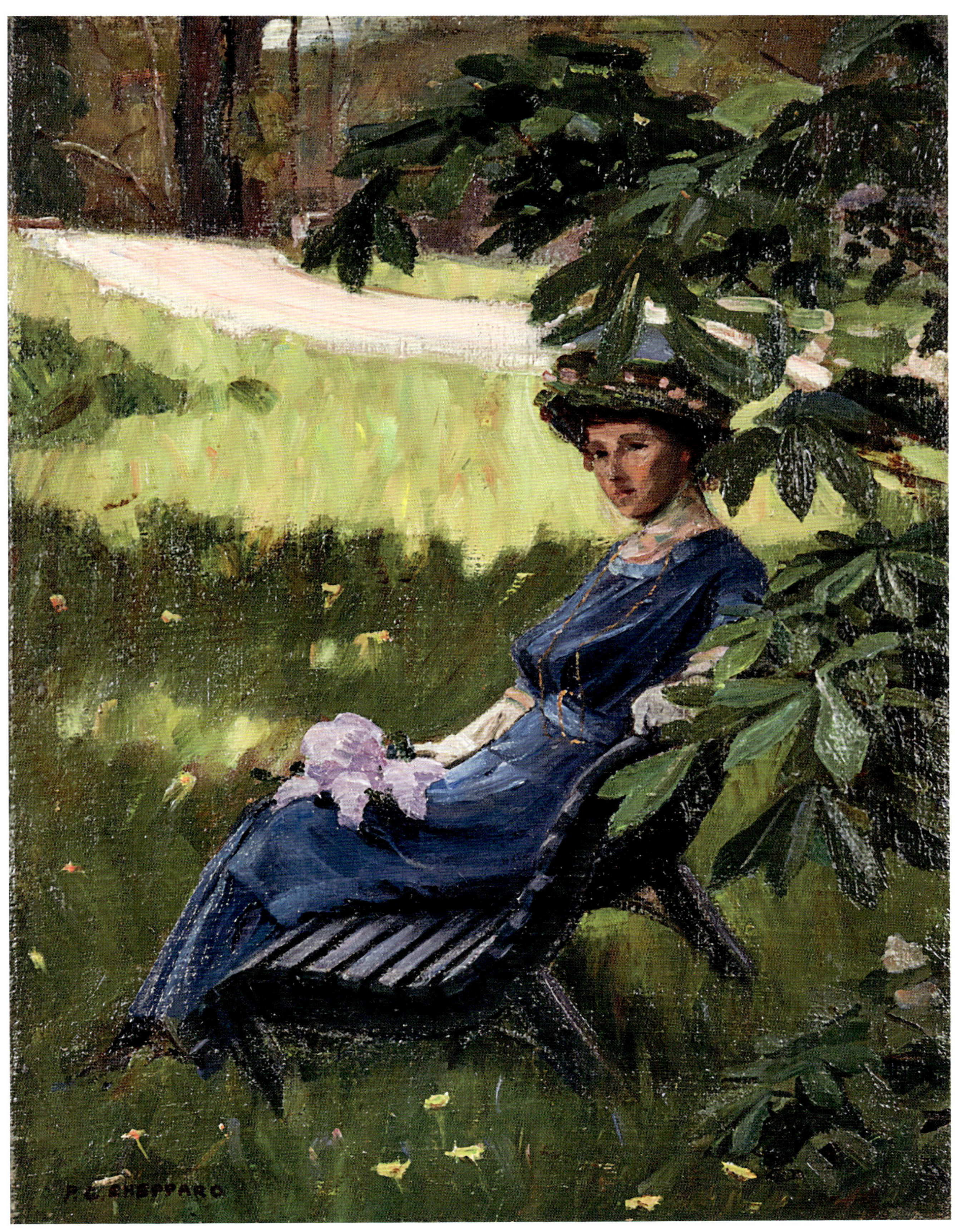

Woman in a Blue Dress.
c. 1910–12. Oil on canvas,
61 x 45.7 cm.

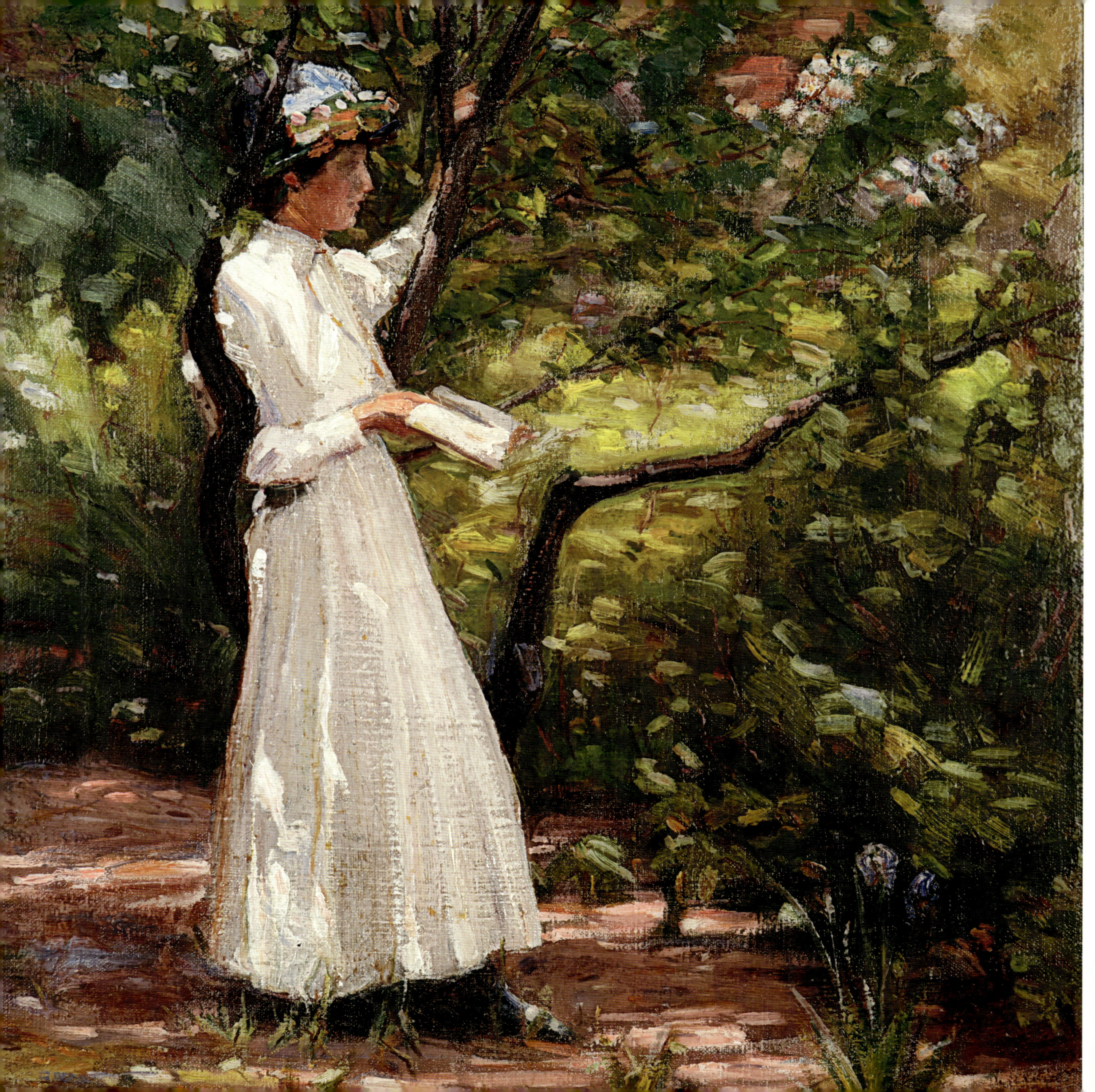

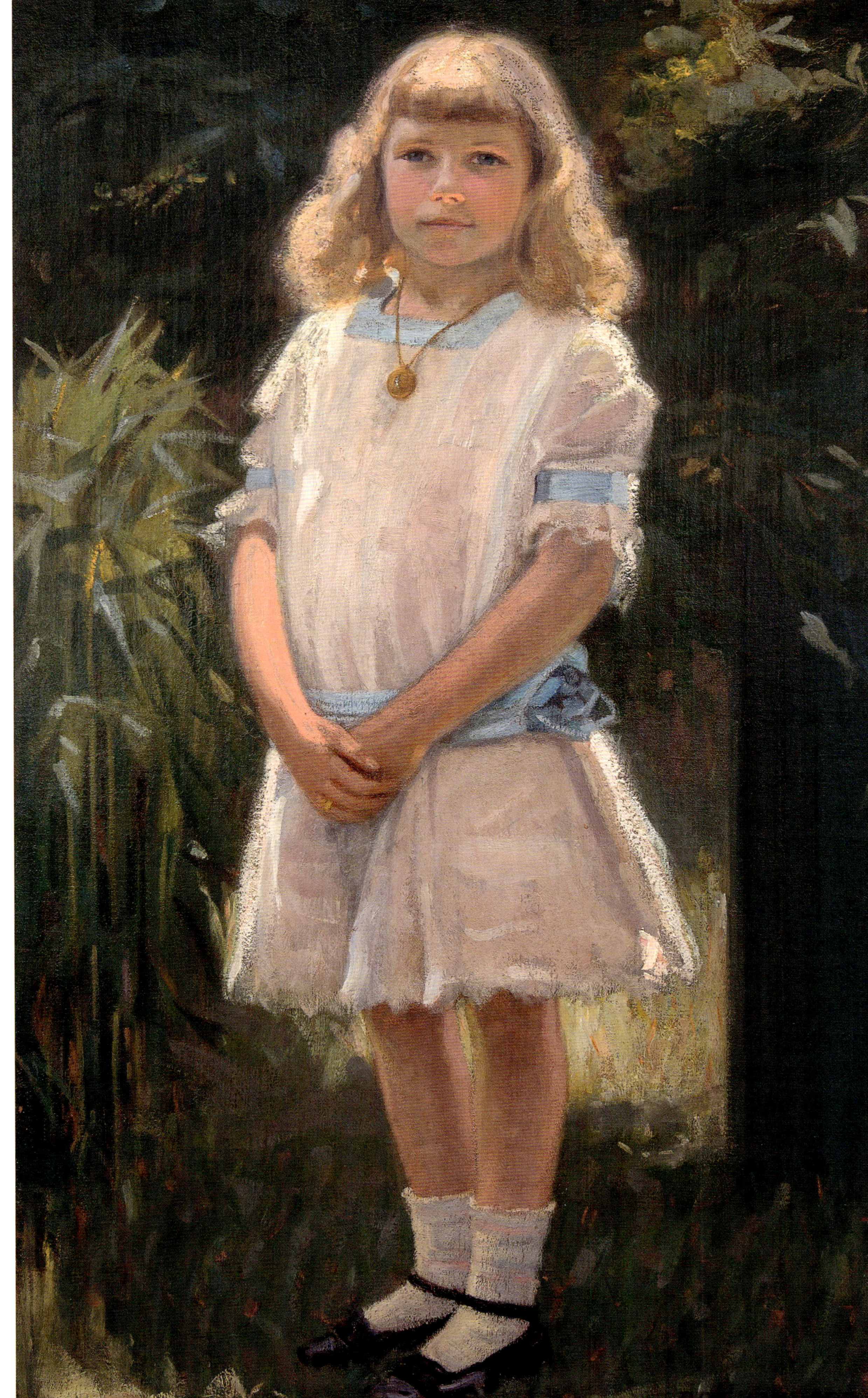

Woman in the Garden, the Grange.
1910. Oil on canvas,
45.7 x 43 cm.

In the Garden.
c. 1912. Oil on canvas,
142 x 81 cm.

is laid on in such a heavy impasto that the image is more a sculpted relief than an oil painting. There is a sense that the impasto around the gas works is the actual subject of the work, one that allows Sheppard to experiment with abstract and formal relationships in and of themselves, particularly the variety of hues and tones in which the atmosphere is described. The edges have been determined by the thick paint incised by brushstrokes, and even by the wooden handle of his paintbrush. The building appears almost as an afterthought, conjured up from the alchemy of pigment and oil as they serve the vagaries of light and atmospheric conditions.

The interpretation of atmosphere, particularly a wintry Toronto day in the industrial district bordered by the rail yards, was also the subject of a painting by another Toronto artist in 1912, one who went on to be a founding member of the Group of Seven, J.E.H. MacDonald. His masterful canvas *Tracks and Traffic* (below) interprets the snowy rail yards nearly enveloped in the expansive steam plume rising from a train's engine. Descriptive and narrative, MacDonald's canvas is, in part, a boastful emblem of the industrial growth of the new country as seen in the never-ceasing activity of the freight yards. Beyond its evident nationalism, *Tracks and Traffic* was a pictorial vehicle for MacDonald to display his handling of the Impressionist mode. The frosty, forward-looking subject matter allowed the artist to combine an advanced painterly method, whose origins lay in Europe, with a decidedly local, resonant Upper Canadian scene. The painting was exhibited at the 1912 OSA exhibition, in which Sheppard also had two canvases: a portrait, *Frederick Ford*, and *In the Garden*.

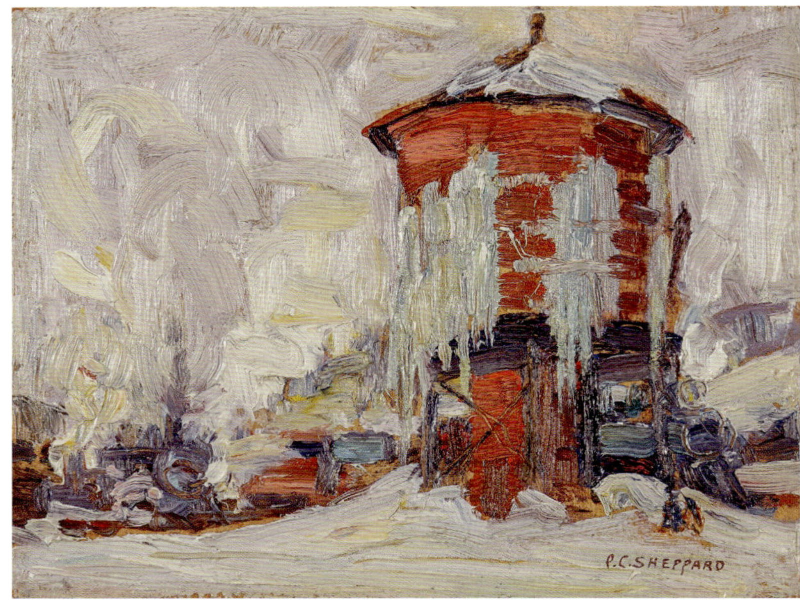

The Gasworks (study).
c. 1912. Oil on board,
15 x 23 cm.

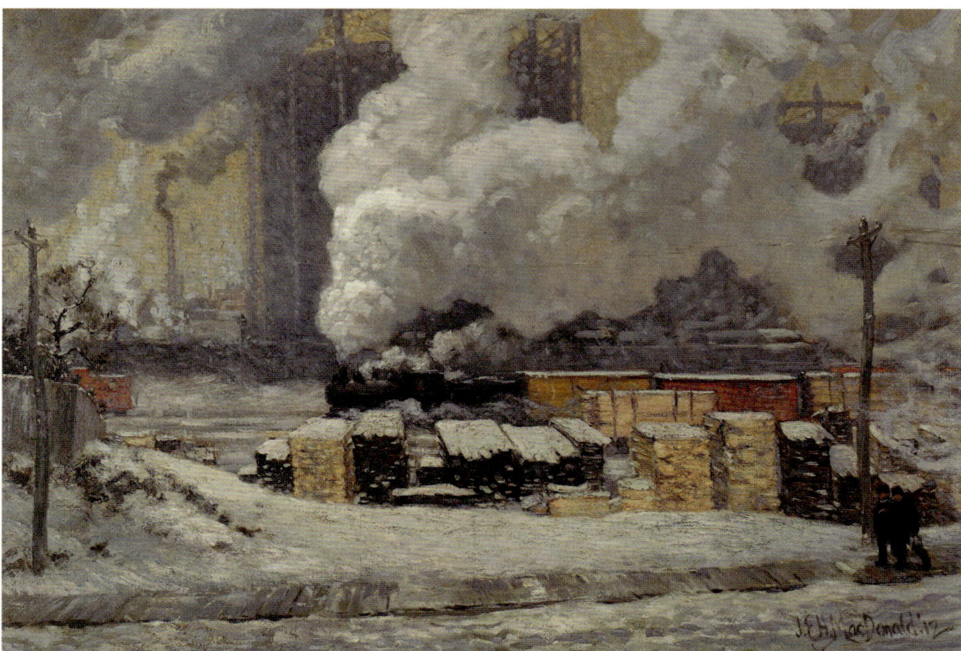

Tracks and Traffic.
By J.E.H. MacDonald.
1912. Oil on canvas,
71.1 x 101.6 cm.

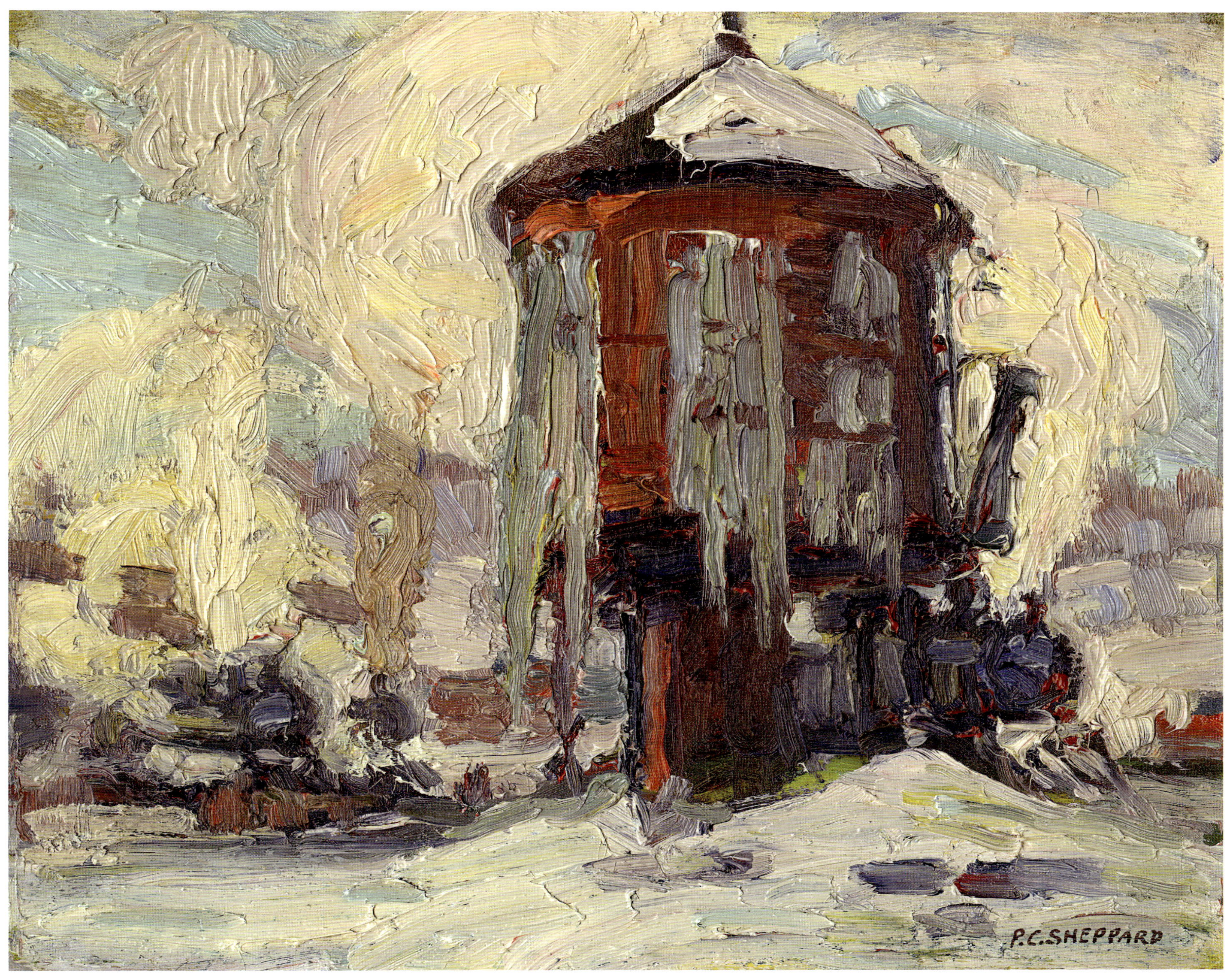

The Gasworks.
c. 1912. Oil on board,
21.5 x 26.7 cm.

Sheppard was certainly aware of the MacDonald painting. In the somewhat modest composition of *The Gasworks*, Sheppard reveals his painterly chops by tackling similar subject matter and glossing it with the same painterly modes as MacDonald. He shows he has learned much from his elder's example in molding the mode to a local subject, but Sheppard restricted himself from layering his interpretation with the pro-industrial development rhetoric that emanates from the MacDonald. Sheppard's approach is more classically formal; his work is a painting first and foremost, and does not carry the burden of narrative content lying outside the pure facts of the object as a painting made with oil pigments, colours, tones and lines. Indeed, in this single painting, Sheppard establishes a close kinship with his French antecedents from Pont-Aven, particularly Paul Sérusier (1864–1927), who admonished artists to divorce narrative from painted imagery and focus instead on the abstract formal properties of media and material. Eyes that fell on Sheppard's *The Gasworks* in 1912 would have seen evidence of an innovator embracing the earliest ideas of abstraction and trying his hand at expressing them through a subject that was rendered in mainly atmospheric tones that seemed to dissolve solids into a colourful visual concoction.

AN ART EDUCATION

For young artists of Sheppard's generation, art schooling generally came in two forms. The first was on-the-job training particular to the firm in which the young charge was employed. Employer-based training was "fertile" in the sense that it provided an apprenticeship in the arts. The growth of the printing trades required that young artists be trained in a manner that would support the needs of the industry. To regularize what was likely a hodgepodge of uneven commercial practices, in 1876 the Ontario School of Art was founded by the Ontario Society of Artists to provide professional training in art to students who wished either to teach in the provincial school system or to work professionally in the arts or printing trades.

In 1886 the Ontario School of Art transformed into the Toronto Art Students' League, an educational centre to teach potential "fine" and "commercial" artists. It lasted a mere four years before evolving into the Central Ontario School of Art and Design, which operated until 1912, when it became the Ontario College of Art.

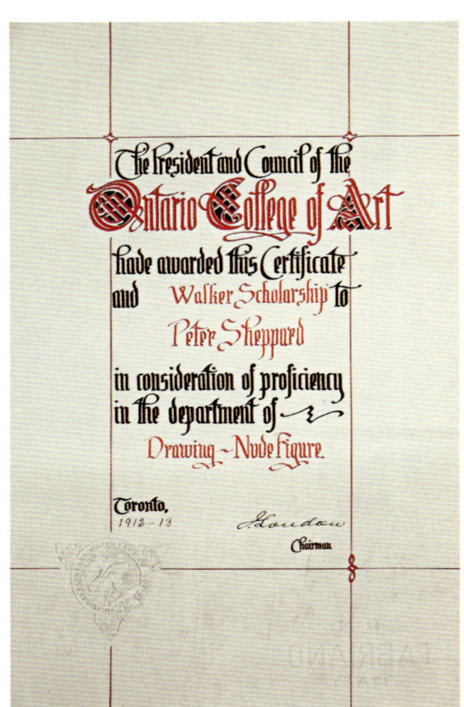

Walker Scholarship:
For Drawing—Nude Figure, 1913–14.

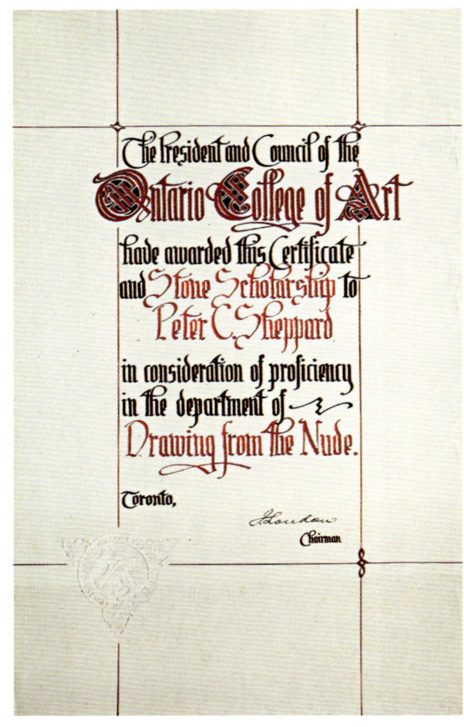

Stone Scholarship:
For Drawing from the Nude, 1913–14.

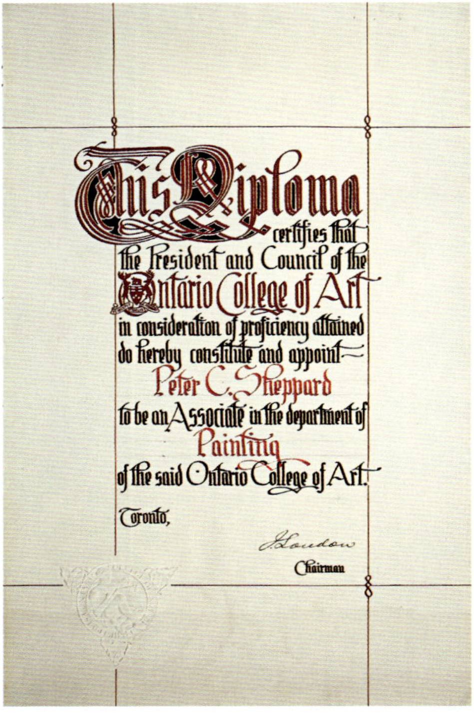

Diploma for Painting, 1913–14.

INFLUENTIAL INSTRUCTORS AT
THE ONTARIO COLLEGE OF ART

Here is what the paper-based evidence of certificates of achievement from the Ontario College of Art tells us about Sheppard's progress as an art student. In the academic year 1912–13 (the first year of OCA's life under that name), he was awarded honourable mention for proficiency in painting from still life; honourable mention for proficiency in painting — portrait and costume; and honourable mention for proficiency in composition. In other undated certificates of merit from the college, he was awarded honourable mentions for proficiency in composition, and in drawing from the draped and nude model. In all, the evidence is of a student who was surely at the top of his class, who learned his lessons well and impressed his instructors with his talent and promise.

Thus, likely in an effort to gain credibility as a fine artist, Sheppard burnished his credentials at the Ontario College of Art, where he studied under several of Toronto and Canada's most important fine artists of the day. In 1920, on a National Gallery of Canada "Information Form," Sheppard listed his teachers at the Ontario College of Art as William Cruikshank (1848–1922),

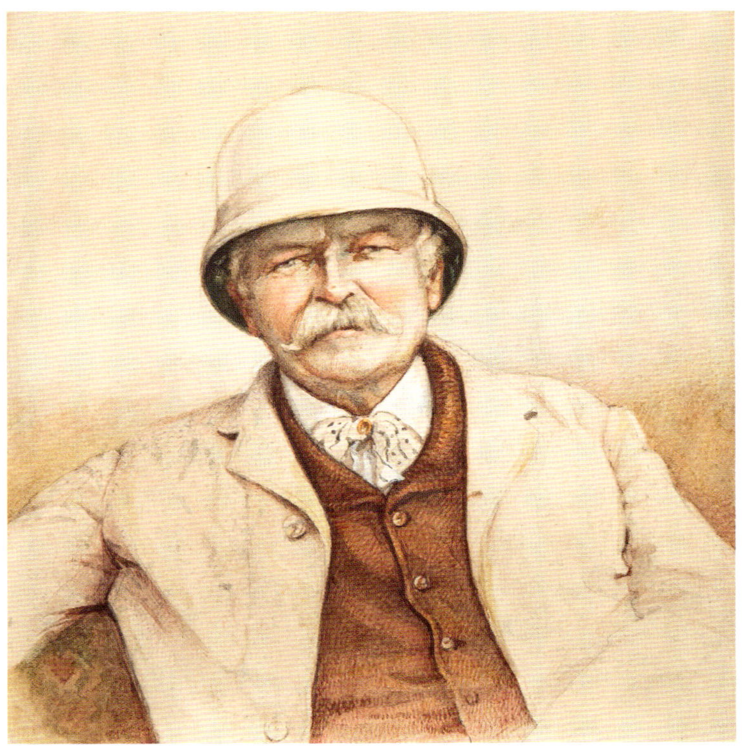

Old Man in a Pith Helmet.
c. 1900. Watercolour,
19 x 16.5 cm.

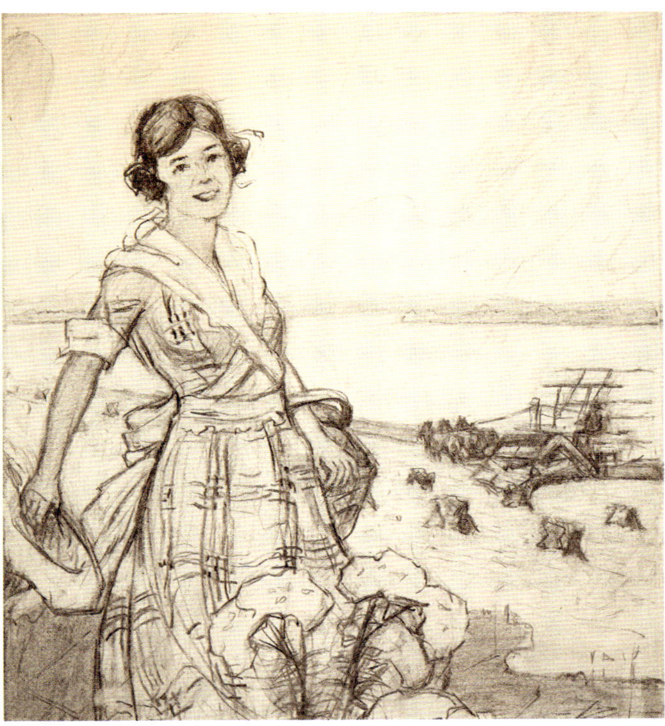

Farm Woman.
c. 1900. Pencil,
30.4 x 26.7 cm.

George Agnew Reid (1860–1947) and John William Beatty (1869–1941).[26] This was a formidable triumvirate. Each brought a different approach to artistic creation and making art — Cruikshank, a respect for tradition; Reid, the expressive properties of colour; and Beatty, the importance of drawing and composition. Each also exerted a different influence on Sheppard when he was a student at the college. Although precise records of the courses Sheppard studied under these artists, and when he took them, are lost, the body of work that exists in the archive provides evidence that each teacher gave Sheppard methods to emulate as he developed his personal style both as a professional fine artist and as a commercial artist. In the studios of the art school, he came under the influence of these professionals and saw in their styles ways to shape his own creative voice, and a way to learn, second-hand, the manners in which modern art was evolving in Europe and in the United States. In addition to the modern, he was schooled in traditional ways, too.

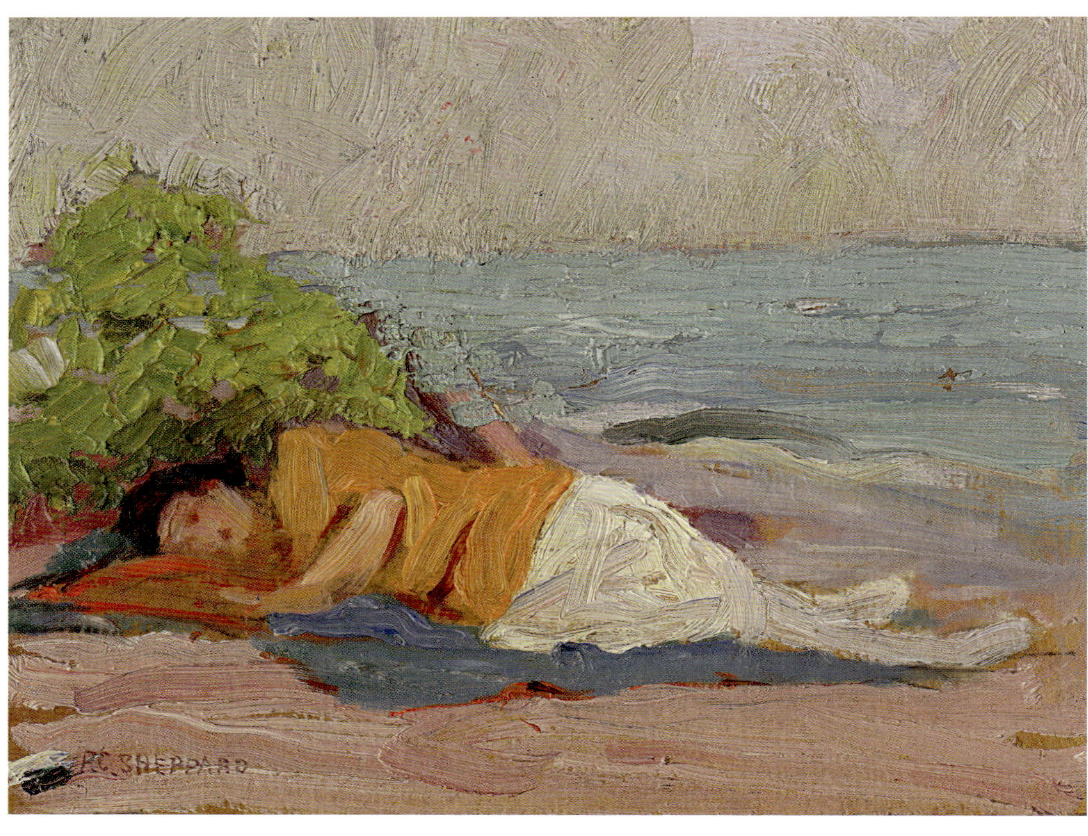

By the Lake.
c. 1910–12. Oil on panel,
14.6 x 24 cm.

Couple, Lakeside.
c. 1910–12. Oil on panel,
14.6 x 24 cm.

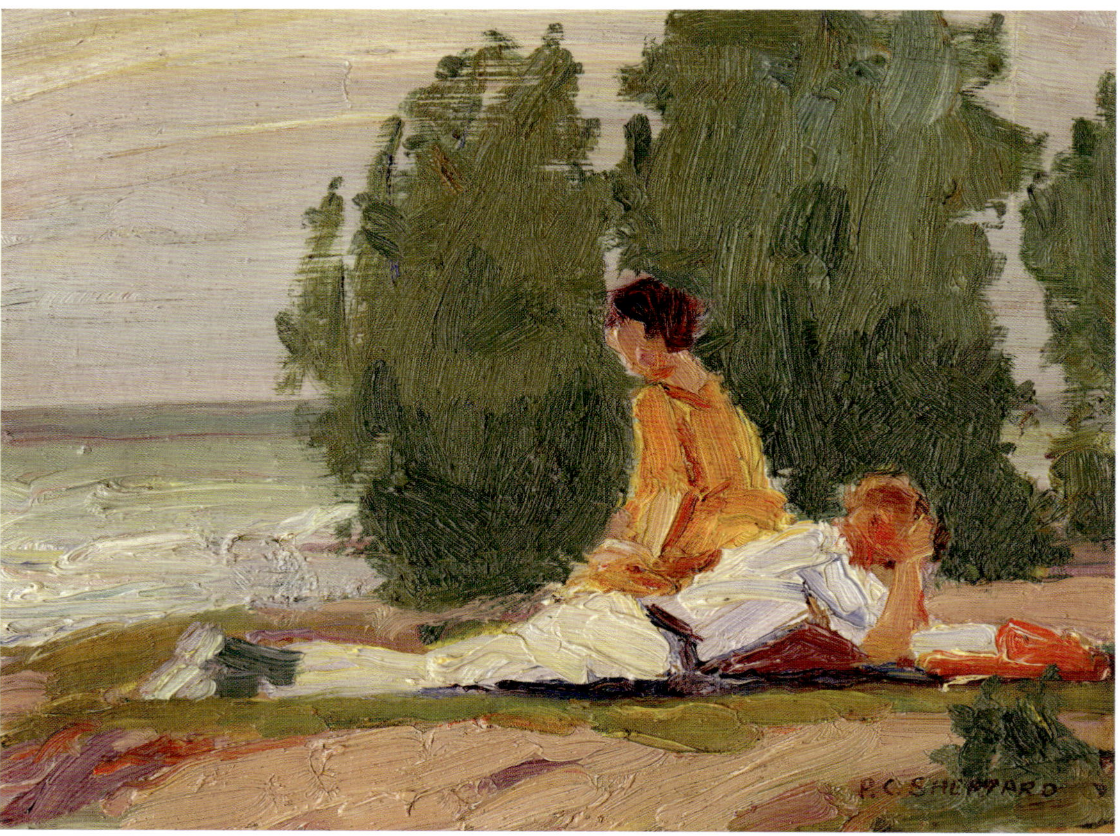

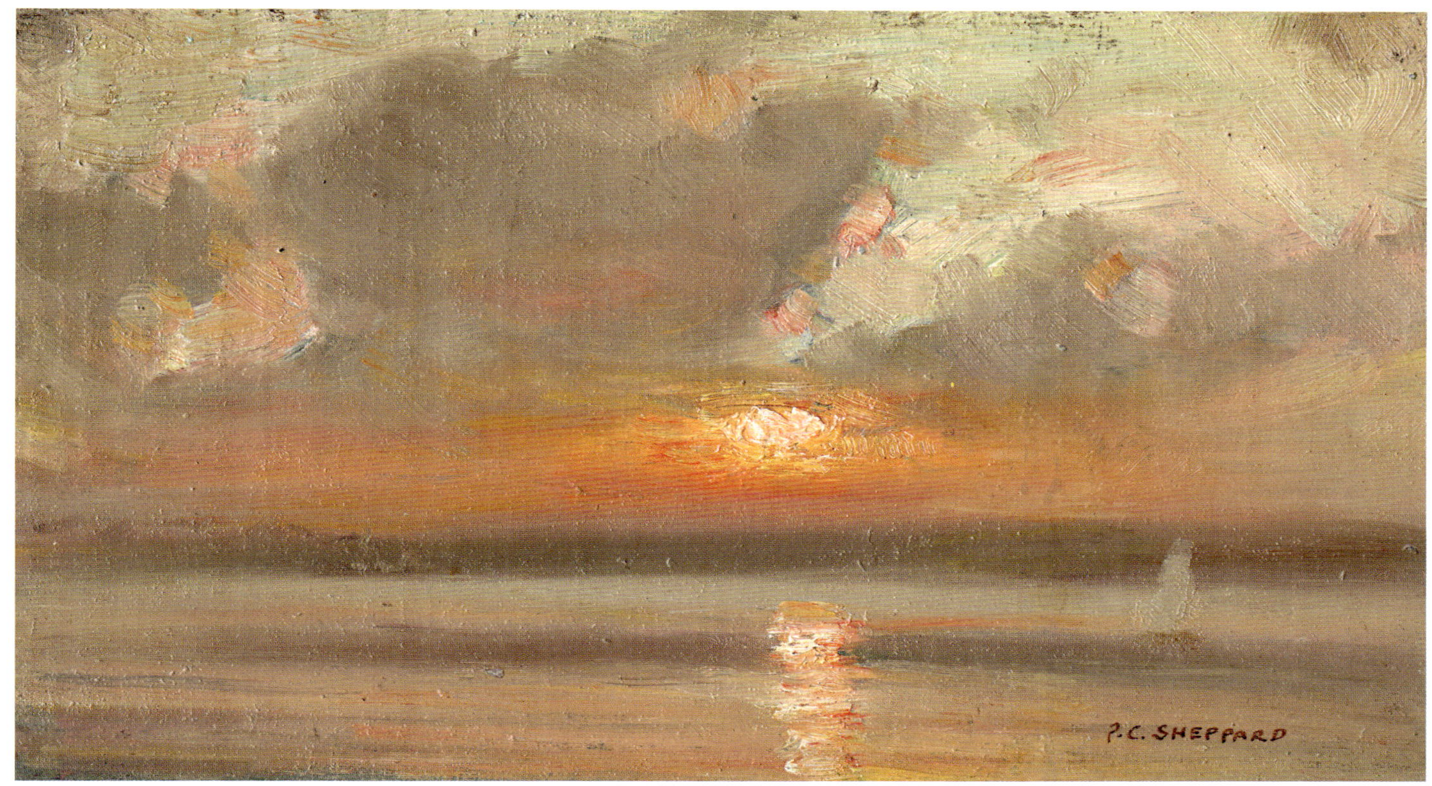

Sunset.
c. 1910–12. Oil on canvas,
14.6 x 24 cm.

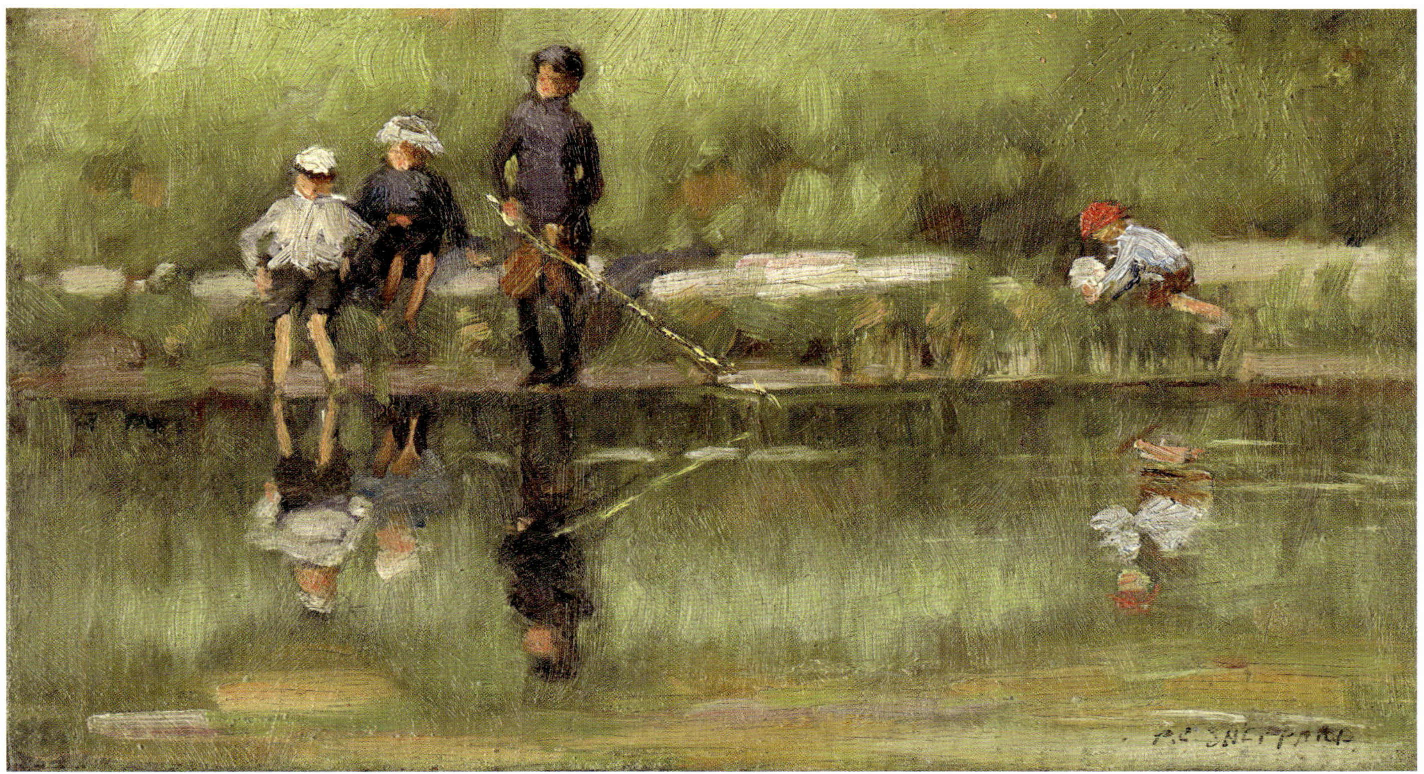

Summer Idyll.
c. 1910–12. Oil on canvas,
14.6 x 24 cm.

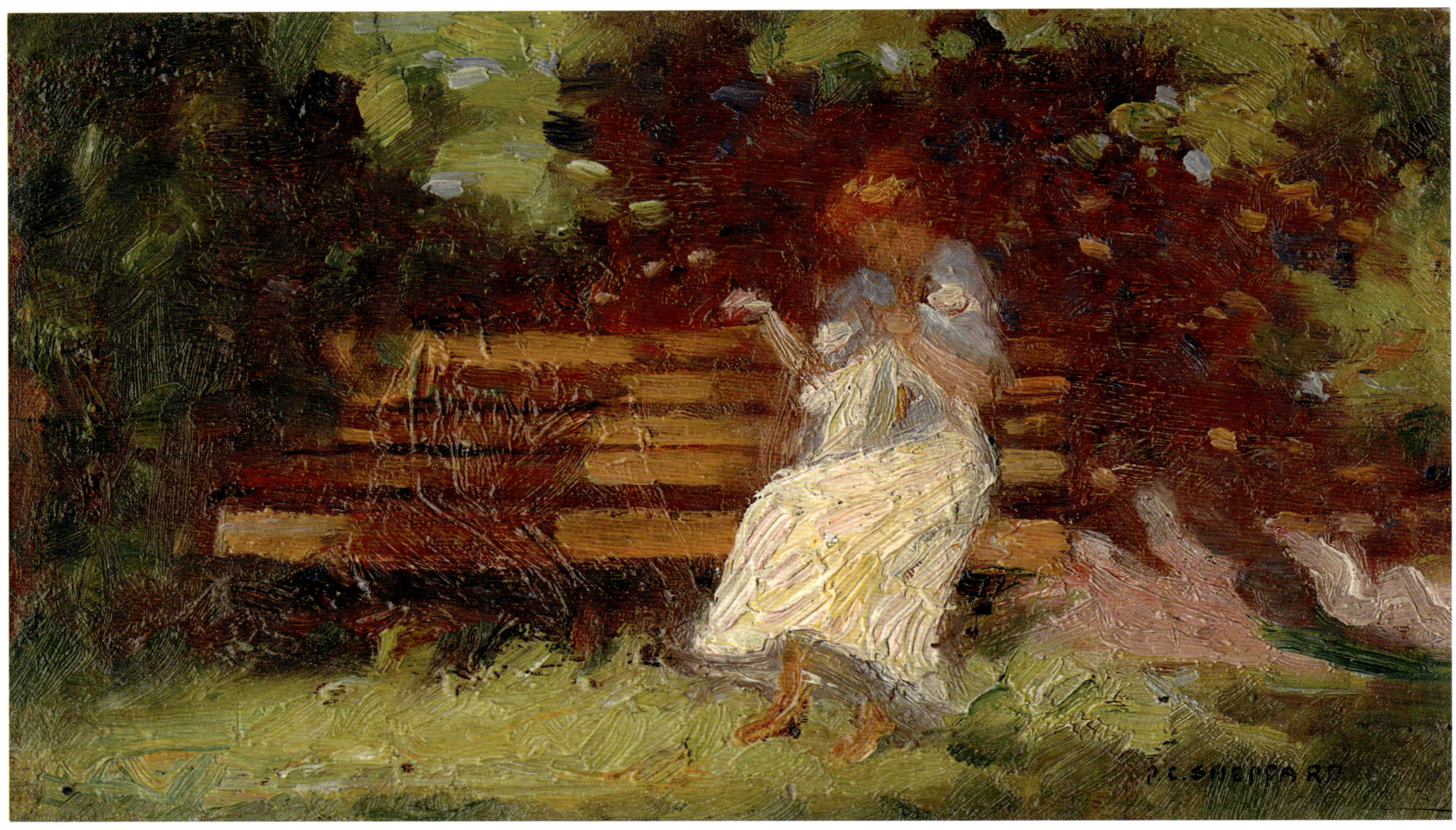

Woman Sewing.
c. 1912. Oil on panel,
14 x 24 cm.

WILLIAM CRUIKSHANK:
RESPECT FOR TRADITION

William Cruikshank, for example, taught Sheppard a so-called traditional way to paint and a manner of description that was suited to the graphic arts trade. Born in Scotland, Cruikshank's great-uncle was George Cruikshank (1792–1878), an artist who illustrated Charles Dickens' works. William Cruikshank came with his parents to Canada in 1857, settling in Toronto. However, in 1864 he returned to Scotland, where he studied art at the Royal Scottish Academy in Edinburgh. While in Europe, Cruikshank also studied at the Royal Academy in London, and at the École des Beaux-Arts in Paris. His education in Paris was interrupted by the Franco-Prussian War, causing him to return to London in 1871 and begin illustrating for London periodicals.

Cruikshank came back to Canada in 1873, and then almost immediately left for New York, where he provided illustrations for *Scribner's* and *St. Nicholas Magazine*. In 1876 he once again returned to Toronto, contributing illustrations to *Canadian Illustrated News* until 1879.

Cruikshank's fine art falls into the category of pictorial narrative that borders on illustration. In his clarity lies an approach to realism that conveys a message, often a moral one, in which the appreciation of art opens onto avenues leading to betterment of character, or to an understanding of something timeless, perhaps even eternal, in a well-described still life, or a study of a dead pigeon or hare.

In 1880 he began teaching classes in sketching at the Ontario School of Art. His students received firm grounding in drawing, a discipline that served them well in the printing trades because he stressed the importance of composition and structure based on hard outlines and linear clarity. Cruikshank's method was easily adaptable to the requirements of linear drawings for lithography and engraving, and without doubt, his purpose was as much to assist his students in honing their commercial skills as to teach them self-expression. In the days before widespread photomechanical reproduction, drawing ability was a marketable skill of use in catalogue and advertising print media, and of use to journalists to document news and current events as they occurred.

What else did Cruikshank teach at the art school? A surviving photograph (see page 76) of one of his studios (one that possibly included Sheppard) shows the class in progress, students drawing studies from plaster casts of antique statues. Cruikshank was the "Instructor, Antique Class," in which, according to the OCA Prospectus, students were "required to make drawings of details of casts of historic ornament and portions of the figure" employing all media, including painting in oil and drawing.[27]

In addition to drawing technique, a class of this sort might also involve instruction on human anatomy and proportion. The modelling of the sculptures was held as an important exercise to study the proportional relationship of one piece of anatomy to another. The plasters often stood in for live models when one might not be available, or the class could have been an introductory drawing class; students graduated to classes with live models only after they had mastered drawing antique subjects.

GEORGE AGNEW REID: THE EXPRESSIVE PROPERTIES OF COLOUR

In contrast to the controlled linear realism of Cruikshank, one of his colleagues at the school, George Agnew Reid, exemplified expressiveness through colour and brushwork. Where Cruikshank was prosaic, composed and precise, Reid opened students' minds not only to Impressionism, but also to mythic narratives and allegory.

Trained in Philadelphia at the prestigious Pennsylvania Academy, Reid was exposed to some of the most progressive, radical theories of the day about art and art education. First of all, the curriculum that was taught in the studios Reid attended at the Pennsylvania Academy was co-educational: men and women shared the same studio space and participated together in field trips and anatomy classes. Reid also learned how to paint directly from nature without an underlying sketch or even a preliminary study.[28] This technique was taught by one of the academy's most influential professors, Thomas Eakins (1844–1916). The art of painting in nature — en plein-air — was an artistic legacy of the work of the French Barbizon painters and of the Impressionists, whose studies — set down in paint directly from nature while literally standing in the field — allowed for a fully engaged approach to subject matter, expressing the immediacy of the experience. The method was ideally suited to capturing the fugitive effects of light falling on subjects, and to conveying the innate vitality of what was being painted. Interpreting in paint what presented itself to the eye in the open air allowed for a seamless, authentic approach to reflecting both the observed objects and the attendant ideas and emotions. Painting done in this way liberated artists from the studio so they could engage directly with the life they saw around them — and paint it.

The consequence of their painting from life is, looking back a century later, an overriding sense in the surviving work that the real daily life of the times — as much as the thought process and creative expression of the artist — had been captured in paint. An archive of paintings whose genesis is the plein-air method gives off an impression of immediacy, as if the distance in time between creation and observation has been elided. Plein-air painting functions as a sort of time machine, seemingly transporting inquisitive viewers back in time. What the paintings show seems true, and the information they offer to a biographer is much more than art historical. As primary research sources they can be plumbed for motives, for intentional ideas, for factual information about the places they describe. For Reid and his contemporaries, the method's foundation in lived experience gave them a means of demonstrating how gesture and colour could convey that experience as well as related thoughts and emotions.

As a student in Philadelphia Reid was also immersed in the study of the human figure and would have spent many hundreds of hours drawing, painting and sculpting from the figure, nude and clothed, and from recast classical Greek and Roman sculptures.

Reid and his fellow students were also aware of the contemporary Tonalist painters of the day, who were schooled in the manner of James Abbott McNeill Whistler (1834–1903) and his American followers, particularly George Inness (1825–1894). Tonalists were interested in creating a resonant atmosphere

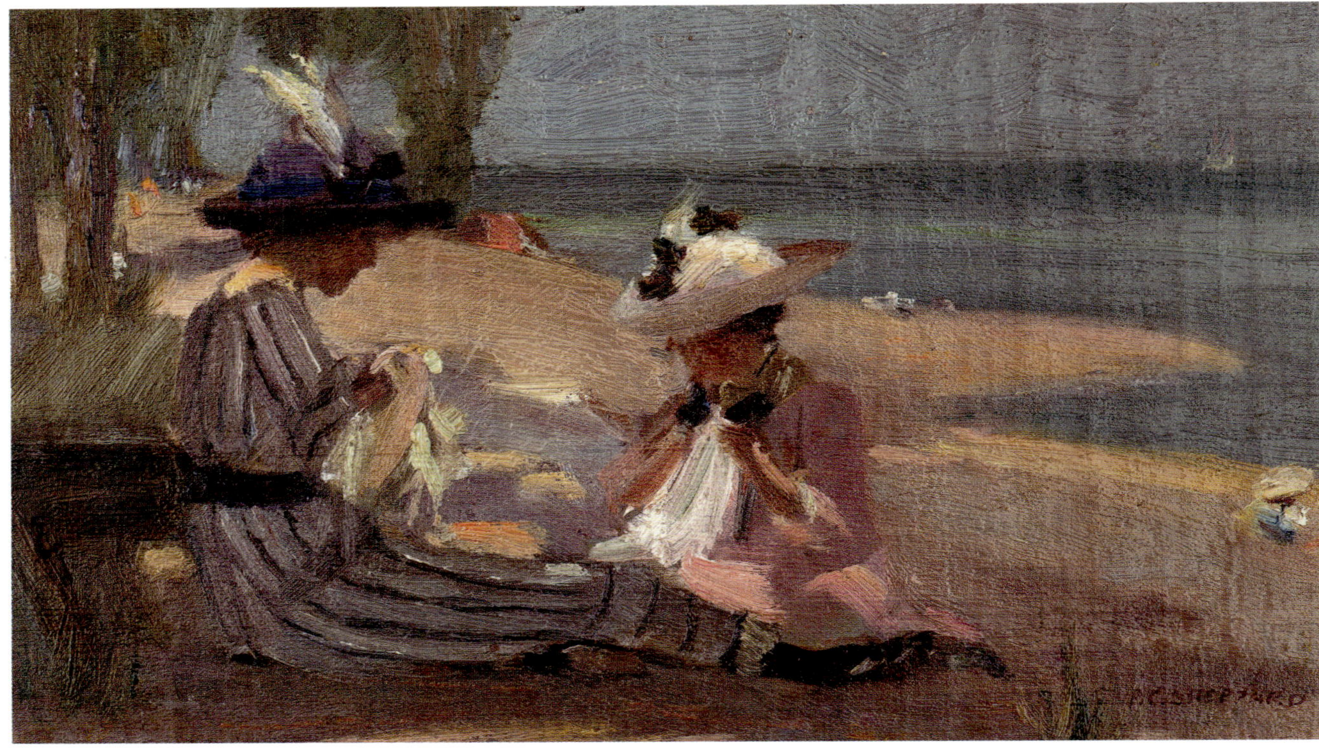

Mother and Child.
c. 1910–12. Oil on panel,
14.6 x 24 cm.

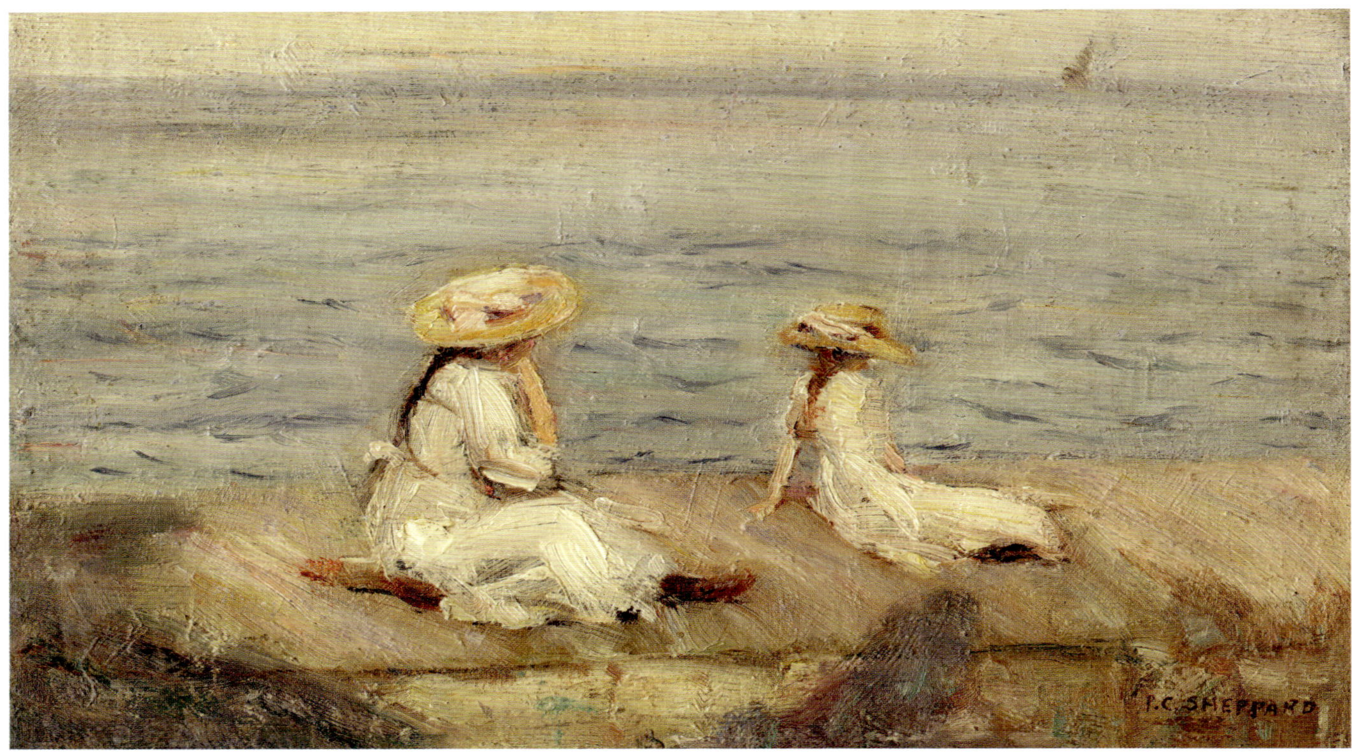

Two Sisters.
c. 1910–12. Oil on panel,
14.6 x 24 cm.

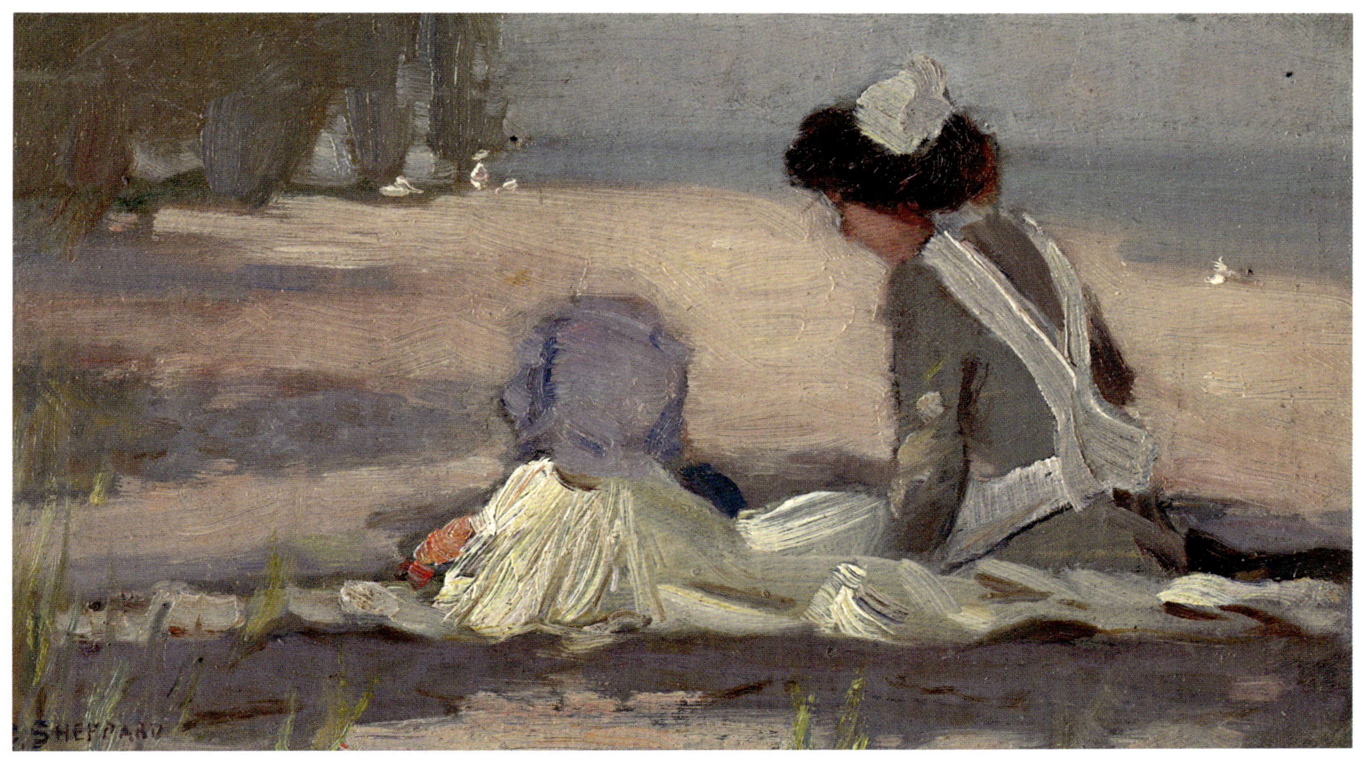

Beachside Idyll.
c. 1910–12. Oil on panel,
14.6 x 24 cm.

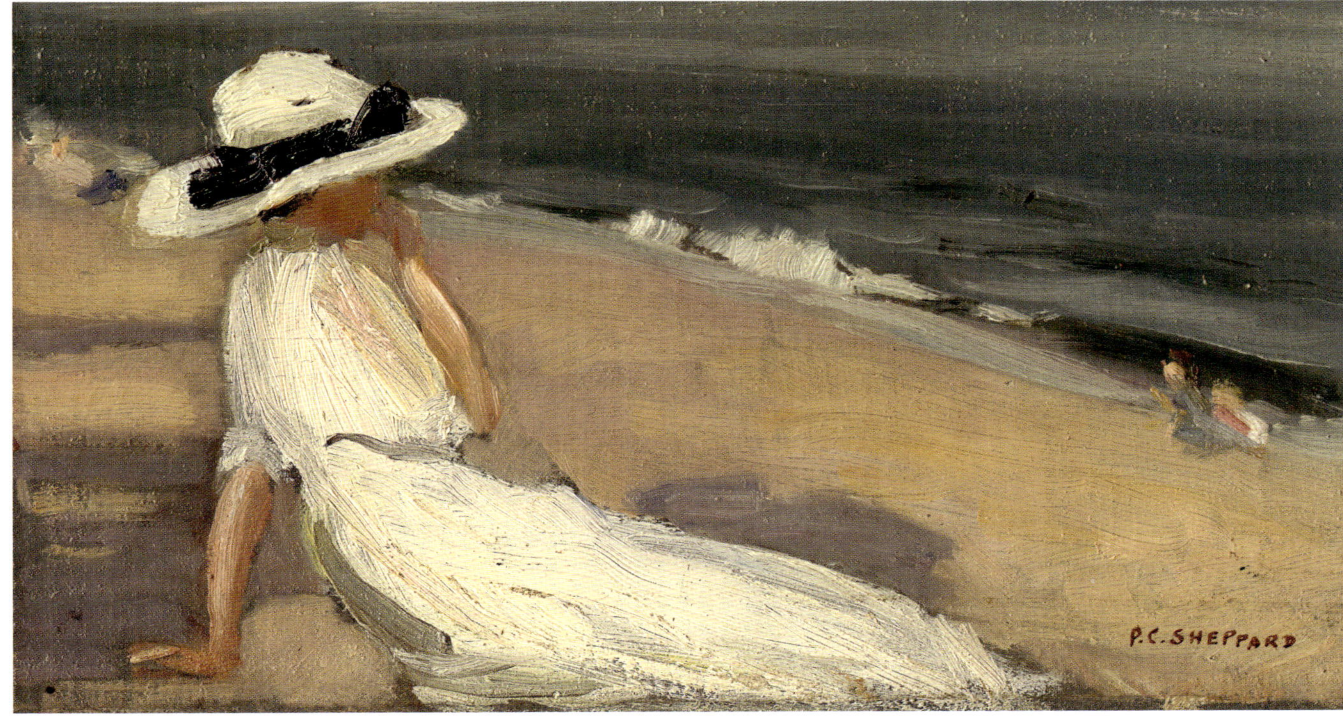

Woman by the Lake.
c. 1910–12. Oil on panel,
14.6 x 24 cm.

of tones in their paintings, to convey mood; the close interactions of hues were effectively the subjects of their compositions. A landscape was reduced to near-abstract description. Reid himself never fully embraced the Tonalist mode.

Reid's tender pastel painting *Reading* (see page 58), discussed earlier in comparison with Sheppard's painting of a woman in blue (page 59) is evidence that he sought to blend his various methods into one composition. The figure is set down in a relaxed profile pose, all the better to emphasize the contemplative theme of the subject: a young woman lost in thought as she ponders the words on the pages of the book that rests on her lap. Reid has used the pose and subject as vehicles to study the effects of the light as it falls on the figure, rendering her in light and shadow. The handling of the medium shows Reid's debt to the Impressionist mode. But a sense of ephemeral mood is balanced by a strong sense of composition. The background is rendered almost as a theatrical tableau; the thoughts of the woman and of the viewer are given space to dissolve in, a poetic vapour in the composition's central area, a brilliant white space that takes eye and thought into infinity.

Reid brought this artistic method — essentially, Impressionism combined with narrative and a strong sense of composition — to his classes at OCA. Sheppard and his classmates embraced this modern (perhaps radical) style as a balance to the linear precision of Cruikshank's teachings. Where Cruikshank prepared his young charges for the requirements of the commercial art, Reid gave these same students an outlet for personal expression and perhaps even poetic interpretation of a subject. The contrast between the two teaching methods underscored the division between commercial art and art for expression that bifurcated the art world at the time when Sheppard was an art student.

J.W. BEATTY: THE IMPORTANCE OF DRAWING AND COMPOSITION

The artist who exerted the strongest influence on Sheppard while he was a student was J.W. Beatty.[29] He was a Torontonian, a complex extrovert of a man possessing a rebarbative character. A braggart, Beatty never felt the warm embrace of the progressive artists of the day, but neither was he entirely rebuffed by them. Caught in some middle ground between imitation and innovation, Beatty followed a path that respected the fundamental elements of drawing and composition even as he gingerly adopted some of the modern notes into his own practice. As the dawning decades of the new century saw modernism increasingly embraced in the studios, Beatty remained steadfast in his

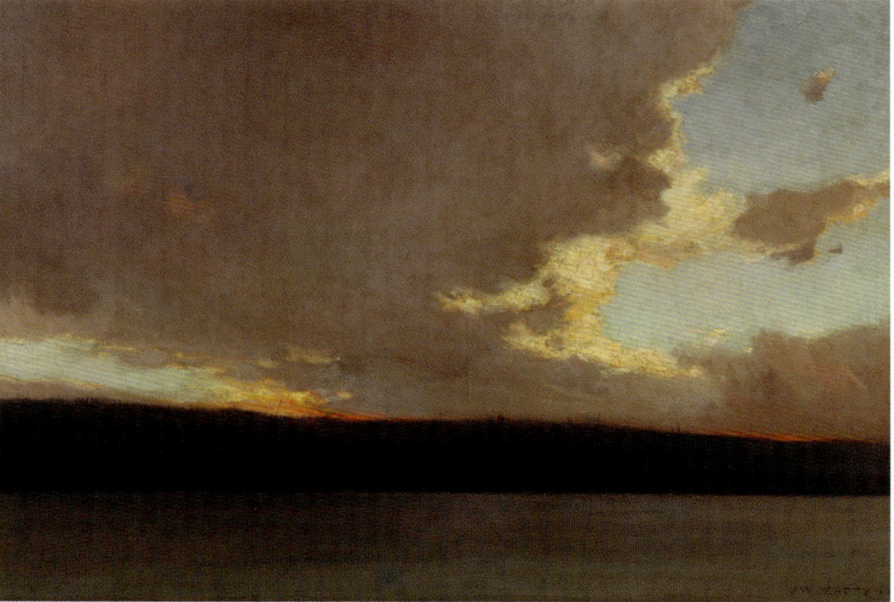

Evening Cloud of the Northland.
By J.W. Beatty.
1910. Oil on canvas,
99.4 x 142.4 cm.

opposition to advances in art, preferring the comfortable attributes of the 19th-century academy in his own work.

Following studies in 1900 at the Académie Julian in Paris (where A.Y. Jackson would study a few years later in 1907) and travels throughout Europe in the first decade of the 20th century, Beatty developed a personal style that owed a considerable debt to the popular Dutch manner of moody, dark-toned paintings that illustrated peasant life. Once in Canada, he put to good use his considerable abilities as a plein-air painter in his interpretations of Algonquin Park, in the hinterland north of Toronto.

He came into his own in the second decade of the century, not least for his expressive manner of depicting the wilderness. His *Evening Cloud of the Northland*, now in the collection of the National Gallery of Canada, won him great praise as attesting to his innovation on a landscape theme. Even though the painting reflects its Dutch stylistic antecedents, it gives a sense of immediacy that is a consequence of its being painted from a sketch made directly from nature. Viewed from the vantage point of today, a little more than a century after the painting was made, the innovations of *Evening Cloud of the Northland* are even more evident than they were when it was painted. It embodies all the compositional qualities that would characterize the northern Ontario landscape paintings of many members of the Group of Seven. The low horizon line, the lyrical interpretation of the sky and clouds almost as elements of an animist interpretation of nature, subordinating the sky itself as a canvas for the performance of an abstract colour essay of close relationships of hue and tone: these among other qualities became closely identified with Beatty's contemporaries in the group. Although he never was a member of the Group of Seven, it is easy to place him at the forefront of their history as either a critical influence or as a fellow traveller and innovator who spawned a Canadian nationalist movement in art.

Beyond his studio practice, however, Beatty's reputation also rests on his "long and influential" career as an art teacher in Toronto.[30] He began teaching private art classes in his studio immediately upon his return from Europe in late 1908, and he also offered courses through Shaw's Correspondence School. These classes included outdoor landscape painting, intaglio printmaking and possibly illustration, thus spanning the distance between the fine and the commercial ends of the professional spectrum. George Reid, then the principal of the Ontario College of Art, hired Beatty in 1912 to teach life drawing, and no doubt Sheppard was one of Beatty's first students in this course (Sheppard won a life-drawing award that year). Reid considered Beatty a born teacher possessing "all the necessary attributes, authority and presence, fondness for people, a natural urge to enlighten and expound, and patience which occasionally exploded in a burst of temperament calculated to arouse the most lethargic student."[31] Beatty taught at OCA from 1912 to 1941, and in 1913 he founded the college's summer school. Classes took place first at Hogg's Hollow in Toronto and then in Port Hope on Lake Ontario. He ran the summer school, which was attended primarily by school teachers, until 1935. He exerted a strong influence on Sheppard, who also taught at the summer school at both locations.

As a fine arts student at OCA, what curriculum would Sheppard have followed in Beatty's studio? We turn to the words of A.J. Casson (1898–1992), a generation younger than Sheppard and an eventual member of the Group of Seven. Casson provides a description of Beatty's studio on the third floor of the Normal School on Toronto's Gould Street; these words very likely reflect the conditions in which Sheppard and his chums drew:

I was in the Life Class which was taken by Bill Beatty … It was a big room and if you were lucky you got under one of those bare bulbs on a cord. Because of the bad lighting and crowded conditions, you almost had to sit down. We all had a thing we called a donkey. It was like a bench with the centre pinched in, and a rail on which you put your drawing board … The old place wasn't dirty but it was untidy and there was an atmosphere.[32]

The innovation that met Sheppard while he was Beatty's life-drawing student was that the models were undraped. Nude. Although this was a common practice in European art schools and teaching academies, it was revolutionary, perhaps even scandalous, in the eyes of prim Toronto. Mixed classes of art students drawing from the nude would have raised many an eyebrow.

The Ontario College of Art Prospectus for 1914–15 provides descriptions of Beatty's role at OCA and the rubric for the courses he taught and which Sheppard attended.[33] As an "Instructor of Drawing and Painting from Life," he based his classes on "general proficiency in drawing as shown by tests made in the Primary and Antique classes." A student in Beatty's studio made use of all media, including "regular-sized" canvas and paper.

Notwithstanding the notoriety of those nude life-drawing models, Beatty's students received sound, helpful instruction in the basic academic curriculum that saw in the study of the figure a firm foundation from which to build a sound professional career. Beatty was respected because he taught technique, while also sharpening the perceptual abilities of his students. Selecting and simplifying naturalistic subjects drawn from life or nature and being attentive to the structural dynamics of a composition supported his methods. He also insisted that his students be sensitive to the play of light on form and the ways it illuminates subjects.[34]

Beatty inculcated in his students the values and principles of academically inspired drawing and painting methods, and was not shy about deriding modern art as so much flimflammery. His stridently expressed prejudice did a disservice to serious art students whose development and knowledge of modern movements of abstraction — Cubism and Expressionism, to give just two examples — were greatly impaired. Sheppard's near peer (and perhaps his classmate — she graduated from OCA in 1918) Yvonne McKague Housser (1898–1996) remarked that one of the legacies of being a student of Beatty was

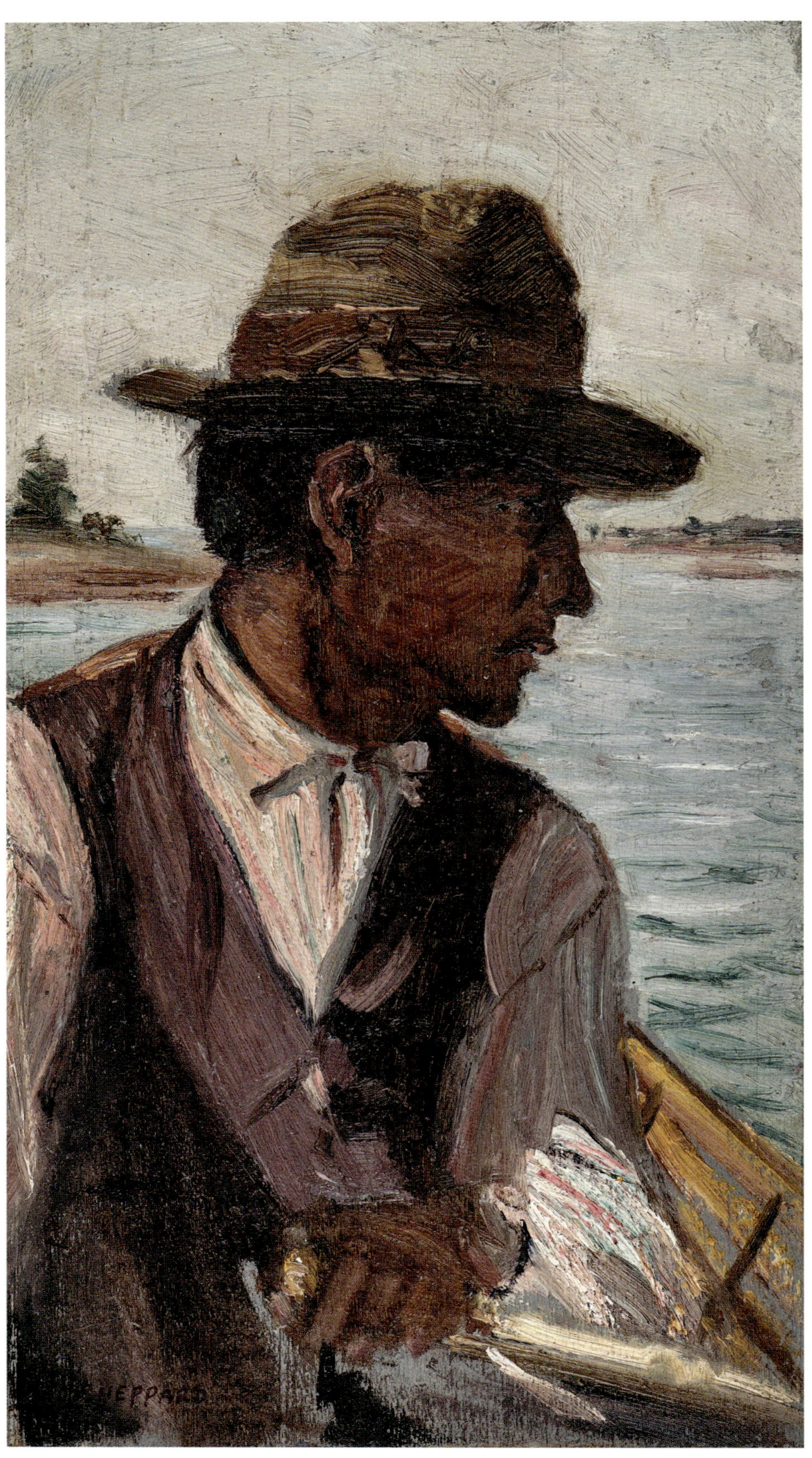

Portrait of a Man in a Rowboat.
(Possibly a portrait of Tom Thomson.)
1910–12. Oil on panel,
24 x 14.6 cm.

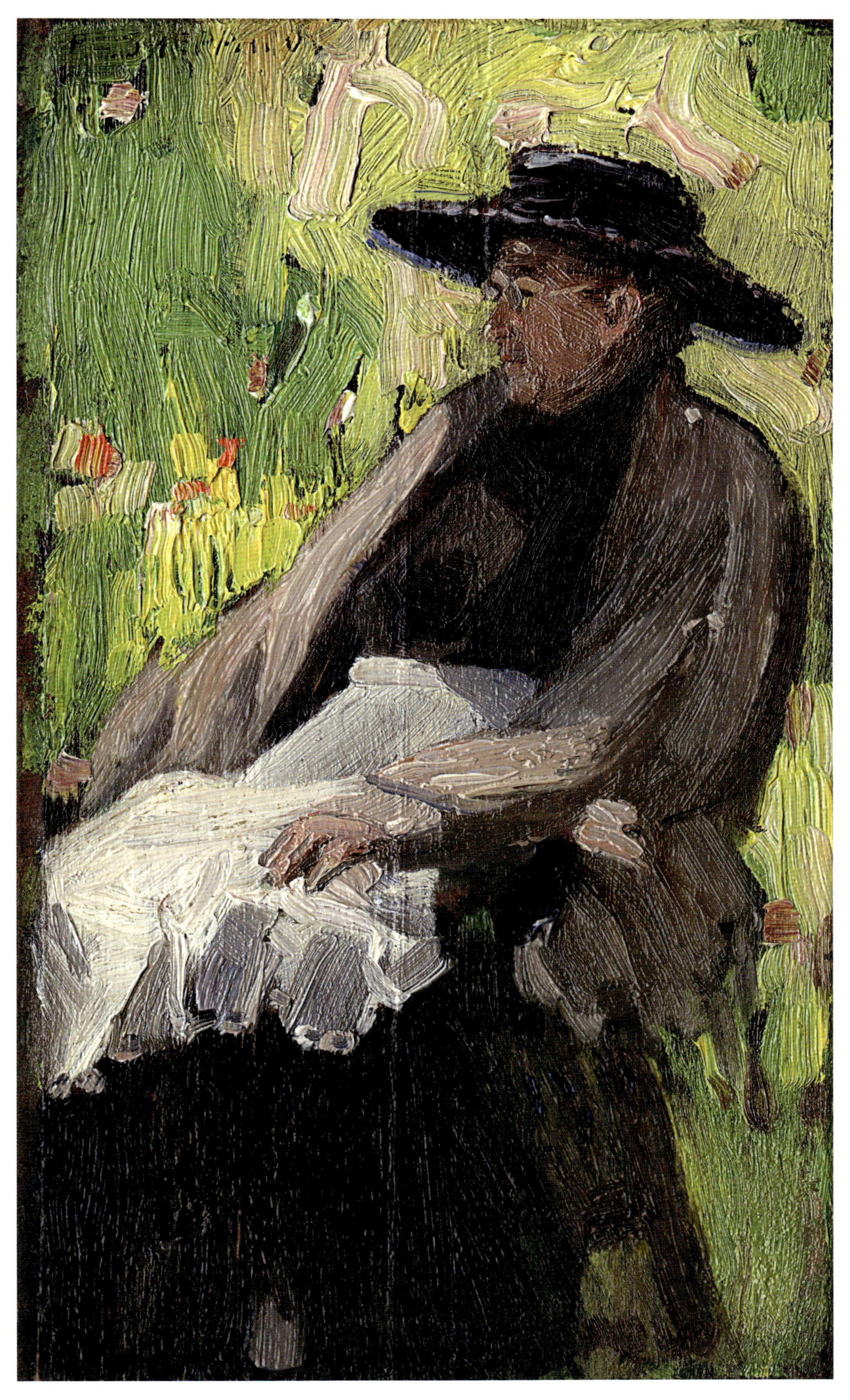

Artist's Mother.
c. 1910–12. Oil on panel,
24 x 14.6 cm.

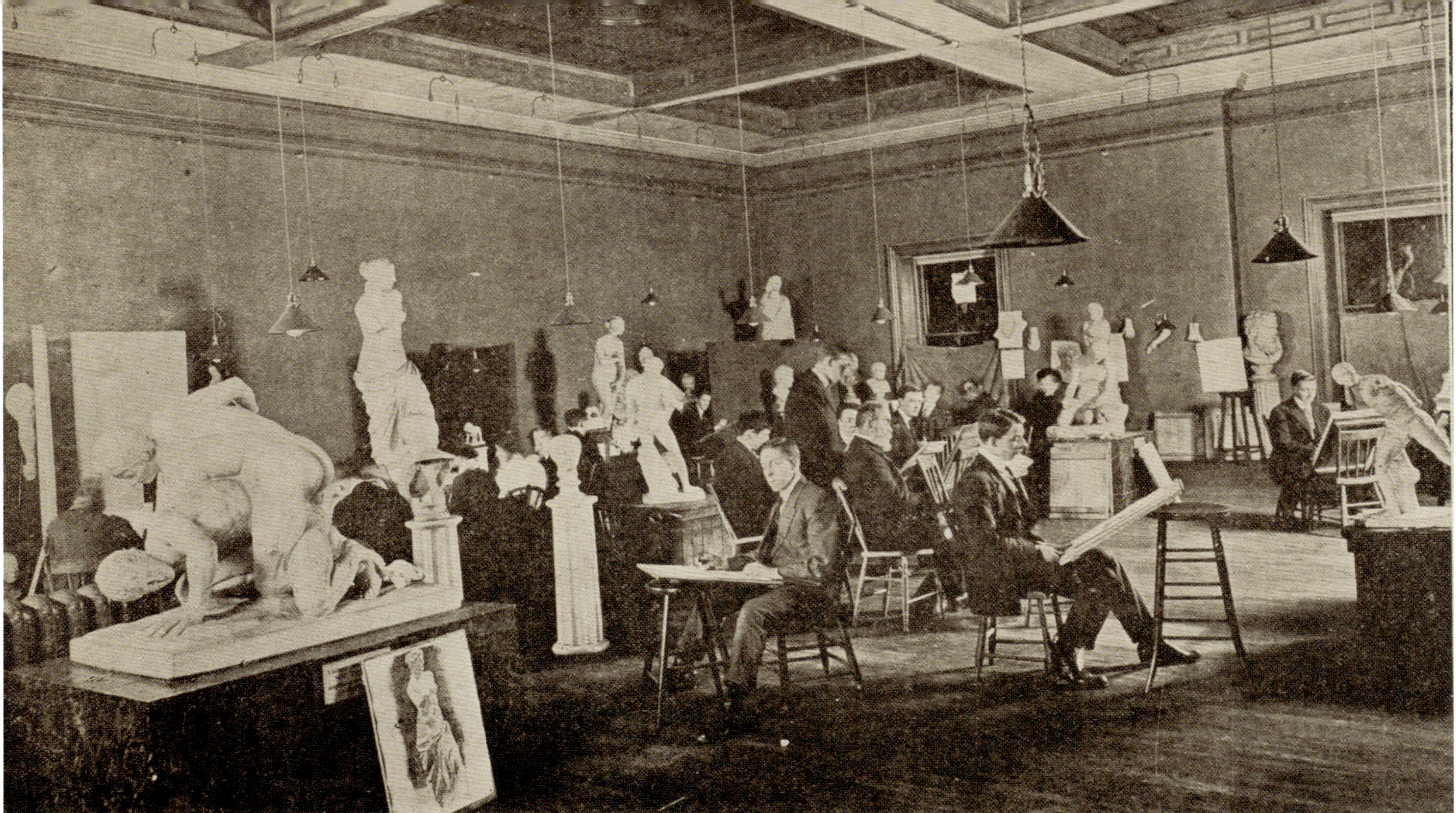

Drawing from plaster casts at the Ontario College of Art at the Normal School, Toronto, 1913. Cruikshank, seated centre, was the instructor.

that she "felt cheated when I arrived in Paris in 1921–1922 — because I had no idea of what was going on in Europe — post impressionists etc. Mr. Beatty's likes and dislikes were very forceful … He wanted me to be a little Beatty."[35]

The archive points to the unquestioned fact that Sheppard learned much from Beatty to the extent that he *was* "a little Beatty." The OCA honourable mention awards Sheppard won in 1912–13 (still-life painting, painting, composition, drawing from the draped model, drawing from the nude), the Stone Scholarship for his "proficiency in the department of drawing from the nude" and the award of a Sir Edmund Walker Scholarship for drawing the nude figure (1913–14) all indicate that Sheppard learned much from this teacher. In fact, throughout the rest of Beatty's life, he and Sheppard remained close friends.

STUDENT WORK AT THE ONTARIO COLLEGE OF ART, AFTER 1912

Sheppard absorbed Beatty's lessons well, particularly those involving drawing from the nude. He clearly had a natural affinity for drawing the figure with a view to capturing its life and energy without diminishing the importance of effectively rendering the model proportionately. He captures the models' languid nature and relaxed posture in ways that are rare among figurative artists, and yet when compared to similar studies by Beatty they display a remarkable affinity to the teacher's work. As a student of Beatty, Sheppard did much more than execute his lessons well; he emulated the master's example, equalling his accomplishment and perhaps even exceeding it.

Without doubt, Beatty gave Sheppard a deep, thorough and rigorous instruction in figuration. The evidence of Sheppard's drawings from nude

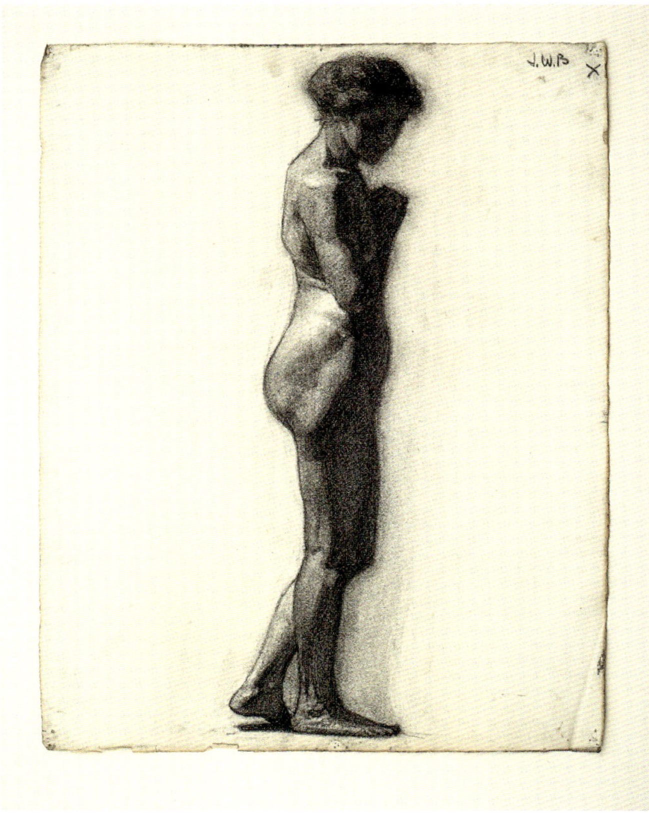

Study from Life.
By J.W. Beatty.
1910–12. Charcoal on paper,
61 x 48.2 cm.

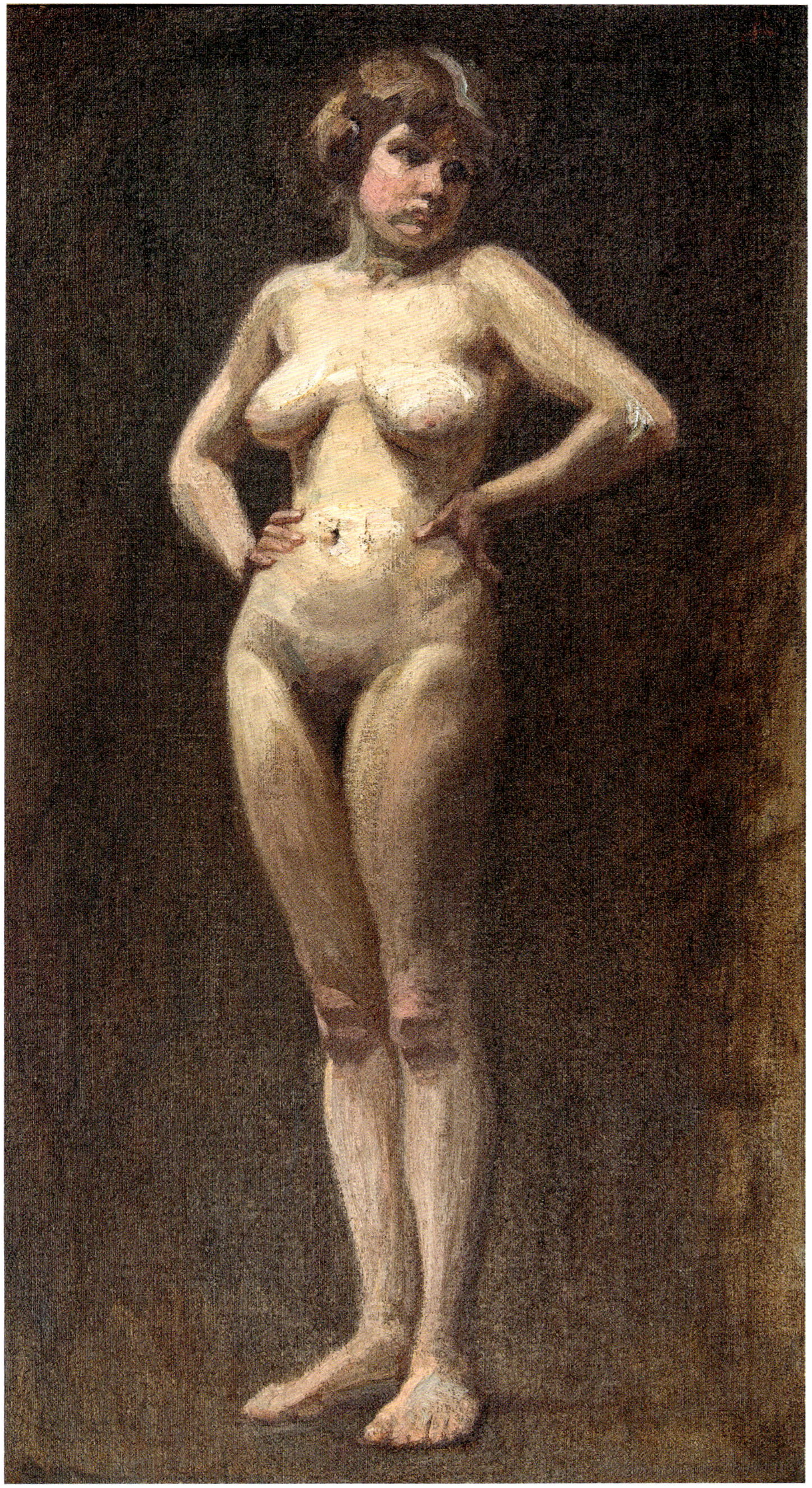

Nude Study from Life.
By J.W. Beatty.
1912–14. Oil on canvas,
94 x 48 cm.

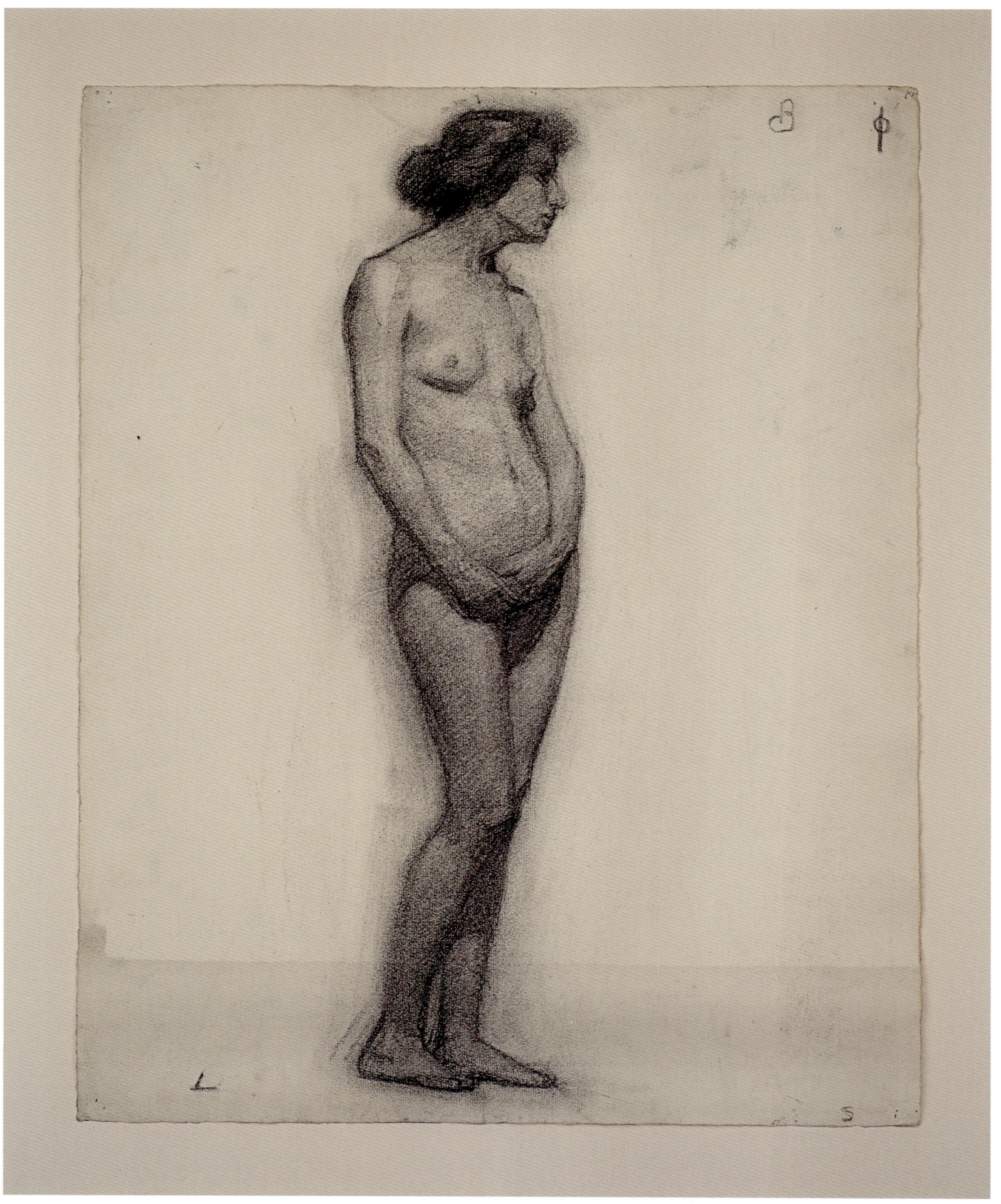

Nude Study from Life.
c. 1912–14. Charcoal on paper,
62.2 x 48.2 cm.

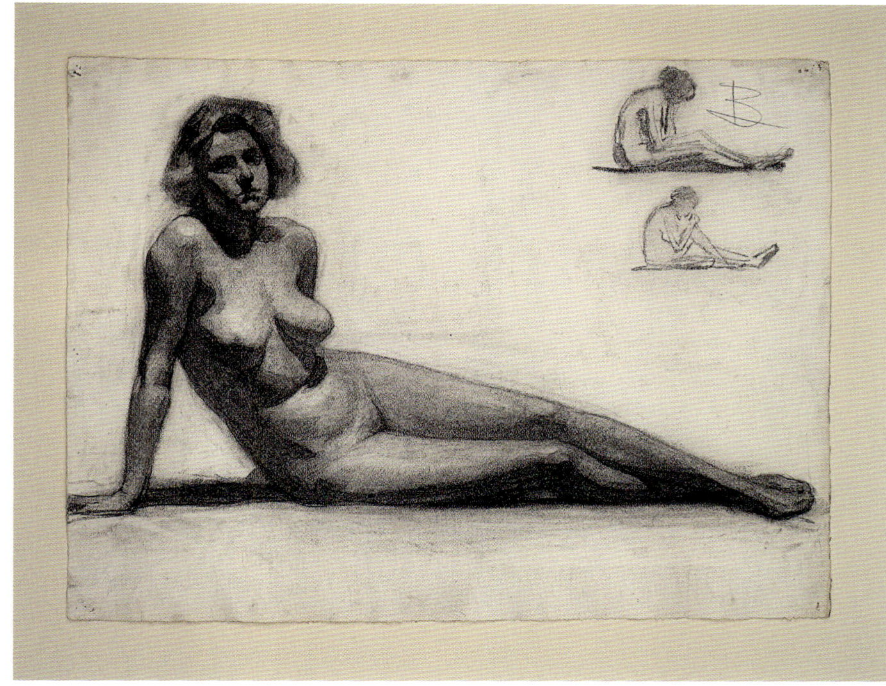

Nude Study from Life.
c. 1912–14. Charcoal on paper,
48.2 x 62.2 cm.

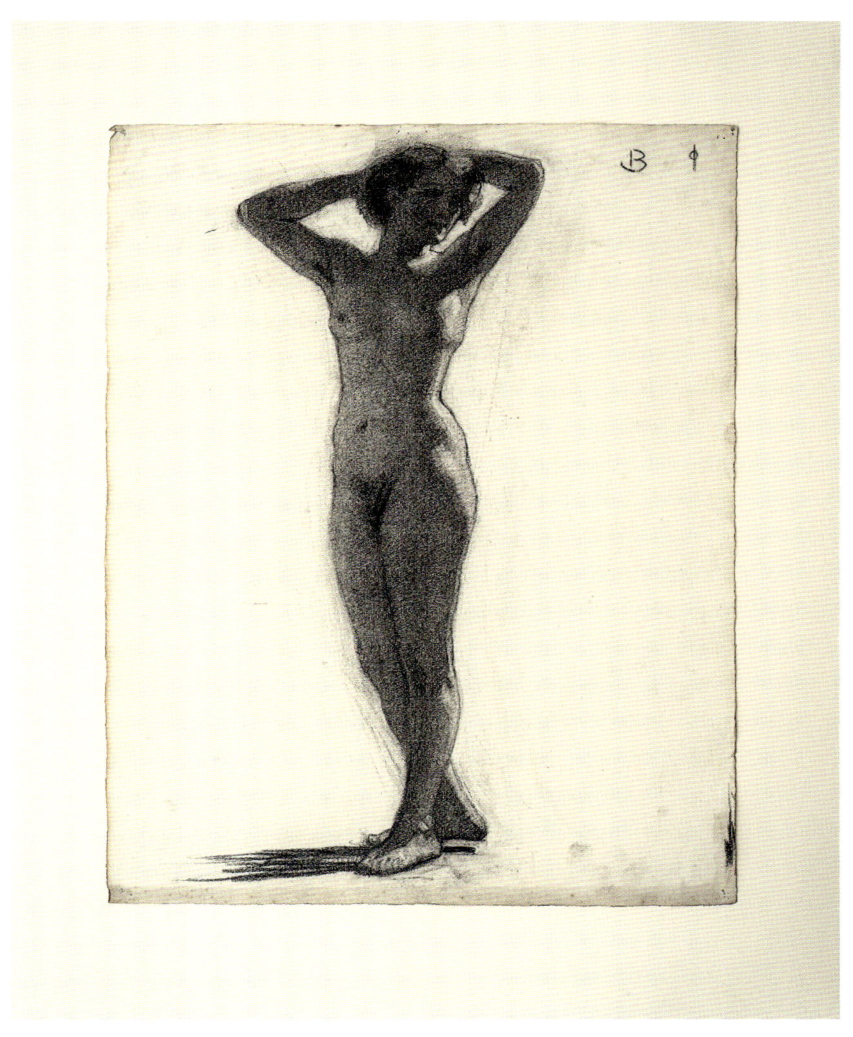

Nude Study from Life.
c. 1912–14. Charcoal on paper,
62.2 x 48.2 cm.

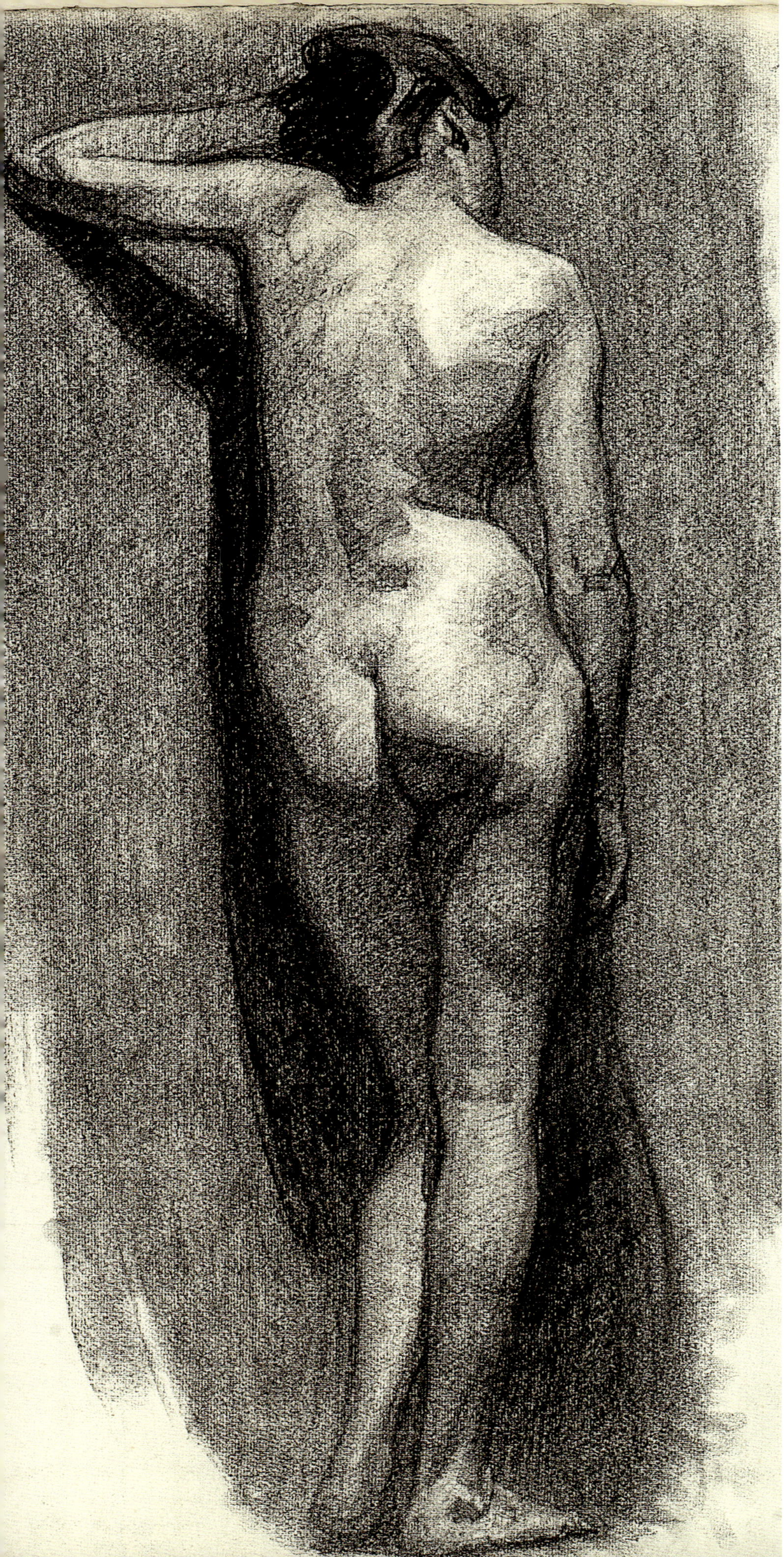

models shows he was adept at understanding and translating information that the model gave an art student into drawings that, in fact, have a liveliness to them. Sheppard's drawn models all retain a human quality because of the manner in which he was able to preserve their gestures throughout the often-long hours of posing and drawing. Take for example two different studies, probably from around 1912, of standing female nudes. One work is a depiction of a model in a relaxed pose, hands clasped in front of her (see page 78), while the second is a tonal study of the model, whose back is to the artist (left). In the former, Sheppard expertly conveys the nonchalance of the pose; the model rests her weight on one leg, the other is slightly bent at the knee, while he focuses on the profile portrait. The languid aspect of the model is preserved through the drawing by the lyricism of the contour lines that delineate the edges of the forms and lift the model ever so gently off the page.

In contrast to the linearity of the former drawing, the latter is a thoughtful visual essay on the way light and tone express the interactions of forms and

Nude Study from Life.
c. 1912–14. Charcoal on paper,
62.2 x 48.2 cm.

masses of muscle. Both drawings also show Sheppard's understanding of ana-
tomical structure, musculature and proportion which, undoubtedly set him
apart from his peers in the studio classes.

In addition to the drawings, the archive contains many examples of his
oil paintings interpreting the nude. Just as his drawings, the paintings display
a precocious talent not afraid to tackle difficult subjects. For example, in the
archive is an oil study of a seated woman viewed from the back and in profile
(see page 84). The light falls on the model's back, emphasizing how the study
is an essay describing the anatomy and musculature of the female form. The
play of light and tone on the model does not obscure the accurate description
of the anatomy, rendered in a nuanced palette of modulated yellows, beiges,
greens and pinks. Beyond the subtleties of shadow and light that define
the forms, the painting emphasizes Sheppard's deft hand at describing the
figure's contours; her left side is delimited by a strong contour line, while
there is a lovely rhythm in the interplay between the dark portrait profile and

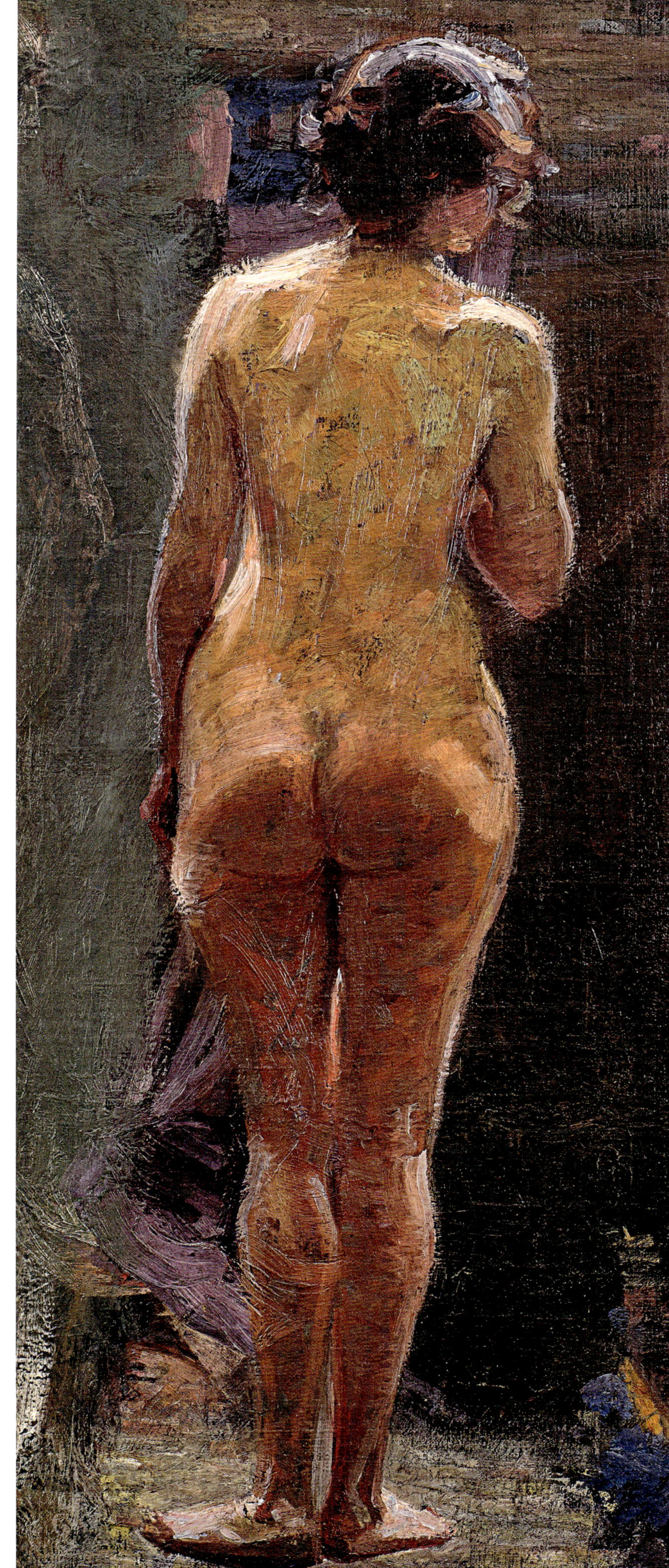

Nude from Life.
c. 1912–14. Oil on canvas,
86.3 x 35.6 cm.

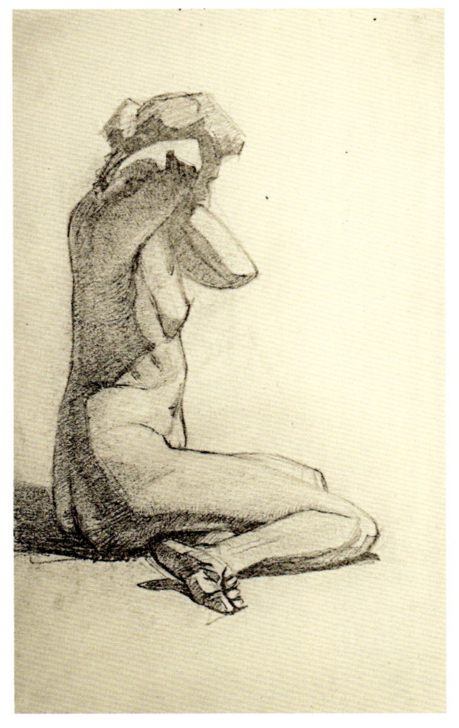
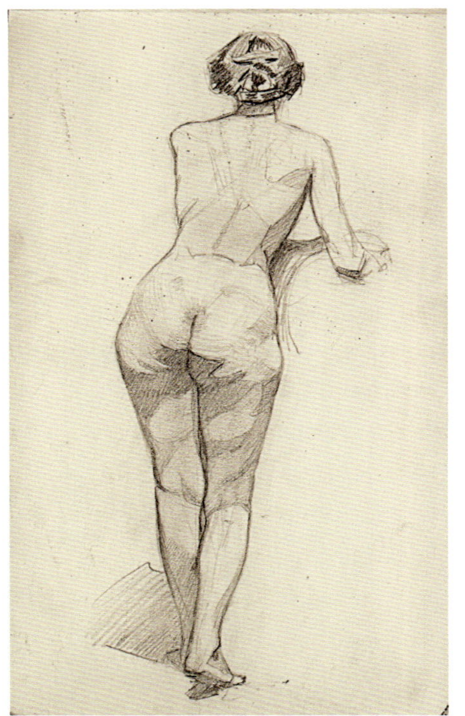
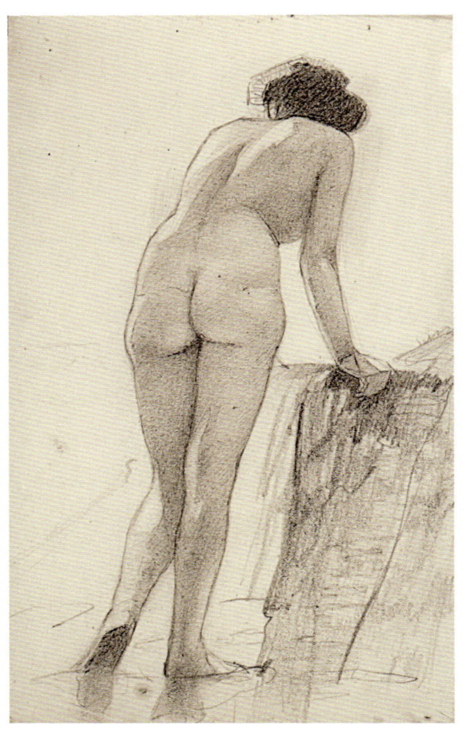
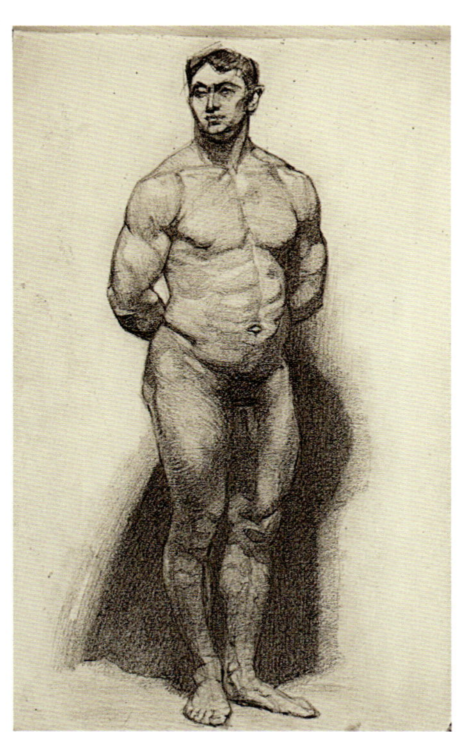
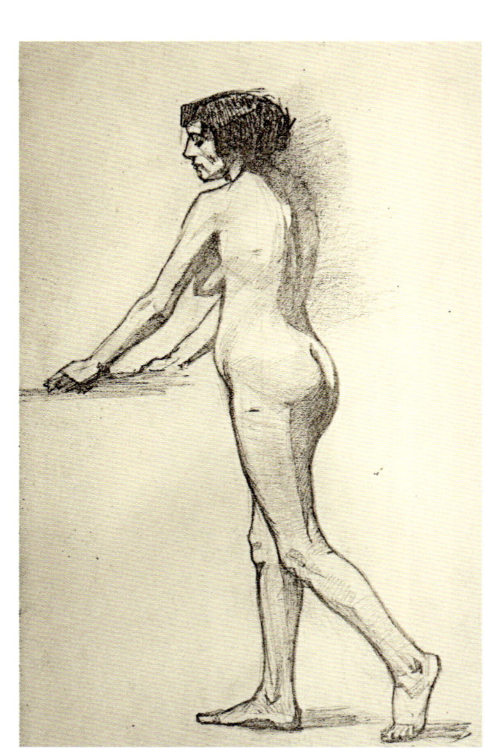
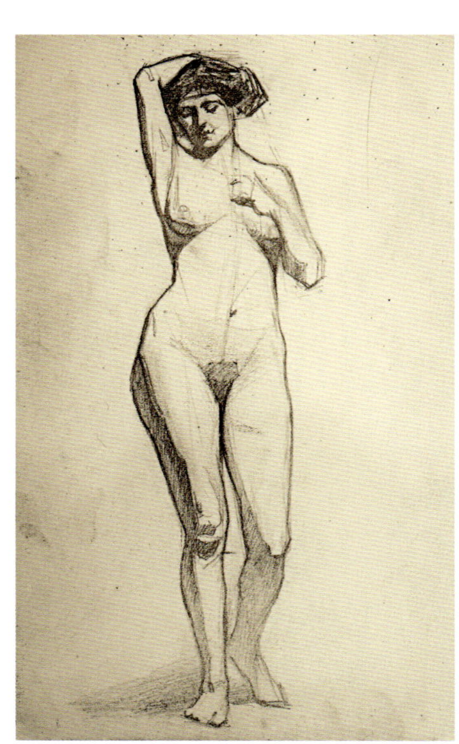

Studies from Life, OCA.
From Sheppard's sketchbook of 1916.
Graphite on paper,
22.2 x 14 cm.

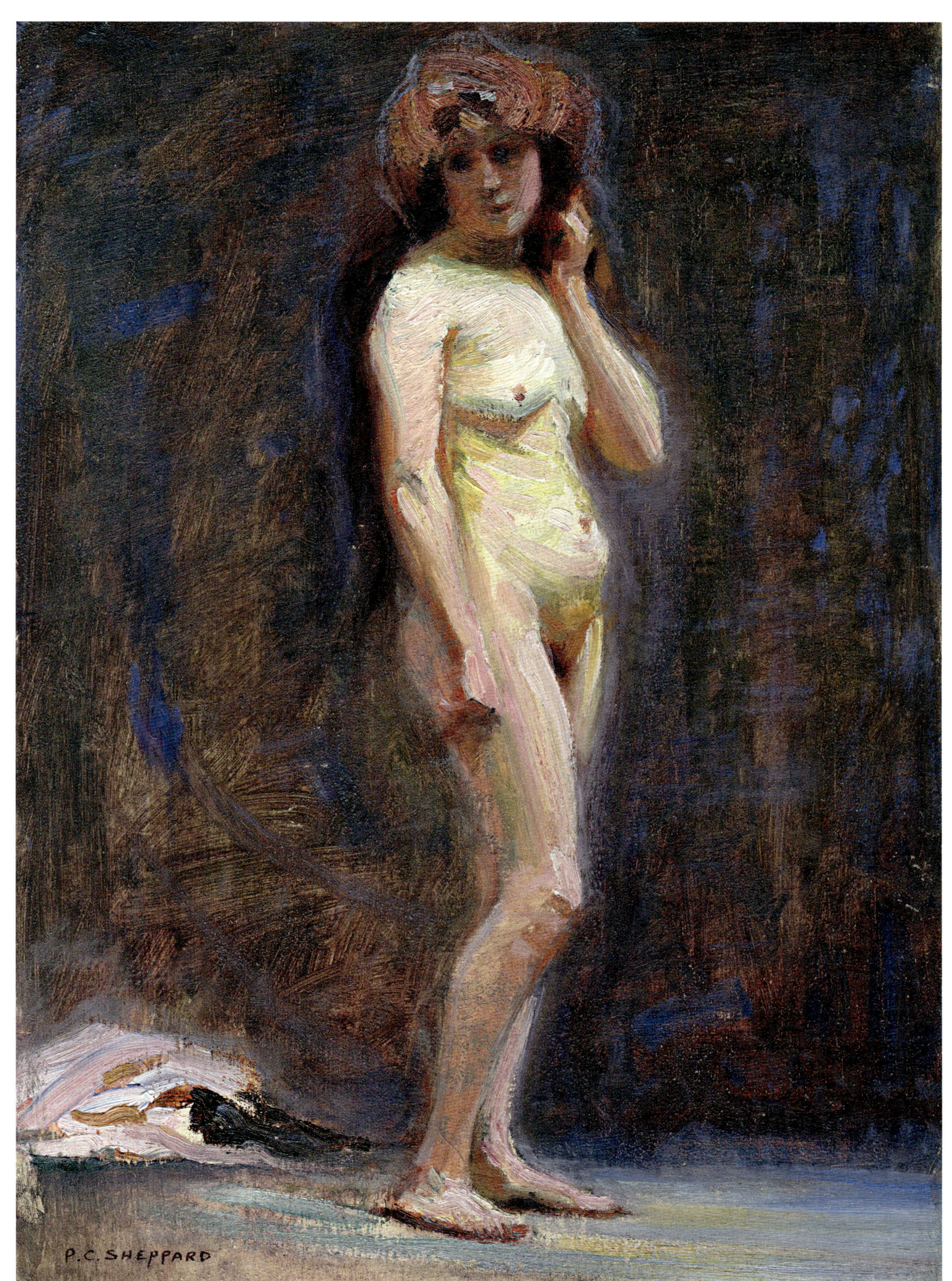

Study from Life, OCA.
c. 1913. Oil on panel,
35.6 x 24.8 cm.

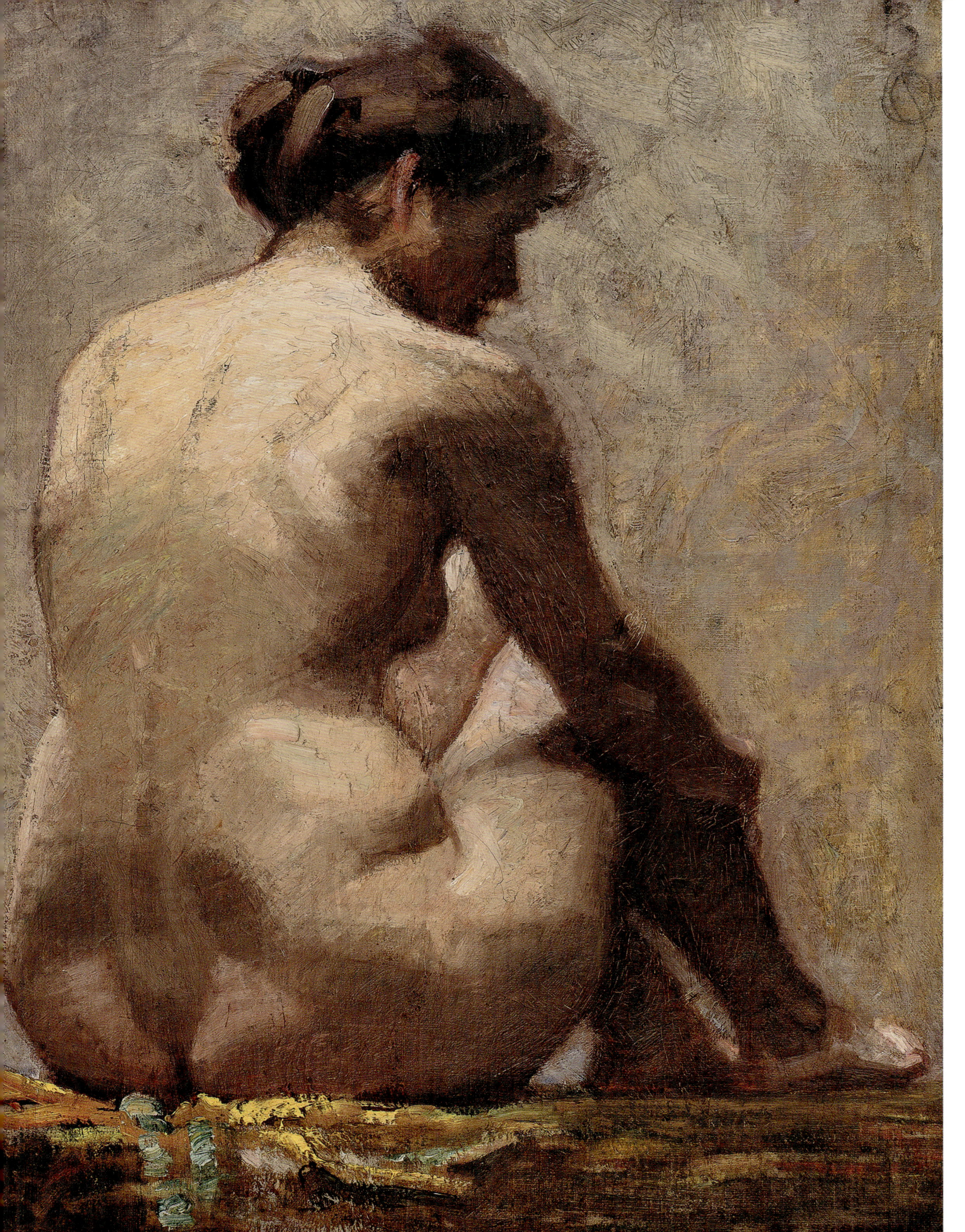

Nude Study from Life.
c. 1912–14. Oil on canvas,
61 x 45.7 cm.

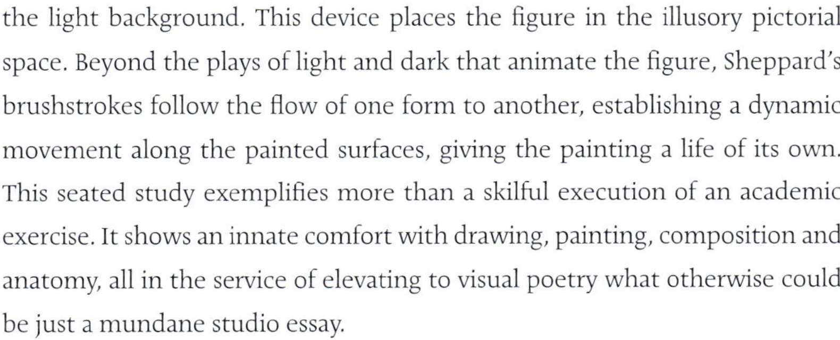

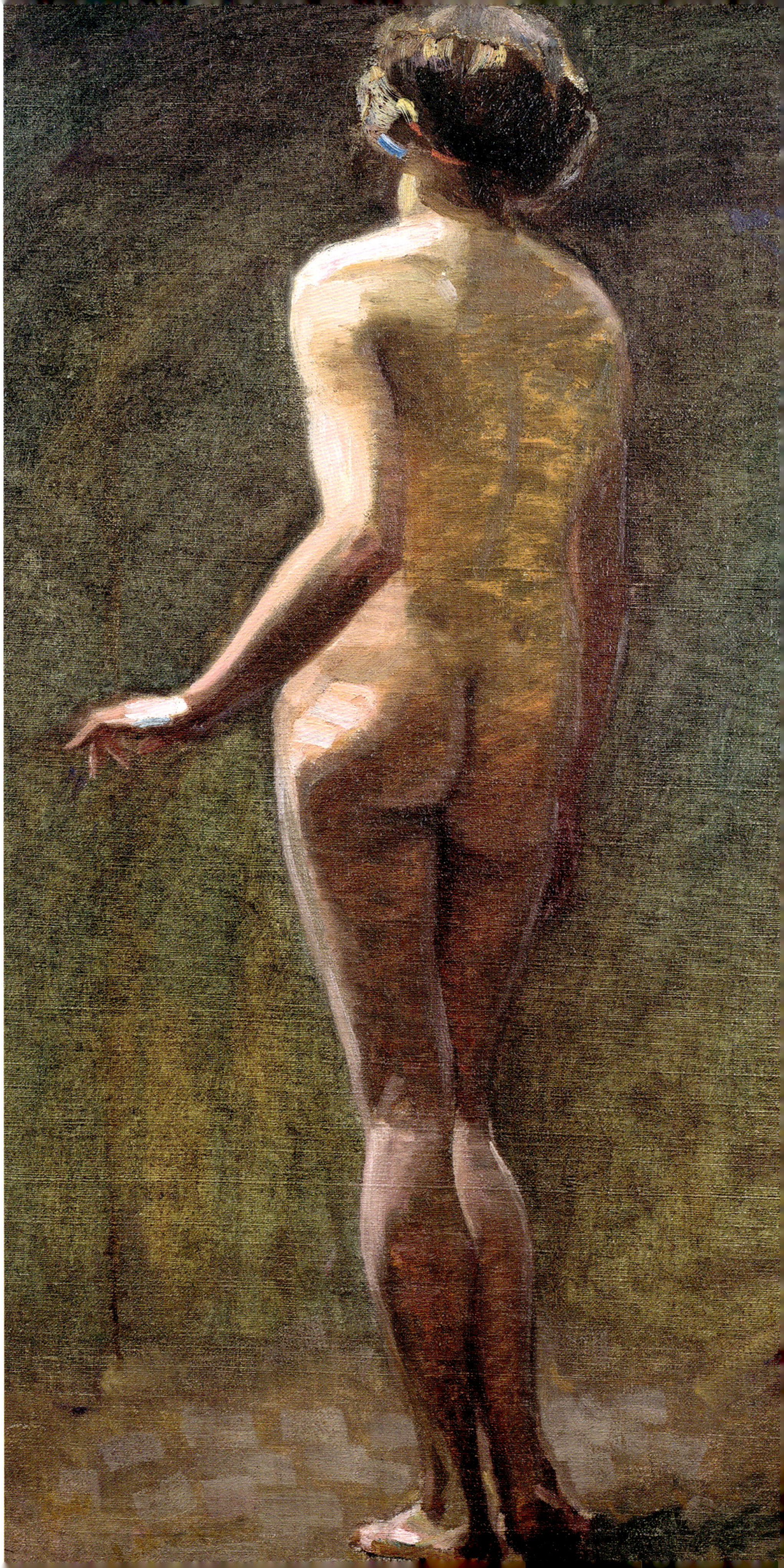

the light background. This device places the figure in the illusory pictorial space. Beyond the plays of light and dark that animate the figure, Sheppard's brushstrokes follow the flow of one form to another, establishing a dynamic movement along the painted surfaces, giving the painting a life of its own. This seated study exemplifies more than a skilful execution of an academic exercise. It shows an innate comfort with drawing, painting, composition and anatomy, all in the service of elevating to visual poetry what otherwise could be just a mundane studio essay.

So, too, a standing nude (right), in a relaxed contrapposto with her weight on the left leg, her back to the viewer, shows a more-than-average handling of the closely related hues that describe the model's back. In its Tonalist palette, this painting points to the effects of Beatty's instruction, but also to the work of Reid and the spell that it exerted on Sheppard. Just as Reid emphasized the allusiveness of tonal essays, Sheppard emphasized the expressive potential of dramatic lighting to animate the illusory space the figure occupies. Sheppard has also applied deft touches of blue and red to establish a visual rhythm beyond the moodiness in the subject matter, and to energize the nude.

In his student paintings, Sheppard describes liveliness. He captures a vital essence radiating from the model that, a century later, can still be seen and felt. There is a visual poetry emanating from the interactions of composition, the placement of the figure in the format and the animation of the gesture. Although Sheppard preferred a restrained palette in his figure studies, he uses line, hue and tone to serve the needs of the particular studio exercise.

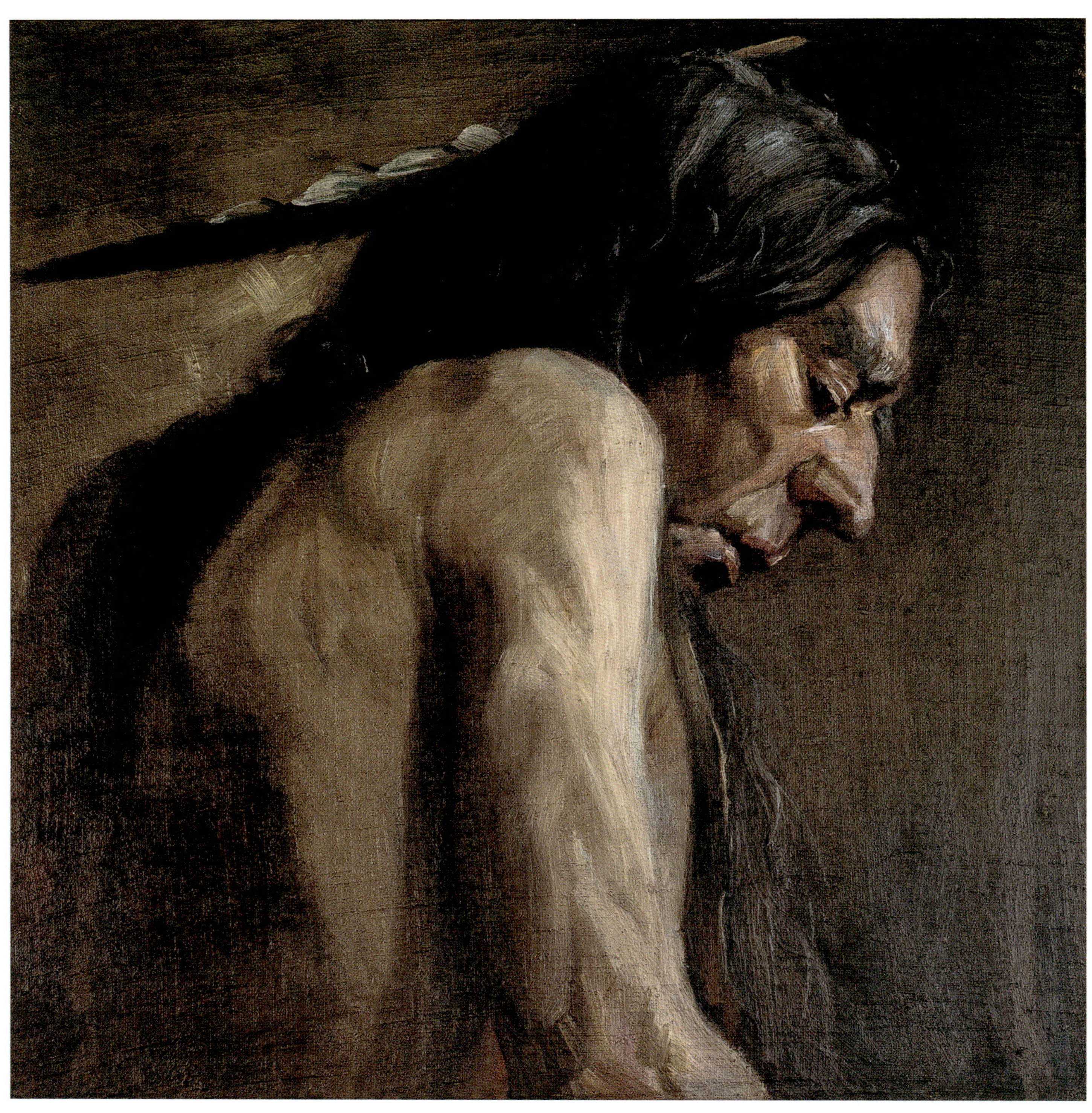

Dominique La Plante, Thundercloud.
c. 1912–14. Oil on canvas,
45.7 x 73 cm.

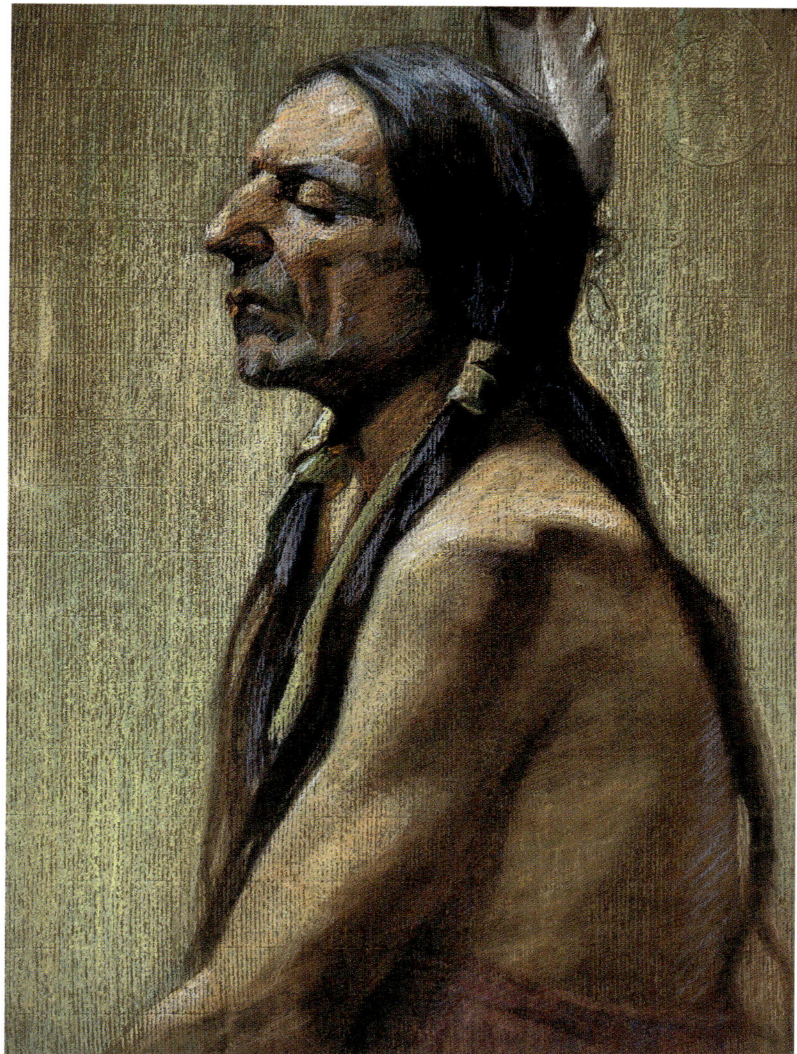

Dominique La Plante, Thundercloud.
c. 1912–14. Pastel on paper,
73 x 45.7 cm.

FIRST NATIONS MODEL: THUNDERCLOUD

As a life-drawing and painting student at OCA, Sheppard (along with his studio mates) also drew clothed and costumed models. One of the more recognizable of these models was known at the time as "Thundercloud," a First Nations man who stood poses in the studios. Sheppard's archive contains many examples of figure studies based on interpretations of this instantly recognizable man. Born Dominique La Plante, "Thundercloud" (1856–1916) was a

popular New York artists' model of mixed Blackfoot and French ancestry. He served as a scout for the United States Army, and at one time was a member of Buffalo Bill's Wild West Show. Reid invited him to Toronto to pose for him and for his students at OCA.[36] Thundercloud also modelled for American artists such as Frederic Remington (1861–1909) and John Singer Sargent (1856–1925), and for many artists in Toronto, including the sculptor Emanuel Hahn.[37]

In the life classes at OCA that Sheppard attended, Thundercloud particularly modelled for portrait-drawing exercises. One profile portrait pastel (left) catches a drowsy man, eyes closed, either lost in a daydream or asleep. The portrait is carefully seen and described resting in the illusory space behind the picture plane. A second, drawn from slightly below (see page 86), looking up at the portrait, similarly catches the model lost in thought (or perhaps also asleep on the modelling podium). Its range of tones from dark to light emphasizes the quality of inwardness through an allusive, moody depiction of spatial depth.

OTHER STUDENT WORK, TO 1914

In the midst of the many portfolios, single sheets of drawings, painted panels and canvases that are safely stored in the archive, a collection of some half-dozen portraits in oil on wooden panel, stand out among the rest as highly accomplished, poetic works of art. They astonish first by their apparent modesty and lack of ostentatious self-confidence. The medium is so expertly applied that the models' liveliness is translated as sensual applications of paint on the wooden surfaces. They are exactly what they set out to be: portraits from life that transcend the particularities of the academic study to be emblems of lives lived.

Take for example the portrait of a costumed woman (see page 89). Its wondrousness is a quality of the lively, dynamic brushwork, which uses impasto to create a relief effect that emphasizes form while moving light along the surface of the model. Sheppard's palette ranges from richly saturated ochres and yellows, violets and crimson to white. His brush sets down the hues with a light touch, all the better to adapt an Impressionist sensibility to the task of interpreting this particular model in her time and place.

So, too, the figure of a seated woman in a hat and coat (see page 88) is a beautifully expressive interpretation of a model surrounded more by colour impressions than by naturalistic depictions of a fur stole collar or another such item of clothing. The figure appears to emerge from the colours laid down with an eye to rendering the effects of light rather than on defining form. In essence, this panel is evidence of a very sophisticated understanding of gesture, composition and how to create the illusion of spatial depth simply by means of colour modulations and tonal variations. These are the same qualities that Sheppard used to interpret a woman dressed in a Breton costume. Rather than exploring the prosaic elements of the subject matter, Sheppard used them as an armature in an essay about composition and brushwork. Through the wonderfully expressive paint handling, it is not difficult to discern an uncommon ability to lay down colour on the panel — the figure is solidly placed on the format and is used as a foundation in a personal statement about the expressiveness of colour and how the brush can preserve a figure's liveliness.

But it is Sheppard's portrait of a man wearing a white hat (page 91) that reveals the artist's unique talents with the figure. This is an expertly painted study that balances lights and darks across the composition. Within this harmonious framework, Sheppard has paid attention to the model's anatomy in descriptive passages. Yet, beyond the formal and factual elements of the subject, Sheppard gives himself the difficult task of describing his subject with the face in shadow, an arrangement that throws the contours of the man's forehead, chin, nose and mouth into sharp delineation. To top it off, Sheppard used the back of the panel to paint yet another superbly seen profile portrait, this one of a woman wearing a bonnet. Just as its painting on the reverse reveals an unusual degree of accomplishment, so, too, this woman's life shines through over the century. It is much more than an academic or formal study. It shows Sheppard comfortable with his medium and mode.

Among the student paintings in the archive are many full-length studies of nudes. These also are evidence of a student with more than a modicum of talent in the demanding discipline of figure painting. They testify to Sheppard's keen sense of observation for form and mass, and for visual rhythms within a composition. Although the canvases also show how he struggled at times with placing the correct temperatures of tone and colour and with describing proportion, an innate talent and apparent ease in portraying his models shine through the paint. This is particularly evident when Sheppard sets his hand to depicting relaxation. He prefers open poses as opposed to closed, densely packed to uncluttered compositions. Their palettes are restrained, laid down to serve the needs of the studio exercise without drawing attention to the interactions of colour. They are muted, nearly monochromatic interpretations of the figure.

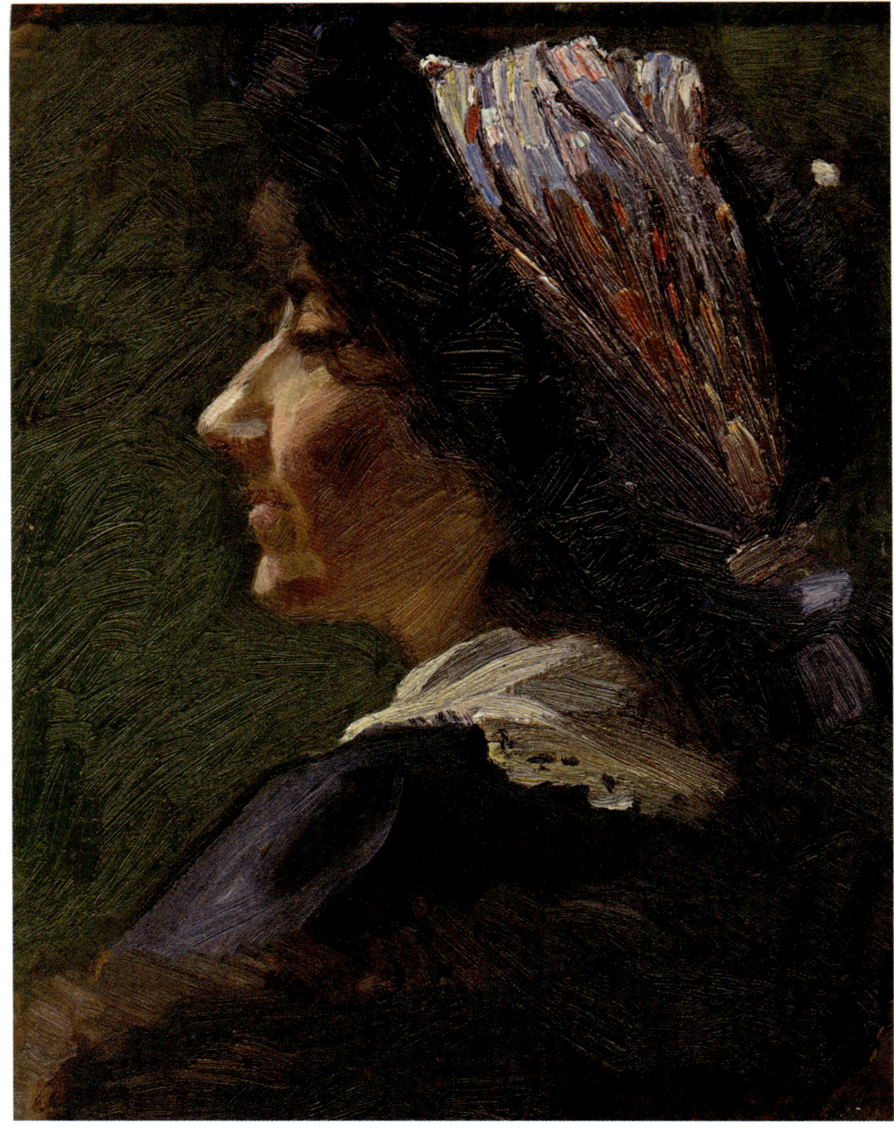

Costume Class, Study, OCA.
c. 1912–14. Oil on panel,
35.6 x 24.7 cm.

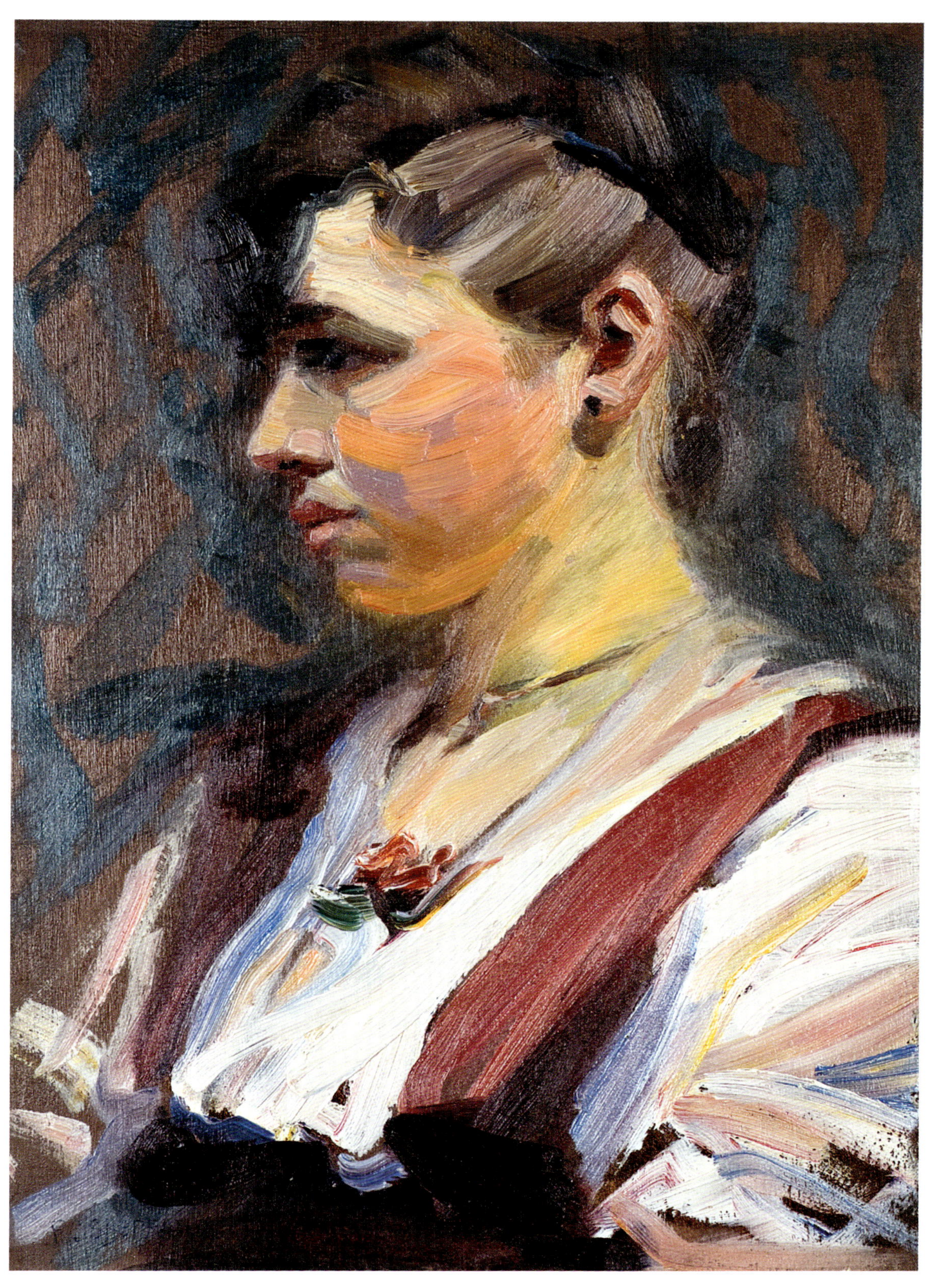

Costume Class, Study, OCA.
c. 1912–14. Oil on panel,
35.6 x 24.8 cm.

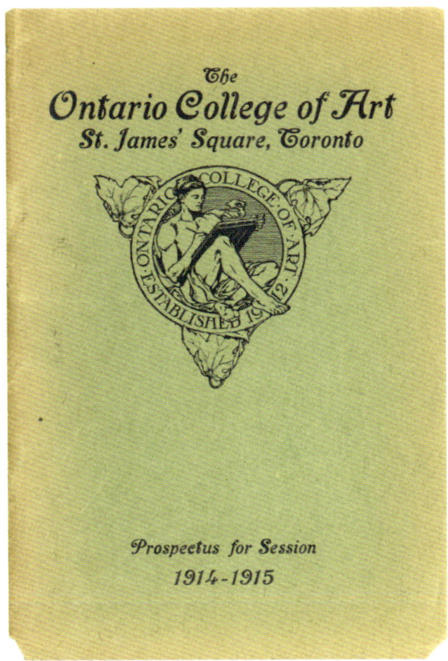 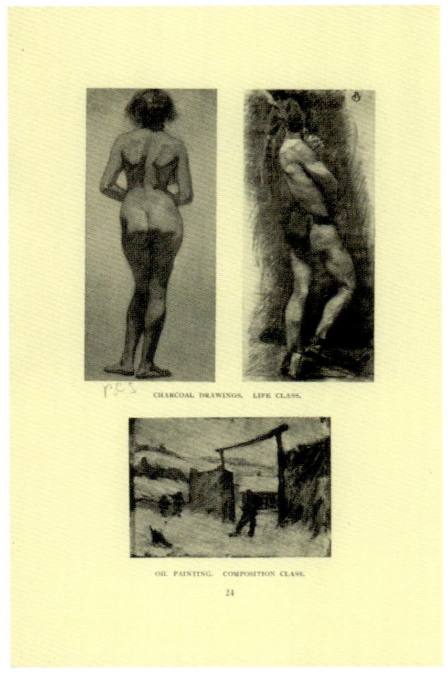 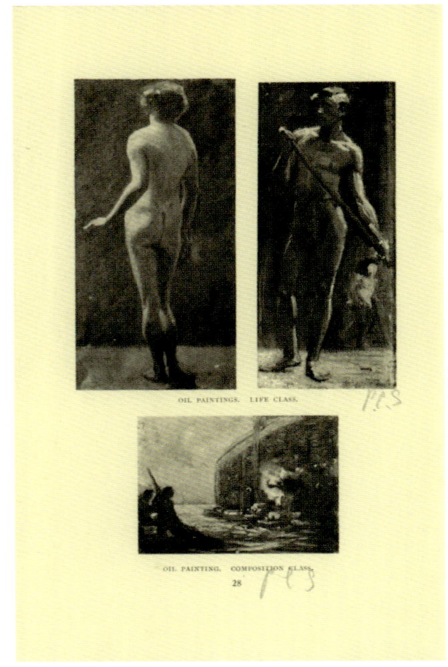

Cover and interior pages of 1914–15 Ontario College of Art Prospectus, featuring some of Sheppard's work in Life Class and Oil Painting Life Classes.

A GRADUATE OF OCA, 1914

By 1914, Sheppard had found a voice and a way of expressing it in paint through the unique vocabulary of figuration. Perhaps acknowledging his distinction among his OCA peers, the prospectus of 1914–15 reproduced two of Sheppard's paintings, which he had completed in Beatty's Life Class studio course.[38] He captures some vital essence of humanity radiating from his models that, a century later, is still evident. Graduating from the college of art, Sheppard was an acolyte of Beatty. He had absorbed his teacher's lessons and personal style and used them as a basis for informing his own expressive language.

These special qualities in the young artist were highlighted in an art review that was published in the *Toronto Sunday World* on February 8, 1914. Sheppard was represented in the OSA exhibition *Little Pictures*, which was on view at the City of Toronto Reference Library. Sheppard, Gordon Payne and Manly E. MacDonald were mentioned in the notice as "Three clever pupils of the Ontario College of Art." [39] The reviewer notes that:

> It is very gratifying to see such excellent work from the brushes of young Canadian artists not yet graduated, and it is a bright promise of the work which they will be doing in the years to come. The sketches are bright, colourful and full of atmospheric charm, and do credit to both teachers and pupils.[40]

Sheppard graduated with the degree of Associate of the Ontario College of Art (AOCA) from the Ontario College of Art on December 18, 1914, at the end of the 1913–14 session.[41] He was one of only two graduates that year, the other being Claude Johnson. In a letter to Sheppard, the OCA's principal, G.A. Reid, informed him that he would graduate from the Department of Drawing and Painting while Johnson would graduate from the Department of Design. Sheppard was also awarded an honorable mention for his work in the Day Costume Class — a class where, possibly, he painted his accomplished portraits-on-panel series. In addition, Sheppard earned a Stone Scholarship for his excellence in Life Classes (see page 64).

In a handwritten note at the bottom of his letter, Reid added this postscript: "I would like if you can come in tomorrow Friday and see me about the summer work for The Teachers Course and if possible to stay and help making some preparations." The note might well have been an invitation to teach in a professional capacity for the five-week summer session of OCA's course for teachers.[42]

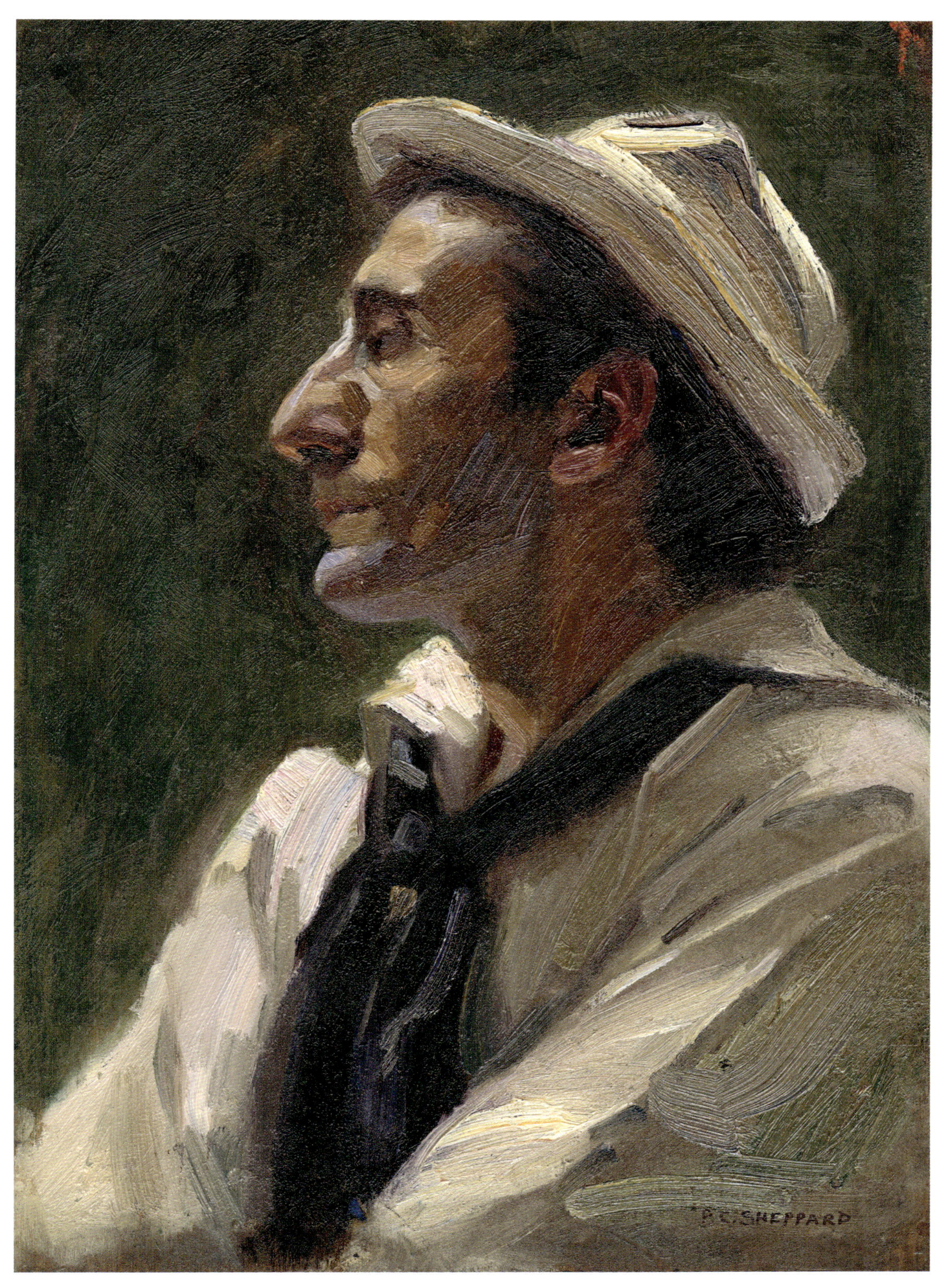

Costume Class, Study, OCA.
c. 1912–14. Oil on panel,
35.6 x 24.7 cm.

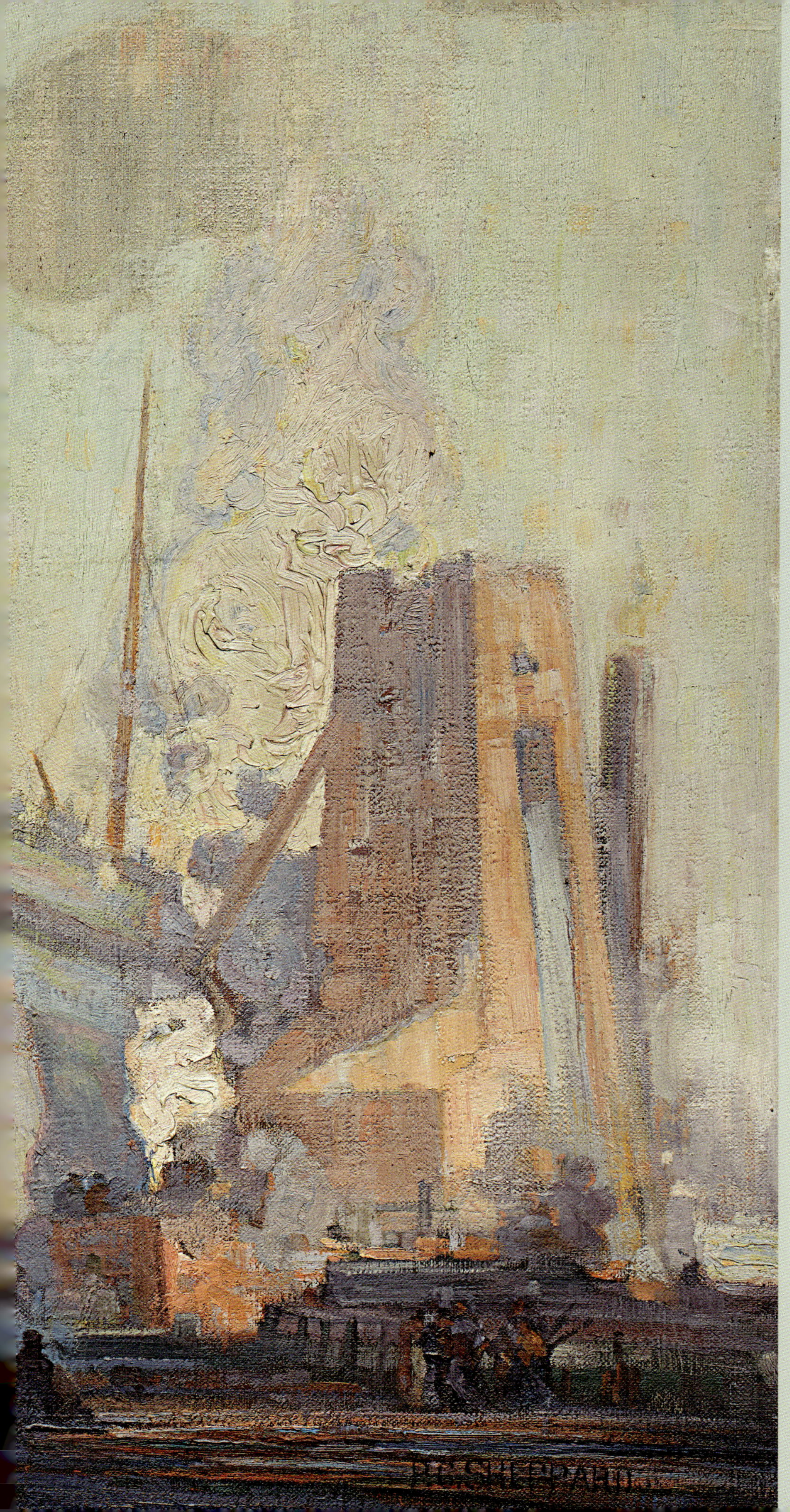

CHAPTER THREE

The City as Subject

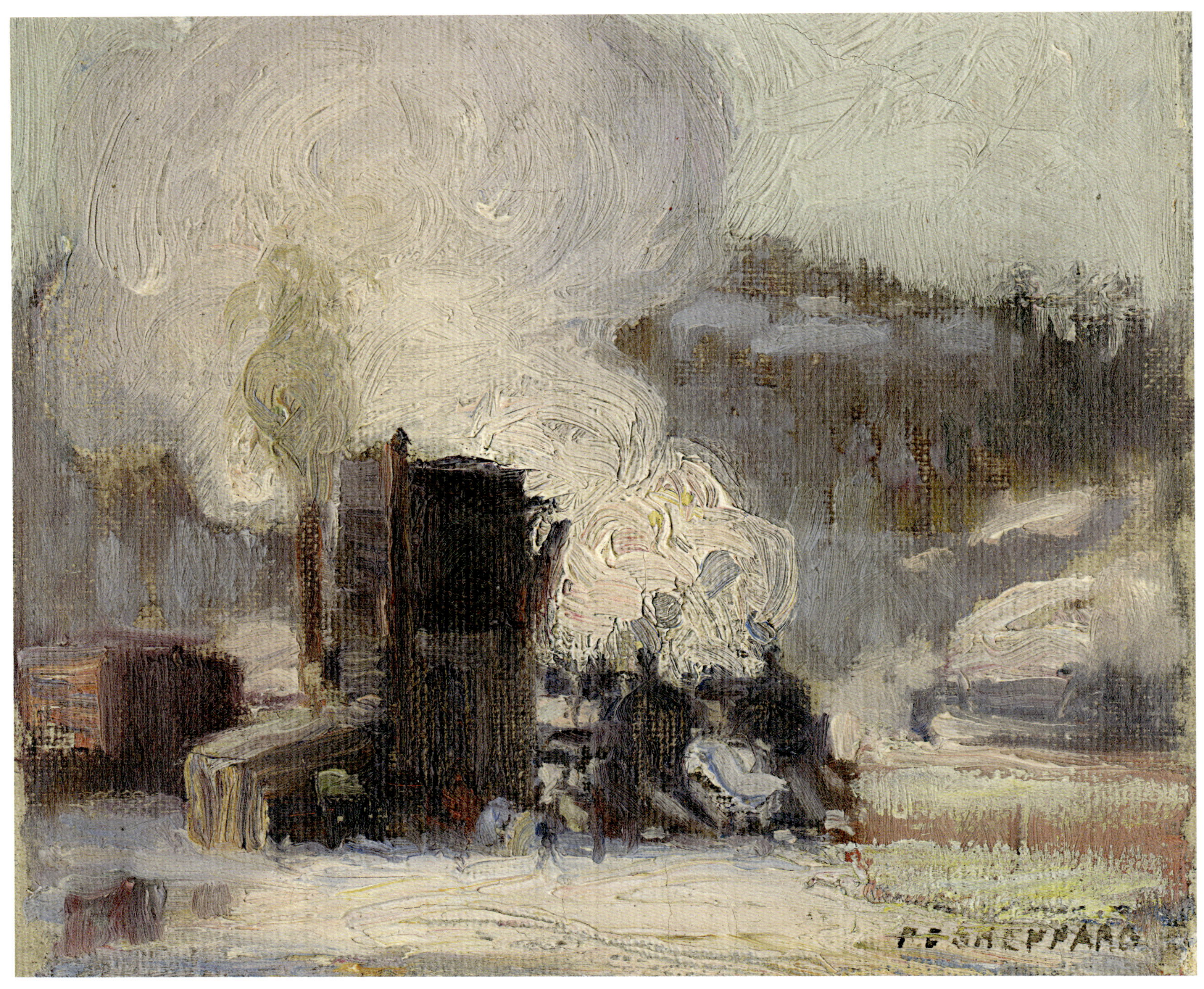

The Two Engines (Locomotives) (study).
1914–15. Oil on canvas,
12.7 x 14.6 cm.

Artists Doing Distinctly Canadian Work

THE STUDIO BUILDING AND THE WINDS OF CHANGE, 1914–15

In the same review noted on page 90, in addition to highlighting the accomplishments of Sheppard and his peers that portended promising futures as professional artists, the author announced the opening of "the first studio building ever built in Canada" on Severn Street in the Rosedale ravine just south of Sheppard's home on Summerhill Avenue. It was also noted that it was "being occupied" by six Toronto artists, Arthur Hemming, J.W. Beatty, J.E.H. MacDonald, Lawren Harris, Curtis Williamson and A.Y. Jackson."

The idea of a building made up of a collection of studios in a purpose-built structure for the making of art was hatched by Lawren Harris (then only 28 years old) and his patron, Dr. James MacCallum. Conceived as "artists doing distinctly Canadian work," the Studio Building was designed by the renowned British-Canadian architect Eden Smith, who, by 1913, when he received the commission, was one of the leading architects working in the city.[43] He had designed many a home in the prestigious Rosedale, Annex, Deer Park and Wychwood Park enclaves of the city, as well as in Cabbagetown, a working-class precinct in the southeast corner of the city, bordering the lakefront and the Don River. Although an acolyte of the British Arts and Crafts movement, Eden Smith's credentials were burnished in Harris' and MacCallum's eyes by his ambition to develop a distinctly Canadian architectural style, an ambition that was absolutely congruent with those of his clients, who were committed to developing a distinctly Canadian art movement. The Studio Building's purpose was to supply domestic and working space for a hand-picked group of artists who had the potential to forge a new national school of painting.

Harris and MacCallum's idea was entirely modern; they wanted the building to reflect an industrial aesthetic, and thereby to stimulate the growth of a modern art movement whose proponents would emulate advanced painting coming out of Europe, particularly Scandinavia, France and Belgium. Sheppard no doubt regarded the project intently. After all, the

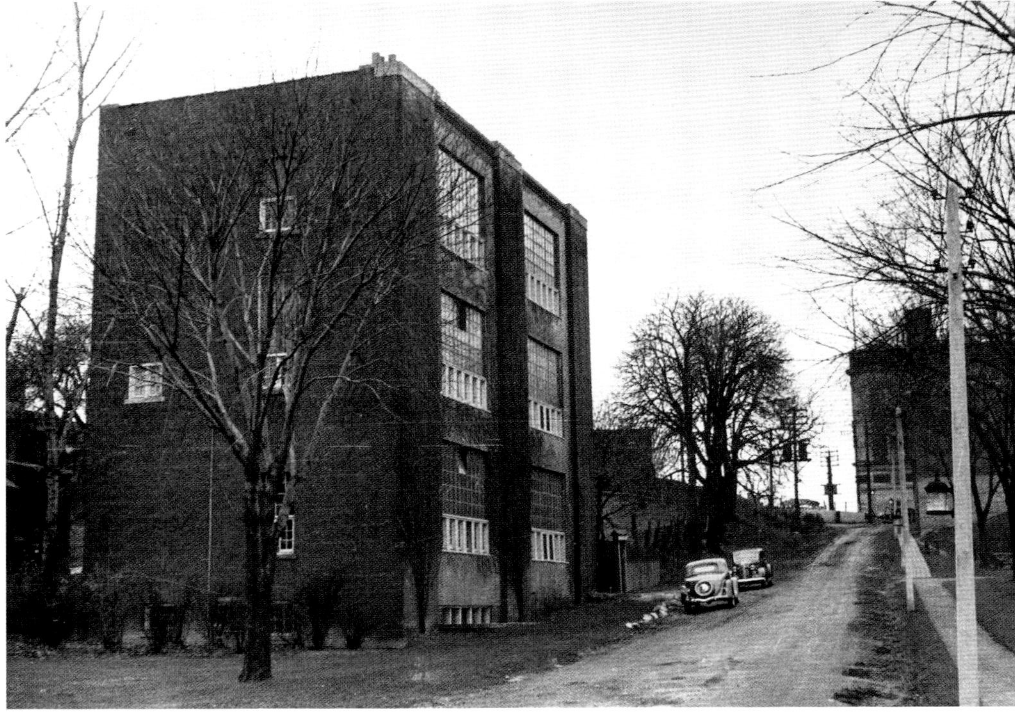

The Studio Building at 5 Severn St., Toronto, opened in 1914.

Studio Building was being constructed not far from his home on Summerhill Avenue. I imagine he and his peers saw the entire project as a beachhead for their own advanced paintings to find their way into Toronto's galleries and salons, and perhaps even for a change in taste — from a tired, hackneyed mode of representing Canadian subjects in an outdated European manner to one that promised authenticity, and even a breakthrough to a national idiom entirely born from the country itself.

These must have been heady times for an artist such as Sheppard. He was poised to inherit the advances of his elders and perhaps even contribute to the project of defining a national school of art in his own way. The Studio Building was certainly a centre, a nexus, a locus of nationalism in art, and it was a symbol of that aspiration as architecture. True to its promise, it did become an aesthetic centre of the national school. By 1917 it could boast a community of tenants that were soon to establish the Group of Seven. They included Harris, MacDonald and Arthur Lismer, founders of the group, and also Williamson, Beatty, Marion Long and Alex Cumming, artists who have been made nearly invisible in the historical narrative due to the ensuing importance — radiance — of their studio colleagues. The tenant roster published in the *Toronto Directory* of 1918 also listed a Thos. Thompson [*sic*], who, although he passed away in July 1917, was a gifted painter whose work and style were emulated by future group members. Together, these artists inspired a resonant movement that reflected a national sensibility that found in the landscape, particularly the northern bush, symbols of Canadian identity. Whatever that meant, the Studio Building had an integral role in birthing modern Canadian art. The sheer boldness of the ambitions that led to its construction certainly rubbed off on Sheppard and his peers, who felt that a career as a fine artist was entirely possible in Toronto. New institutions and supports were being built. The foundation for professional development seemed sure.

PATRIOTIC FERVOUR

In 1915 Sheppard continued to live at 63 Summerhill Avenue and to list his profession as "lithographer." As a note of context, his contemporary Thomas Thomson, who soon would also launch a brief career as a painter, was noted in the *City of Toronto Directory* as a "painter" living at 33 Davenport Road, in the same general vicinity as Sheppard on Toronto's northern edges. Thomson was also listed as an "engraver" at Randall and Johnston Ltd., located downtown at 119 Dundas Street. The year 1915 must have been professionally satisfying

for Sheppard the recent graduate, whose two paintings *The Water Trough* and *The Two Engines* were selected by the jury of the Royal Canadian Academy for exhibition in its annual exhibition that year.[44]

The archive is silent on how the Great War might have touched him. By 1915 the war was being fiercely waged in Europe, and recruitment in Canada, and in Toronto, reflected full patriotic fervour. I wonder about the extent to which it affected Sheppard, then 36 or 33 years old, depending on which birthdate we use, 1879 or 1882. Perhaps he felt he was too old to enlist in the army; there is no record to let us know why he was not recruited or conscripted.

There is also no hint of the war going on in Europe in his work of the period of 1914–18, although there is an emphasis on industrial themes, urban development and economic vitality. For example, in 1916 he exhibited *The Two Engines* at that year's Canadian National Exhibition, likely the very same painting that he showed in the Royal Canadian Academy Exhibition a year earlier. Could this be the same painting, the sketch of which I find in the archive, listed in its inventory as *Study for the Two Engines (Locomotives)* (page 94), a small-format oil painting of two locomotives lined up at the water tower in a winter landscape that appears to be in a rural, not urban, setting? This small essay is a nearly abstract impression of the engines. Sheppard has made the steam cloud the focus of the composition; he uses the subject as an excuse to experiment with pictorial abstraction of the monochromatic and closely related tones and values of the steam. Although small in size, the painting has an unusually thorough sense of completion, balance and well-established structure.

Is it in any way alluding to the conflict overseas? Although I would like to find the subject symbolic of what is going on outside the edges of the frame, the painting seems to function in a contextual void. It is simply an interpretation of its subject, and if anything a pictorial and representative basis that allows the artist to experiment with abstract painting that is still anchored to something, in this case steam vapourizing and condensing above the engines. According to Bernice Martin's biographical sketch, Sheppard shows in this painting that he found a creative outlet in expressing "the unusual in strong, vigorous patterns of singing color and bold design," while maintaining distance between what he saw and weighting it with symbolic meaning. It is true enough, as Martin writes, that "his creed was to observe and paint the world around him, without becoming a participator in the passing scene. He believed artists should be ... apart and not let themselves become involved with those things which tend to distract from their creative work." *Locomotives* is a perfect exemplar of this personal philosophy and creative attitude.

SKETCHBOOKS, 1916

A surviving sketchbook from this time reveals much about Sheppard's drawing interests and abilities. He took the idea of "drawing from life" beyond the walls of the studio and into Toronto's streets, parks and harbour. Martin wrote on her "biographical data" sheet that Sheppard "carried a small sketchbook, pens, pencils, etc. at all times, tucked away in a pocket (even in his dress suit) for jotting down an idea or a sketch of any unusual subject, or phase of light, which might present itself." This exactly describes one such modestly formatted sketchbook with a canvas cover that is tagged "1916," which can be found in the archive. Signed on the cover "Peter C. Sheppard/63 Summerhill Av.," the book has a charming lack of pretension about it. Its crumpled cover and traces of past folds attest to the fact it was likely carried, used and pocketed, just as Martin noted. Inside its covers, the pages are filled with figure and portrait studies laid down in lead or graphite pencil (see page 82). The intimate, small sketches catch the gestures and liveliness of the subjects in ways that make the pictures come alive when looked at a century later. This quality is what attracts me to Sheppard's work in the first place: his uncanny ability to capture life in the intent, inquisitive gazes of his models, in the relaxed way they take their unselfconscious poses before the artist. Sheppard clearly set his subjects at ease and was able to express the comfortable relationship between artist and model.

As pictorial essays, the drawings represent studies of modulated tones from light to dark to show volume while not having the shadows distort the forms — not a simple task since it involves a sophisticated understanding of what is going on below the skin anatomically, and how this architecture is echoed on the surfaces of the skin and in the attitudes of the pose. Even though in a strict sense many pages of the sketchbook are quickly rendered academic studies, they nevertheless also convey individualism traced through beautifully handled gestures, lines and tones.

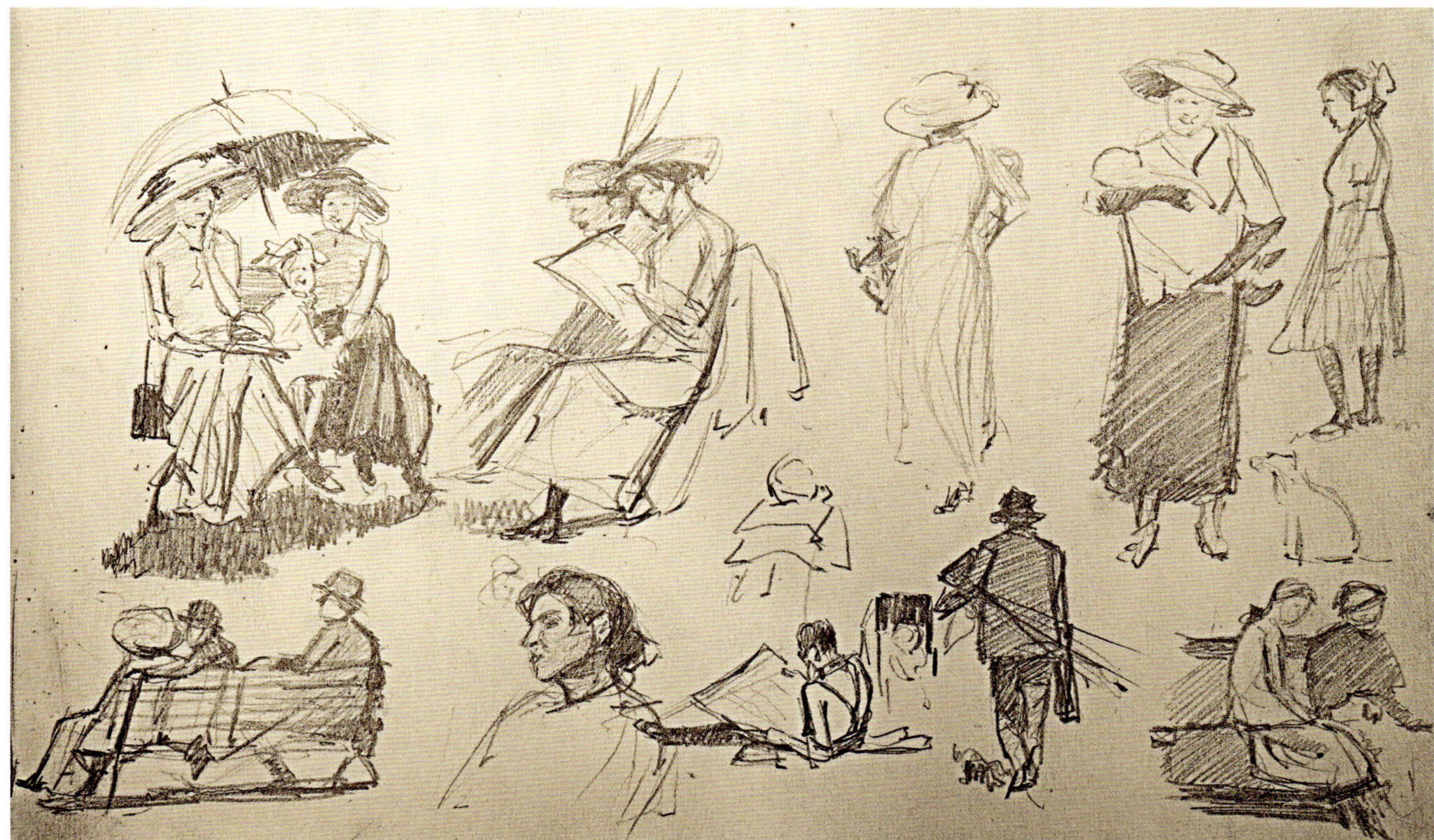

Outdoor Sketches.
1916. Pencil on paper,
12.7 x 14.6 cm.

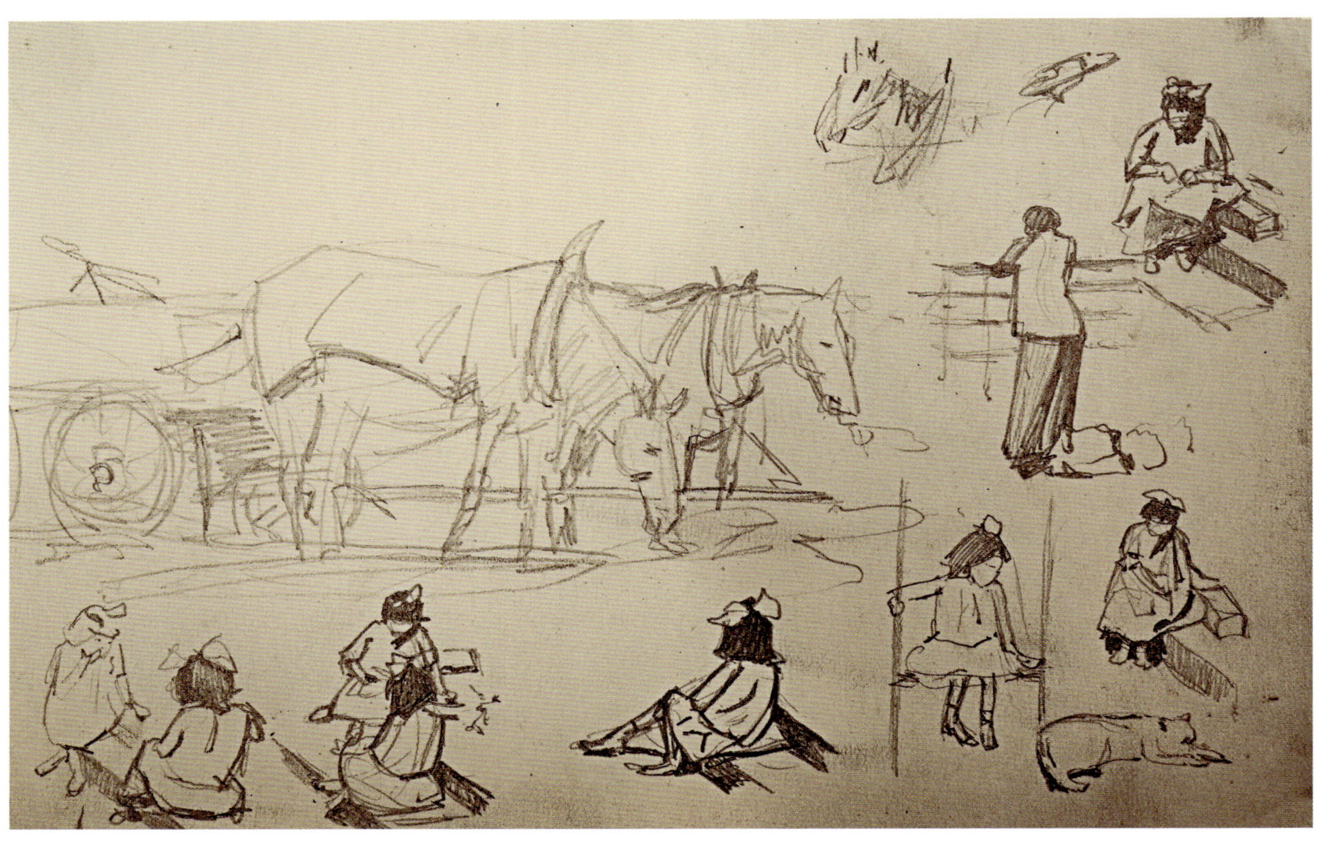

Outdoor Sketches.
1916. Pencil on paper,
12.7 x 14.6 cm.

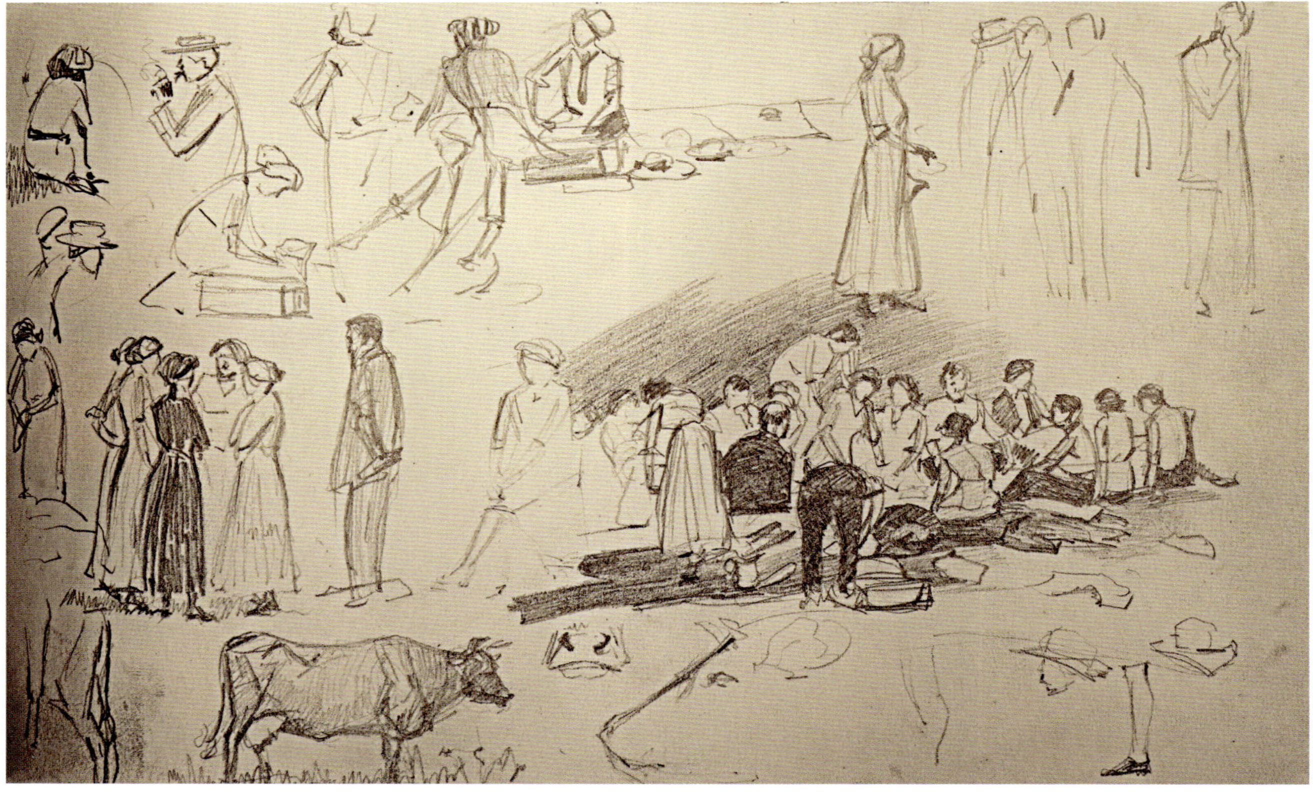

Outdoor Sketches.
1916. Pencil on paper,
12.7 x 14.6 cm.

Another sketchbook, similarly inscribed "PC Sheppard/63 Summerhill Ave" and tagged with auction lot "1106 Waddington's," opens to pages of drawings from plaster reproduction statues of antique and Renaissance sculpture, among them Michelangelo's *River Gods,* cast from his Medici Tomb ensemble in Florence (see page 100). As with the former sketches, Sheppard places his pencil's emphasis on rendering deep shadows cast by the figure and falling on the sculpted forms. In addition, this book contains a charming array of thumbnail sketches of people going about their business out-of-doors (pages 97–99). Here are impressions of picnics and people sitting on park benches, children playing, boats, barges and crowds on the ferry to the Toronto islands, including Hanlan's Point. All attest to Sheppard's keen eye for rendering light and shade without obscuring the very human element expressed in the posed attitudes and gestures. And all of this is evident in lively jottings not much larger than a postage stamp. True to Bernice's portrait of her friend, these are sketches by an artist who clearly saw himself as an observer of the world around him; the point of view is of an outsider on the edges of a "passing scene."

A third sketchbook, also from around 1916 (perhaps even containing sketches from 1919 and 1920), is a modest bound book in a green canvas cover, that could easily be held in the left hand, thus freeing the right to do the drawing or painting. It contains more outdoor sketches, of carousels along with studio drawings of nudes. Curiously enough, I turn a page and discover watercolour wash sketches of either a theatrical performance or rehearsals for the popular romantic musical comedy *Chu Chin Chow* (see page 101). Sheppard's drawings suggest that he was recording the action on the stage from the theatre's wings; his pages contain what appear to be candid scenes of actors in their costumes, and stagehands erecting sets and painting scenes.

This begs the question as to whether Sheppard was involved in a production of the play. The point of view of the sketches from backstage suggests that he may have had privileged access to the actors and stagehands, and I would like to think that this was the case because he may well have been a scene painter. There are several lovely watercolour sketches in this book that appear to show the theatrical scenery being set in place on riggings in the fly tower behind the stage proscenium.

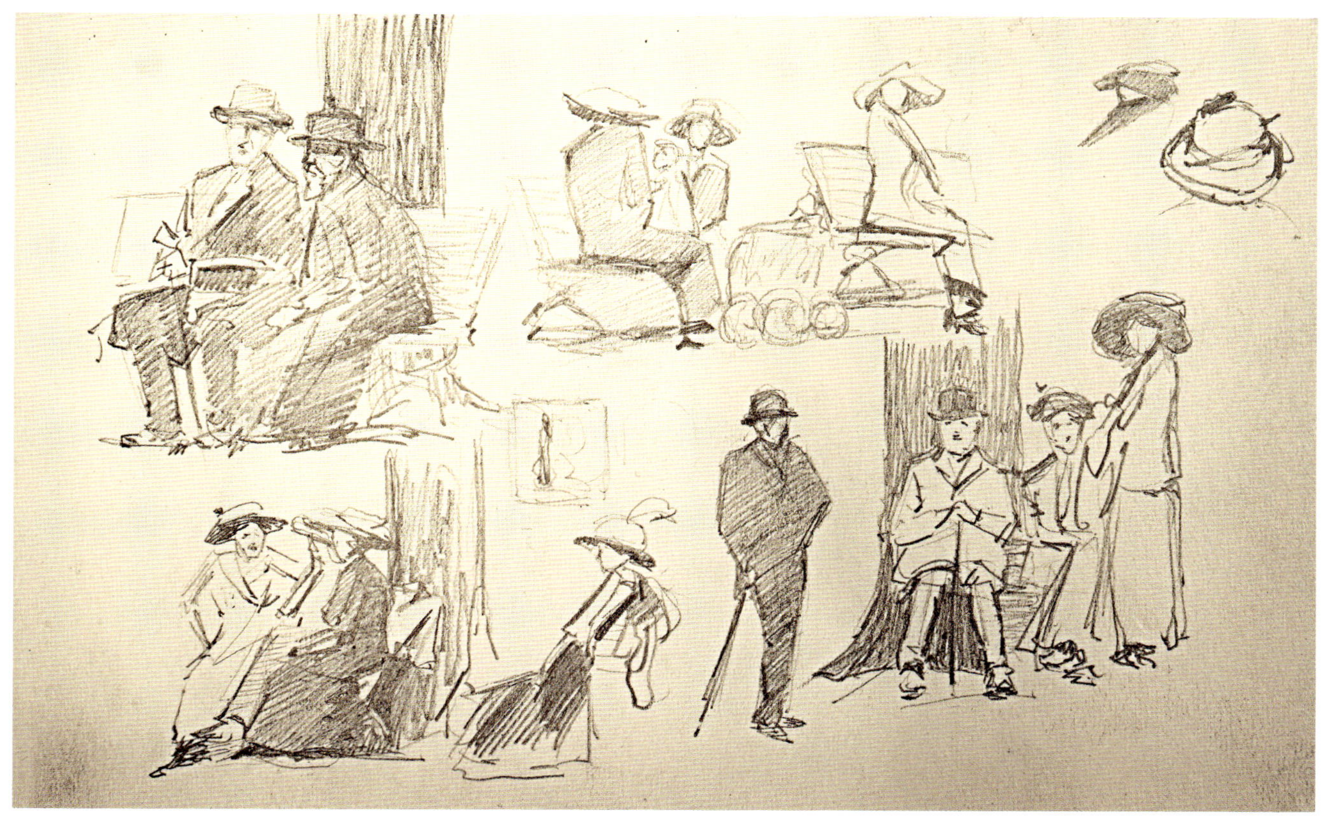

Outdoor Sketches.
1916. Pencil on paper,
12.7 x 14.6 cm.

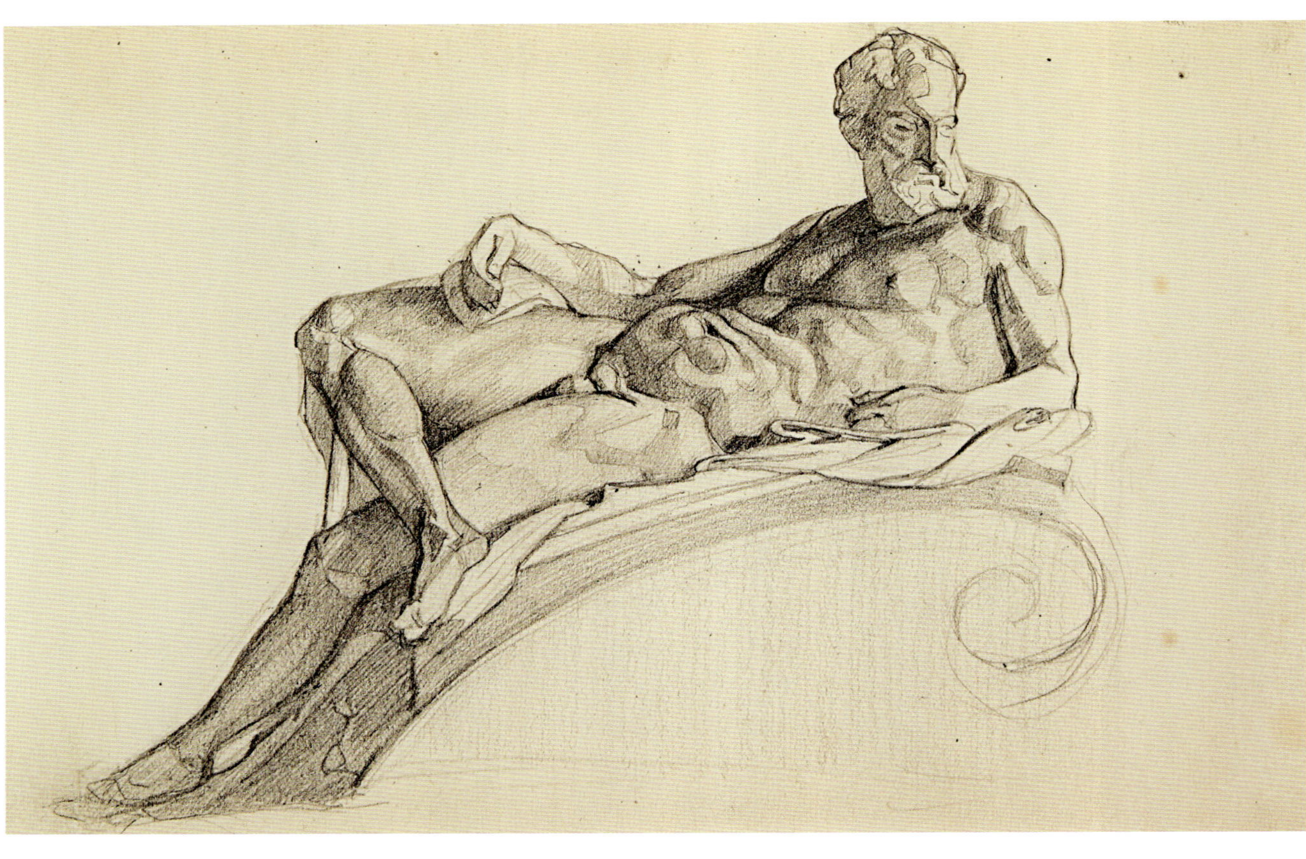

Sketch.
1916. Pencil on paper,
12.7 x 14.6 cm.

Sketch.
1916. Pencil on paper,
12.7 x 14.6 cm.

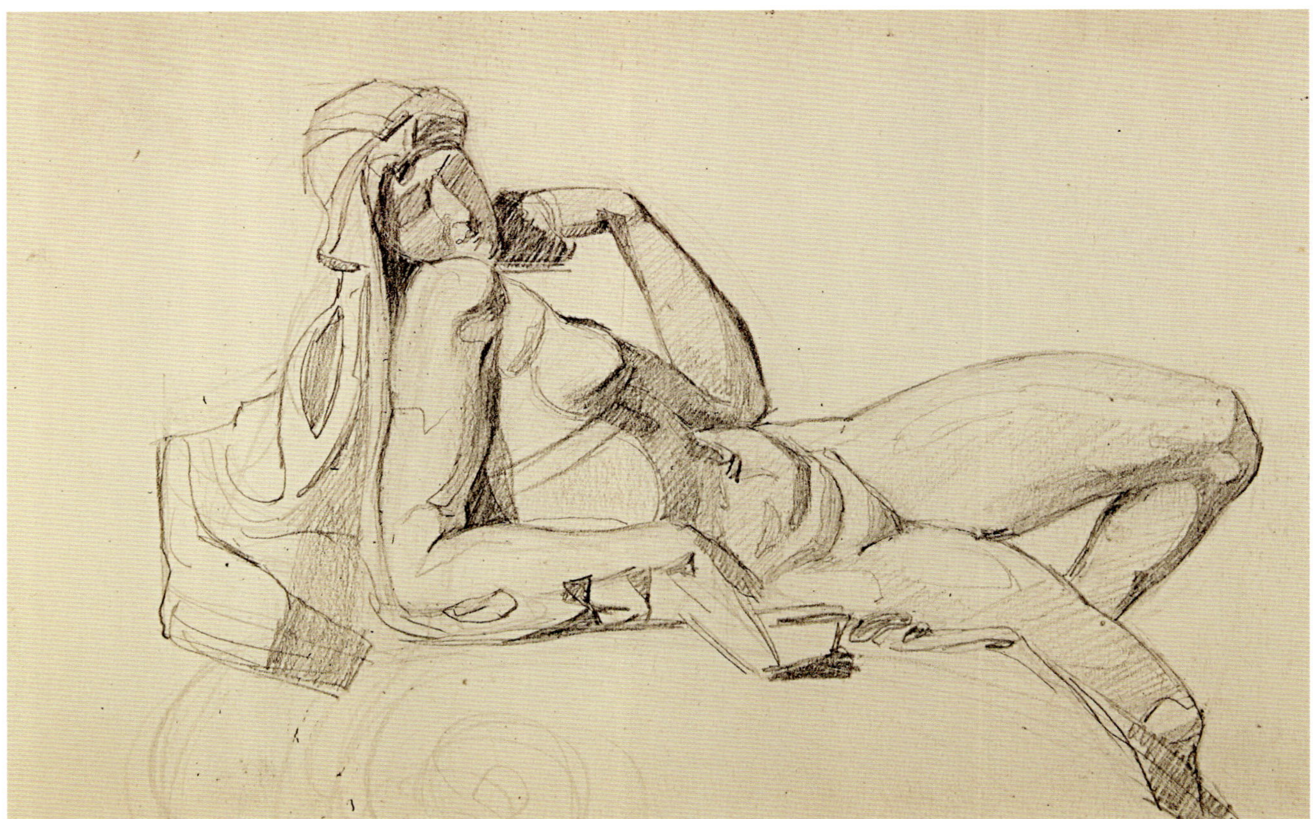

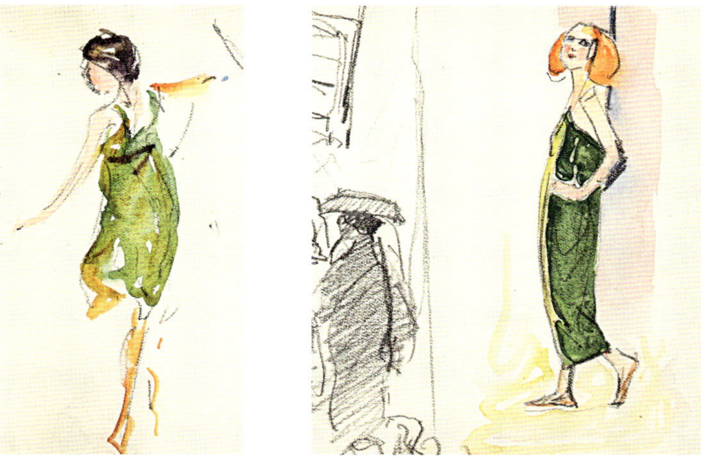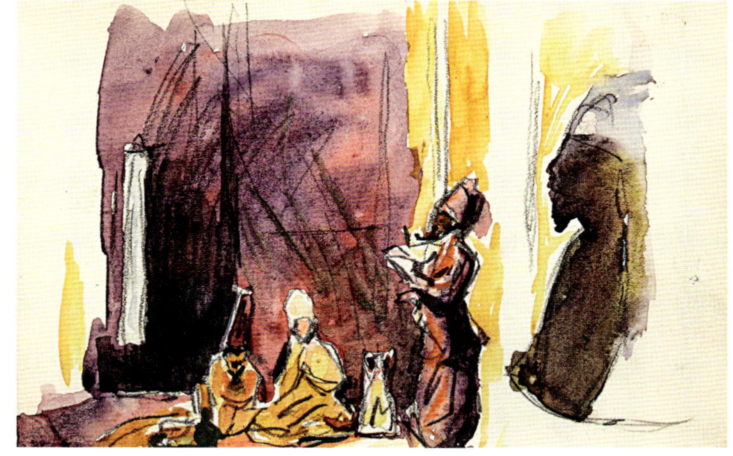

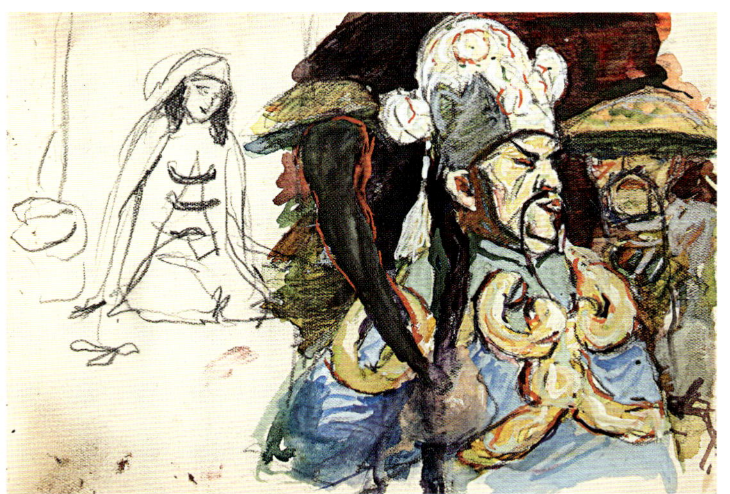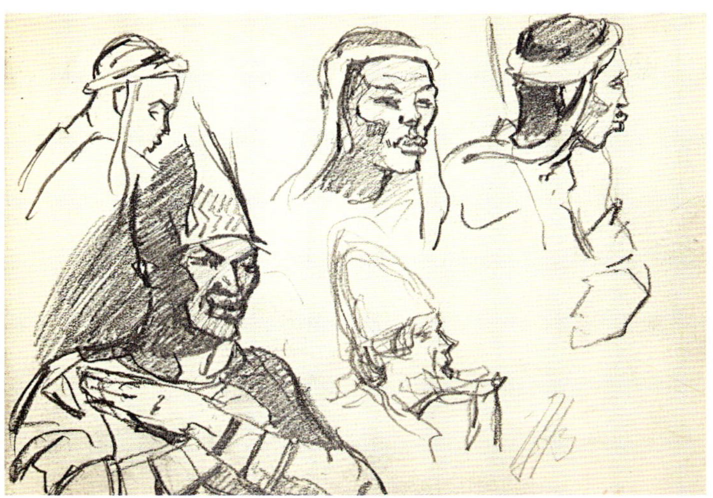

Sketches from Sheppard's green canvas sketchbook of 1919–20. He has mixed his pencil work with watercolour wash in sketches of a theatrical performance or rehearsals of the popular romantic musical comedy *Chu Chin Chow*. Sheppard's drawings suggest that he was recording the action on the stage from the theatre's wings. The two images at top left show audience members in fancy dresses of the time.

Here is where circumstance needs to be described to flesh out the biography. Although the sketchbook has "1916" on it, this may have been added at a later date, reflecting an imprecise recollection by the recorder. I sense that the drawings were done when the play was being prepared for presentation at Toronto's Royal Alexandra Theatre in 1920, a production that included the actor Lionel Braham. Braham's name is listed on a page in this sketchbook. If Sheppard was involved in painting the backdrops, or in making the props, he was given anonymous recognition and high praise in a contemporary review of the production that was festooned with "Magnificent scenery, gorgeous costumes, [and] a series of wonderful pictures of oriental life … The scenic effects are among the finest ever presented, and the playgoer passes a veritable evening in fairyland."[45] Braham played the role of the villain Abu Hasan, "robber of mankind."

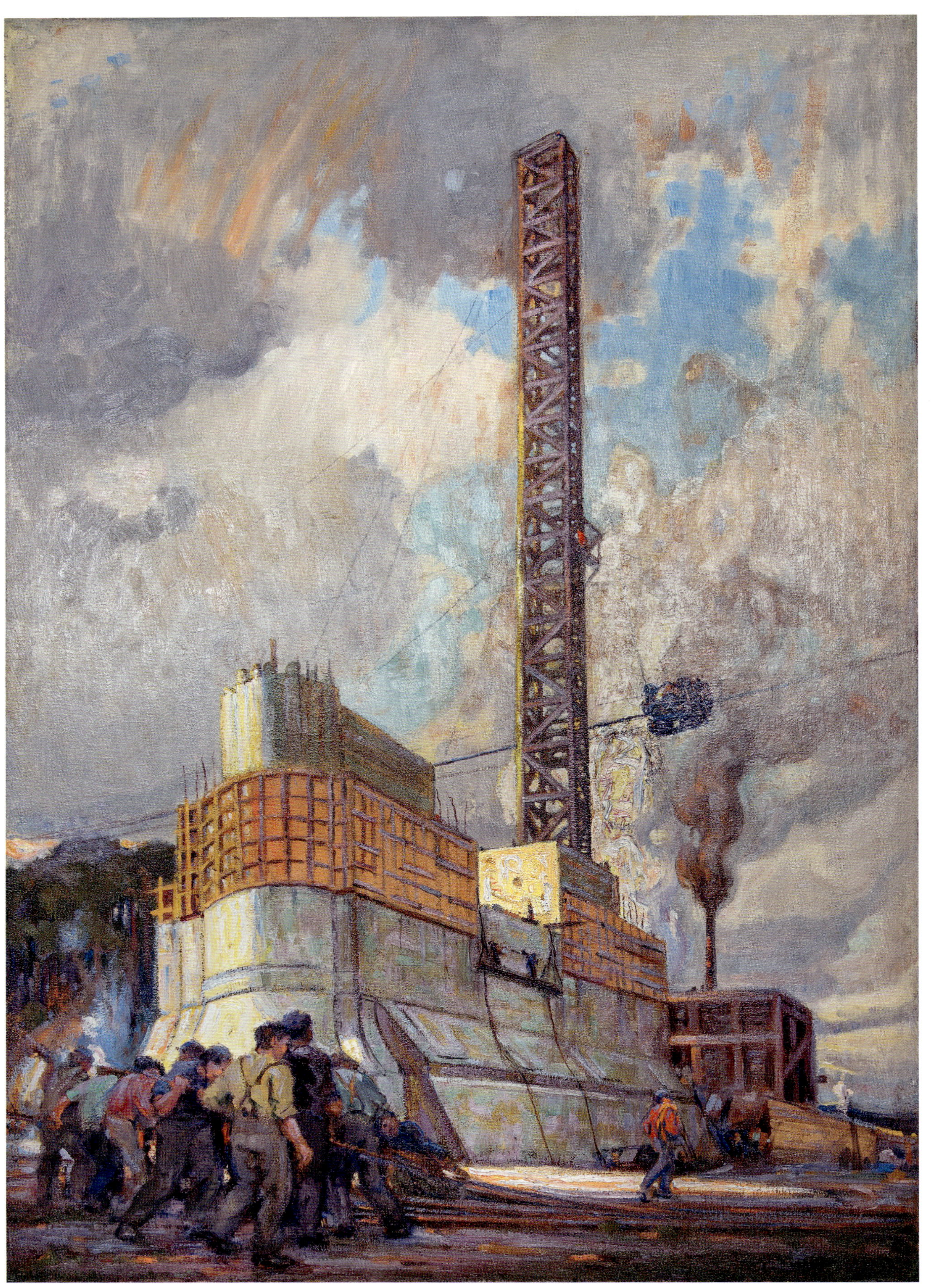

The Bridge Builders, Construction,
Bloor Street Viaduct.
1915. Oil on canvas,
147.3 x 101.6 cm.

CONSTRUCTION OF THE BLOOR STREET/
PRINCE EDWARD VIADUCT, 1915

The most ambitious painting of Sheppard's career up to 1916 was his large-format canvas *The Bridge Builders, Construction, Bloor Street Viaduct*, a dynamic composition showing the construction of a massive pier that supports one of the series of connected steel arches. The bridge itself was one of Toronto's more ambitious civil engineering projects; its purpose was to span the Don River and Rosedale Valleys.[46] The bridge was under construction by 1913 and was opened in 1918; Sheppard's view interprets, from ground level in the river valley, the construction of Pier D.

Before starting his large studio canvas of the subject, Sheppard made sketches of the construction site from the floor of the valley. Two of the surviving outdoor studies that are in the archive are remarkable for the ways they convey the immediacy of the scene, drawing the viewer into the compositions with several clever devices and a vibrantly keyed colour palette. Holding a couple of the sketches in my hands, I am convinced that Sheppard felt a deep connection with the subject matter, particularly the ways that the human scale is dwarfed by the monumentality of the built structures and by the sheer au-

dacity of the project, which pitted human ingenuity against a geographical feature that needed to be spanned to connect two different precincts of the city. Indeed, the ambition of the project (and the proximity of the construction to the Studio Building) likely attracted the attention of Sheppard's peer and neighbour Tom Thomson, a tenant of the wooden shack behind the building, whose modest untitled oil panel sketch of a construction shed and crane on a ravine hillside very likely also interpreted a viaduct pier being built.

Sheppard's *Study for Bloor Street Viaduct* (page 104) is composed in two parts: a study of the crane and a pictorialization of the intersecting rail lines at the crane's base. Sheppard has cleverly emphasized the curves of the rails and their merging together to lead the eye into the composition's imaginary space. The foreground shadow is contrasted by the middle ground's sunlight to accelerate my movement into the space as if suggesting the hustle and noise of the construction of the pier. Sheppard has laid in a sky of muted mauves with yellow highlights to interpret the interactions of the straight, curved and diagonal lines, all of which lend the subject rhythm and lyricism.

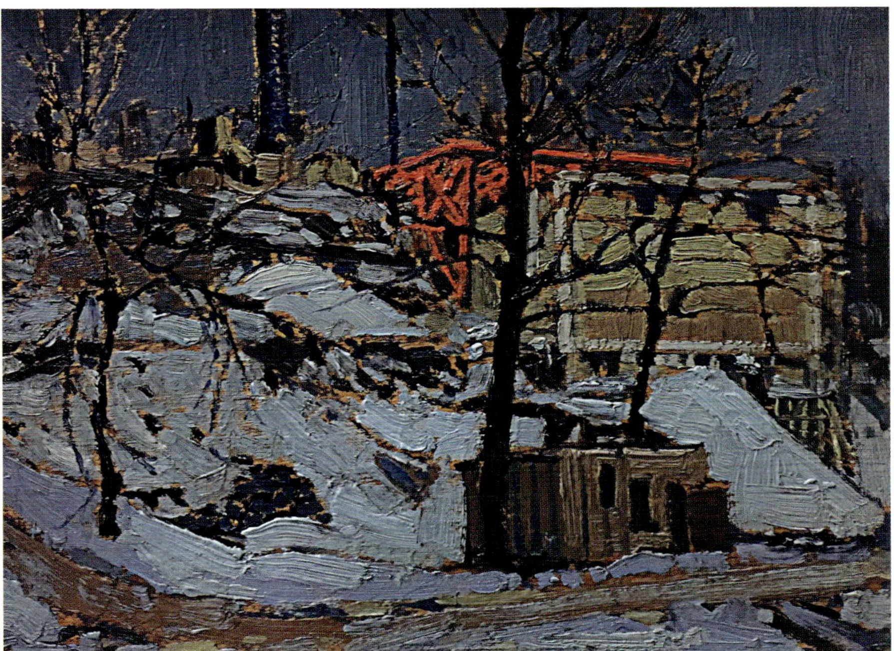

City planning photograph of Bloor Street Viaduct, Pier D, 1915, with typewritten note.

Twilight.
By Tom Thomson.
1915. Oil on panel, 21.3 x 28 cm.

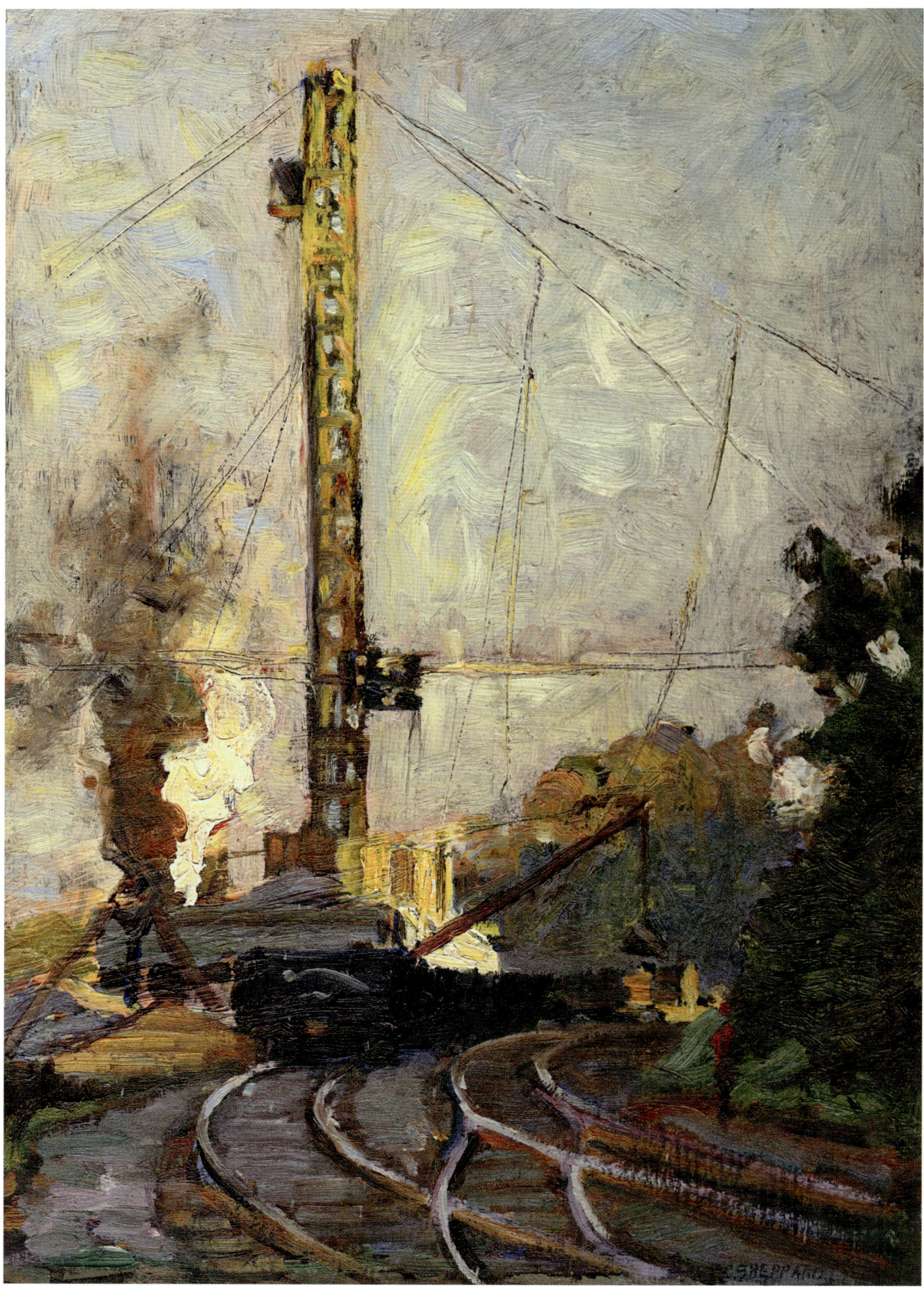

Bloor Street Viaduct (study).
1915. Oil on panel,
26.7 x 21.6 cm.

I can imagine hearing the noise of the site as this compact sketch uncannily activates several of my senses at the same time in startling ways.

A second sketch on canvas board of the same subject (page 106) is a dense, compact picture about the confrontation of humans and nature epitomized in the viaduct project. Small-format, vertical in orientation, this sketch is notable for how Sheppard has not used local colours to depict the forms. His purpose is not to illustrate, but to describe mood in the ways the colours and lines are selected and laid down in the composition. The outcome is a striking composition with complementary contrasts of oranges and reds with blues and greens, and an interplay of lines — horizontals, verticals, diagonals and arcs. Even in its compact size, I am taken with the vibrant way that Sheppard gives me a sense of the subject's dynamic potentialities. Its immediacy is transmitted not just in the sketch's formal elements of colour, line and composition. The disparities in scale, particularly in the way that humanity is dwarfed by the magnitude of the constructed forms, point sharply to Sheppard's awe at the boldness of the ambition encapsulated in the very genetics of the construction project.

A third sketch that is undated but that I am inclined to see as from this time because of its composition and the feeling it conveys, is unrelated to the actual construction of the viaduct, but nevertheless has a similar theme and mood. It shows a young artist interested in exploring how monolithic built structures dwarf human beings. A looming, shadowy industrial structure is an enigmatic presence that overwhelms the foreground figures, which are presented as not much more than brushstrokes of paint. In the way it is handled, this modest yet monumental painting treats the industrial theme almost as a symbolic abstraction.

These several impulses that are evident in the manner of the sketches' execution are translated in Sheppard's large-format studio canvas of the subject (see page 102). Although much, much larger than the compact, lap-sized paintings done on-site in the open air, the studio painting shows that Sheppard zeroed in on interpreting the scene in heroic terms as a struggle between builders, materials and forces. There is no one-to-one correspondence between sketches and painting; Sheppard did not simply copy one of the sketches into a larger format. Rather, he translated the sketches' information in a larger variation on the same themes. The big painting is a separate, yet related, construction in its own right. In its foreground a gang of bridge builders struggles to overcome the inertia and weight of materials while their project — the massive pier — looms in the distance surmounted by a crane

tower. The dynamism of the composition essentially arises from the series of large and small triangles faceting the pictorial space while also animating it.

Just as his contemporary *Locomotives* served as a means for expressing abstract qualities of colours and tones in a recognizable substance (vapour), so, too, the Bloor Street Viaduct subject gave him much with which to explore purely abstract values within a representational image. On the one hand, the crossing lines — verticals, diagonals, horizontals — all could be conscripted to piece up the picture plane's illusory space into a complex web of lines and angles. Moreover, the large fields of sky, the monumental planes cast up by the concrete pier, and the foreground all define zones for Sheppard to convey different moods largely through the interaction of hues (laid down in an Impressionist manner), tones that create dramatic effects while amplifying the exertions of the construction workers, and the massive strength of the pier that dwarfs the scene below. The strong verticality of the crane not only bisects the composition, it also draws attention to the height of the project, contrasting lightness to heaviness. Overall the pictorial elements play off contrasts and paradoxes.

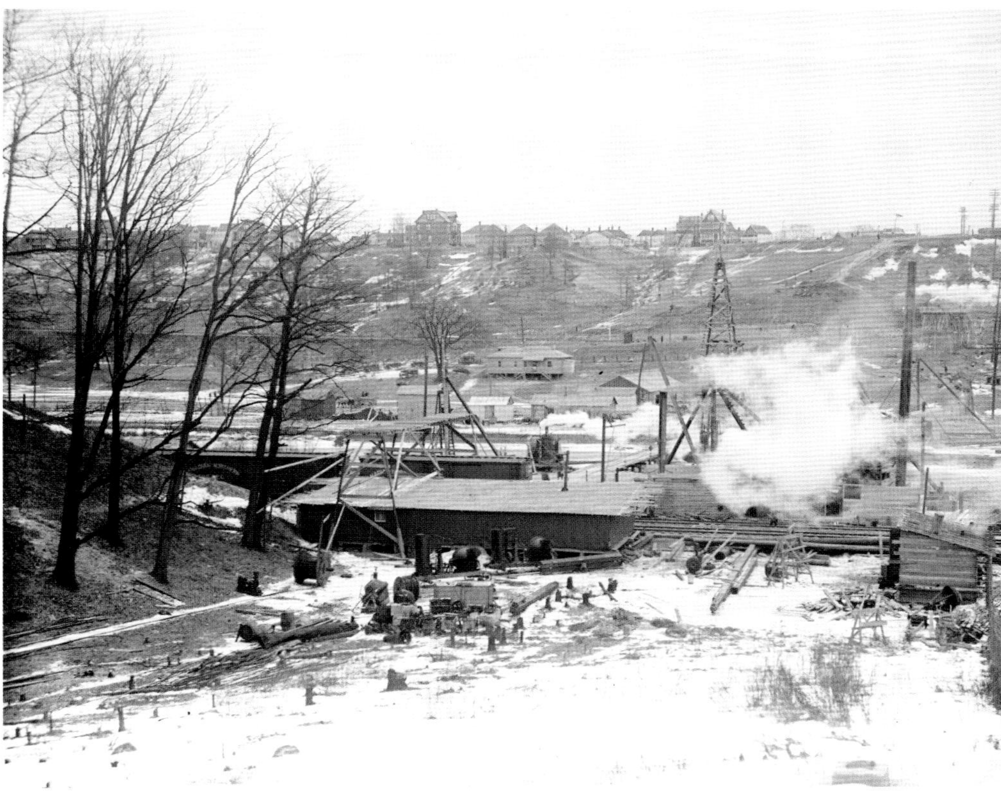

Bloor Street Viaduct construction, 1915.

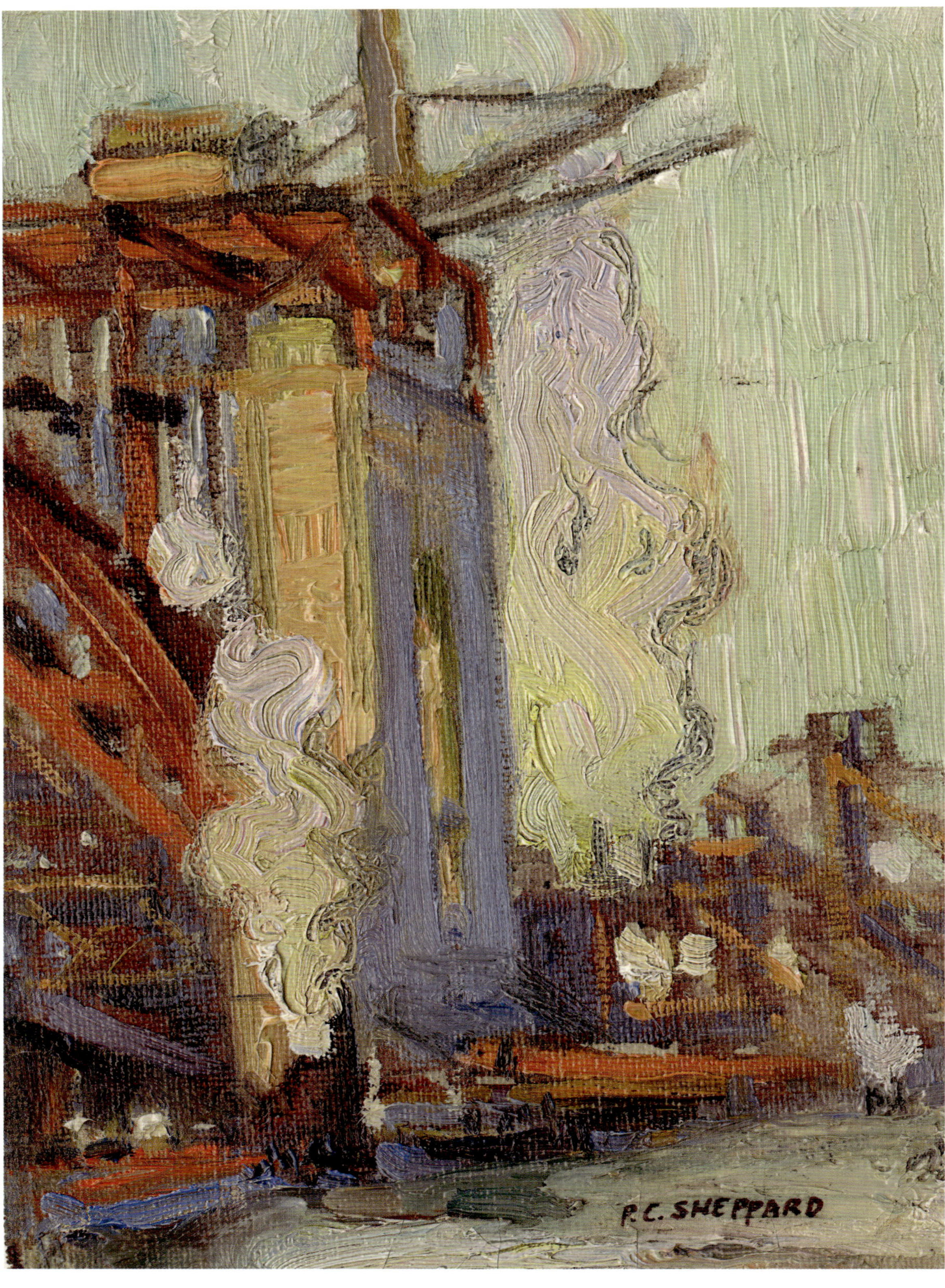

Bloor Street Viaduct (study).
1915. Oil on canvas board,
26.7 x 21.6 cm.

While the view is based on the actual construction details as can be seen preserved in photographic archives, Sheppard has not slavishly created an illustration of the construction process. Rather, his purpose was to blend the formal elements of the composition with the powerful exertions of the workers and thereby distill the project as an emblem of heroic might directed by civic development. The bridge was an ambitious engineering project, an effort to join east and west Toronto to encourage future growth, and the entire image as Sheppard presents it is indeed a powerful and positive symbol of growth and development. Surely, at the time of its construction, coinciding exactly with the years of the Great War, the Bloor Street Viaduct represented hope in future prosperity and signified a young country and city poised on the brink of self-defining growth. Sheppard catches the civic mood of pride in accomplishment, taking the specific event of a massive piece of urban-development's civil engineering and re-presenting it as a graphic display. In this context the painting might be seen as an emblematic response to the war. Although far away in Europe, its impact on the lives of Toronto's citizens was being keenly felt in 1915. The painting interprets a specific local project with no direct connection to the war, but metaphorically it could be an au-dacious statement of civic and national resolve to overcome the tragedy of war through bold, positive action. Sheppard captures these heroic qualities in this painting that is much more than it shows; it can be read as his response to war's destruction. By signifying growth rather than defeat, the painting mirrors the accomplishments of Thomson, whose contemporary painting *The Jack Pine* signifies this same symbolic and nationalistic intent.

Once again, the archive is silent on how Sheppard's work was received when first viewed by the public. *Bloor Street Viaduct* was exhibited at the OSA annual exhibition from March to April 1916, and then again that autumn in Montreal at the annual exhibition of the Royal Canadian Academy, although Sheppard was neither an academician nor an associate of the RCA. All the same, I can imagine that it caught the attention of the public in an exhibition that also featured scenes of exotic foreign locations — for example, in the work of J. Ernest Sampson interpreting Tangier, Venice and Capri — and of northern Ontario hinterland forests.[47] That same year, Thomson exhibited paintings of birches, spring ice, moonlight and hardwood trees. Sheppard's works, in some respects, expressed similarly exotic themes, but where Sampson and Thomson depicted visual and moody metaphors of escape and transcendence, Sheppard harnessed his metaphors to the heroic struggle of overcoming inert forces and obstacles to progress in an urban setting. Yet what strikes me most

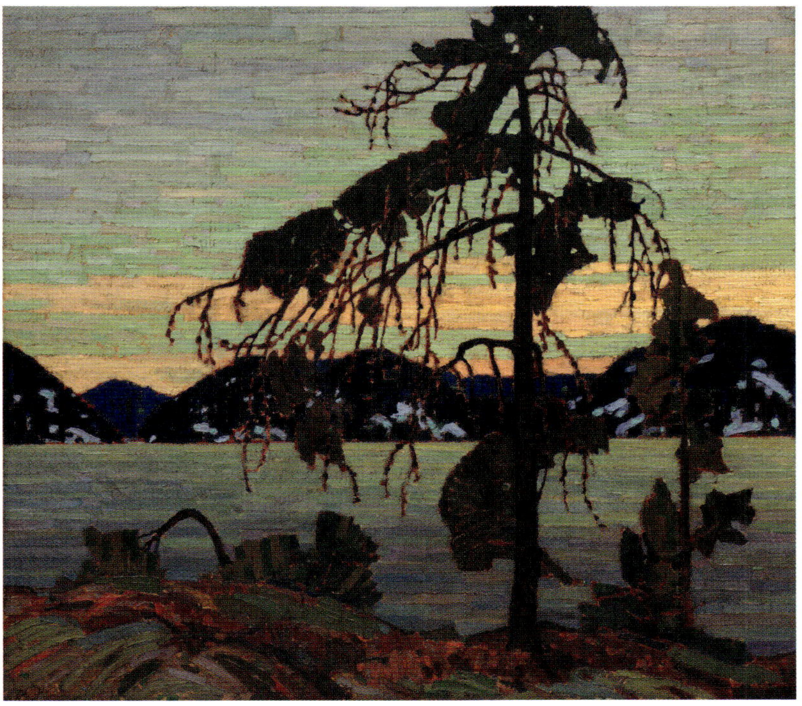

The Jack Pine.
By Tom Thomson.
1916–17. Oil on canvas, 127.9 x 139.8 cm.

as I page through the RCA exhibition catalogue, scanning the illustrations, is that Sheppard's viaduct painting is very different from the majority of what is being shown that year. A large majority of the exhibitors have interpreted the landscape in a picturesque manner. There are plenty of paintings of rivers and fields, shorelines and views, along with portraits of record and society paintings. The energy of Sheppard's submission and its elegant compositional formality mark it as one of the more progressive offerings of the 1916 season, and this quality might well have contributed to its being selected as worthy of illustration in the booklet, surely an honour for an aspiring painter who was not even a member of the academy.

What I can well appreciate is that in 1916 Sheppard was on his way in the field of the "fine" arts. In addition to being exhibited in that year's OSA and RCA exhibitions, he had a painting selected by the jury for the annual art exhi-bition at Toronto's Canadian National Exhibition. His work in that prestigious show is listed in the records at the CNE as *"The Two Engines,"* a descriptive title that applies to a few paintings that are preserved in the archive.[48]

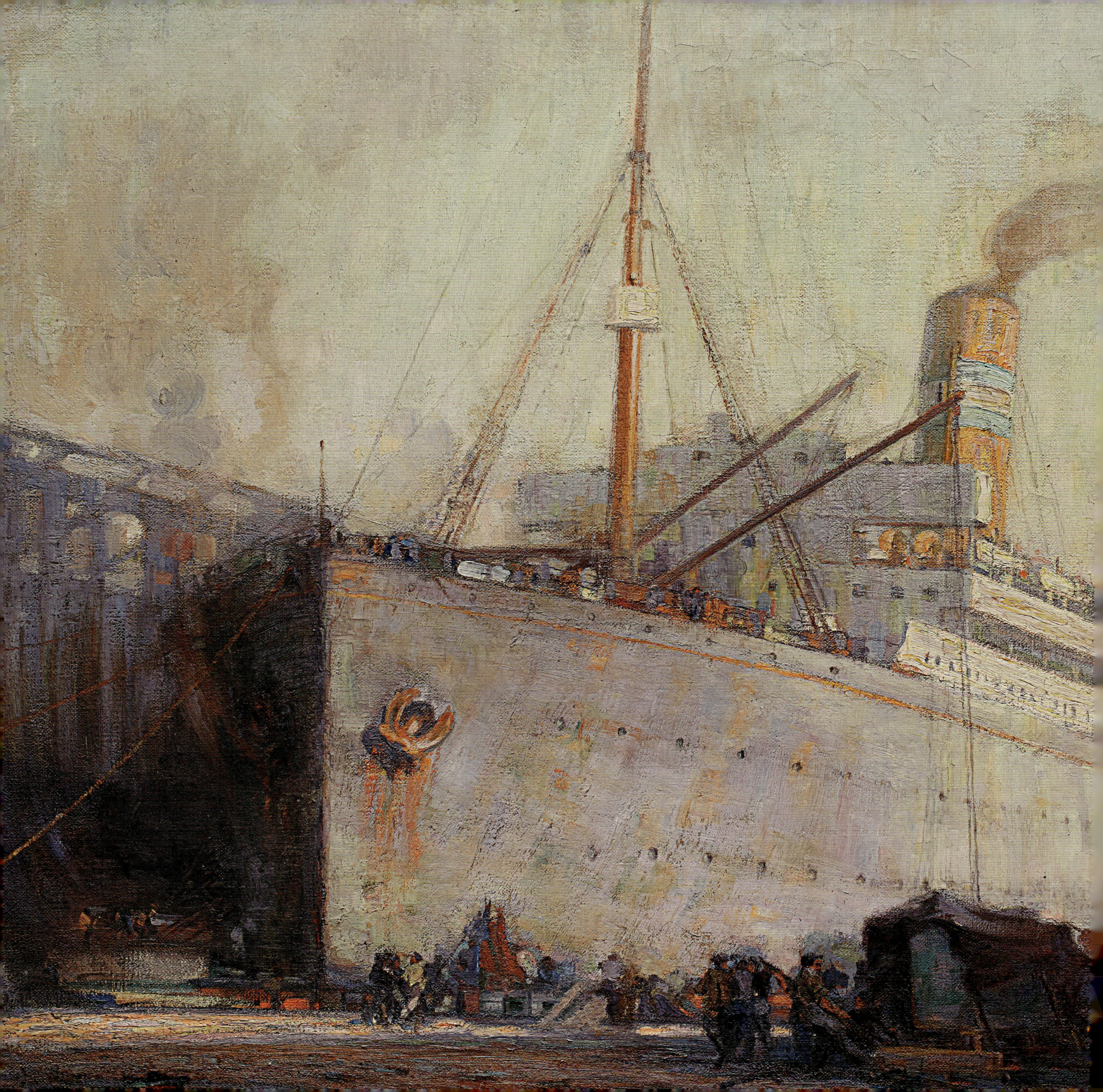

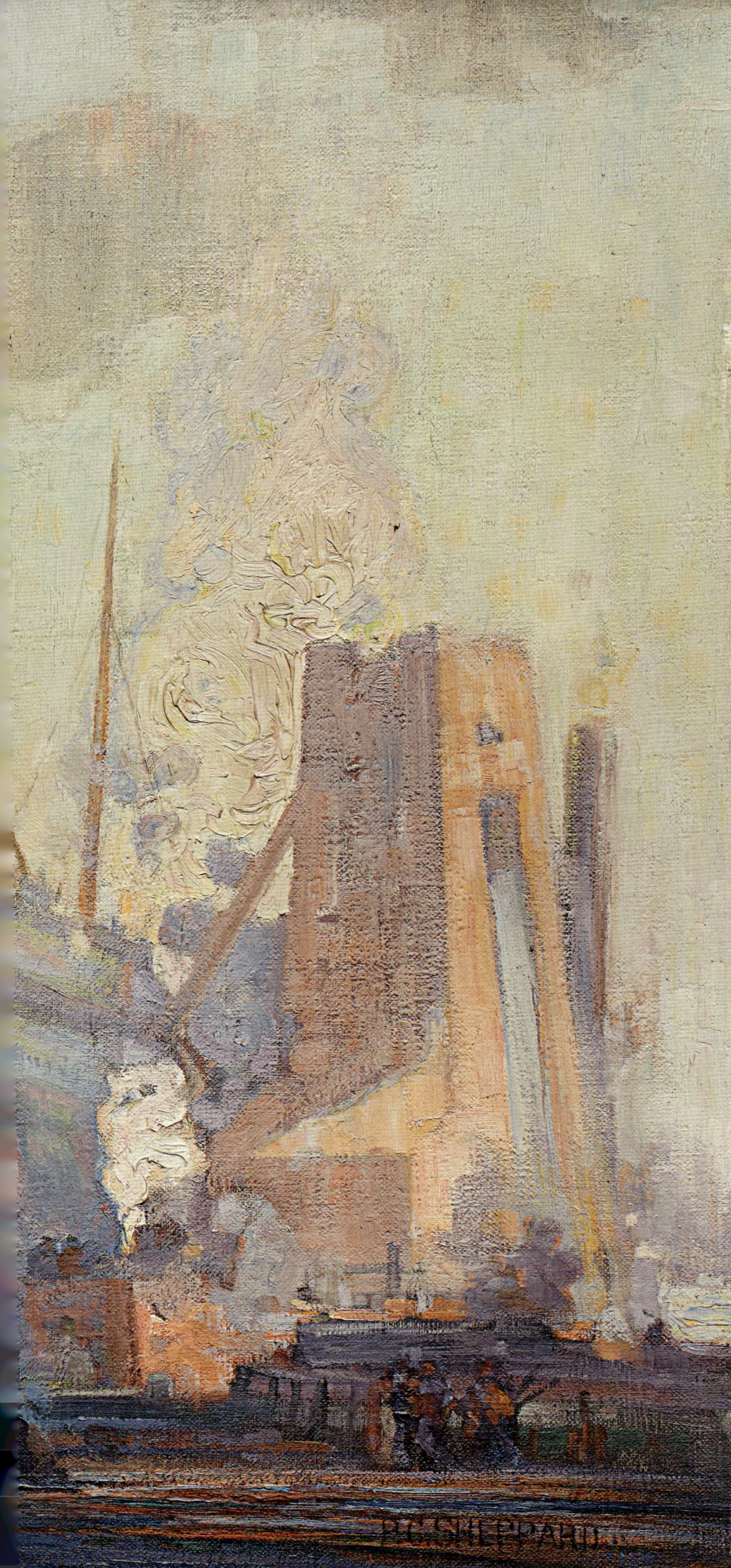

Morning on the River.
1917. Oil on canvas,
101.6 x 147.3 cm.

MAKING A LIVING AS AN ARTIST, 1917 ONWARD

The vexing question that becomes ever more evident as I work in the archive is: how did Sheppard make a living? Surrounded by the fruits of his studio practice, I am aware that these works of art were not sold during his lifetime. Many of the paintings were exhibited in important exhibitions in their day — exhibitions that encouraged the public to purchase the art and even supplied or published price lists. On the evidence that surrounds me, it is clear that Sheppard did not sell much of his studio production. How did he afford to live?

On this question (as on so many others) the archive is silent and I am left to piece together circumstances to guess at how he earned a living. The *City of Toronto Directory* shows that between 1913 and 1918 Sheppard transitioned from the profession of "Lithographer" to that of "Artist." In 1919 he is listed as an "Artist," a profession he would have worked at through 1918. He occupied a downtown Toronto studio at 101½ King Street West, surely a move that was made after careful consideration of the prospects of leaving gainful for precarious employment. The 1919 *Assessment Roll* shows that he was not the only artist at this address; John Thackings (no dates available) and Frances M. Geddes (1888–1947) shared the building's second floor with Sheppard and

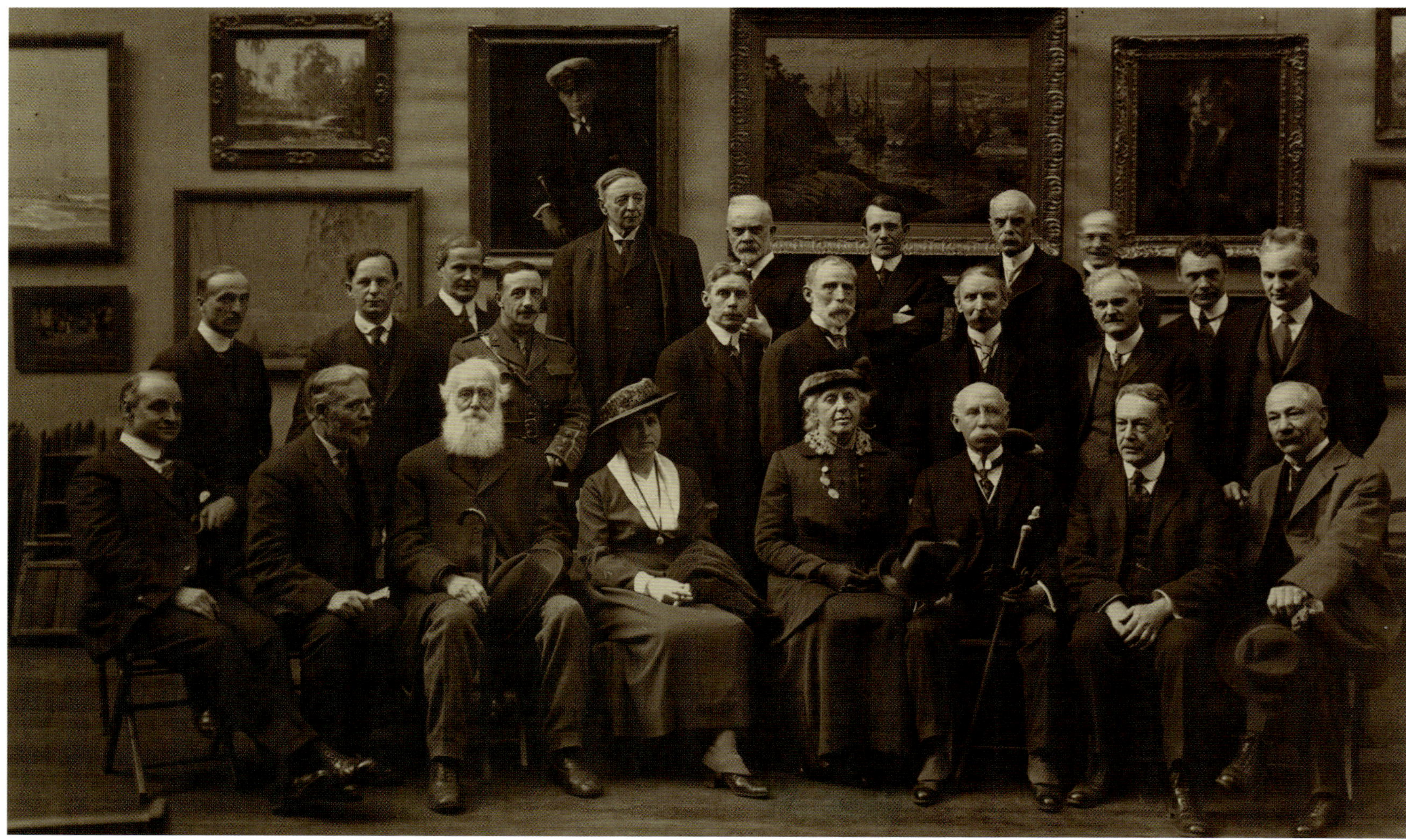

Opening of the Art Gallery of Toronto, 1918. While Sheppard is not in this photograph, these are the shoulders on which he and his cohort rested, benefitting from their pioneering work to establish a cultural outpost in the colony.

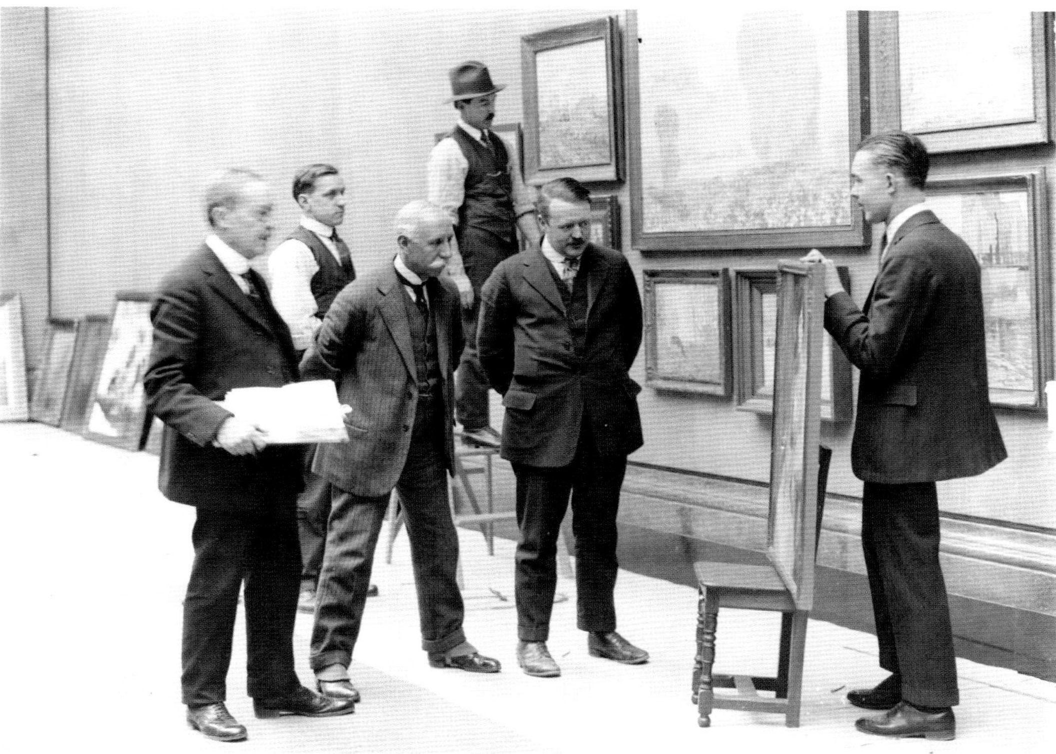

Ontario Society of Artists hanging committee, 1919. Left to right: W. Downard, A. Boughten, R.F. Gagen, E. Wyly Grier, Francis H. Johnston and Lawren S. Harris, holding painting.

had studios there, too, as did John Kennedy, a photographer.[49] An unidentified photocopy of a page from what appears to be a dictionary of painters allows that Sheppard was, "For some years … secretary of night classes at O.C.A." and that he "taught at O.C.A summer school."[50] An undated note attached to the back of a photographic portrait of Sheppard offers a bit more information about his teaching in that he "now has several pupils of his own at his Toronto studio," and that "one year he painted 'Midway' figures at the Canadian National Exhibition." What does this latter statement suggest, that Sheppard painted gaudy billboard attractions that were meant to entice visitors into sideshow attractions at the CNE? I am left with the impression that whatever living Sheppard made it was a meagre, perhaps even a hardscrabble one that combined fine art painting, commissions and sales with teaching, college administration and odd assignments that called for a figurative artist and a commercial illustrator not afraid to take a job for hire.

Around 1916–17, Sheppard sold some of his paintings to what were then important collections. For example, in 1917 he exhibited a large oil painting entitled *Morning on the River* at the Ontario Society of Artists annual exhibition and at the Canadian National Exhibition.[51] It was purchased by the CNE, presumably for the listed price of $400. A full catalogue entry for this painting, now at the Art Gallery of Ontario (then the Art Gallery of Toronto), indicates that the Canadian National Exhibition Association gave it to the AGO in 1965.[52]

Morning on the River (see pages 108–109) shows that Sheppard continued to explore industrial subjects that both pointed to economic development and gave him the latitude to veer away from pictorialism to paint in an abstract mode, albeit lashed to a mast of representation. In a manner that recalls his Bloor Viaduct paintings, *Morning on the River* monumentalizes the subject of the passenger boat. The vessel fills the composition, defined by a stable foundation of triangles, squares and rectangles. Although the ocean liner is set at a perspective angle to the picture plane, implying depth into the imaginary space, Sheppard has flattened the planes of sky and hull all the better to use them as expressive fields. And he does riff on these fields to good effect in abstract forms. The boat's hull contains beautiful passages of purples, mauves

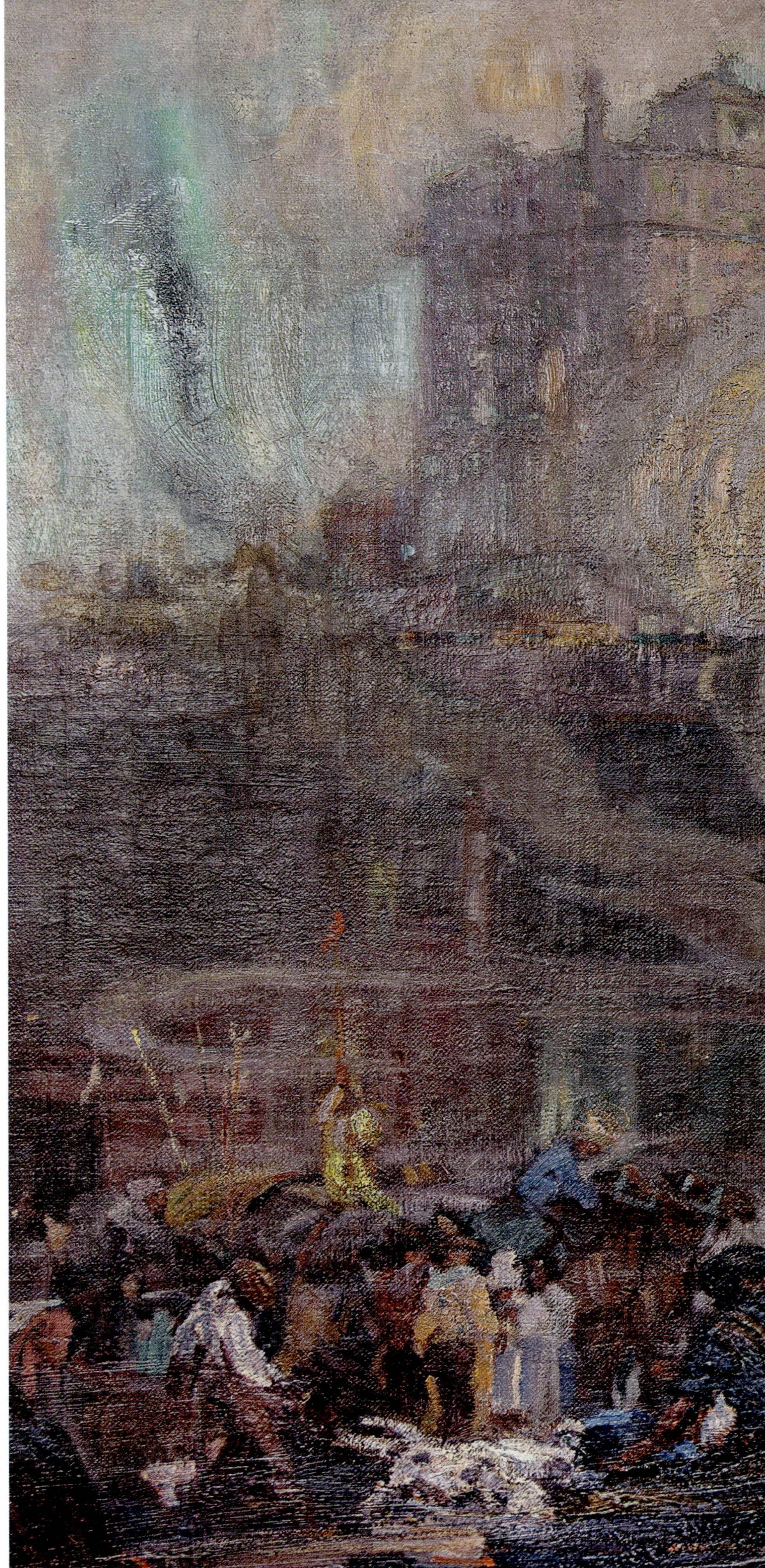

Arrival of the Circus.
c. 1919. Oil on canvas,
101.6 x 147.3 cm.

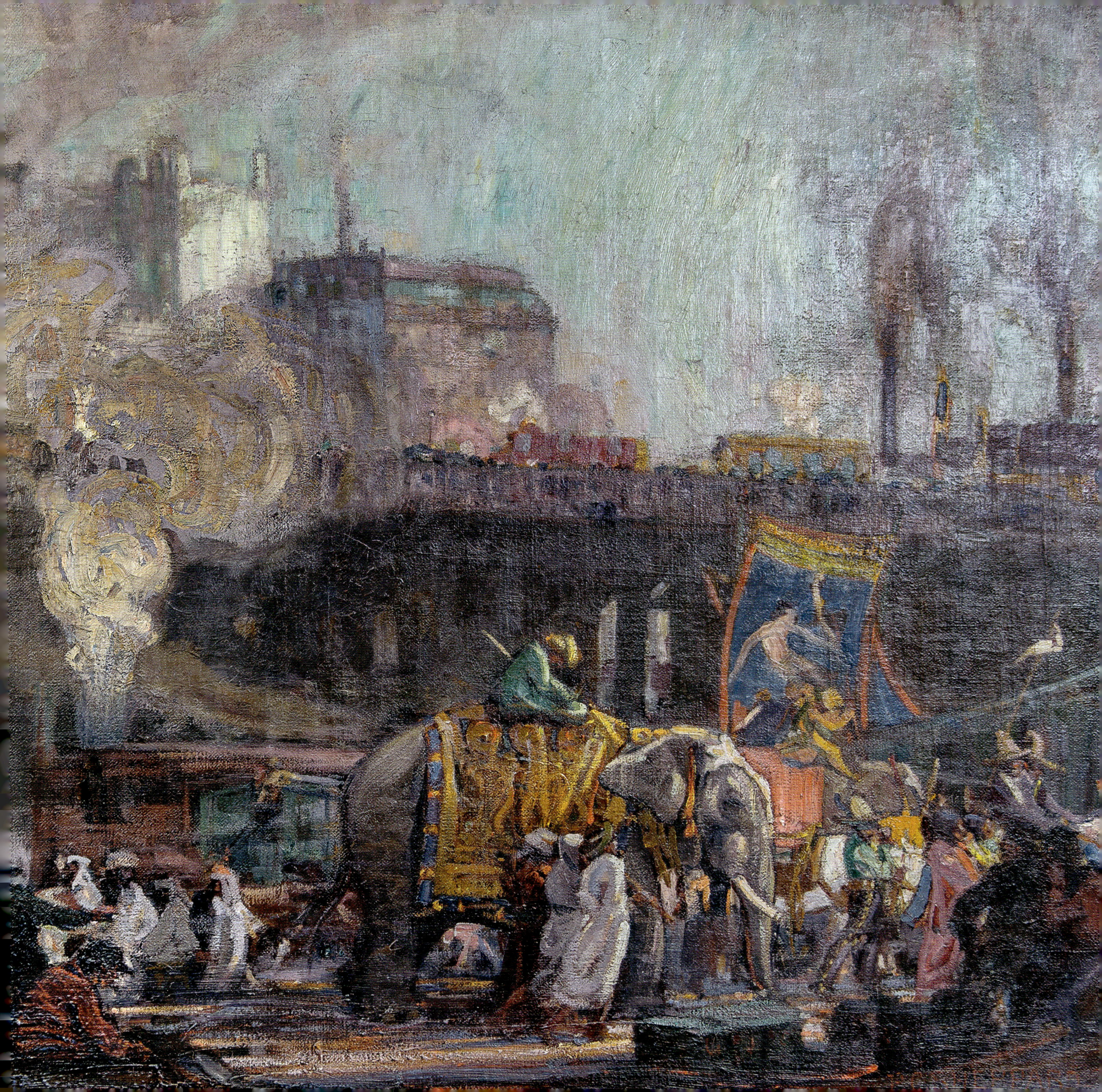

and blues, and these are contrasted with the carefully delineated foreground action of the stevedores working in the shadows as the crane lifts the cargo onboard. The sky is accented by non-local variations of greens. All these effects appear to be aimed at portraying the humid air at dockside to the extent that, although appearing to be an interpretation of a boat, the true subject is light; boat, crane, sky are armatures that anchor Sheppard's abstract forays to recognizable references, yet allow the painter's expressiveness to unfold. The scene is simply a convenient excuse to paint purely.

In 1918 prospects began to look much better for Toronto and Ontario artists because the Art Museum of Toronto opened in April of that year. The construction of a purpose-built art museum was certainly tangible recognition of the arts in the life of a modern, growing urban centre. It also gave the city's artists a forum for the exhibition and promotion of their work, while also providing impetus for the further development of provincial art societies and educational institutions, among them the OSA and OCA. In the dour, be-whiskered "notable gathering of Canadian artists" on the occasion of the opening of the art museum there is a sense of self-congratulation and satisfaction in attaining something important. While Sheppard is not in the photograph published in the *Toronto Star Weekly,* these are the shoulders on which Sheppard and his cohort rested, benefitting from their pioneering work to establish a cultural outpost in the colony (see page 110). The efforts of those who established the museum made making a living as a professional artist somewhat less onerous and precarious for Sheppard than it likely had been when they were at the beginnings of their careers. Membership in the OSA and exhibiting in its annual exhibitions conferred status on any artist, especially those who were in the early stages of their professional careers as was Sheppard, and provided a forum for the promotion and sale of their art.

ARRIVAL OF THE CIRCUS, 1919

Sheppard's membership in the OSA was affirmed at the association's annual meeting that was held on March 11, 1919. He was among three of that year's "accessions," which included two fellow artists, Harry Britton (1878–1958) and Manly MacDonald (1889–1971).[53] Things appeared to be going Sheppard's way that year; as one of the new generation of artists, he was viewed as being among a small cadre of painters who found their inspiration in gritty urban subject matter. I am intrigued by the possibilities packed up in a statement published in 1932 by artist and author A.H. Robson in his book *Canadian Land-scape Painters.* Robson writes of Sheppard that after studying at OCA, he "then began exhibiting pictures with a breadth of brush handling and a brilliancy of colour which attracted favourable attention."[54] This is true. He was even singled out in a review published in Toronto's *Globe* newspaper, its author writing:

> What seems to the unseeing the garish commonplace of Exhibition crowds and colors spurred a little group of young artists last fall into most interesting activity, one of the immediate results of which appears in a clever study of "The Balloon Booth" by Vivien Logan, while less directly it is manifest in Frances Geddes' "A Chinese Fantasy" and P. C. Sheppard's "Arrival of the Circus." In the latter, against a background of skyscrapers and over a gray railway bridge veiled with wisps of lavender smoke trails the circus parade with its gaudily-glad people, its gaily-caparisoned elephants and all its color and allurements.[55]

Beyond the specific mention of Sheppard in this review, I am also drawn to the name of Frances Geddes, who was at that time Sheppard's studio neighbour at 101½ King Street West. A sketch of Geddes' biography gives context in showing what one of Sheppard's peers was doing at the time and subsequently sheds light on their knowing each other as neighbours. Geddes, born in Clyde, New York, was the daughter of a British father and a Canadian mother. Although she grew up in England, where she studied at Oxford and then at the Slade School of Art in London with Sir Henry Tonks (1862–1937), she came to Toronto and continued her art education at OCA under Reid and Beatty. Indeed, it is entirely possible that she and Sheppard were classmates, and that she is one of the anonymous student artists seen working over her drawing board in the surviving photographs of OCA studios in which we can identify Sheppard.

Following her work in Toronto she moved on to New York and the Art Students League, where she studied with Kenneth Hayes Miller (1876–1952) and Dimitri Romanovsky (1887–1971).[56]

At the time that Sheppard and Geddes occupied studio space in the same building in 1919, he (and according to the reviewer) and Geddes were interpreting the "garish commonplace" of the annual late summer Canadian National Exhibition, and it was this interest that no doubt also drew Sheppard to interpret the arrival of the circus in town. A surviving sketch in the archive is of a view backstage of the CNE's grandstand, where Sheppard paused to draw elephants and figures, some on horseback, set on a dais or stage, where

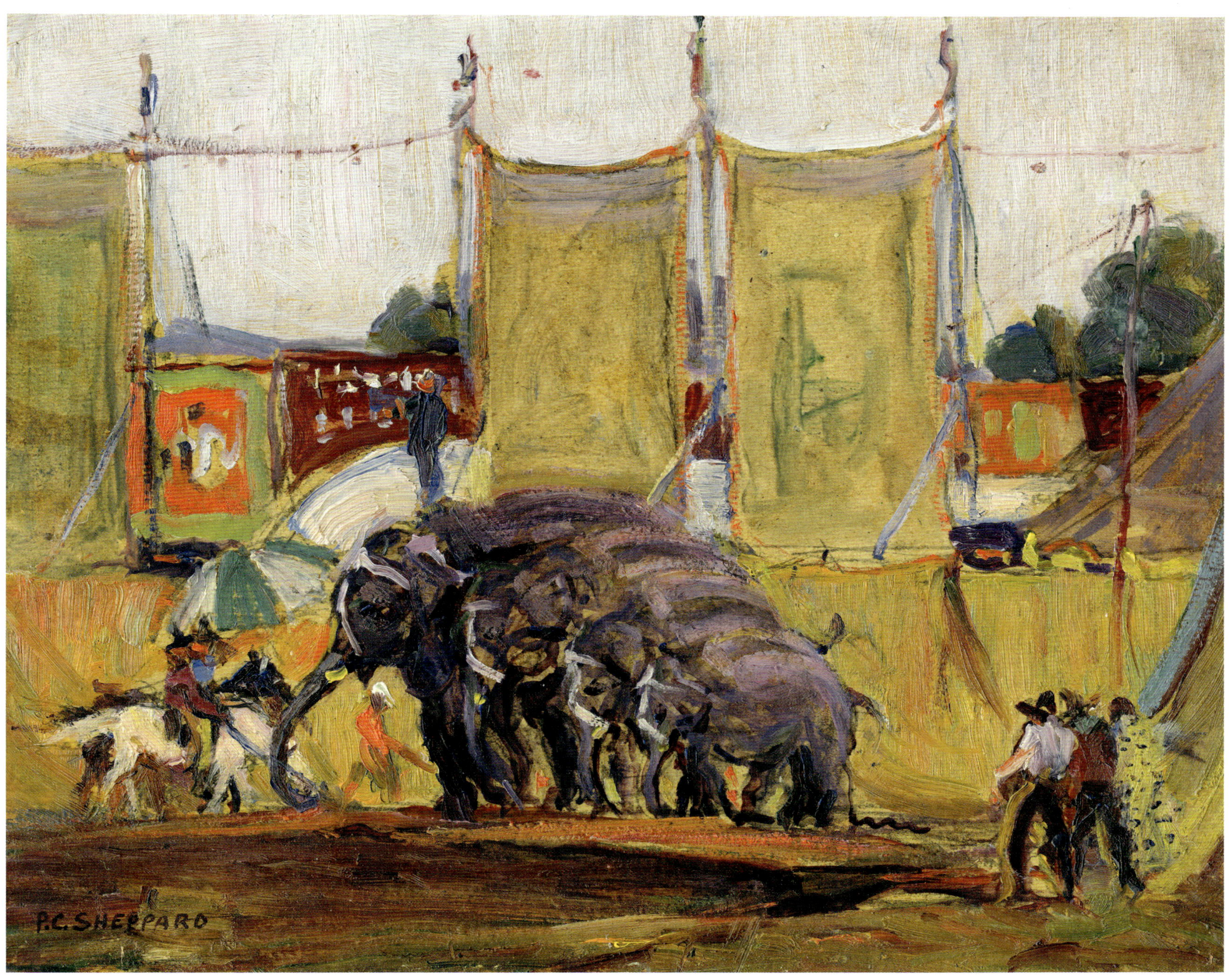

Circus (study).
c. 1919. Oil on board,
21.6 x 26.7 cm.

the elephants are grouped in a cluster at the composition's centre. As troubling as the subject is to contemporary eyes attuned to the barbaric treatment that was accorded to circus animals, particularly elephants, Sheppard approached his subject with a light touch, more on-the-spot reportage, in which he records what appears before his eyes and sketch pad.

Sheppard also made several other sketches of the CNE, likely from notes he set down during a visit to the 1918 exhibition grounds (and as alluded to by the reviewer). Take, for example, his sketch of the CNE's horticultural building, in which the figures assembled in the foreground (possibly attending a wedding) are depicted with a deft handling of the brushstrokes in the foreground to such an extent that they are not much more than impressions. The building itself, whose dome-like roof overlooks the scene, acts almost as a backdrop that sets the stage for the Toronto-based *fête champêtre.*

His small-format panel *The Promenade* (pages 22–23), also an on-the-spot oil sketch, provides a dynamic and vivid impression of the crowds enjoying a sunny day at the CNE. But I prefer to imagine that the subject, the light and the blaze of colours radiating in the late-summer sun all gave Sheppard a basis for luxuriating in setting down an abstracted interpretation of the scene. In the handling of colour, Sheppard establishes a pleasing use of complementary blue and ochre, and a description of the way light moves in the immediate foreground. It was probably these very paintings, among others by his painter friends, that prompted the reviewer to mention how Sheppard and the others approached the "garish commonplace" subjects of the CNE, and in the end turned them into sensitive pictorial statements that were both beautiful and made in a manner that showed more than a fleeting kinship with a mode of abstract painting and a sensibility that scoured the urban maelstrom for subjects to interpret as paintings.

The circus, however, gave Sheppard a subject for his first ambitious, large-format, multi-figured tableau that is remarkable for its originality and sheer ambition. Although the painting appears to be unfinished, it evidently was worked up to a point that made him satisfied that it was complete enough to exhibit in the 1919 CNE and OSA exhibitions, and also good enough to

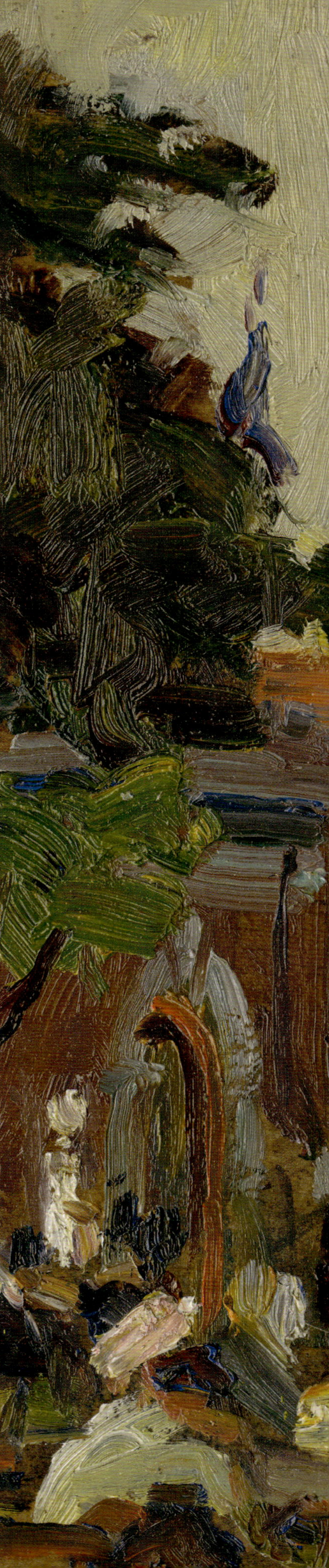

Horticultural Building,
Canadian National Exhibition.
1919. Oil on panel,
21.6 x 26.7 cm.

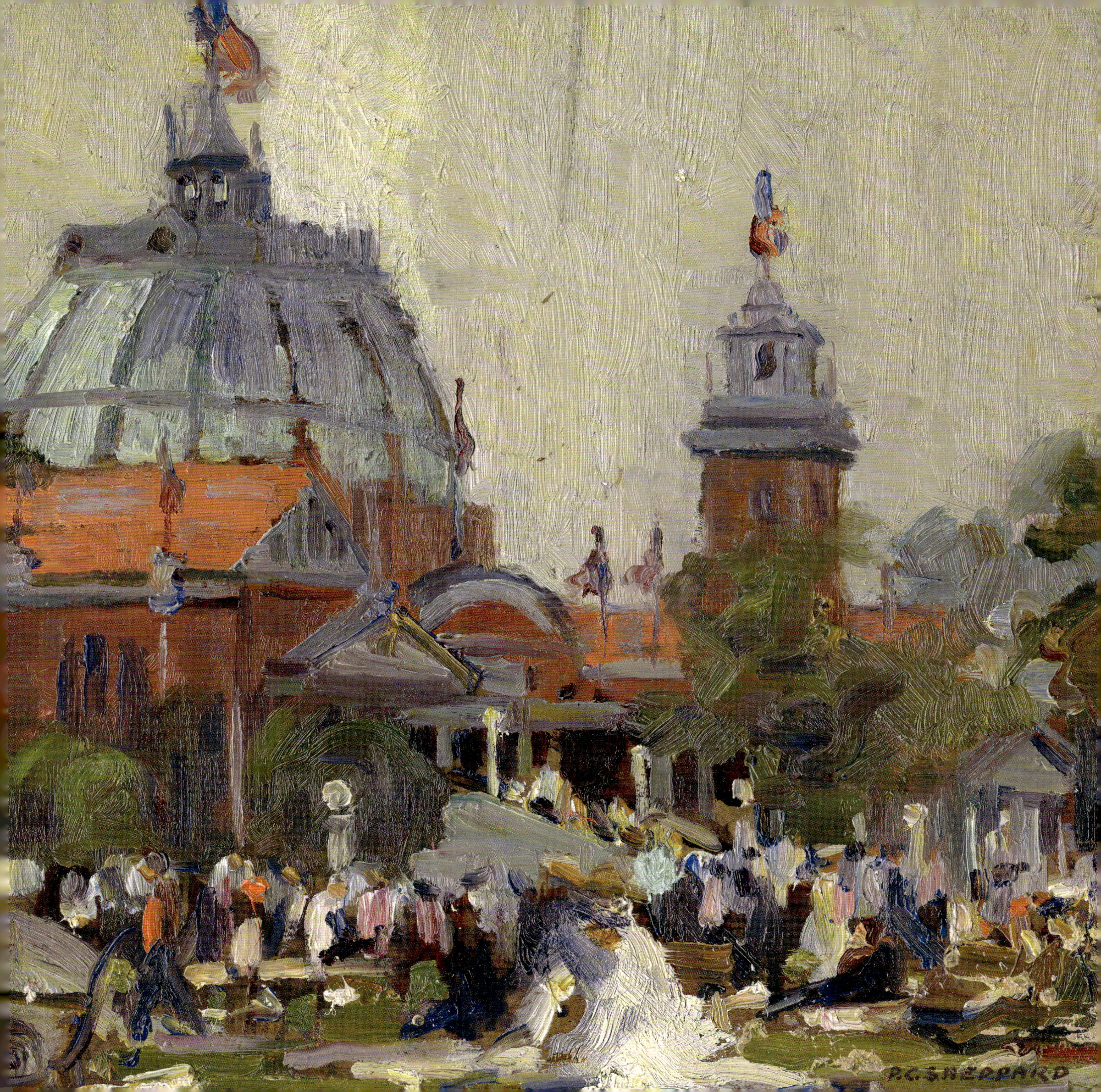
P.C. SHEPPARD

pass muster with an august hanging committee (page 111) of none other than W. Downard, A. Boughten, R.F. Gagen, E. Wyly Grier, Francis Johnston and Lawren Harris, the latter two of whom would soon become founding members of the Group of Seven.

What survives today is a painting that contains energy and vitality, and Sheppard's ambitions. The scene is dominated by action in the bottom right corner of the composition showing elephants and performers parading to the circus grounds at a site on the waterfront below the city, adjacent to a popular boardwalk that gave way to the beach and shallow waters. Sheppard has imbued his band of gypsies and acrobats with a whiff of the underworld; there is definitely a sense that the horde is parading to a place in the shadows, below ground, on the margins of society. To enhance the effect of an underworld, the boardwalk neatly divides the composition into two horizontal registers. In the gloaming, the figurative elements are described with not much more than brushed impressions. Whereas, in contrast, the city is a brightly lit background, itself depicted as complex fields of greens and purples and tenebrous tones. It seems that Sheppard wants to give an effect of movement and transience by describing parts of the picture through different levels of refinement, giving the sense that the painting is unfinished. The lower right quadrant creates an exotic tableau of bohemian pageantry tinged with that special dinginess and seediness associated with a transient circus troupe peddling a mirage of mystery, amusement, spectacle, chance, risk and perhaps even vice.

THE GROUP OF SEVEN

Among the many circumstances that give a context for Sheppard's life, the most important for him and for his cohort of artists working in Toronto particularly was the Group of Seven. The artists who formed and were members of this collective cast a very long shadow over the lives and art of their contemporaries in ways that were certainly not appreciated at the time of their emergence. An unknown consequence of their ascent and radiance in the cultural firmament of post–World War I Toronto is that, over the succeeding decades and into the new millennium, they made many of their contemporaries vanish from public consciousness. This was Sheppard's unfortunate fate. Although he continued to paint in a style and mode that rivalled some of his peers' in the group, for a complex set of reasons his light dimmed next to theirs, and his expressive skills and innovations were diminished and underappreciated.

Why did this occur? On the one hand it might well have been the result of being in or out of a club. A select group might have the patina of being open and democratic, but the truth is that a group by definition is exclusionary. Insiders were a phalanx that valued privileged inclusion, but were protective of their corporate status. You were let in to the company. You did not join it. The Group of Seven modelled itself as a band of like-minded individuals whose aims were to define a national school of art, and this academy was based almost exclusively on interpreting the landscape, urban and wilderness. Their artistic aims were tempered by circumstances as well. In the aftermath of the Great War, in which several of the members served in the armed forces, and which had a catastrophic effect on the members' peer group, many of whom who were either killed or wounded in battle, the group looked to the landscape as a way of coming to grips with the trauma of war and the aftermath their generation inherited. They looked to the hinterland — the landscapes of northern Ontario — for subject matter, and to northern European schools of painting for stylistic influences in an effort to paint a new utopia of unspoiled nature that could replace the outmoded norms and perhaps help order the chaos of the present days.

Their efforts struck a chord with the viewing public. Their popularity was also supported by the cultural institutions of the day, which exhibited and promoted their art at home and abroad. In the first place, as members of the OSA, the group enjoyed the support structures and relationships that were afforded by membership in that society. Exhibiting in the annual shows ensured that their paintings were seen and noticed by contemporary reviewers. Moreover, the RCA and the National Gallery of Canada added their considerable influence by also continuing to exhibit, collect and promote their work.

The institutional heft that the group received contributed to their ubiquitous presence in the cultural landscape of the third decade of the 20th century, and it is against this backdrop that Sheppard plied his trade. In retrospect, a key reason Sheppard was on the outside looking in at the group's efforts is that his artistic intentions did not align with theirs. He did not seek out or describe nationalistic symbols or utopias in the northern landscape. His was a very different source of inspiration, articulated in a form of urban pastoral and in scenes of economic growth embodied in civil engineering projects and in the rail yards. Rather than identifying with the Group of Seven, Sheppard saw his art as better aligned with the two groups of contemporary American painters, the Eight and the Ashcan School.

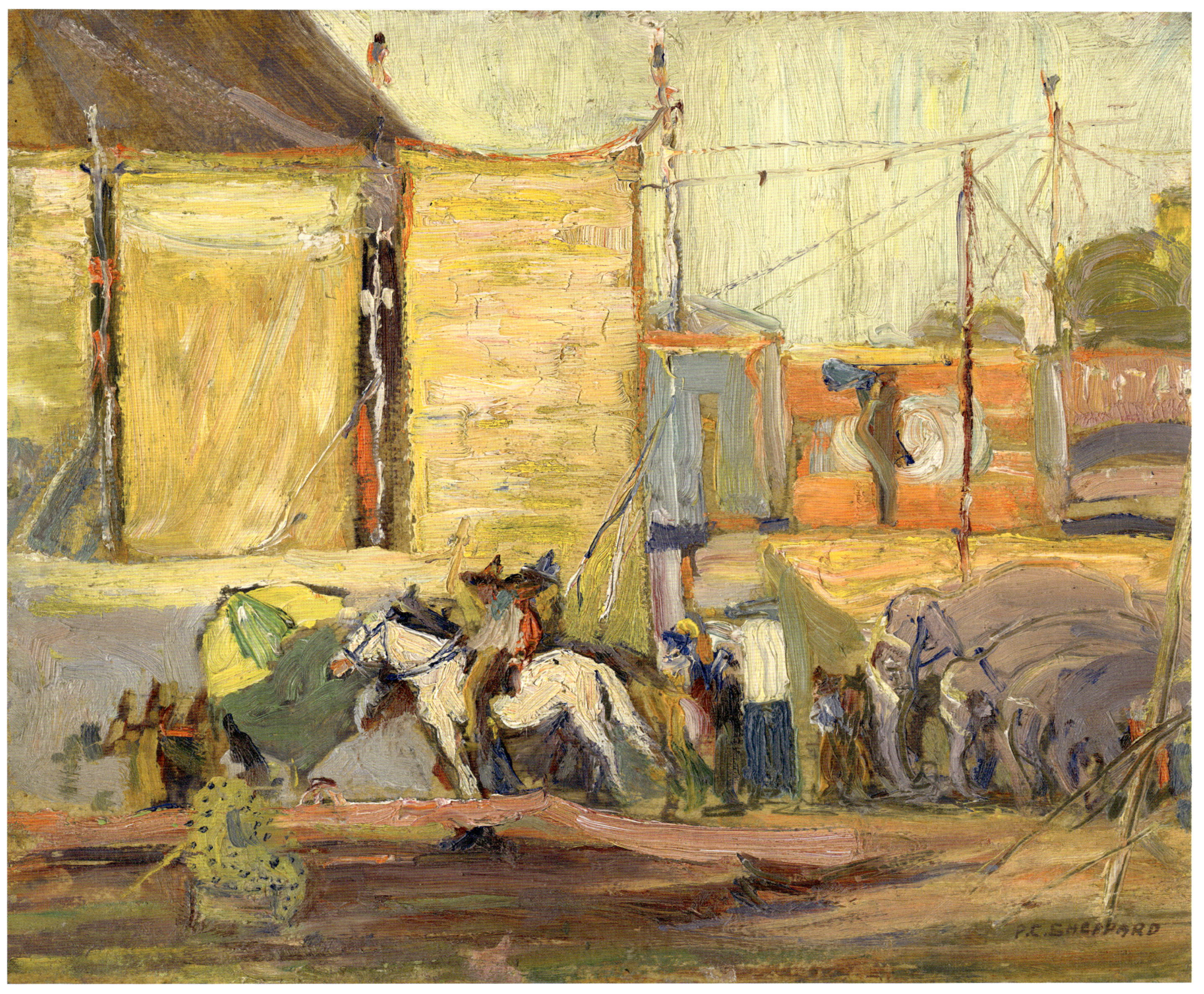

Circus (study).
c. 1919. Oil on board,
21.6 x 26.7 cm.

The Tramp (detail).
1921–22. Oil on canvas,
86 x 96.5 cm.

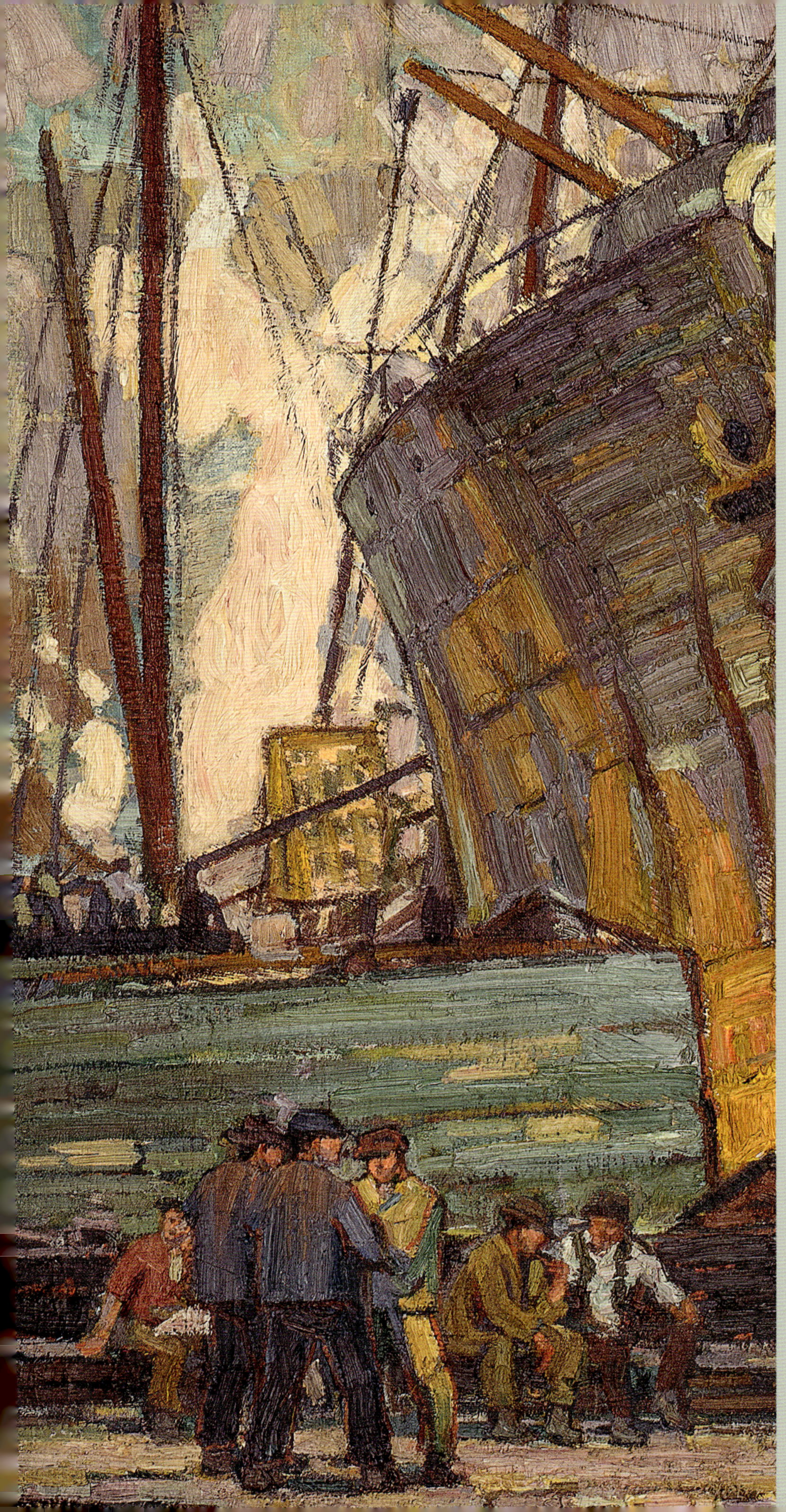

Working Beyond Toronto

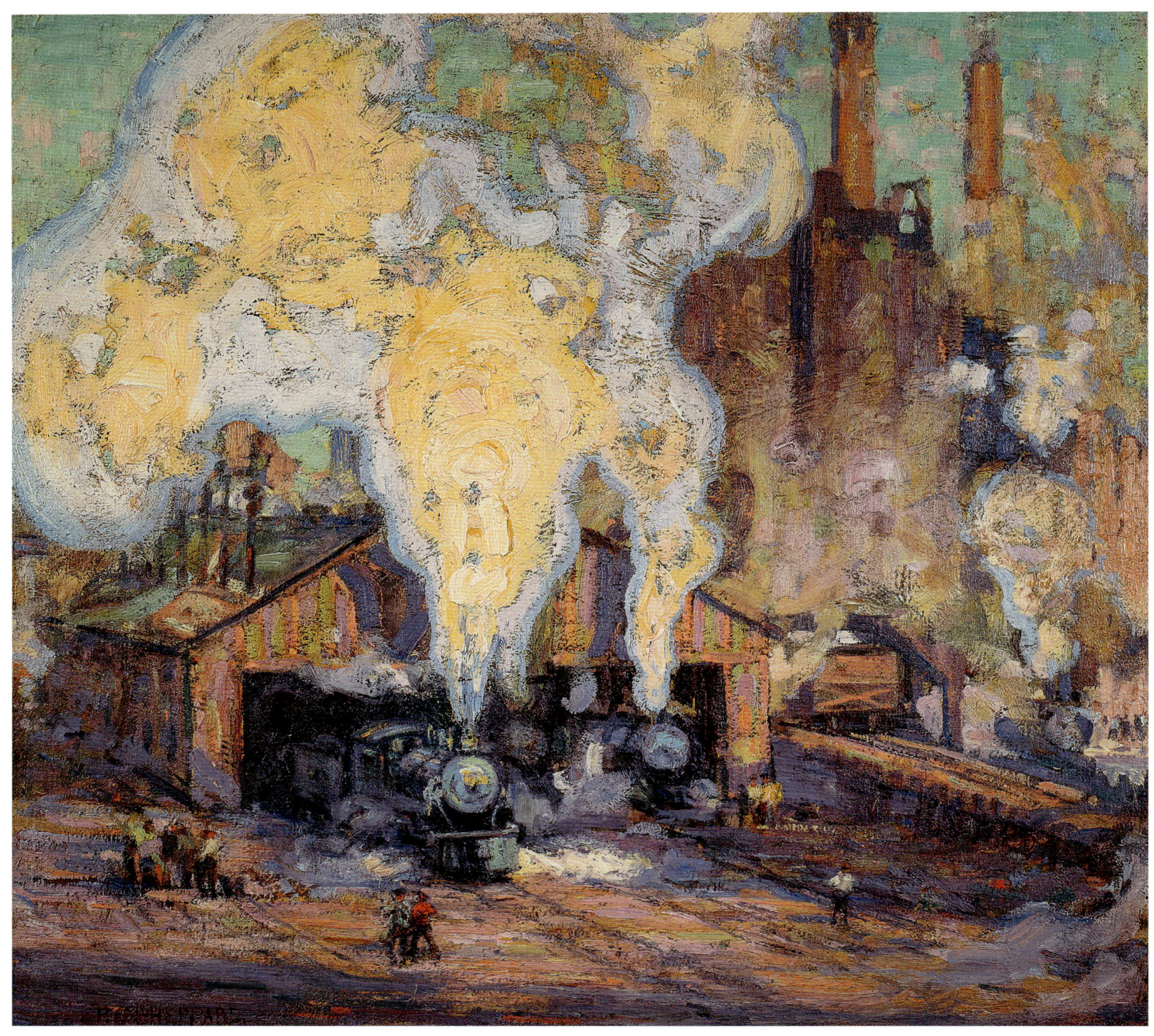

The Engine Home.
 c. 1919. Oil on canvas,
84 x 91.4 cm.

New York and Montreal

TRANSITION, 1920s

The record of where Sheppard lived and worked around 1920 becomes less well defined than it had been in the *City of Toronto Directory* and in the *Assessment Roll.* What we know from these records is that sometime in 1919 the Sheppard home at 63 Summerhill Avenue changes ownership; in the 1920 *Directory* the property is registered in the name of Robert Bourne. That same source shows that Sheppard still occupies the 101½ King Street West studio, and he continues to do so through 1920. Yet it is not clear where he lived. If it was at the Summerhill address, perhaps he rented the premises from Bourne. In 1921 he is not listed in the *Directory* at all either as an artist on King Street, or as living on Summerhill. This evidence points to him leaving Toronto sometime around 1921, and perhaps even as early as 1919. Based on the paintings that are in the archive, we can assume Sheppard travelled (perhaps frequently) to New York City and Montreal in the early 1920s.

NEW YORK INFLUENCES

The archive holds some clues as to Sheppard's travels and artistic influences at this time. By 1920 he was taken with subjects involving the figure. He was by now a talented draftsman, a skilled commercial artist and a developing fine artist.

There is an affinity in his work to that of his American contemporaries who were members of the Eight, an early 20th-century society of artist brethren who looked to the streets of New York City, its hustle and bustle, its cacophony, as fertile subject matter all the better to reflect the close relationship between life and art. Its members included Robert Henri (1865–1929), Maurice Prendergast (1859–1924), John Sloan (1871–1951), Arthur B. Davis (1862–1928), William J. Glackens (1870–1938), Everett Shinn (1876–1953), Ernest Lawson

(1873–1939), George Luks (1867–1933) and George Bellows (1882–1925), who joined the group later, a ninth member. All were intent on creating a distinctly American school of painting that did not ape aestheticism or academicism. They approached their subjects directly and on their own turf in Gotham's bustling neighbourhoods. Their approach to painting was direct and expressive; their gritty realism is characterized by vibrant brushwork all the better to simulate in paint the action of the common scenes in front of them.

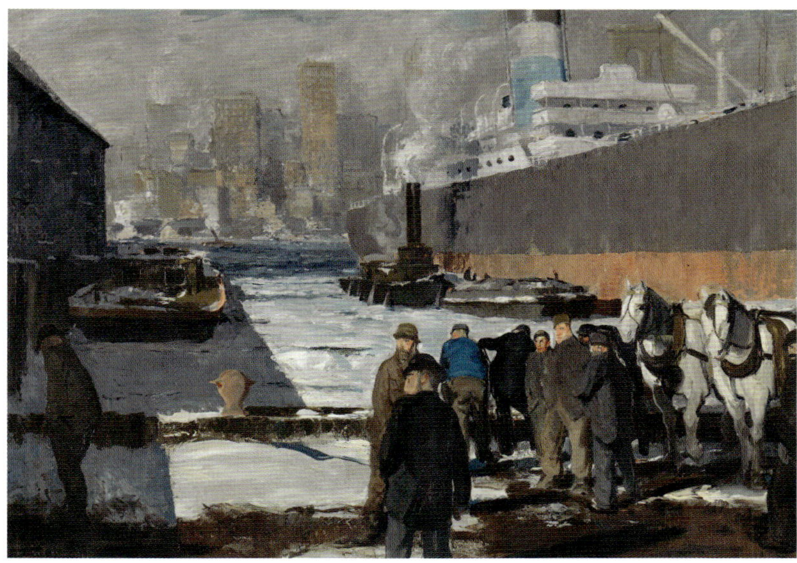

Men at the Docks.
By George Bellows.
1912. Oil on canvas, 114.3 x 161.3 cm.

The Eight transitioned into the Ashcan School, whose artists were more strident in their artistic aim of painting urban realities in a manner that was decidedly anti-aesthetic. Their intentions were to reflect contemporary life and illustrate it more accurately than their academic peers, and not to be afraid of offending the protectors of official taste. They responded to Henri's call to turn their eyes and brushes to capturing in paint the realities of working-class and middle-class urban subjects. These, Henri pronounced, provided more appropriate material for modern painters than the genteel subjects that adorned the walls and salons of the upper classes.

Sheppard was primarily a figurative artist. While landscape did feature in his paintings of the late 1910s, it was treated more as a convenient means for developing painterly idioms independent of subject matter — as if the landscape merely served as a visual anchor for his forays into expressive experiments with colour. His wide brushstroke, his subtle use of close colour harmonies and complements betray an artist pushing convention and adapting the landscape subject, making it submit to the requirement of being a visual touchstone that supported an impulse to explore the purely expressive properties of colour.

A case in point is his lyrical oil painting *River Pattern* (below). A landscape sketch of the snowy bank of a stream or freshet that he worked up into a studio canvas (*River Pattern* study, below right), it shows that the traces of figurative art are embedded into his stylistic genetic code. The ghost of the figure lurks in the manner in which he depicted the landscape. In *River Pattern*, the wintry landscape seems not much more than an excuse for Sheppard to explore the expressive abstract potentials of brushwork and non-local colours. Blues and greens are juxtaposed with oranges, while blues, violets and mauves describe the shadows made on the snow. But it is in his delineation of the stream's contours that Sheppard, perhaps unknowingly, shows his interests as a figurative artist first and foremost. The shore's contours give up a spectral outline of the human form; the turn of line, its cadence and lyricism all point to a hand that cannot help but conform to the rules of figurative description.

It is no stretch to state that Sheppard's sensibilities as a figurative artist infused his expressive mode. From his abstracted handling of form and contour to his selection of subjects and his narrative voice, Sheppard used the full range of the figurative language. The examples of his New York counterparts provided him with models to emulate in describing the full spectrum

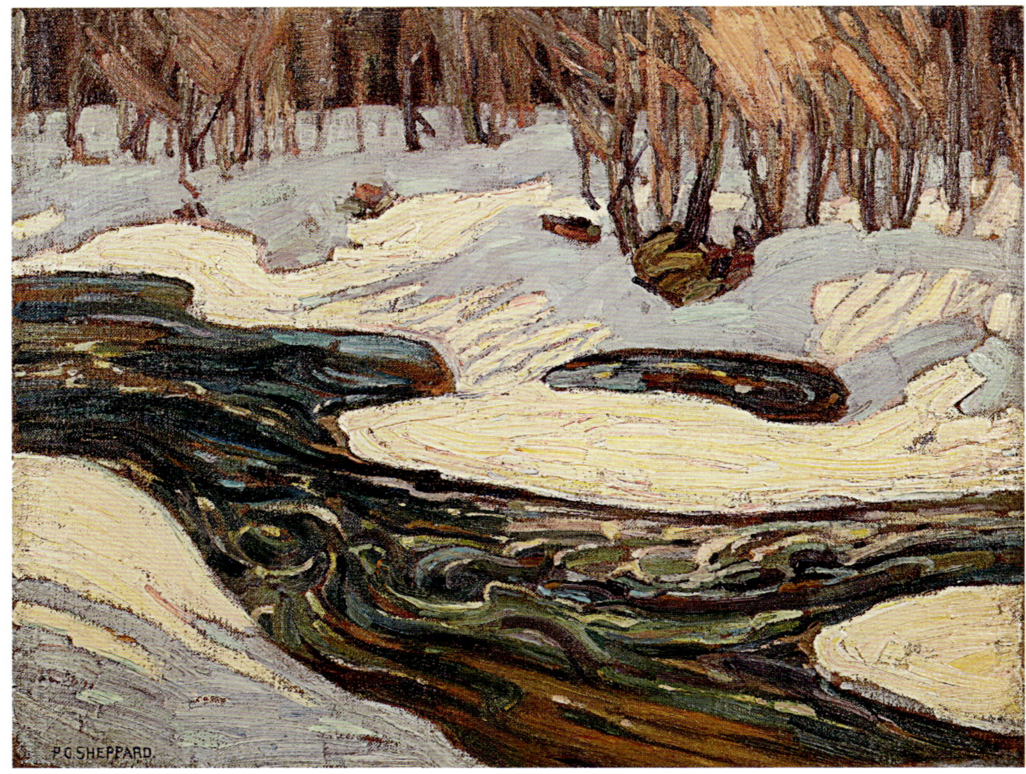

River Pattern.
1920. Oil on canvas,
71 x 91.4 cm.

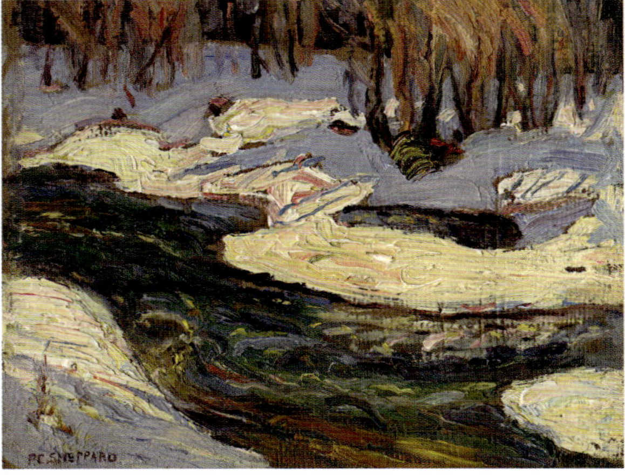

Study for River Pattern.
1920. Oil on panel,
21.6 x 26.7 cm.

of the life of the city. The maelstrom of crowds and activity, the contrast of a monolithic metropolitanism with the hubbub of life in the boroughs lying in the shadows of commercial towers, these themes attracted Sheppard as did the innovative modes of representation that were being devised in the loft studios of Bellows, Henri, Glackens and Lawson. Sheppard faced admiringly the example of eight or nine Americans and their acolytes who reached for an American reality by immersing themselves in the untidy, densely, diversely populated urban avenues, markets and harbours. In artistic terms, Sheppard identified with human subjects in gritty urban settings.

No matter where he actually lived, Sheppard continued to exhibit in the annual OSA exhibitions. His 1920 contribution was *The Engine Home* (page 122), a scene of two locomotives tucked into a shed (their "home") in a rail yard. But the title does absolutely no justice to the innovative interpretation that Sheppard brings to the subject. True to the direction in which his interest has been developing as a painter of dynamic energy and its sources, Sheppard preferred to concentrate more on expressing the abstract potentialities rather than the purely picturesque qualities of a scene — a distinguishing feature of his in the crowd of painters in which he moved and measured himself.

The Engine Home is a pictorialization of the ephemeral nature of steam and smoke. In Sheppard's hands and under his brushes, the plumes are treated as abstracted studies of vapours set down in multi-tinted hues of yellow, white-greys and greens that drift over the engines. In the way he glories in capturing the ever-changing and ephemeral forms of the smoke and steam, I am convinced that Sheppard gravitated to this perhaps difficult subject for the simple reason that it gave him the opportunity and licence to explore abstraction through the Impressionist mode. The referential anchor that loco-motive steam lent him made sure that his advances into non-representation were somehow anchored in a natural (or mechanical) phenomenon.

I marvel at a purely abstract passage along the painting's right edge, a sensi-tively seen arrangement of colours that are entirely non-imagistic, indicative of Sheppard's nod to non-representation as a crucible for personal expression. The concrete and the ephemeral: in the interplay of this paradox Sheppard found a way to create pictorial tension. For example, in contrast to the indefiniteness of the steam and the depiction of the city's buildings behind and above the rail yard, the engines are described more as impressions than definite things. Not much more than brushstrokes' traces, they signify a human (if mechani-cally human) presence that contrasts with machine-generated energy. In their relative diminutiveness they nevertheless suggest that power and energy are

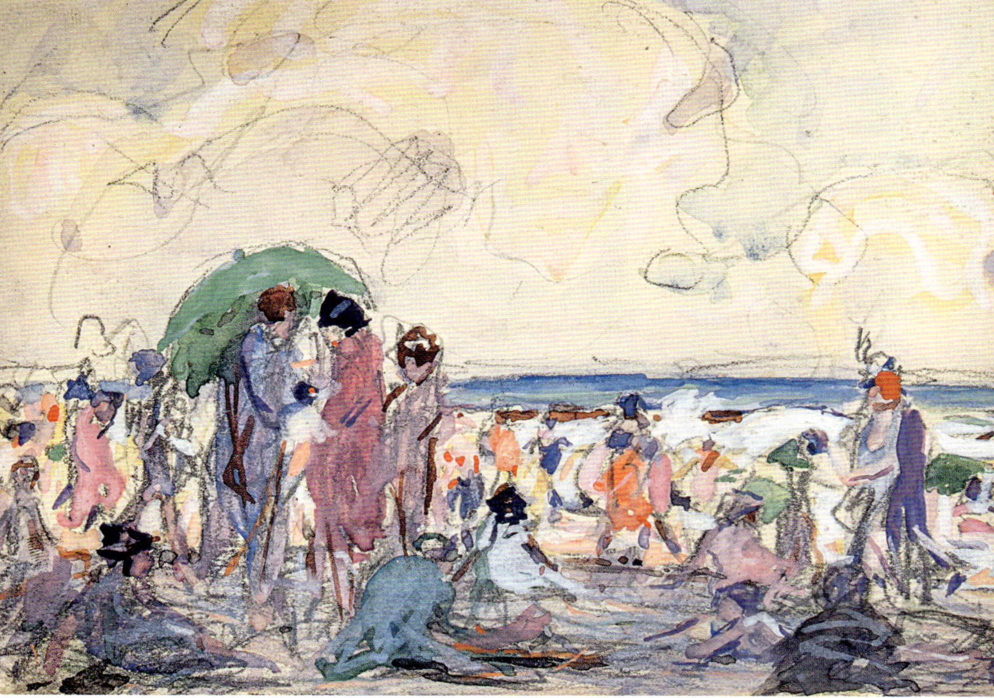

On the Beach, New York.
c. 1919–23. New York City Sketchbook.
Watercolour and graphite on paper,
9 x 12.7 cm.

both harnessed in the pursuit of growth and development. In its totality, Shep-pard's painting spans the poles of order and chaos, substance and formlessness, as they interact in an "engine home" on the edges of the metropolis.

I expect that the device of a referential anchor was also a comfortable touchstone for the contemporary viewing public. Sheppard, it seems, was a latent abstract painter who found in colour relationships in and of themselves, and in the underlying balances and geometries of a composition, exciting and dynamic subjects that satisfied his inner expressive compulsions. Yet, he was not innovative enough to jettison representational subjects and dive into for-malist or colour-centred abstraction. That breakthrough had to wait for a later generation and its Painters Eleven, artists who in 1916 were mere babies, if they were even born yet.

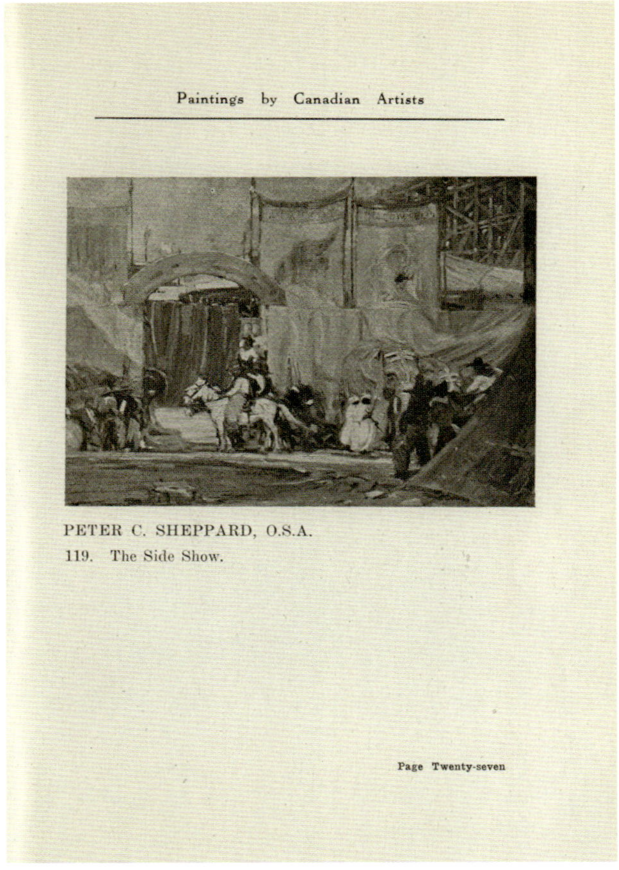

The Side Show, c. 1919. This painting (now lost) was reproduced in the OSA exhibition catalogue of works shown at the CNE in 1920.

Sheppard also painted a canvas that was exhibited at the 1920 CNE entitled *The Side Show.* The painting is not a part of the archive (and is perhaps lost), but fortunately it is reproduced in the exhibition catalogue.[57] Based on the black-and-white reproduction in the catalogue, it can be seen that Sheppard has revisited the theme of the circus in this canvas that shows the midway banners and some of its spectacles. There is an air of the exotic about this piece — horsemen placed in the middle ground with what might well be costumed performers, granting a patina of carnival orientalism to the sideshow alley. It is not surprising that a reviewer of the OSA exhibition echoed the sentiments of a year earlier that this "circus scene ... is full of the garish colour of the fair.[58]"

I suspect, too, that Sheppard likely continued to maintain ties with his alma mater, OCA. Its Prospectus for Session 1920–21 reproduces one of his 1912 oil paintings of the female nude (refer to Chapter 2) amidst the syllabus describing "Course for Teachers."[59] Sheppard, who might have been one of the instructors, plumped for having one of his paintings reproduced. He would have wanted to be clear about the kind of instruction that lay in front of a prospective art teacher who had to take the five-week-long OCA summer session consisting of, as the Prospectus notes, "work in Drawing, Modelling, Composition and Design; the practice of various mediums of expression. Lectures, demonstrations and [a] reading course in the History of Art."

From the evidence published in the OSA and CNE exhibition records, as well as in the *Toronto City Directory*, Sheppard occupied the 101½ King Street West studio in 1922 (perhaps he re-rented it), and lived at 39 St. Clair Avenue East, an address registered in the name of William Sheppard (a cousin?), a labourer in the roadway section of the Department of Works, just a few blocks north of Summerhill Avenue.

In 1924, Sheppard seems to have moved once again: there is no listing in the *Directory* indicating he continued to occupy the King Street studio, now registered in the names of Everett Stationery and Loose Leaf Co., Ltd., and to the architectural firm Burden & Gouinlock. The OSA catalogue, however, gives Sheppard's address that year as 39 St. Clair Avenue, even though he did not exhibit any paintings at their annual exhibitions in 1923 or in 1924. The

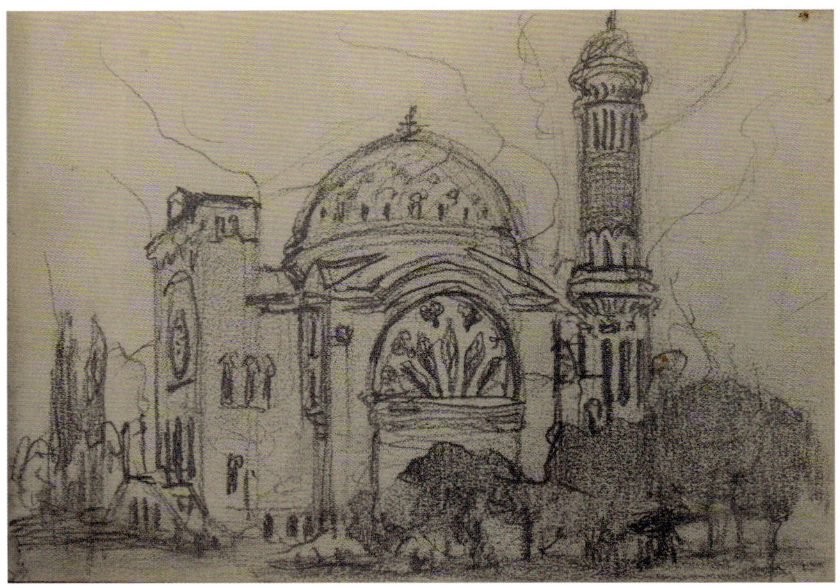

Church of St. Michael and St. Anthony, Mile End, Montreal.
1920. Garner Street Sketchbook.
Graphite on paper,
9 x 12.7 cm.

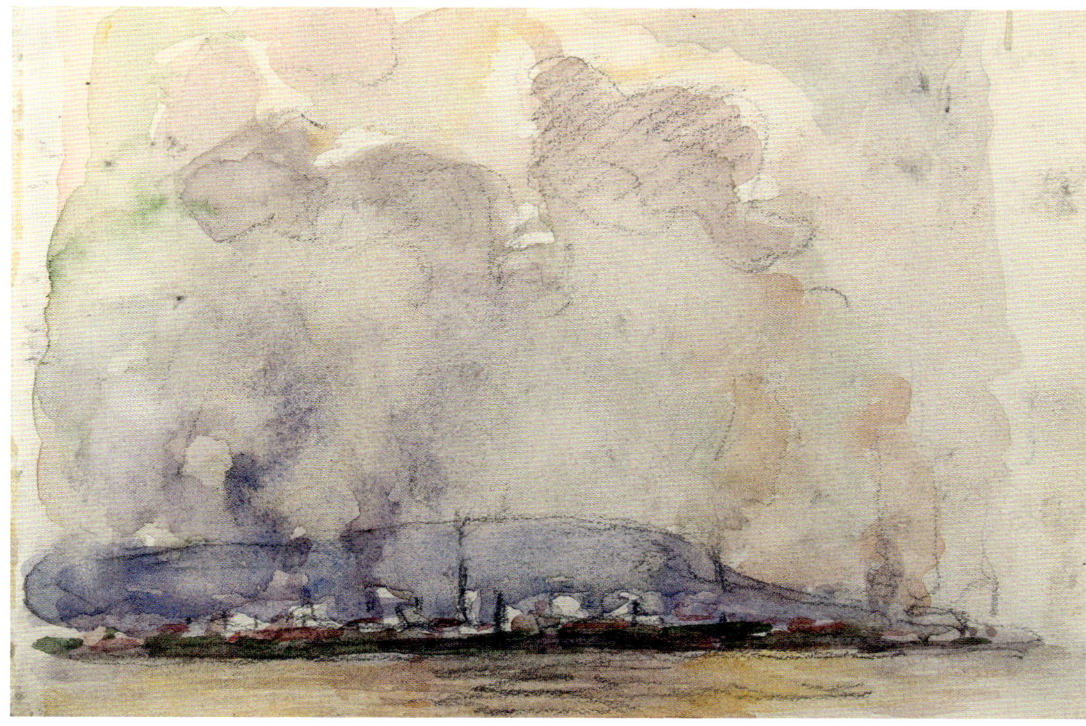

Montreal Port.
1920. Garner Street Sketchbook.
 Watercolour and graphite on paper,
9 x 12.7 cm.

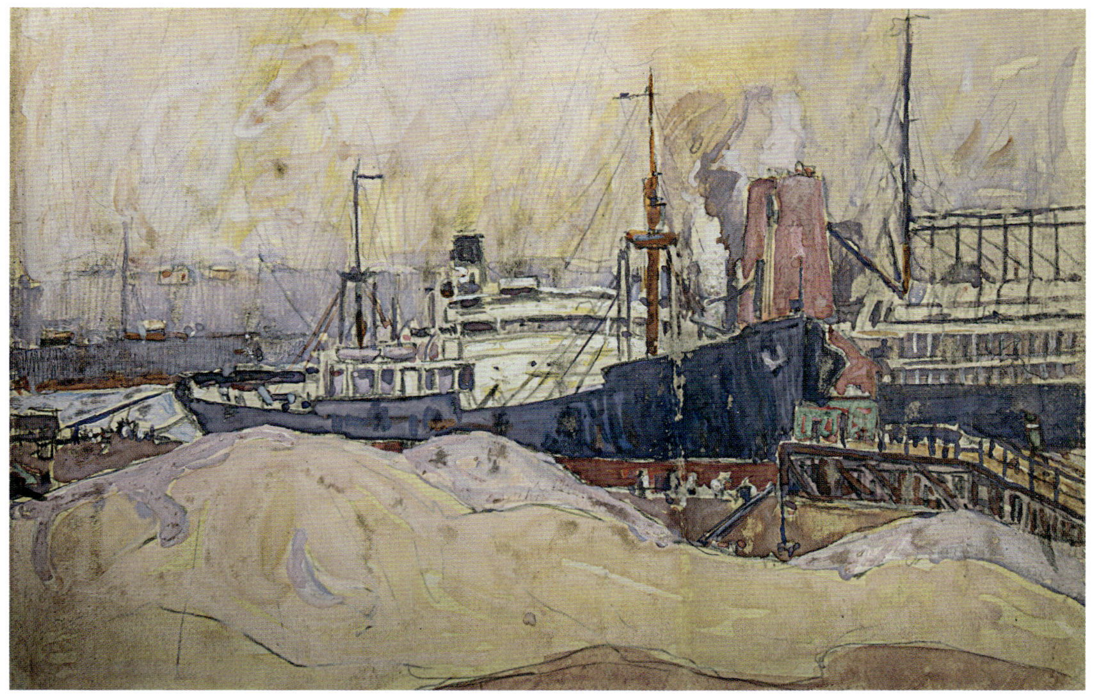

Montreal Port.
1920. Garner Street Sketchbook.
Watercolour and graphite on paper,
9 x 12.7 cm.

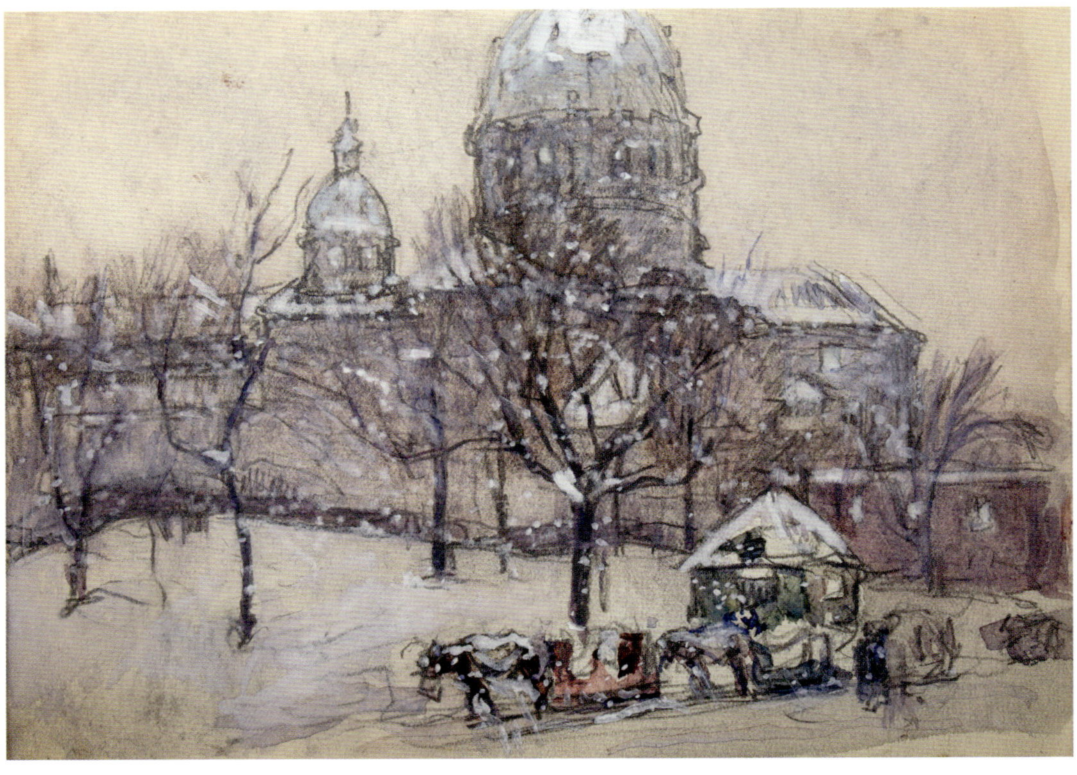

Montreal Cabstand Near the Oratory.
1920. Garner Street Sketchbook.
Watercolour and graphite on paper,
9 x 12.7 cm.

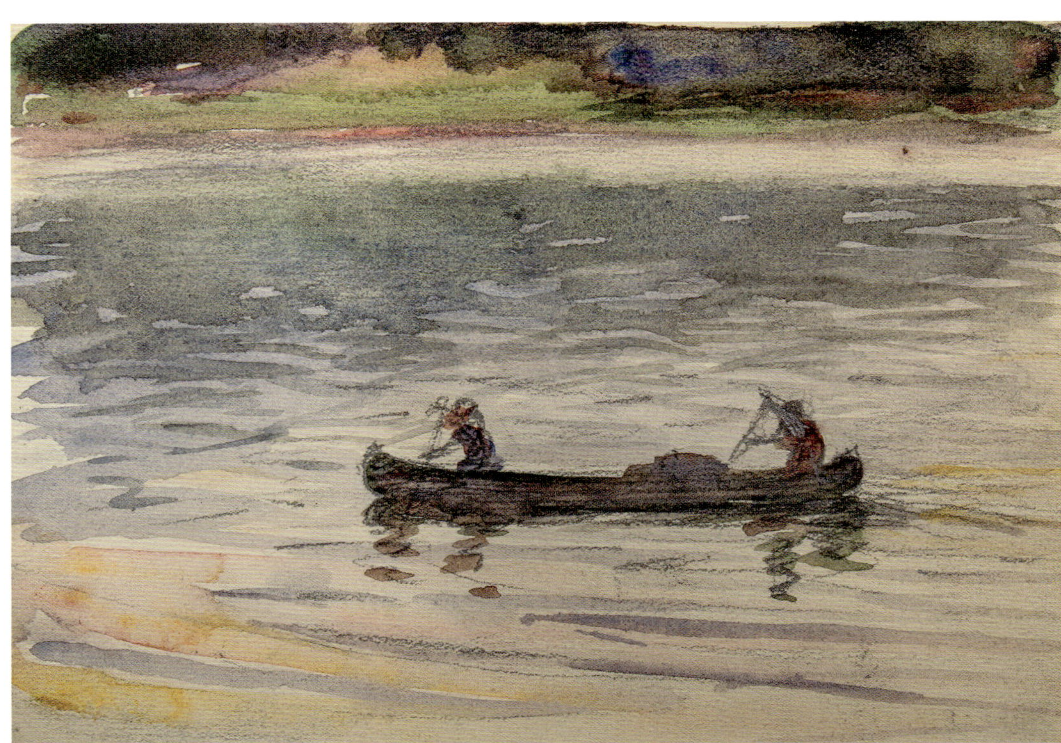

Canoeists.
1920. Garner Street Sketchbook.
Watercolour and graphite on paper,
9 x 12.7 cm.

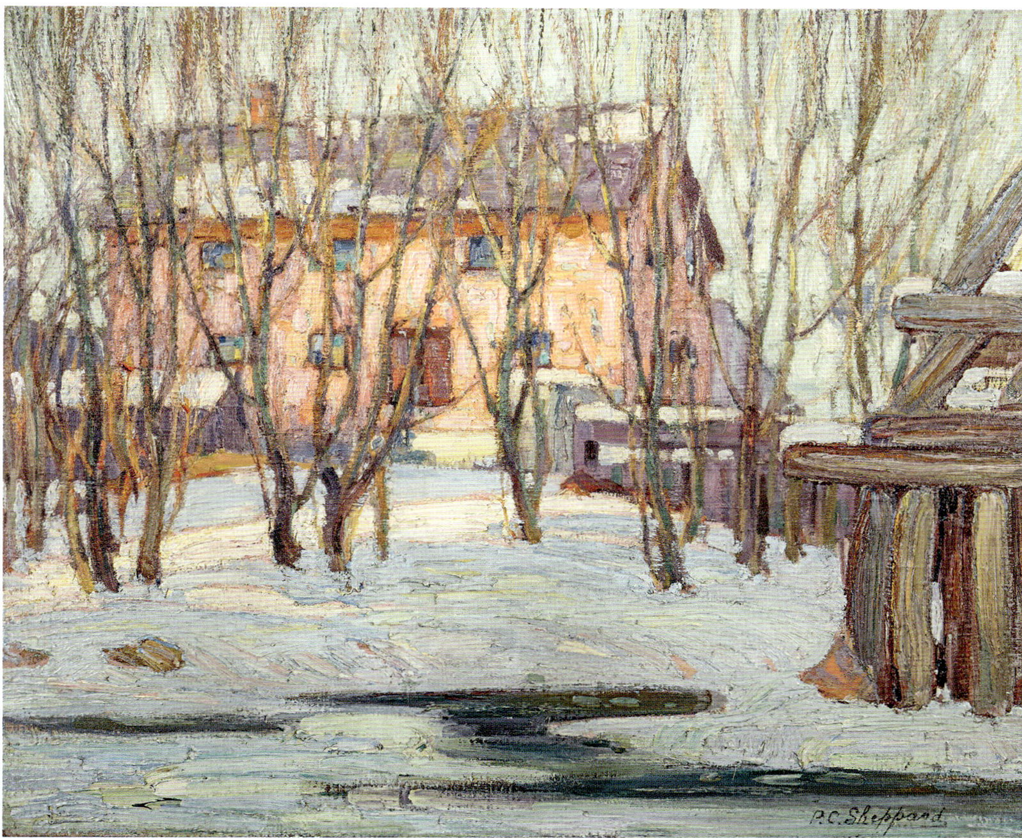

Wheat Elevator, Montreal.
1920–21. Oil on canvas,
76 x 91.4 cm

same is true in 1925, 1926, 1927 and 1928: Sheppard, it appears, is absent from Toronto in these years. In 1929 he is back in Toronto; the 1930 *Directory* lists his profession as "Artist" and notes him as a "Homeowner" at 70 Oakwood Avenue, in the city's west end. Given the gaps in the chronology of addresses, I search for clues to his comings and goings in the early 20s.

MONTREAL

One such clue to where Sheppard most likely spent time (and perhaps may even have lived for a few months) is found in the 1921 OSA exhibition: Montreal. This is not the first time Sheppard was in that city; the clue appears in one of the very few letters and postcards in the archive, indicating that on July 19, 1921, Sheppard was staying in "Room 14, 204 St. James Street, Montreal."[60] But the rest of this thin source is mute on how long he stayed or even what he did while he was in the city. On the inside cover of a sketchbook containing evocative, tonal watercolours of Montreal river scenes, studies of

ships, the Oratory and Lachine Rapids, Sheppard writes that he was staying at "505 Garner Street" (possibly Garnier) and that, should the sketchbook be lost, he would pay a reward if it were returned to that address.[61] Notwithstanding the fact that the catalogue lists his address as the King Street West studio (a fact corroborated by the *Toronto Directory* listing), Sheppard exhibited four paintings at that year's (1921) OSA exhibition, held from May 7–29, of which two are given titles indicating that they are Montreal or St. Lawrence River subjects. It is noteworthy to point out that during this same month-long time period at the Art Gallery of Toronto (where the OSA exhibition was being held), an exhibition of paintings by the Group of Seven was also being presented. Sheppard's contributions (and their sale prices) were listed in the catalogue as *The Mill* ($300); *Down the St. Lawrence* ($400); *Behind the Scenes* ($600); and *Wheat Elevator, Montreal* ($250).[62] The latter painting (see above), which is in the archive, is a moody winter landscape scene punctuated by the imposing presence of what appears to be a water-powered mill behind a sparse screen of bare-branched trees.

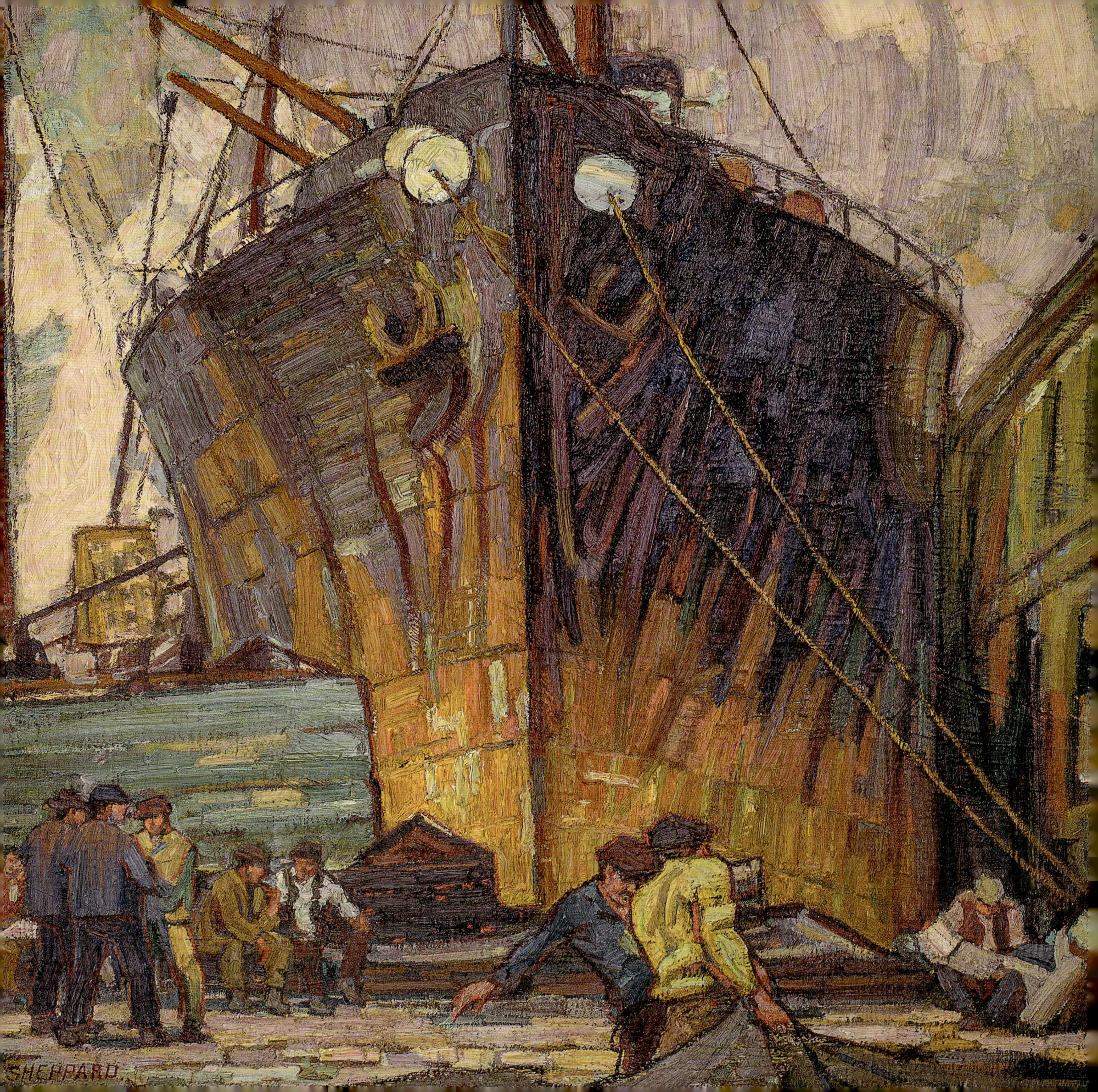

SHEPPARD

The OSA exhibition of 1922 included three Sheppard canvases of Montreal urban scenes and one, entitled *The Tramp,* of a New York subject. *The Tramp*, whose preliminary drawing is found in one of Sheppard's New York sketchbooks, is an object lesson in all the various influences that coalesced in Sheppard's career. It is a kind of summation piece, while signalling the direction that Sheppard promised to advance along. It is a gorgeous painting of a ship's hull, whose prow, seen nose on, is pointing straight out from the middle ground and into the viewer's space. The stevedores in the foreground are carefully delineated in a way that shows the important debt Sheppard owed to his sketchbook drawing practice. They could have been lifted in their entirety from the sketchbook pages. So what the record shows is that in 1920 and 1921, Sheppard stayed in Montreal (and may have made a trip to New York) or travelled there on occasion and found in that city subject matter for his work.

As I explore the exhibition history and the reviews of this period I come across a peculiar circumstance. The catalogue for the 1923 OSA exhibition does not list Sheppard as one of the exhibitors that year. Yet in a review of the exhibition, Sheppard received a very good notice by the *Toronto Mail and Empire* writer, who notes that he "is working doggedly to his goal as an interpreter of industrial life in big cities. Every year he makes a steady advance in his mastery of subject. His scenes grow in clarity and reality. His study of a snow storm on a crowded street shows him at his best."[63] This note foreshadows successes that awaited him just a few years hence. Could the reviewer be referencing an understated Montreal snow scene that I come across in a corner of the archive (see page 16)? With no inventory number and seemingly to have been forgotten in the accumulation of artworks, it is a wonderfully expressive impression of a snowfall on a street buttressed by a church's outside wall pierced by a series of Gothic-arched windows. Sheppard has used this out-of-the-way corner of the urban landscape to turn his hand to a composition in greys, blue-greys, green-greys and violets, setting off the energetic depiction of the snowsquall. The figures are rendered as not much more than daubs of pigment. Altogether the elements convey the energy of a squall in a well-composed, theatrical tableau.

The Tramp.
1921–22. Oil on canvas,
86 x 96.5 cm.

NEW YORK CITY, 1923–24

The record of the paintings also shows that, possibly following the example of his studio colleague Frances Geddes (who went to New York City to study at the Art Students League sometime in 1921 or 1922), Sheppard travelled to and stayed in New York, possibly through 1923 and perhaps into 1924. Based on his absence from the 1925 *Directory* (which reflects addresses in 1924), New York is a not surprising destination, given his affinity for the paintings of members of the Eight and of the Ashcan School. Following their example of directly interpreting the city by sketching from life, Sheppard filled many a sketchbook with vivid drawings and watercolours of what came before his eyes and fell under his pencil and brush. On the inside cover of a few of these palm-sized sketchbooks, there is still the faint pencilled-in trace of Sheppard's New York address: "127 West 75th New York."[64]

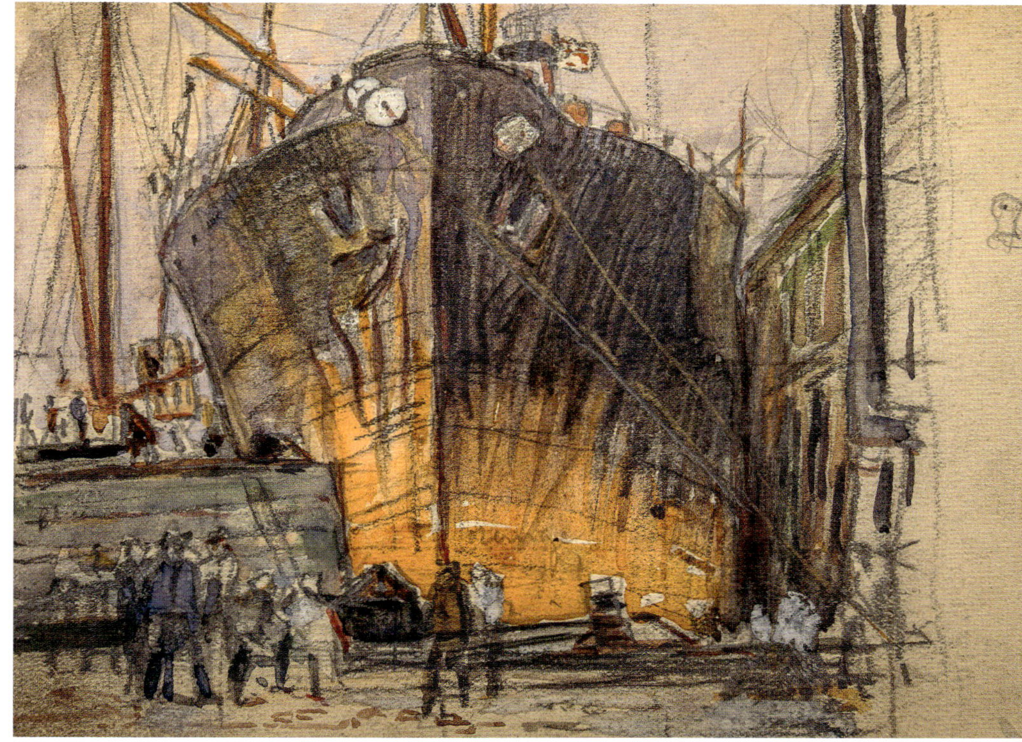

The Tramp (study sketch).
1920–21. Watercolour, graphite, charcoal on paper,
76 x 91.4 cm.

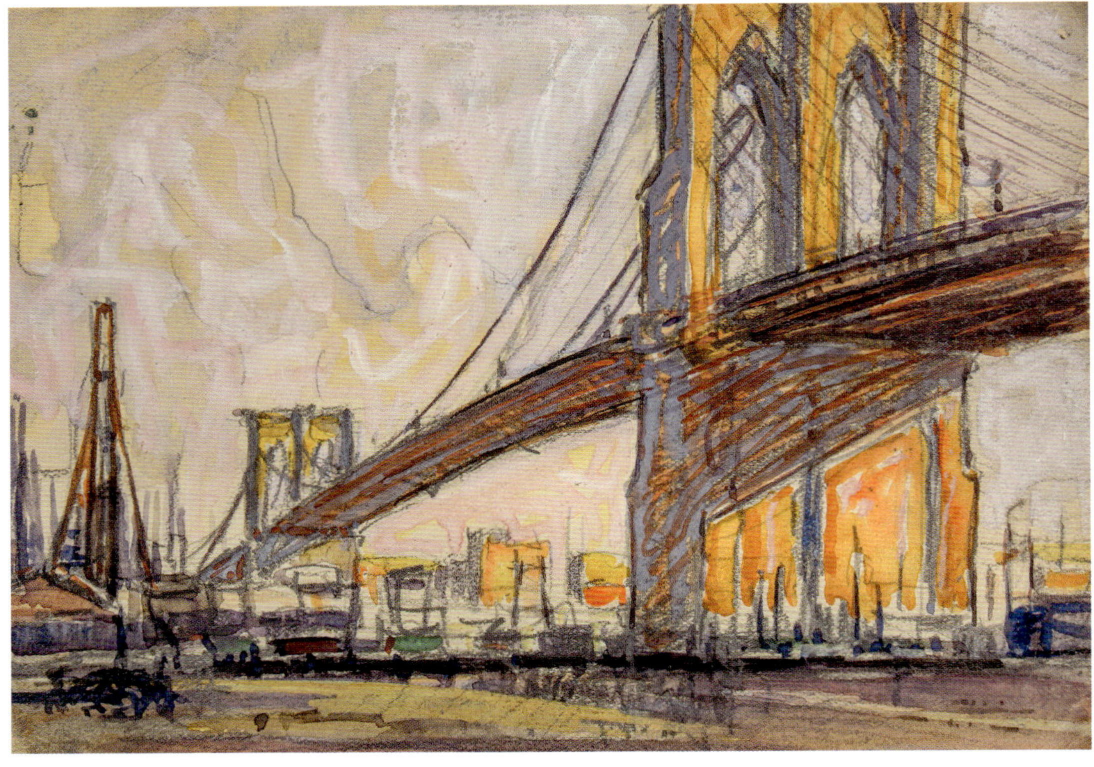

Brooklyn Bridge.
c. 1923. New York City Sketchbook.
Watercolour and graphite on paper,
9 x 12.7 cm.

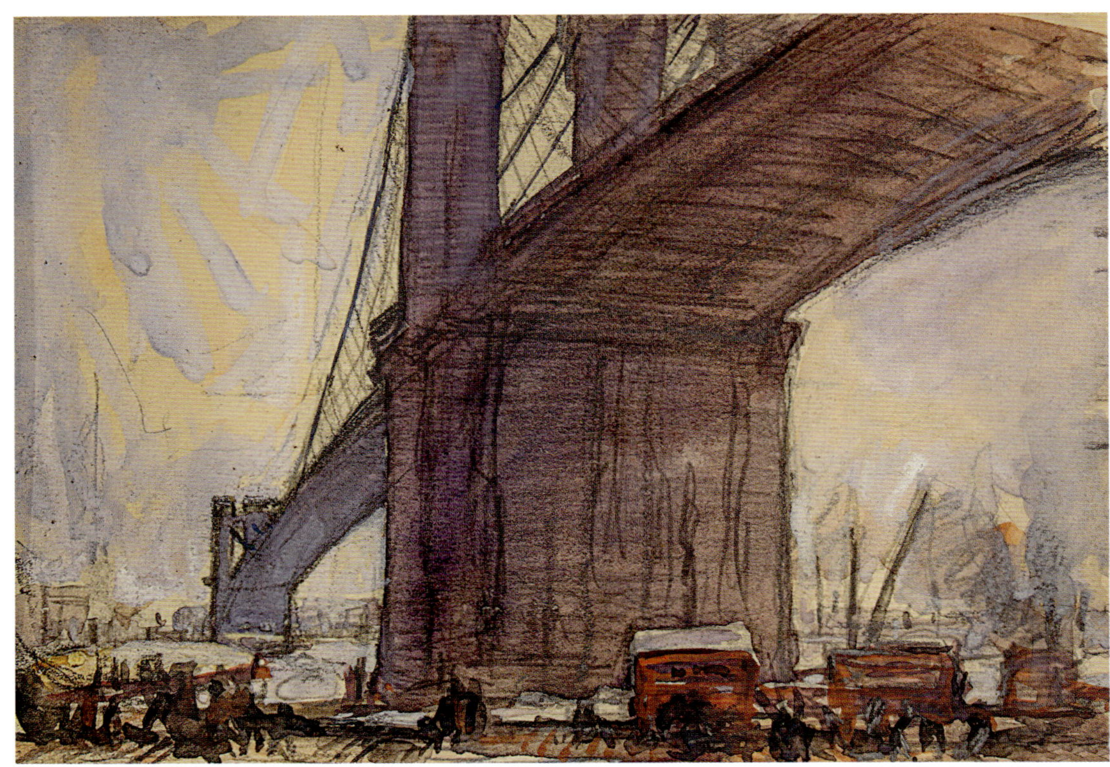

Brooklyn Bridge.
c. 1923. New York City Sketchbook.
Watercolour and graphite on paper,
9 x 12.7 cm.

The surviving New York sketchbooks that I leaf through on a pleasant summer evening at the archive contain page after page of scenes of boats, ocean-going vessels, and tugboats moored at docks. One page opens to reveal a depiction of the Brooklyn Bridge. Another gives way to the Manhattan skyline. Landscapes of the river, the countryside up the Hudson, even portrait studies and rapid studies of horses and carts reveal Sheppard to have not only the unusual capacity to capture the specifics of the scenes, but also an uncanny knack for conveying the energy of the city and figures animating his views. Almost all the scenes are set down in a controlled, careful manner, using opaque gouaches and transparent watercolours. Interspersed with these vivid studies are finely rendered pencil drawings of men working.

The impression I form from "reading" the sketchbooks is that by the mid-1920s Sheppard had developed a multi-faceted artistic practice built on the foundation of draftsmanship. He was able to translate visual information into pencil drawings and plein-air sketches. Beyond the expert technical capacity to which his drawings are testaments, Sheppard captured an essential liveliness, apparently easily. Gesture and the rhythms of line and colour simulate as if by magic the cacophony and harmonies of his subjects. Much like a jazz musician, Sheppard built his compositions on an onomatopoeic motif; his sketchbooks show him as an artist who could orchestrate colour and line to such a complex degree that the baseline of his practice was the ability to create painted and drawn analogues to the energy and life that was taking place around him at the very moment he was drawing the city's racket and melodies.

As I close the sketchbooks my impressions of the man are that he began to find his artistic voice in Montreal and in the New York City of the early 1920s, when his innate gift as a sketch-maker gave him confidence to explore a modern way to paint in a manner that emulated that of his New York contemporaries. His sketches gave him much — from visual information, a means of ideation, to an agile creative outlet whose hallmarks were directness and immediacy. They freed him from the studio, while also providing him with research notation that could later be worked up in the studio into large-format oil compositions on board and canvas.

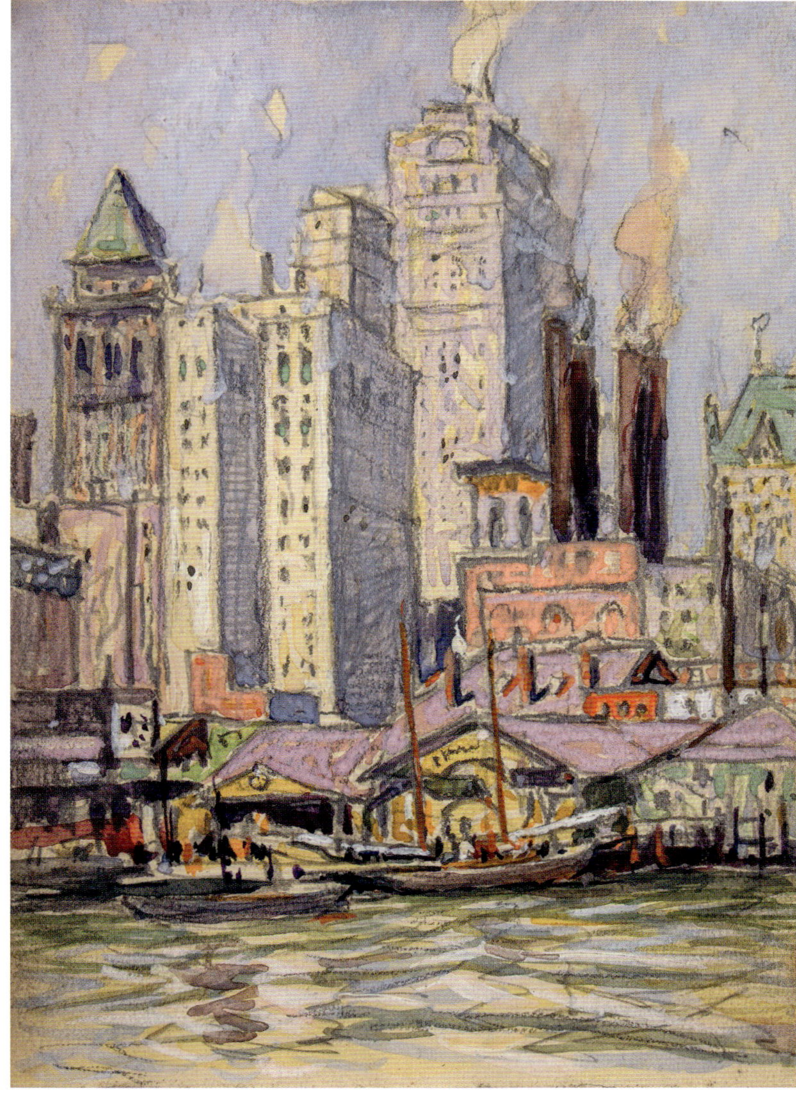

Harbour Sketch.
1919–23. New York City Sketchbook.
Watercolour and graphite on paper,
12.7 x 9 cm.

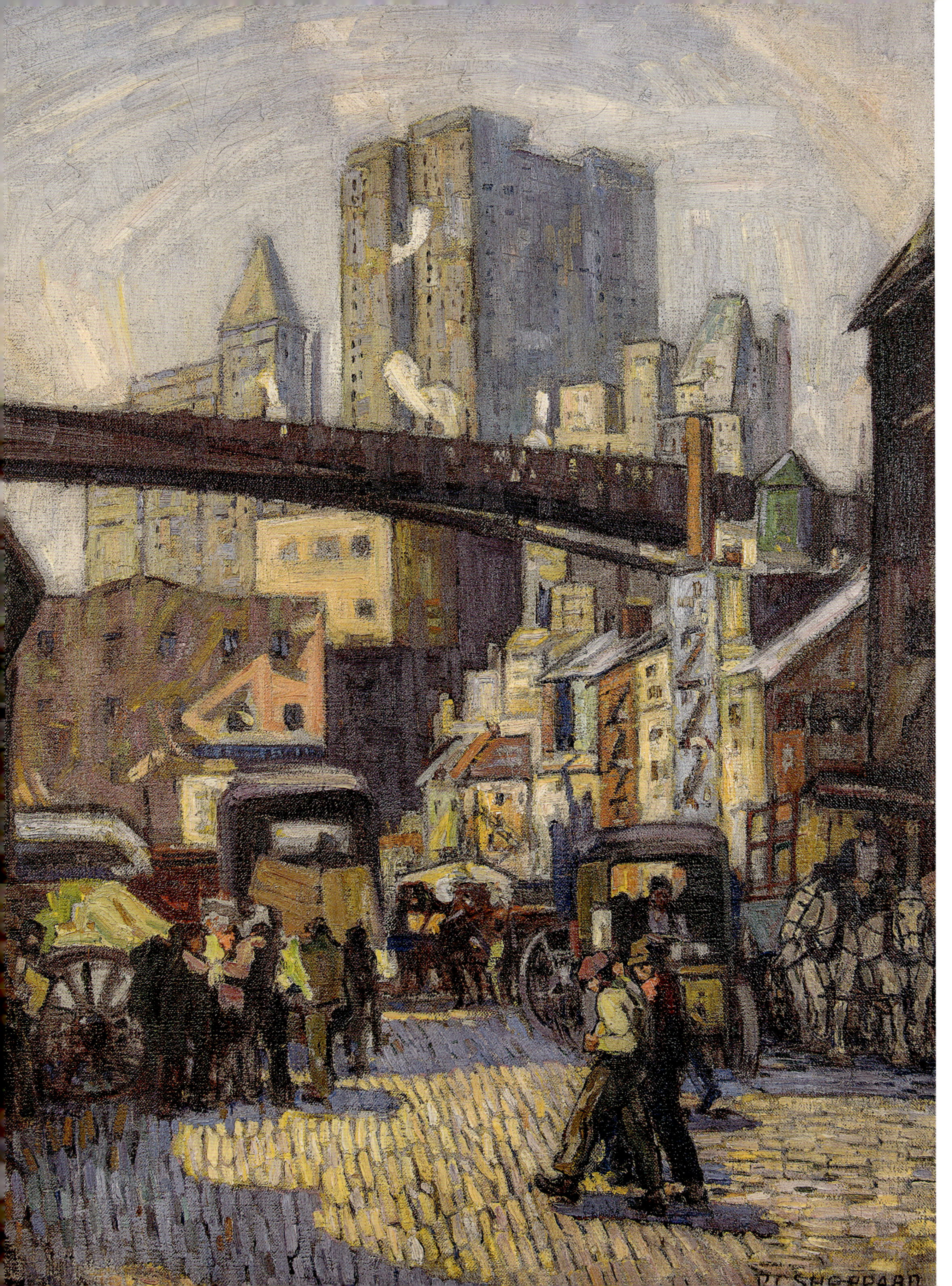

Lower New York.
1922. Oil on canvas,
122 x 89 cm.

INFLUENCE OF JOHN SLOAN

In a manner that is entirely innovative for Sheppard, in many of his early and mid-1920s paintings he has set himself the task of presenting visual essays on striking contrasts of hue that he has hung on a pictorial armature of decidedly non-picturesque subject matter and compositions. He makes vibrant use of a dynamic palette of deep blues and violets, contrasted with yellows and oranges. Large swatches of paint have been laid on with a broad brush. His backgrounds and skies are delicious arrangements of whites and greys that have been given definition by the addition of mauve, blue-green and brown tones. While the compositions are stable and balanced visually, paint is laid on to emphasize expression; you might even consider the application slapdash relative to his other paintings. As for his New York subjects, it is not difficult to imagine that Sheppard had his eye on the work of Glackens and Bellows. Was Sheppard trying his hand at their painterly licks? Likely so, but whether he knew it or not, he might well have been under the spell of ideas promoted by Sloan, a founding member of the Ashcan School and an influential teacher at the Art Students League.

A maverick in his day, Sloan's reputation is partially based on his subject matter drawn from contemporary urban life. He is equally respected for the value he placed on the formal aspects of painting: brushwork, colour, line and composition. Beyond subject and formalism, Sloan also pushed his students and viewers of contemporary art to look beyond the formal elements of painting and drawing to represented ideas. "Art is an ideograph," wrote Sloan.[65] "So long as you are not making ideas you are not making art," he declared in studios, where he urged students to look beyond pure technical expertise to create art that springs from an interest in life. Sloan's emphasis as a teacher and as a painter was to express the "art life" of a subject, which he believed came through the use of symbolic images. Such images, when expressed in an easily readable and understandable form — and largely through figuration — elevated the creations to the level of works of art. Although Sloan held to the notion that the representation of form — what he termed "realization" — was a fundamental principle in visual art, he also sought to transcend the limits of form, mass, bulk and weight. Yet he never championed pure abstraction either. The goal of all great art, according to Sloan and his acolytes, was to express the life of form in all its fullness, and to give the senses and reason intelligible images upon which to ponder the immutable essence at the core of the image.

Sloan also taught that drawing is the cornerstone of art. Drawing was the coordination of line, tone and colour into "formations that express the artist's thought," a principle that creates an equivalency between draftsmanship and composition, two elements of graphic art that could not exist separately. Together the elements create a sense of order on the two-dimensional plane that, for Sloan, is a key requirement of image making. "To formulate his visual images," Sloan averred, "[the artist] must have order in his thinking and order in his expression. A sense of the structure of things, of their geometrical composition, the ability to see order in nature, and then the technical ability to compose these plastic ideas is essential."

Sheppard's ideas on art, drawing and painting as he expressed them entirely in pictorial terms, whether deliberately or by chance, exactly accord with Sloan's. It is not a leap to imagine that Sloan provided an aesthetic framework for Sheppard that guided his development and self-education particularly while he was in New York in 1922. On the basis of the visual evidence that is in the archive, I imagine that for Sheppard, Sloan's "art life" theory and the pronouncement that an artist must articulate visually a personal, symbolic pictorial language had the ring of truth. While there is no written testament of artistic faith in the archive either, the circumstantial evidence points to a debt to Sloan's ideas that Sheppard may have taken as permission to deviate from the current Canadian orthodoxy of finding meaningful ideographs in unpopulated northern lakes and forests.

What the evidence shows is that, circumstances aside, Sheppard's New York paintings are among the most ambitious and advanced that he had made to that point in his career. *Lower New York* (pictured left), for example, is a carefully controlled and rendered urban scene under the spans of an elevated road or tramway. In this painting we find some of the devices that he would return to for the next several years. The composition divides the format horizontally into two ranks: above the divide is an anonymous cityscape of towering commercial buildings and skyscrapers, while below is the urban hurly-burly of boisterous activity, horse-and-carriage traffic and pedestrians. In the foreground a group of people, well drawn, march toward the action while also serving as a convenient means of drawing the viewer into the scene. The deeper one moves into the pictorial space, the less distinct becomes the drawing, which gives way to passages of colours laid down as blocks and facets in an Impressionist manner. The roadway is described using strokes of colour that further direct the eye into the space and eventually

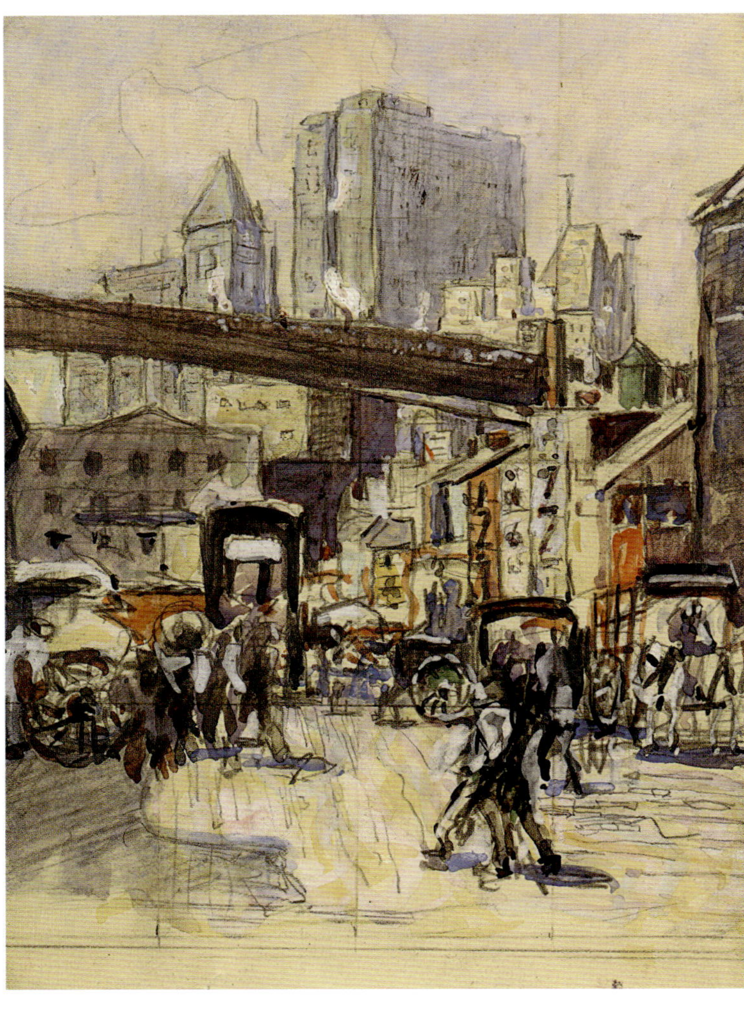

Lower New York (study).
1922. Watercolour,
19 x 12.7 cm.

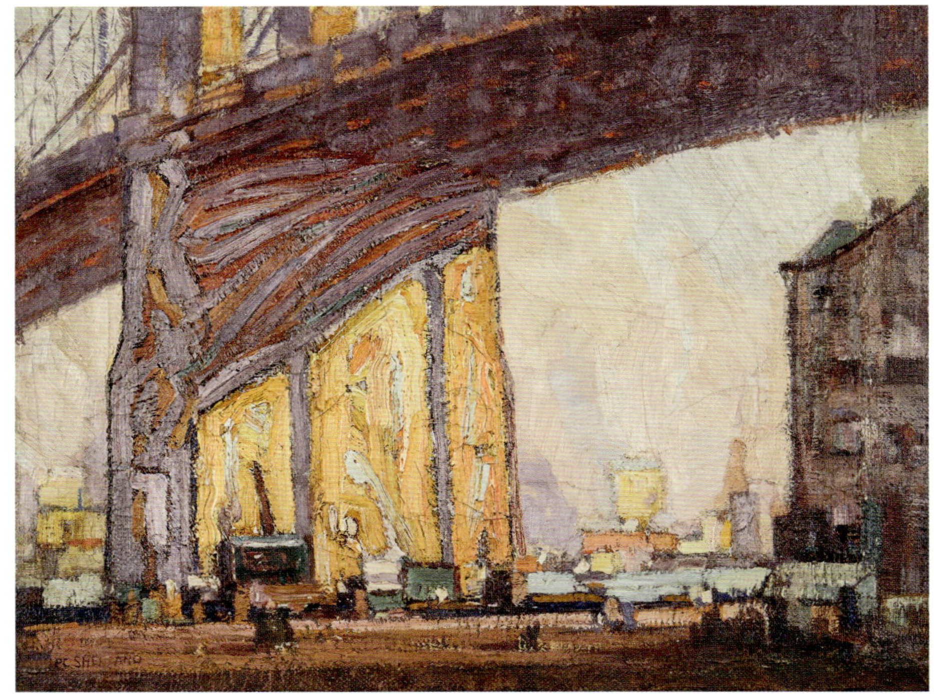

The Brooklyn Bridge.
1922. Oil on canvas,
35.6 x 47 cm.

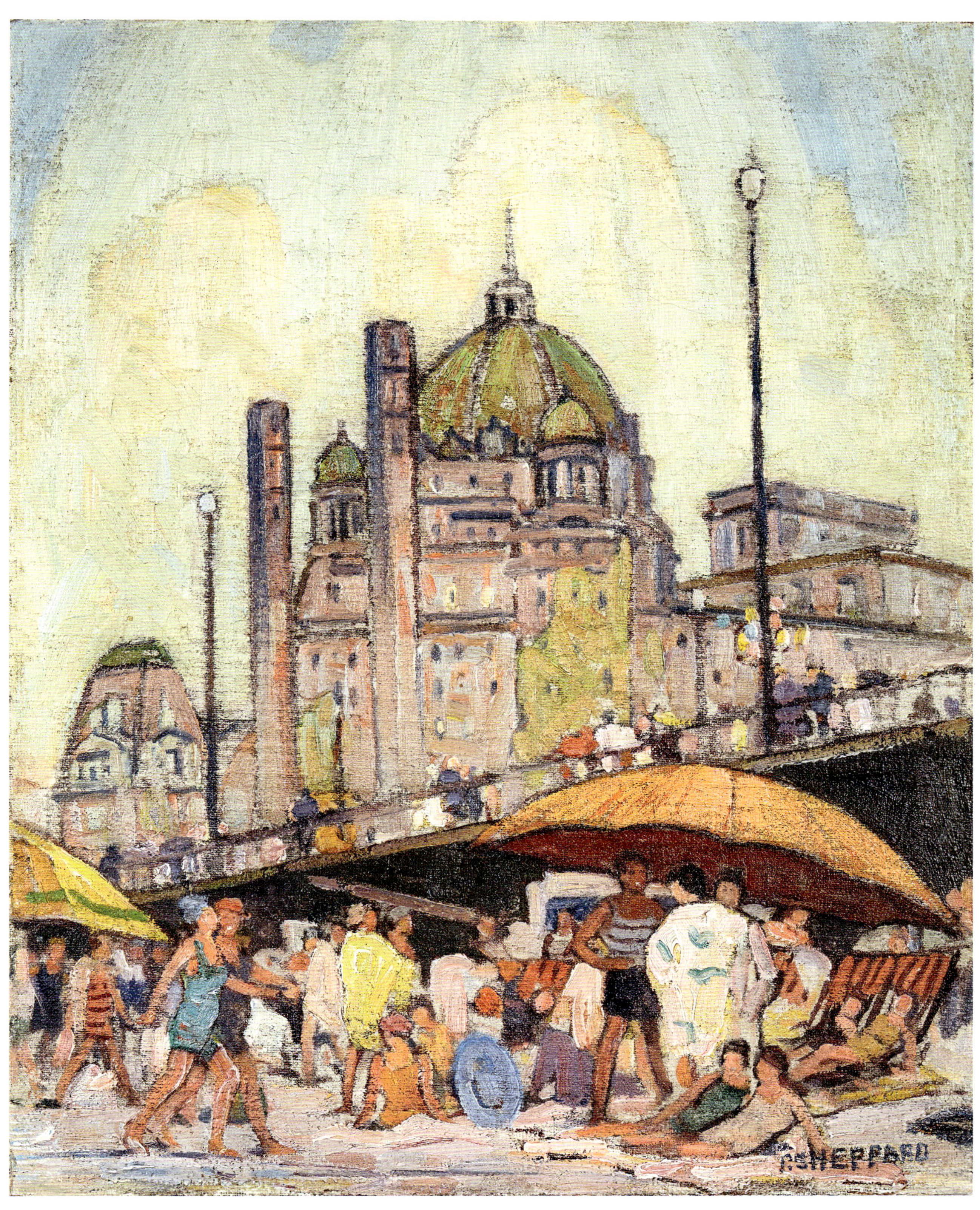

The Boardwalk, Atlantic City.
1922. Oil on canvas,
53.3 x 43 cm.

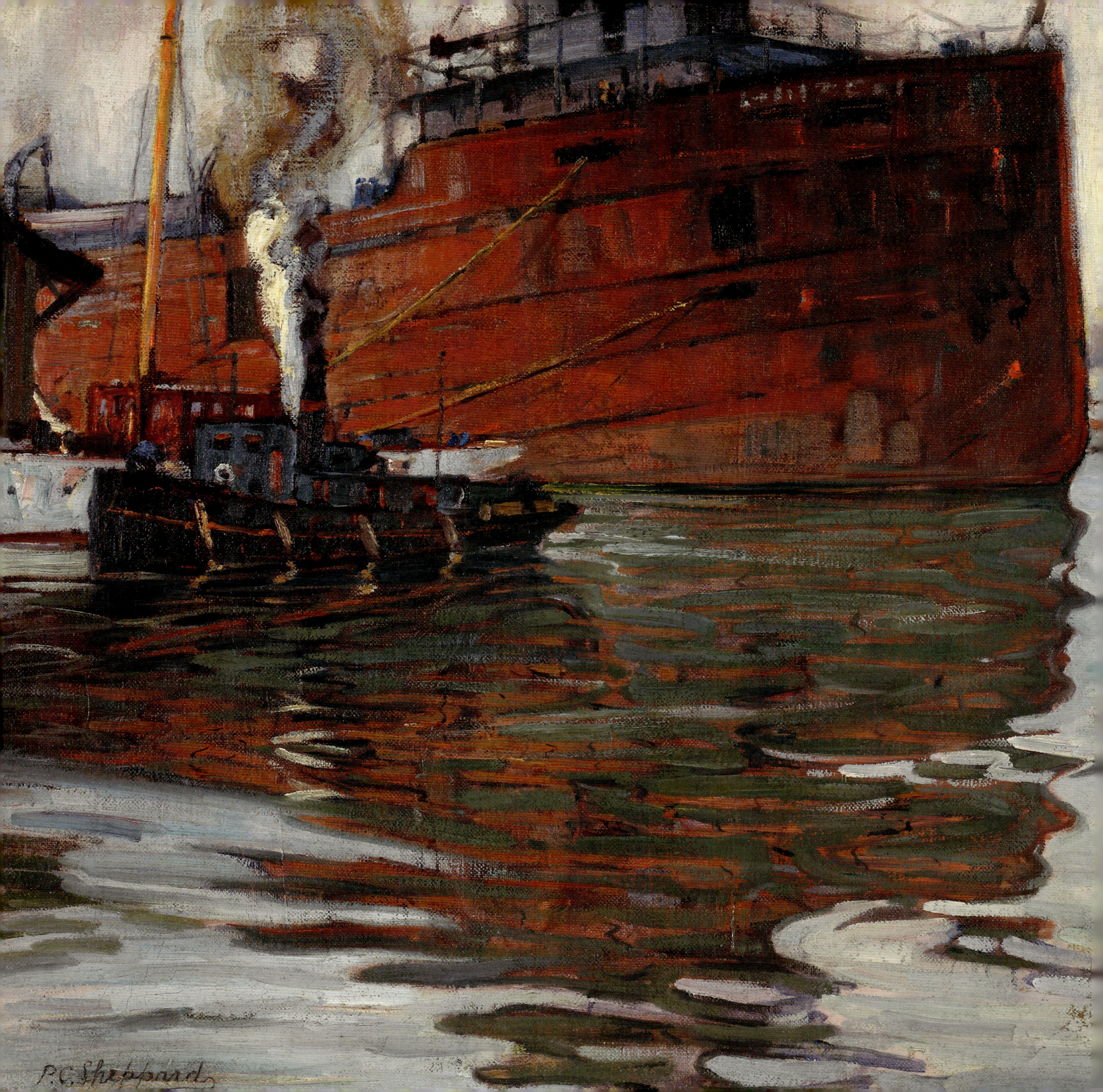
P.C. Sheppard

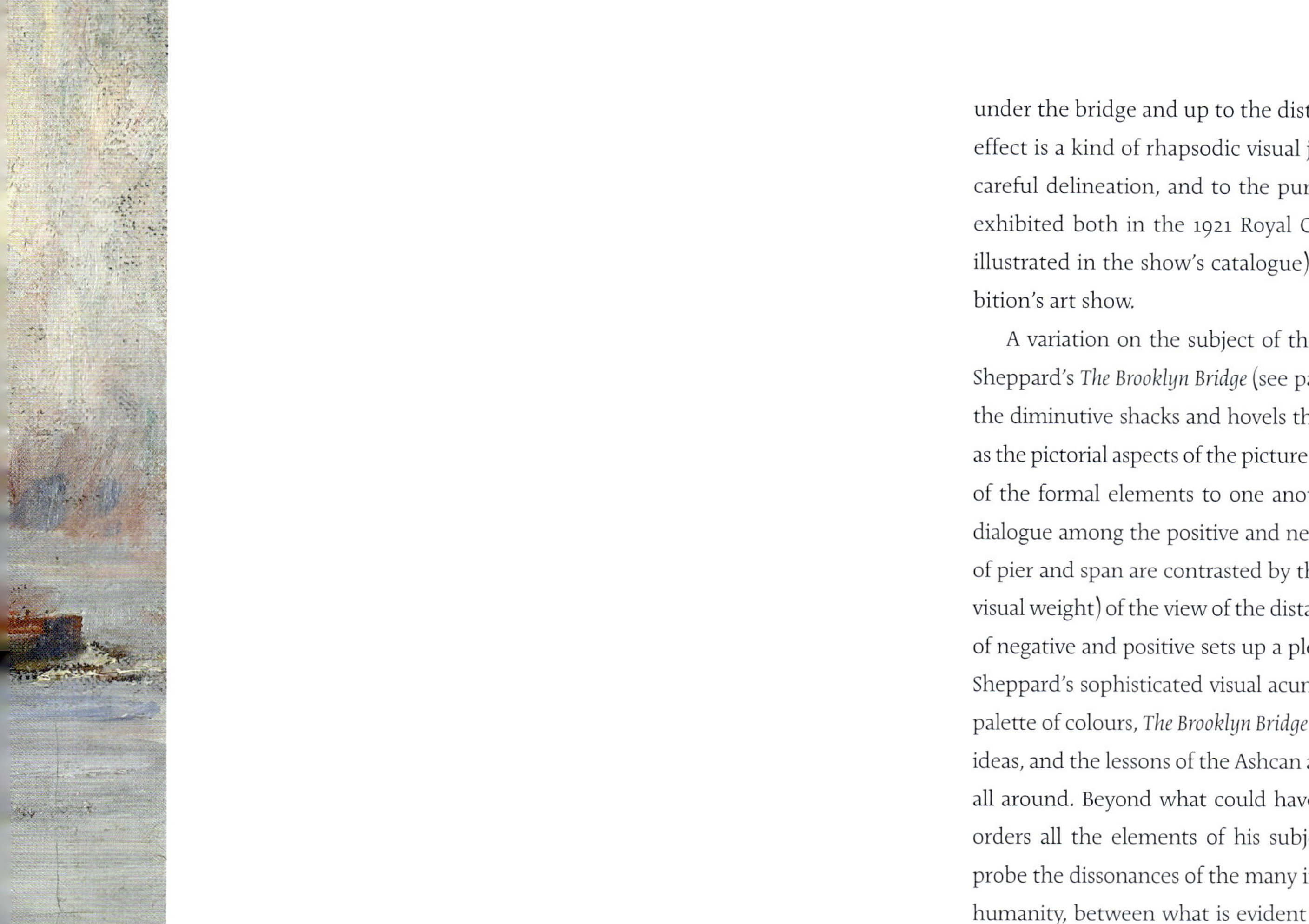

Lake Traffic.
c. 1920. Oil on canvas,
83.9 x 91.5 cm.

under the bridge and up to the distant Gotham spires and crenellations. The effect is a kind of rhapsodic visual jazz owing to the rhythmical contrast and careful delineation, and to the purely colouristic effects. *Lower New York* was exhibited both in the 1921 Royal Canadian Academy's *Special Exhibition* (and illustrated in the show's catalogue), and in the 1922 Canadian National Exhibition's art show.

A variation on the subject of the life of the city under a bridge is seen in Sheppard's *The Brooklyn Bridge* (see page 136), in which the bridge's span dwarfs the diminutive shacks and hovels that cluster in the span's shadow. As elegant as the pictorial aspects of the picture are, the painting explores the relationships of the formal elements to one another. Sheppard has crafted a sophisticated dialogue among the positive and negative elements of his subject. The solidity of pier and span are contrasted by the piercing negative space (of almost equal visual weight) of the view of the distant city across the river. Indeed, the balance of negative and positive sets up a pleasing asymmetrical pattern that speaks to Sheppard's sophisticated visual acumen. Well drawn, painted in a non-specific palette of colours, *The Brooklyn Bridge* is a striking, practical application of Sloan's ideas, and the lessons of the Ashcan artists of finding meaningful subjects in life all around. Beyond what could have been simple prosaic narrative, Sheppard orders all the elements of his subject into a symbolic personal grammar to probe the dissonances of the many inherent contrasts between anonymity and humanity, between what is evident and what is sensed, and between uncompromising ugliness transformed through the magic of colour, line, light and interval and a satisfying and beautifully lyrical visual poem.

Sheppard makes good use of the similar two-ranked composition in his *Boardwalk, Atlantic City* (page 137), a painting that recalls the ambitions of *Arrival of the Circus* with its heavily populated foreground overshadowed by an elevated avenue separating the maelstrom from the built structures looming over everything. Sheppard's emphasis in both *Brooklyn Bridge* and *Boardwalk, Atlantic City,* is the portrayal of city life. The figure groupings are carefully composed and delineated, all with an eye to mitigating the dehumanizing force represented in the background buildings. *The Waterfront, New York City* (page 20), a painting exhibited at the CNE in 1924, similarly explores the dichotomy between human-scaled objects and the almighty dehumanization of the modern city. In its composition, Sheppard has established an array of contrasts, not the least of which is the difference between the tugboat nudging the house barge to shore, and the impersonality of the city looming in the background.

As avatars for the attentive viewers to occupy and animate imaginatively, the foreground vessels are the very epitome of personal sanctuary in an otherwise heartlessly cold city that dwarfs the human scale. A variation on this same theme is transcribed in *Lake Traffic* (see page 138), in which the scale of a tugboat is contrasted with the overwhelming presence of the lake freighter's hull. Although a favourite subject of Sheppard's — depictions of boats of all shapes and sizes — in light of the contexts and apparent influences that he is absorbing, he is no doubt intending the familiar to take on a nuanced and different meaning. Although set down realistically, and interpreted in light of modern abstract principles, Sheppard, I am convinced, is anthropomorphizing his boats, intending them to be vessels of the imagination as much as they may simply be illustrations of a common sight that drew him in again and again.

I wonder if Sheppard is conveying a thinly disguised political message in his New York paintings, much in the same way that his American artist-cousins were intending their paintings to be read? For the Eight and for the Ashcan artists (and for Sloan himself) the choice of urban, commonplace subjects was filtered through an egalitarian lens, one that reflected a socialist point of view. It is not difficult to project socialist principles onto Sheppard's art. Although once again the archive has no political tracts penned by the artist, the circumstantial evidence of the paintings provides more than a hint of an affinity for honest humanism without inflecting their reading with stereotypes of class struggle. Sheppard, it appears, took another tack at pointing to class division in his New York paintings. His symbolic language involved the coded grammar and structure of the bifurcated composition, the insistence that ugliness be the foundation for splendid, beautiful applications of pigment that were meant to be appreciated simply on their own terms. Abstract formalism, laid down in a mode of realism to depict subjects that had a covert socialist message: this was the syntax of Sheppard's "ideographs" as they emerged in his New York paintings.

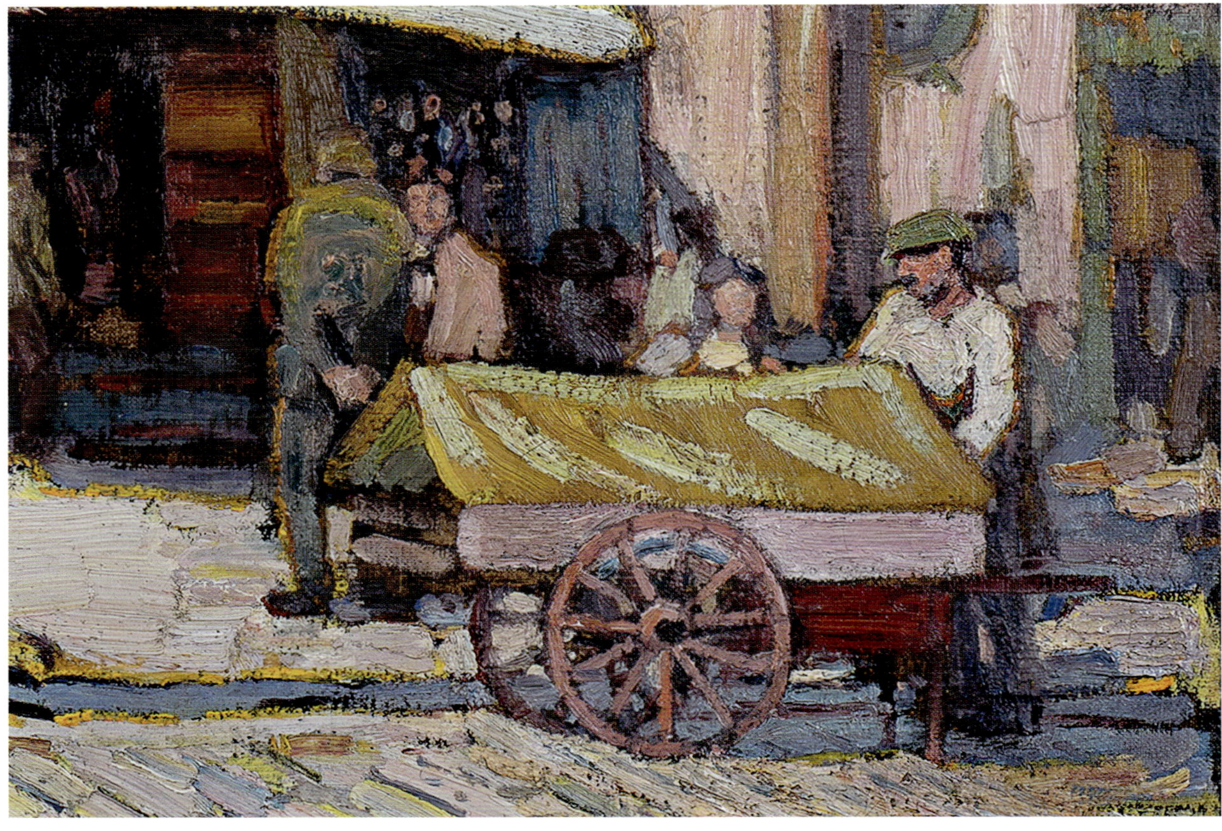

Old Store, Craig Street (detail).

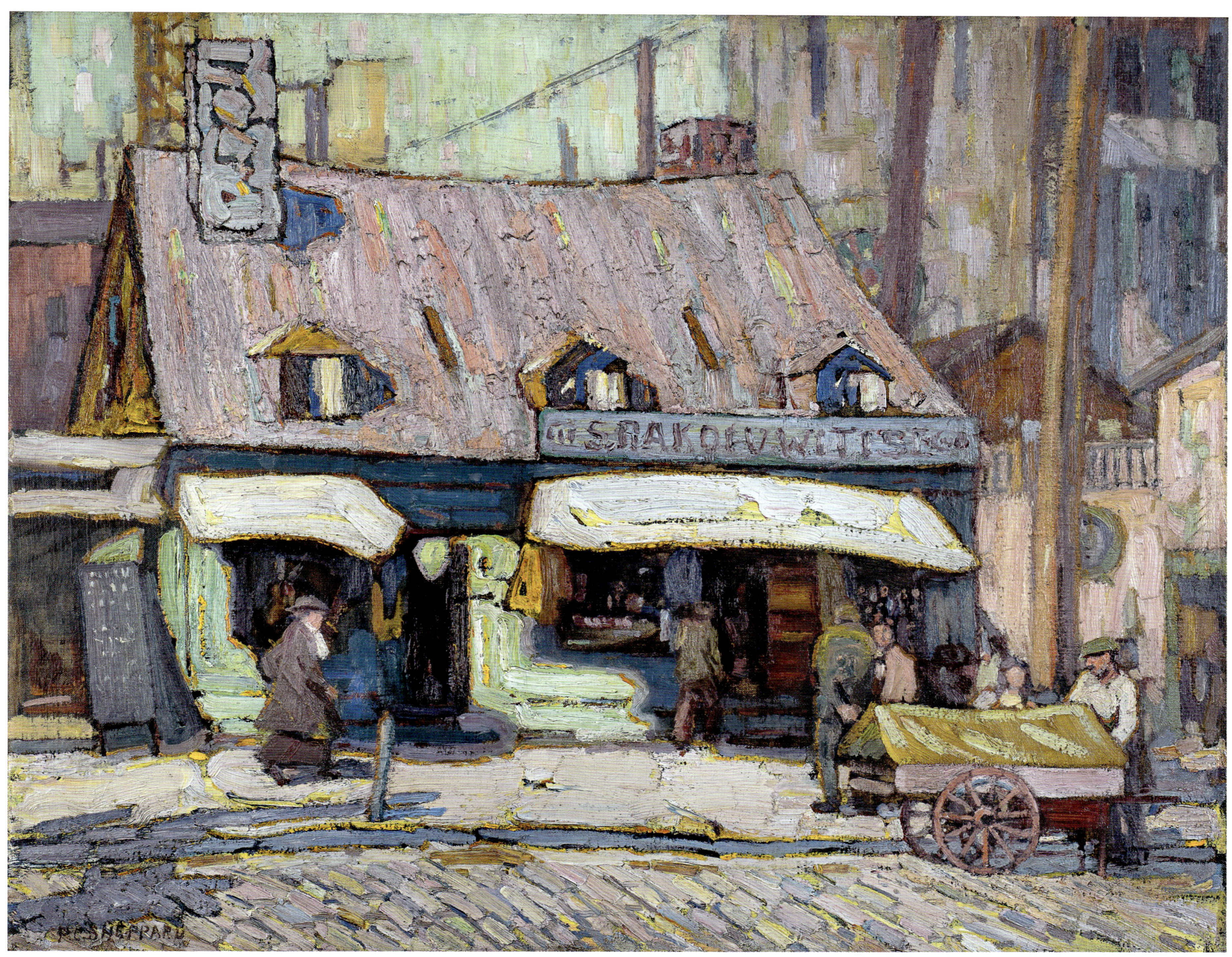

Old Store, Craig Street.
c. 1925. Oil on canvas,
61 x 80 cm.

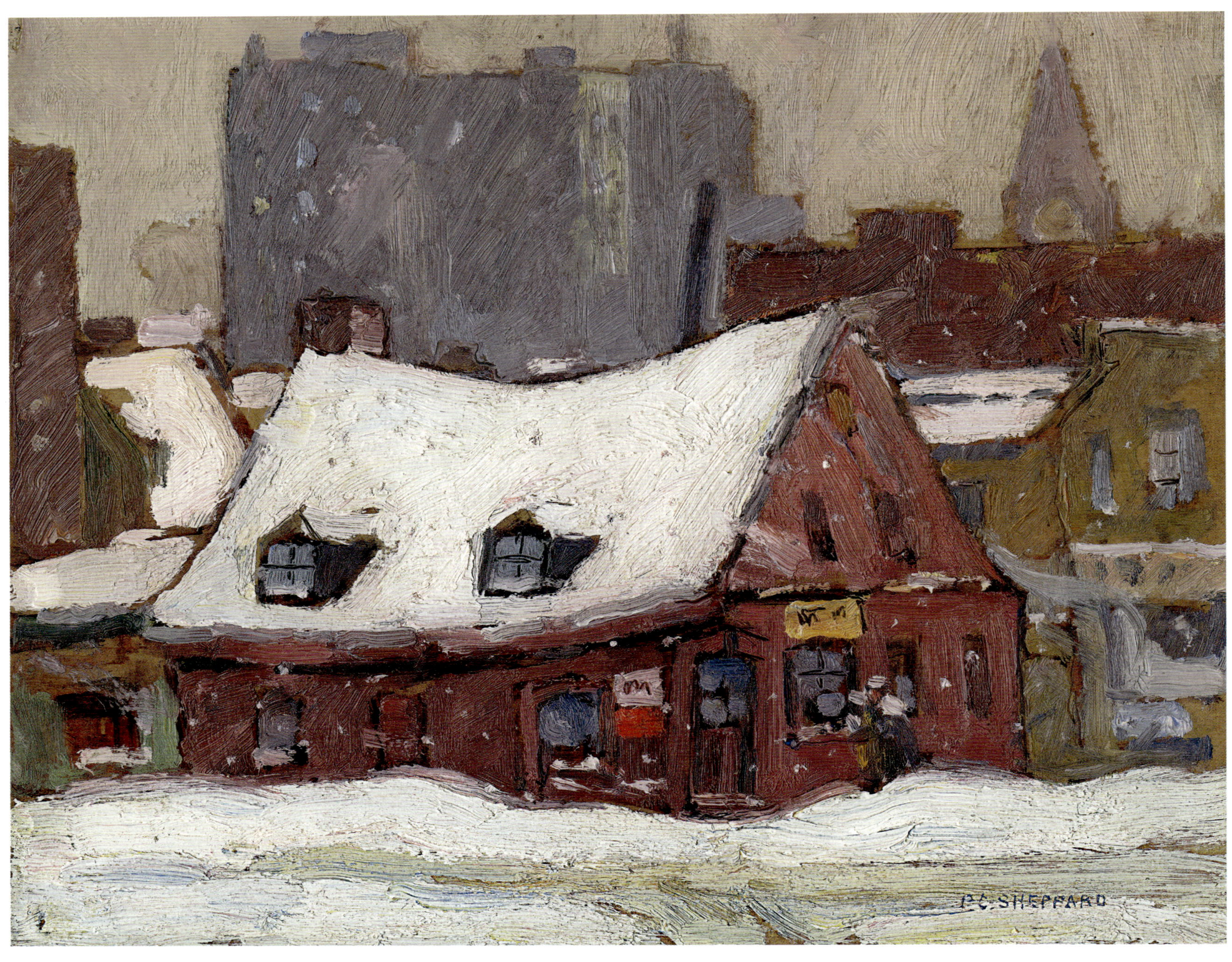

Old House, Winter (The Ward, Toronto).
c. 1921. Oil on panel,
21.6 x 26.7 cm.

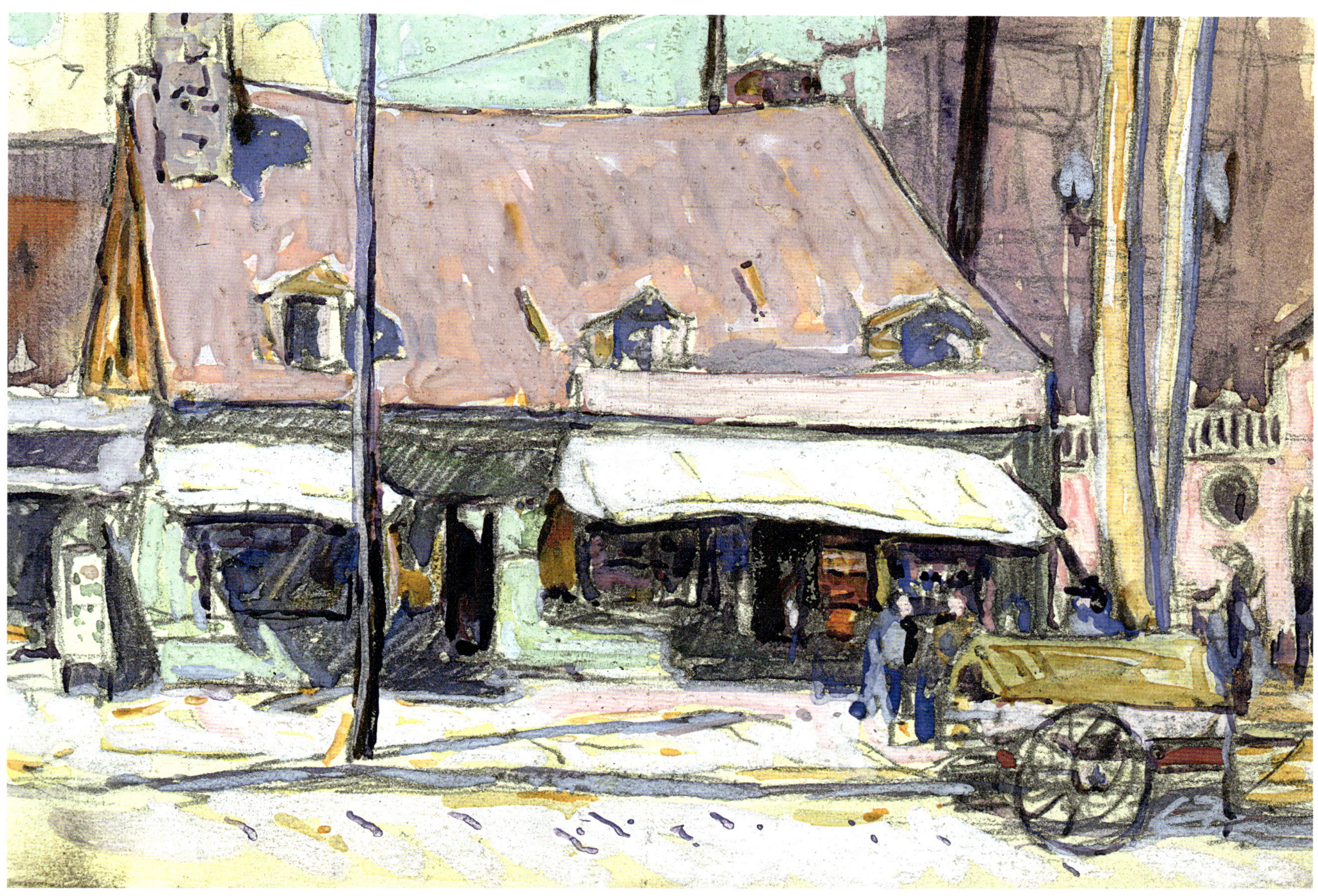

Old Store, Craig Street (study).
c. 1925. Watercolour,
9 x 12.7 cm.

OLD STORE, CRAIG STREET, 1925

Of all Sheppard's paintings of the early 1920s, his *Old Store, Craig Street* (see pages 140, 141, 143) announces him as an artist with an uncommon ability to marry formalism to an ability to capture the spirit of an entire neighbourhood. The question arises, though, whether this is a Montreal or a New York scene. A torn label attached to the back of the canvas provides a hint as to the subject matter's location beyond the descriptive "Craig Street." The label indicates that this canvas was exhibited at the National Gallery of Canada's *Special Exhibition of Canadian Art* in 1926 — an exhibition that Eric Brown, the gallery's director, declared as showing "the best work produced in 1925." [66] The 1926 exhibition catalogue indicates that the subject is a Montreal storefront, suggesting that in 1925 Sheppard spent time not only in New York City, but also in Montreal.

In its mood and in the handling of the subject of an old house, this painting echoes an earlier, undated painting that is contained in the archive. *Old House, Winter* (see page 142) interprets a dilapidated, bent and broken house from some woebegone neighbourhood. Rendering it in a palette of warm reds, violets and oranges, Sheppard emphasizes the swaying rhythms of the windows and dormers and the gentle degradation of the structure, which he sets down in lines that seem to breathe and groan, lending the forlorn subject a human spirit.

I wonder, though, if the record accurately reflects Sheppard's movements at the time? Is the location accurate? My questions stem from a sketch contained in one of Sheppard's New York sketchbooks that records the scene that was clearly the subject of *Old Store, Craig Street* (see page 143). While the scene's location is unidentified, the watercolour is among pages on which Sheppard set down his impressions of New York.

New York or Montreal — notwithstanding its source's location, the humble storefront is described in a sympathetic manner. With its open foreground giving way onto the doorstep of the establishment, and the subtle diagonal shadow of the hydro pole leading the eye in the same direction, the composition's open, welcoming nature provides easy visual and imaginative access to the subject. Despite a rundown nature and commonplace features that no doubt rendered this storefront invisible, anti-picturesque in its day, Sheppard gives it an attractive, even sympathetic, humanity. The curved lines and gentle horizontal arcs testify to the artist's hand making the sketch, lending it vitality while perhaps subliminally telling anyone who cares to notice that this place is worth looking at closely, intently. A portrait of a specific New York building, the subject could also reflect Sheppard's identification with the working class and their neighbourhoods. The sketch reflects as much affection for place as it does its author's clear talents for lifting what could have been mere documentary illustration to a level of symbolic emblem about vibrant inner-city enclaves.

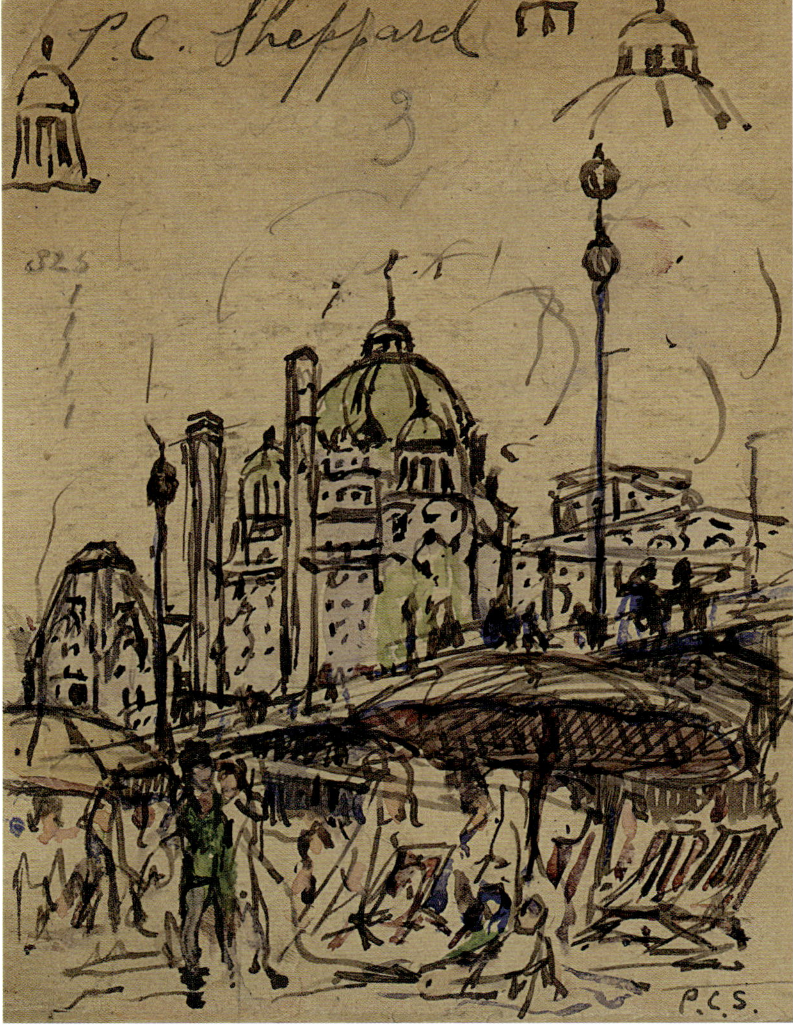

The Boardwalk, Atlantic City (study).
1919–22. New York Sketchbook.
Watercolour, graphite and ink on paper,
12.7 x 9 cm.

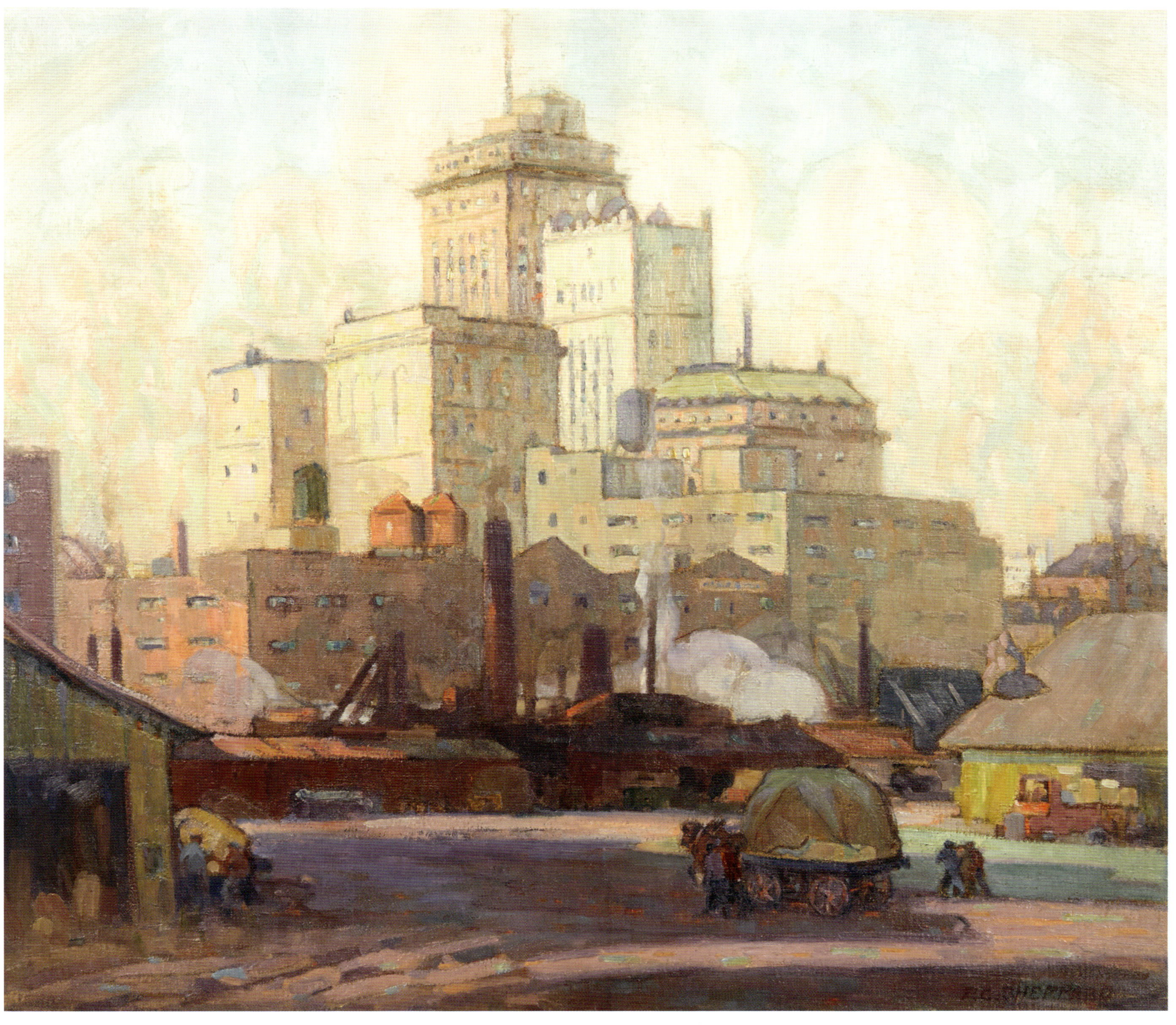

The City.
1925. Oil on canvas,
86 x 96.5 cm.

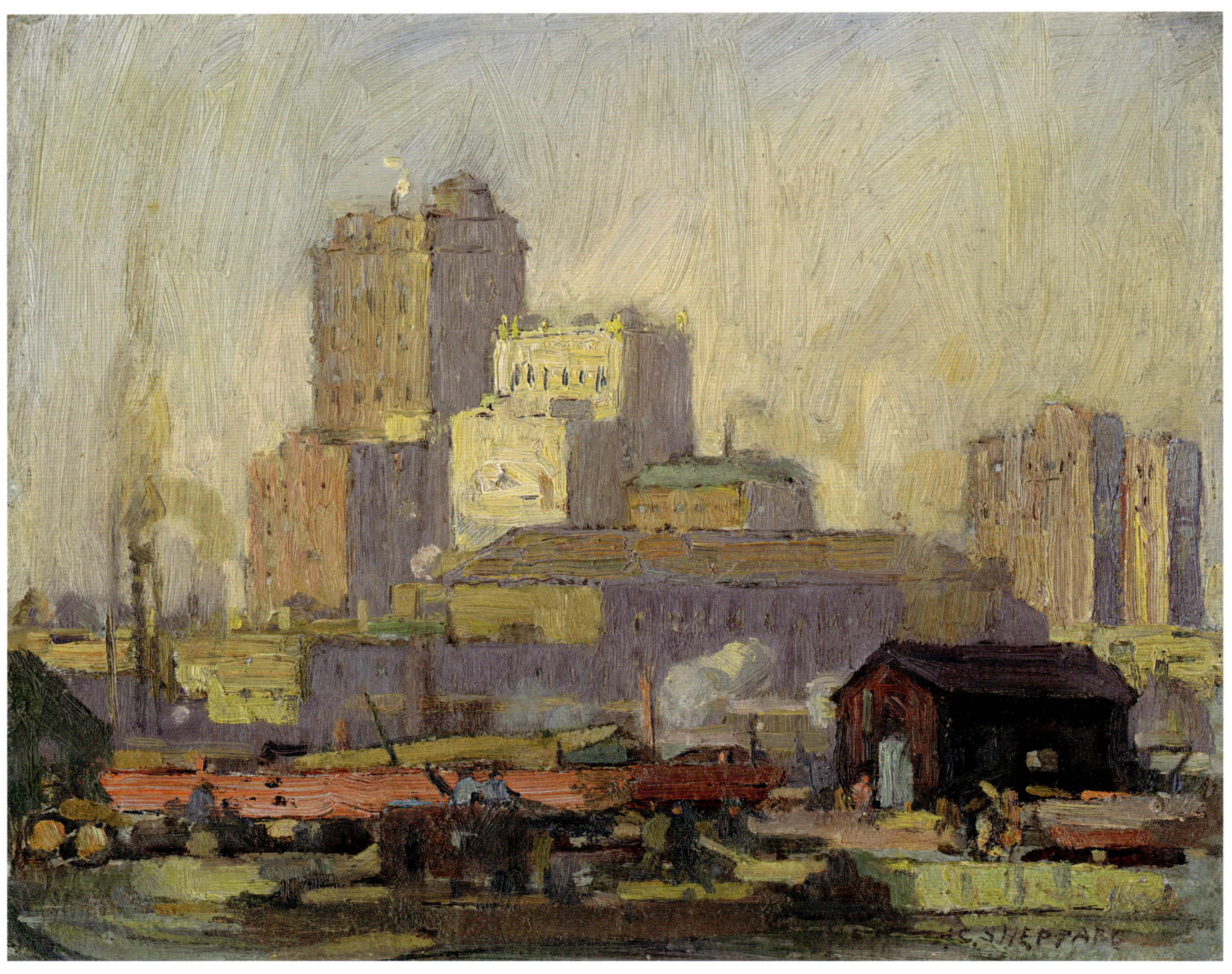

The City.
1925. Oil on panel,
21.6 x 26.7 cm.

Even though Sheppard adjusted the composition and elements of the scene when he worked the sketch into a large-format studio canvas, he successfully preserved the dynamism and energetic gesture of the sketch in the finished painting. His is a marvellously spirited handling of the paint. The complex palette of pinks, oranges and yellows is contrasted with a spectrum of cool blues, mauves, greens and violets, all in the service of conveying the commonplace narrative of neighbourhood folk going to a store to shop. In addition to the action established by the colour contrasts, the brushwork and the direction of the daubs of paint all amplify the energy of the scene as well as direct the eye in and around the composition. The ensemble of colours, brushstrokes and lines brings to mind musical riffs; the painting seems to exude a visual energy whose analogue is syncopated and contrapuntal rhythms.

As a whole, I find *Old Store, Craig Street* to be one of the more ambitious of Sheppard's urban paintings. It blends his innate talents as a draftsman with his acutely sharp sensibilities as a colourist. The foreground passage of a horizontal line of blue-grey oil paint sets up an electric charge of potential energy that animates the whole painting. Descriptive, prosaic, the narrative is further animated by the anonymous figure of the striding woman on the left side of the composition. Even more, the painting embodies a telling social critique, subtly stated, but nevertheless evident, in the way Sheppard valourizes what was certainly a marginal, invisible fragment of the bustling metropolis in the first quarter of the 20th century. By pointing to the store in such a finely crafted composition, Sheppard directs a light on the underclass that, while living in the shadows of the city, drives its engines of progress.

Was Sheppard an Impressionist? The answer is that in 1925 he was on the verge of adopting an Impressionist mode as his own. In the first place, Sheppard was aware of the French artists who had developed the movement a generation and a half earlier. Their style and influence were seen and felt not only in Western Europe, but also in Canada and the United States. By 1925, an Impressionist mode could be seen in the work of many Canadians — Maurice Cullen (1866–1934), Clarence Gagnon (1881–1942) and James Wilson Morrice (1865–1924) being three of the more important; in fact, it's even seen in the work of the relatively younger Sheppard, whose studies of women on park benches, in gardens and relaxing in the outdoors could claim in their style an affinity to the work of Impressionist antecedents. Just as the primary aim of the French painters was to capture light effects as they fell on the landscape or on figures, so, too, Sheppard's paintings in this mode could claim a similar intention. He sought to paint the light on his subjects.

But where the Impressionists also sought to incorporate into their work theories of optical colour mixing, particularly contrasting complementary colours, Sheppard can be seen to have placed less emphasis on this practice. Instead, he put down colour in ways that were non-specific to the subject. In other words, as a colourist, Sheppard was less interested in capturing in paint the fugitive qualities of light, as he was in using colour as a vehicle for expressing mood and emotion, or for accentuating formal relationships in compositions. True, in the backgrounds of his cityscapes the optical blending of highly tinted hues may be said to have been inspired by an Impressionist sensibility, but for the most part, colour passages in a Sheppard painting are freighted more with the requirement to convey expressions than to capture impressions. By the mid-1920s, Sheppard had a foot in both camps; he made use of aspects of the Impressionist mode, but also saw colour as an instrument for making visible his feelings.

BRITISH EMPIRE EXHIBITION, 1925

By the mid-1920s Sheppard had hit his creative stride, the best evidence being the self-evident accomplishment of his New York scenes, which display confidence and rigour, as well as resonance in the context of the modern figurative movements emanating from the United States. However, despite the pull of New York, Sheppard was not forgotten at home. He continued to be a member of the OSA and to exhibit (irregularly) in its annuals. In the 1925 OSA show the judges selected three of his canvases — *The Fair, Freighters in Harbour* (see page 164) and *The City* (see page 146). The latter is a variation on the familiar theme of a faceless metropolis made up of a sequence of interlocking skyscrapers. The "city" literally rises up in the distance in a blocky pyramid, dwarfing and shadowing the humble enclave of a neighbourhood and factory in the foreground.

In a review that dwelt upon the quantity and quality of portrait paintings in the exhibition, the influential critic Hector Charlesworth gave Sheppard a mention as exhibiting "some clever urban studies."[67] The reviewer in the *Toronto Mail and Empire* was more vociferous than Charlesworth, declaring that:

> Peter C. Sheppard is becoming almost entirely an interpreter of cities and crowded commercial centres. There is a certain brutal strength in the colors that he uses which might be regarded as symbolic. One would feel inclined to say that his three canvasses, 'The Fair', 'Freighters', and 'The City' are over-crowded, but then the life that he presents is that way. [68]

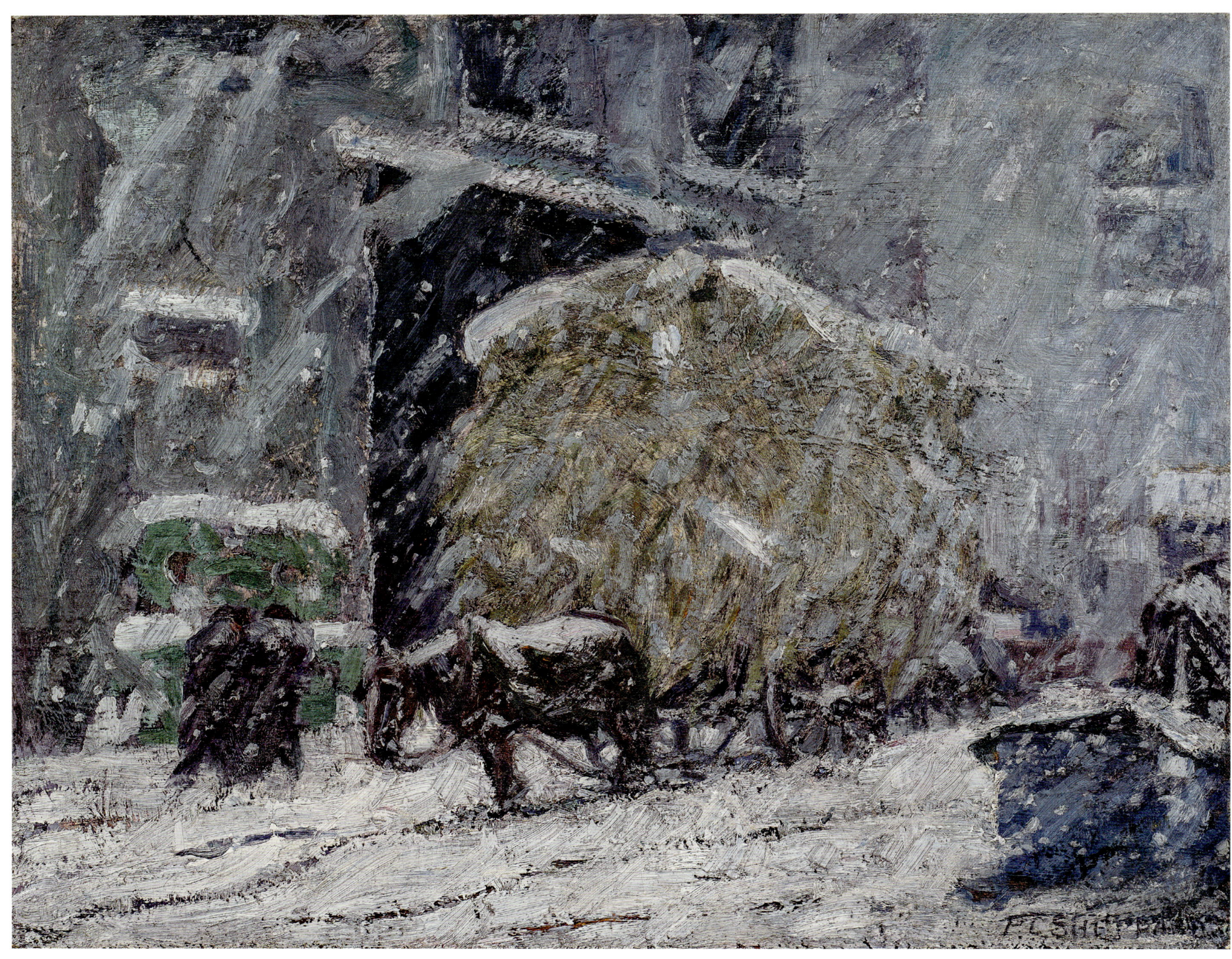

Early Snow, Montreal.
1924–25. Oil on canvas,
61.6 x 77 cm.

Sheppard also enjoyed the further recognition of his peers by being selected for the important international exhibition of paintings that were part of the 1925 Canadian Section of Fine Arts at the British Empire Exhibition held at Wembley in London, England, that year. His entry in the show was *Early Snow, Montreal* (see page 148), a canvas that the archive had just recently acquired — repatriated — while I was researching its holdings.

The 1925 iteration of the Wembley exhibition was the second in two years. The 1924 presentation, whose selection of work was made by a jury overseen by the National Gallery of Canada, is recognized as a milestone in the history of Canadian art. This is largely because it allowed some 267 pieces of Canadian art, including 215 paintings, particularly those of the Group of Seven, to be seen in an international forum. In fact, it offered "one of the few stages — and a major one at that — on which they [the Group of Seven] might prove themselves."[69] Eric Brown, Director of the National Gallery of Canada, pronounced the exhibition "the most important exhibition of Canadian art ever held outside the Dominion."[70] The bombast was correct, too; many British critics proclaimed that Canadian painting generally and the landscapes of the Group of Seven particularly could be counted as among the more significant expressions of modernist painting at the time.[71] The Canadian critics, however, particularly the authoritative if pontificating Charlesworth, derided the accomplishments of the group.

The claim that the 1925 exhibition reflected a "justifiable feeling of confidence" that Canadian art in the previous year's exhibition had "earned praise from all critical judgment for its qualities of originality, frankness and an indigenous Canadianism," was a matter for extreme satisfaction throughout Canada.[72] Believing that the 1925 exhibition "outclassed" its predecessor "in every quality of originality and nationalism," it was the fervent hope of the Canadian organizers that this exhibition in particular would further advance the fame and fortunes of Canadian artists "in the eyes of the Mother Country" and would encourage "a wider interchange of art within various parts of the Empire."

Sheppard found himself in good company in the 1925 exhibition, which included all the significant artists of the day, ranging from Impressionists Clarence Gagnon and James Wilson Morrice; to members of the Group of Seven; sculptors Frances Loring (1887–1968), Florence Wyle (1881–1968) and Emanuel Hahn (1881–1957); Sheppard's peers as interpreters of modern life in the city, Kathleen Moir Morris (1893–1986) and David Milne (1882–1953); and landscapists such as the Saskatchewan-raised Frederick Loveroff (1894–1959); among others whom the jury selected as reflecting the best work being done in Canada at the time.

Sheppard's contribution to the British Empire Exhibition, *Early Snow, Montreal,* showed him embracing Impressionism as a means of capturing the light and energy of an unexpected snowstorm enveloping a horse-drawn hay wain. Rather than treat the scene with his characteristic manner, delineating the forms and applying the paint to support and intensify foundational drawing, Sheppard has approached his subject with a view to interpreting it in a more experiential manner, and the Impressionist mode provided a way to do this. The paint surfaces are heavily roughed-in to such a degree that the impasto gives an effect of a textured ground that conveys a sense of the snowstorm's building energy. This is a painting of a phenomenon rather than just a depiction of place, or the telling of a visual narrative. With a palette of blue-greys and greys, the overall application of media intensifies the feeling of the wagon's heavy load made all the more burdensome by the increasing impenetrableness of the snow accumulating on the roadway. The forms are indistinct owing to the sense of pelting ice and snow that Sheppard describes through vigorous, energetic brushstrokes. The figures on the left, leaning into the storm, are mere daubs of paint.

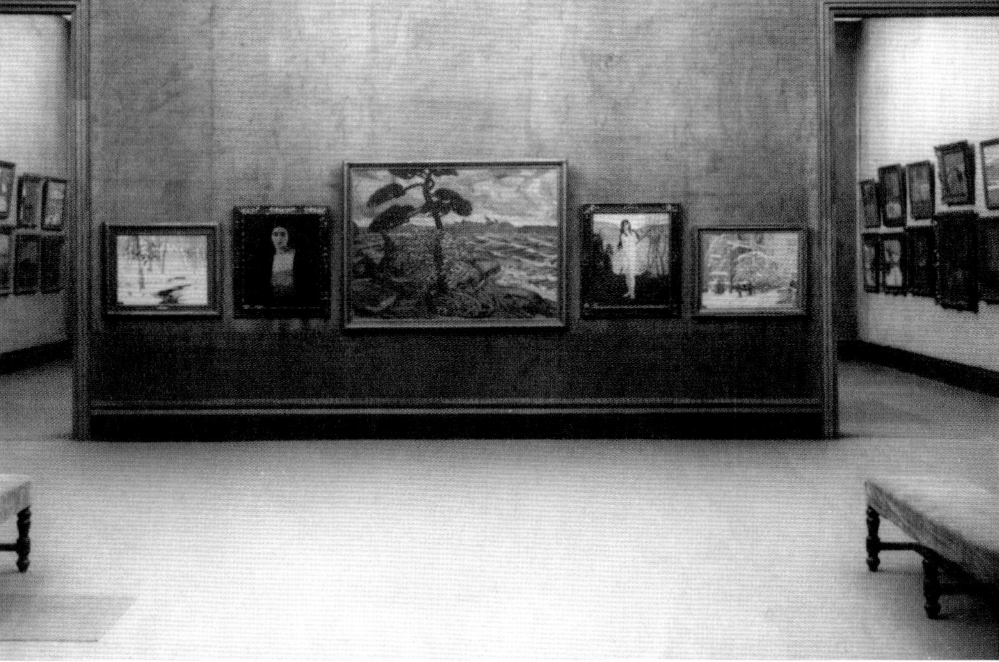

Exhibition at the Musée du Jeu de Paume, Paris, May 10, 1927. Sheppard's *Early Snow, Montreal,* is on the far right. At the centre is Arthur Lismer's *September Gale,* borrowed for the occasion from the collection of the National Gallery of Canada.

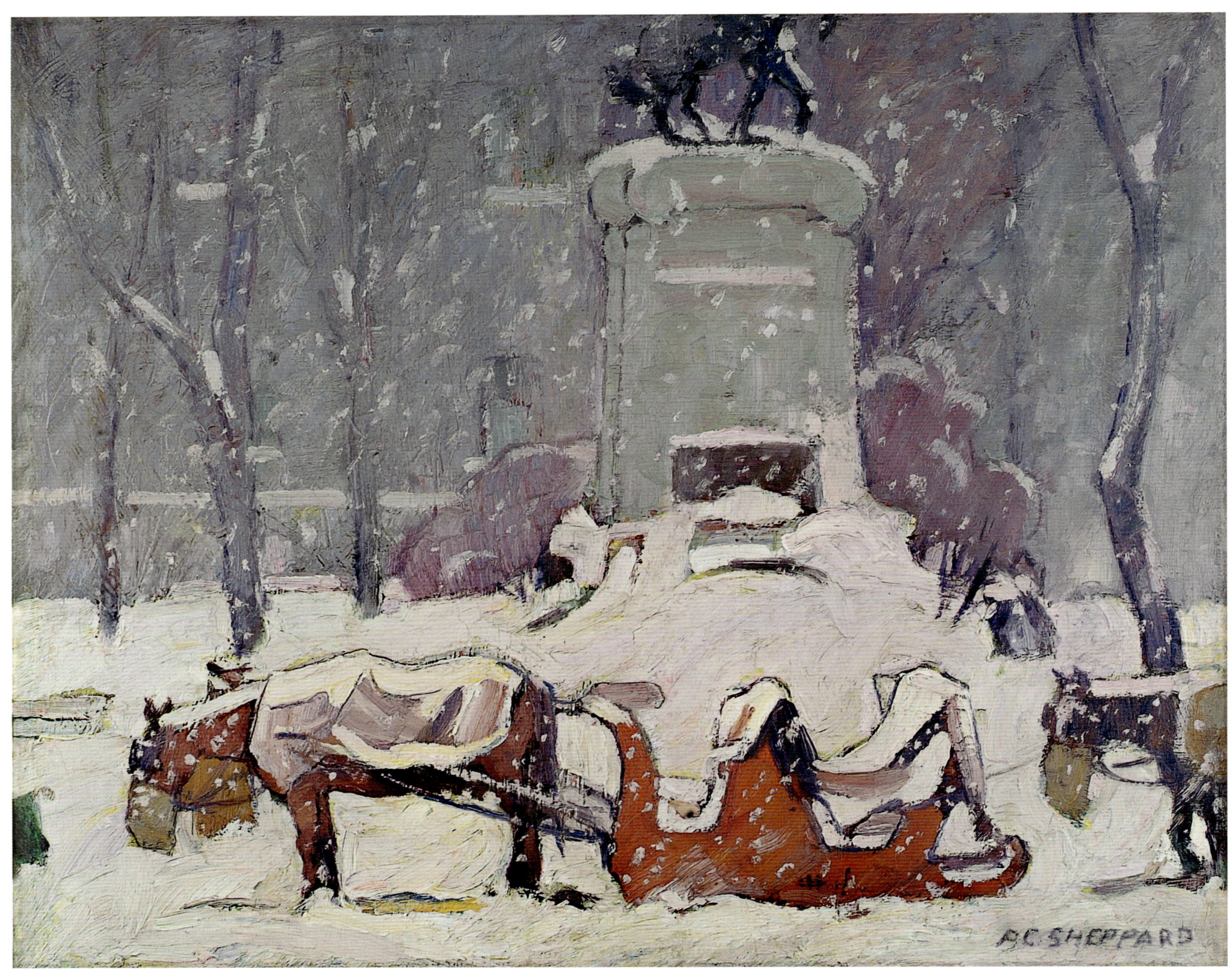

The Cabstand, Dominion Square, Montreal.
c. 1926. Oil on canvas,
50.8 x 61 cm.

A "RADICAL" IN MONTREAL, 1925–27

Through this simple painterly iconography, Sheppard expresses life and humanity. Beyond the subject matter, through his expert handling of colours and textures, Sheppard has created a beautiful evocation of the atmosphere of an early winter's day in Montreal. *Early Snow, Montreal,* also provides an important piece of information concerning Sheppard's comings and goings in 1924: he evidently spent time there, probably in the autumn. His carefully delineated *Market Scene, Montreal* of 1926 (page 161) reflects the hand of a skilled draftsman who set down accurately what took place in front of him, all the while establishing a composition that emphasized an innate theatricality in the action of a busy market. *Early Snow, Montreal* was also exhibited in the Exposition d'art canadien at the Musée de Jeu du Paume in Paris in the spring of 1927, an exhibition based on the two previous Wembley exhibitions, while also billing itself as the first exhibition of Canadian art in France.[73] An installation photograph of the exhibition shows that Sheppard's painting was hung on the same wall *September Gale,* an icon and masterful painting by the Group of Seven's Arthur Lismer. Lismer's contribution to the exhibit was borrowed for the occasion from the collection of the National Gallery of Canada, which had purchased it only a year earlier.

While working in Montreal in 1925 and 1926, Sheppard developed as an Impressionist.[74] It seems from the surviving paintings — some in public collections, and others in the archive — that he found in the city's winter landscapes evocative themes and subject matter that adapted well to being presented as impressionistic paintings. Just as spring and summer inspired Monet's paintings of his garden at Giverny, so winter spoke to Sheppard in a language of light and colour rather than strictly of form.

The Cabstand, Dominion Square, Montreal (see left), for example, is a measured, gently lyrical study capturing the quiet solemnity of a winter's afternoon below the Boer War monument in the square. There is a dab of humour, too, in Sheppard's depiction of the subject as a contrast between life and art. The lassitude of the blinkered cab horses, their noses in the feedbags, standing at the edge of a snowdrift is elegantly suggested by the rhythms of curves and arcs lending the foreground a sense of easy humanity. In contrast, the heroic, majestically striding bronze horse atop the cenotaph appears to mock the tired swaybacks that stand in its shadow.

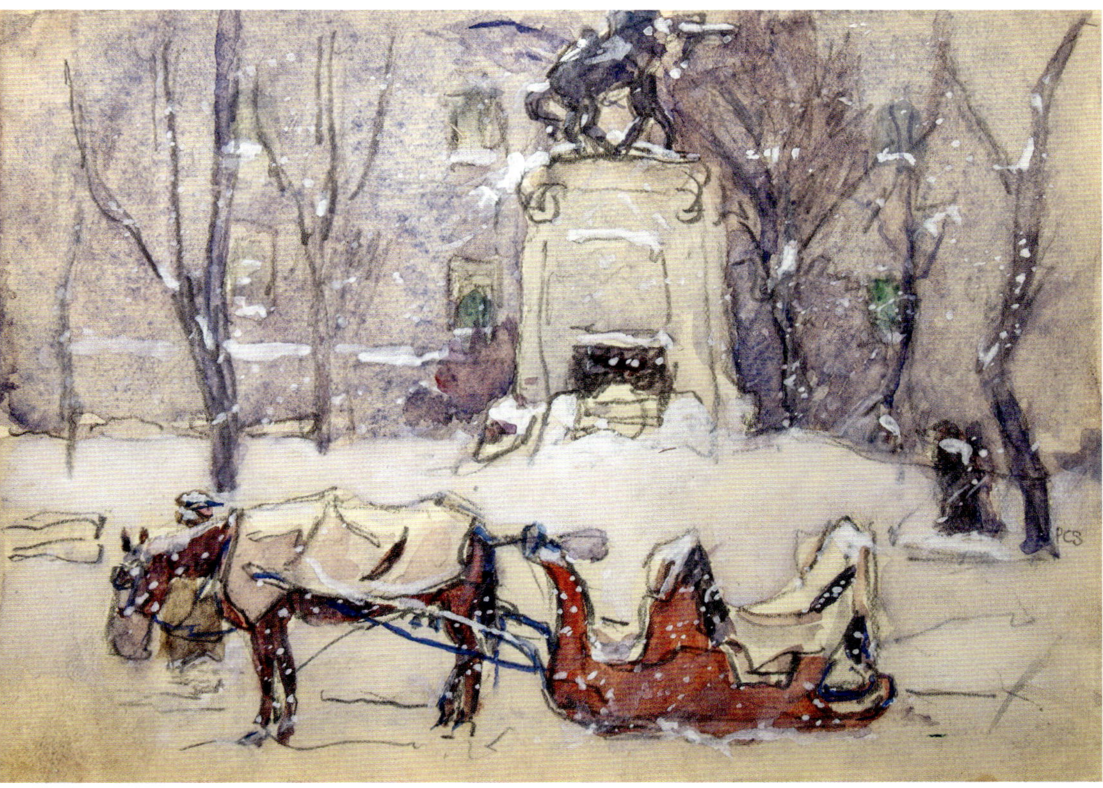

The Cabstand, Dominion Square, Montreal (study). 1926. Watercolour, 12.7 x 17.8 cm.

Sheppard tackles the slice of life with a highly refined colour essay that effectively lifts the scene from the doldrums of ordinariness, making it more than a humorous visual episode in the life of the city. His painting is an exploration of impressionistic colour relationships that, when combined with a refined sense of the expressiveness of line, create a simulacrum of a winter's day in Montreal. Looking at the colour alone, there is a pleasing abstract patterning to the way the muted hues are laid down to suggest depth and atmosphere. The blue-grey parentheses on either side of the grey stone plinth and the snowdrift are painted punctuation marks that the neutral tones set off in an understated fashion. The building facades are described in cool greys and mauves that push the whites and creams of the snow into the foreground that is occupied by the musical cadences of the cabs and their notes of warm browns, oranges, reds and ochres. In this composition of colour relationships, Sheppard displays an innate sense of how harmonies can be set off by highly keyed secondary colours. The feeling of perceptual reality is made all the more tangible by the inflections of white dabs that not only describe the falling snowflakes, but also accentuate the impression of the scene as emerging and receding.

The Cabstand, Dominion Square, Montreal was likely a rehearsal, a study, for one of the more important paintings of Sheppard's career, entitled *Midwinter* (see page 155). This painting is now a part of the permanent collection of the National Gallery of Canada. When exhibited in the 1927 OSA annual, *Midwinter*

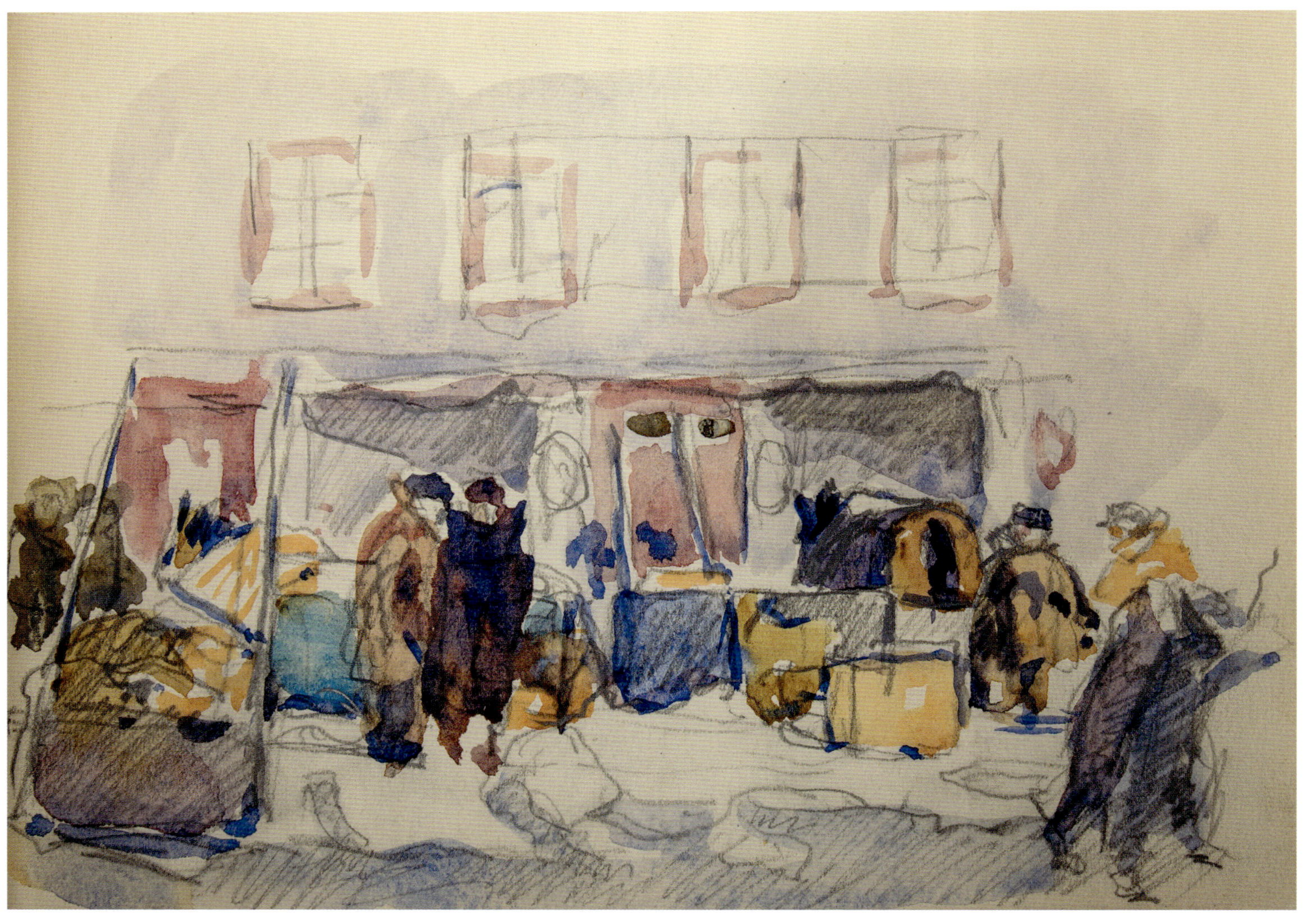

People on the Street.
c. 1925–26. Montreal
Sketchbook.
Graphite and watercolour,
12.7 x 17.8 cm.

met with critical praise. It was described as "a fine, tightly cold thing" in an exhibition that the *Toronto Star*'s critic characterized as a "bold advance on any previous show in color, variety, vibration and virility."[75] Sheppard, from the tone of the review, was situated with the more advanced painters working in Canada in the mid-20s in a creative terrain described as "everyman's land between the impressively stereotyped academy and the insurgent Group of Seven." In fact, according to the *Toronto Mail and Empire* reviewer, the 1927 OSA exhibition was hailed as being superior to the previous year's annual exhibition of the RCA, and Sheppard was corralled with a group of "radical painters."[76] Colour, according to the reviewer, distinguished the work of the "radicals" — "youngsters and experimenters" — from that of the traditionalists. "There

is something startling and challenging wherever you look," intoned the reviewer, "not only in theories or coloring, but in the general theories of art." Abstraction, colour effects for their own sakes — these innovations were all in evidence at the OSA annual. In other words, the reviewer suggests that rather than falling solely under the spell of the advances signalled in the work of the Group of Seven, the exhibition was featuring canvases that evidenced the influence of Impressionism (colourists). The artist heralding this trend was identified as Winnipeg man Bertram Brooker (1888–1955). In the context of this exhibition, Sheppard was hailed as having "never done anything better than 'Midwinter' and 'Lower Town' … [he] has acquired a marked skill as a painter of snow. The pictures have atmosphere."

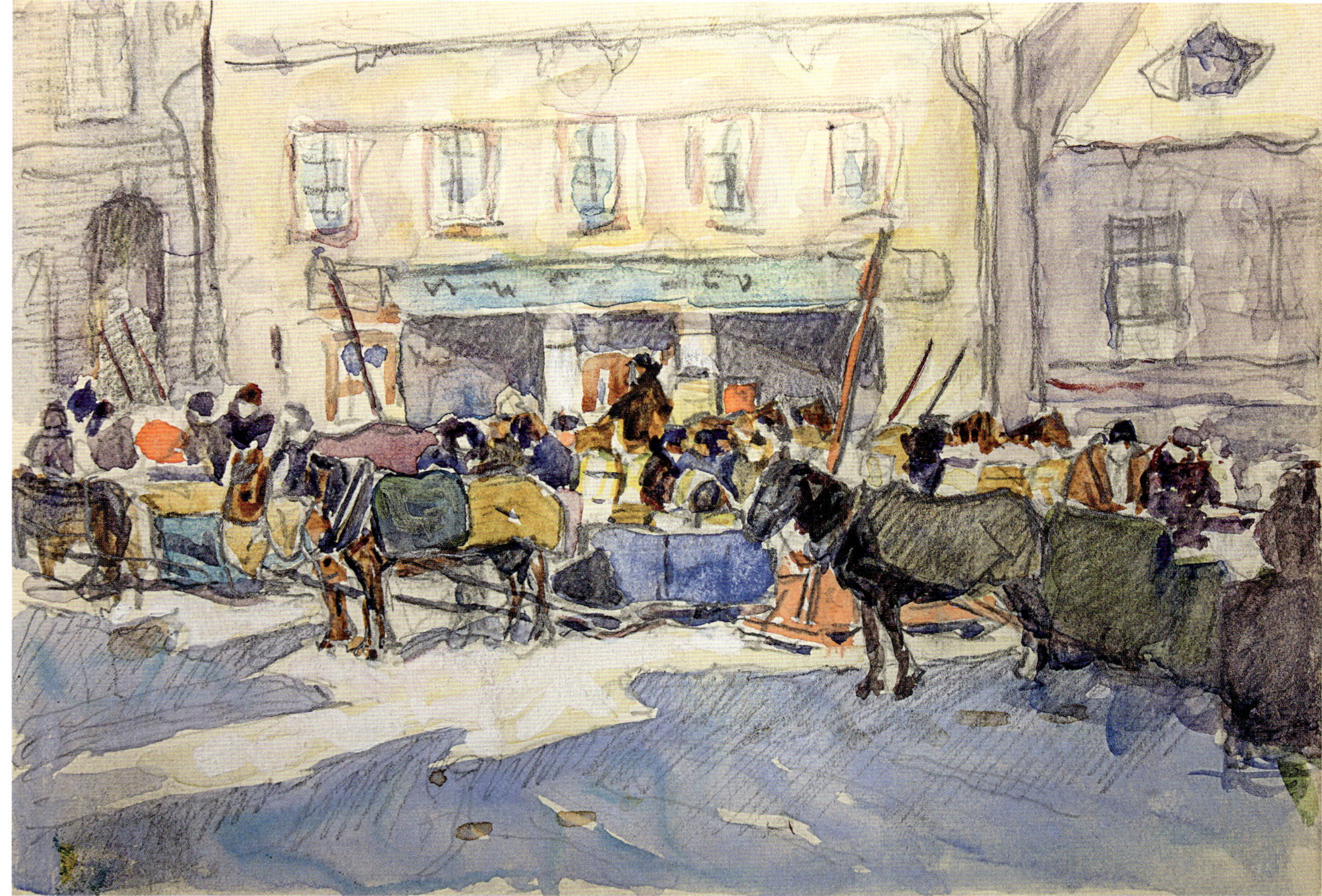

Parking on the Street.
c. 1925–26. Montreal
Sketchbook.
Graphite and watercolour,
12.7 x 17.8 cm.

Atmosphere and snow: if *Midwinter* has a subject, it is certainly encapsulated in these two nouns. The painting, a variation on the *Cabstand*'s subject, exemplifies the sense and experience of a Montreal winter day, while showing Sheppard confident in his interpretive skills and entirely comfortable creating a harmonious composition of the formal elements of a painting. Not evident in *Midwinter*'s narrative is the tincture of humour in the conversation between the live horses and the bronze one. This has been replaced with a moody meditation on the Dominion Square Park. Absent, too, is the familiar crisp, draftsman-like delineation of form in favour of a painterly style that owes a debt to Impressionism. The diagonal foreground leads the eye into the composition and into its painterly translation of form as an array of colours laid on the canvas to emphasize feeling over form and to provide a painted simulacrum of the experience of the scene. The two figures in the lower right quadrant of the composition serve as colourful, indistinct avatars for viewers to project their imaginations and memories into, all the better to engage with the subject for a fulsome aesthetic encounter with a midwinter snowstorm.

Sheppard mitigates the picturesque qualities of the subject in *Midwinter* by intensifying the effect of the tree limbs that overhang the cabstand. In one sense the trees, particularly the large crooked-limbed hardwood behind the cabs, serve as framing devices that draw the eye around and through the composition as a hand or an arm might direct the gaze of a passive viewer. To be sure, Sheppard has anthropomorphized the branches, and in this subtlety he has made the branches appear menacing. The wall of the city that forms the backdrop to the square is a dazzling abstract field of deeply toned purples, greys and blues. The pictorial space is more a stage on which the meteorological event occurs, rather than just an interpretation of place. The interaction of the colours and lines results in a multi-sensory experience that conjures emotion and memory from the impression of a familiar event (a snowstorm) and place, amplified as the painting compels the viewer to give in to the magic of colours, lines and light. In every sense, *Midwinter* qualifies as an Impressionist painting, and further gives Sheppard "cred" as a "radical" in the context of the more academic painting of his time.

Midwinter is a summing-up piece in Sheppard's career to that point. It embodies his interest in urban scenes that are attuned to giving a human, common point of view. He structures the visual narrative as a set of contrasts, particularly the one between his evident personal affection for the working class and the impersonal nature of the world of commerce signified by the city. The painting also advances Sheppard as a technical artist. He downplays a natural inclination for a strongly stated foundational drawing that organizes the composition in favour of a loose, expressionistic handling of drawing that reinforces mood rather than structure. And perhaps its most innovative aspect is that it finds in the particular event an essential humanity, all of which he puts down in a dazzling, nearly abstract performance of colours. The *Mail and Empire* reviewer was correct: Sheppard and the radicals of his cohort were declaring themselves as colourists, perhaps even abstractionists at a time when Canadian art was in flux. He was correct in another way: Sheppard had never done anything better.

OTHER CABSTANDS

Having achieved a new level of painting with *Midwinter,* Sheppard did something unexpected. He fell back on his reliance on drawing. The Montreal-based Impressionist canvases promised innovation and development away from a personal style based on observations of the life around him, to abstractions that luxuriated in the pure poetry of colouristic effects, hung on the armature of recognizable subjects yet whose meanings arose from the interactions of formal elements in a composition. But this development did not occur. Was

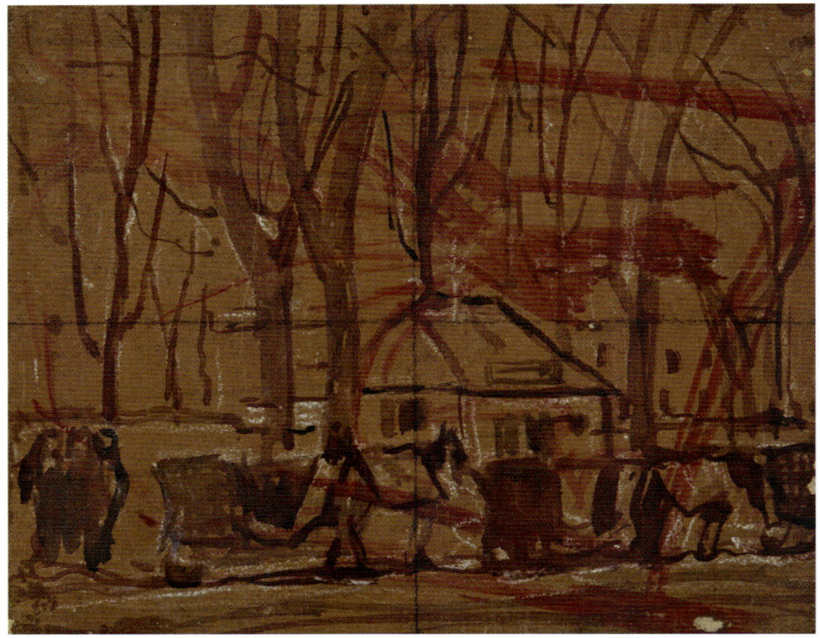

Cabstand, Montreal (study).
c. 1926. Oil wash on board,
21.6 x 17 cm.

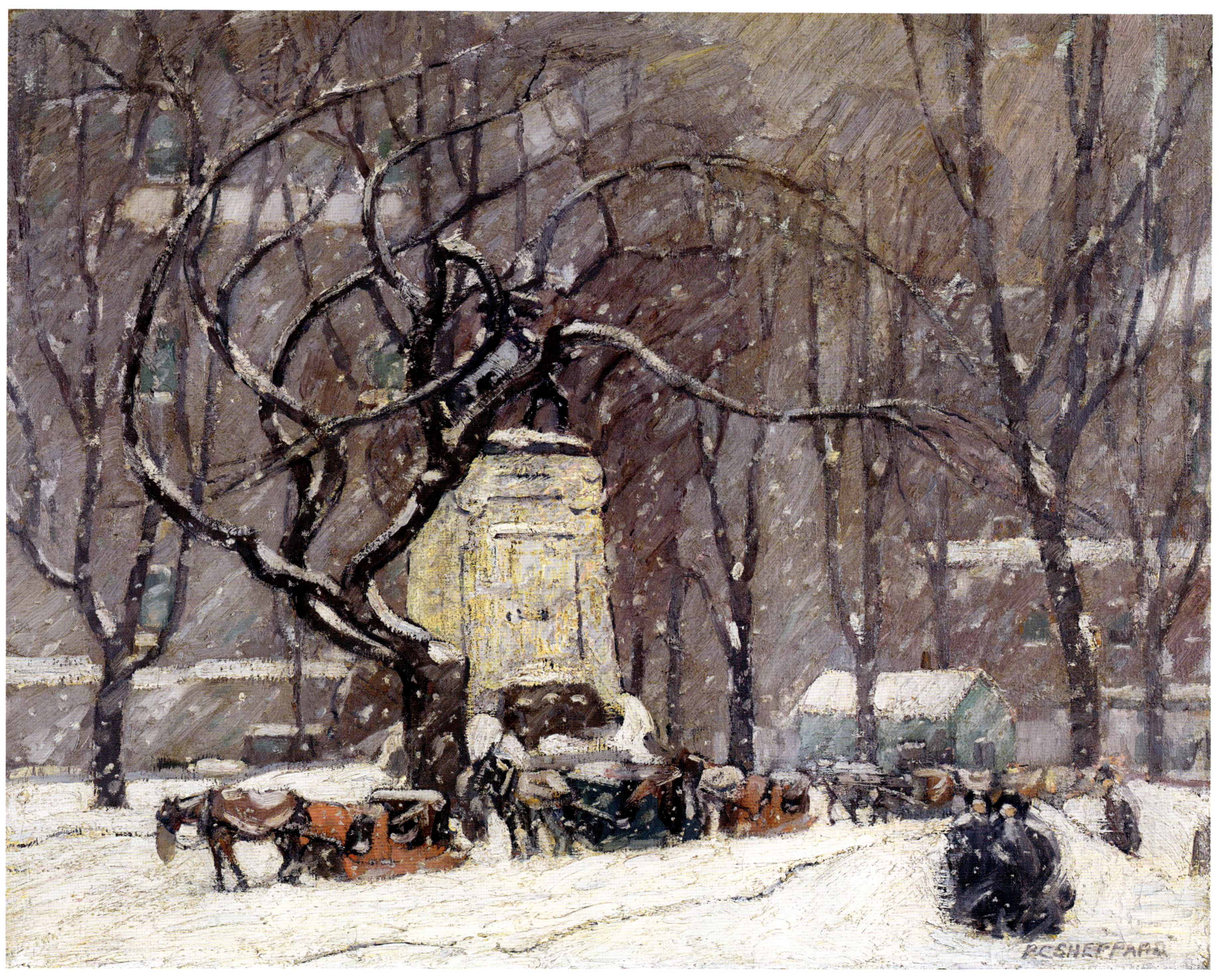

Midwinter.
1927. Oil on canvas,
76.2 x 91.9 cm.

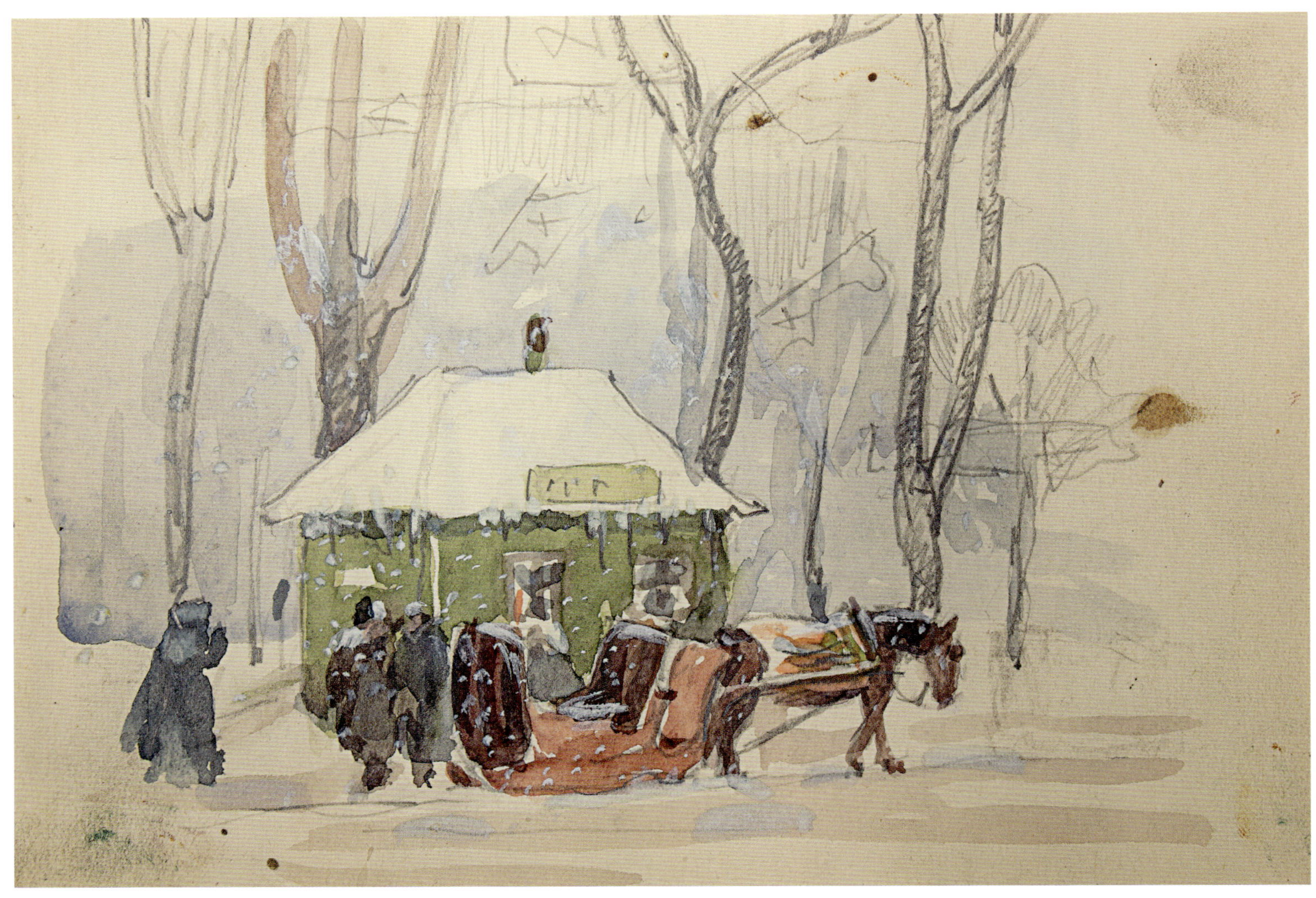

Cabstand, Montreal.
1926. Montreal sketchbook.
Watercolour,
12.7 x 17.8 cm.

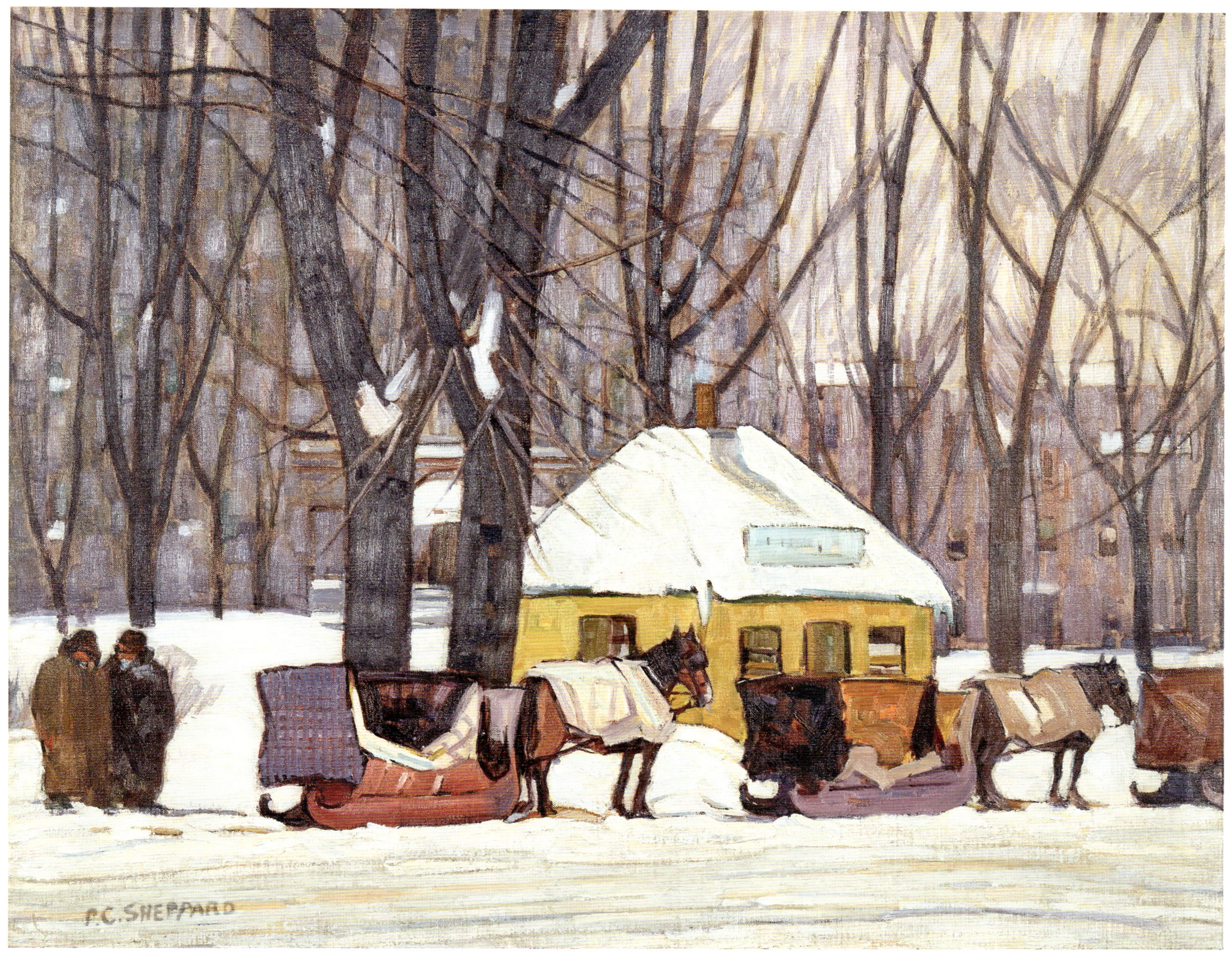

Cabstand, Montreal.
c. 1927. Oil on canvas,
61 x 76 cm.

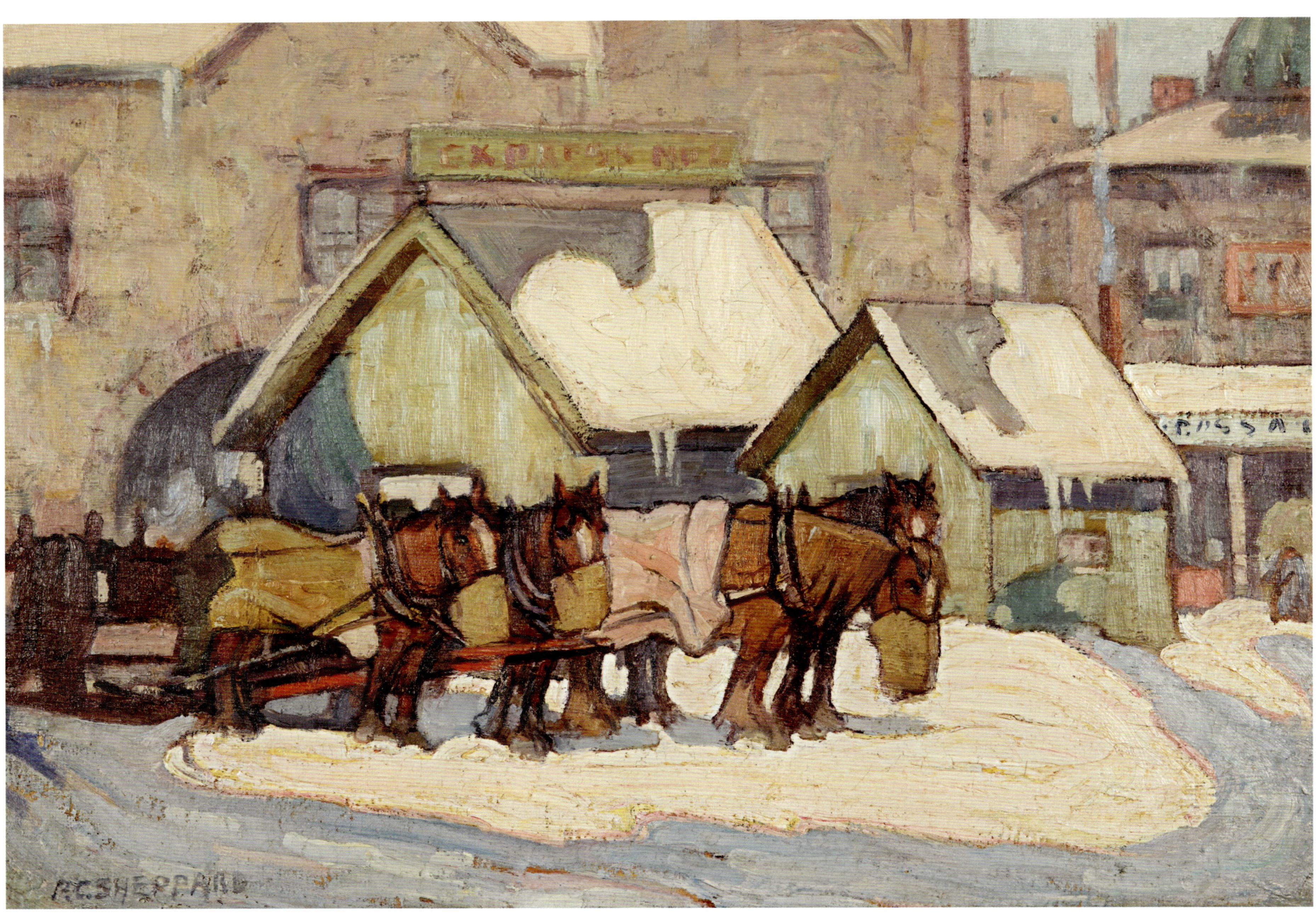

Cabstand, Old Quebec.
1926. Oil on canvas,
61 x 86 cm.

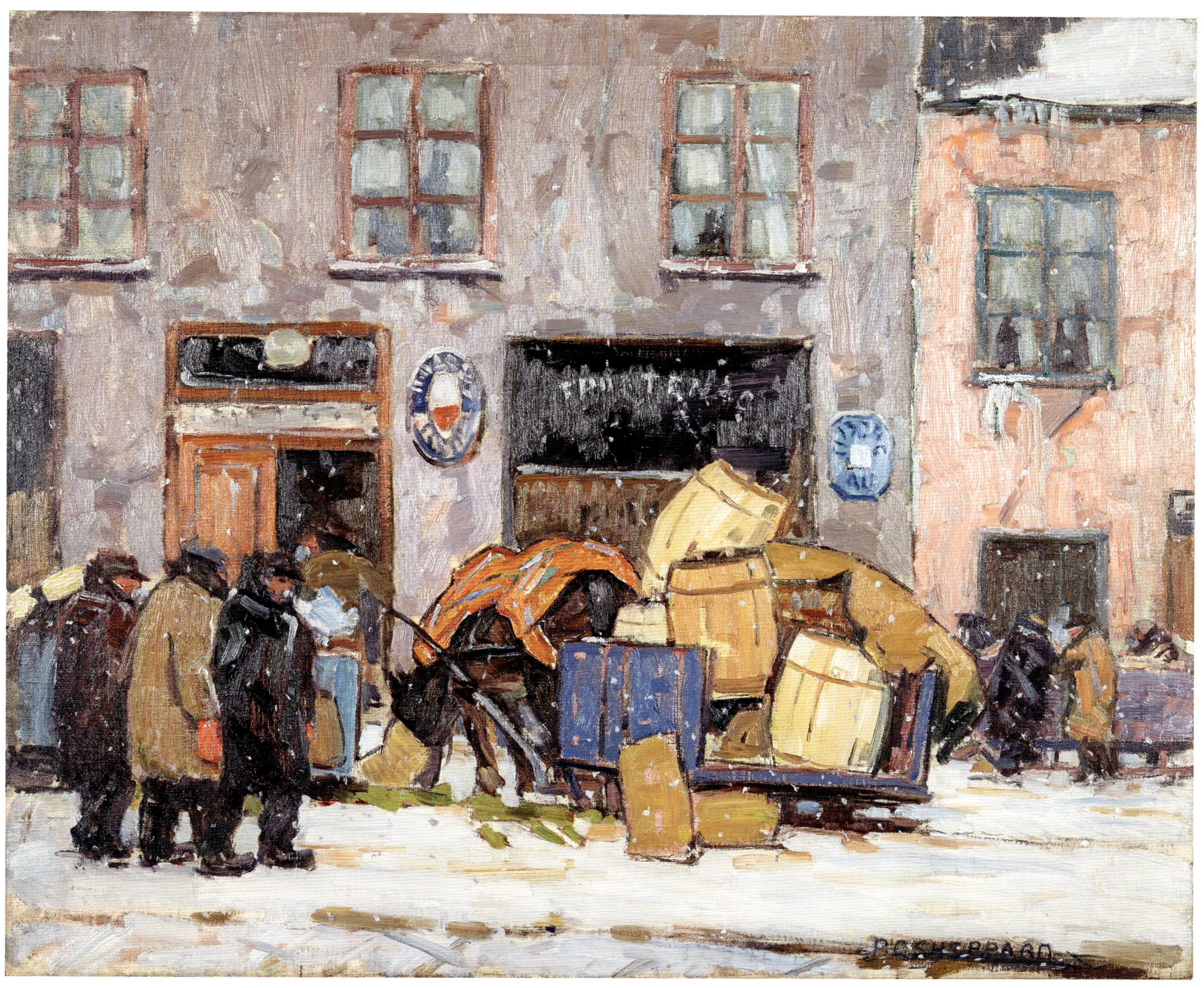

The Inn Yard.
1926–27. Oil on canvas,
91.4 x 76 cm.

Sheppard timid? Did he need to order his aesthetic impulses by anchoring them to an artistic practice that proceeded from sketches of life to studies and then to finished compositions? Did he have the temperament to cast off from the safe place of naturalism, of recognizable subjects, of figuration and of a documentary (almost illustrative) impulse? I suspect that in 1927 he asked himself the same questions; he likely knew he was at a watershed moment in his artistic development as a 48-year-old man who represented himself as being 45.

Sheppard was drawn to cabstands as a subject. The archive contains several paintings and sketches of them, particularly in winter. I imagine that his attraction to them reflects more his affection for the horses that pulled the cabs through the snowy streets. There are many pages in his sketchbooks that offer up depictions of horses parked in front of stands, but also beside markets and outside taverns. The subject appears to have given Sheppard excuses to explore a picturesque mode rather than push himself artistically and out of his comfort zone as a painter. A 1927 cabstand (see page 157), for example, is a case in point. It was originally thought that this tidy, balanced canvas showed a Toronto streetscape, but a sketch places it in Montreal (page 156). Pulling back from the Impressionist style, Sheppard has set down this scene first as a clear, crisp sketch taken from life; he stood a short distance from the rank of cabs and carefully (if also quickly) put down his impressions in pencil and opaque watercolour paints on a cold afternoon.

The oil painting that is based on this sketch shows a clean, clear delineation of all the pictorial elements. The horses and cabs (there are two more than are seen in the sketch) remind me of the work of Sheppard's Montreal contemporary and a member of the Beaver Hall Group, Kathleen Moir Morris, who showed a similar affection for Montreal and its familiar, perhaps overlooked, sites, such as ordinary cabstands. The cityscape beyond, much in the manner of many a Sheppard canvas, is described more as a vague, indistinctly coloured field rather than an identifiable location. With a composition revolving around the mustard-coloured cottage, the painting's visual tension is established by the subtle complementary colours of the cabs contrasting with the background phalanx of buildings. There is a beautiful lyricism in the undulating rhythms of the horses and cabs; the two figures at the left animate the scene while also providing a prosaic narrative gloss to it as an ordinary Montreal winter day.

Ordinariness, where the New York paintings embodied a thinly veiled critique of class status by ennobling in paint slices of life of the working classes. Sheppard's Montreal paintings radiate warmth that conveys not criticism so much as fondness. They exude affection. To my eye, Sheppard keenly associated with the Montreal off the beaten path, down avenues away from the commercial core, to the places where plain folk shopped and enjoyed each other's company in the open air or in taverns. A winter view (see page 158) is a finely seen study of four parked horses with feeding bags patiently waiting in a snowy Montreal alley. The warmth of the mood is reflected in a palette keyed to green-greys with light blue-grey and pink highlights. It is as if Sheppard composed the scene as a theatrical tableau where the building facades are backdrop to a stage on which the horses serve as mute characters. Control and clear delineation define the hallmarks of Sheppard's style, where every turn of line and subtle element in the ensemble has importance. The composition's geometry is reinforced by the way the landscape has been laid in as a series of squares, triangles and faceted rectangles.

Altogether, these elements establish a dynamic surface rhythm as well as create visual interest. The pitch-roofed houses, in particular, are affectionately described, not in an impressionistic manner, but virtually as living, breathing things, an effect that is made all the more evident when it is juxtaposed with the crisp linearity of the background buildings. Above all else, this painting exemplifies what a reviewer of Sheppard's work wrote in 1919, that he found something interesting in "garish" and "commonplace" subjects. What could be more common than the narrative that unfolds in this composition? Rather than seeing it as garish, Sheppard interprets it as compelling, vital — and by painting it he tells his viewers that it is worth contemplating.

The same sentiments are evident in *The Inn Yard* (see page 159), describing an out-of-the-way Montreal corner in front of a tavern, a composition that gave Sheppard the latitude to show off his talents as a draftsman in the handling of the foreground figures and sleighs full of barrels. Without a doubt, all the hours of study and observation of the urban scene served him well when it came to composing and delineating this subject, about as commonplace a subject as could be found at the time — horses idling in front of a tavern.

Midwinter, The Inn Yard and a third painting, *Lower Town, Montreal* were all selected for the 1927 OSA annual exhibition. In his self-congratulatory report, Fred Brigden (1841–1956), the OSA president at the time, stated that although 1926 had been a year of "dissension and bickering in the varied ranks of art," the past year had seen greater recognition of Canadian art on the international stage.[77] *Midwinter* was also exhibited in the RCA annual, and at the CNE. It was acquired by the National Gallery of Canada in 1928. Sheppard had revealed himself as an artist with a range that showed him on the one

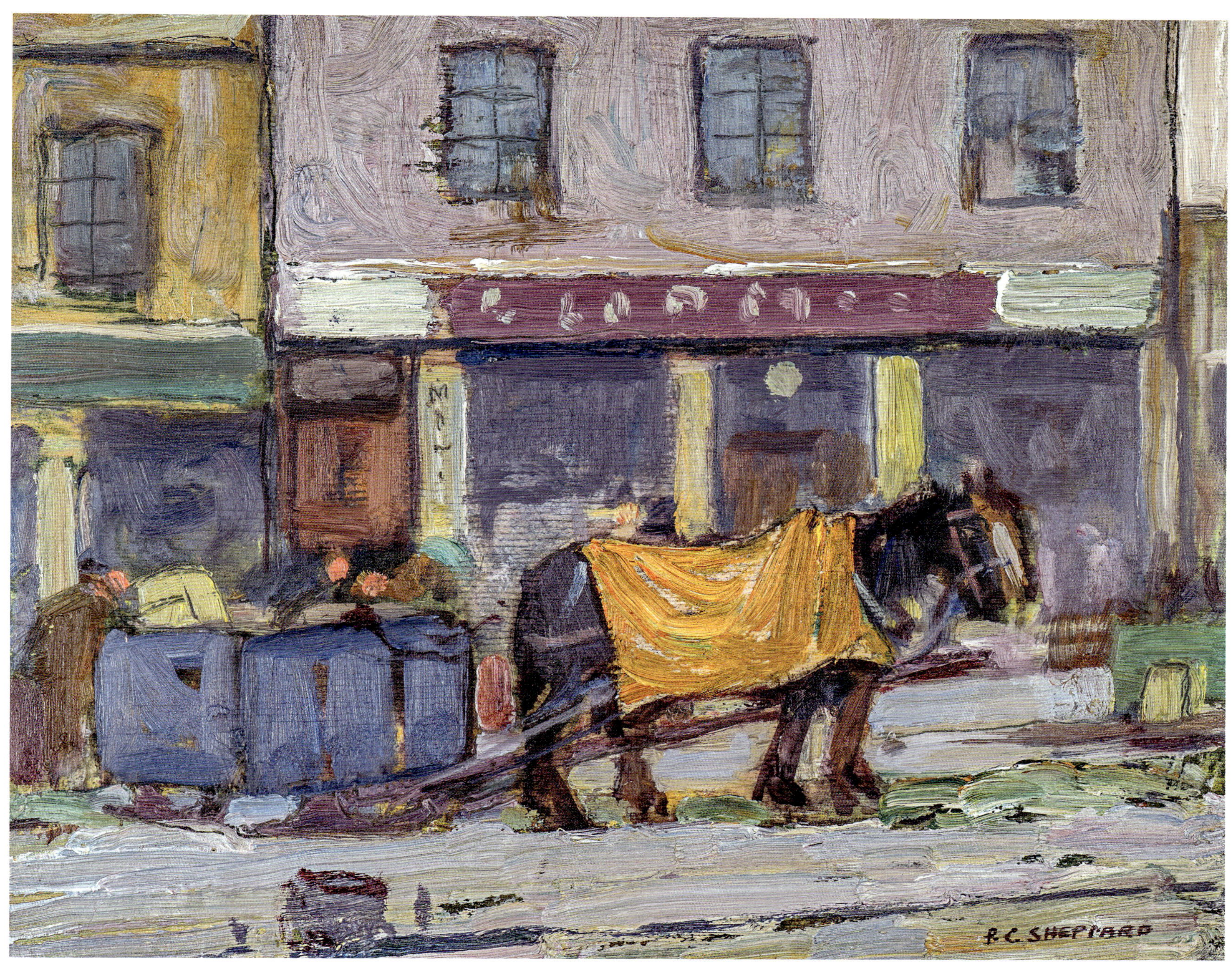

Market Scene, Montreal.
1926. Oil on board,
21.6 x 26.7 cm.

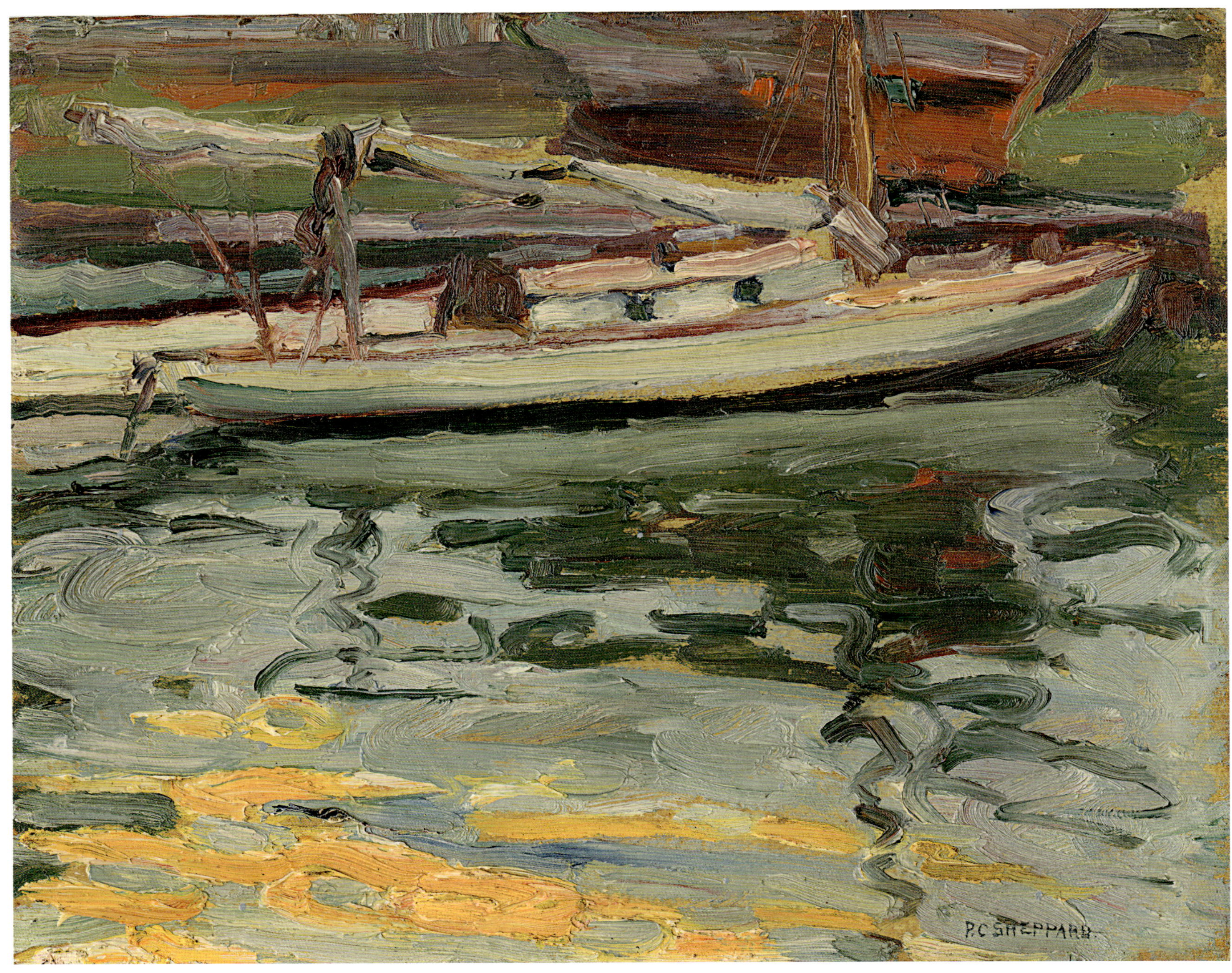

Sailboat at Dock.
1921. Oil on board,
21.6 x 26.7 cm.

hand as more than capable of painting in the advanced Impressionist manner, and on the other as being attuned to developments in New York City that valourized subjects drawn from and reflecting contemporary life in the city. The challenges that lay before him were: Would he continue to develop along the twin streams? Would he embrace only one? Or would he branch out and explore another painterly avenue, one that held equal sway in the Canadian art world? His oil sketches show the many directions he explored atistically and simultaneously.

INTERLUDE: OIL SKETCHES ON WOOD PANELS, 1920s

The broad spectrum of Sheppard's artistic practice is also well served by the collection of oil paintings on wood or paperboard panels that are held in the archive, which number well over 65 paintings, completed throughout the 1920s. With very few exceptions, the panels measure 21.6 x 26.7 cm, a size that was ideally suited to portability; the artist could easily carry them into the field and paint directly from nature. It is not an exaggeration to say that oil on panel was an emblematic medium of its time — the 1910s and 20s — a time in Canadian art when a generation of artists painted nature directly, honestly and as a conduit to transcendence and national identity. Intense study of nature, as is afforded in this painting technique, could give the sensation of being absorbed directly into the interpreted subject to such a degree that the artist's ego dissolved, allowing a kind of mystical intermingling of subject with object.

More than other transcendent processes, painting with a wood panel on your lap or easel had the capacity to deliver a sense of this intercommunion, and this promise no doubt attracted Sheppard and his peers to exploring panel painting ardently. Given the nature of the wooden paintboxes of the day — they were about the size of a typical leather briefcase and had slotted grooves cut into the inside frame of the box's top — the wood panels, when completed, could be filed in the grooves in a way that the wet paint surface of one panel would not touch the back of the next. This system of panel painting and paintbox filing ideally suited the hunger for plein-air painting that many a Canadian favoured, including the members of the Group of Seven. Sheppard, too, adopted this portable system, which allowed him to satisfy his own need to paint in the open. The resulting paintings almost all reflect an expressionistic manner that conveys a vividness and directness that contrasts with the more

controlled nature of his studio paintings. Small-format paintings served several purposes: they were not only traces of experiences with the land and the views in front of the easel, but also preliminary studies that were later worked up into studio works; as well, they were autonomous expressions in their own right.

When looking through the stacks of panels in the archive, leafing through them one after another, I become ever more absorbed by the evident ease with which Sheppard set down his thoughts and experiences in paint. The pigment is laid on in a manner that says he was comfortable with his media; Sheppard luxuriated in the stuff with which he made paintings. The oils are brushed on in ways that take full advantage of their subtle viscosity to suggest the movements, rhythms and textures of the components of his subject matter. Expressive, sensual, lyrical and, at times, visually simulating a kind of musical cadence — Sheppard released uncanniness in his materials. The panels speak to me with a directness that compresses the decades between Sheppard and me to such an extent that, perhaps more than all the other work of art in the archive, they give me a window on the man as an expressive individual: an artist.

The panels are not only landscapes; there are also boats, harbour views and lake views, underscoring Sheppard's abiding interest in interpreting urban life and the commerce of the lakes. These paintings range from studies of water — eddies and ripples — to picturesque views of sailboats and steamers that allowed for lovely painterly handling of media and colours.

There are vivid, clear pictures of freighters set against expressive skies lusciously described by the gestures of brush and pigment. One panel, a lakeside view with freighters in the distance (see page 164), depicts a gorgeous, sensual, light-palette rendering of the boats as indistinct impressions set off by a radiant, dynamic sky where the brush has laid on paint to give a sense of the air's humid density. Another concentrates on a side view of a passenger steamer with tugs in the foreground (see page 165), which serve as supports for the interplay of wonderfully dynamic colour relationships involving purples, yellows, greens and reds. A third subverts the expected representation of a freighter's hull, making it a metaphor of a painter's canvas or panel (see page 168). In a fourth, the hull is a stand-in for a painter's canvas or board (see page 169). Yet another depicts a tugboat as an anthropomorphized form (see page 172) — a sturdy presence in an industrial, lakeside landscape. In contrast to the usual painterly look of the panels, several in the collection, among them a view of two freighters (see page 173), seem more drawing than painting.

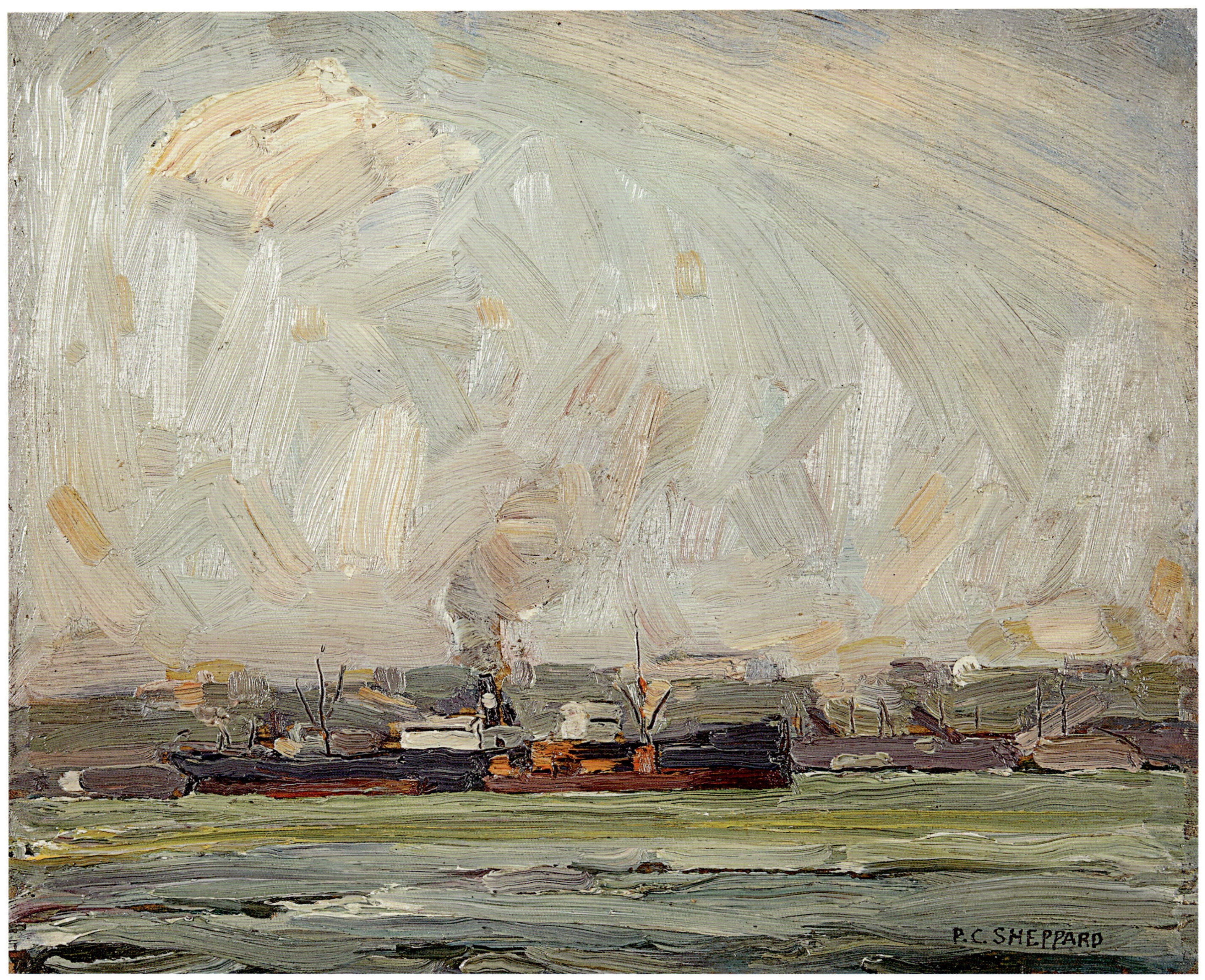

Freighters in Harbour.
1921. Oil on board,
21.6 x 26.7 cm.

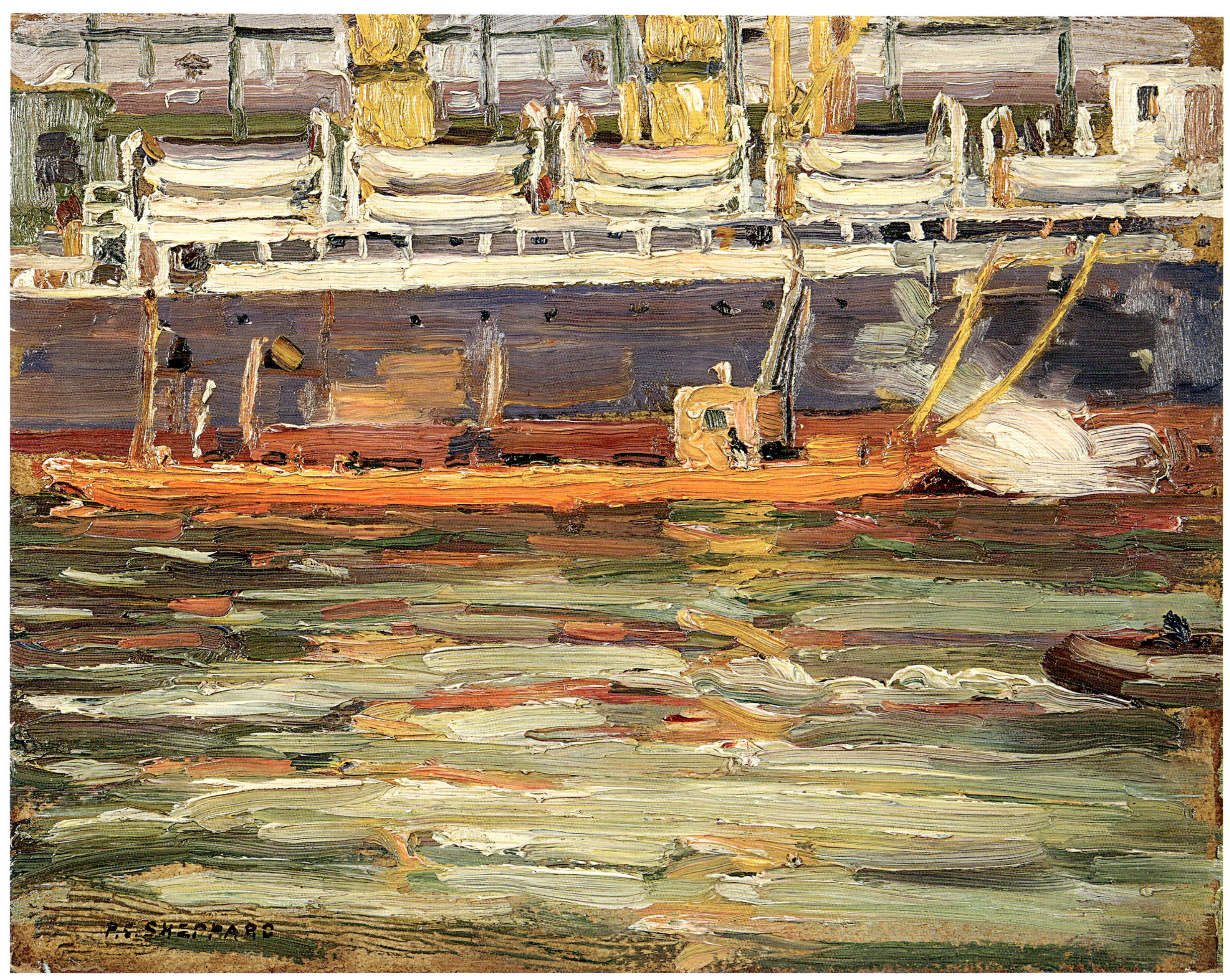

Ships in Harbour.
1921. Oil on board,
21.6 x 26.7 cm.

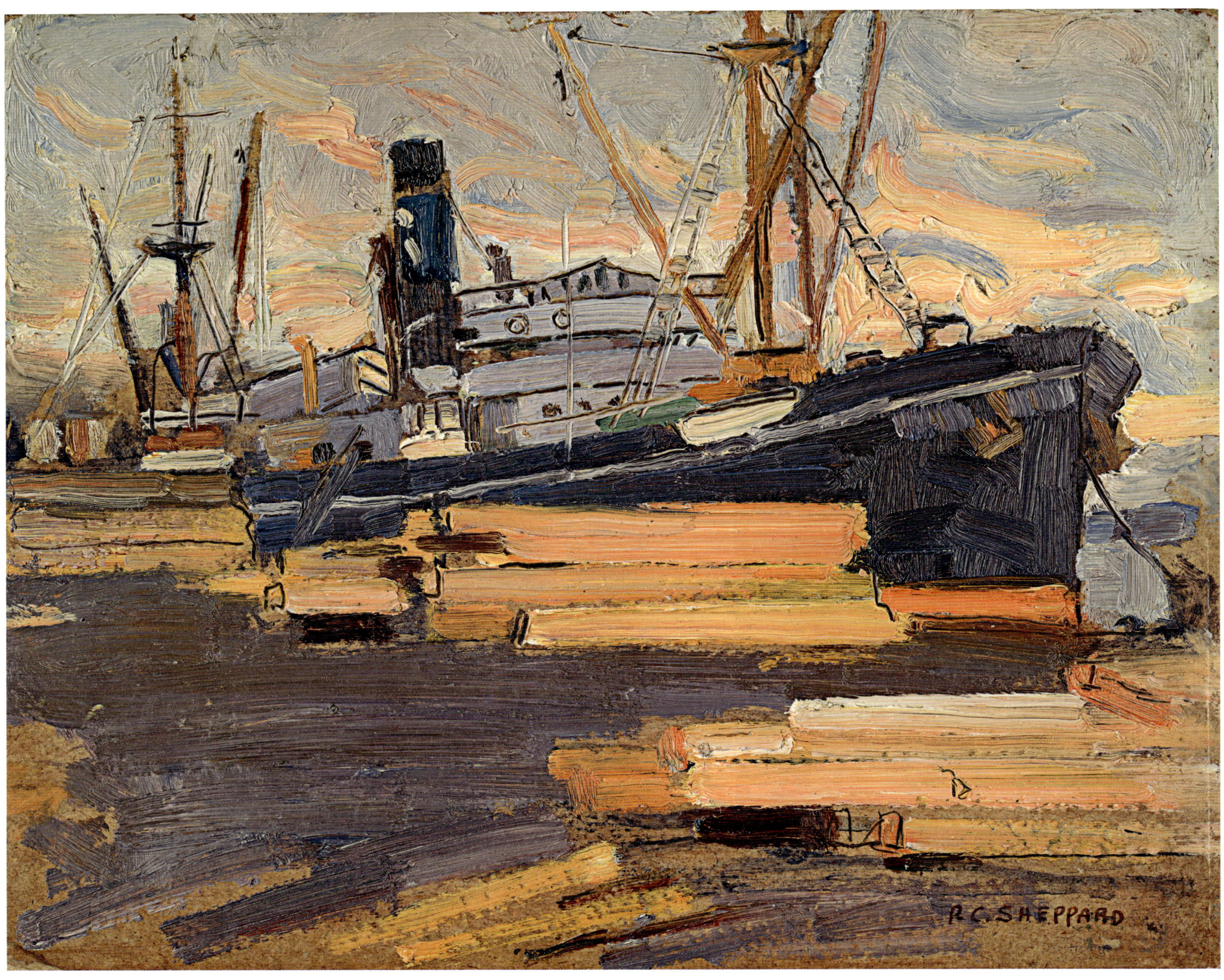

Ships in Harbour.
1922. Oil on board,
21.6 x 26.7 cm.

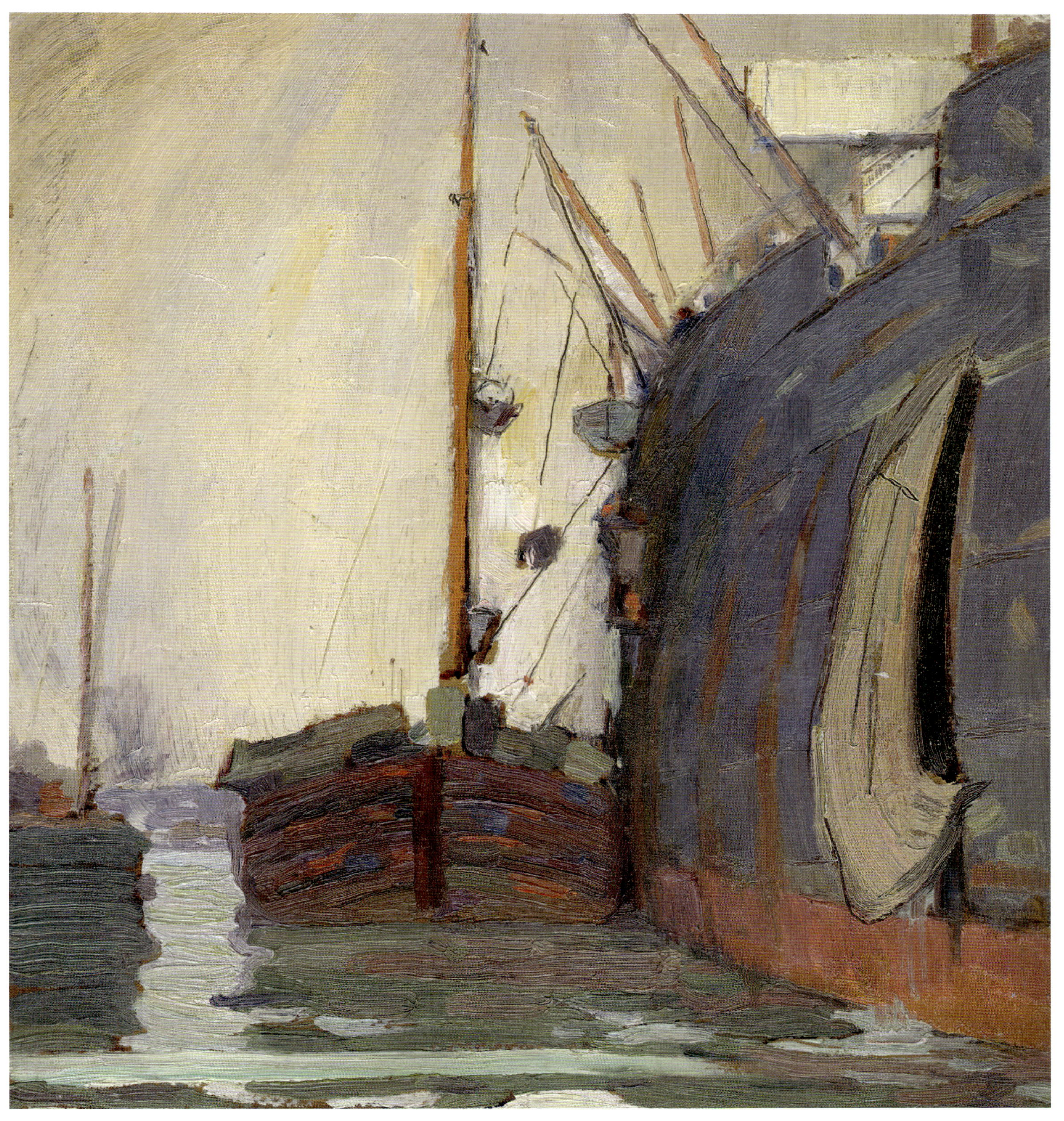

Ship Offloading.
1921. Oil on board,
30.4 x 28 cm.

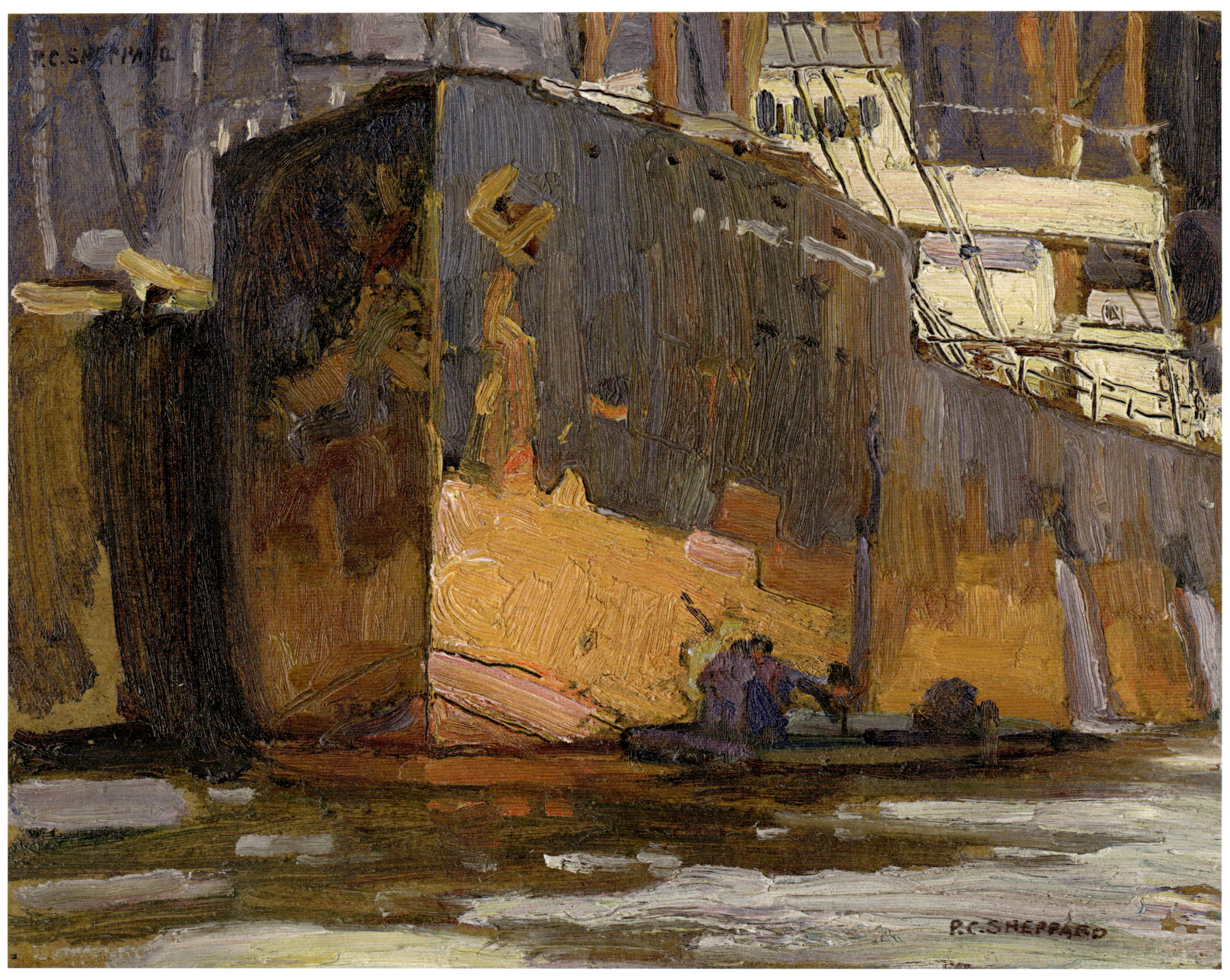

Oiling Up.
1922. Oil on board,
21.6 x 26.7 cm.

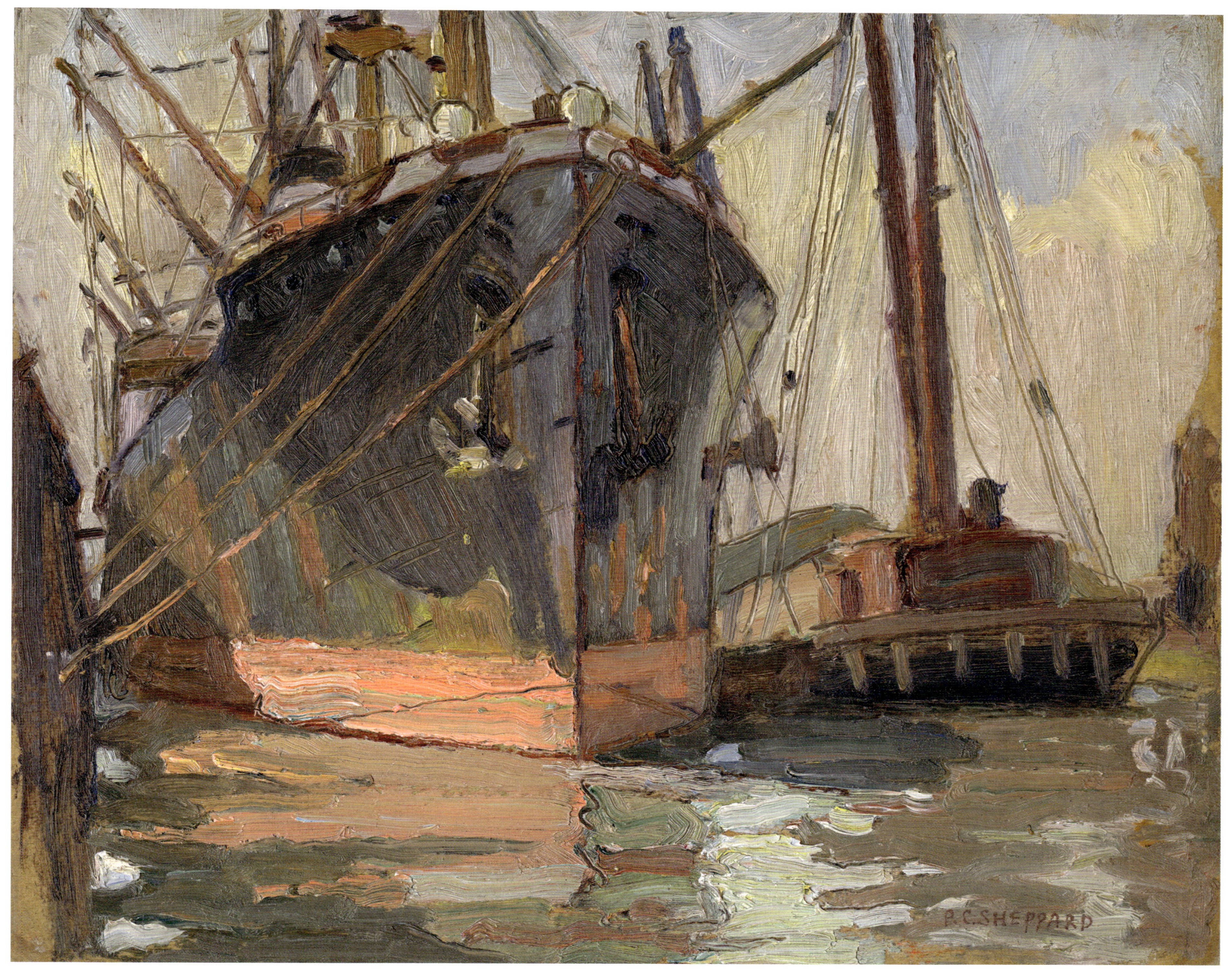

Freighter.
1922. Oil on board,
21.6 x 26.7 cm.

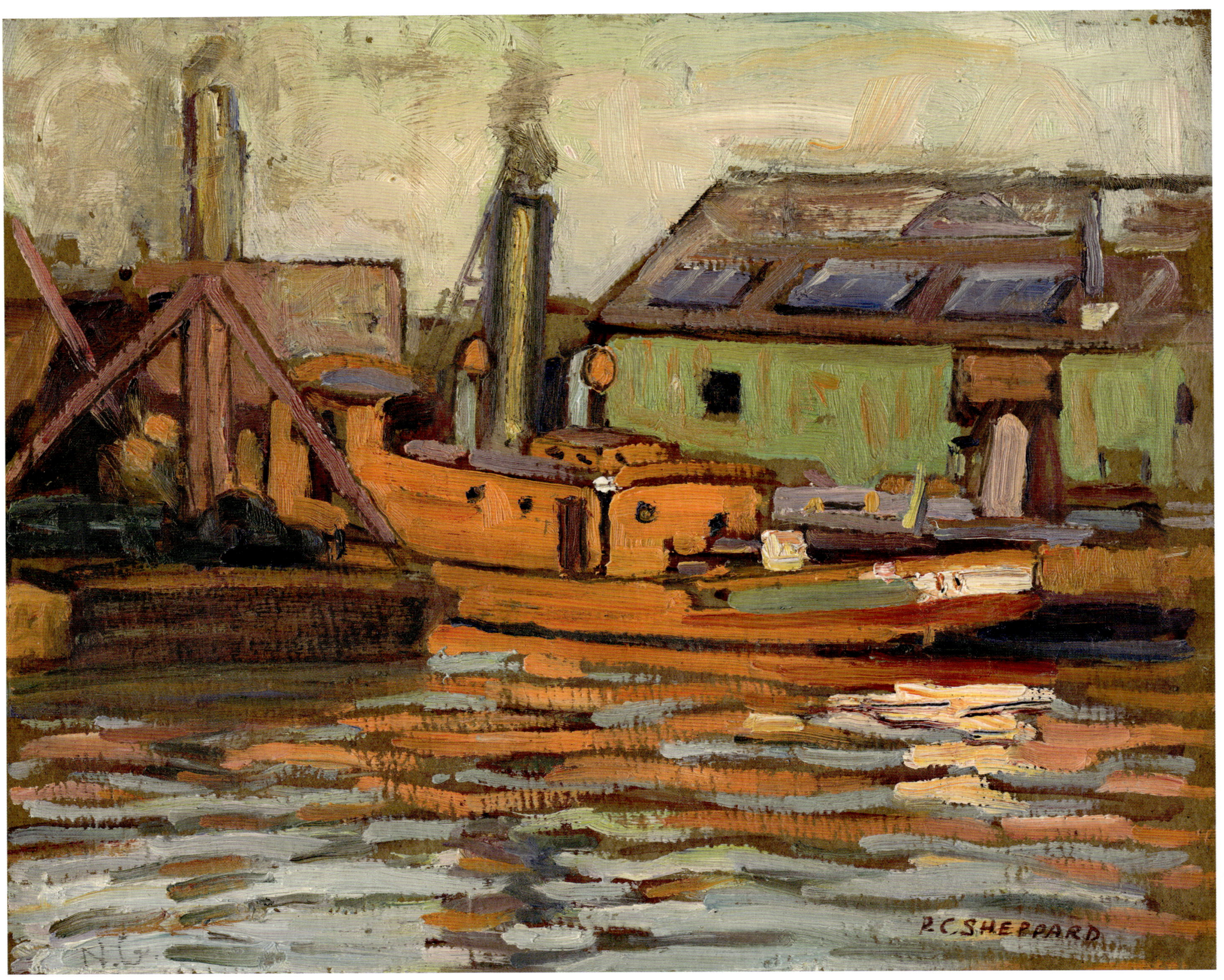

Tugboat at Dock.
1926. Oil on board,
21.6 x 26.7 cm.

Indeed, Sheppard's approaches to the conventions associated with an open-air oil panel painting reflect his creative agility and sheer technical aplomb. In terms of relegating the subject a mere excuse for abstraction, to many of the paintings are analytical in the way Sheppard takes down his subjects. For example, a hillside landscape (see page 174) serves the purpose of a visual analysis of how a landscape can be broken down into ever-smaller cubes and triangles arranged on a colour-field hillside. A market scene (page 175) is a dynamic Impressionist interpretation of the subject where two horizontal bands of light pigment are emphasized to signify snow; they also double as elegant framing devices for depicting the theatre of the street. A painting of an orange tugboat (see page 170) betrays a sensibility that accentuates expression rather than a mere desire to convey an impression, a prosaic subject or a piece of illustration; Sheppard wants the boat to be weighted with allusiveness and emotional baggage.

Just when the artist appears to be a latent abstractionist closeted inside the skin of a realist, he sets down his interpretation of dories and a fish plant as a gorgeously descriptive composition in which a large dark doorway sucks the eye into the scene and also into the painterly space (see *The Red Boathouse,* below). A scene of men in a rowboat at the bow of a freighter (see page 178) shows Sheppard's chops as a colourist. Here, hues are applied in strong passages to lend an effect of expression in an abstracted composition where forms have been flattened into dynamic shapes that drift away from specific references. Synaesthesia also seems to have attracted Sheppard. In a painting of rapids (see page 179), he captures the rhythms of rushing water cascading over rocks in a way that simulates sound waves. Similarly, a study of pine trees (see page 186) shows how he subverted brushstrokes and the depiction of the trees themselves to give a painted trace of wind gusting in the sunlit landscape. In the heavenly shades of blues, ceruleans and lapis the wind is strongly suggested as a visible, living presence.

Sheppard could not help but be an artist of his time, when the panel sketch was much in vogue as a means of painting in and from nature. An autumn landscape (see page 176) shows a debt to the work of his Group of Seven peers, especially A.Y. Jackson, who turned his hand to many a similar view. Was Sheppard aping a group style in his autumn landscape, which

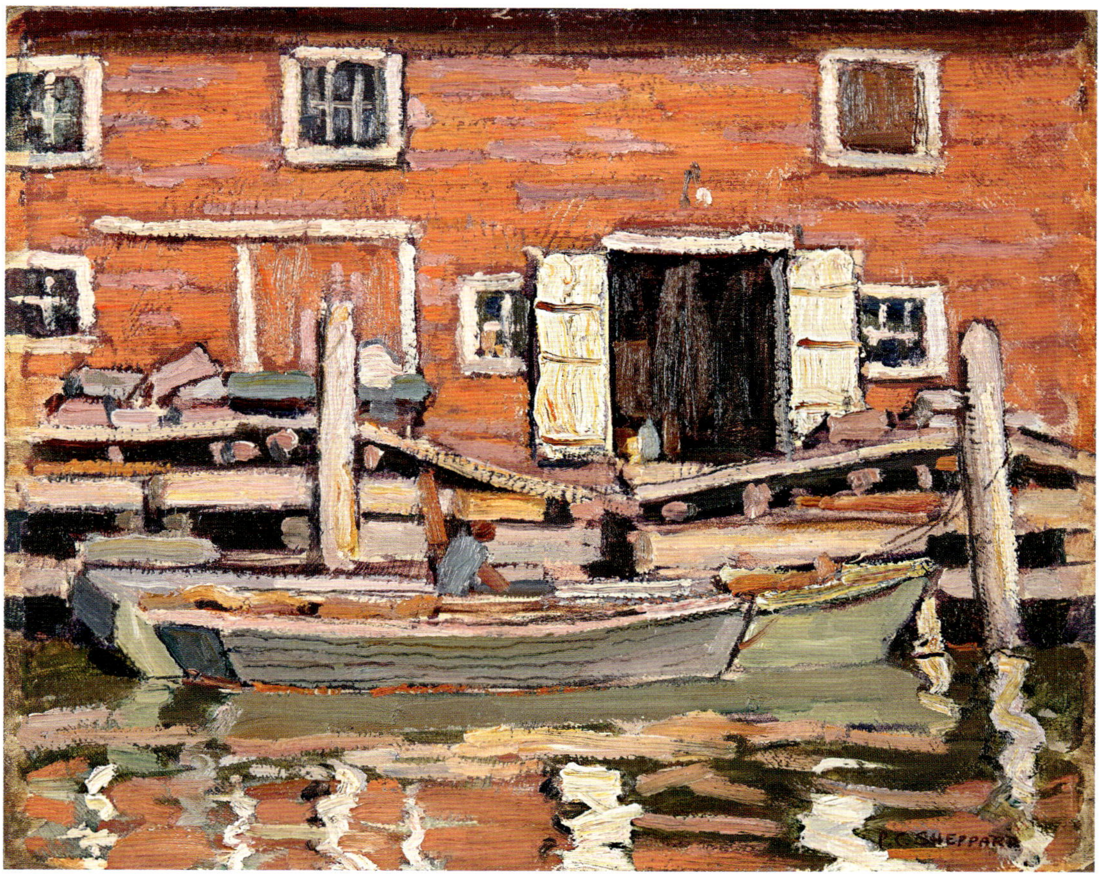

The Red Boathouse.
1926. Oil on board,
21.6 x 26.7 cm.

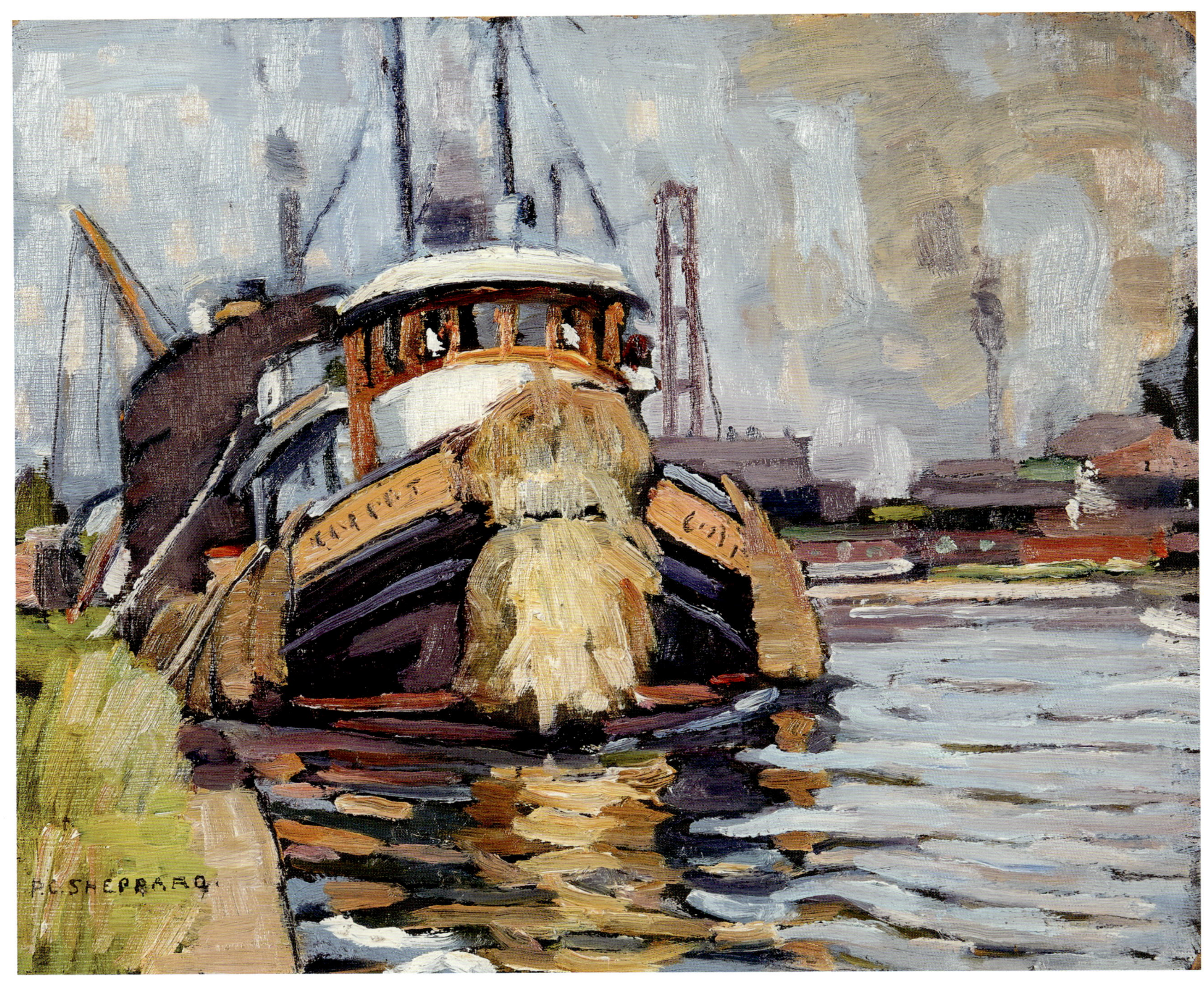

Tugboat.
1922. Oil on board,
21.6 x 26.7 cm.

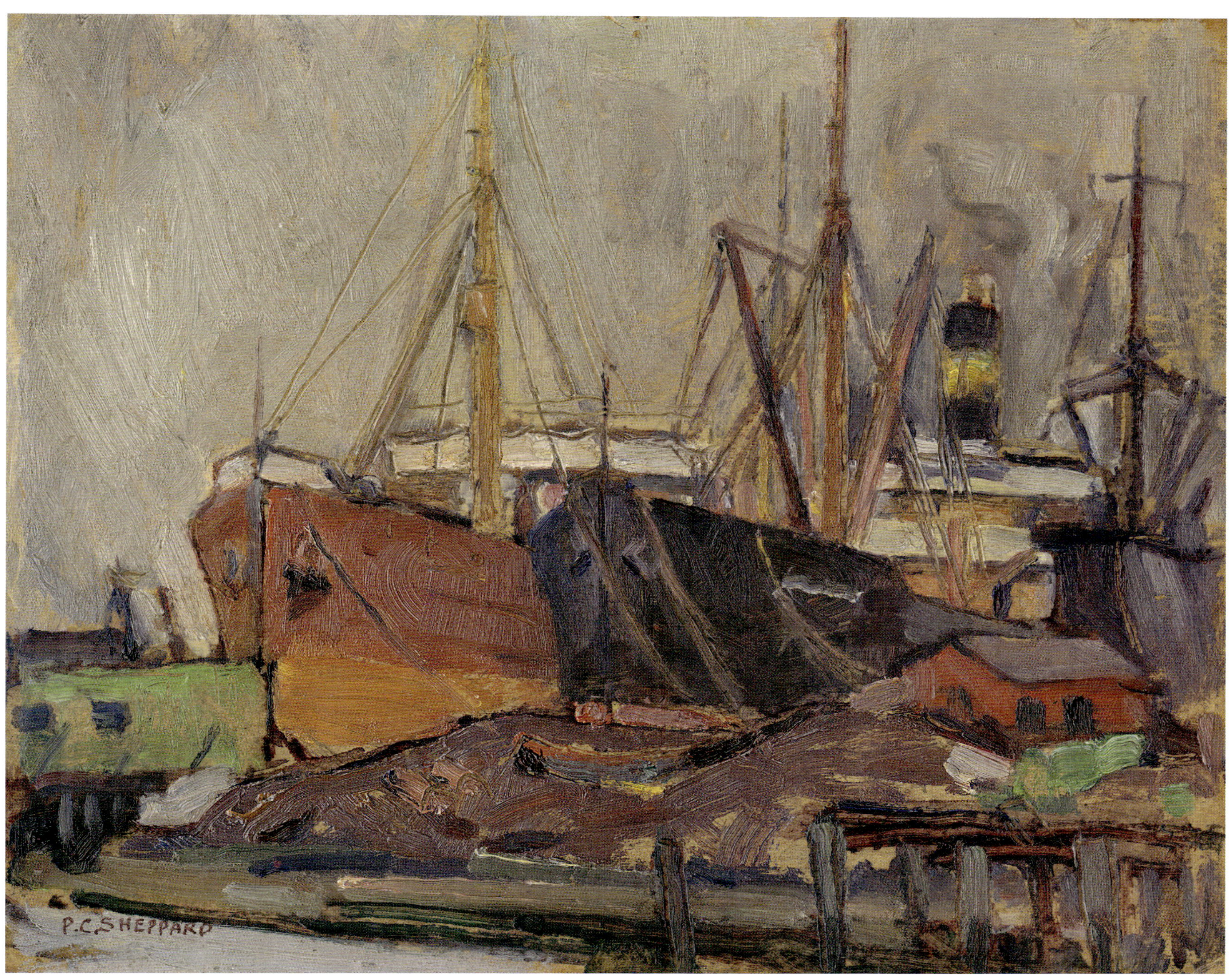

Ships in Harbour.
1922. Oil on board,
21.6 x 26.7 cm.

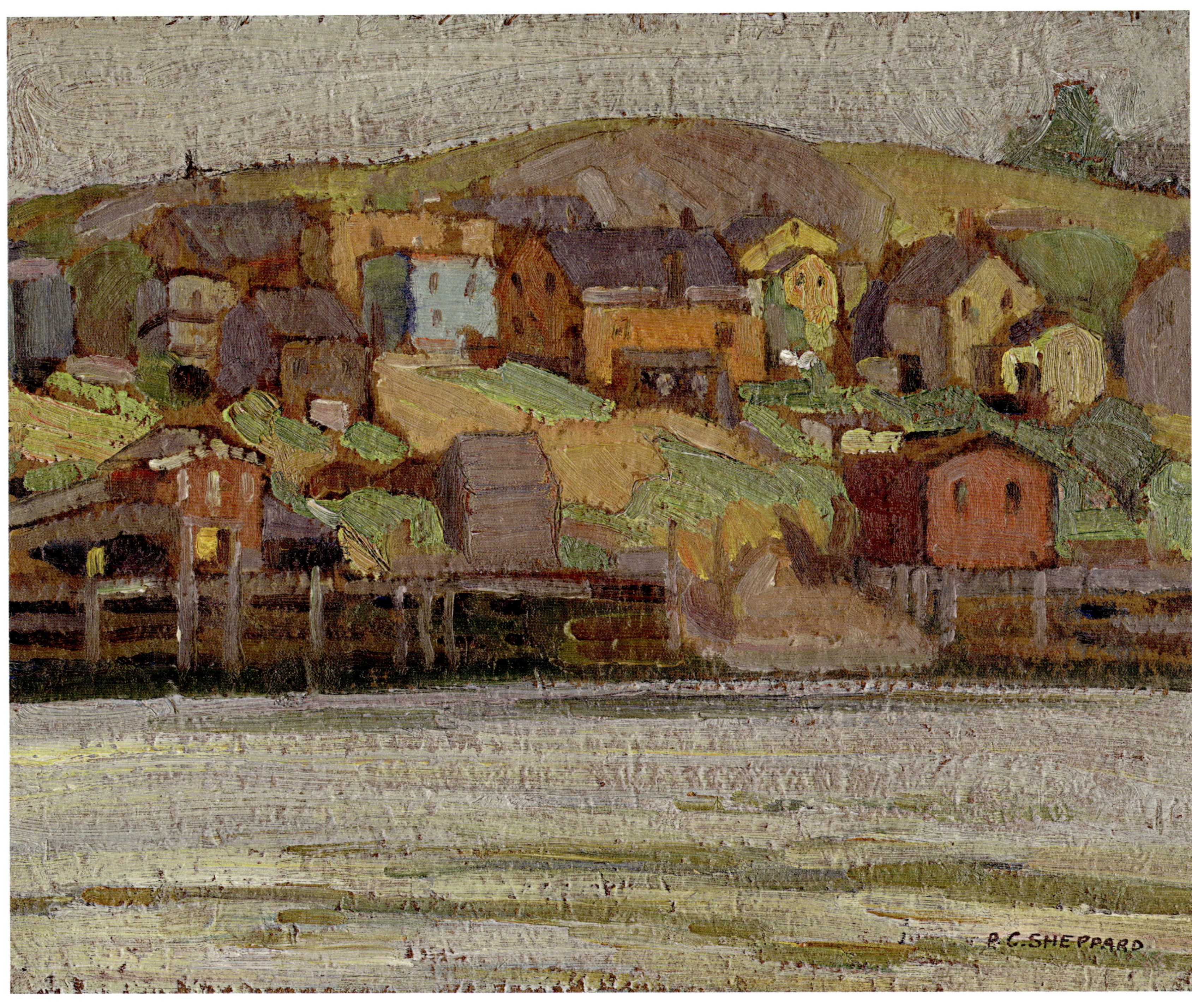

Lunenburg, Nova Scotia.
1924. Oil on board,
21.6 x 26.7 cm.

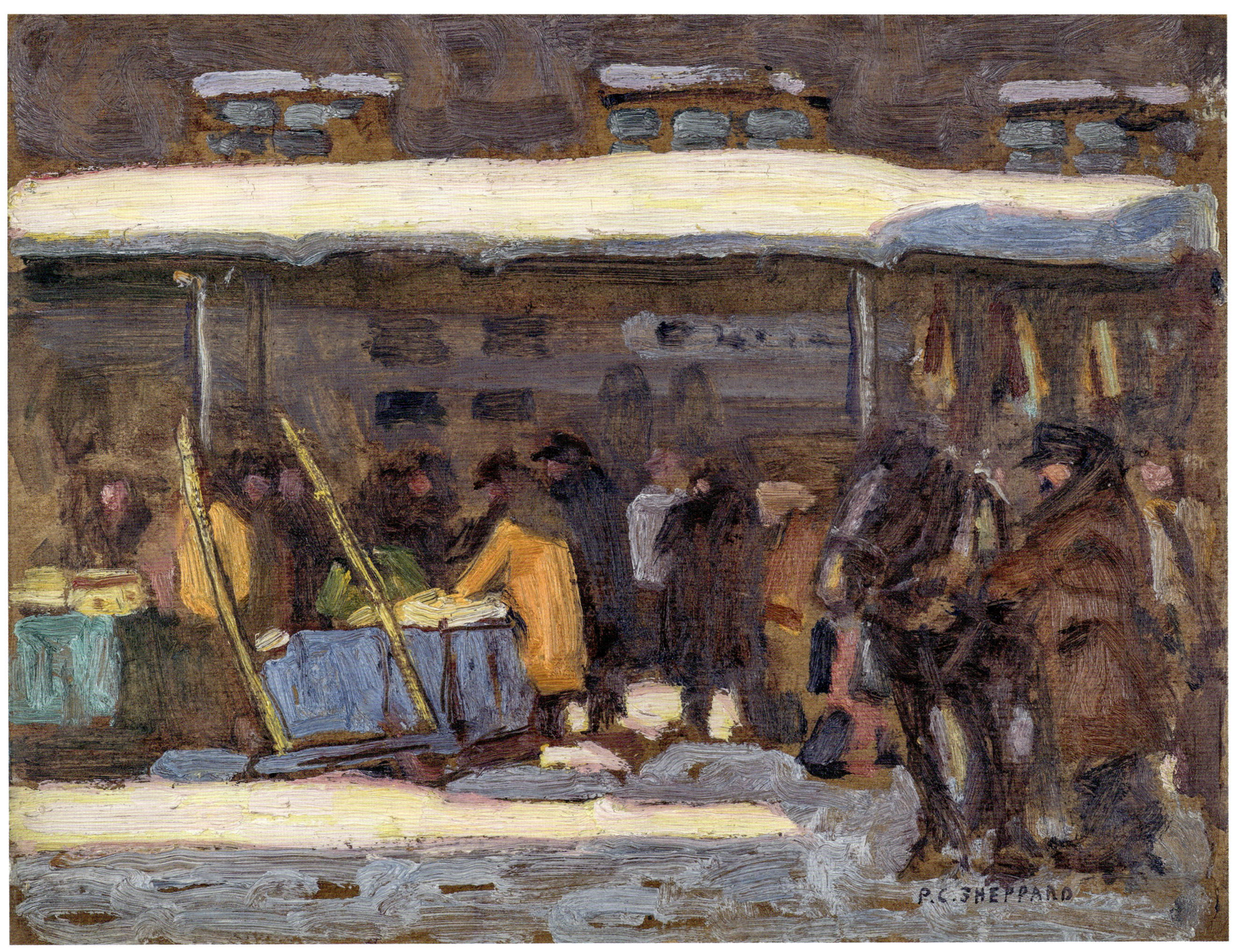

Market Scene, Montreal.
1926. Oil on board,
21.6 x 26.7 cm.

shows a controlled handling of paint in an uncharacteristic manner, even for Sheppard? To my eye this panel bears the unmistakable spectres of the styles and manners not only of Jackson, but also of J.E.H. MacDonald and Tom Thomson. A study of sky and shore (page 177) looks like a Franklin Carmichael painting in the ways it delineates the separations of colour zones. Even so, Sheppard appears to have rejected this manner because, for him, the way the paint is laid on lacks forcefulness. And, not to limit his art history allusions to Canadian antecedents, the artist shows himself emulating the example of the late 19th-century French Post-Impressionist painter and member of the Nabis movement, Émil Bernard (1868–1941); Sheppard's forest interior and tree trunk (see page 180), rendered in sharp yellows set off against the dark grey foil of the trunk, has a clear echo in the work of this French near contemporary. The Norwegian Edvard Munch (1863–1944) also appears to have influenced a Sheppard panel; the moody landscape of a church spire silhouetted against an evening sky (see page 187) recalls Munch's treatment of colours and forms to create sensate visual analogues of sounds and smells.

Just when it seems that Sheppard's work is formulaic, even rote, in the way it set down subjects and experiences, a panel appears from the archived stacks to show that he was an original voice in a crowded theatre of landscapists. His study of water patterns (see page 184) is a masterwork, a beautiful sketch that seeks to capture abstract qualities liberated by light and water bordered by a rocky shoreline. I find this a very satisfying painting in all the multi-hued cacophony of sketch panels. It is tightly composed around a white splash of paint in the upper left quadrant, and energized by jagged ochre passages of pigment

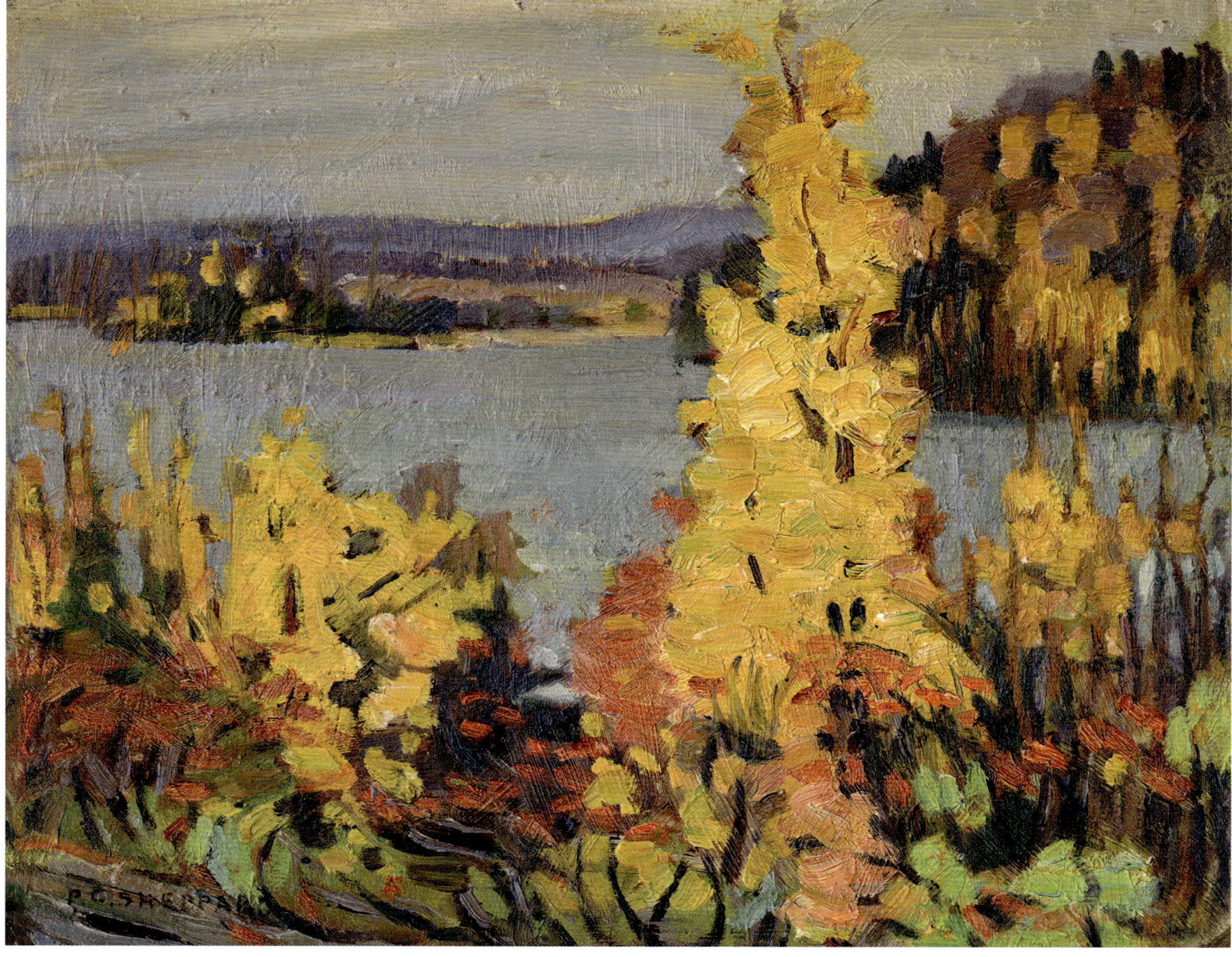

Lake View, Autumn.
1928. Oil on board,
21.6 x 26.7 cm.

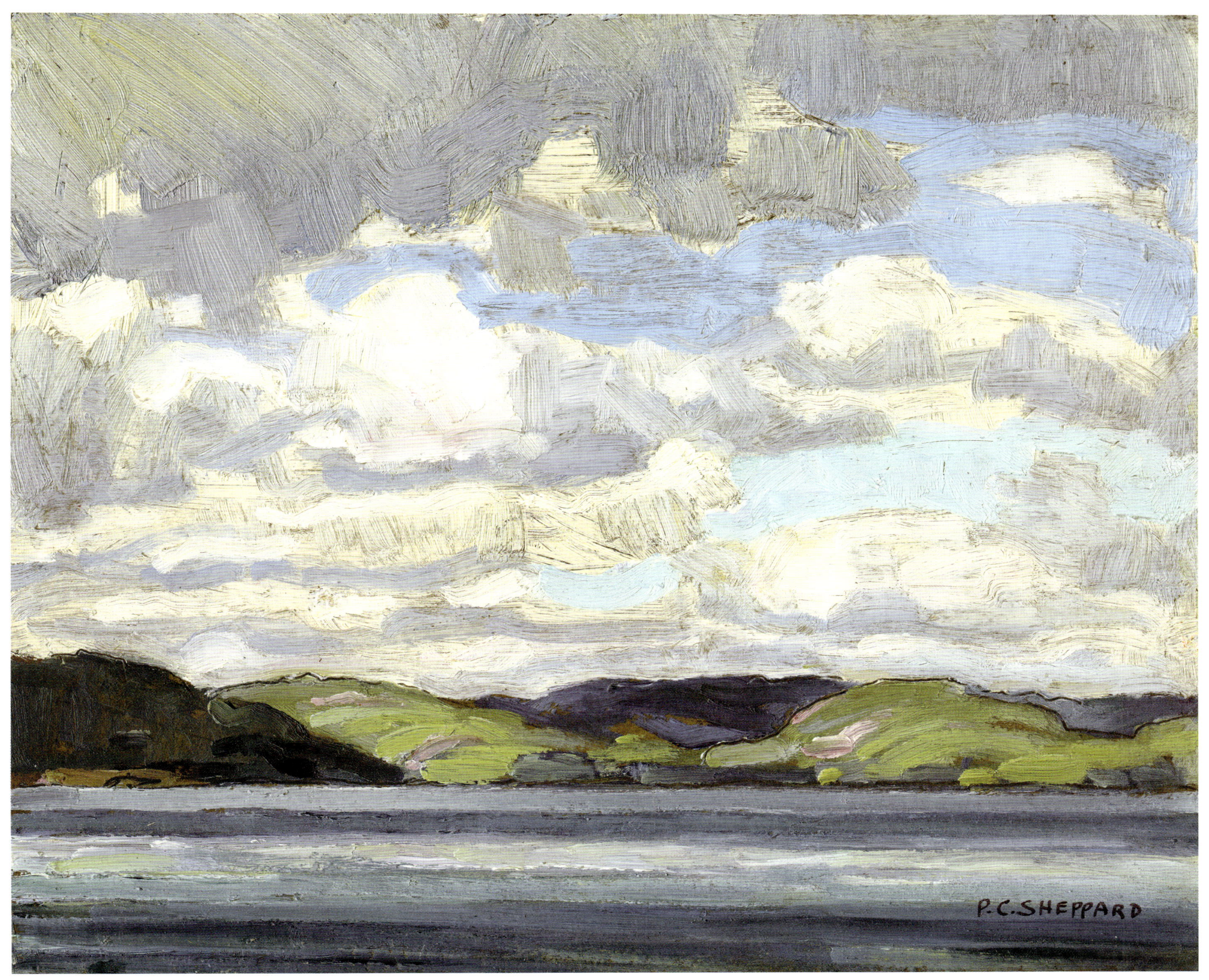

Cloudscape over Lake and Hills.
1928. Oil on board,
21.6 x 26.7 cm.

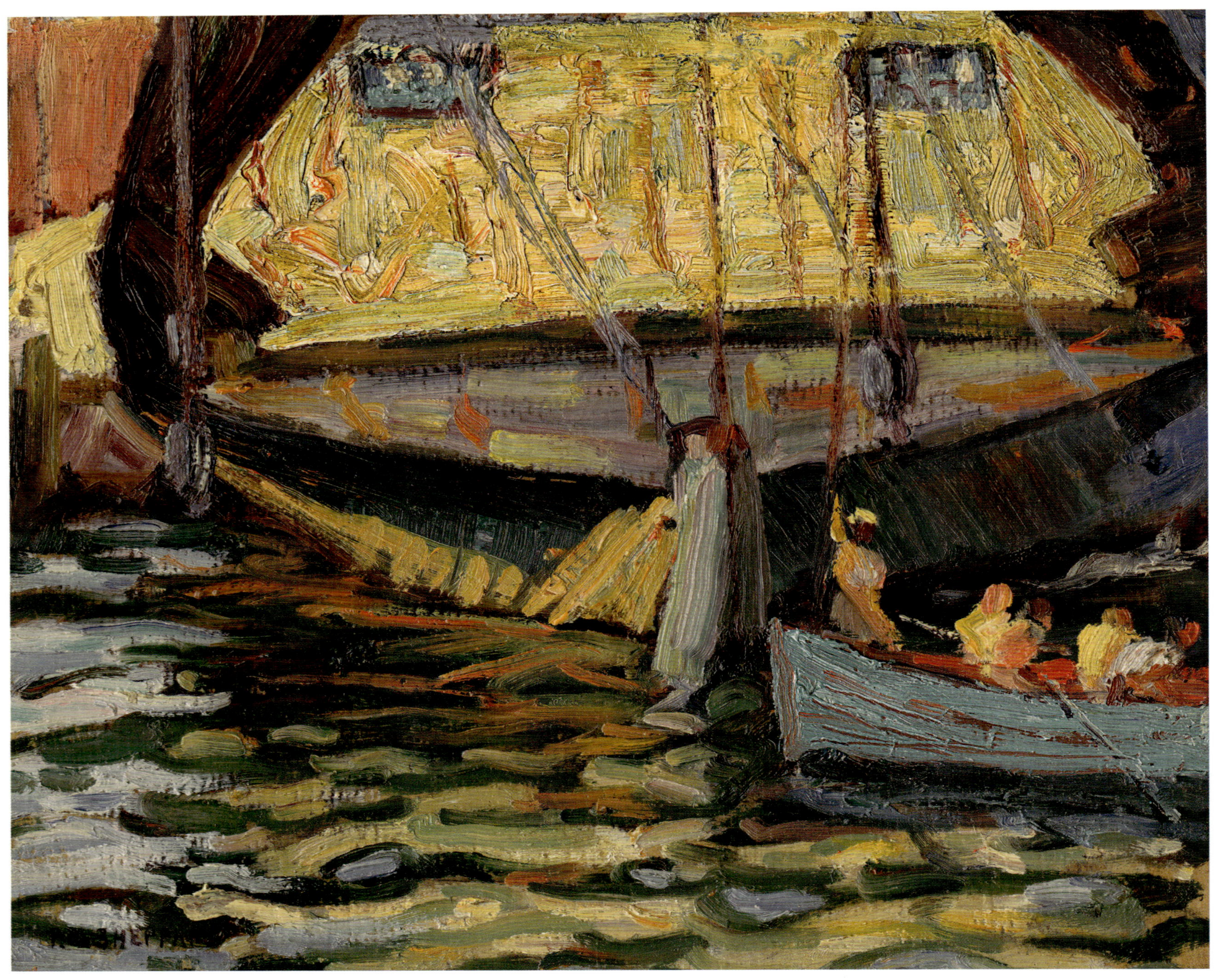

Oiling Up.
1926. Oil on board,
21.6 x 26.7 cm.

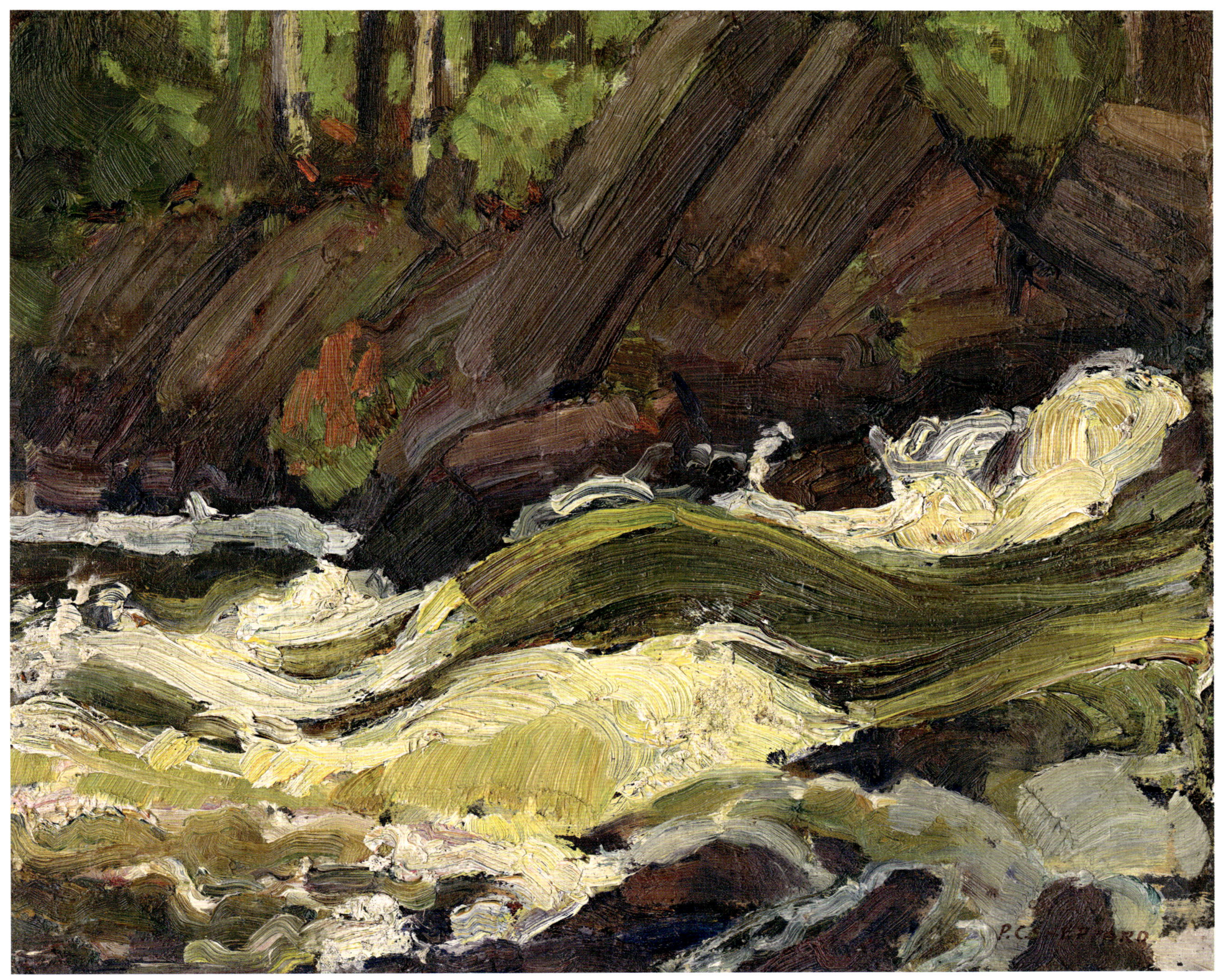

Hollow River.
1926. Oil on board,
21.6 x 26.7 cm.

at the upper right. *Waterfall* (see page 185) is an exceptional painting in the portfolio of panels. It is analytical and expressive, referential yet abstracted, energetic and beautifully painted. In aggregate, its many attributes signify Sheppard's affection for this wilderness idyll and this time in Canadian art. A similar complex vivacity is evident in another forest scene involving rapids (see page 181). A remarkable painting, this small panel is a compact, crackling composition that is more abstract than referential, incorporating dynamic brushstrokes in a composition that radiates around an electrical spark of a painted passage that is no more than a speck of pure orange.

The selection of panels is not limited to shorelines, riverbanks and forest floors. Sheppard also painted close to home, being inspired by locations not too far removed from Toronto. A set of panels of the Scarborough Bluffs on Lake Ontario (see pages 182 and 183) is gorgeously rendered to convey the expansive lake view through very few visual references. The scenes are

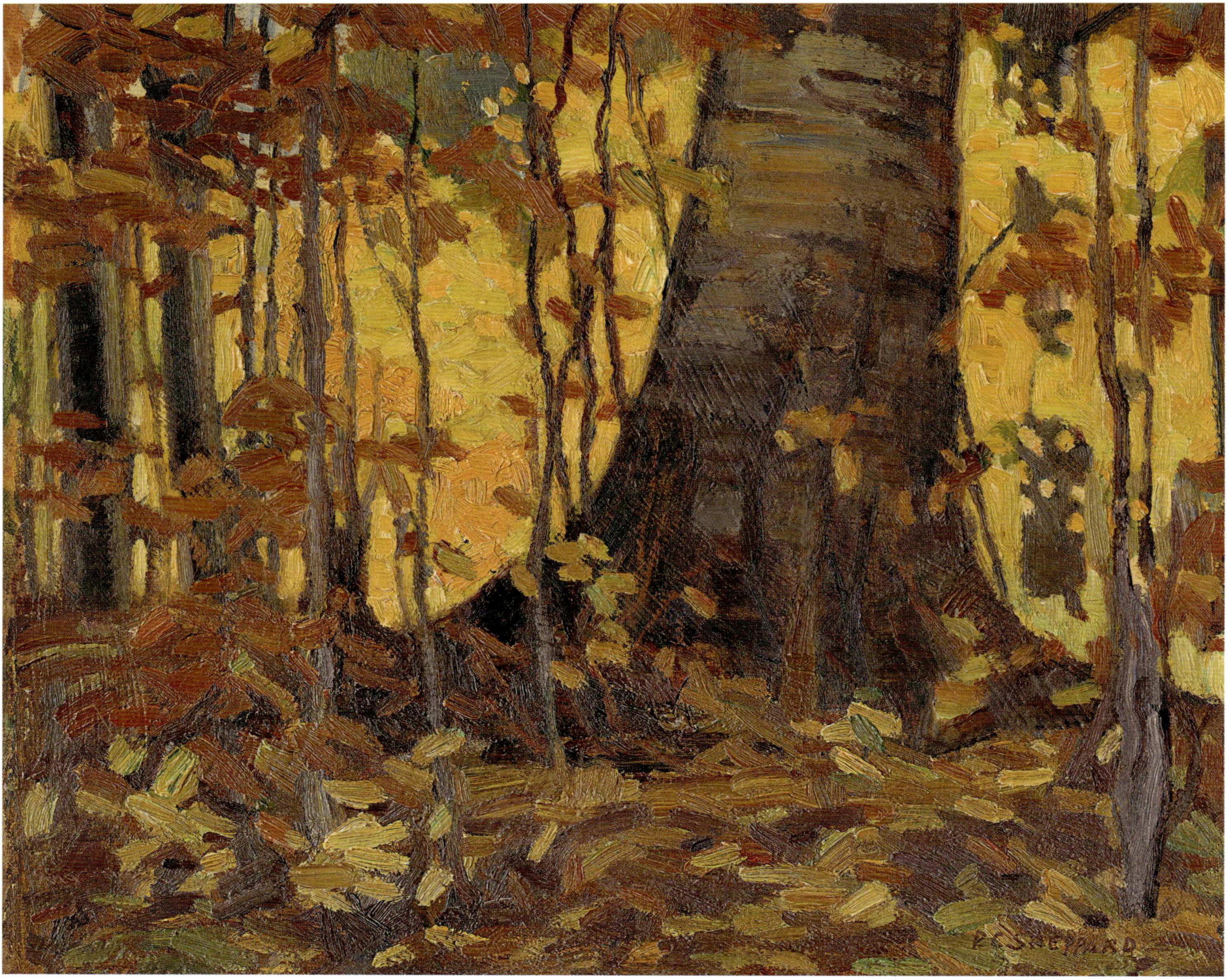

Forest Floor, Autumn.
1928. Oil on board,
21.6 x 26.7 cm.

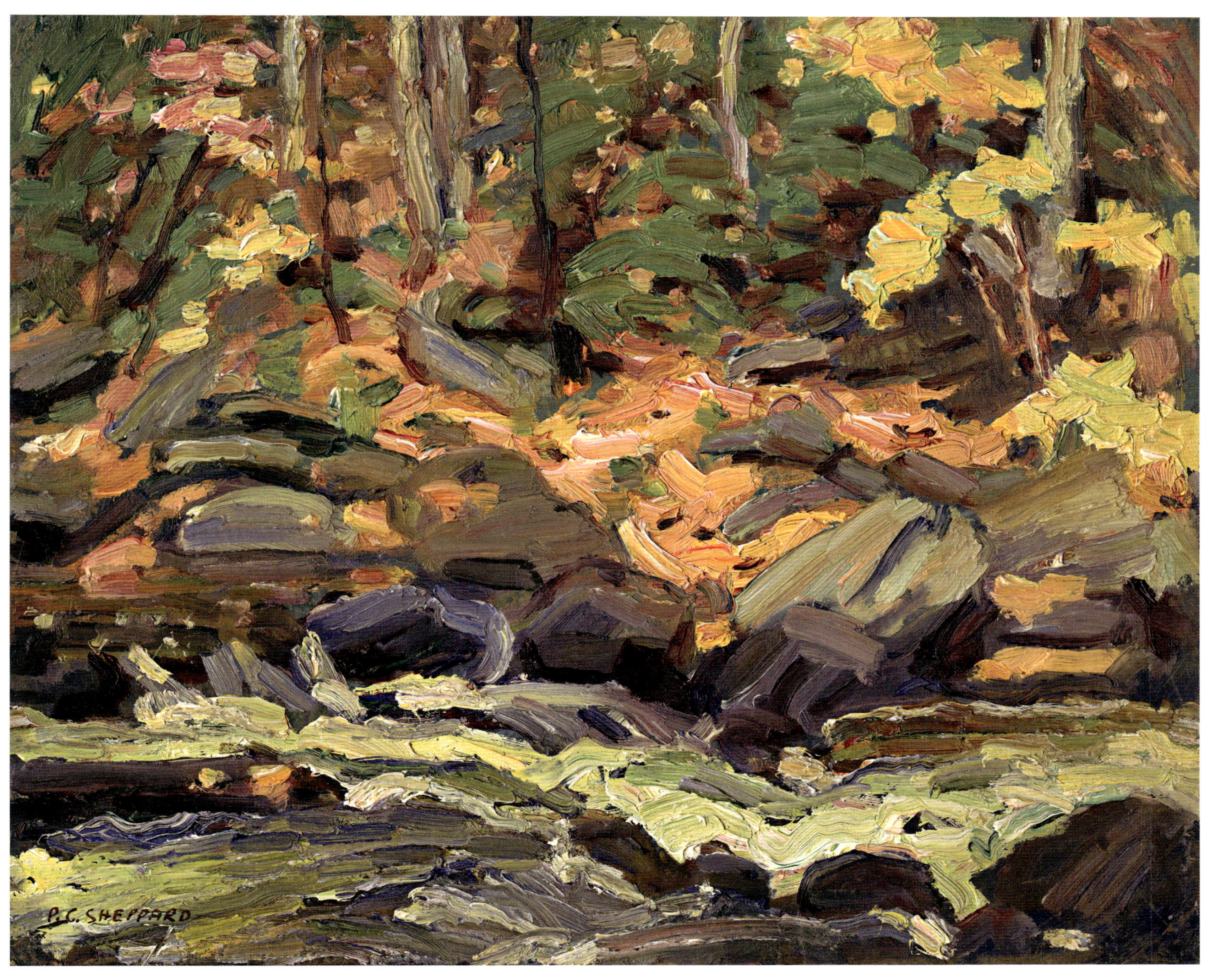

Northern Rapids and Forest, Autumn.
1929. Oil on board,
21.6 x 26.7 cm.

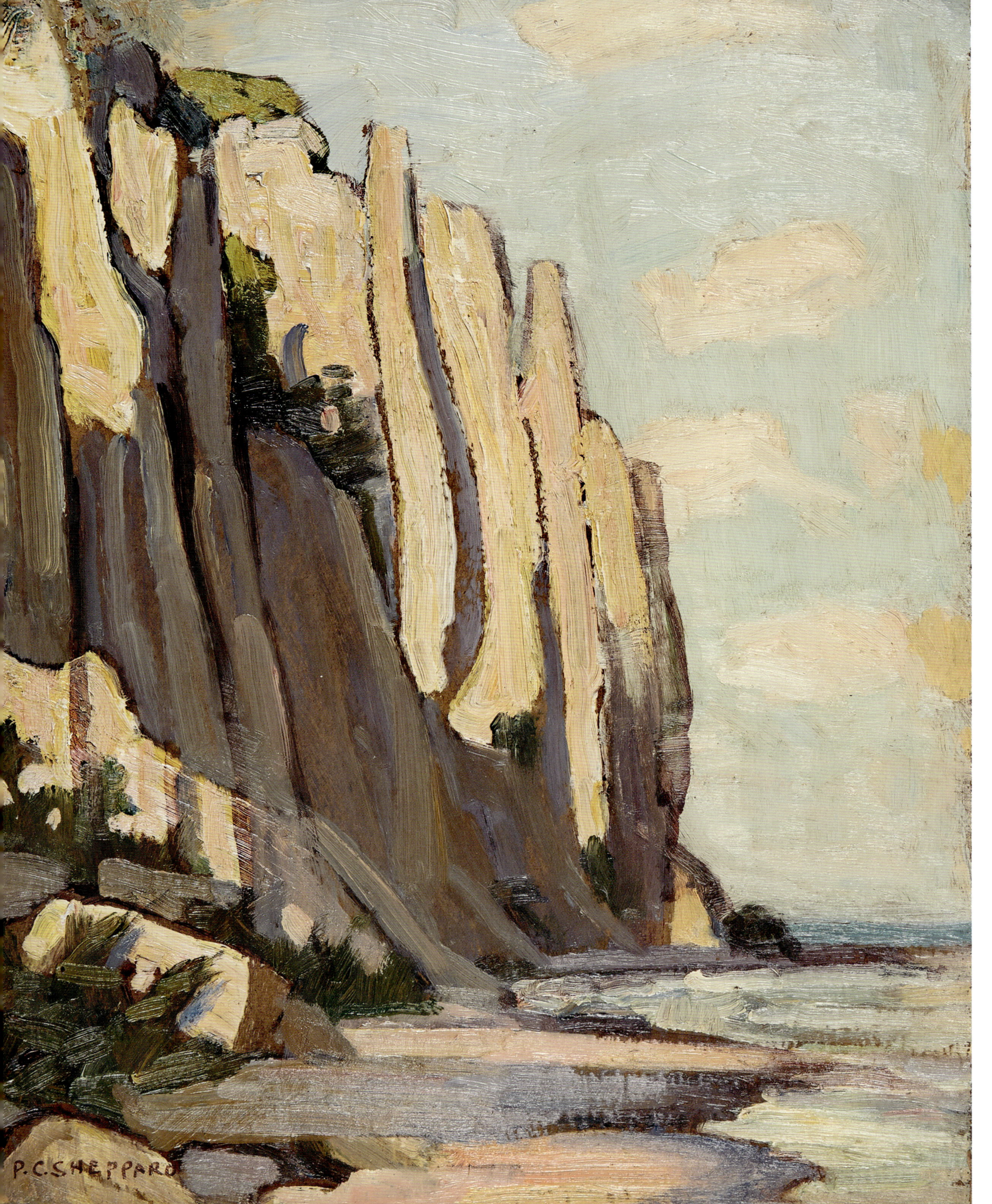

Scarborough Bluffs.
1929. Oil on board,
26.7 x 21.6 cm.

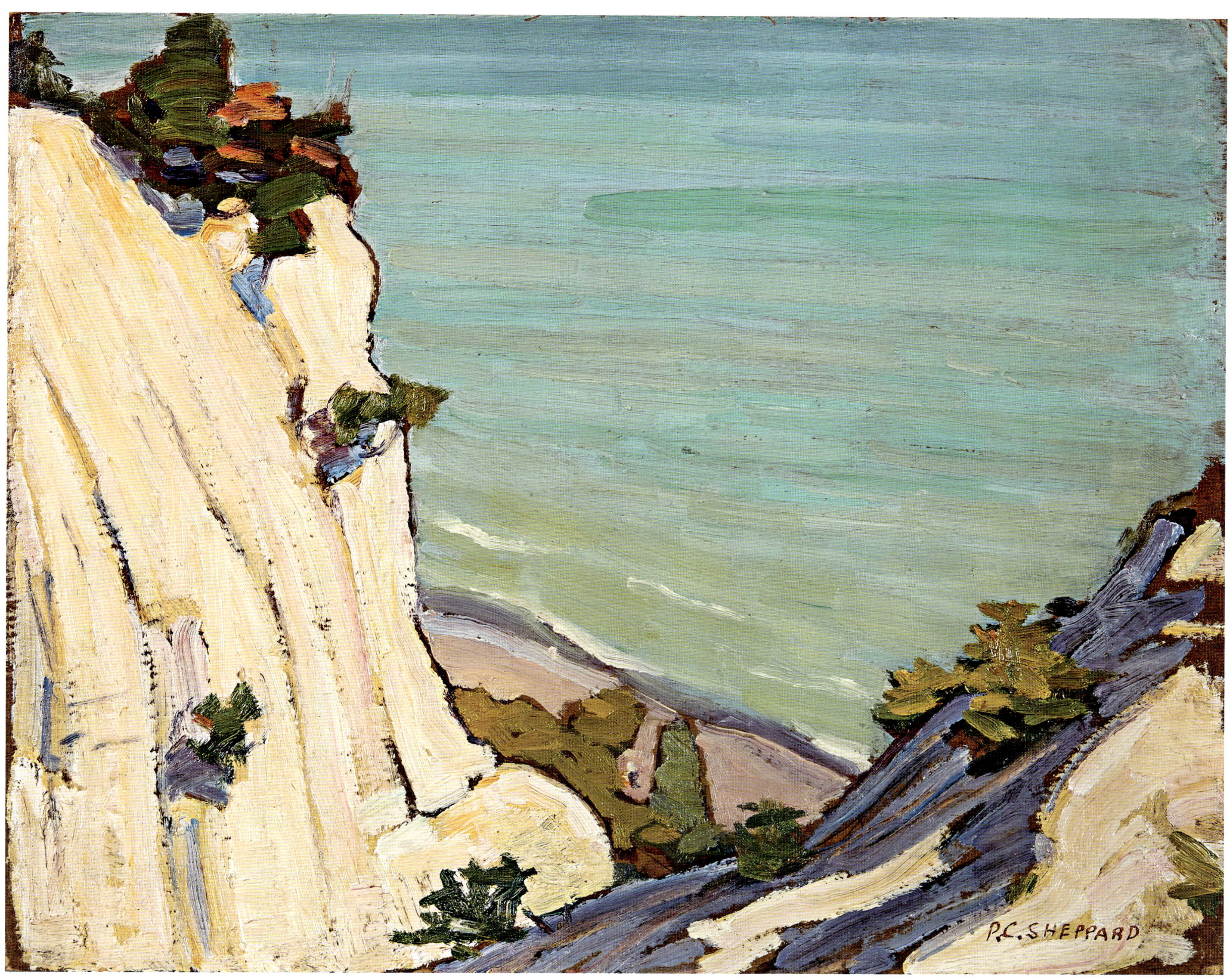

Scarborough Bluffs, Lake Ontario.
1929. Oil on board,
21.6 x 26.7 cm.

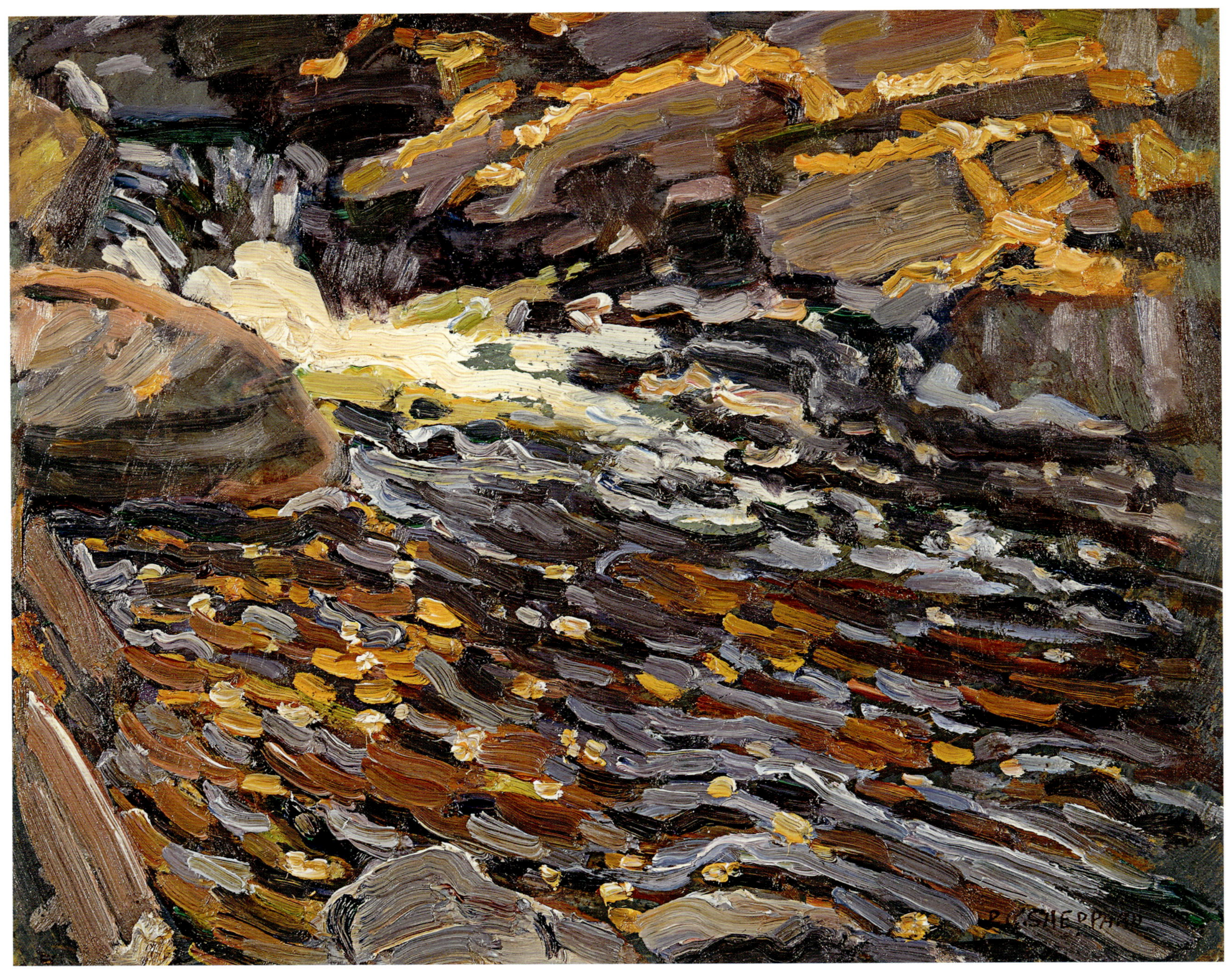

Rushing River, Muskoka.
1929. Oil on board,
21.6 x 26.7 cm.

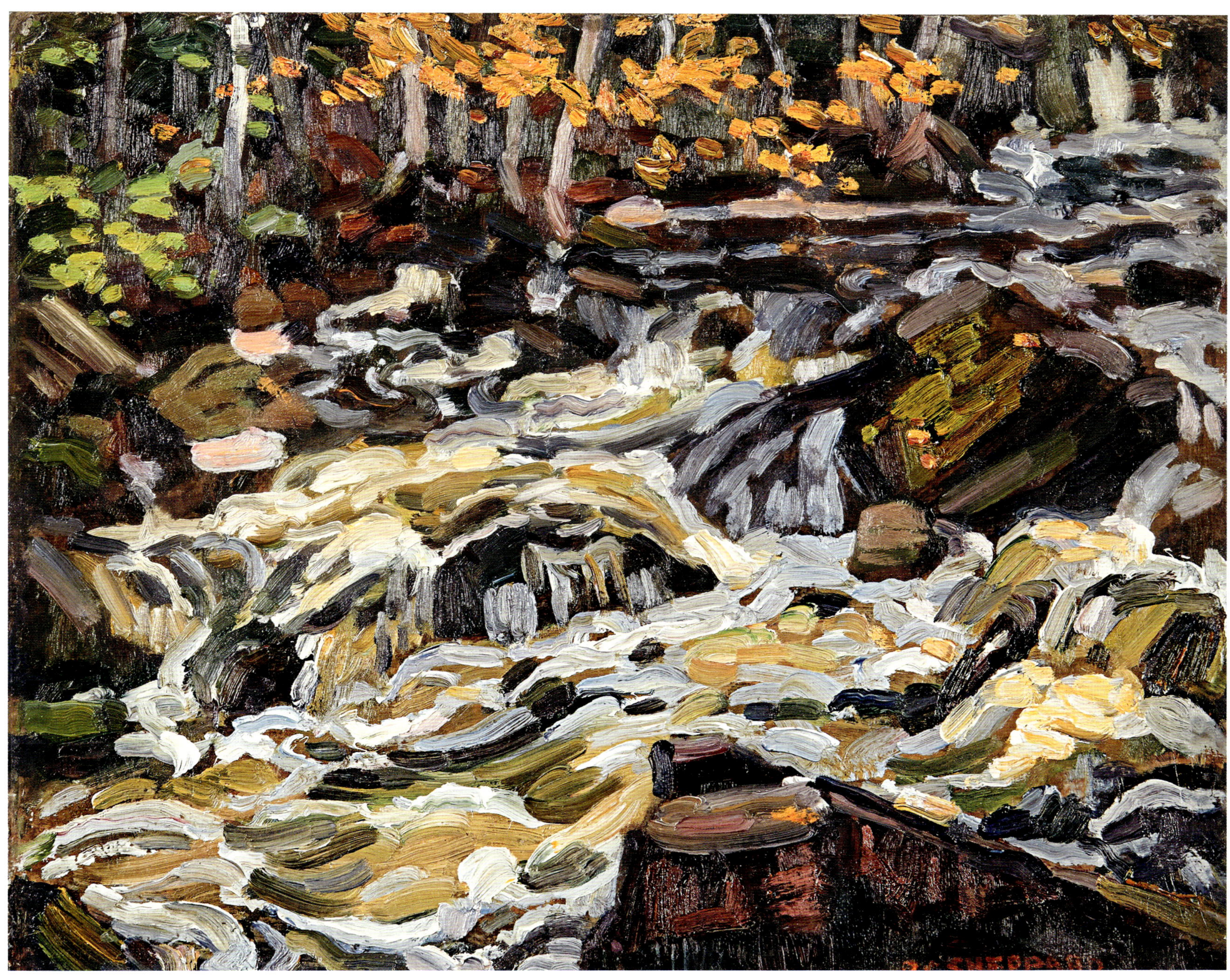

Waterfall.
1929. Oil on board,
21.6 x 26.7 cm.

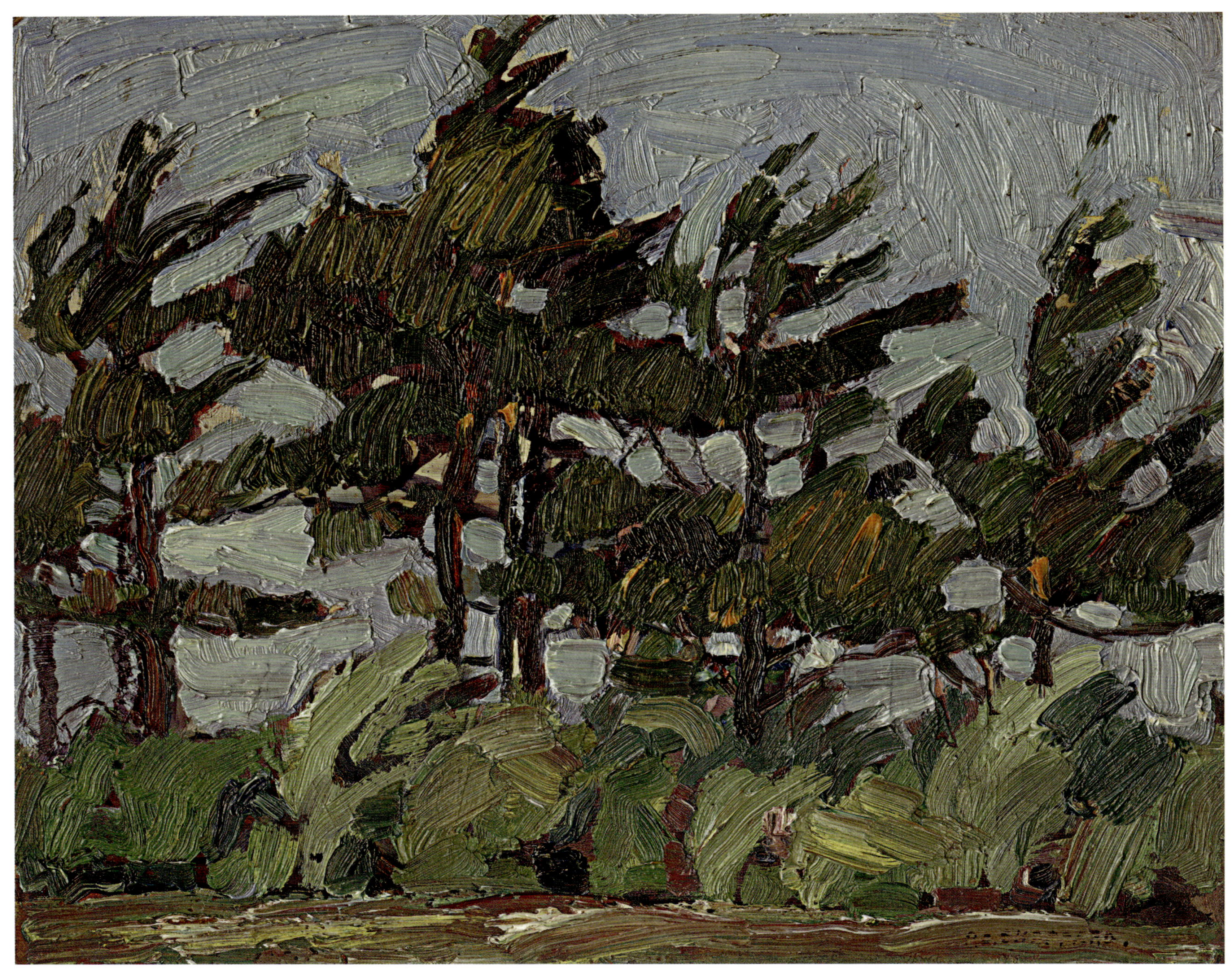

Pines, Windy Day, Georgian Bay.
1929. Oil on board,
21.6 x 26.7 cm.

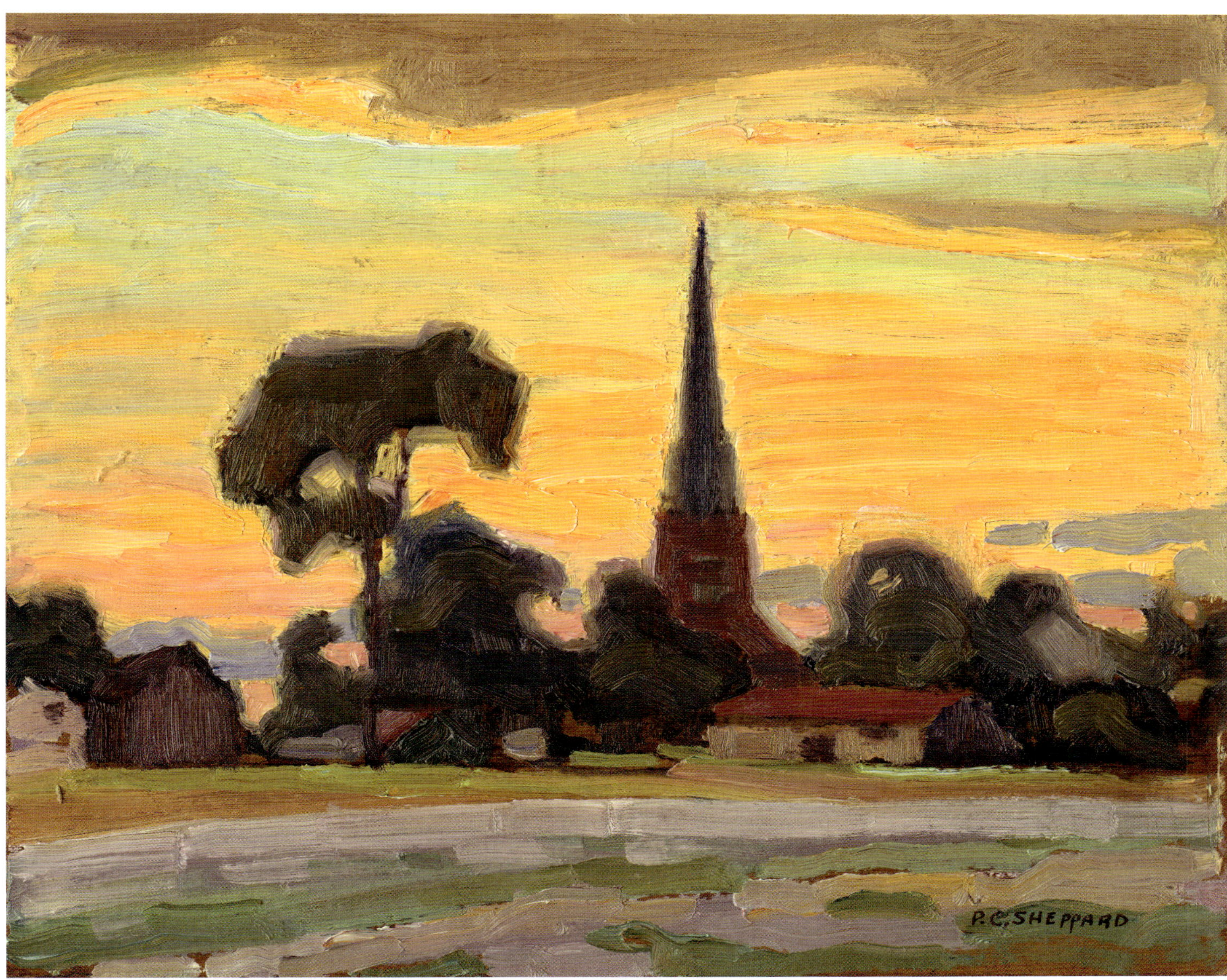

Church, Evening.
1929. Oil on board,
21.6 x 26.7 cm.

suggested through economic means; his iconography is not much more than modulated blue-green fields signifying water beyond foregrounded hills that are lovingly described.

As much as Sheppard could rise to a highly accomplished, even masterful, level as a panel painter, the archive is also unforgiving in that it holds examples of less successful paintings. In some, the forested complexity utterly defeats Sheppard and dissolves into a mishmash of browns and duns. So, too, in his analytical zeal, Sheppard denudes many a subject of its vitality, setting the subjects down as merely "nice" paintings, prosaic or lifelessly descriptive. Nevertheless, these few paintings aside, the panels are evidence of a subtle yet wide-ranging talent. Sheppard was a painter who was more than ordinarily comfortable with the integrity of the oil paint that he used in ways that uniquely took advantage of its expressive properties. His panels tell me much about how Sheppard saw and how he translated his perceptual experience and its latent mysticisim into a painted picture.

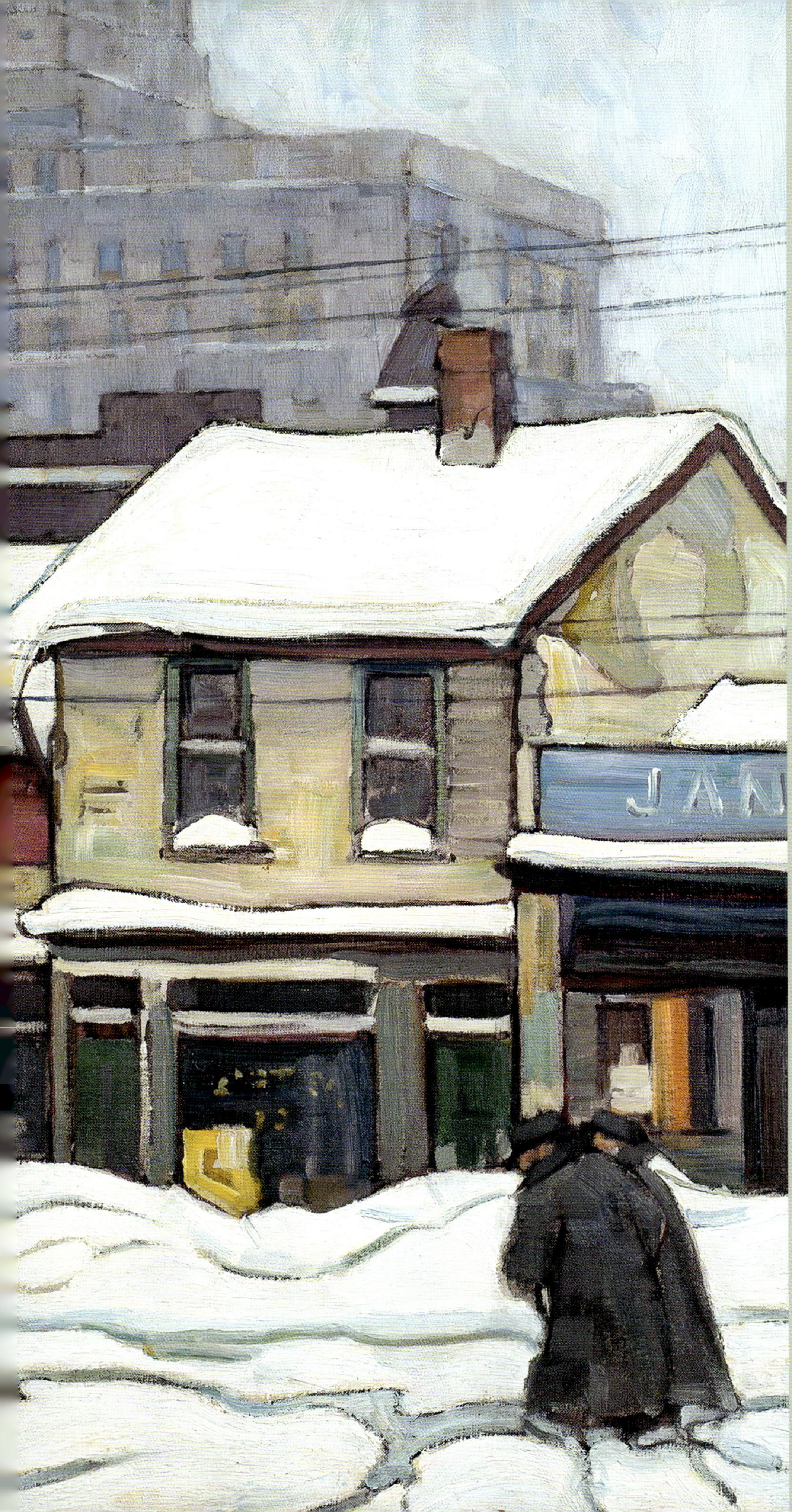

CHAPTER FIVE

Toronto

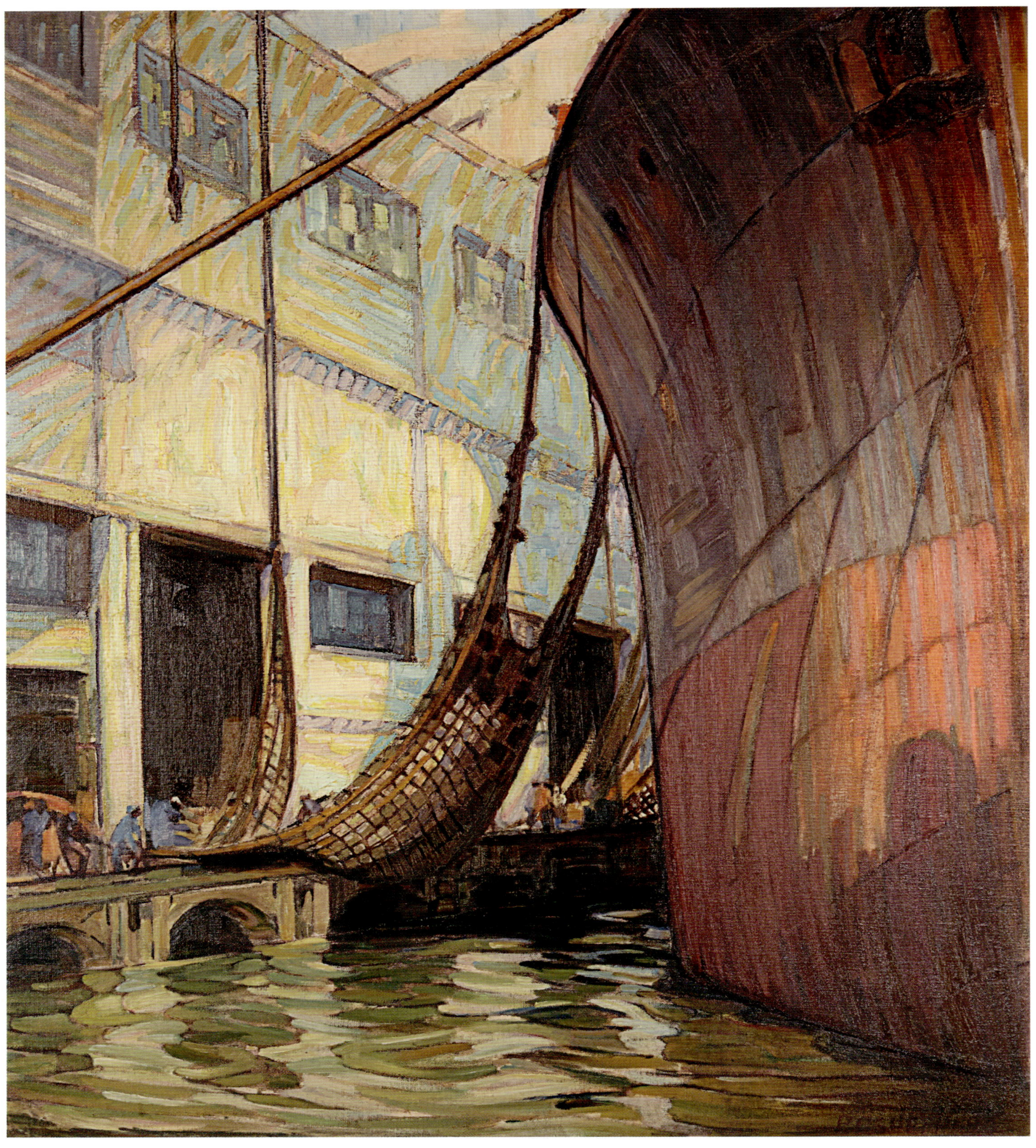

Sea Port / Ocean Freighter.
1929–30. Oil on canvas,
96.5 x 86.3 cm.

Return to Toronto, 1929

Sheppard moved back to Toronto sometime in 1929. The *Toronto Directory* of 1930 (reflecting addresses in 1929) lists him as living at 70 Oakwood Ave, close to the Arts and Crafts Wychwood Park, where G.A. Reid continued to live. Evidently, he also continued to travel to find subjects. In the early 1930s he went to the Muskoka area of central Ontario near Rabbits Bay (adjacent to Dorset), where he painted a small oil of its church (below, right) that was exhibited in the 1932 CNE exhibition. He also went to Montreal and to Canada's east coast. The 1931 catalogue of the exhibit *Little Pictures by Members of the OSA,* held at the Art Gallery of Toronto in November 1931, included *Winter, Bonsecours Market* (see page 206); the catalogue also shows that he exhibited the painting *Old Houses, Yarmouth, N.S.*

Back in Toronto he indulged himself in painting his favourite subjects: ships and their rusty hulls. His *Sea Port/Ocean Freighter* (left) (perhaps not an ocean freighter but a lake freighter) is an example of how his approach had changed over the years.[78] Gone is the aggressive painting marked by gestural brushstrokes and vivid, non-specific colours. Rather than approach his subject with an eye to interpreting it, he used the subject in the formal sense as a way to develop an interesting approach to composition. The square format has been segmented into a series of large planar areas — one defined by the curvilinear side of the ship's hull, another by the triangles, and a third by the shape of the water at the foreground. Sheppard hangs his analysis on the referential subject matter more than on the geometrical arrangements, and I wonder how much more visually arresting the entire ensemble might have been if the picture had been released from the restriction of being recognizable. Sheppard is certainly working toward abstraction, but he maintains a representational basis for the work.

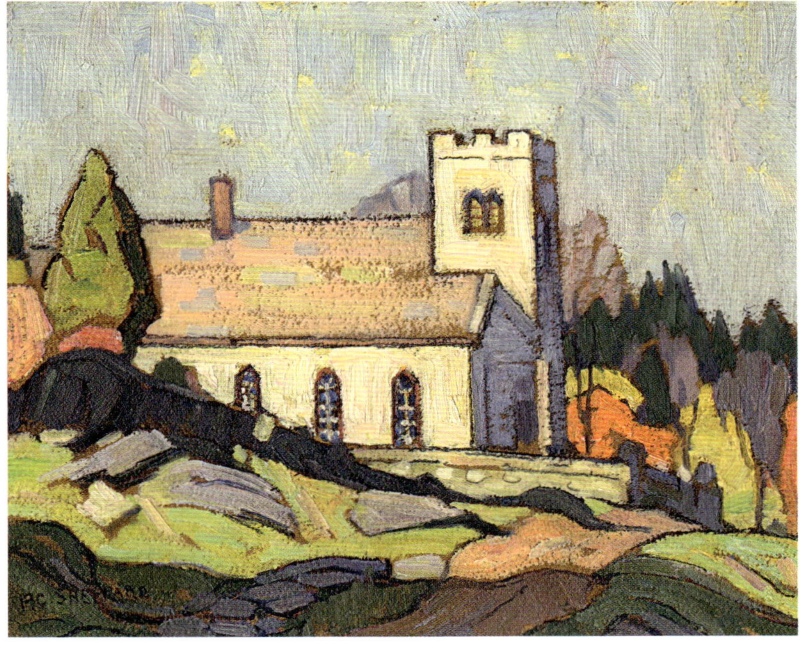

Dorset.
1930. Oil on board,
21.6 x 26.7 cm.

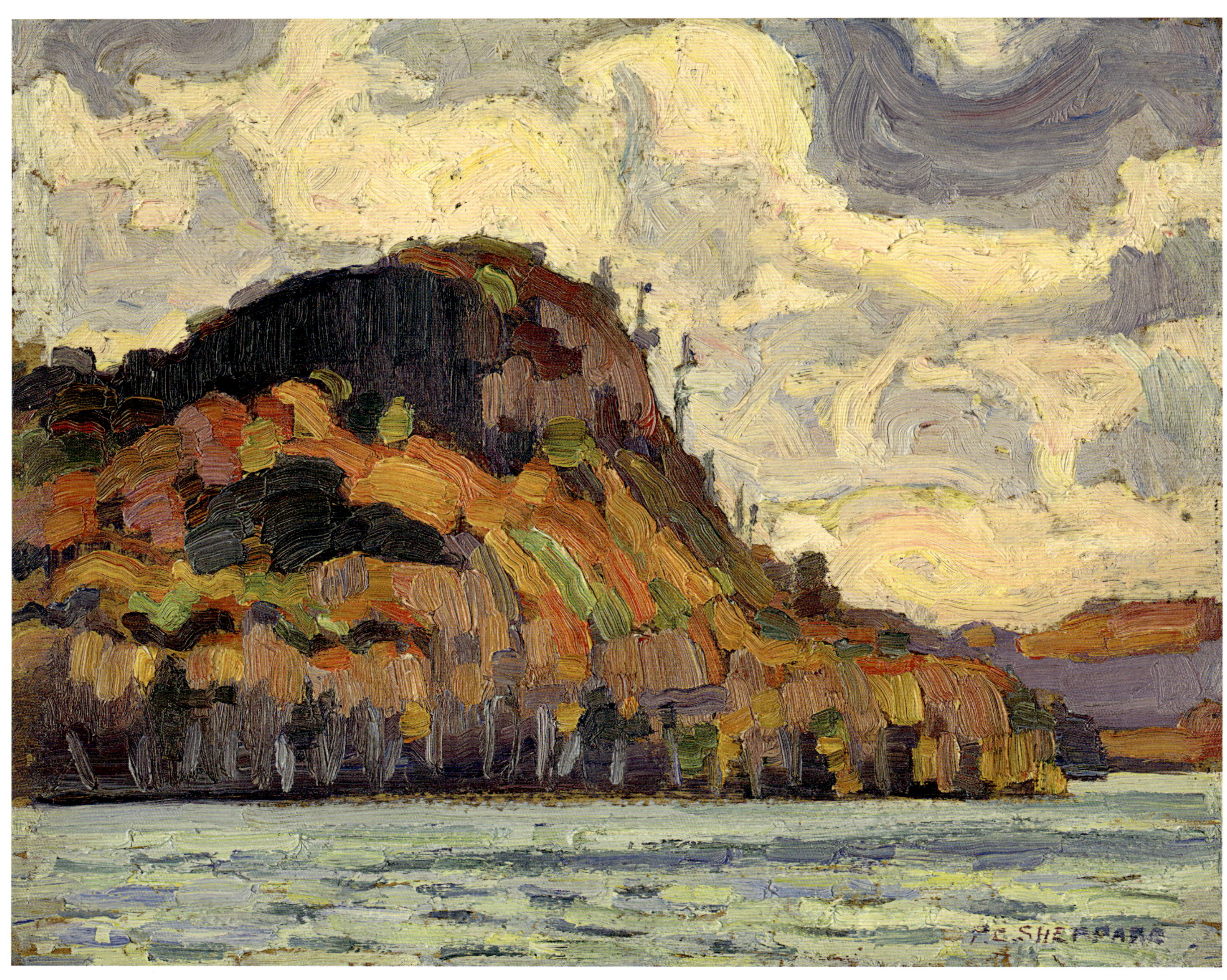

Autumn Hillside.
1931. Oil on board,
21.6 x 26.7 cm.

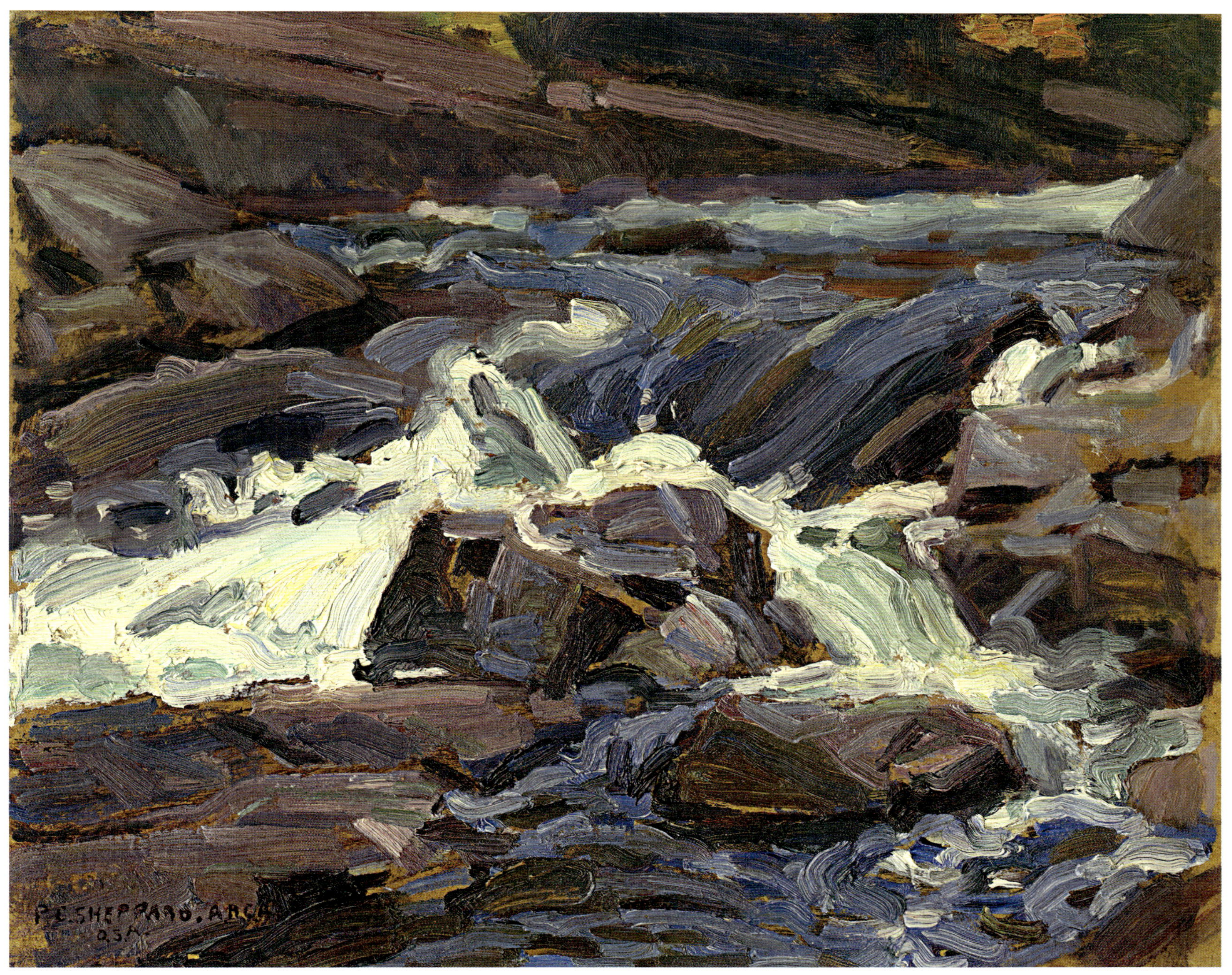

Rapids, Hollow River.
1931. Oil on board,
21.6 x 26.7 cm.

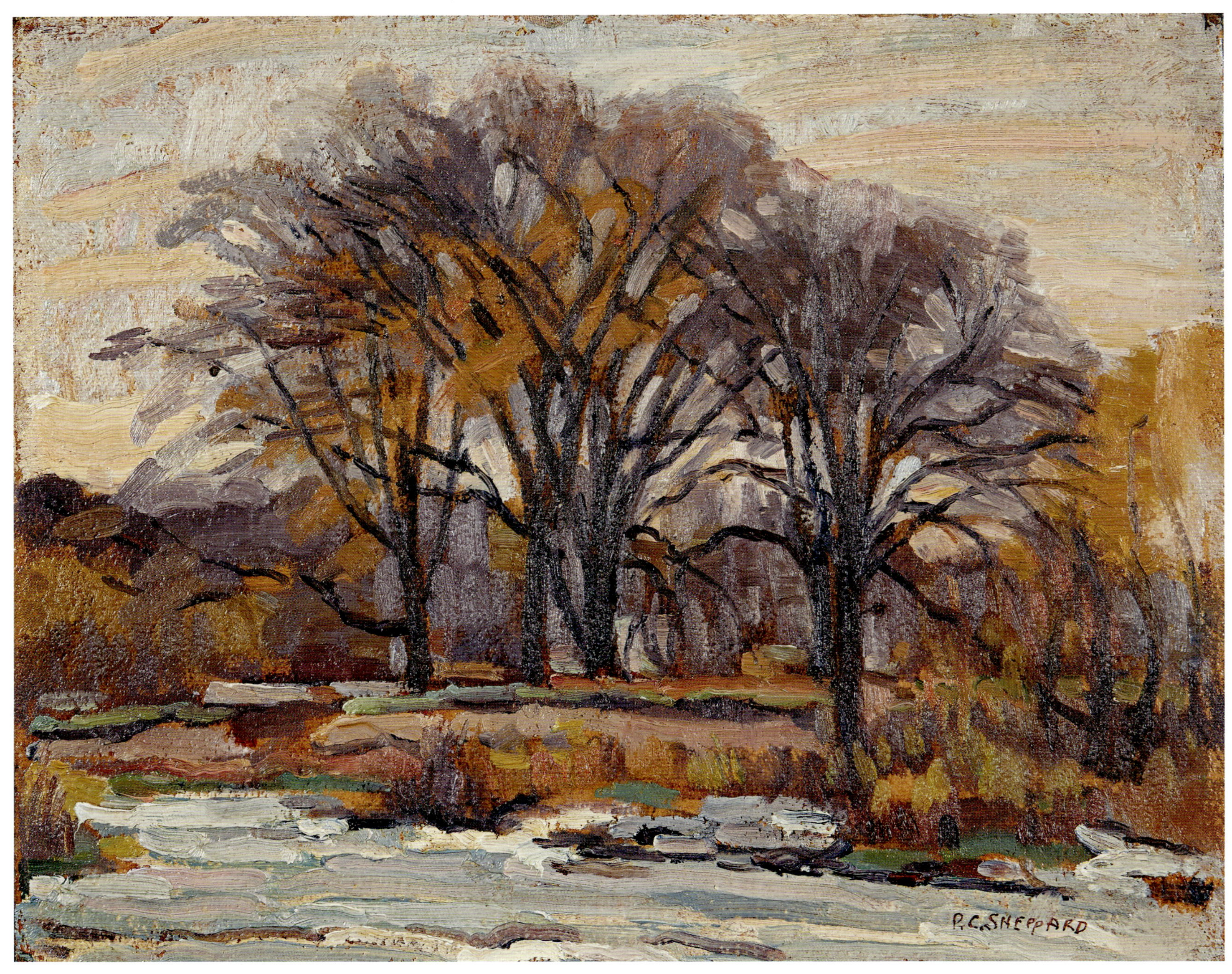

The Three Sisters, Humber River, Late Fall.
1931. Oil on board,
21.6 x 26.7 cm.

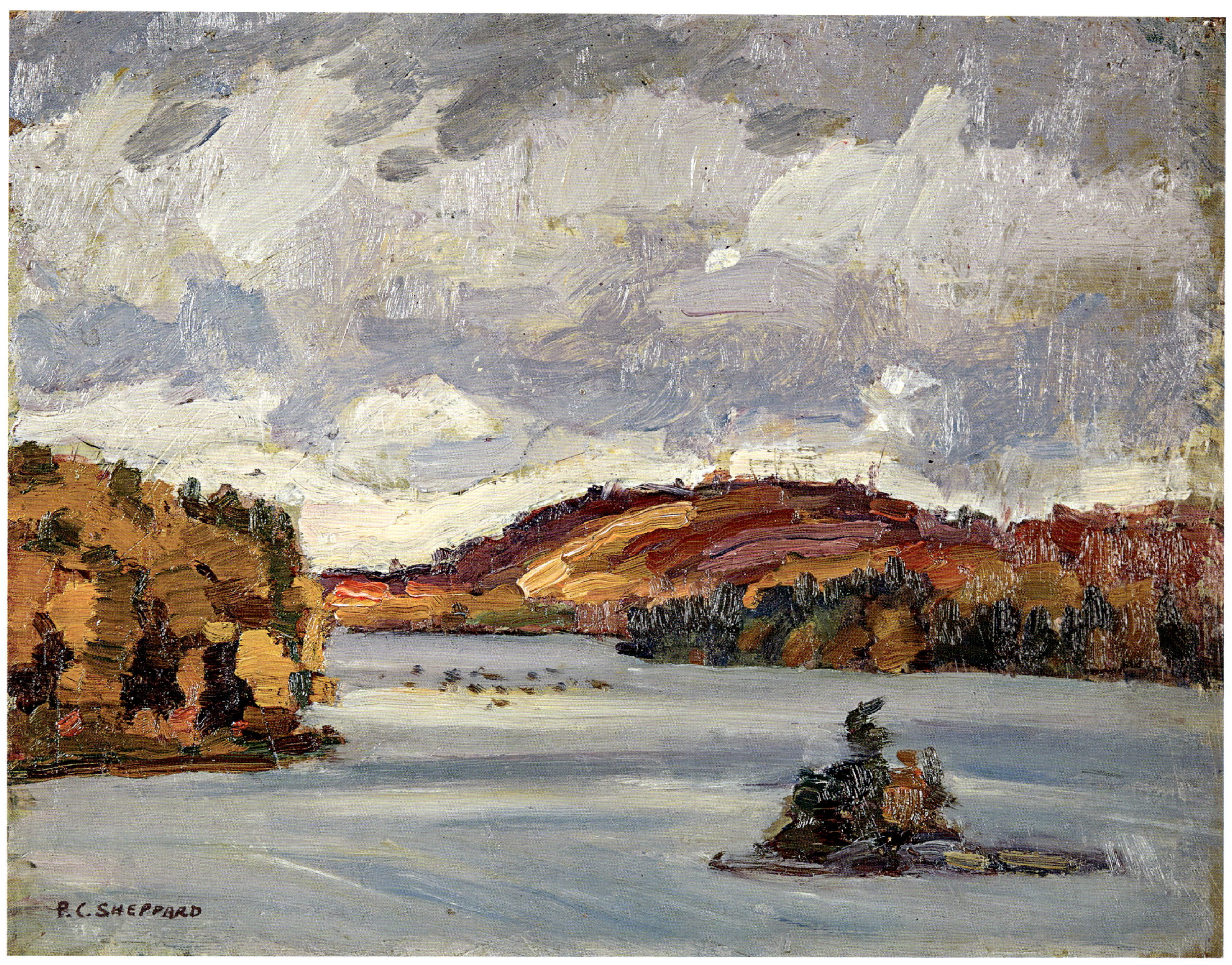

Lake Landscape.
1932. Oil on board,
21.6 x 26.7 cm.

Even though Sheppard pulled his aesthetic punches with *Sea Port/Ocean Freighter,* the work was well exposed in 1930 and 1931. It may be that this painting was his ticket to membership in the Royal Canadian Academy, where Sheppard was elected as an Associate (ARCA) in 1929 in Montreal.[79] *Sea Port/Ocean Freighter* was exhibited in the 1930 RCA exhibition and illustrated (as *Sea Port*) in the exhibition catalogue,[80] and it was subsequently featured in the RCA's 1931, 1954 and 1955 exhibitions. The OSA exhibited the canvas as *Ocean Freighter.* (See photograph on page 18 of Sheppard with the painting on his easel.)

PAINTED PANELS AND SKETCHBOOKS OF THE 1930s

When looking at Sheppard's sketchbooks, oil panels and studio oil paintings of the 1930s, I feel there is a shift in the way he engaged with his subject matter. It is as if he had had a change of artistic persona, from an active participant in the scenes to someone slightly less directly and passionately involved in his subjects.

For example, a painted panel study of a hillside in the autumn (see page 192) — a panel that was shown in the 1931 OSA *Little Pictures* exhibition, is a plein-air sketch displaying a beautiful application of colours and brushwork, particularly in the sky and along the cliff's edge. This modest study is a unique interpretation of the sky. *Rapids, Hollow River* (see page 193), also shown in the 1931 exhibition, is a complicated study of a waterfall and rapids set down in blues, greys and greens. The dynamic, radiating composition revolves around the white cascading water. In contrast to the vitality of *Rapids, Hollow River,* the painting *The Three Sisters, Humber River, Late Fall* (see page 194), is an understated depiction of a river landscape in a muted palette that heightens an overall feeling of decline that emanates from the subject and its handling. So, too, Sheppard's *Lake Landscape* (see page 195) is more moody tone poem than a representation of a specific place. In this study, linearity gives way to brushed passages of greys and earth tones. There is no sense of an underdrawing. Rather, the emphasis is on painterliness, not delineation or contour outlines. These sketches provided Sheppard with the opportunity to show his mettle as a painter who could handle colour passages. His *Houses on the Edge of a Lake* (see page 197) is composed crisply and geometrically. The houses are set on a complex ground of yellows, oranges, greens and azure, which all interact with degrees of autonomy, so much so that the palette never darkens to browns and greys, despite the close relationships of complementary colours.

So it goes with the collection of dozens of painted oil panels from the 1930s that are in the archive. The handling of many of the paintings is intended to convey mood and emotion — a river scene (see page 198) is a case in point, where the subject is rendered in pinks, mauves and intense yellows. A variation on this is evident in several evocative cloud studies that appear to have loosened the artist, opened up his handling of the ephemeral nature of the cloudscape to experiment in abstract painterly licks. *Cloudscape* (see page 199) in particular is practically a study in colour interactions; the image's abstract heart is defined by the deep greys, purples and light blues that animate much of the format, while the spare landscape is described in a cryptic iconography of coloured dabs and marks. The small format seems to have given Sheppard creative licence to untether prosaic or recognizable subjects from the formal conventions of putting paint on wooden rectangles.

Just when it looks like Sheppard will unmoor himself from narration and give himself over to a kind of non-referential formalism, he steps back into his comfort zone of crisp linearity and expressive draftsmanship, all in the service of setting down in paint what he perceives in front of his eyes. Three examples, among many, illustrate this expressive paradox. A farm landscape with a barn (see page 200) gives a sense of the rhythms that are attendant upon the geometry of the barn's distinguishing feature — its gambrel roof, set off in profile by the lovely light blue sky. *Sawmill, Ontario* (see page 201) is picturesque, descriptive, and yet it is rescued from cliché by the pictorial poetry in the patterning and rhythms of the woodpiles. And *Wharf, Parry Sound* (see page 202) is a beautiful study of the buildings, the water and the reflections. In the emphatic descriptiveness of the prosaic, picturesque subject matter there is no sense of moodiness or poignancy.

Among the dozens of panels, two are special and to my eye convey something deeply felt in their subject matter. They are two scenes (see pages 204 and 205) of a carnival that has set up in Christie Pits, a gully of a park on Bloor Street West near where Sheppard lived. Both are wonderfully evocative, showing the view as seen from the eye of a curious observer, but one who prefers the position at the margins of the activity, in this case from the edge of the park, where he could look on and interpret a Ferris wheel, amusement rides, tents, caravans and midway rides, all establishing an air of late-summer festiveness in which the people depicted in the scenes are enjoying an afternoon at the fair. Time capsules, hypnotic, these two modest panels seamlessly transport a contemporary viewer back to another time in Toronto's history.

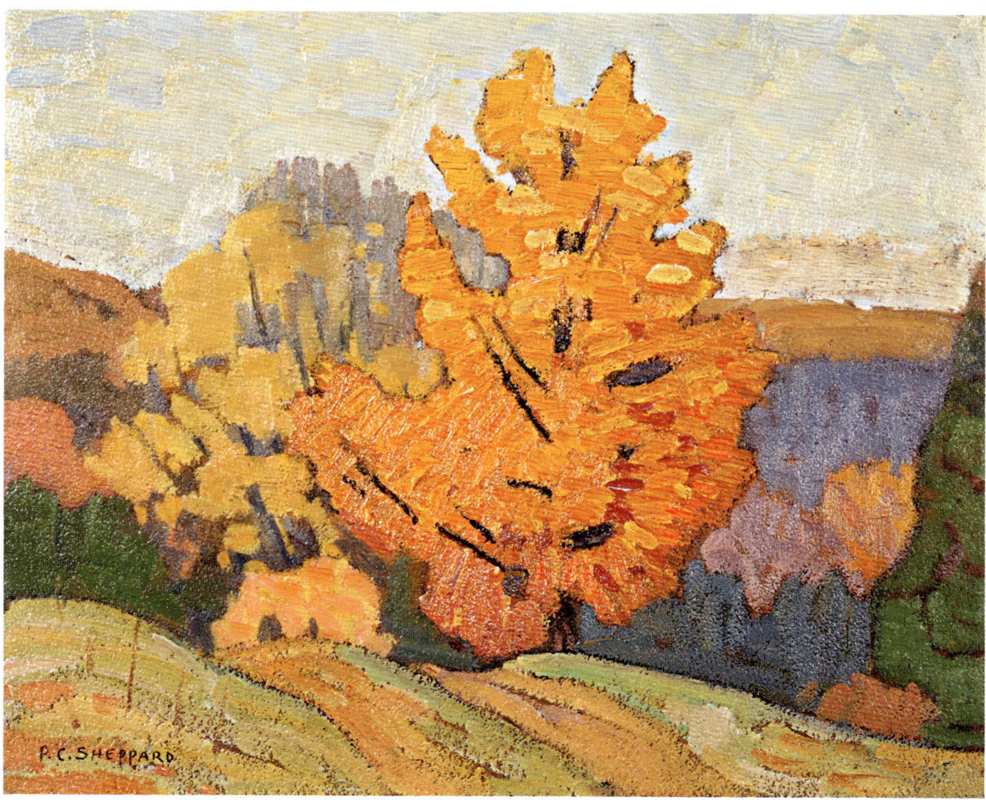

Autumn Landscape.
1937. Oil on board,
33 x 40.6 cm.

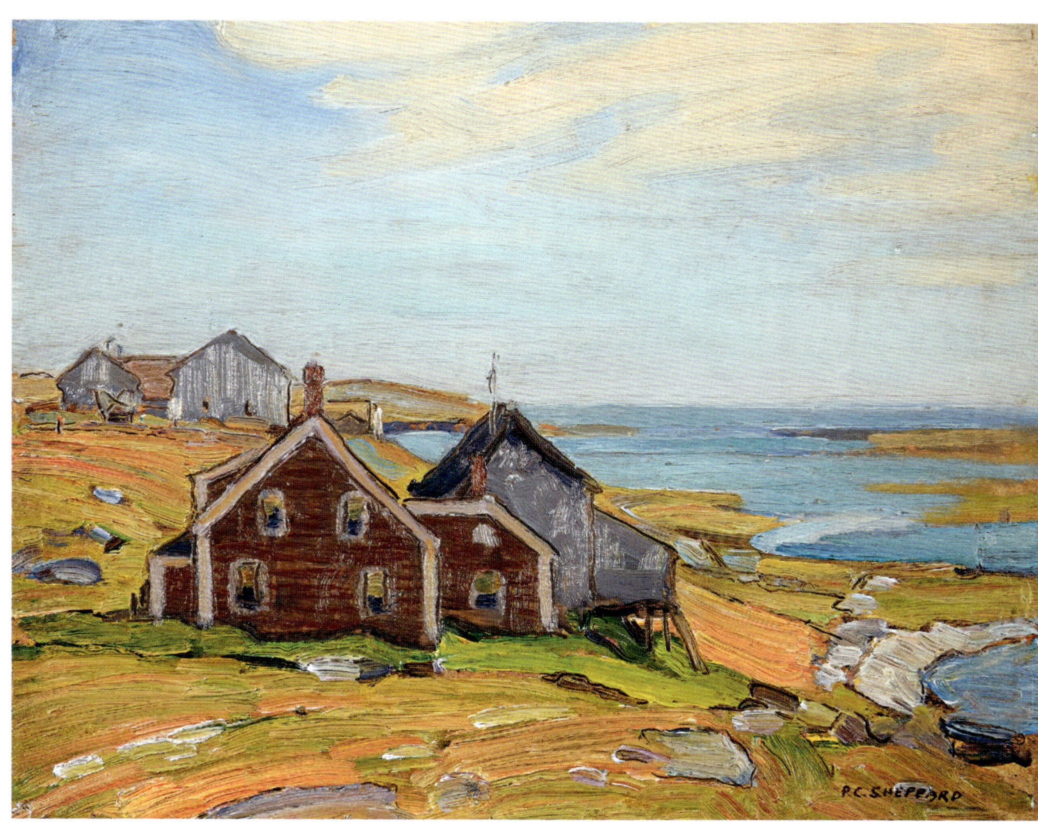

Houses on the Edge of a Lake.
1932. Oil on board,
21.6 x 26.7 cm.

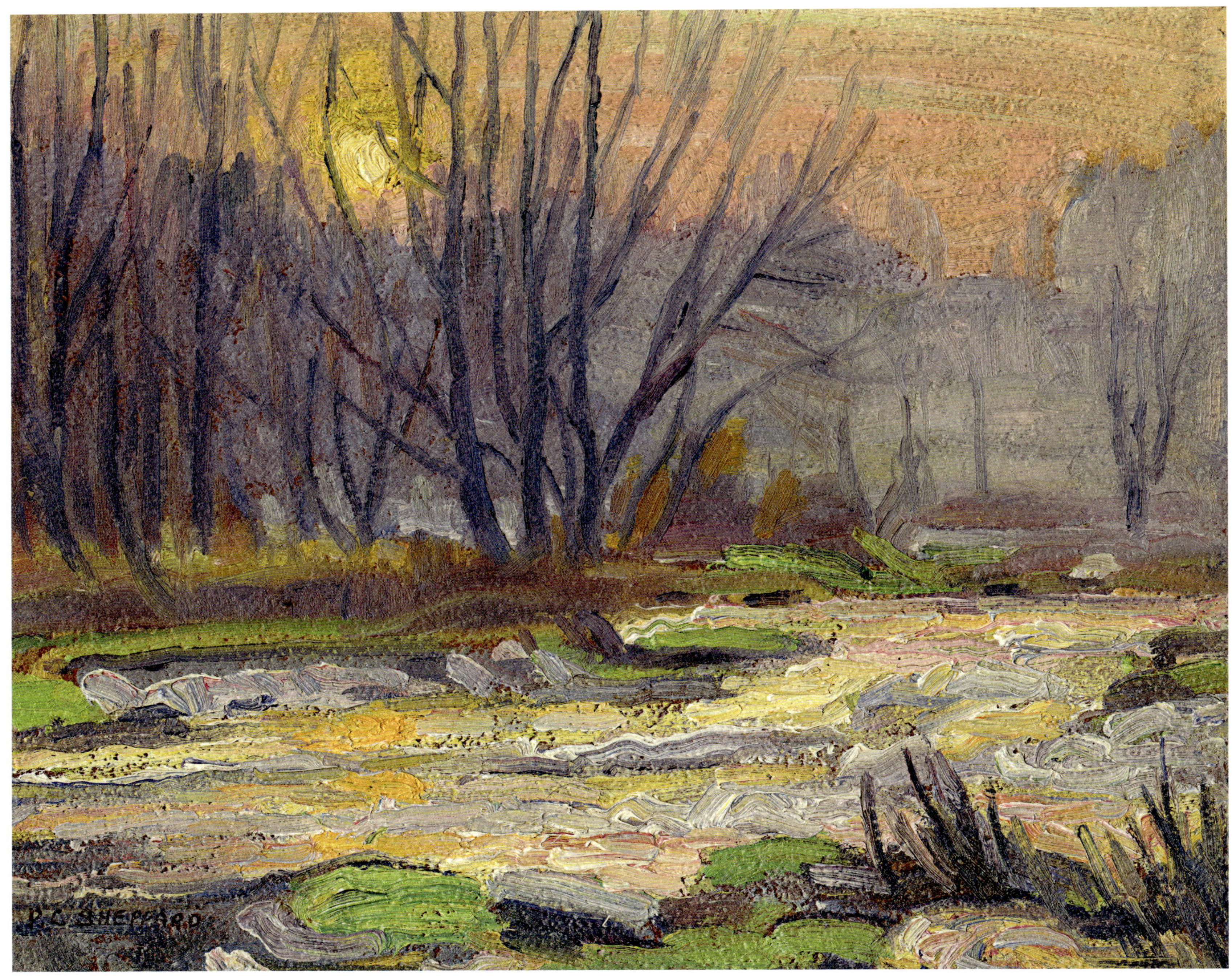

River Scene, Dusk.
1931. Oil on board,
21.6 x 26.7 cm.

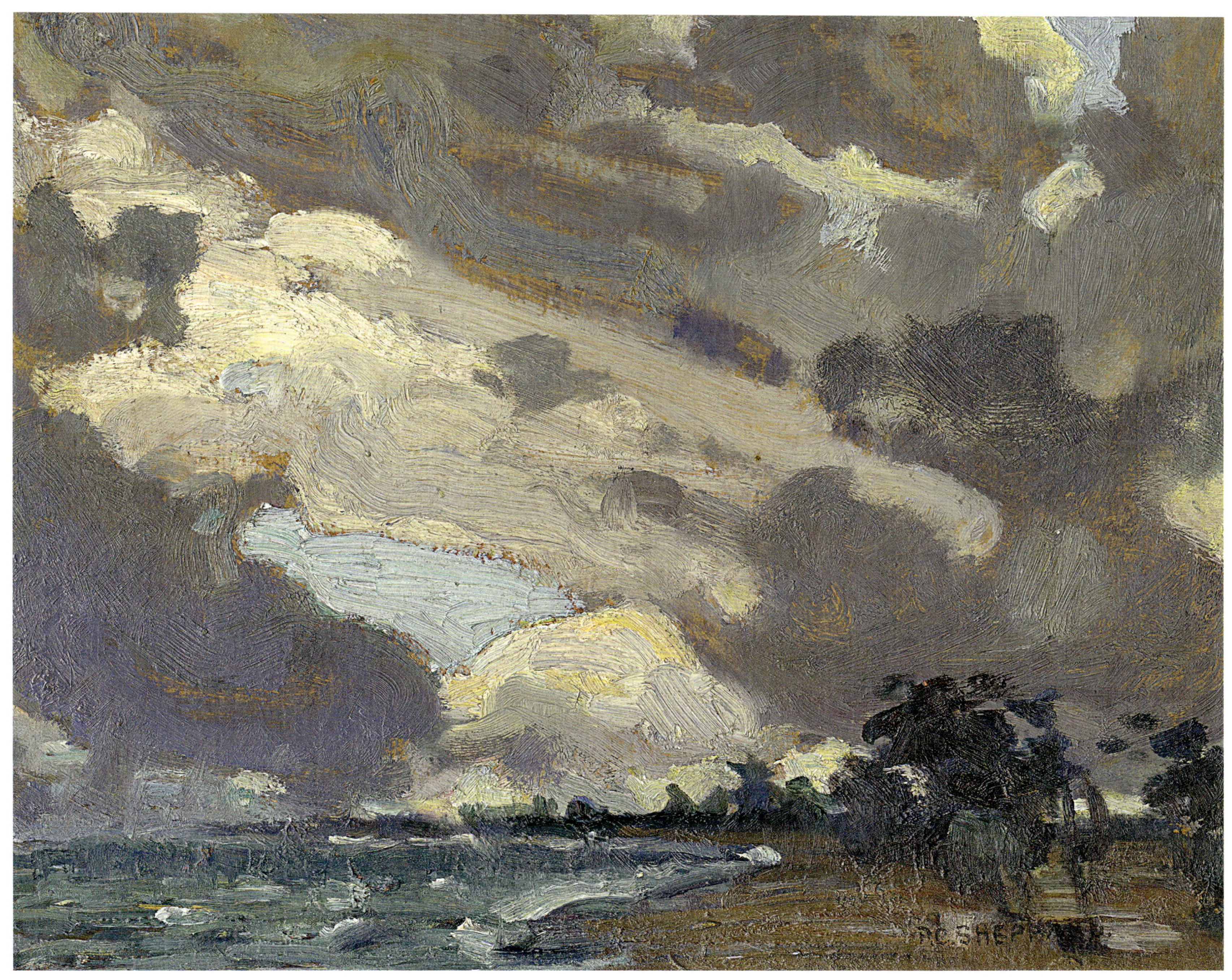

Cloudscape.
1934. Oil on board,
21.6 x 26.7 cm.

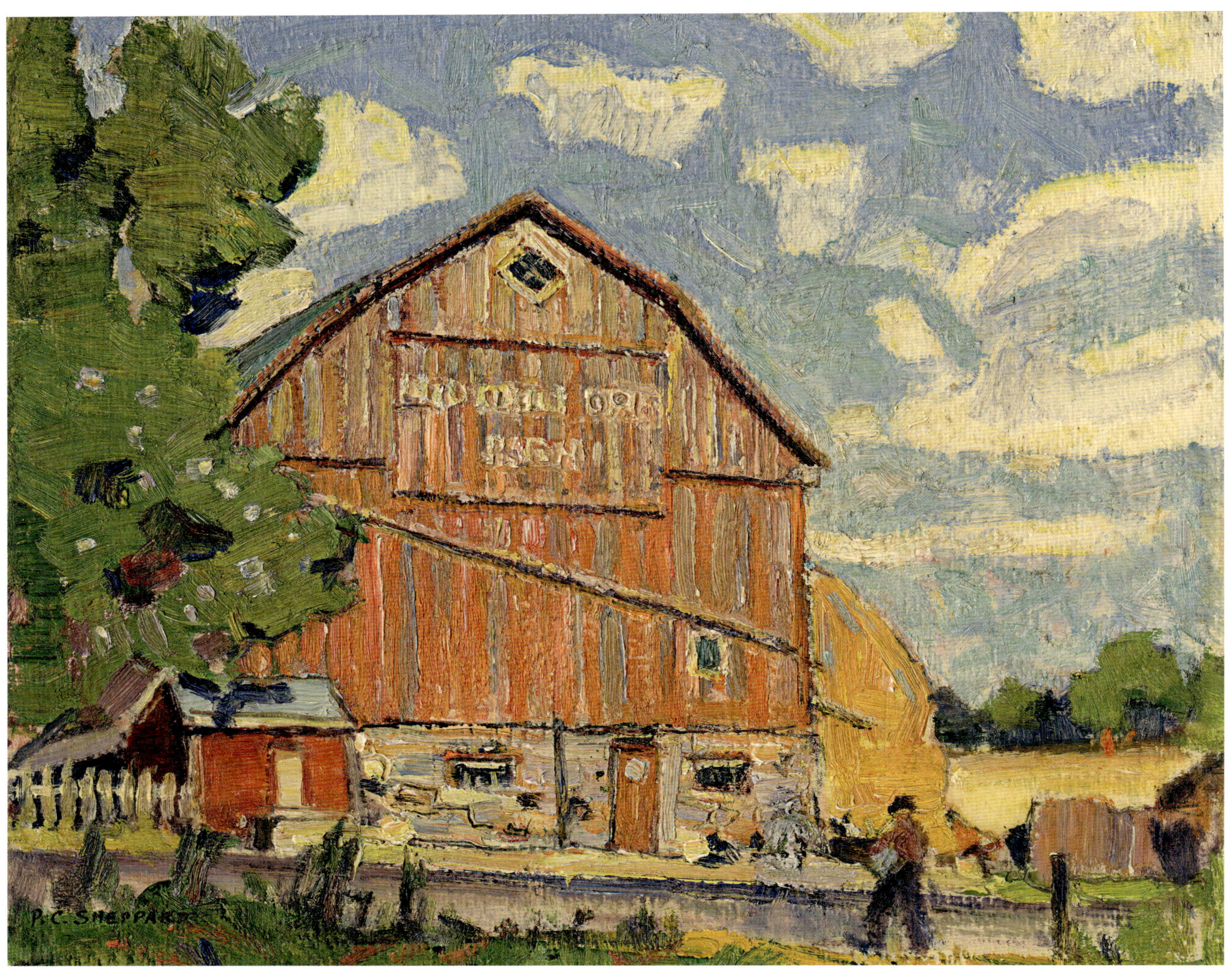

Red Barn, Ontario.
1934. Oil on board,
21.6 x 26.7 cm.

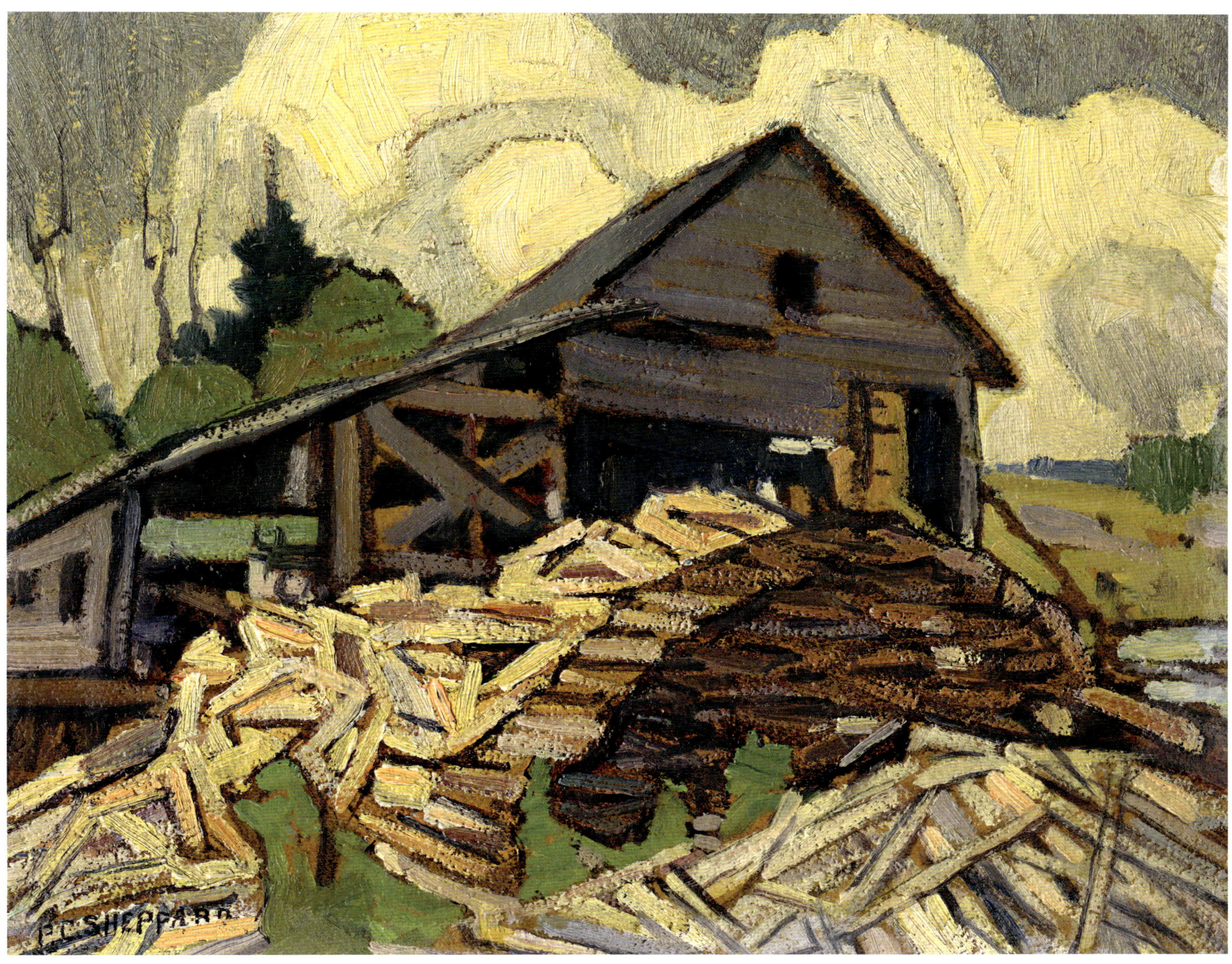

Sawmill, Ontario.
1934. Oil on board,
21.6 x 26.7 cm.

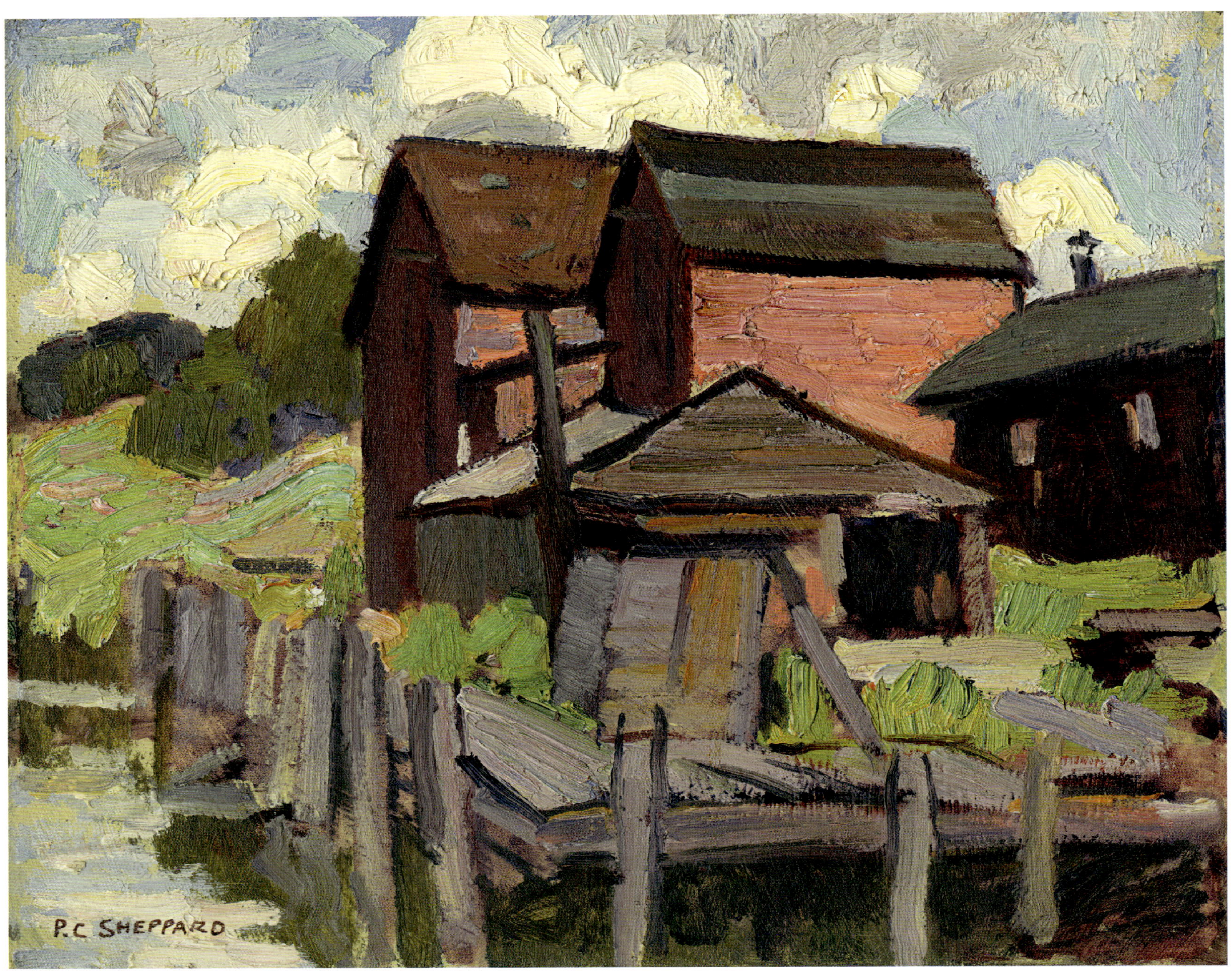

Wharf, Parry Sound.
1934. Oil on board,
21.6 x 26.7 cm.

The character of these modestly scaled carnival studies can be seen and sensed in his contemporaneous large-format canvas *Side Show, Canadian National Exhibition* (see right), painted around 1930. The scene shows a degree of control and stylization that is unique in Sheppard's output up to this time. There is a patterned mannerism in the way he has set down the midway crowd standing in front of the sideshow carneys hawking their spectacles in front of colourful banners, to such a degree that it appears that Sheppard may have been experimenting with turning these subjects into mural-like tableaux. He has taken this scene and elevated it to a near mythic-level so that the subject is more emblem than representation or illustration. He has distilled an essential quality of the carnival and set it down as an allegory of a slice of Toronto's late-summer life presented as a truthful, universal interpretation of the subject.

As Sheppard's sketchbooks show, it is as if he takes the attitude in his work of an observer, a chronicler watching life around him from the edge of the scene — on a park bench, in a corner of a tavern, perhaps from an out-of-the-way vantage point. Surreptitious notation takes on an elevated importance in his artistic alphabet, and to my mind, this is where I find the inquisitive, probing eye of the artist. Where in the 1920s his work traces a kind of exploding extroversion, an energetic embrace of the experience of subject and place, in the 1930s the fire cools and so does his relationship to subject. Yet the passion does not drain from his art. Rather it flows into another media and mood. The 1930s, as Sheppard moves into his 50s, is a decade marked by an honest interest in conveying emotion through tone and ephemeral forms, and a honing of his pencil- and watercolour-sketching techniques, all the better to set down the deeply human and timeless qualities of the subjects. Sheppard's creative action is traced in his sketchbooks.

One of the latter types of painting is the winter scene of Montreal's Bonsecours Market (see page 206), painted in 1931 and exhibited in that year's OSA *Little Pictures* exhibition. Sheppard's handling of the paint in this small picture shows that he is still adept at depicting a scene in an impressionistic mode. The horse-drawn sleigh is burdened by a jauntily set down blaze of yellow hay offset by a contrasting blue sign, which creates a dynamic, vivid complement that dazzles in front of the eye. The background is a flat tableau organized as a series of squares and rectangles that provide the space and context in which the sleigh and its horse rest.

To what end was Sheppard's analysis? The archive offers a clue, once again, to an artist who had a creative foot in several camps. A realist who

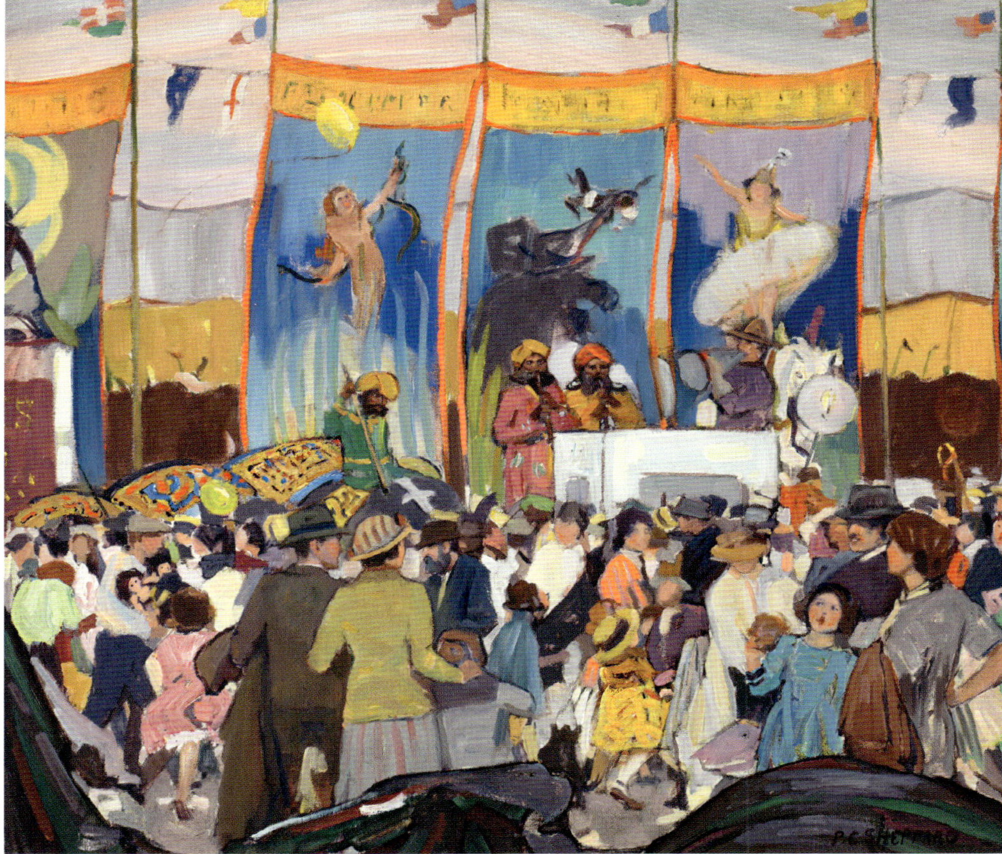

Side Show, Canadian National Exhibition.
1930. Oil on canvas,
86.3 x 96.5 cm.

captured the life and times of his people and city; an Impressionist who sought to picture the effects of light and weather in an urban context, particularly a winter snow squall or blizzard; a plein-air painter who worked to capture the experience of place in cedar shingle–sized paintings done on-site in all weather conditions; and a latent abstractionist whose sharp eye could also be turned to reducing landscape elements to essential shapes and significant forms, and in the process could flatten the picture plane into arrangements of colours, shapes, lines and textures. In fact, his predilection for abstracting a landscape subject by flattening pictorial space emerged as a strong interest in the 1930s.

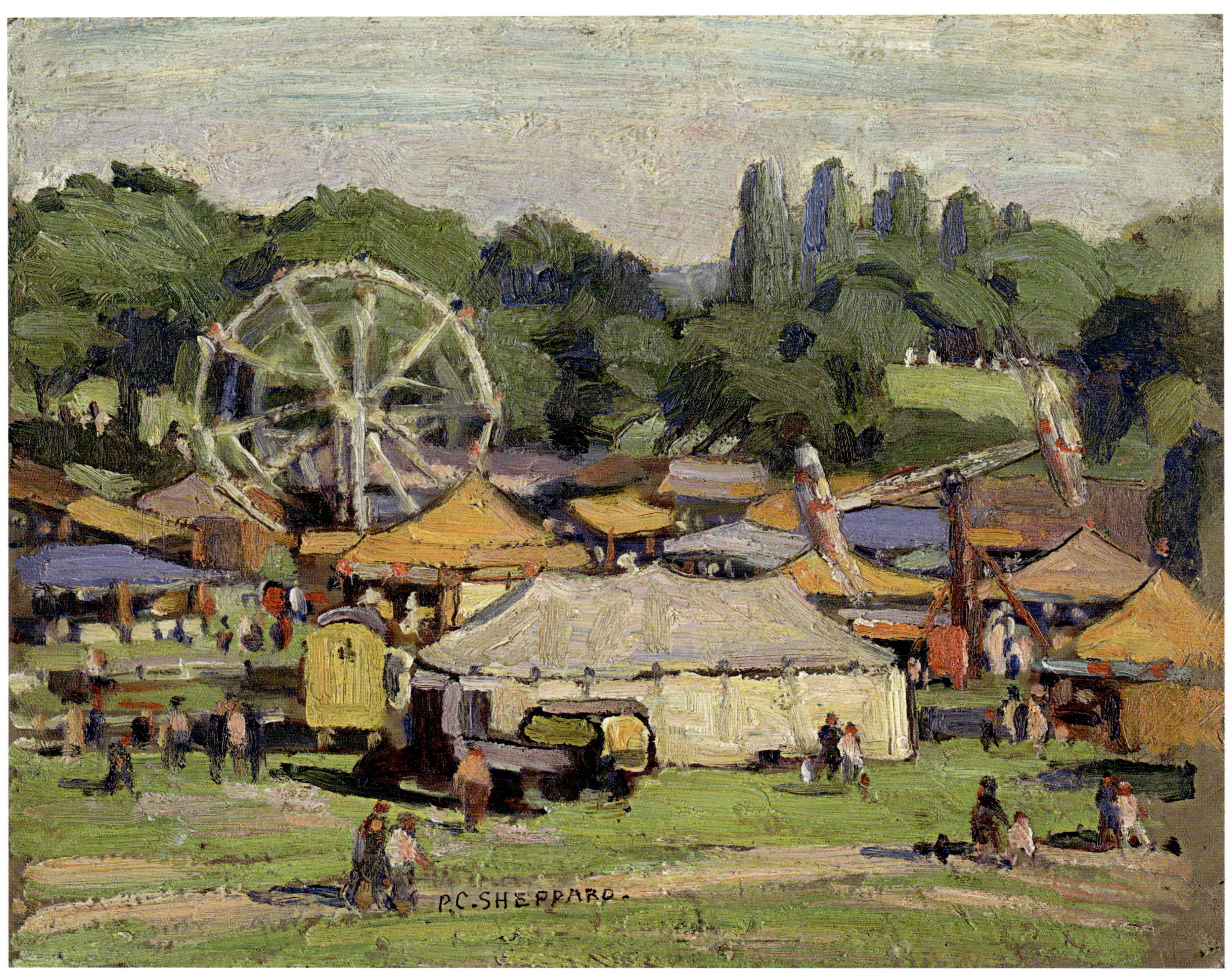

Christie Pits, Toronto.
1936. Oil on board,
21.6 x 26.7 cm.

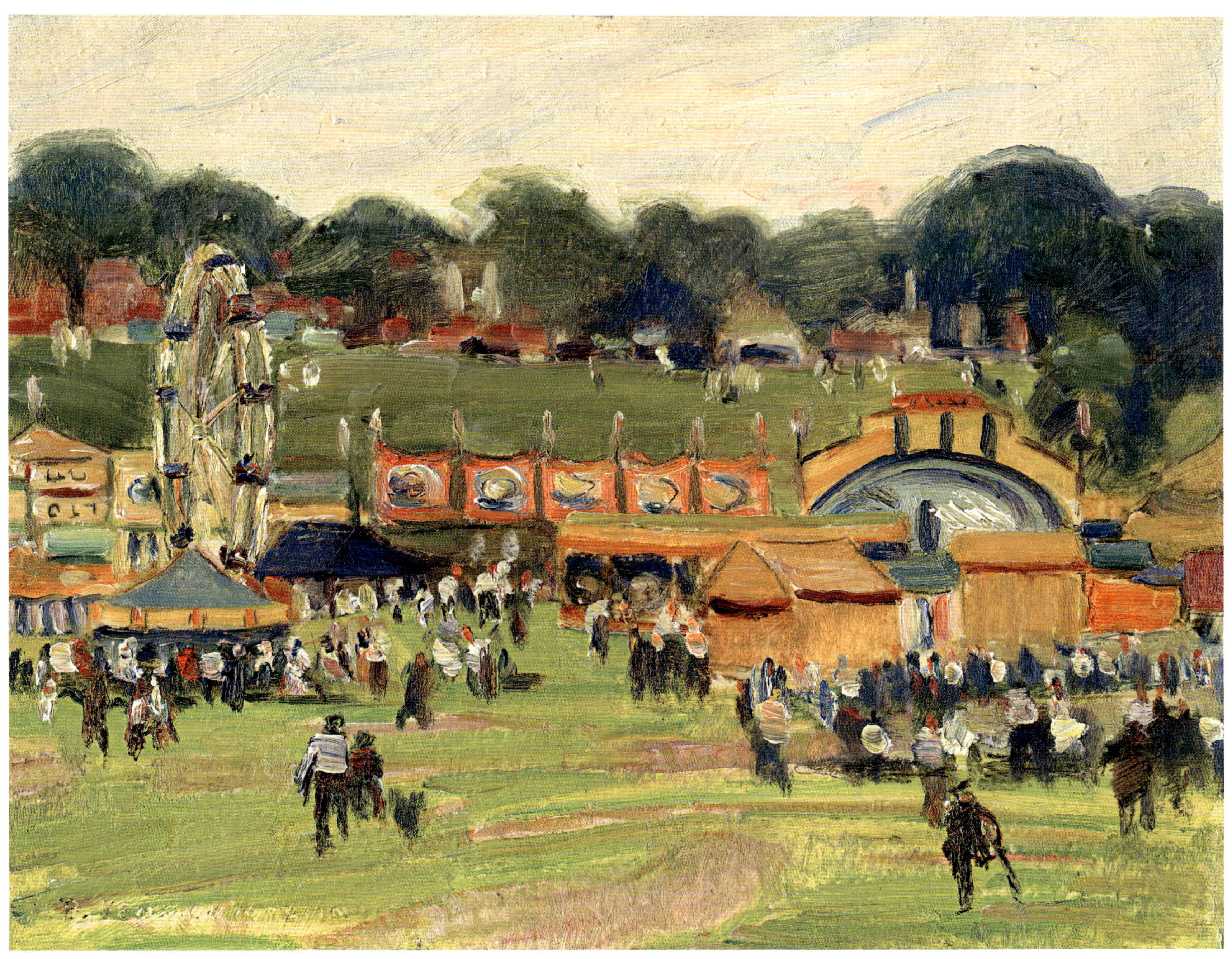

Christie Pits, Toronto.
1936. Oil on board,
21.6 x 26.7 cm.

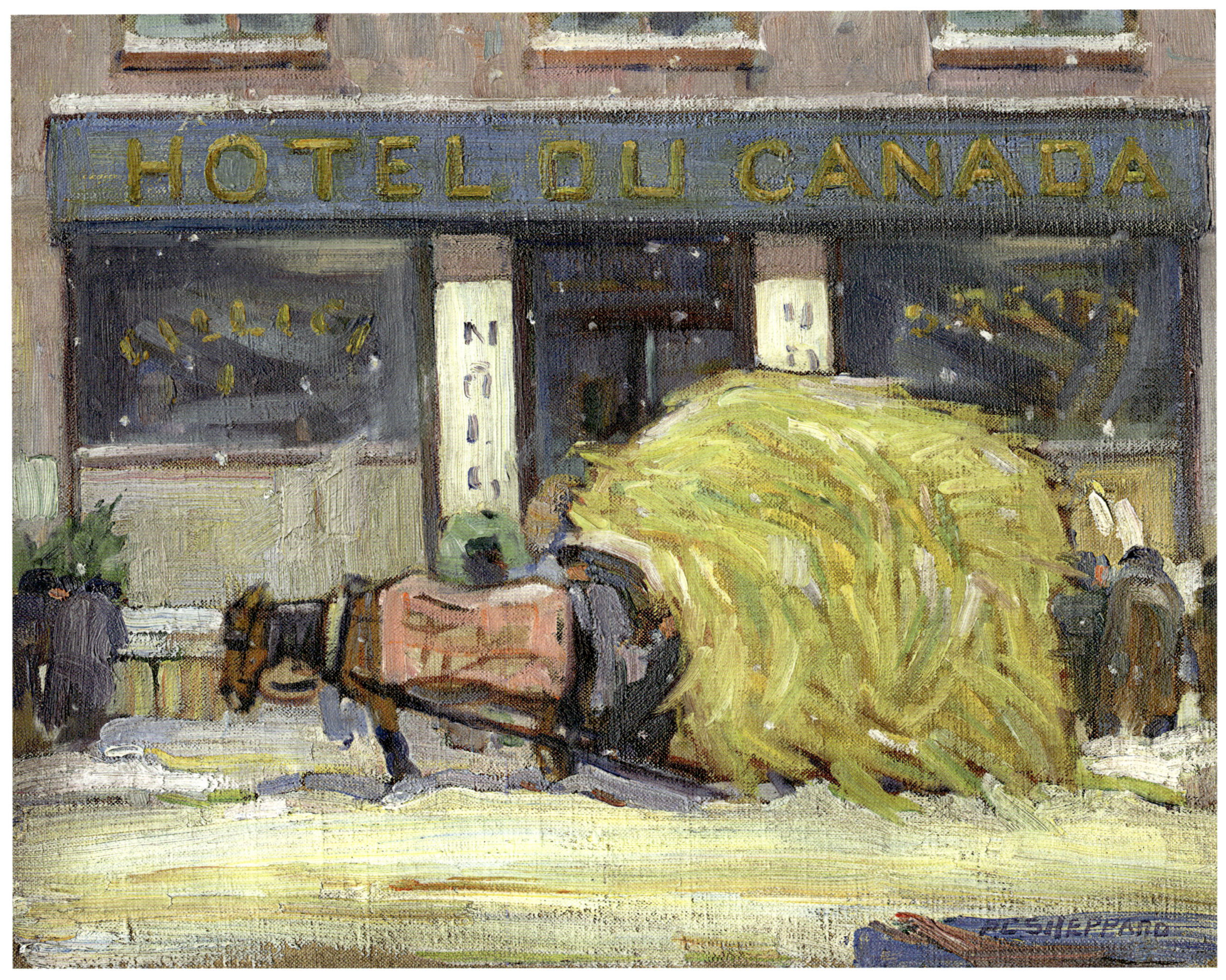

Winter, Bonsecours Market.
1931. Oil on canvas,
33 x 40.6 cm.

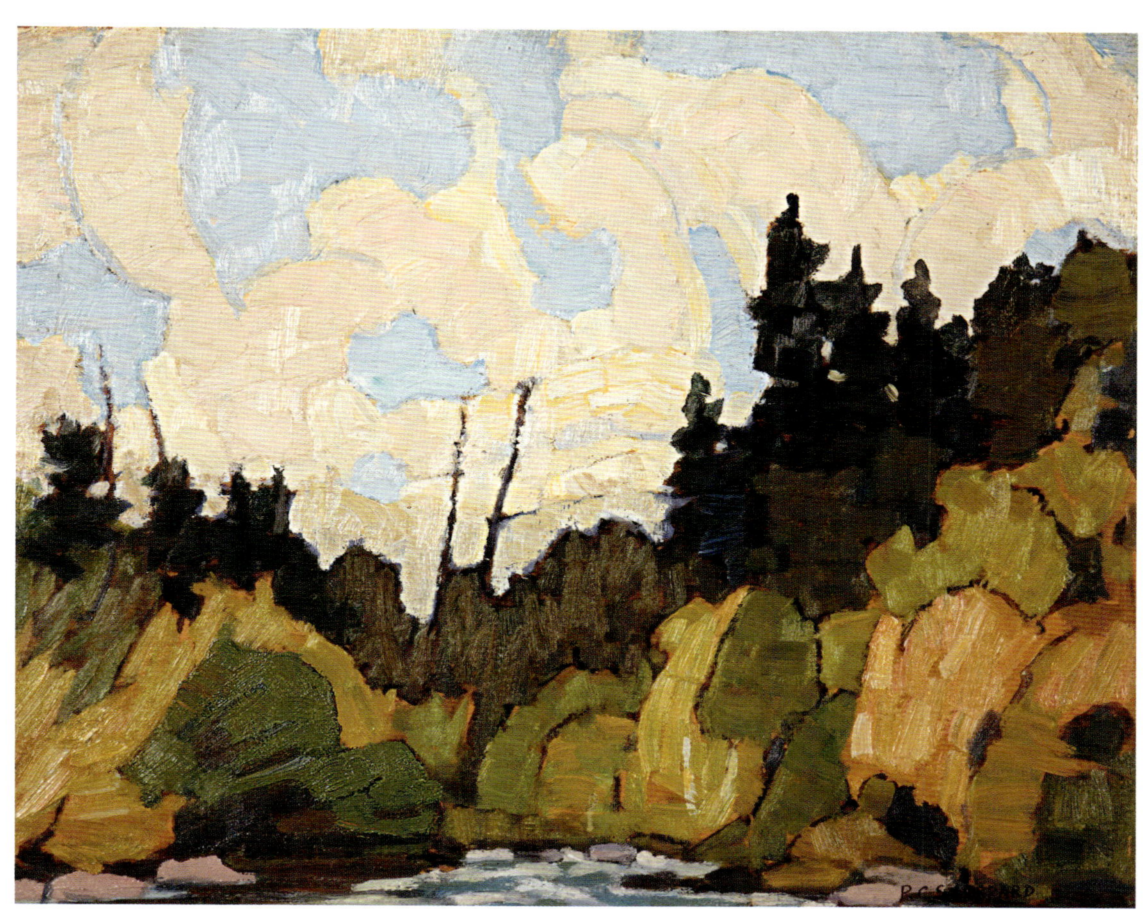

Wooded Landscape.
c. 1936–37. Oil on board,
33 x 40.6 cm.

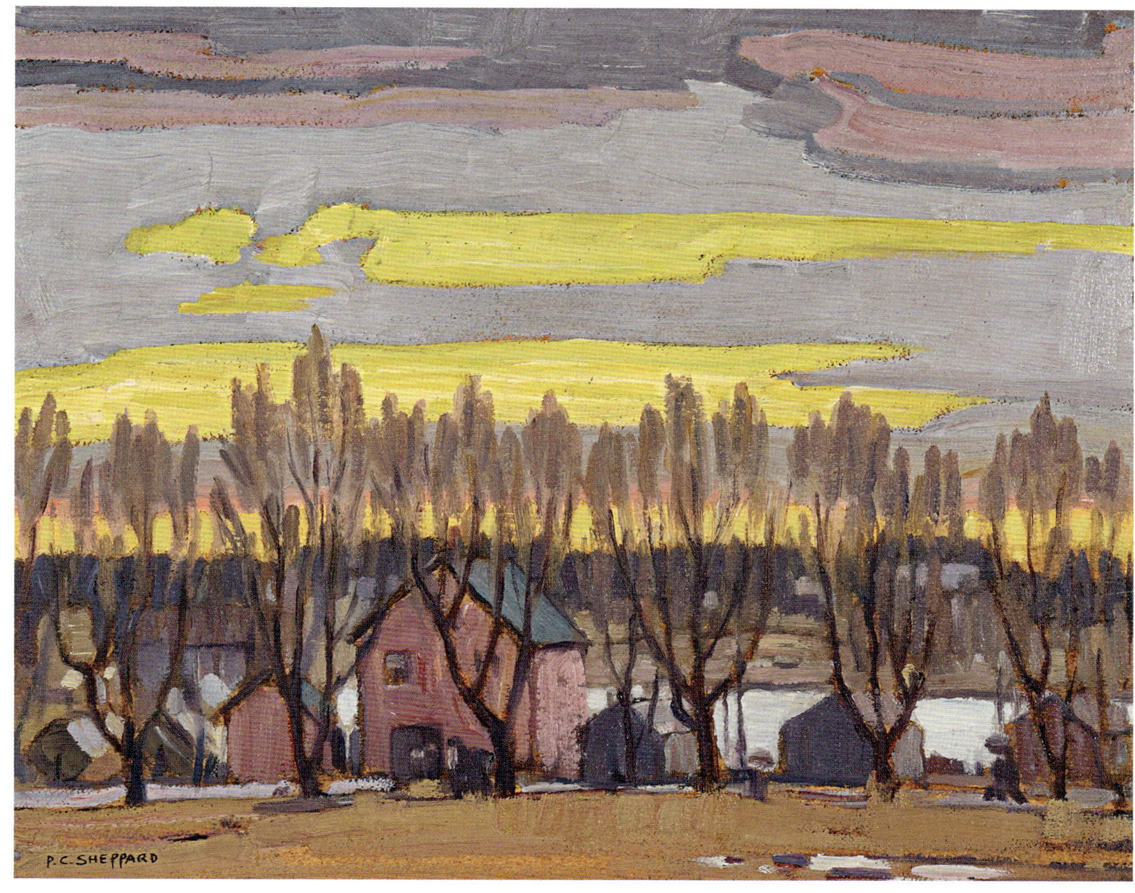

Late Autumn Sunset.
c. 1936–37. Oil on board,
33 x 40.6 cm.

The evidence to my eye rests in two landscapes in the archive. *Wooded Landscape*, a forest view with shoreline in the foreground (see page 207), simplifies the complexities of forest and rocks by defining them as areas of pure colour separated and delineated by contour lines. The effect of Sheppard's organizational sensibilities is that the spatial relationships are compressed, despite the device of a single-point-perspective triangular shape leading the eye into the painterly space. So, too, his *Autumn Landscape* (see page 197) is a carefully composed, analytical colour study, and an asymmetrical arrangement of significant forms that, while alluding to landscape, is an abstract diagram exposing the interplay of colour harmonies and contrasts, and rhythms. The effect pushes the pictorial space to the picture plane, but Sheppard once again mitigates this by using illusionistic devices (a triangle, for example) to fight the flattening of depth.

A CALCULATED RISK–TAKER

At his best, Sheppard is a calculated risk–taker, content to use one or more visual languages to render a subject. And with this tendency, he might have put himself in an awkward place in Toronto's art scene, which was still dominated by the stringent aesthetic orthodoxies of the OSA, the RCA and the very few artists up-to-date in contemporary artistic trends who were working both inside and outside the societies and academies in the early 1930s. To be sure, Sheppard was at home under the roofs of the OSA and the RCA; he was featured in their increasingly predictable annual exhibitions, nurtured in that comforting embrace.

For Sheppard, this was both a snare and a delusion — a snare in that qualification for continuing membership did not include stylistic innovation, and to a degree Sheppard may therefore not have felt the urgency to develop artistically by absorbing contemporary styles and conventions. A delusion because, as his work shows, Sheppard had the interest and painterly capacity to adapt and adopt advanced styles that reflected more than a passing acquaintance with new painting movements. His move to abstraction and his ease working in an Impressionist mode indicate a creative agility that was, no doubt, rare.

But where did this stylistic and aesthetic polymath feel most comfortable? Did he have one particular natural voice or was he fluent in a number of artistic languages? The evidence in the archive suggests that by the early 1930s Sheppard's talents were wide ranging, so wide ranging that he set himself apart as unique, maybe even in a class of his own; he moved easily among the orthodoxies, but did not abide strictly by their rules.

As a result of speaking in many voices, Sheppard may not have been fully understood by his peers and contemporaries. Perhaps he himself second-guessed his approach to such an extent that he sometimes showed a split of intentionality in a single painting. Take for example *Late Autumn Sunset* (see page 207). The composition is lit by an evening sky defined by bands of greys and dark violets, and also by sharply delineated yellow passages. While the handling of form moves in the direction of abstraction, the painting also shows that the artist may have felt uncomfortable letting go entirely of the crutch of tangible references.

TORONTO WARD PAINTINGS, 1930s

While Sheppard continued to live on Oakwood Ave, in 1932 he appears also to have established a studio nearby at 982 Bloor Street West, in a commercial property owned by Hastings Wainright, which also accommodated dentists, a Fuller Brush distributor, a chocolate maker and James R. Tate, another artist (see page 225). Although he was now situated relatively far north of the largely immigrant neighbourhood known as "the Ward," Sheppard turned his attention to interpreting its gritty, working-class streets (notably Louisa and Elizabeth Streets), alleys, houses and shacks as portraits of resilient survival in places defined by transition and impoverishment.

By the early 1930s Sheppard likely did not have to look far for subjects that were emblems of poverty, a condition of the times brought about by the sudden economic downturn of the late 1920s and the subsequent Depression of the early 1930s that hung as a pall over the city. For an artist with Sheppard's abilities and aesthetic turn of mind, it must have seemed a small step to turn to subjects that reflected a mood of downcast melancholy brought on by straitened circumstances. There are several paintings in the archive that attest to Sheppard's sympathetic portrayal of the poverty that disrupted the lives that fell within his gaze. His painting *Hard Times* (page 209) is an evocative composition showing a couple of men sitting on a bench apparently lost in thought, perhaps even aimlessly passing the time. In his handling of the pigment, even Sheppard's treatment has a haphazard feel about it, possibly reflecting a cast of indigence and drift. His drawing is unusually clumsy. In fact, it appears as if Sheppard abandoned the painting while it was in its early stages; the painting that survives in the archive seems to be not much more than an underdrawing, yet one with a compelling presence that, deliberately or not, speaks to a kind of hopelessness as a consequence of being poor.

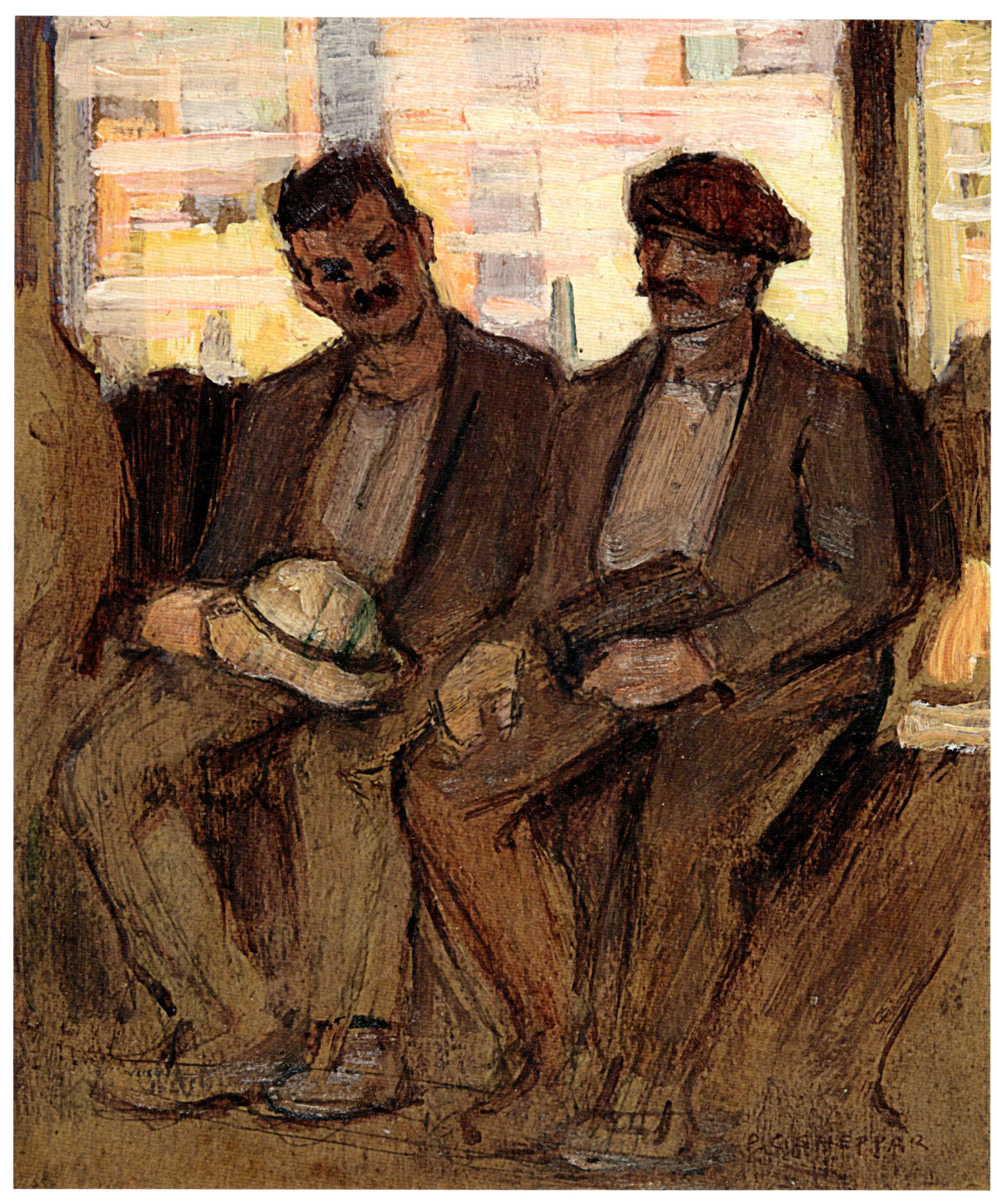

Hard Times.
1932. Oil on board,
26.7 x 21.6 cm.

Sheppard's *Knife Sharpener* (see page 211) is also emblematic of listless in-activity that might well be a condition of indigence. The painting is more tonal drawing than a colourful picture; its bold contours define a figure — a transient knife sharpener — asleep on a park bench in the shadow of a tree. The figure has been carefully foreshortened, reflecting the keen eye of the artist, who appears to also have had a good deal of time to lay in the figure in the composition as he lay fast asleep. The shadowed man is rendered in a rich array of duns and green-greys. The landscape beyond the gloaming radiates with light that throws the man into a sharp silhouette. A portrait of a down-and-out fellow, the painting is also a metaphor of hard times, of drift as a condition of unemployment.

LOUISA STREET AND ELIZABETH STREET SKETCHES AND PAINTINGS, EARLY 1930s

Sheppard's studies and paintings of a series of houses on Louisa Street provide a way of seeing how he continued to use sketches and drawings made in the field as sources of information to be edited and amended in the studio for creative and expressive ends. In the early 1930s, the Ward in general, and Louisa Street in particular, drew his attention as resonant subjects. He meandered through the Ward, a transitional working-class neighbourhood of

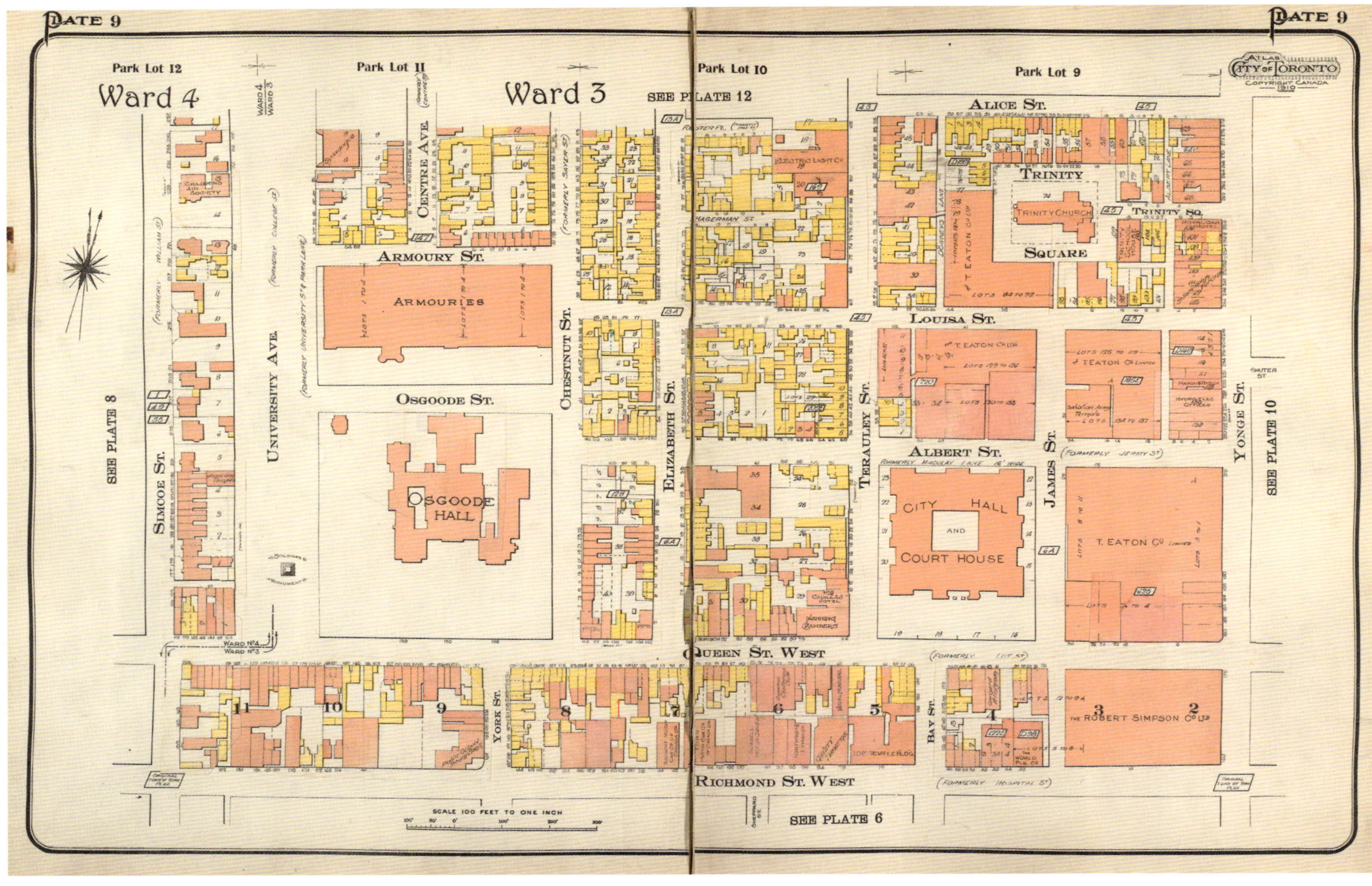

Map of the Ward, Toronto, 1913.

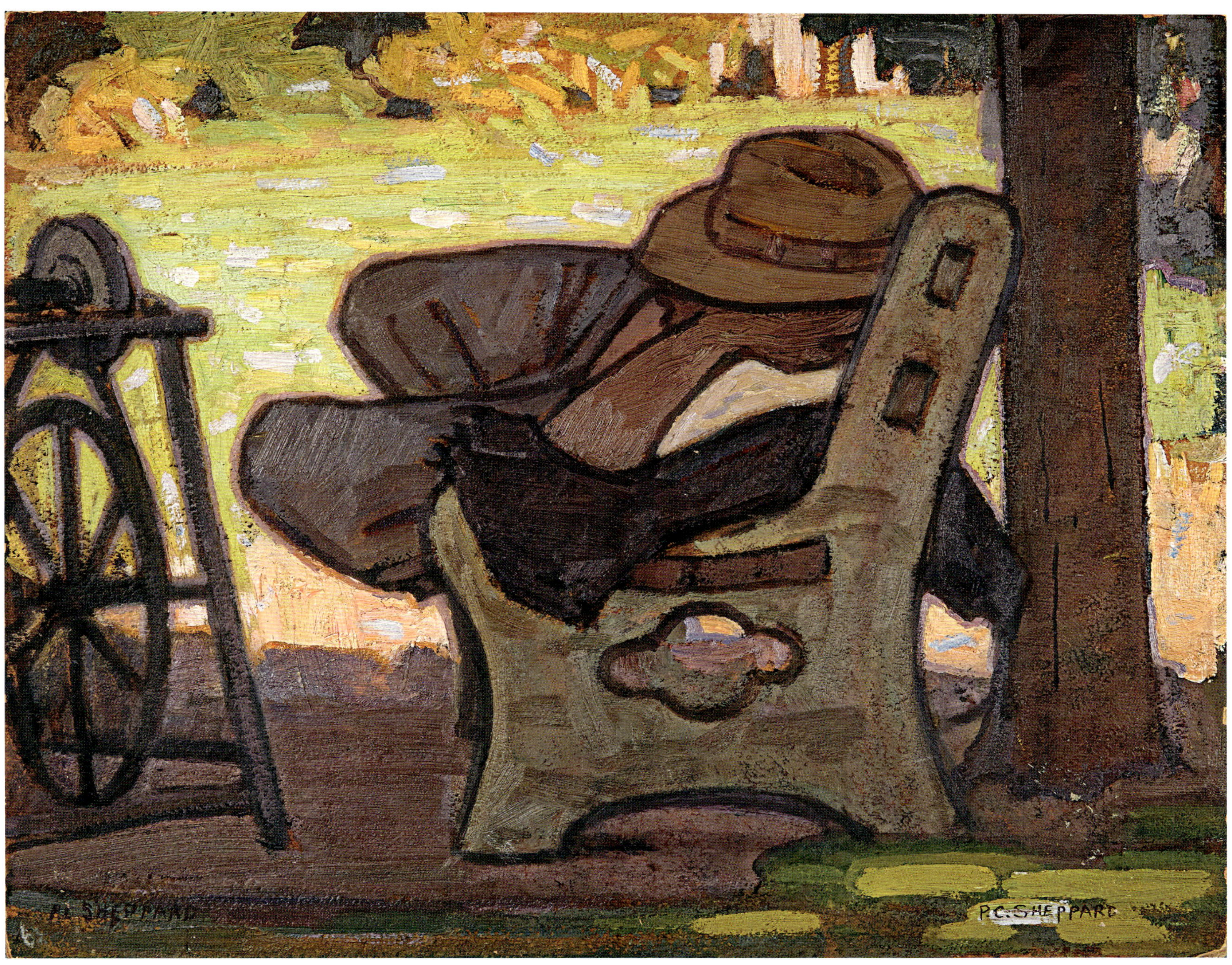

The Knife Sharpener.
1932. Oil on board,
33 x 40.6 cm.

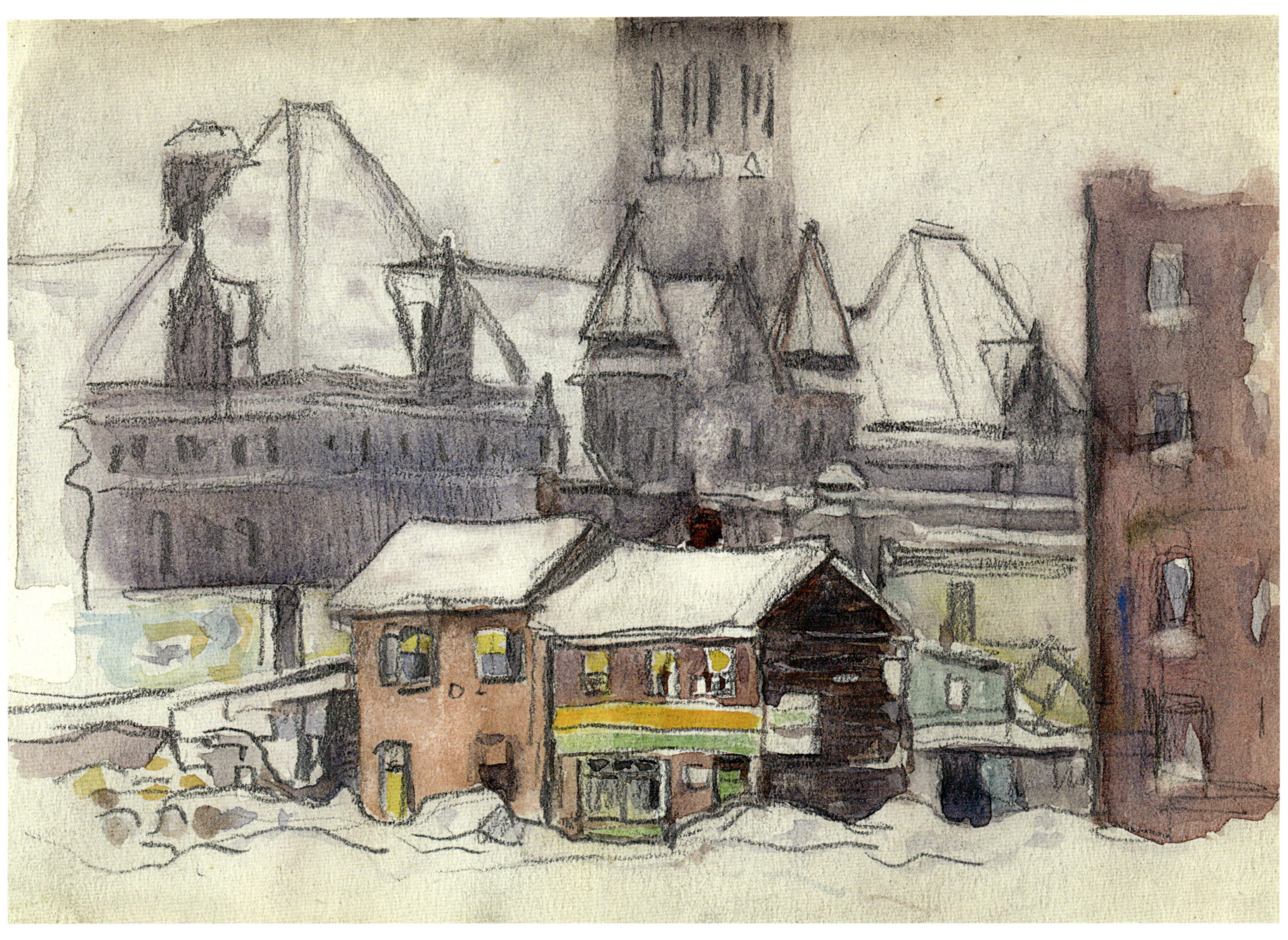

Louisa Street.
1930–31. Watercolour,
12.7 x 17.8 cm.

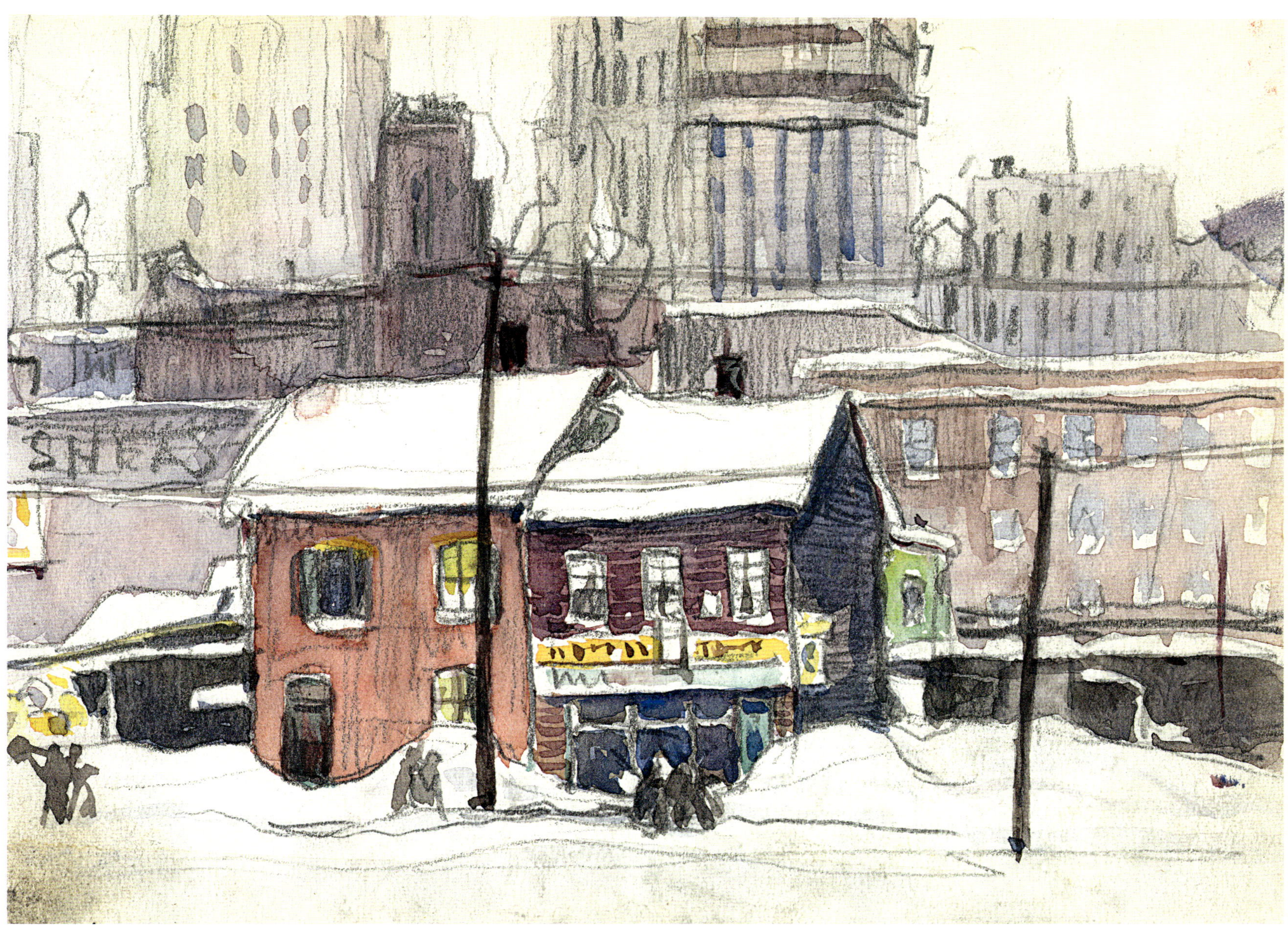

The Ward.
1930–31. Watercolour,
12.7 x 17.8 cm.

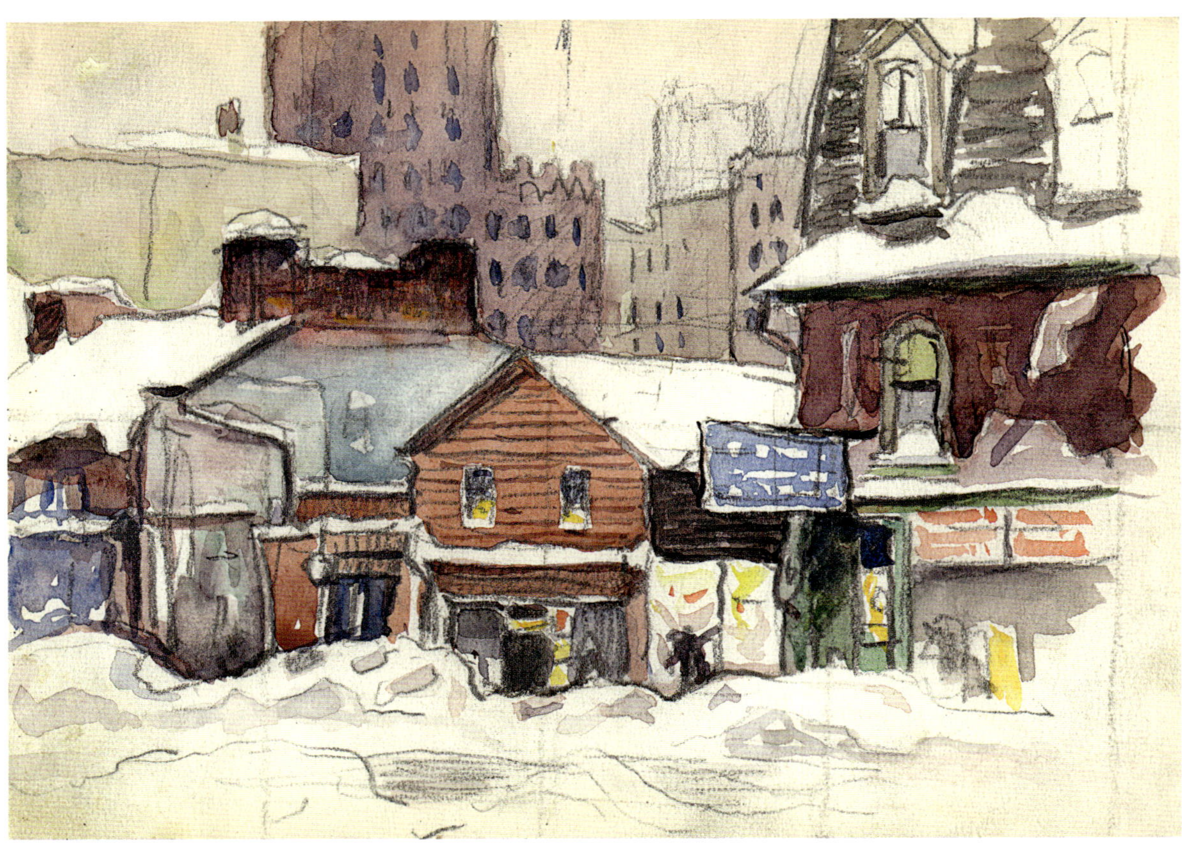

The Ward.
1930–31. Watercolour and graphite, 12.7
x 17.8 cm.

Elizabeth Street.
1930–31. Watercolour and graphite,
12.7 x 17.8 cm.

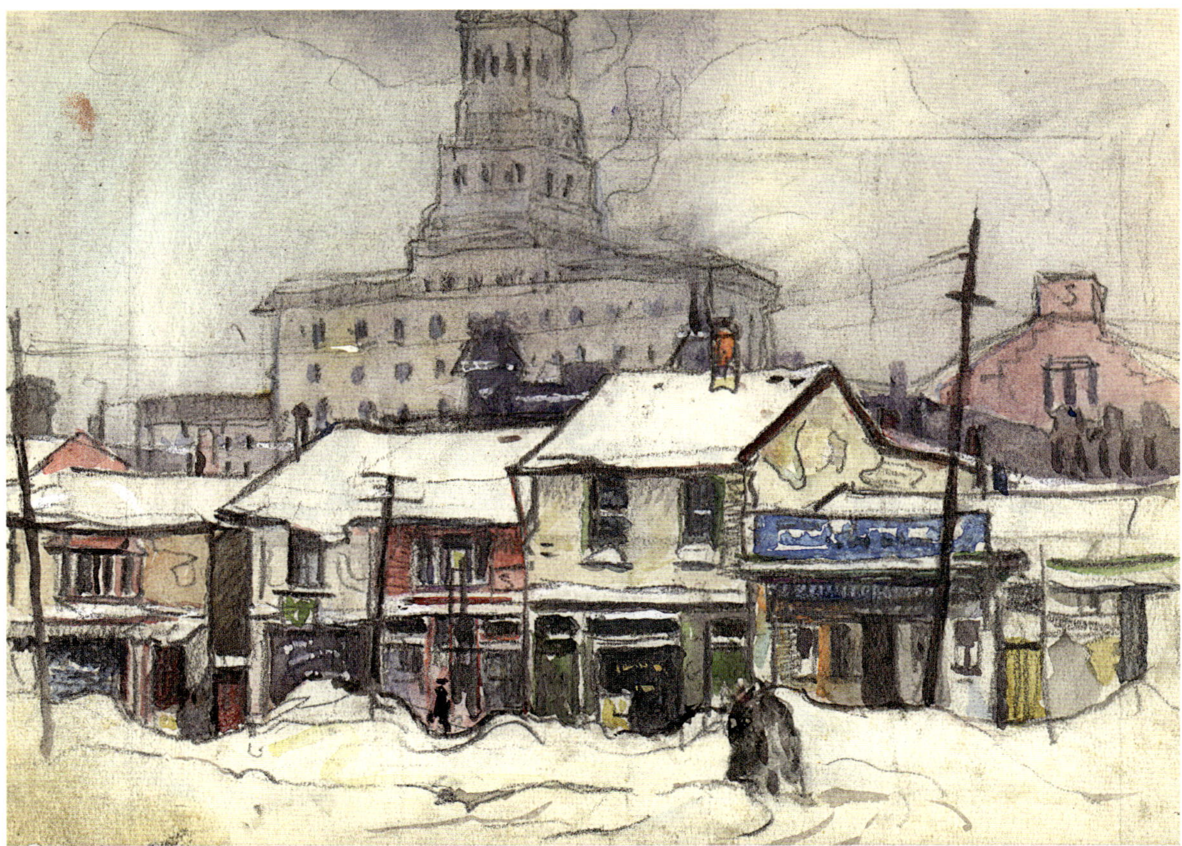

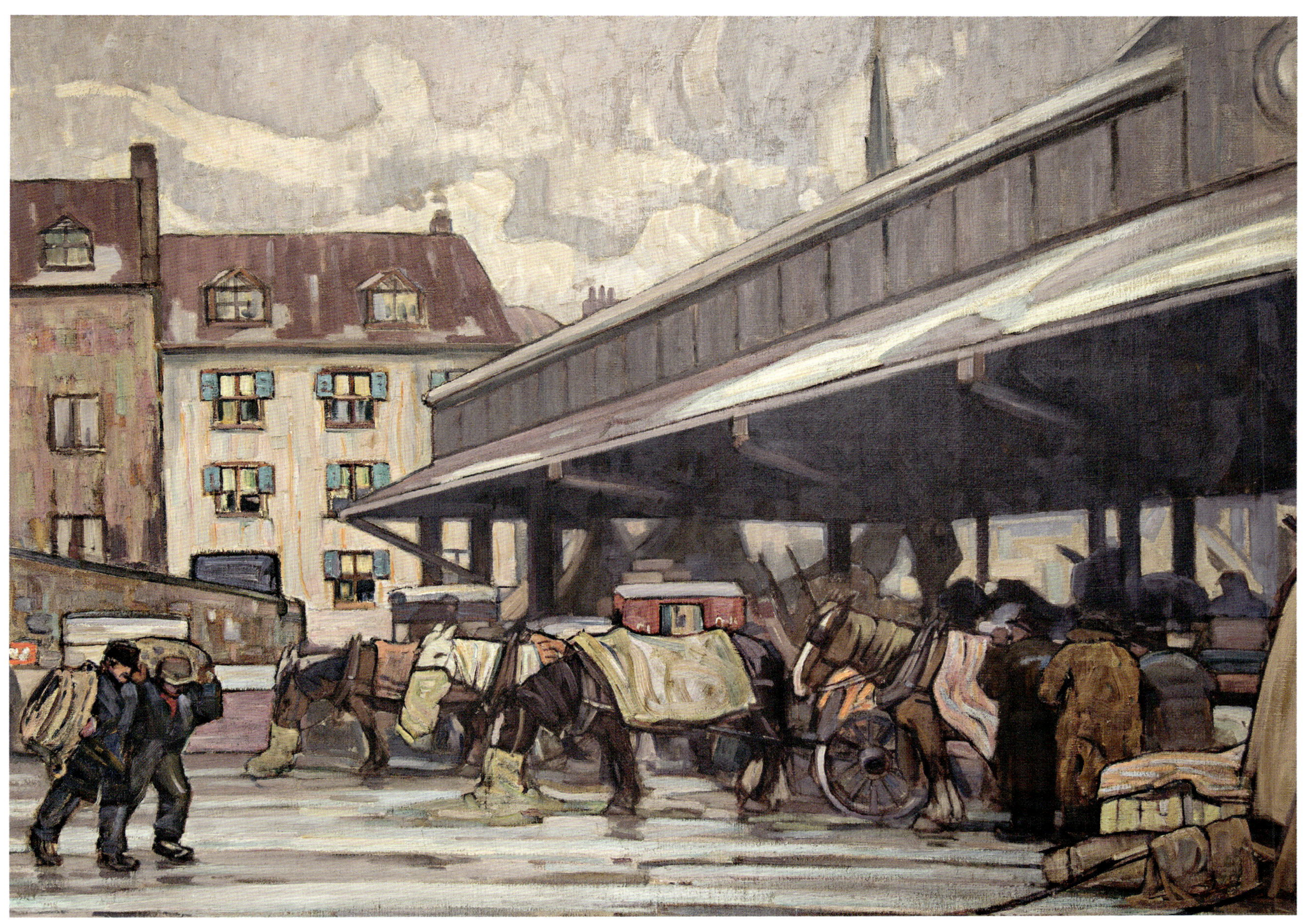

The Market, November.
1929. Oil on canvas,
90 x 122 cm.

cottage-lined streets and lanes thrown together in the late decades of the 19th century. The place had the feeling of buildings being squeezed into a parcel of land between the commercial district and the university on the western city limits in the shadow of the City Hall (and where the present-day City Hall now stands), in which predominantly Italian, Chinese and Jewish immigrants settled in after arriving in their newly adopted country. It was a place of poverty, disease and hardship as its citizens strove to stake their claims in the rapidly expanding city and country.[81]

The Ward's first and most renowned artist interpreter was Lawren Harris, who, even before he helped to found the Group of Seven, painted scenes and urban views of the Ward. Fascinated by subjects that related to all aspects of the modern city, Harris painted them with a focus on drawing out a beauty found in the patterns, colours and rhythms of the houses and streets. In fact, he imbued the Ward with such beauty that it entirely disguised the place's Dickensian squalor. His first known Ward painting was completed in 1912, well before Sheppard took on the same subjects some two decades later. By 1913, Harris' take on the neighbourhood was characterized by a highly keyed, bright palette and an impressionistic mode. Where he included figures they were laden with a kind of moral baggage that was meant to exemplify the artist's concern for documenting an aspect of the human condition, notably alienation, as it was seen in the Ward.[82] By 1926 Harris had ceased painting urban subjects in favour of landscapes that drew him further into an abstract mode.

In the early 1930s, Sheppard made pencil and watercolour sketches of the Ward, among them an affectionate study of two houses on Louisa Street portrayed as domestic oases in an impassive urban desert of commercial and public buildings (among them Toronto's City Hall) dwarfing the human-scaled houses (see page 212). This watercolour among the booklet of sketches was used as a reference in his studio when he made not only direct portraits of the streetscape but also other streetscapes, based on Louisa Street's buildings, that were intended to be general metaphors of the modern, if downtrodden, city.

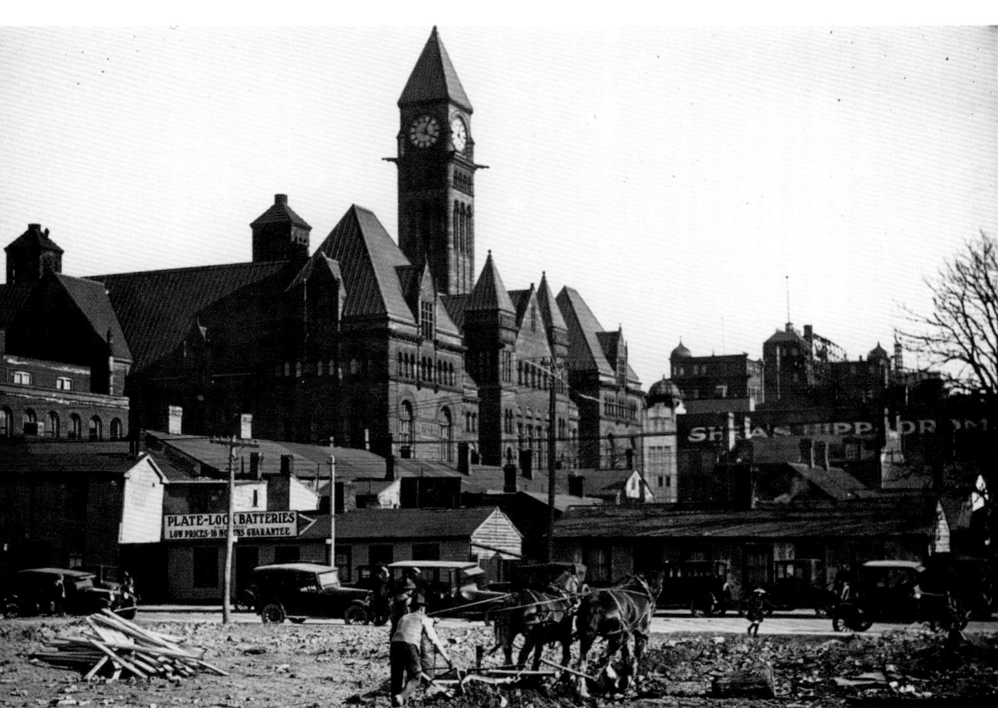

Compare the *Louisa Street* sketch (page 212) with this archival photograph of Toronto City Hall, c. 1918.

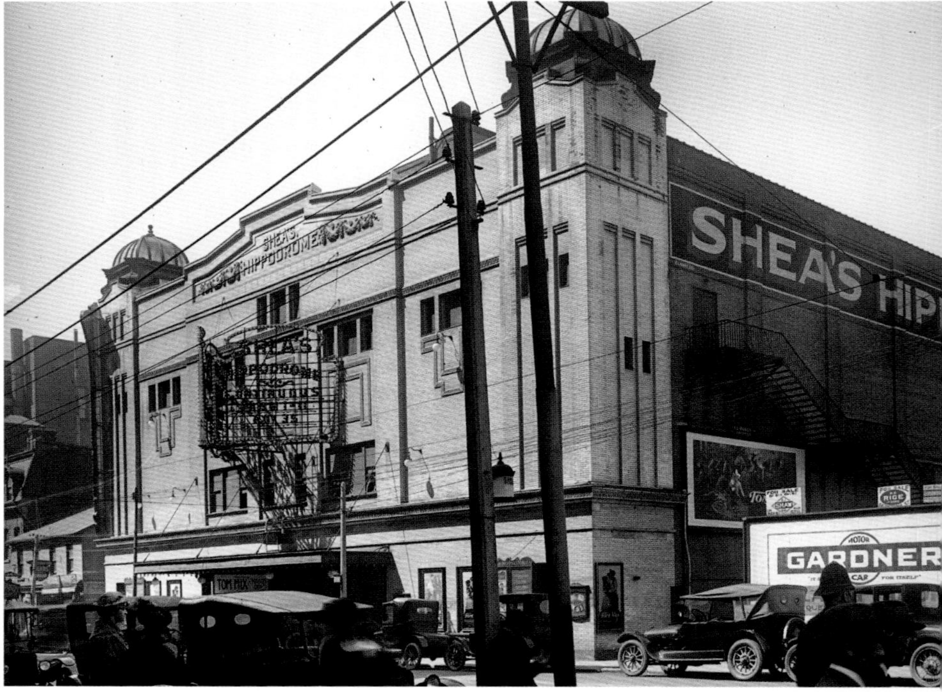

Shea's Hippodrome Theatre, Toronto, c. 1920. Opened in 1914, the Hippodrome, located at Queen and Teraulay Street, could seat 3,000 and was the largest vaudeville theatre in Canada. By 1920 it was ranked among the top vaudeville houses in North America. The building was demolished in 1957.

His *Three Old Houses, Louisa Street* (see page 218), a studio canvas based loosely on the sketch on page 212, blends an overall feeling of heaviness, world-weariness, with a sense of a living, breathing and vital neighbourhood that is hibernating in the winter. The formal rank of three ramshackle Louisa Street houses is contrasted with the large commercial skyscrapers rising up in the background, which serve as backdrops to the domestic architecture. Although it is a humble subject, Sheppard nevertheless brings to it his gifts as a visual storyteller and composer. The snowbanks in the foreground act as a screen to overcome before entering the scene itself. The actual Louisa Street view, looking south and east, of two mid-block houses at lots 61 and 63, near the corner of Teraulay Street, has been altered to include three, rather than two, structures. And the actual background view of City Hall's steeply pitched roofline has been replaced by commercial towers and what appears to be the silhouette of Shea's Hippodrome, whose uniquely designed corner tower is rendered in Sheppard's fanciful cityscape background.

Pedestrians trudge through the snowdrifts mimicking the way the eye moves in and along the street. Beyond the descriptive elements of the composition, Sheppard glosses the view with a prosaic narrative. His handling of the snow lends it an almost human presence. The folds of the drifts suggest a breath-like rhythm and flow. In this, Sheppard echoes the work of contemporary and Group of Seven member A.Y. Jackson. In contrast to these anthropomorphic stylizations, the built structures are linear, crisply defined in colours associated with old houses — oranges, reds, purples, greens and greys. All of these elements animate the houses in a kind, affectionate way, leaving the viewer with the impression that the subject in all its dimensions engaged the artist deeply. The Louisa Street sketch also served as a source for Sheppard's painting *Old Houses* (see page 219), a painting that similarly looks south but has a different arrangement of buildings forming the background cityscape. City Hall has been replaced by an accumulation of commercial buildings and possibly a structure based on Shea's Hippodrome, signified by the "EAS" lettered on the side of the building to the left of the composition. This painting was exhibited at the 1934 CNE exhibition and reproduced in its catalogue.

Just as Sheppard made use of the Louisa Street sketch as a source for several paintings that derived from it, he also adapted an Elizabeth Street sketch (see page 214) in the service of interpreting not only a particular piece of a Ward neighbourhood, but also the city generally. Similar to its close cousin on Louisa Street, the Elizabeth Street watercolour-and-graphite sketch juxtaposes the domestic and commercial nature of the subject: a row of hardscrabble houses and businesses cobbled together in a rank are weighted down by the heavy burden of the snowfall as well as by the looming towers of the commercial district beyond. The edifice in the distance is the newly constructed Canada Life Building, which opened in 1931. Sheppard's canvas *Elizabeth Street* (see page 220), which is based on the sketch, is very similar in style and mood to the Louisa Street paintings, although there is a stronger linearity in the former painting than in the latter. As with the Louisa Street painting, this scene is entered visually by passing over the screen of the snowdrift through which two men trudge. These anonymous forms are convenient stand-ins for the viewers to occupy imaginatively and animate. In contrast to the flowing, almost figurative, lines of the snowfall, the row of built structures establishes a visual rhythm based on the interrelationships of rectangles and triangles that are ever more intricately facetted. The background is beautifully coloured and brushed in with a palette of blues, mauves and pinks, whites and greys. Contrasts abound in this painting between the natural and the built: the human-scaled houses and the gargantuan commercial buildings; snow and stone; geometrical and lyrical lines. The electrical utility pole shown slightly akimbo at the right of the composition lends the work a prosaic touch and humanity. Through it Sheppard appears to identify (or at least to interpret) the Ward as being more humane than megalithic.

Elizabeth Street was exhibited in the 1933 OSA exhibition along with two other Sheppard paintings — *The Market, November* and *Sea Port/Ocean Freighter.* Of these two canvases, I pause over *The Market, November* (see page 215), because the overwhelming feeling I have is that its foundation shows Sheppard's capacity to draw very well. The various vignettes framed in its composition and under the market's open-air canopy are attentively laid into the composition. Men shouldering their goods, a sack of grain, a washtub and affectionately described horses all attest to the artist's keen observational skills. The colour palette is intentionally subdued in a way that allows for the contour lines to be more evident than if they were under a layer of heavy, opaque pigment. And the framing device of the canopy also allows Sheppard to develop a visual patterning based on the rectangles that subdivide into ever smaller sections, establishing a pleasing abstract rhythm all its own, separate from the narrative of the market's activity.

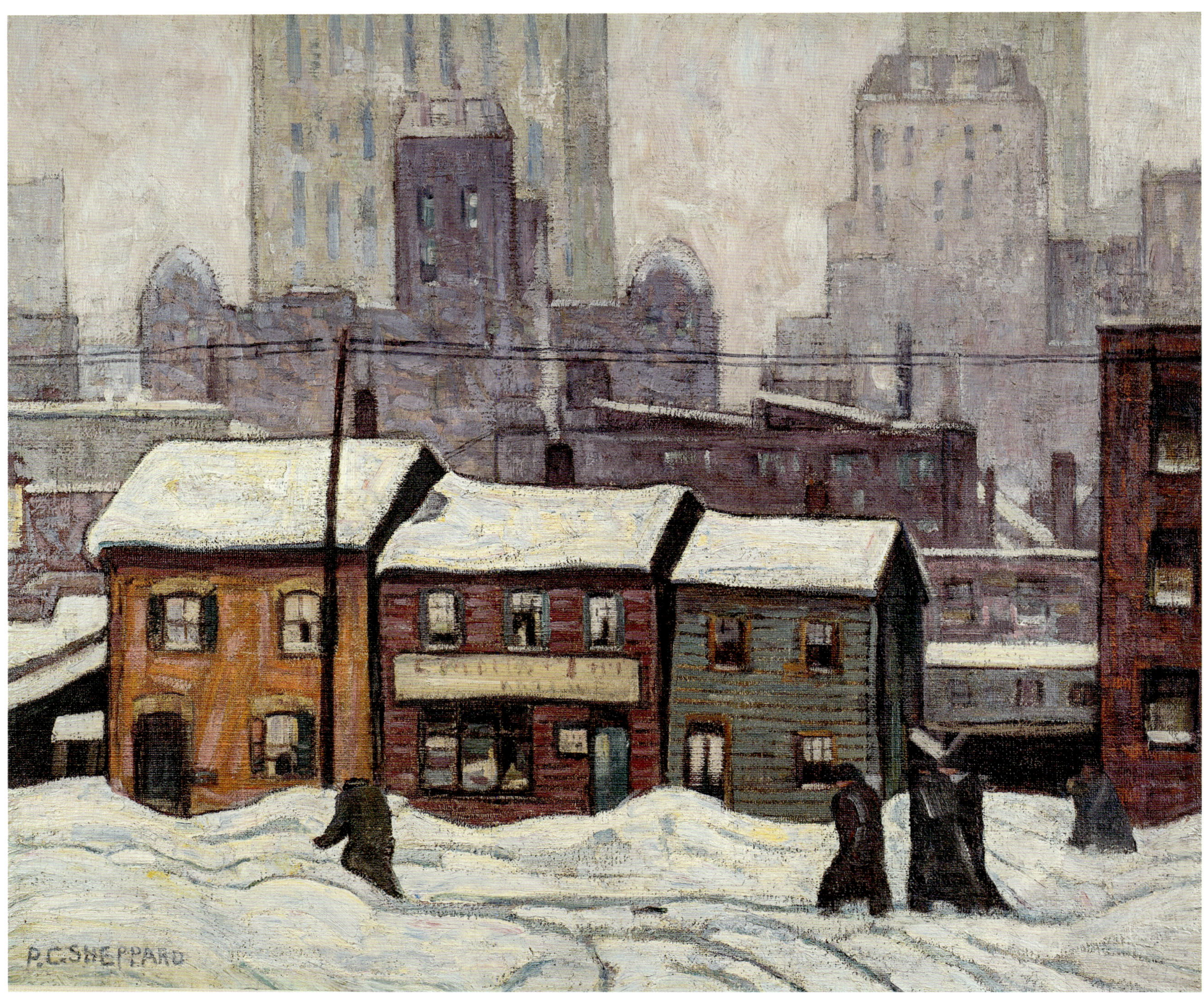

Three Old Houses, Louisa Street.
1930–31. Oil on canvas,
76 x 91.4 cm.

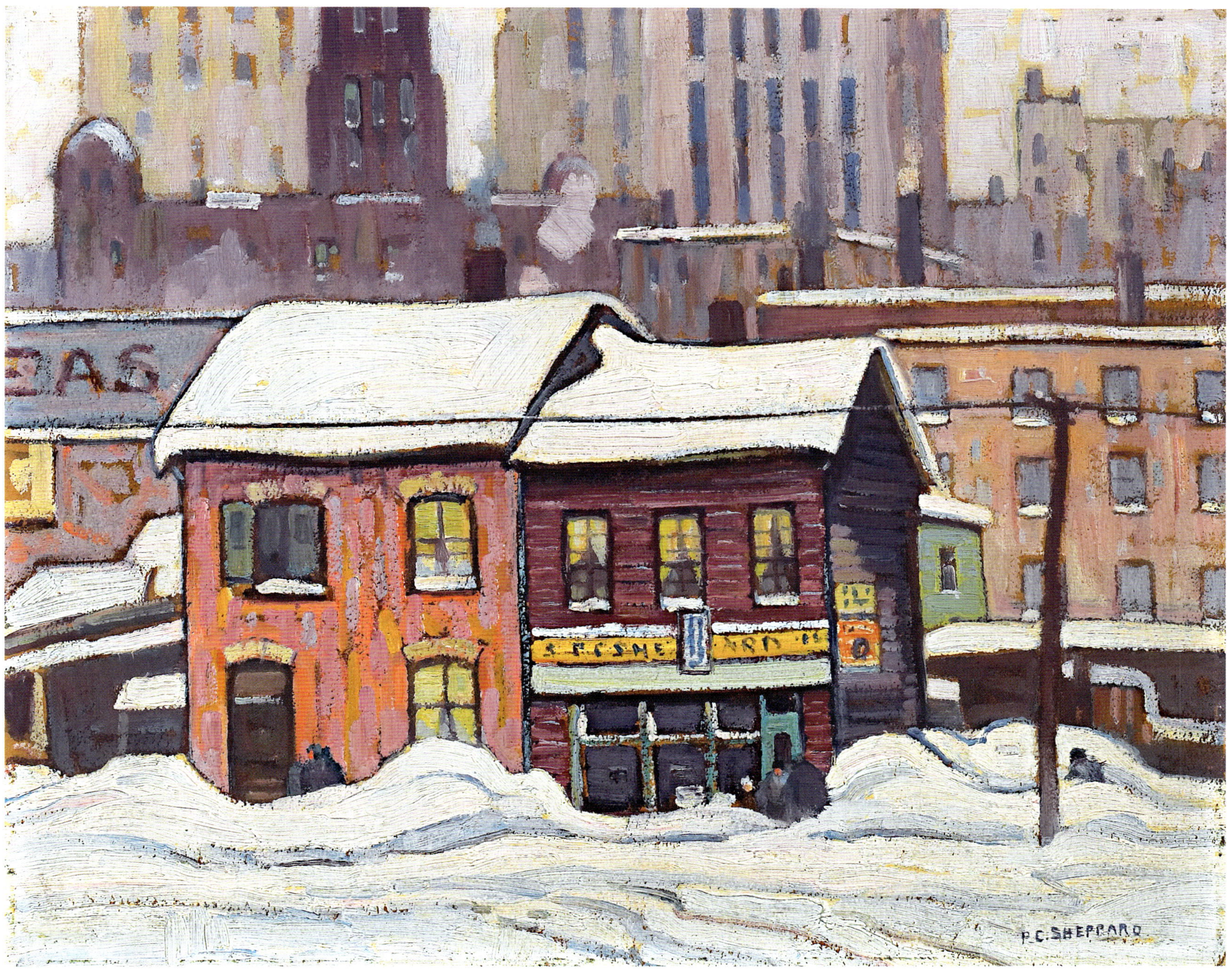

Old Houses.
1931. Oil on board,
33 x 40.6 cm.

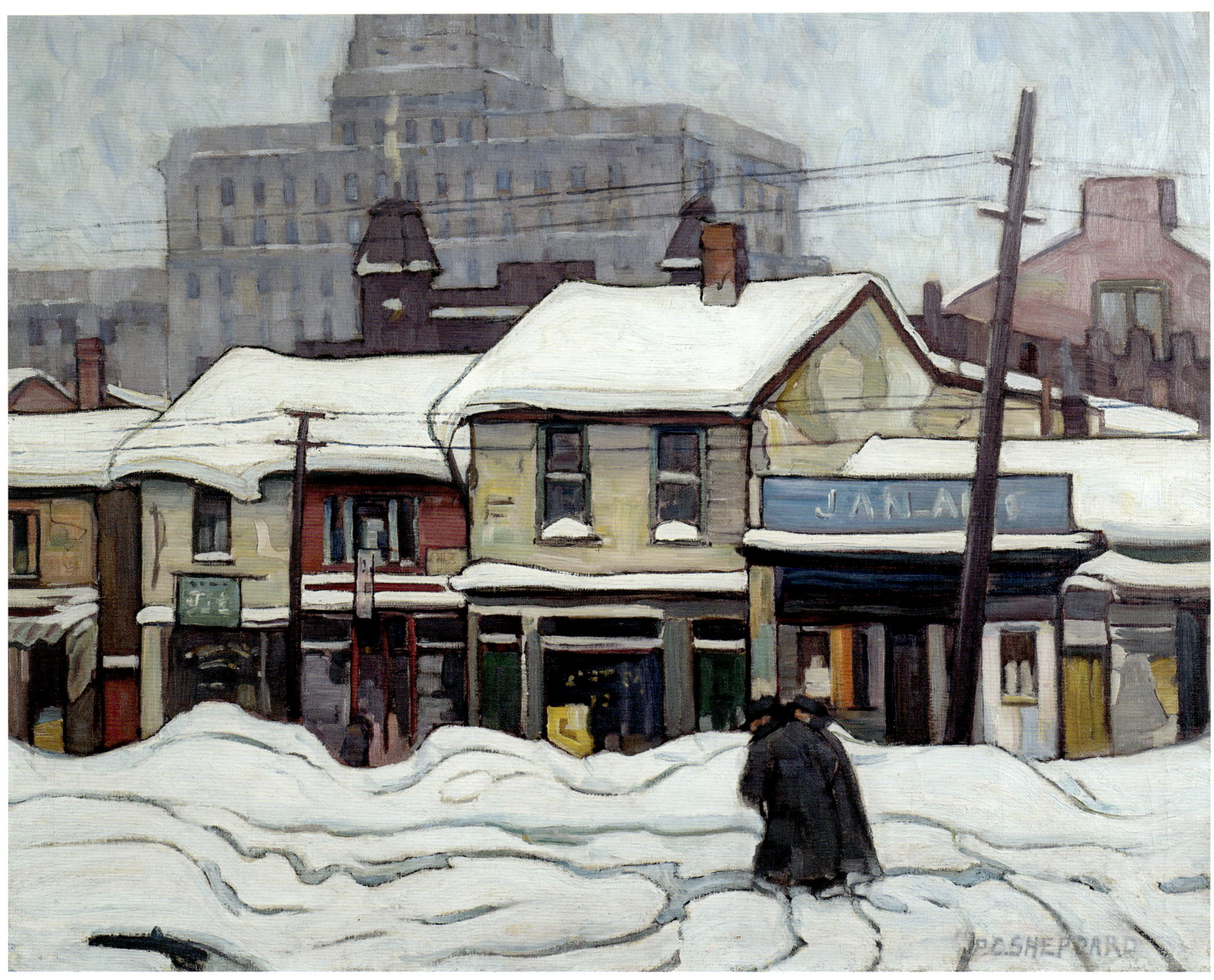

Elizabeth Street.
1930–31. Oil on canvas,
76 x 91.4 cm.

IMPARTIAL ECLECTICISM, 1934

A middle-aged man of 55 now, Sheppard was comfortably part of the art establishment of his time. A regularly exhibiting artist in the annual OSA and RCA exhibitions, he was swept up in the smooth machinery of these professional societies and basked in the acclaim membership accorded him. He also benefited from the patina of development and artistic growth that they offered him and his associates when their work that was rounded up and put on view every year. Indeed, the critics recognized his creative range as demonstrated in the Ward paintings. Graham Campbell McInnes writes in a review that Sheppard is:

> at his best among the skyscraper and the docks. "Queen Street" and "Louisa Street" bring out admirably the desolation and oppressiveness not only of the snow-laden streets, but of the frowning towers of commerce behind them. But that Mr. Sheppard can vary both subject matter and technique is shown by his "Springtime," a riot of color, and a bowl of "Marigolds" with some of the strength and directness of Van Gogh sunflowers.[83]

By the mid-1930s I imagine Sheppard was comfortable as a professional, and enjoyed his status as one, a feeling likely reinforced by the tone of the introductory message to the 1934 OSA exhibition (its 62nd) noting that this iteration of the annual "forms the third of a series of unusually interesting displays of recent months." (The series included the retrospective exhibitions *Canadian Art of Early Days* and *French Impressionists of the Last Century*). "From each of these periods of artistic activity," the OSA's president L.A.C. Panton stated, "modern art in Canada received much inspiration; and its development, while slow and reserved, bears evidence of the tendency to combine the fine qualities of pioneer art with the newer emotional expressions and technical practices of the more advanced French school." Panton pointed to two "sources of influence" in the modern scene. The first he dubbed "tradition" and the other he characterized as displaying "adventure and experiment"; he also said the two were often "in decided conflict." But, he added, Canadian painters found middle ground between the two poles, seeking "to present the life and character" of the country "unhampered by any slavish respect for established idioms of other schools." "Impartial eclecticism": that was the fundamental quality of painting of 1934 in Canada, according to Panton, a tendency to draw from a range of influences and sources to define, depict and interpret the Canadian experience, landscape and people. Sheppard, as an exhibiting member of the OSA show, was brushed with this rhetoric that "mark[s] a new advance in the interpretation of the Canadian scene."[84]

Sheppard's four entries — *The Hunter, St. John River, Island Ferry* (*Toronto*) and *Harbour Scene* (*Halifax*) — suggest that he preferred to stay on familiar terrain with landscapes and water scenes. He was still accorded a level of respect in the catalogue; *Halifax Harbour* (see page 222) was reproduced in it. The painting is tightly composed with all the linear relationships well balanced — two masts bisect the format, while the houses, warehouses and church steeple establish a geometrically organized landscape and convincing spatial depth. The schooner in the foreground is crisply rendered and set off from the background. Overall, the treatment of the subject shows a draftsman-like sensibility in rendering the scene primarily using contour lines. The painting was also mentioned in a review of the RCA exhibition (in which it was also included); the critic noted that on the whole, among the selection of paintings "there is nothing that shocks nor strains credulity too far." Indeed, the reviewer goes on, "Wharfside scenes have long interested Peter C. Sheppard, A.R.C.A, and the diversity of such subjects have lured him to the waterfront in 'Harbour Scene, Halifax' and 'St. John River.'"[85]

IN THE COMPANY OF "GOOD PICTURES"

By the mid-1930s, if Sheppard had an identity in the Ontario and Canadian art scenes, a good part of it was based on his membership in the art societies and the loyal support of their members not only as an exhibitor, but also as a participant in their administration. One example of his dutiful involvement in the smooth running of the OSA's annual exhibitions is his place on the "competent and representative" 1936 "Selection and Hanging Committee" alongside C.W. Jefferys and Fred Brigden, who were busy that year accepting 215 works to the exhibition ("eighty-one being by forty-five members; one hundred thirty-four by ninety-seven non-members").

But Sheppard's close connection with the OSA, while it had advanced his career as a young artist 20 years earlier, did not do him any favours in the mid-1930s. Increasingly, as newer modes of representation and progressive styles began to hold sway in more advanced artistic circles in Canada and the United States — and in Toronto — the OSA could not shake its hidebound, conservative identity.

A younger generation was moving on into ever more creative territories, leaving the OSA in its wake. Rather than be content with working in a pictorial mode, making well composed formalist constructions that solely interpreted the landscape (as did the Group of Seven and their acolytes), progressive Canadian artists were engaging with society and with internationalism in

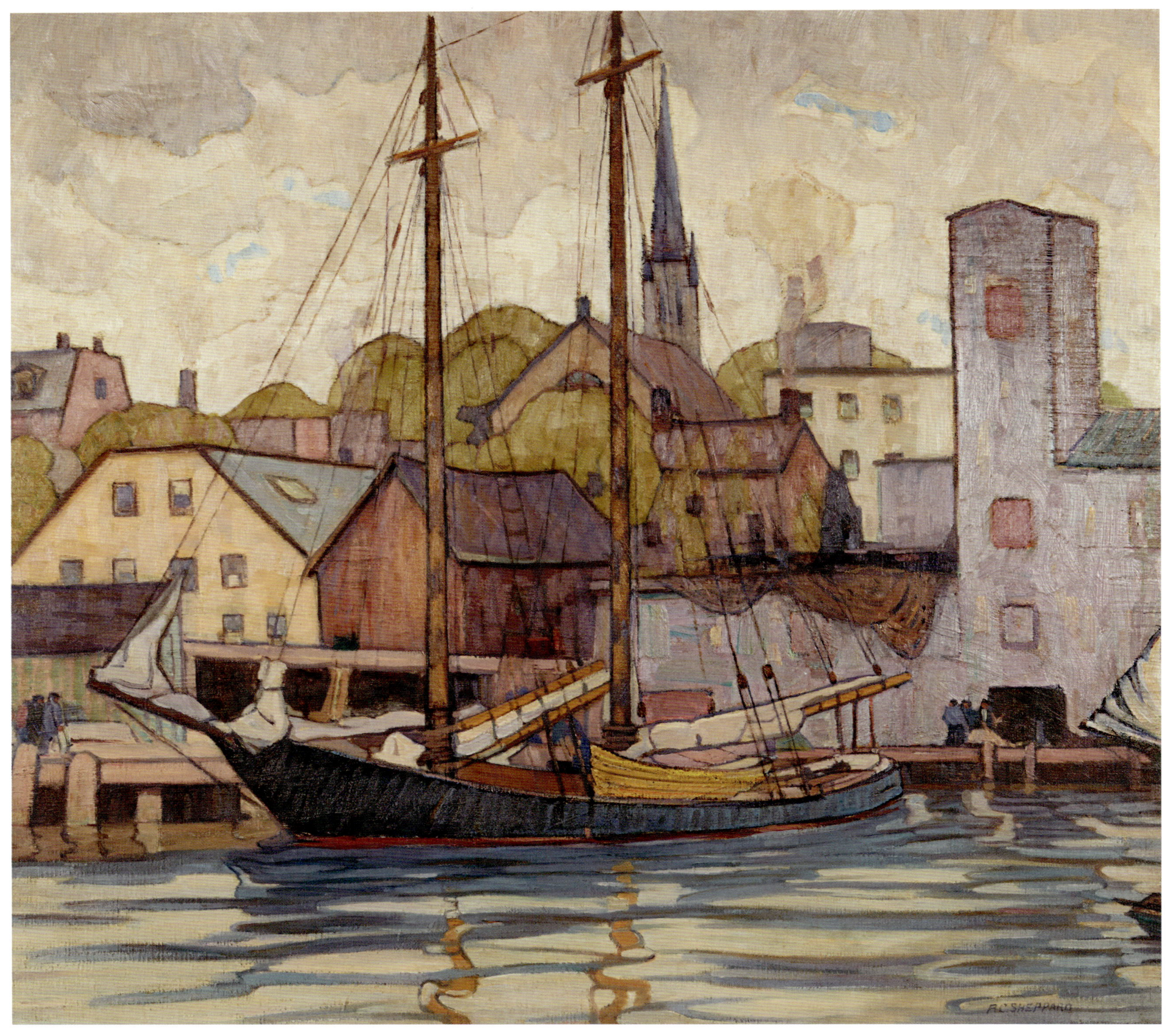

Harbour Scene (Halifax).
1934. Oil on canvas,
85 x 95 cm.

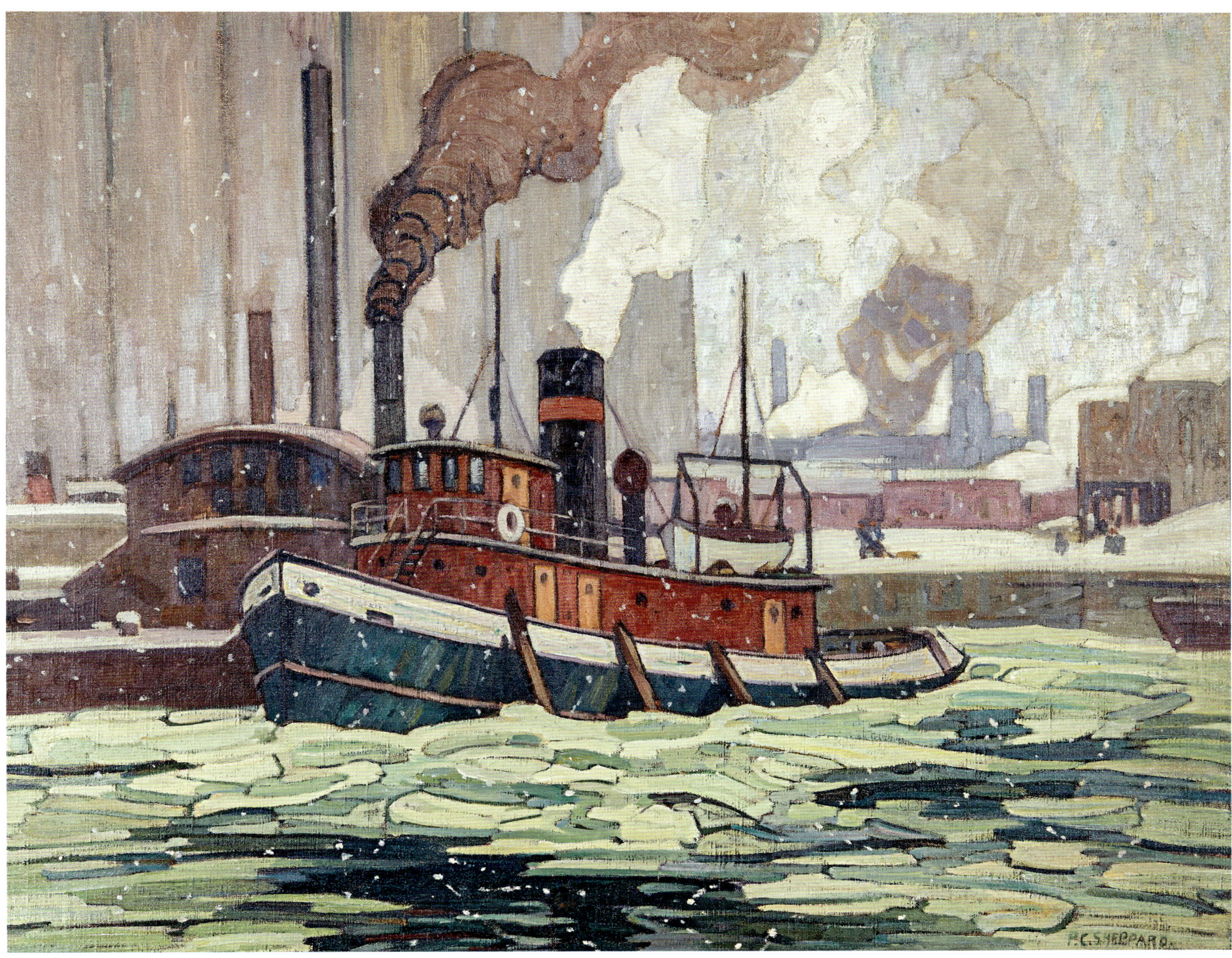

Winter Ferry/City Docks.
1935–36. Oil on canvas,
89 x 111.8 cm.

ways that put stresses on Sheppard's generation of artists, and their paintings increasingly became irrelevant. They did not speak in a resonant voice to the difficult economic conditions facing many Canadians in the 1930s. Neither did they embrace a form of strident nationalism that sought to find a unique Canadian identity in cultural products. They also did not adopt international styles and translate them as an urgent language that voiced Canadian themes.

The Contemporary Arts Society, formed in Montreal in 1939, represented a need among the younger artists to band together in their own exhibiting society, in which they presented advanced abstract, non-figurative and Surrealist-inspired art to the public. Other artists sought ways to adapt the lessons of the American Regionalists into their art — work that reflected social conditions, impoverishment and the necessity of communal action to combat society's ills. Social commentary, industrial landscapes, still lifes, emblematic figurative art, symbolism: these forms, genres, conventions and modes supplanted the tired riffs that were predominantly promulgated by the OSA and RCA.

What brought artists together was a need to find an economic and social model that not only valued the place of art in society, but also rewarded its artists with respect and a living wage. In the midst of this turbulence, Sheppard's generation was under pressure either to transform themselves and the institutions that they had built, and which had served them well, or risk being cast aside, to disappear from notice and from history.

The evidence in the archive points to Sheppard choosing to follow the creative path that he knew best. While the winds of change were blowing through the art world, inside his studio at 982 Bloor Street West, not far from his home at 48 Oakwood Avenue, where he appears to have been living with his elder sister, Adelaide, Sheppard took comfort in his several subjects: forested landscapes, remote rivers and lakes, and his beloved views of ships plying the waters of Lake Ontario. Among the latter subject matter, Sheppard's *Winter Ferry/City Docks* (see page 223) from around 1936 is an accomplished performance by an adept practitioner of this kind of painting. Well composed and clearly delineated, the painting of a sturdy ferry working the waters has a monumental quality about it, even though the subject is a workhorse of the dockside fleet. As a subject and composition, it echoes one of the earliest works of art in the archive — a 1910 etching of a tugboat. This sense is due to how Sheppard has laid in the outlines of the forms so deliberately and confidently, and then coloured the painted drawing in a way that makes

it easy to imagine he was emulating the way a large-format mural might be painted. There is also an emblematic quality to the boat, as if it were symbolic of something else, as if it were, in fact, the personification of a character who embodied the qualities of strength, endurance and dependability when a confluence of forces and currents might threaten to throw a lesser vessel (or person) off-kilter. *Winter Ferry/City Docks* might have autobiographical overtones reflecting the enduring spirit and character of its creator. The painting did well for Sheppard, appearing in the 1937 RCA and OSA annuals, and it was also displayed in 1939 at the New York World's Fair *Exhibition of Canadian Art,* alongside similar workhorse portraits, landscapes and seascapes.

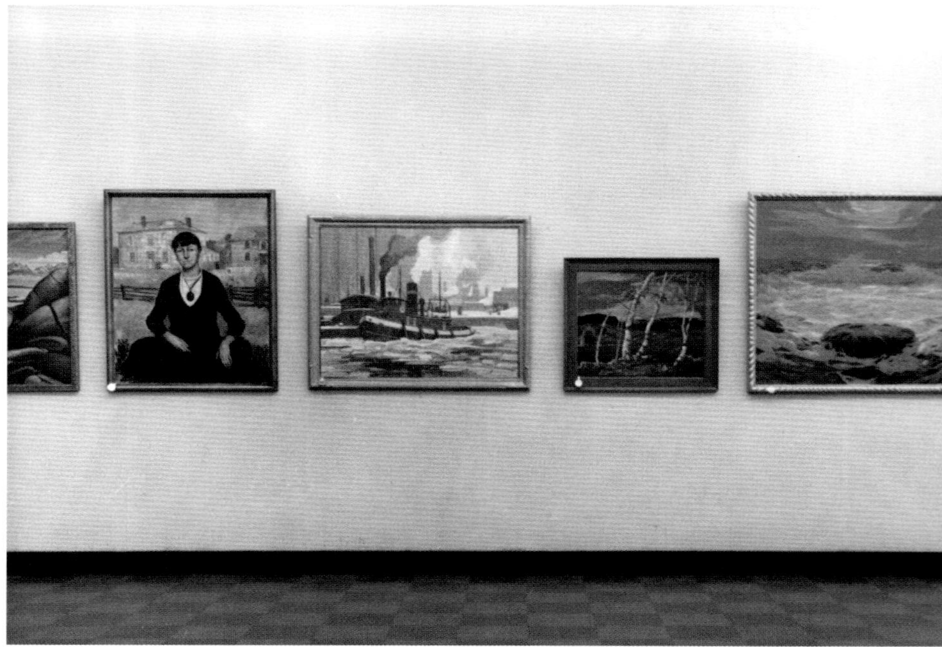

RCA Travelling Exhibition, New York World's Fair, 1939. Sheppard's *Winter Ferry/ City Docks* is shown alongside other Canadian paintings.

A KIND OF RETIREMENT

While Sheppard continued to paint into the 1940s, the archive shows that he took comfort in the ways he had always used to produce paintings. Modernism did not advance either his creative approach or his personal style. It is not difficult to imagine that in his 60s, Sheppard's most innovative years were behind him. He painted for the pleasure of it. How could he do otherwise? In effect, he retired, and went to a creative place where he could satisfy whatever inner compulsion he still had to express himself, and which gave him the means to indulge his habit: painting outdoors and in his studio.

Even though the archive has no written documentation of these years, I imagine a man at ease, content to sit before his easel beside a Muskoka waterfall or on a hillside looking across a field to a rural village. I see him taking on the occasional student, passing on to them the tradecraft of an approach to art that spoke deeply to him, and whose genetic code lay in both the commercial and the fine arts.

Whatever fight might have been left in him to advance the cause of Canadian art, Sheppard now chose not to engage in it, and so faded from public notice. He lived with his younger sister, Jessie, in the late 1940s and 50s, and he maintained a studio at 8 Albany Street in Toronto's Annex neighbourhood until 1952 or 1953, when, at 74 years old, he disappears from the *City Directory*, in which up to this point he had been listed as an "Artist." He was sustained in these years by his friend Bernice Fenwick Martin, a former student and an artist in her own right. Based on the stories that Louis has passed on to me, it seems Peter and Bernice were close friends. She attended to and watched out for him as he grew older and feeble. Near the end, she saw to his comforts and found an institutional home for him when he needed nursing care.

Bernice also looked after his artistic affairs. She kept the contents of his studio safe. When Sheppard passed away on April 24, 1965, she inherited the studio archive and continued to be its watchful, attentive curator until Louis assumed its ownership in later decades. Upon Sheppard's passing, the OSA *President's Annual Report* noted that "shy and retiring in temperament, he nevertheless won students by his understanding and patience. To his few close friends he was of warm affection and humour."

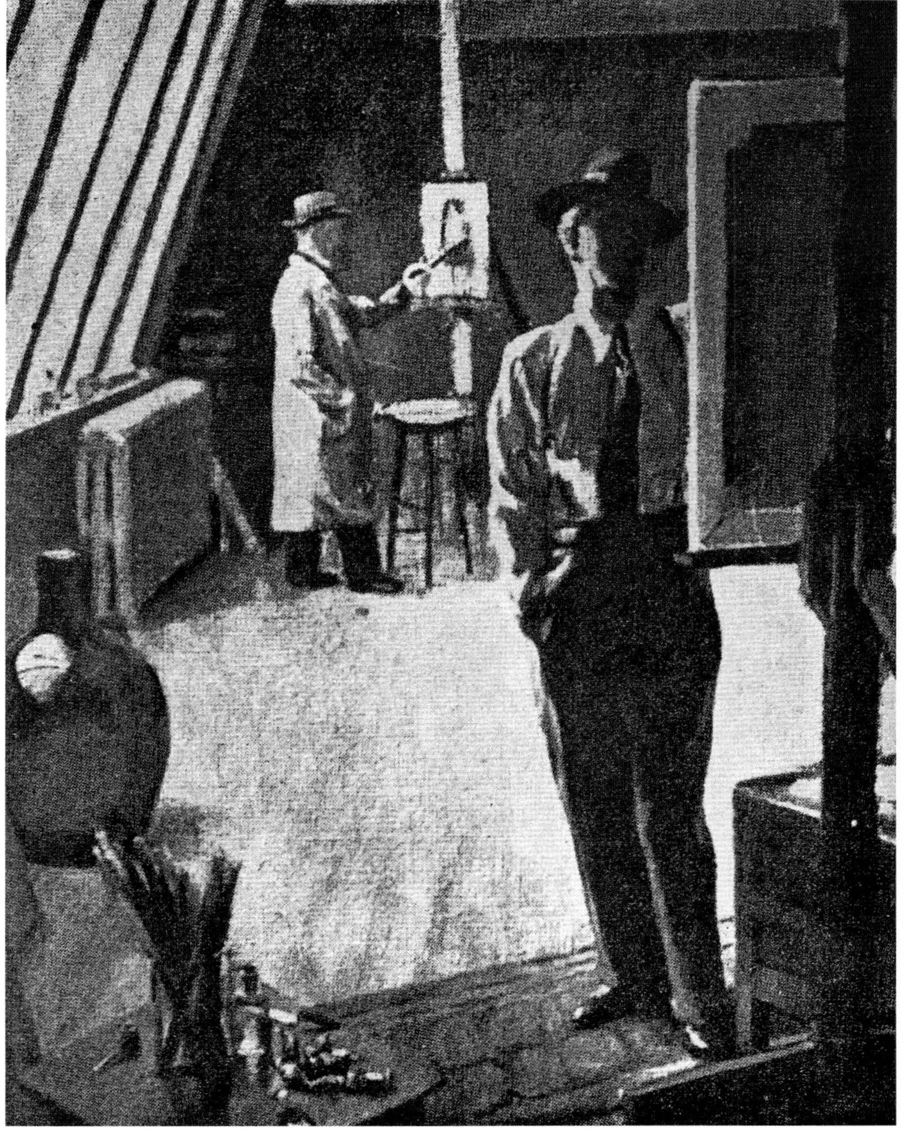

In My Studio Mirror.
By James R. Tate.
In this painting by James R. Tate, one of Sheppard's students, Sheppard is shown painting in the background.

VISIBILITY

As a man of his times, Peter Sheppard ventured out: into the bustling city, into the woodlands of central Ontario and to lakesides and seashores returning with compelling images of his encounters with humanity and nature. Among his peers who took on the themes of inter-war urban and industrial development and immigration, Sheppard worked at a level of ambition and accomplishment that gave lasting visual interpretations to those societal advancements. He was also among the finest figurative draftsmen of his time, practising this most unforgiving pictorial language with poetry and lyricism. Above all, his paintings of the ports of New York, Montreal and Toronto, of the crowded avenues of inner cities and wards, and of the forests and lakes, show a deep love of the land, the city and its people, expressed with sensitivity and passion.

Sheppard found his creative touchstones, influences and identity in a different version of modernism than the Group of Seven's. He was sustained and inspired by urban life, translating his experiences of it into paint. As an observer and interpreter of humanity, he found his artistic voice — his presence, his visibility — in urban scenes at a time when many Canadian artists were finding meaning in the wilderness.

By moving against the Canadian artistic tide, by looking to figuration, to New York schools of painting and to Impressionism, Sheppard experimented, widening the spectrum of subjects that resonated to contemporary eyes.

The Sheppard archive reveals much about the man and his art, about his times, and about the worlds in which he moved and practised his craft. It is a different kind of archive, one in which voice and detail are expressed mainly in visual imagery, in artworks. A circumstantial archive, the material in it gives us a portrait (if an incomplete one) of an artist, yet sheds almost no light on his personal life. But the artist we've come to know is one who observed the world around him deeply and depicted it largely by engaging at arm's length with the environment — urban, rural and wilderness.

The traces of this perspective are in the art that has come down to us, rendering the artist visible across the century as a curious, adventurous, quizzical observer, distancing himself from what he sees, yet embracing it, making it his own through his art.

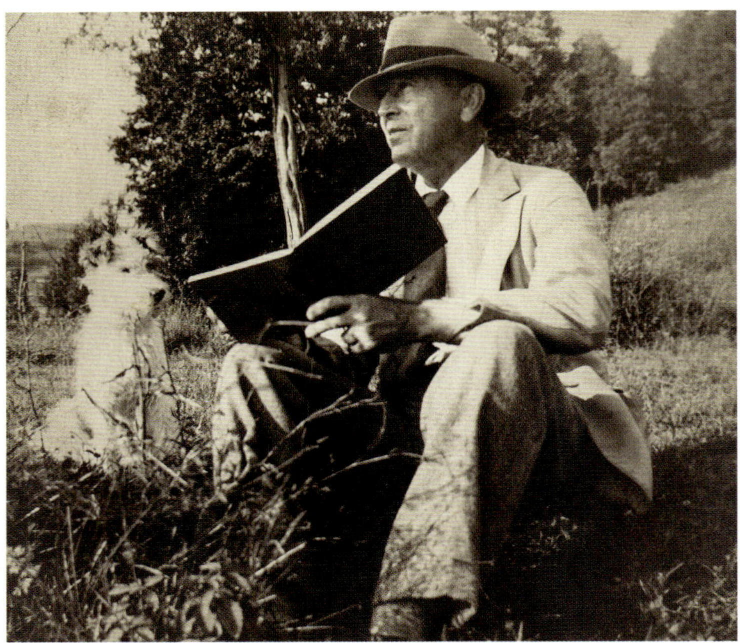

Sheppard painting *Haliburton Waterfall*, October 1941.

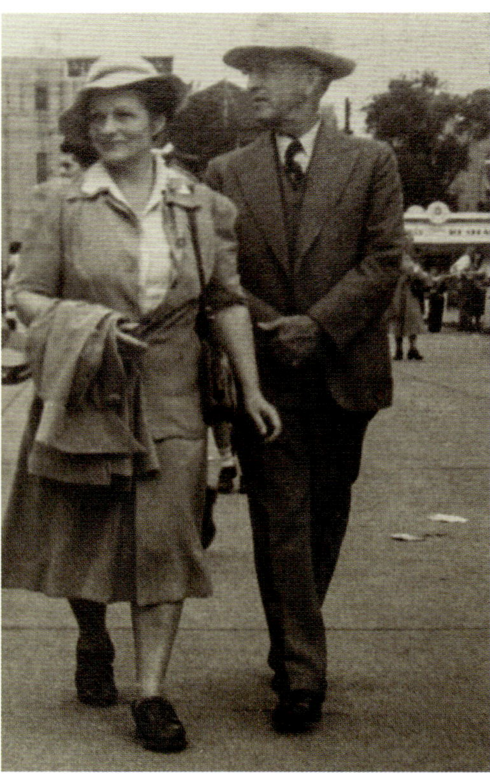

Bernice Fenwick Martin
and Peter Clapham Sheppard.

Notes to the Text

1. Bernice Fenwick Martin, C.P.E.. "Biographical data: Sheppard, Peter Clapham, R.C.A; O.S.A" (c. 1965).

2. L.A.C. Panton. "The O.S.A.," The Ontario Society of Artists: 75th Annual Spring Exhibition, Including a Retrospective Group of Paintings Selected from Works Exhibited During the First 50 Years of the Society's History (1946–47), pp. 6–20.

3. National Gallery of Canada "Information Form" from 1920. Sheppard gives his birthdate as "Oct. 21st, 1882." This date is also listed in "Biographical Data for the Records of the Art Gallery of Toronto" (May 1, 1923), and on a "Data Questionnaire" for *Who's Who in American Art* (August 1946).

4. National Gallery of Canada "Information Form" from January 1944. Sheppard gives his birthdate as "Oct. 21st, 1881."

5. Ontario, Canada, Births, 1869–1913 [database online]. Provo, Utah, USA: Ancestry.com.

6. *City of Toronto Directory* (1894).

7. *City of Toronto Directory* (1895).

8. Ibid.

9. *City of Toronto Directory* (1897).

10. Peter Clapham Sheppard Archives [hereafter cited as PCS Archives].

11. *City of Toronto Assessment Rolls* (1896) and (1897); Ward III, Div. 1.

12. 1901 Census of Canada.

13. Angela E. Davis. *Art and Work: A Social History of Labour in the Canadian Graphic Arts Industry to the 1940s* (Montreal and Kingston: McGill-Queen's University Press, 1995).

14. The range of printed material is illustrated in a 1912 advertisement in the Toronto Directory for Rolph & Clark Ltd, one of the city's larger printing establishments, which employed Sheppard that year; the ad gives the range of the firm's commercial services as: "Artistic lithographers, engravers, stationers, die sinkers and embossers." The printer produced products as diverse as: "bill heads, letter heads, envelopes, notepaper, business cards ... pamphlets, circulars, folders, seals, invitation cards, visiting cards ... book plates ... calendars, posters."

15. Davis, pp. 3–4.

16. Davis, p. 5.

17. Davis, pp. 83–84.

18. Davis, p. 12.

19. Davis, p. 90.

20. Ibid.

21. This information is taken from listings in volumes of the annual *City of Toronto Directory.*

22. Elizabeth Hulse. *A Dictionary of Toronto Printers, Publishers, Booksellers and Allied Trades, 1798–1900* (Toronto: Anson-Cartwright Editions, 1982). Provides a history of the industry in Toronto at this time.

23. Ontario Society of Artists 39th Annual Exhibition. (March 31st–April 29th 1911). Sheppard exhibited two portraits (catalogue #172 and #173).

24. For a historical sketch of the OSA, refer to Robert Stacey, *Ontario Society of Artists: A Brief Historical Outline* (http://ccca.concordia.ca/history/osa/english/).

25. E. Wyly Grier. Ontario Society of Artists President's Annual Report, 1911 (http://ccca.concordia.ca/history/osa/english/references/1911-rpt.html).

26. "Information form for the purpose of making a record of artists and their work," National Gallery of Canada (date-stamped: "Rec'd Dec 30" [1920]).

27. Ontario College of Art Prospectus for Session 1914–15.

28. Muriel Miller. *George Reid: A Biography* (Toronto: Summerhill Press, 1987).

29. Sheppard acknowledges Beatty as a "prominent art teacher" under whom he acquired "special training," on a "Data Questionnaire" for *Who's Who in American Art* (August 1946). On a National Gallery of Canada "Information Form" (1920), Sheppard lists that he studied under G.A. Reid, J.W. Beatty and W. Cruikshank at the Ontario College of Art.

30. Dorothy M. Farr. *J.W. Beatty: 1869–1941* (Kingston, ON: Agnes Etherington Art Centre, Queen's University, 1980), p. 32.

31. Farr, pp. 33–34, quoting Dorothy Hoover. *J.W. Beatty* (Toronto: Ryerson, 1948), p. 17.

32. Farr, p. 33.

33. Ontario College of Art Prospectus for Session 1914–15.

34. Farr, p. 35.

35. Farr, p. 35, quoting Yvonne McKague Housser from correspondence with her (October 18, 1979).

36. Victoria Baker, Emanuel Hahn and Elizabeth Wyn Wood. *Tradition and Innovation in Canadian Sculpture* (Ottawa: National Gallery of Canada, 1997), p. 26; fn. 87.

37. Undated email correspondence from Sarah E. Boehme and John S. Bugas, Curators, Whitney Gallery of Western Art, Buffalo Bill Historical Center, to Louis Gagliardi.

38. Ontario College of Art Prospectus for Session 1914–15, pp. 24, 28.

39. Ontario Society of Artists: Second Annual Exhibition of Little Pictures by Canadian Artists, Art Galleries of the Public Reference Library, Toronto (February 7–28, 1914).

40. Irene B. Wrenshall, "The Field of Art: Women's Art Association Opens Exhibition in New Galleries Feb. 28 — Young Artists Show Splendid Work — Canada's First Studio Building Is Being Opened — News and Notes of Artists and Collectors," *The Toronto Sunday World* (February 8, 1914).

41. Ontario College of Art Presentation of Awards Session 1913–1914. (December 18, 1914).

42. Letter from G.A. Reid to Peter Sheppard, Esq., A.O.C.A. (June 2, 1914), PCS Archives.

43. Andrew Waldron, "The Studio Building, 25 Severn Street, Toronto," *JSSAC* 31: no. 1 (2006), pp. 65–80 (http://dalspace.library. dal.ca:8080/bitstream/handle/10222/70780/vol31_1_65_80. pdf?sequence=1&isAllowed=y).

44. *The Water Trough* (RCA catalogue #197); *The Two Engines* (RCA catalogue #198).

45. "First Nights at Toronto Theatres. Large Audiences Greet Popular Attractions for Initial Week of Exhibition. 'Chu Chin Chow' Success," *The Toronto World* (Tuesday, August 31, 1920), p. 4.

46. Phyllis Rose, "Into the Twentieth Century — Two Toronto Bridges" (http://www.nrcresearchpress.com/doi/pdf/10.1139/l84-105).

47. Ontario Society of Artists, 44th Annual Exhibition (March 11–April 15, 1916), catalogue #117; Catalogue of the 38th Annual Exhibition of the Royal Canadian Academy of Arts held in the Art Association Galleries, 679 Sherbrook Street West, Montreal … (November 16–December 16, 1916), catalogue #212, illustrated in catalogue as *The Bridge Builders.*

48. *The Two Engines,* exhibited as item 413. It was listed for sale at $200.

49. *City of Toronto Assessment Roll*, 1920, Ward 3, Div. 2. This *Assessment Roll,* made in 1919 as a basis for calculating taxes in 1920, lists "Peter Shepherd" [sic] as occupying a studio at 101½ King Street West, 2nd Floor. The 1919 *Assessment Roll* does not provide a listing for Peter Clapham Sheppard.

50. Based on the statement in this same source that "At present, painting in studio — 8 Albany Ave., Toronto," this note was written sometime between 1946 and 1953, when his studio was located at this address.

51. Ontario Society of Artists, 45th Annual Exhibition (1917), catalogue #125. Listed for sale at $400; at the 1917 CNE exhibition it was listed as item 209, for sale at $400.

52. Object registration entry, Art Gallery of Ontario (accession number 92).

53. Ontario Society of Artists President's Annual Report, 1920 (http://ccca. concordia.ca/history/osa/english/references/1920-rpt.html).

54. Albert H. Robson. *Canadian Landscape Painters* (Toronto: The Ryerson Press, 1932), p. 164.

55. "O.S.A. Annual Exhibition. Color, Vigor and Originality Chief Characteristics of the Works. Great War Records," *Globe* (Toronto), March 8, 1919, p. 8.

56. http://www.askart.com/artist_bio/Frances_Mildred_Lithecke_ Geddes/10019767/Frances_Mildred_Lithecke_Geddes.aspx.

57. The Side Show, exhibition catalogue of the Canadian National Exhibition (1920), #119, illustrated.

58. "Many Picture by Canadians on Exhibition. Ontario Society of Artists Has Opened 48th Annual Display. Wide Variety of Style. Work of Old and Modern Schools Is Well Represented," *Globe* (Toronto), March 6, 1920.

59. Ontario College of Art Prospectus for Session 1920–1921. Sheppard's painting is reproduced on p. 21.

60. Postcard in the PCS Archives (July 19, 1921).

61. Small-format sketchbook labelled "Works dated between 1920–1929," PCS Archives.

62. Ontario Society of Artists, 49th Annual Exhibition (1921), catalogue #130, 131, 132, 133.

63. Review in the curatorial files at the National Gallery of Canada, *Toronto Mail and Empire,* March 10, 1923.

64. Sketchbook labelled "New York Scenes, 1910–1919," PCS Archives.

65. John Sloan. *Gist of Art: Principles and Practise Expounded in the Classroom and Studio* (New York: Dover Publications, 1939), p. 18.

66. Eric Brown. Preface to Special Exhibition of Canadian Art, National Gallery of Canada (January 21–February 28, 1926). Sheppard exhibited *The Blue Sleigh* (cat. #149) and *Old Store, Craig Street, Montreal* (cat. #150).

67. Hector Charlesworth, "Ontario Society of Artists. Brilliant Portraiture the Outstanding Feature of This Year's Show," *Saturday Night*, March 14, 1925, p. 3.

68. Review in the curatorial files at the National Gallery of Canada, *Toronto Mail and Empire,* March 14, 1925.

69. Ross King. *Defiant Spirits: The Modernist Revolution of the Group of Seven* (Kleinburg, ON: McMichael Canadian Art Collection in partnership with Douglas & McIntyre, 2010).

70. Press Comments on the Canadian Section of Fine Arts, British Empire Exhibition (London, 1924–25), unpaginated; as quoted in King, p. 402.

71. King, p. 404.

72. Foreword, Catalogue of the Canadian Section of Fine Arts, British Empire Exhibition, (London, 1924–25).

73. Eric Brown, "Quelques mots sur l'histoire de l'art Canadien," in Exposition d'art Canadien, Musée du Jeu de Paume (April 10–May 10, 1927), p. 12.

74. The 1926 OSA exhibition catalogue lists these two Toronto addresses for Sheppard: 39 St. Clair Avenue East, and 70 Oakwood Avenue.

75. "Progressive Group Takes Hold of Ontario Artists," *The Toronto Star,* March 5, 1927.

76. "Radical Painters Showing Their Work. Annual Show of Ontario Society of Artists Now on View," *Toronto Mail and Empire*, March 5, 1927.

77. Ontario Society of Artists President's Annual Report, 1927 (http://ccca. concordia.ca/history/osa/english/).

78. This painting was exhibited under both titles — *Sea Port* and *Ocean Freighter.*

79. Letter from Sheppard to H.O. McCurry, Assistant Director of the National Gallery of Canada (February 19, 1930). Sheppard writes: "Dear Mr. McCurry … was elected an A.R.C.A. 1929 Montreal …"

80. Catalogue of the 51st Annual Exhibition of the Royal Canadian Academy of Arts (November 1930), illustrated on p. 18.

81. John Lorinc. *Introduction to The Ward: The Life and Loss of Toronto's First Immigrant Neighbourhood* (Toronto: Coach House Books, 2015), pp. 11–23.

82. Jim Burant. "Lawren Harris's Ward Period," *The Ward: The Life and Loss of Toronto's First Immigrant Neighbourhood* (Toronto: Coach House Books, 2015), pp. 84–87.

83. Graham Campbell McInnes, "World of Art," undated and unattributed [review in the files of the PCS Archives].

84. Introductory statement from L.A.C. Panton, OSA Catalogue (March 1934), p. 5.

85. "Art Gallery Scene of R.C.A. Exhibition: Paintings and Other Works from Various Canadian Points Total 444. Much Good Portraiture," *Gazette* (Montreal), November 23, 1935, p. 19.

Exhibition History

Abbreviations:
AGH: Art Gallery of Hamilton
AGT: Art Gallery of Toronto
CNE: Canadian National Exhibition
MCAC: McMichael Canadian Art Collection
NGC: National Gallery of Canada
OSA: Ontario Society of Artists
RCA: Royal Canadian Academy

The Bridge Builders, Bloor Street Viaduct, Toronto
Exhibited: RCA 1916, OSA 1916, CNE 1922, OSA 1922,
MCAC 2010
Cover

Lower New York
Exhibited: RCA 1921 (illustrated), AGH 1922, CNE 1922
Page 8

Autumn Landscape
Exhibited: MCAC 2010
Page 14

The Waterfront, New York City
Exhibited: OSA 1923, RCA 1924, CNE 1924
Page 20

The Promenade
Exhibited: CNE 1919
Page 22

In the Garden
Exhibited: OSA 1912
Page 61

The Gasworks
Exhibited: MCAC, 2010–11.
Page 63

The Bridge Builders, Construction, Bloor Street Viaduct
Exhibited: RCA 1916, OSA 1916, CNE 1922, OSA 1922,
MCAC 2010–11
Page 102

Morning on the River
Exhibited: OSA 1917, OSA 1927
Pages 108–09

Arrival of the Circus
Exhibited: OSA 1919, CNE 1919
Pages 112–13

Horticultural Building, Canadian National Exhibition
Exhibited: OSA 1919, CNE 1919
Pages 116–17

The Engine Home
Exhibited: OSA 1920, MCAC 2010
Page 122

Wheat Elevator (Montreal)
Exhibited: OSA 1921
Page 129

The Tramp
Exhibited: OSA 1922 (illustrated)
Page 130

Lower New York
Exhibited: RCA 1921 (illustrated), AGH 1922, CNE 1922
Page 134

Lake Traffic
Exhibited: RCA 1920
Pages 138–39

Old Store, Craig Street
Exhibited: NGH Special Exhibition of Canadian Art, 1926
Page 141

The City
Exhibited: OSA 1925
Page 145

Early Snow, Montreal
Exhibited: British Empire Exhibition, Wembley 1925 (RCA)
Exhibition of Canadian Art, Jeu du Paume, Paris, 1927 (RCA)
Page 148

Midwinter
Exhibited: RCA 1927, OSA 1927
Page 155

The Inn Yard
Exhibited: OSA 1927
Page 159

Sea Port/Ocean Freighter
Sea Port also exhibited as *Ocean Freighter*, 1929–30.
Exhibited: RCA 1930 (illustrated),
AGT 1930, RCA 1931. OSA 1933, RCA 1933
Page 190

Dorset
Exhibited: CNE 1932 (illustrated)
Page 191

Autumn Hillside
Exhibited: OSA 1931
Page 192

Rapids, Hollow River
Exhibited: OSA 1931
Page 193

Winter, Bonsecours Market
Exhibited: OSA 1931
Page 206

Three Old Houses, Louisa Street
Exhibited: RCA 1932 (illustrated)
Page 218

The Market, November
Exhibited: OSA 1929, OSA 1933, CNE 1933
Page 215

Old Houses
Exhibited: CNE 1934 (illustrated)
Page 219

Elizabeth Street
Exhibited: OSA 1933
Page 220

Halifax Harbour
Exhibited: RCA 1935, OSA 1935 (illustrated).
 Also illustrated in *Canadian Art – Its Origins and
Development*, William Colgate, Ryerson Press, Toronto, 1943. p. 146
Page 222

Winter Ferry/City Docks
Exhibited: NGC 1936, RCA 1937, OSA 1937, CNE 1937,
New York World's Fair 1939
Page 223

Image Credits

Pages 6–7 and 155
Midwinter, 1927. Purchased in 1928 by the National Gallery of Canada. Ottawa. NGC 3536.

Page 38
Beverly Street, Toronto, 1911. Courtesy of the City of Toronto Archives. Series 372, S 0372, SS0058, Item 0032.

Page 54
Life Drawing Class, Ontario School of Art, the Grange, 1911. *Toronto Star Weekly.* Courtesy of the City of Toronto Archives. Fonds 1244, Item 703K.

Page 55
Exhibitors at the Ontario Society of Artists Exhibition, 1911. *Toronto Star Weekly*, April 8, 1911. *Toronto Star* Photograph Archive. Courtesy of the Toronto Public Library.

Page 58
Reading. George Agnew Reid. Purchased by the Government of Ontario from the 28th Annual OSA Exhibition, 1900. Government of Ontario Art Collection. Courtesy of the Archives of Ontario, Item 623112.

Page 62
The Gasworks (study). Private collection, Toronto.

Page 62
Tracks and Traffic. J.EH. MacDonald. Art Gallery of Ontario. Gift of Walter C. Laidlaw. Toronto, 1937. 2435, Image c 2017.

Page 72
Evening Cloud of the Northland. J.W. Beatty. Acquired in 1911. Courtesy of the National Gallery of Canada. NGC41.

Page 76
Drawing from plaster casts at the Ontario College of Art at the Normal School, Toronto. *Toronto Star Weekly,* February 8, 1913. *Toronto Star* Photographic Archives. Courtesy of the Toronto Public Library.

Page 90
Ontario College of Art Prospectus, 1914–15. OCAD University Archives/ Visual Resources.

Page 95
Studio Building, Severn Street, Toronto. April, 1938. Private collection. Courtesy of the National Gallery of Canada Library and Archives.

Page 103
Photo of Bloor Street Viaduct, Pier D. T.T. Black. City of Toronto Archives. Fonds 1181, Item 13.

Page 103
Twilight. Tom Thomson. Courtesy of the Samuel E. Weir Collection, Riverbrink Art Museum.

Page 105
Bloor Street Viaduct construction, 1915. City of Toronto Archives. Fonds 1231, Item 1869.

Page 107
The Jack Pine. Tom Thomson. Purchased in 1918 by the National Gallery of Canada. NGC 1519.

Pages 108–109
Morning on the River. Art Gallery of Ontario. Gift of the Canadian National Exhibition Association, 1965.

Page 110
Opening of the Art Gallery of Toronto, 1918. JRR4387. *Toronto Star* Photographic Archives. Courtesy of the Toronto Public Library.

Page 111
Ontario Society of Artists Hanging committee, 1919. Ontario Society of Artists Collection. Archives of Ontario. F1140-7-0-1.

Page 123
Men of the Docks. George Bellows. The National Gallery, London. NG6649 Bought with a grant from the American Friends of the National Gallery, made possible by Sir Paul Getty's fund, and by a donation from Mark Getty, 2014.

Page 126
The Side Show. CNE Catalogue of Paintings by Canadian Artists, Toronto, Aug 28 to Sept 11, 1920. P. 27., Item 119. Courtesy of the Archives of Ontario.

Page 138
Lake Traffic. Purchased in 1920 by the National Gallery of Canada, NGC 1707.

Page 149
Photo of Exhibition at the Musée du Jeu de Paume, Paris, May 10, 1927. Charles Berthelomier. Visual Resources Collection, National Gallery of Canada Library and Archives.

Page 150
The Cabstand, Dominion Square. Private collection.

Page 155
Midwinter. Purchased in 1928 by the National Gallery of Canada. NGC 3536.

Page 203
Slide Show. Canadian National Exhibition, Private collection.

Page 210
Map of the Ward, Toronto (PDP). C. Goad's, Vol. 1. Central City, 1913. Plate 9. City of Toronto Archives. Fonds 200, S.372, SS.10, Item 187.

Page 216
Old City Hall. City of Toronto Archives. Fonds 1244, Item 1002.

Page 219
Old Houses. Art Gallery of Ontario.

Page 224
Royal Canadian Academy Travelling Exhibition, New York World's Fair, May 1 – June 15, 1939. Visual Resources Collection, National Gallery of Canada Library and Archives.

Page 225
William Colgate. *Canadian Art: Its Origin and Development.* Toronto, Ryerson Press, 1943, page 146.

Selected Bibliography

Baker, Victoria. *Emanuel Hahn and Elizabeth Wyn Wood: Tradition and Innovation in Canadian Sculpture*. Ottawa: National Gallery of Canada, 1997.

Burant, Jim. "Lawren Harris's Ward Period." *The Ward: The Life and Loss of Toronto's First Immigrant Neighbourhood*. Toronto: Coach House Books, 2015.

Davis, Angela E. *Art and Work: A Social History of Labour in the Canadian Graphic Arts Industry to the 1940s*. Montreal and Kingston: McGill-Queen's University Press, 1995.

Farr, Dorothy M. *J.W. Beatty: 1869–1941*. Kingston: Agnes Etherington Art Centre, Queen's University, 1980.

Hoover, Dorothy. *J.W. Beatty*. Toronto: Ryerson Press, 1948.

Hulse, Elizabeth. *A Dictionary of Toronto Printers, Publishers, Booksellers and Allied Trades, 1798–1900*. Toronto: Anson-Cartwright Editions, 1982.

King, Ross. *Defiant Spirits: The Modernist Revolution of the Group of Seven*. Toronto: McMichael Canadian Art Collection, in partnership with Douglas & McIntyre, 2010.

Lorinc, John. "Introduction." *The Ward: The Life and Loss of Toronto's First Immigrant Neighbourhood*. Toronto: Coach House Books, 2015.

Miller, Muriel. *George Reid: A Biography*. Toronto: Summerhill Press, 1987.

Robson, Albert H. *Canadian Landscape Painters*. Toronto: Ryerson Press, 1932.

Rose, Phyllis. "Into the Twentieth Century – Two Toronto Bridges." http://www.nrcresearchpress.com/doi/abs/10.1139/l84-105.

Sloan, John. *Gist of Art: Principles and Practise Expounded in the Classroom and Studio*. New York: Dover Publications, 1939.

Stacey, Robert. *Ontario Society of Artists: A Brief Historical Outline*. http://ccca.concordia.ca/history/osa/english/.

Waldron, Andrew. "The Studio Building, 25 Severn Street, Toronto," *JSSAC* 31: No. 1 (2006), pp. 65–80. http://dalspace.library.dal.ca/handle/10222/70780.

Index

In the index, page numbers in boldface refer to reproductions of images. Dates for artworks are included only when needed to distinguish two works with the same title. Where artworks have the same title and the same date, a number has been placed in parentheses after the title to distinguish the two (or more) by order of appearance in this book.

A

academic art and academicism, 37, 41, 73, 85, 107, 123, 124, 154
Académie Julian, Paris, 72
Adams Chiclets gum, advertisement, **37**
Algonquin Park, 72
Annex (Toronto), 38, 95, 225
ARCA, **18**, 221, 231, 196
Arrival of the Circus, 19, 28, **112**, 114, 116, 118
Art Gallery of Ontario, 111
Art Gallery of Toronto, **110**, 111, 129, 191, 229
Artist, The, **32**
Artist's Mother, **75**
Art Museum of Toronto, 114
Art Students League, New York, 114, 131, 134
Arts and Crafts, movement and style, 95, 191
Ashcan School, 86, 118, 124, 131, 135, 139, 140
Assessment Roll. See City of Toronto Assessment Roll
Autumn Hillside, **192**, 232
Autumn Landscape (1922), **14,** 232
Autumn Landscape (1937), **197**, 208

B

Barbizon painters, 69
Barclay, Clark & Co., 39, 40, 42
Beachside Idyll, **71**
Beatty, Bill. *See* Beatty, J.W.
Beatty, J.W., 43, 50, **55**, 65, **72**, 72–73, 76, **77**, 85, 88, 95, 96, 114, 229

Beaver Hall Group, 160
Bellows, George, 123, **123**, 125, 135
Belmont Street. *See* Sheppard, Peter Clapham
Bernard, Émil, 176
Beverley Street. *See* Sheppard, Peter Clapham
Bloor Street Viaduct, 28, 103, **103**, 105, **105**, 107, 111
Bloor Street Viaduct (study) (2), **104**
Bloor Street Viaduct (study) (3), **106**
Bloor Street Viaduct, The (1), 19, 107
Bloor Street West. See *Christie Pits*
Boardwalk, Atlantic City, The, **137**, 139
study, **144**
Bonsecours Market. See *Winter, Bonsecours Market*
Boughten, A., 118
Boys by a Pond, **30**, 47
Boys Playing, **31**, 47
Braham, Lionel, 55, **57**, 101
Bridge Builders, Construction, Bloor Street Viaduct, The, cover, **102**, 103, 105
Brigden, Fred, 160, 221
British Empire Exhibition, Wembley, 19, 147, 149, 151, 231, 232
Britton, Harry, 114
Broadhead, W.S., **55**
Brooker, Bertram, 153
Brooklyn Bridge (1), **132**
Brooklyn Bridge (2), **132**
Brooklyn Bridge, The, **136**, 139
Brown, Eric, 144, 149, 231
Burden & Gouinlock, 126
By the Lake, **66**

C

Cabbagetown, 38, 95
Cabstand, Dominion Square, Montreal, The, 19, **150**, 151–52, 233
study, **151**
Cabstand, Montreal, **157**
studies, **154**, **156**
Cabstand, Old Quebec, **158**
cabstands, 154
Calton Hill Cemetery, Edinboro [sic], 46, **46**
Canada's national identity, 25, 163
Canadian Magazine, 43
Canadian National Exhibition (CNE), 51, 96, 107, 111, 114, **116**, 126, **126**, 139, 160, 191, **203**, 230, 232
exhibition at the CNE, 217
Canadian Section of Fine Arts, British Empire Exhibition, 149, 231
Canoeists, **128**
Carmichael, Franklin, 176
Carr, Emily, 25
Casa Loma, 86
Casson, A.J., 73
Challener, Fred, 43
Charlesworth, Hector, 147, 231
Child on a Hobby Horse, **47**
Christie Pits, Bloor Street West, 196
Christie Pits, Toronto (1), **204**
Christie Pits, Toronto (2), **205**
Chu Chin Chow (musical comedy), 99
sketches of, **101**

Church, Evening, **187**
Church of St. Michael and St. Anthony, Mile End, Montreal, **126**
Circus (study), **115, 119**
City, The (1), **33**, **146,** 147
City, The (2), **145**
City of Toronto Assessment Roll, 40, 110, 123, 229, 230
City of Toronto Directory (also, *Toronto City Directory*), 37, 39, 40, 96, 110, 123, 126, 129, 131, 191, 225, 229
Clark Lithographing Co., 47
Claudius, Marcus, 54
Cloudscape, **24**, **199**
Cloudscape over Lake and Hills, **177**
CNE. *See* Canadian National Exhibition
Commercial Illustration [beaver], **41**
Construction, **26**
Contemporary Arts Society, 224
Costume Class, Study, OCA (1), 87, **88**
Costume Class, Study, OCA (2), 87, **89**
Costume Class, Study, OCA (3), **91**
Couple, Lakeside, **66**
Credit River, 38
Cruikshank, William, 65, 68–69, 72, **76**, 229
Cubism, 73
Cullen, Maurice, 147
Cumming, Alex, 96
Currie, Herbert, 40

D

Davenport Road, 39, 46, 96
Davis, Arthur B., 123
Death of Virginia, 54, **57**

Deer Park, 95
Dominion Square. See *The Cabstand, Dominion Square, Montreal*
Dominion Square Park, 154
Dominique La Plante. See *Thundercloud*
Don River, 38, 95, 103
Dorset, 191, **191**, 232
Down the St. Lawrence, 129
Downard, W., **111**, 118
Durand, William, 40

E

Eakins, Thomas, 69
Early Snow, Montreal, **148**, 149, **149**, 150, 232
Eight, the, 86, 118, 123–24, 131, 140
Elizabeth Street, 208, 210
Elizabeth Street, 217, **220**
  detail, **189**
  sketch, **214**, 217
Elliot, J.E., **55**
Engine Home, The, **frontis.**, 19, **122**, 125, 232
  detail, **35**
Evening Cloud of the Northland, **72**, 72–73
Everett Stationery and Loose Leaf Co., Ltd., 126
Expressionism, 73
expressive properties of colour, 65, 69, 124

F

Fair, The, 147
Farm Woman, **65**
Field and Crows, **48**
Field and Trees, **49**
Figure with Child in Pram, **23**
First Nations. *See* Thundercloud
First World War. *See* Great War
Ford, Harriet, **55**
Ford, Jesse (Sheppard), 38
Forest Floor, Autumn, **180**
Frederick Ford, 62
Freighter, **169**

Freighters in Harbour, 147, **164**
French school, 221

G

Gagen, R.F. (Robert), 50, **55**, **111**, 118
Gagliardi, Louis, 19, 27, 230
Gagnon, Clarence, 147, 149
Gasworks, The, 58, **63**, 64, 232
  detail, **45**
  study, **62**
Geddes, Frances M., 110, 114, 131, 230
Girl with Dog and Gifts, **47**
Glackens, William J., 123, 125, 135
Globe newspaper (Toronto), 114, 230
Goldike, George, 40
graphic arts industry, 41–42
Great War, 19, 96, 107, 118
Grier, Edmund Wyly, 50, 51, **55**, **111**, 118, 229
Group of Seven, 19, 25, 27, 62, 73, 96, 118, 129, 149, 151, 153, 163, 171, 216, 217, 221, 226, 231

H

Hahn, Emanuel, 86, 149, 230
Haliburton Waterfall, **226**
Halliday, F.R., **55**
Harbour Scene (Halifax), 221, **222**
Harbour Sketch, **133**
Hard Times, 208, **209**
Harris, Lawren, 50, **55**, 95, 96, **111**, 118, 216, 231
Hemming, Arthur, 95
Henri, Robert, 86, 123–125
Hogg's Hollow, 73
Hollow River, **179**
Horticultural Building, Canadian National Exhibition, 116, **116**, 232
Houses on the Edge of a Lake, 196, **197**
Housser, Yvonne McKague, 73, 230
Hudson River, 133
Humber River, 38
Hunter, The, 221

I

In My Studio Mirror, **225**
In the Garden, 58, **61**, 62, 232
Inn Yard, The, **10**, **159**, 160, 232
Inness, George, 69
intaglio printmaking, 73
Island Ferry (Toronto), 221

J

Jack Pine, The, 107, **107**
Jackson, A.Y., 72, 95, 171, 176, 217
Jefferys, C.W., 43, 50, **55**, 221
Johnson, Claude, 90
Johnston, Francis H. (Frank), 50, **55**, **111**, 118
Johnston, Mabel A., 50, **55**
Johnston, W.C., **55**

K

Kallymeyer, Minnie, **55**
Kennedy, John, 111
Knife Sharpener, The, 210, **211**

L

La Plante, Dominique. See *Thundercloud*
Lake Landscape, **195**, 196
Lake Ontario, 38, 54, 73, 180, 224
Lake Traffic, **139**, 140, 232
Lake View, Autumn, 171, **176**
Late Autumn Sunset, **207**, 208
Lawson, Ernest, 123, 125
life drawing, **54**, 73, 86
Lionel Braham, **57**
Lismer, Arthur, 96, **149**, 151
Locomotives. See *Two Engines*
Logan, Vivien, 114
Long, Marion, 96
Loring, Frances, 149
Louisa Street, 208, 210, 216, 217, 218
Louisa Street, 221
  sketch, **212**, **216**
Loveroff, Frederick, 149
Lower New York, 19, **134**, 135, 139, 232
  detail, **8**, **13**
  study, **136**

Luks, George, 123
Lunenburg, Nova Scotia, **174**

M

MacCallum, Dr. James, 95
MacDonald, J.E.H., 50, 55, **62**, 64, 95, 96, 176
MacDonald, Manly E., 88, 114
Market, November, The, **215**, 217
Market Scene, Montreal (1), 151, **161**
Market Scene, Montreal (2), **21**, 171, **175**
Martin, Bernice Fenwick, 27, 36–37, 96, 97, 99, 225, **226**, 229
McInnes, Graham Campbell, 221, 231
McLean, T.W., **55**
McMichael Canadian Art Collection, 27, 231, 232
Men at the Docks, **123**
Michelangelo
  River Gods, 99, **100**
Midwinter, 152–54, **155**
Miller, Kenneth Hayes, 114
Milne, David, 149
Monet [Claude], 151
  Giverny, 151
Montreal Cabstand Near the Oratory, **128**
Montreal Port (1), **127**
Montreal Port (2), **127**
Morning on the River, **109**, 111, 232
  detail, **93**
Morrice, James Wilson, 147, 149
Morris, Kathleen Moir, 149, 160
Mother and Child, **70**
Mueller, A., 40
Munch, Edvard, 176
Musée du Jeu de Paume, exhibition, **149**, 151, 231, 232
Muskoka, 191, 225

N

Nabis movement, 176
National Gallery of Canada, 19, 65, 72, 118, 144, 149, **149**, 150, 152, 160, 229–232
New York World's Fair *Exhibition*

of Canadian Art, 224, **224**, 232
Normal School, 51, 73, **76**
northern Ontario, 72–73, 107, 118
Northern Rapids and Forest, Autumn,
    181

O

OCA. *See* Ontario College of Art
October, **15**
Oiling Up (1922), **168**
Oiling Up (1926), **178**
*Old Church (Yonge St. and Davenport
    Rd., Toronto)*, 39, **39**, 46
*Old House, Winter (The Ward,
    Toronto)*, **142**, 144
Old Houses, 217, **219**, 232
Old Houses, Yarmouth, N.S., 191
Old Man in a Pith Helmet, 47, **65**
Old Store, Craig Street, **141**, 144,
    146, 231
        detail, **140**
        study, **143**
On the Beach, New York, **125**
Ontario College of Art (OCA), 51,
    64, 65, 73, 76, **76**, 88, 90, 114,
    229, 230
        Prospectus, 69, 73, **90**, 126,
            229, 230
Ontario School of Art, **54**, 64, 69
        the Grange, **54**
Ontario Society of Artists (OSA),
    18, 38, 43, 50, 51, 58, 62, 88,
    111, **111**, 107, 114, 116, 118, 125,
    126, **126**, 129, 131, 147, 152–153,
    160, 191, 196, 203, 208, 217, 221,
    224–225, 229–231
        exhibitors, 1911 exhibition,
            55
        Little Pictures, exhibition, 88,
            191, 196, 203, 230
OSA. *See* Ontario Society of
    Artists

P

Painters Eleven, 125
Palmer, H.S., **55**
Panton, L.A.C., 38, 221, 229, 231
Parking on the Street, **153**

Payne, Gordon, 88
Pellatt, Sir Henry, 86
Pendleton, D.R. (S.K.), 40
Pennsylvania Academy, Philadel-
    phia, 69
People on the Street, **152**
Phaendtner, Otto, 40
Pines, Windy Day, Georgian Bay, **186**
plein-air painting, 69, 72, 133, 196,
    203
Port Hope, 73
Portrait of a Man in a Rowboat, **74**
Post-Impressionist, 176
Prendergast, Maurice, 123
Prince Edward Viaduct. *See* Bloor
    Street Viaduct
Profile Portrait: Mata, **40**
Promenade, The, **23**, 116, 232
Provincial Art School, 39

Q

Queen Street, 221

R

Rapids, Hollow River, **193**, 196, 232
RCA. *See* Royal Canadian
    Academy
Reading, **58**, 72
Red Barn, Ontario, 196, **200**
Red Boathouse, The, 171, **171**
Reid, George Agnew (G.A.), 50,
    55, 58, **58**, 65, 69, 72, 73, 85, 86,
    90, 114, 191, 229, 230
Reid, Mary H., 50, **55**
Remington, Frederic, 86
River Pattern, 124, **124**
        study, **124**
River Scene, Dusk, **198**
Robson, Albert (A.H.), 43, 114
Rolph, Clark, Stone Ltd., 36, 43
Romanovsky, Dimitri, 114
Rosedale, 95, 103
Royal Canadian Academy, 43, 96,
    107, 118, 139, 153, 160, 196, 208,
    221, 224, 230, 231, 232
        exhibition, 107, 221, **224**,
Rushing River, Muskoka, **184**
Ruskin, John, 19

S

Sailboat at Dock, **162**
Sampson, J. Ernest, 107
Sawmill, Ontario, 196, **201**
Scarborough Bluffs, 180, **182**
Scarborough Bluffs, Lake Ontario,
    180, **183**
Sea Port/Ocean Freighter, **18**, **190**,
    191, 196, 217, 231, 232
September Gale, **149**
Sérusier, Paul, 64
Shea's Hippodrome Theatre, **216**,
    217
Sheppard, Adelaide (sister of
    Peter), 39, 224
Sheppard, Charles (brother of
    Peter), 39
Sheppard, Jessie (sister of Peter),
    39, 225
Sheppard, Jesse (née Ford)
    (mother of Peter), 38
Sheppard, John (paternal grand-
    father of Peter), 38
Sheppard, Peter Clapham
        1930, **27**
        Albany Street studio, 225
        art school certificate, **39**
        at work in Toronto studio,
            18
        Belmont Street, 39
        Beverley Street, 38, 38, 39
        birth, 38
        Bloor Street West studio,
            208, 224
        commercial art, 25, 36,
            40–43, 46–47, 65, 111,
            123, 225, 229
            advertisements, calendars,
            labels, playbills, 40
        Diploma for Painting, **64**
        friendship with Bernice
            Fenwick Martin, 225
        Garner Street Sketchbook,
            126–128, 129
        graduate of OCA, 88, 90
        industrial themes, 27, 28,
            64, 95, 96, 105, 111, 131, 226
        journeyman lithographer,
            27

        King Street West studio,
            110, 114, 123, 126, 129
        lithography, 36, 39, 47
        Methodist, 40
        Montreal Sketchbook,
            152–53
        New York/New York City
            Sketchbooks, **125**, 131, **132**,
            133, **133**, **144**
        Nude/Study/ies from Life
            [various], **50–53**, **78–85**
        Oakwood Avenue, 129, 191,
            208, 224, 231
        painting *Haliburton
            Waterfall*, **226**
        Provincial Art School
            Certification, 39
        Sir Edmund Walker
            Scholarship, **64**, 76
        sketchbooks, 97ff
        Sketch/es [untitled, various],
            97–101
        St. James Street, 129
        Stone Scholarship, 76, **64**,
            90
        Summerhill Avenue home,
            46, 50, 96, 97, 99, 123
        Toronto studio, **18**, 111
        with Bernice Fenwick
            Martin, **226**
        young man, **41**
Sheppard, William (cousin? of
    Peter), 126
Sheppard, William (father of
    Peter), 38
Shiner, H.E., 40
Shinn, Everett, 123
Ship Offloading, **167**
Ships in Harbour (1921), **165**
Ships in Harbour (1922) (1), **166**
Ships in Harbour (1922) (2), **173**
*Side Show, Canadian National Exhi-
    bition*, 126, **126**, 203, **203**, 230
Singer Sargent, John, 86
Slade School of Art, 114
Sloan, John, 123, 135, 139, 140, 230
Smith, Eden, 95
Snowstorm, Montreal, The, **6–7**
St. John River, 221

St. Lawrence River, 129
Staples, Owen, **55**
Studio Building, Severn Street, 95
Study from Life (drawing), **28**
Study from Life (painting), **11**
Summer Idyll, **67**
Sunset, **67**

T

Tate, James R., 208, **225**
Thackings, John, 110
Thompson [*sic*], 96
Thomson, Tom, 25, 55, 58, **74**, 96,
    103, **103**, 107, **107**, 176
        Davenport Road, 96
        Randall and Johnston Ltd.,
          96
Three Old Houses, Louisa Street, **18**,
    217, **218**, 232
Three Sisters, Humber River, Late Fall,
    The, **194**, 196
Thundercloud, 86
        Blackfoot and French, 86
        Buffalo Bill's Wild West
          Show, 86
        First Nations, 86

Thundercloud, **86** , **87**
Tonalism, Tonalist, 58, 69, 72, 85,
Tonks, Sir Henry, 114
Toronto Art Students' League, 64
Toronto City Directory. See *City of*
    Toronto Directory
Toronto Mail and Empire, 131, 147,
    153, 154, 230, 231
Toronto Reference Library, 88, 230
Toronto Star/Weekly, 114, 153, 231
Tracks and Traffic, **62**
Tramp, The, 19, **130**, 131, 232
        detail, **121**
        study, **131**
Trott, Herman, 40
Tugboat (1910), 51, **56**, 224
Tugboat (1922), **172**
Tugboat at Dock, 163, **170**, 171
Twilight, **103**
Two Engines (Locomotives), The
        study, **94**
Two Sisters, **70**

U

Upper Canada, 38, 62
        Provincial Exhibition, 50

V

Vickers, Henrietta, **55**
Victoria Rugby Club, **42**
Victoria Rugby Football Club, **43**

W

Waddington's, 99
Wainright, Hastings, 208
Ward, The (1), **213**
Ward, The (2), **29, 214**
Ward, the, Toronto, 38, 208, 210,
    216–17, 221, 231
        immigrants, Chinese,
          Italian, Jewish, 216
        map of, **210**
        proximity to City Hall, 216
Waterfall, 180, **185**
Waterfront, New York City, The, 19,
    20, 139, 232
Wharf, Parry Sound, 196, **202**
Wheat Elevator, Montreal, 129, **129**, 232
Whistler, James Abbott McNeill,
    69, 86
Williamson, Curtis, 95, 96
Winter, Bonsecours Market, 191, 203,

    206, 232
Winter Ferry/City Docks, **223**, 224,
    224, 232
Woman by the Lake, **71**
Woman in a Blue Dress, **59**, 72
Woman in the Garden, the Grange,
    58, **60**
Woman Sewing, 58, **68**
Wooded Landscape, **207**
Wrinch, Mary E., **55**
Wychwood Park, 95, 191
Wyle, Florence, 149

NOTES ON THE DESIGN

The text for this book was set in Cartier Book and Cooper Hewitt Sans, selected for their complementary style and elegant design. Cartier was designed in 1967 by Carl Dair to celebrate Canada's centennial. I thought it would be fitting to use this typeface in 2017, Canada's 150th birthday.

Rod McDonald created the digital version of Cartier Book by carefully assembling Dair's ideas into a fully developed typeface family that refines the original's distinctive character shapes, creating engaging and distinctive text copy that is both legible and uniquely Canadian. I chose the contemporary sans serif Cooper Hewitt typeface for the subheaders and captions. Cooper Hewitt's characters are composed of modified geometric curves and arches that complement the edges and curves of Cartier Book.

In creating the design I considered that many readers would be reading this book in pieces, snatching moments and flipping through the pages. The page design needed to be open and reader-friendly, with adequate leading (space between lines of text) and margins, as well as breathing room around art and captions. I think the square shape of the book helps to feature both the portrait and landscape orientations of the art as well as providing a pleasing shape for the reader. I hope you enjoy this layout as much as I did making it.

George A. Walker

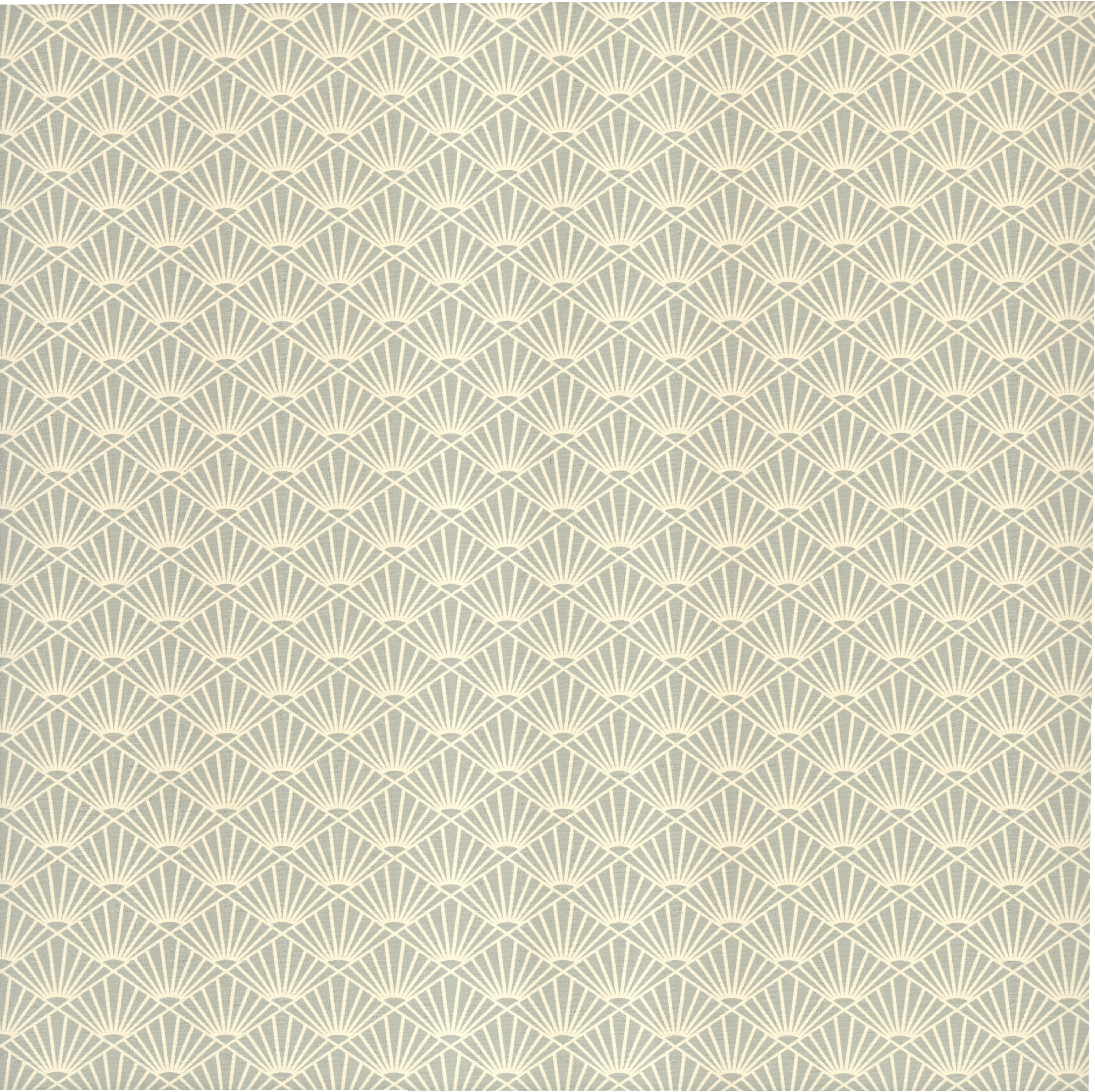